D0896223

The Hidden Heritage

BY JOHN HOWARD LAWSON

Theory and Technique of Playwriting
Film: The Creative Process

PLAYS

Roger Bloomer
Processional
Nirvana
Loudspeaker
The International
Success Story
The Gentlewoman
The Pure in Heart
Marching Song
Parlor Magic

JOHN HOWARD LAWSON

The Hidden Heritage

❦ A REDISCOVERY OF THE IDEAS AND FORCES THAT LINK THE THOUGHT OF OUR TIME WITH THE CULTURE OF THE PAST

The Citadel Press NEW YORK

First revised paperbound edition, 1968

 Published by Citadel Press, Inc., 222 Park Avenue South, New York, N. Y. 10003. In Canada: George J. McLeod Limited, 73 Bathurst St., Toronto 2B, Ontario. Manufactured in the United States of America by The Haddon Craftsmen, Inc., Scranton, Pa.

INTRODUCTION (1968)

A NEW EDITION of *The Hidden Heritage* gives me an opportunity to re-examine the book in the light of what I have learned since its first publication. In my introduction in 1950, I wrote that the work is "unfinished . . . tentative and exploratory. . . . It poses many questions concerning historical relationships. But it is easier to ask questions than to offer definitive answers. In some cases, the answer can be no more than another question."

The questions have multiplied in these eighteen years, the search for answers has become more baffling. If I have acquired more wisdom, I may be able to state the theme and purpose more clearly. At the same time, I feel obligated to indicate changes in my viewpoint, assumptions that require modification, generalizations which now seem to me too sweeping.

There is a four-fold design: first, I undertook a personal voyage of discovery, to find out what the past meant to me (if it meant anything at all) and how it affected my identity as an American. Second, since I could not identify myself, or my sense of present reality, with what I read in history books, I had to search for hidden facts or meanings, which could be traced in certain specialized studies and original documents. Third (this brought me to the heart of the matter), I had to explore the development of culture and the arts, to explain the way in which our concepts of man and society, freedom and law, democracy and power, peace and war, relate to the "reality" of history, including its hidden aspects. Fourth, I came back to the first question, but it no longer concerned me alone: whether the people of the United States and the world's people could understand and control their present history was a question of survival. The problem

of consciousness would determine whether human consciousness would continue at all.

1. *Personal Report*

In 1934, at the age of forty, I had a superficial acquaintanceship with American literature and an almost complete ignorance of American history. Washington crossing the Delaware was as remote as Caesar being stabbed in ancient Rome. In fact, Caesar's death made more sense, because Shakespeare had written a play about it.

I had begun to study Marxism, and I found it difficult but enormously rewarding as a revelation of the development of human society and the possibilities of a more rational social order. But Marxism provided only fragmentary clues to the role of culture and the arts. I was primarily concerned with my own work in the theatre, and I undertook a systematic study of the evolution of dramatic art: *Theory and Technique of Playwriting,* published in 1937, mentions Marxism only once (as an aspect of nineteenth-century thought). I avoided Marxist phraseology, because I believed my use of the theory was original, rejecting the conventional emphasis on politics and the primacy of "content," and insisting instead that the *form* of a work of art determines its meaning.

My work on dramatic history made me painfully conscious of my historical illiteracy. The vast drama of events approached a climax: the agony of Guernica was a trial run for the destruction of civilians in the coming global conflict, which became inevitable with the victory of fascism in Spain.

I had plunged into a study of the ideas and forces which had created the United States and placed the nation in its present relationship to a world in crisis. I raced against time, but time overtook and passed me. The world changed and my perspective changed. I found that "ideas" and "forces" are unmanageable terms; it is hard to tell which is which or how they collide or when an "idea" becomes a "force."

I wrote eight or nine versions, with different titles—*The Bridge of History, Western Star, Patterns of Change, The Golden Fleece, The Web of Time.* I had to go back, because the roots of American experience lay in Europe; I could not deal with the English colonies without going back to Skakespeare and the Elizabethans, which made it necessary to go further back to the European Renaissance and then to the Middle Ages, which in turn imposed the need to explore the expansion of Europe, to travel with the explorers and colonizers of the Western Hemisphere.

Thus *The Hidden Heritage* is largely an examination of origins, and ends with the first settlement of Jamestown and New England. When I completed it in this form, I had to publish it without further ado, because I was about to serve a year's sentence in a federal penitentiary for "contempt of Congress." I need not comment on the irony of my conviction, as the culmination of a fifteen-year search for the creative values in my country's history. The publication of the book seemed to me an important affirmation of the meaning of the work. Entering prison in June, 1950, I left the manuscript with Dr. Philip Foner. I was not permitted to correspond with him. We had agreed that the manuscript must be heavily cut and reorganized, and he made editorial decisions without consulting me. There are no words that can adequately express my gratitude to him; the best tribute I can pay to Dr. Foner is to say that every change he made was exactly what I would have done myself.

When *The Hidden Heritage* appeared, the prison authorities allowed me to have one copy. It circulated among the inmates until it was worn out. Many who could not read wanted to thumb over the pages and stare at my picture on the back of the dust-jacket. It was important to them that one of *us* had his name and picture on a book. I watched others who were able to read, following each line with a finger, trying to understand the unfamiliar phrases.

It seemed to me that this was what the book was about. Yet it was not *their* heritage, and when I tried to explain it, they were puzzled and skeptical. The promise of justice seemed to them absurd. One man said, "Not in a million years." He said it softly, and others joined him. . . . "Not in a million years . . . Not in a million years."

If I had written the book after my stay in prison, it would be a different book. If I had finished it today, it would be even more different. Yet I believe today, more surely than ever in the past, that the basic thesis is sound.

2. *What Is Hidden?*

When I began *The Hidden Heritage* in 1936, there were only two books about the American past which made a serious impression on me—D. H. Lawrence's *Studies in Classic American Literature* and Vernon Louis Parrington's *Main Currents in American Thought*. They are astonishingly different, and in a sense they crystallize the thought of two decades. It is curious that an Englishman could distill the American mood of the early twenties better than any American writer—perhaps because it was an alien mood. Lawrence wrote of Melville:[1]

> Doom! Doom! Doom! Something seems to whisper it in the very dark trees of America. . . . Melville knew. He knew his race was doomed. His white soul doomed. His great white epoch doomed. Himself, doomed. The idealist, doomed. The spirit, doomed!

I felt premonitions of doom. I responded to Lawrence's Freudian approach, his concept of a psychic wound. But when disaster came, in the economic crash of 1929, there was commotion and anger, protest and organization. Parrington's work was still unfinished when he died in 1928, but his view of American history as a "conflict between man and the dollar, between democracy and property," was attuned to the temper of the thirties. Parrington revealed a conflict between democratic ideals and plutocratic practices which began in the colonies and became more violent and inescapable as the natiion grew and the system of power became more entrenched.

Yet I was disturbed: although Parrington speaks of "class struggle," his concept of human rights is intellectual and moral, a body of ideas derived from English and French sources. The integrity and ethical value of these ideas are strengthened by American thinkers. But Parrington does not relate the labor of thought to the labor and life-patterns of the people. Since Parrington does not discuss, and possibly does not know, the scope or effectiveness of popular movements, the conflict between man and the dollar is treated abstractly: to be more precise, man is an abstraction—the dollar is formidably real. Parrington was guided largely by the theory of economic determinism; like all determinisms, it led to a bleak conclusion. His final "Chapter in American Liberalism" proposes that we "put away all profitless romanticism and turn realist." But property is real: "If property is the master force in every society, one cannot understand American institutional development until one comes to understand the part property played in shaping the fundamental law." Parrington sees no counter-force. The future, he writes at the end of his last pages, "lies in the lap of the Gods."[2]

Another kind of realism was manifest when I read *Black Reconstruction,* by W. E. B. Du Bois. Here again there is a final summary:[3]

> In propaganda against the Negro since the emancipation in this land, we face one of the most stupendous efforts the world ever saw to discredit human beings, an effort involving universities, history, science, social life and religion. . . . In Africa, a black back runs red with the blood of the lash. . . . Flames of jealous murder sweep the earth.

The fires are still burning, in distant lands and in our smoldering ghettos. Du Bois accused scholars of perpetuating lies: "This is education in the nineteen hundred and thirty-fifth year of the Christ; this is modern and exact science; this is the university course in 'History 12.'"

It is unjust to place the whole blame on the university or to argue that History 12 is unchanged in 1968. There is a healthy turmoil in educational institutions, spates of disorder which question the whole system of order and power. Students and teachers begin to confront authority. The confrontation relates mainly to the way in which institutions of learning are organized and controlled; this is the immediate issue. But underlying and justifying the structure of power is a structure of ideas. Racism is built into the structure; our culture is not accidentally or occasionally racist; prejudice against the Negro is part of an over-all pattern of myth and misrepresentation.

The pattern, still unbroken, treats art and thought as the exclusive domain of artists and thinkers. Historical studies of what are loosely called "the Humanities" tend to exclude a considerable part of humanity. This can be defended on the ground that, while anthropology and sociology are concerned with masses of people, aesthetic and intellectual history is properly restricted to the small more or less privileged groups who have created works of art and promulgated ideas.

The people of the lower depths—slaves and serfs, peasants and poor farmers, laborers and industrial workers—have built civilizations, including our own. The dominant culture has celebrated their dreams in pageants and rites, and erected temples for their prayers. "The people" have originated folk arts and oral traditions. They have rebelled and fought their rulers. They have been defeated and sometimes they have conquered.

The problem which has received almost no attention is the extent and kind of influence which the lower classes, the people in limbo, exert on the dominant culture. We can readily grant that the most exploited people are not direct participants in the blessings of art or the wonder of books. Yet the people of the abyss are not literally separated from the exploiters: on the contrary, they are present and indispensable. For example, the Negro is so much and so threateningly a presence in the South that he has shaped and possibly dominated the consciousness of Southern whites. The continuing exploitation of the Negro has an incalculable effect on attitudes, ideas and arts in the Northern United States. But this is part of a whole web of exploitation in which we are all entangled.

No one in an exploitative society is truly ignorant of its character. The pretense of innocence is itself a symptom of moral sickness. But there is also danger of over-stressing or sentimentalizing the role of "the people." It is misleading to talk of "the power of the people," a phrase which presupposes victories that were not achieved and minimizes the ability of ruling classes to exploit the lower orders. There are several passages in *The Hidden Heritage* which err in this respect: I cannot defend the statement that "the people are the makers of their own history." The bloody realities of history were not made by the victims.

3. *Images and Symbols*

While the people did not make their history, it is truly *theirs:* civilization could not develop without their labor; wars could not be fought without their dying; Spartacus was not the first organizer of slaves to challenge an empire, and Nat Turner was not the last.

In guarding against idealization of the revolutionary role of slaves and peasants and workers, it is also necessary to avoid over-simplification of the way in which religion and philosophy and all the arts serve the dominant culture, creating myths and illusions which conceal or idealize the structure of power, and at the same time express the dreams and hopes of the masses. In performing this function the priest or thinker or artist experiences *within himself* the conflict between two realities—the barbarous reality of power and the human reality of aspiring and enduring humanity struggling to survive.

We know very little about this cultural conflict. It is a subtle and variable undercurrent of feeling, an elusive moral dilemma, in great works of art. I disassociate myself from so-called "Marxist" views of culture which insist on an "objective" or sociological interpretation of the arts. George Lukacs tries to avoid what he calls "vulgar sociology" by attributing to certain novelists the ability to encompass the whole "reality" of a given epoch, to reproduce the "complex and ramifying totality with historical faithfulness."[4]

Lukacs' theory leads to his incomprehensible admiration for Sir Walter Scott's Tory romanticism and colorless characterization. Even more misleading is Lukacs' artificial separation of historical fiction from other novels: *Madame Bovary* is dismissed because it is not "historical," but neither is Balzac's *Eugénie Grandet* or Dostoyevsky's *Crime and Punishment* or Tolstoy's *Anna Karenina,* to mention a few of the great nineteenth century novels which probe aspects of human experience, insoluble and tragic conflicts. *Totality* puts the writer in the position of a super-sociologist, who is above class conflict and free of its pressures; it is the lack of this freedom which tortures and drives the artist. Lukacs speaks of a "total picture of objective reality,"[5] "crystallizing the really typical,"[6] "reproducing reality realistically."[7] Again, we are told that "the author must honestly record, without fear or favor, everything he sees around him."[8]

How can an artist or a man be without fear? Has he no compassion, no tragic vision, no knowledge of the irony and misery of wasted lives? How is his sight blurred by tears? Is there nothing hidden in the history and belief of his time?

The artist works with specific materials and forms—the primary reality for the artist is the stuff with which he creates structures, paint and canvas, or chisel and stone, or musical sounds, or words, or bodies in movement. With these he endeavors to interpret realities which are not fully known, which impend and threaten, seen or imagined painfully and under emotional stress.

There is a growing literature devoted to the psychological processes that bring a work of art into being. These studies tend to ignore the reality of exploitation and class differences; they continue to hide what has always been hidden, in aesthetics as well as in historiography. But in spite of this limitation, the examination of the artist's function yields rewarding insights.

Herbert Read writes: "We must recognize, with the Marxists, the historic nature of human consciousness and, with certain psychologists, the ambiguous nature of this evolutionary acquisition. In terms of art, it gave us the symbol where hitherto there had been only the image." Read describes the co-existence of image and symbol as "an unresolved dialectical contradiction."[9] Modern theories of aesthetics rely on various formulations of the conflict between objective representation and symbolic expression, often placing major emphasis on the symbol.

It seems to me that Marxists are obligated to investigate the interaction of image and symbol, not as an abstract opposition, but as a means of dealing with reality. When reality is unbearable, it is transfigured or humanized or given mythic meaning by the symbol. The symbol (the work of art) becomes the mediator between Man and his intolerable condition, between the artist's restricted consciousness and his torn and bleeding conscience.

Hamlet is not a realistic image of the time. But the play symbolizes the desperate choices that confront modern Man. In the following pages, I describe Hamlet as "divided against himself, because there is no order or unity in the society in which he lives."[10] I find almost the same words in the introduction to a recent collection of specialized studies of *Identity and Anxiety:* "Central to Hamlet's character is the search for personal reality in a society where collective reality can no longer be taken for granted."[11]

I have tried to suggest the evolution of Shakespeare's thought until at last he imagines an island in the Western seas, ruled by the magic of science (Prospero), threatened by the monstrous figure of the servant-slave (Caliban). There is no wholeness here, but rather a structure of symbols, an "insubstantial pageant—" yet it speaks to us across the centuries.

When Melville, preparing to write *Moby Dick,* circled a passage in his copy of *The Tempest*—"O brave new world,"—and commented on its irony—"how terrible!"—he groped for the hidden roots of conflict between the half-mythic "New World" and its terrifying reality.[12]

4. *The Past Is Prelude*

This book is only a beginning: it comes to the threshold of American experience, and to the threshold of our divided and tortured consciousness. Our most elementary and precious symbols are words—

violence, democracy, brotherhood, power, peace. Each of these words involves a cruel contradiction; the myth is at war with reality, yet they are interlocked and inseparable.

We have imperfect images of reality, which are history; and a conglomeration of symbols, which are historiography. It is imperative to expand our consciousness, to decipher the symbols so that we are masters of our past and present. What is hidden in our history is the essence of it—the conflict between moral pretentions and the brutal exercise of power. Today the conflict threatens disaster. Either we learn to use our consciousness creatively or doom engulfs us.

In the middle of the nineteenth century, Melville's Ahab proclaimed his personal identity—"I'd strike the sun if it insulted me." But the swirling waters close over him and his ship and his crew. A symbol and a portent. The same cry of despair echoes through our contemporary culture. Robert Lowell ends his adaptation of *Prometheus Bound* with the defeat of the fire-bringer. . . . "All standing here, all descending, all standing here again, we will be stopped, blocked, frozen in our suffering."

But there are other voices. In the middle twenties, Scott Fitzgerald looked back to our past as a wondrous vanished dream. But it was a nightmare, a sojourn in Hell, for millions and millions, Negro and white. This new sense of the past began to emerge in the thirties. Thomas Wolfe imagined a new role for the artist: "He is the tongue of his unuttered brothers, he is the language of man's buried heart . . . the tongue that will express the buried treasures in the hearts of men, that *all* men know and that no man has a language for. . . ."[13] Shortly before his death in 1938, Wolfe spoke of our "self-destructive" past and our "undying and immortal" people, whose future is "as certain as the morning."[14]

Maxwell Geismar wrote of this last passage and this moment: "Standing thus at the threshold of the door, Wolfe was halted."[15] Can we cross the threshold?

JOHN HOWARD LAWSON

May 1, 1968

REFERENCES

1. D. H. Lawrence, *Studies in Classic American Literature,* New York, 1953, p. 173.
2. Vernon Louis Parrington, *Main Currents in American Thought,* Vollume III, New York, 1930, pp. 408-413.
3. W. E. B. Du Bois, *Black Reconstruction,* New York, 1935, pp. 727-728.
4. Georg Lukacs, *The Historical Novel,* Boston, 1963, p. 167.
5. *Ibid.,* p. 90.
6. *Ibid.,* p. 140.
7. *Ibid.,* p. 255.
8. Georg Lukacs, *Studies in European Realism,* New York, 1964, pp. 137-138.
9. Herbert Read, *The Philosophy of Modern Art,* Cleveland and New York, 1962, p. 10.
10. See below, p. 144.
11. *Identity and Anxiety,* edited by Maurice R. Stein, Arthur J. Vidich and David Manning White. Introductory essay by Stein and Vidich, Glencoe, Illinois, 1960, p. 17.
12. See below, p. 428.
13. Thomas Wolfe, *Of Time and the River,* New York, 1935, p. 551.
14. Thomas Wolfe, *You Can't Go Home Again,* New York, 1962, p. 669.
15. Maxwell Geismar, *Writers in Crisis,* New York, 1963, p. 234.

"If Man will strike, strike through the mask! How can the prisoner reach outside except by thrusting through the wall? . . . Talk not to me of blasphemy, Man, I'd strike the sun if it insulted me . . . Who's over me? Truth hath no confines."

Herman Melville, *Moby Dick*, 1851

"As the moon rose higher the inessential houses began to melt away until gradually I became aware of the old island here that flowered once for Dutch sailors' eyes. . . . For a transitory enchanted moment man must have held his breath in the presence of this continent, compelled into an aesthetic contemplation he neither understood nor desired, face to face for the last time in history with something commensurate to his capacity for wonder."

F. Scott Fitzgerald, *The Great Gatsby*, 1925

"I believe that we are lost here in America and that we shall be found. . . . I think the life which we have fashioned in America, and which has fashioned us—the forms we made, the cells that grow, the honeycomb that was created—was self-destructive in its nature, and must be destroyed. I think those forms are dying and must die, just as I know that America and the people in it are deathless, undying and immortal, and must live."

Thomas Wolfe, *You Can't Go Home Again*, 1938

TABLE OF CONTENTS

PART III
The Colonial Pattern
1492–1600

PART IV
The European Background of English Colonization
1593–1607

PART V
The European Background of English Colonization
1607–1618

PART VI

The English Colonies 1618–1628

PART I

The Decline of Catholic Power

1075–1434

1 : THE CATHEDRAL

In its physical appearance, the medieval town suggested a fortress, a city of God, an ant-heap of crowded humanity. The grim walls faced the countryside. The tangled thoroughfares made defense easier: "Crooked streets, salients, sudden openings, made hand-to-hand street fighting difficult for invaders who did not know the town." [1] The cathedral, the center of the city's life, flung sculptured beauty against the sky. Around its base, interwoven with its flying buttresses, crowded houses spawned poverty and disease. The house of God overshadowed the town. Indeed, it sometimes seems to overshadow the life of the Middle Ages, standing as an enduring monument in the stream of history, above the miseries that swirled around it.

What were the forces that built the cathedral? What was its relationship to the human mass that moved within sight of its towers?

The social theory on which Catholic power was based was formulated by St. Augustine at the beginning of the fifth century. However, Augustine did not invent a new philosophy, nor was his thought mainly derived from Christian sources. He transmitted and clarified the neo-Platonic mysticism which was widely accepted by the scholars and thinkers of the Roman world. The structure of the Augustinian *City of God* was already established in Plato's *Republic*.

Writing in the first half of the fourth century B.C., at a time when the Athenian society based on slave labor faced economic disintegration and moral bankruptcy, Plato proposed government by an elite class as the means of stabilizing the state. He posed the problem with admirable frankness. It was necessary, he said, to "devise one of those needful falsehoods . . . just one royal lie which may deceive the rulers, if that be possible, and at any rate the rest of the city." As part of the lie, the citizens were to be told that "their youth was a dream," their education and training "an appearance only." They were to believe that "they were formed and fed in the womb of the earth, where they themselves and their arms and appurtenances were manufactured." One need not stress the similarity between the Platonic idea and the Nazi myth of the Volk united by blood and rooted in the soil. In both cases, the aim is to combine the concept of brotherhood and defense of the country with obedience to the dominant class. The next passages in Plato's dialogue make the purpose clear:

> You had good reason, he said, to be ashamed of the lie you were going to tell.
>
> True, I replied, but there is more coming; I have only told you half. Citizens, we shall say to them in our tale, you are brothers, yet God has framed you differently. Some of you have the power of command, and in the composition of these he has mingled gold, wherefore also they have the greatest honor; others he has made of silver, to be auxiliaries; others again who are to be husbandmen and craftsmen he has composed of brass and iron. . . . And God proclaims as the first principle to the rulers, and above all else, that there is nothing which they should so anxiously guard, or of which they are to be such good guardians, as of the purity of the race. . . . For an oracle says that when a man of brass or iron guards the State, it will be destroyed.[2]

Early Christianity was the direct antithesis of the Platonic theory of an elite class. Developing in the crowded poverty of the cities of Asia minor, Christian doctrine found its first adherents among craftsmen and laborers, many of them slaves. Its revolutionary affirmation of human rights found practical implementation in the organization of the oppressed. Jesus lived at a period of intense social ferment throughout the Roman empire. There were gilds of workers in many places. Even on the sea of Galilee, fishermen and boatmen were members of a secret religious-economic association.[3] The great revolt of slaves led by Spartacus conquered most of southern Italy and threatened Rome in the century before Christ.[4]

The persecution of the Christians was regarded as a social necessity by the rulers of Rome; the spread of the doctrine nourished dangerous discontents and provided new and effective channels of organization for the lower classes. Pliny the Younger, who was governor of Bithynia in the early years of the second century, wrote to the emperor concerning the troublesome activity of Christians in forming *collegia* or gilds, and he told of torturing two maidservants in order to get information about these associations.

As Christianity developed, it gained adherents among well-to-do craftsmen and merchants, especially in the cities of the eastern Mediterranean; economic interest made it imperative for these classes to oppose the corrupt and oppressive power of the empire. In joining the Christian movement, they could restrain its more radical tendencies, and utilize its organized strength as a defense against imperial restrictions. The disintegration of the imperial system forced Constantine to abandon Rome and move his capital to Byzantium in order to control the eastern areas of trade. At the same time, he had to adopt Christianity, as the best means of maintaining his authority over the urban centers which were the key to the economic existence of the empire.

The adoption of Christianity as a state religion required a fundamental change in its class character and ideology. But this was not an easy task. It could not be accomplished without a violent conflict between the patrician class which ruled the empire and the majority who took Christianity literally as a gospel of equality and brotherhood. By the time of Augustine, the conflict had reached a stage of crisis, which threatened to disrupt the empire.

In his early years, Augustine was associated with the Manichaeian heresy, against which he thundered so furiously in his later controversial writings. In preaching the doctrine of original sin, the absolute corruption of man and the absolute authority of God, he laid the foundations of the hierarchical church-state, converting the brotherhood of the martyrs into a divinely ordained structure of power.

Augustine's polemics did not obliterate the heretical movements. The Circumcellions continued their program of agrarian communism in North Africa. Popular heresies retained their hold on the urban populations of the eastern Mediterranean. The seeds of the medieval revolt against the church were already planted in Augustine's time. But he was successful in consolidating the church as a disciplined organization. Behind the mystical phraseology of the *Confessions,* we can discern the practical outlines of the economic plan. In order to build the ecclesiastical edifice, it was essential that the church take craft production and trade out of private hands. Augustine showed the way, giving constant and detailed attention to the monastic movement. People of the lower classes flocked to the monasteries as the means of gaining subsistence by collective work. Augustine knew that these institutions could be troublesome unless they were brought under rigid discipline. But he saw the limitless possibilities of the system. As Max Beer observes, "the communists in the cloisters seemed to him less dangerous than those outside." [5]

Augustine's efforts bore fruit a century later, when St. Benedict founded the monastery at Monte Cassino in Italy, which became the headquarters of a growing economic organization. The Benedictine rule that artists "shall in all humility practice their arts" [6] made the monasteries centers for the development of craft industry and the concurrent diffusion of art forms, over the whole area from the Black Sea to Ireland. The impressive record of cultural contacts may be traced in architectural remains. Early religious edifices in Italy combined Roman traditions with Oriental and Saracenic influences. Intercourse between Rome and Constantinople brought the Byzantine decorations that appear in the Italian structures of the fifth and sixth centuries. These forms were carried—perhaps by St. Patrick—to the green hills of Ireland, where the sculptured crosses of the ninth and tenth centuries exhibit Byzantine symbols and geometrical designs.[7]

The same forms appear in Southern Russia, where the civilization of the Kiev Rus was enriched by contact with the Eastern Mediterranean and Europe. The mosaics and frescoes that decorate St. Sophia Cathedral at Kiev, started in 1037 and completed in 1049, show the Byzantine influence. The huge blocks of marble for the edifice came from the Marmora quarries in the suburbs of Constantinople, being transported across the Black Sea and up the Dnieper River to their destination.[8]

The western church, with headquarters at Rome, functioned as an international business enterprise, combining centralization of power with independent operation of subsidiary units to secure maximum efficiency and low-cost operation. Monasteries were engaged in agriculture, viniculture, and the raising of livestock, as well as in industrial production that required the services of large numbers of metal workers, wood-carvers, shoemakers, weavers, and furriers. The Christian fellowship did not preclude the employment of slaves and serfs. The militant doctrine of brotherhood was translated into the code of submission; the flesh must labor without complaint in order that the spirit might be free. In Charlemagne's time, priests were allowed two slaves, a man and a woman, and the laws provided that soothsayers and diviners were to be assigned to the church as slaves. The growth of feudalism reduced the general use of slave labor, but the church, enlarging its monastic enterprises, opposed emancipation. Bishops were forbidden to free slaves unless they repaid the value of human chattels out of their own funds.[9]

In short, the church—bishops, monasteries, orders, etc.—was a landlord like the feudal aristocracy, and in that role behaved in exactly the same way, exploiting free and slave labor to the same degree by the same means. Clergy and nobility upheld the same system.

Coulton, Sombart and other scholars have stressed the role of the Benedictines as the founders of modern capitalism.[10] Their historical contribution is more clearly defined if it is related to specific characteristics of the capitalist mode of production: the Benedictines were large-scale enterprisers and business organizers; they attempted to establish a monopoly of international trade and industry; they accumulated capital from the values created by unpaid labor. However, these tendencies toward capitalism were restricted by the Benedictine mode of production, utilizing the voluntary work of monks in conjunction with servile and slave labor. This "Utopian" form of intensive exploitation could exist only in a self-contained and rigidly disciplined network of communities. Karl Marx notes: "the production of commodities does not impose itself upon the whole society until wage-labour becomes its basis. And only then does it unfold all its powers."[11] The Benedictines could not impose their system on the whole society; even in the ninth and tenth centuries, the monastic exploitation of labor was restrictive and retrogressive in terms of the existent forces of production. These forces were concentrated in the towns, where artisans developed specialized skills and merchants introduced the rich and varied products of the more advanced civilizations of the eastern Mediterranean and the Mohammedan empire.

The origins of the medieval town are obscure. Many of the Mediterranean seaports had a continuous existence that antedated the Roman empire. In the interior, the urban centers that developed along the main arteries of trade were often built around monasteries and churches. Episcopal authority supplemented monastic rule. The bishop exercised jurisdiction over the inhabitants who were outside monastic discipline. In these cases, the whole population was "dependent more or less directly upon the church."[12] However, even when the town was born within the orbit of feudal or ecclesiastical authority, it manifested, almost from the moment of its birth, a tendency toward independent organization. The tendency, which reflected the aims and needs of merchants and craftsmen, was reinforced by social traditions that went far back into the past. The appearance of similar types of local government in widely separated areas suggests that urban organization may have been influenced by vestiges of the primitive agrarian society, with its common ownership of land and control by an assembly of freemen, which had formerly existed in many parts of Europe. Whatever the town's debt to the agricultural past, it seems to have owned a larger and more direct debt to the gild form of association.

Combinations of workers, artisans or traders are as old as civilization, and appear wherever handicraft production reaches a certain level of development. There is fragmentary, but valid, evidence that the gild tradition was maintained during the centuries that followed the disintegration of the Roman empire. The architects who built the early cathedrals seem to have been members of a gild which originated in the Roman period, preserving its secrets at its headquarters on Lake Como, and sending its members to undertake commissions in all parts of Christendom.[13] The occasional mention of gilds in the early Middle Ages shows that the term was applied to any association that sought to defend the economic interests of a class. A Carolingian capitulary issued in 884, at a time when the free peasantry was being reduced to serfdom, prohibited villeins from joining associations "vulgarly" called "gilds," to oppose "those who have despoiled them." A gild of knights existed in London in the days of King Canute, holding a grant of land at the east gate of the city.[14]

We do not find any record of the gild as a municipal association until the eleventh century. It then appeared as a fraternity of traders, the gild merchant, generally forming a part of the administrative machinery of the town.[15] But the manner in which it functioned at that time shows that it was not a novelty; it was rooted in the system of municipal organization that developed during the tenth century, and it emerged as a separate association when the interests of the wealthier merchants no longer corresponded to the interests of the whole body of traders and craftsmen.

The essential factor in the growth of the medieval town is the organized opposition of the townspeople to the dominance of the ecclesiastical and monastic system. The economic power of the church may be illustrated in the case of the Abbey of St. Riquier in northern France. In the ninth century, it commanded a town of 2,500 inhabitants, with artisans grouped in streets according to crafts, all working under a collective obligation to furnish wares to the abbey.[16] The social conditions under which these people labored encouraged organization, and made it inevitable that they would sooner or later throw off the clerical yoke.

The founding of the Abbey of Cluny in 910 inaugurated a vigorous drive on the part of the church to meet, and if possible eliminate, the increasing competition of craftsmen and traders operating outside the orbit of monastic power. Located in east central France, where commerce from Geneva met goods moving northward from Provence, Cluny became the headquarters of a network of 314 religious houses. The Cluniac reform of the Benedictine rule was intended to insure the more efficient practice of the arts and crafts, and tighter administrative control. Some of these establishments employed as many as 500 artisans. The leaders of the order tried to avoid a direct clash with civilian enterprise by locating most of their monasteries outside urban areas.[17]

In safeguarding the farflung business interests of the church, Cluny introduced the peace, or truce, of God, adapting the uniform law of the Roman empire, the *Pax Romana,* to the social confusion of feudal Europe. The peace was first proclaimed in 990 in southern and central France, in the area which was the nerve center of the Cluniac system. It proclaimed the right of sanctuary for persons on religious premises, protected classes engaged in useful work—clerics, pilgrims, merchants, women, peasants—from the violence of feudal warfare, and prohibited depredations against cattle or agricultural implements. All warfare was forbidden from noon on Saturday until Monday morning, and the period was gradually extended until it covered four days of the week.

The law was a tremendous boon to the whole population. But in asserting its right to enforce social order, the church proclaimed its continuing control over the whole economic life of society. This was the price which the nascent town was asked to pay for peace during at least a part of the week, protection on the roads and sanctuary in the churches. It may be argued that the law was mainly directed against the feudal barons. But the curb on indiscriminate warfare was welcomed by the more powerful lords, who were anxious to maintain order, to prevent local disputes and the unprofitable plunder of the countryside. The period of the Truce of God was characterized by intimate political cooperation between the rulers of Cluny and the Norman aristocracy.

Feudal and ecclesiastical lordship were two aspects of an interdependent system. There was no class demarcation between the church and the secular power. The military caste and the priestly caste came from the same families. The hierarchical organization of the church was duplicated in the feudal structure. Although investiture was a civil ceremony, the right of the lord to the homage, obedience and tribute of the vassal was mystically ordained, deriving its ultimate sanction from the church as the guardian of a divinely-appointed social order.

There was no disagreement between the lords of the land and the ecclesiastical power concerning the exploitation of the peasantry. The agricultural labor of the serf formed the productive base of feudalism. Difficulties between the two groups arose when craft production, and the trade that accompanied it, had reached a point of development which carried it beyond the control of the priesthood and its martial allies. The lords of the land needed the products of commerce and industry. They could conquer a town and exact tribute from its inhabitants. But the craftsman could not be made a serf, because he owned two inviolable properties, his skill and his tools. The merchant owned the goods he had traveled to acquire. If the craftsman's products or the merchant's wares were appropriated by force, the supply of commodities would be cut off.

From the viewpoint of the nobility, the monastic system was the safest and most efficacious method of organizing industry and commerce. The Cluniac reforms came at a time when the Dukes of Normandy were consolidating and extending their power. Their generosity in founding and supporting monasteries was motivated by their class interest.

But the class interest of the town could not be reconciled to the feudal-ecclesiastical alliance. Only a few years after the proclamation of the Truce of God in 990, we find the first recorded use of the word *burgher*. It occurs in France in 1007. The name refers to the growth of a separate district inhabited by traders outside the walled enceinte called the burg. The external area became known as the new burg, and its inhabitants were called burghers. The word appears at St.

Omer in Flanders in 1056, and at Huy in the Moselle region in 1066.[18]

We are accustomed to associate the burgher with sedentary pursuits, but he appears on the stage of history in armed revolt against the authority of the church. The most important eleventh century rising occurred at Milan in 1057. The city was strategically important as the main depot for Italian trade across the Alps. The insurrection was suppressed, but the spirit of independence moved over the mountain passes, touching off a series of uprisings, exploding in a chain reaction along the routes of trade: Cologne, 1074; Cambrai, 1076; St. Quentin, 1080; Beauvais, 1099; Noyon, 1108; Amiens, 1113; Laon, 1115.[19]

These urban disorders were accompanied by a revival of the heretical activities which had been outlawed with such vigor and apparent finality in the time of St. Augustine.

The urban disorders were an embryonic, but nonetheless serious, threat to the structure of church power. They were, in fact, the harbingers of the general European rebellion against sacerdotal authority that was to reach a climax in the Reformation. When Hildebrand became the head of the western church as Gregory VII in 1073, his most pressing task was the maintenance of ecclesiastical control over the expanding urban economy. He may not have understood the historical significance of the unrest in the towns, but he knew well enough that clerical absolutism rested on an economic base, and that the political authority of the church would be undermined if it lost its stranglehold on the economic life of Europe.

Above all, the pope had to control Milan, because it was the gateway to the Alpine passes, giving access to the Rhineland, Germany, Flanders and northern France. The situation in Milan, which was duplicated in other towns, was responsible for Gregory's attack on the financial and moral corruption of the clergy. In outlawing simony and concubinage, the Vatican assured the town population that it would be protected against the most notorious clerical abuses. On this basis, Gregory was able to win the support of the prosperous merchants, and detach them from their more militant followers.

In 1075, Pope Gregory VII issued a decree prohibiting lay investiture. It had been customary for kings or princes to invest church dignitaries with their fiefs and appurtenances. In prohibiting the intervention of secular rulers in ecclesiastical appointments, Gregory entered into the bitter controversy with Emperor Henry IV.

The investiture controversy was not conducted in a vacuum, nor did it relate to formal honors and prerogatives. It was about Milan, although, of course, the issue of lay investiture arose in many countries, not just in Italy. Control of the city had somewhat the same international importance that is attached today to control of the industrial Ruhr. When Henry IV invested his own candidate with the archbishopric of Milan in 1075, he signified his intention of bringing the whole system of western European trade under the aegis of the empire. Gregory could hardly have debated the question in moral or psychological terms. He had to stop the seizure of the most important trading center of Northern Italy. He therefore asserted the papal right to appoint the ruler of Milan. Henry replied by encouraging the Rhineland cities to throw off the episcopal authority. In return for imperial charters, the communes protected the emperor in his struggle with the pope.

Henry's course of action foreshadowed the future development of national power. In seeking more concentrated control, he made concessions to the cities. But the concentration of power in the hands of the emperor was objectionable to the feudal barons as well as to the Vatican. Therefore, the aid which he received from the cities in the investiture controversy was counterbalanced by baronial opposition. The revolt of the barons forced Henry to capitulate. Within a year, the pope seemed to have won an impressive victory; in January, 1077, Henry made the journey to Canossa in order to receive papal absolution. The report of the incident has been embroidered (in Gregory's own boastful and questionable account of the episode) with the picture of the penitent standing for three days barefoot in the snow of the courtyard before the pope would admit him to his presence. The unlikely story has become a potent myth, because it symbolizes so perfectly the concept of Catholic supremacy.

In reality, Canossa was not so much a symbol of Catholic supremacy (Catholicism as a doctrine was not being challenged) as of the Empire's failure to vindicate claims beyond its politico-economic power to realize. In any event, Henry's abasement was brief. Having gained the time he needed by the display at Canossa, he assembled an army and drove the pope out of Rome in 1084. Gregory died at Salerno in the following year.

At this point, the huge economic and political resources of the Cluniac system entered the dispute. Cluny represented the only power that could cope effectively either with the imperial opposition or the growing strength of the cities. The reality of power was recognized in the election of a French Cluniac pope as Urban II in 1088. Urban possessed the means to conduct the struggle that Gregory had initiated. But the battle between the Vatican and the empire was only an aspect of the larger economic problem. The church wanted to retain a virtual monopoly over the European economy. The commerce that flowed through the cities came from the rich marts of trade in the eastern Mediterranean. Conquest in the east was the answer to the problem of continental power.

In the following year, Urban II journeyed to France, proclaiming the Holy War at a gathering of nobles and clergymen at Clermont. The location of the meeting near the Abbey of Cluny is significant. The plan of eastern conquest was based on an alliance between Cluny and the feudal lords of Normandy, France and Provence. Normandy was at the height of its power, having conquered England in 1066. At the same time another group of Norman adventurers subjugated Sicily and secured a hold on Southern Italy.

The crusade was not a new idea. The knowledge that European supremacy depended on mastery of the Mediterranean basin was a political truism in the eleventh century. But the decision in 1095 to launch the great venture was determined by the general European crisis, the growth of the cities, and the papal conflict with the empire. In proclaiming the crusade, the pope extended The Truce of God throughout Europe. But the Roman imperium was to be reconstructed *without* the participation of the Holy Roman Emperor. The most powerful ruler in Christendom was excluded from the call for Christian unity.

The crusades offered a solution to another pressing problem. While an active and ambitious life developed in the cities, the feudal order showed signs of serious social disorganization. Constant warfare created an increasing dispossessed and migrant population. The serf's use of the land depended on the lord's military fortunes, and if the lord met with reverses, the peasant was driven from his home or forced to labor for a new master under heavier burdens. The low level of the economy deprived the wandering poor of any possibility of securing employment. Beggars crowded the roads and gravitated to the cities.

But it was not only the lower classes who suffered from the prevalent insecurity. Wars and shifting allegiances deprived many members of the lower nobility of their estates. As the more powerful nobles expanded their holdings, primarily by war but also by negotiation and marriage, they dispossessed the landholders who held fiefs from their enemies and replaced them with their own followers. These shifts were inherent in the personal bond between vassal and liege. The contract was vacated when the mutual obligations could no longer be performed.

The knights were the class that suffered most seriously from the results of the warfare in which they were the active participants. In order to maintain their social status, they had to give their services wherever there seemed to be a chance of gain. They suffered the vicissitudes of irregular employment. These professional warriors were described in the language of chivalry as *knights errant;* they were really de-classed aristocrats possessing nothing but a horse and a suit of armor, looking for the only kind of work for which they were fitted.

Social disorganization was aggravated by the plagues that swept the continent at frequent intervals. Lack of medical knowledge made it impossible to cope with the pestilence, which was nourished by poverty, lack of sanitation, and shifts of population. In 1094, one of the most virulent of the frequent epidemics spread across Europe from Flanders to Bohemia.

To the majority of the European population, many of them unemployed, driven from the land, consigned to beggary and starvation, the crusade offered an illusory hope. The church justified the proposed conquest of Jerusalem by a religious appeal which had convincing economic implications. The assurance that the march to the east would bring salvation, and assuage poverty and suffering, evoked a mass response. Before the military crusade could be organized, the Beggars' Crusade started eastward under the leadership of Peter the Hermit and Walter the Penniless. The description of the crusade as a march of beggars is somewhat misleading. It seems probable that it was made up very largely of knights, feudal retainers, and military adventurers looking for booty.[20] Nonetheless, it expressed the social sickness of the period.

The participation of lawless and criminal elements was probably responsible for the pogroms that accompanied the march through the Rhineland. The propaganda for a crusade was implicit encouragement to anti-Semitism. Hatred of the infidels who held the Holy Sepulchre was directed against their only European representatives, the Jews. All the social ills of Christendom, unemployment and plagues and human degradation, were explained by the failure to retain Christian possession of Palestine. Anger against the rich cities was real enough. But anti-Semitism served its perennial purpose in divorcing this anger from any connection with its actual causes, and deflecting it to an attack on the population of the ghettos. The story was the same in all the towns from Metz to Spires, Worms, Mayence, Treves, Cologne, Ratisbon. In many cases, the Jews offered armed resistance, and fought until they were overpowered. It is estimated that ten thousand were murdered.[21]

The attackers soon shared the fate of their victims. Many of the beggars were killed as they fought their way through Hungary. Those who reached Constantinople and crossed the Bosphorus were annihilated by the Seljukian Turks. The cohorts of chivalry that came later were the products of the same social system that produced the Beggars' Crusade. The men who slaughtered their way through the streets of Jerusalem in 1099 were the lumpen-aristocracy, the military fortune hunters who had at last found an enterprise worthy of their talents.

The crusades brought a great expansion of the European economy. But the effect was not at all what the first organizers of the Mediterranean adventure had intended. Instead of building a Catholic empire, the profits of the enterprise flowed to the cities. From the beginning, the armies had to rely upon the Italian seaports for transports and supplies. Venice and Genoa served the crusaders, in return for commercial privileges. The Fourth Crusade, managed by Venice and resulting in the capture and sack of Constantinople, was "a very orgy of capitalism,"[22] the means of founding immense fortunes. The chronicler Villehardouin wrote: "Never since the world was created, had so much booty been won in any city."[23] Venice celebrated the occasion by bringing the four bronze horses, originally carried from Rome to Constantinople by the emperor Constantine, back to Italy to grace the facade of St. Mark's.

The peregrinations of the bronze horses (they turned up six centuries later in Paris to honor Napoleon's victories) bring us back, after an excursion over centuries of history, to the building of cathedrals. We can now place the medieval churches in the social and economic setting that explains the apparent miracle of their construction.

The social disintegration of the crusading period supplied a migrant population that could be drafted for unskilled labor. The limited trading and craft economy of the towns had no means of utilizing this dangerous surplus of workers. But the priesthood was eager to use it, for its own profit, and as a means of securing a larger control over the life of the cities. Although the towns were born out of conflict with the church, the more substantial burghers were frightened by social unrest. They were not slow to learn the lesson of the Beggars' Crusade, and to realize that the anger deflected to the ghettos might on other occasions be directed against their homes and counting houses. Furthermore, the growth of craft industry brought the skilled artisans into conflict with the ruling mercantile group.

The clergy offered their services in solving these difficulties—if the people of wealth would pay the cost of cathedral building. The use of surplus manpower for this purpose accomplished three objectives: it established a measure of social control over the migrant unemployed; it diverted a goodly share of the profits of commerce and industry to the clergy; it conciliated many of the craft gilds by giving them the chance to use their skills at gild rates. The gain for the clergy was enormous, being the difference between the total amount collected and the cost of production with unskilled labor that was reduced virtually to a slave status.

The use of serfs or subject populations for unpaid work on building projects was common in the Middle Ages. The corvée, the requisition of labor as a feudal right, was frequently utilized by bishops or abbots for construction purposes.[24] Homeless wanderers had no legal status. They could be drafted on any terms decreed by the church or the community, and the bare cost of keeping them alive was regarded as alms rather than as wages.

The location and architecture of cathedrals follows the economic progress of European cities. The Romanesque and Byzantine architecture of the eleventh century testifies to the growing influence of the culture of the Middle East, as a result of Mediterranean trade. The profits of commerce were enhanced by the booty of war. Military victories were often the occasion for initiating new churches. The cathedral of Pisa was begun in 1063, after the Pisans had secured rich spoils from the capture of Palermo. The transformation of St. Mark's into the five-domed structure with which we are familiar was begun at about the same time as a by-product of Venetian maritime conquests.

As cathedral building moved westward to the transalpine centers of trade, the architecture changed from Romanesque to Gothic, indicating a break with Mediterranean influences and the rise of a distinctive urban culture in Germany, Flanders and northern France. The growth of the town's culture was not a peaceful process. The conflict of classes centered around the cathedral, often interrupting its construction, and bringing outbursts of anticlericalism that reflected the contradiction between the interest of the clergy and the necessities of urban development.

It is sometimes said that the cathedral refutes the Marxist thesis that human society is a system of productive relationships. The opponents of Marx argue that in an age of insecurity and want, man devoted prodigious energies to the building of a monument from which the majority derived no profit. The travail produced nothing tangible for man's subsistence. The profit was reverence.

Henry Adams took this view when he journeyed from Paris to Chartres in the first decade of the twentieth century. It seemed to him that there was a meaningful contrast between the industrial wonders displayed at the Paris Exposition in 1900 and the unworldly majesty of the cathedral.

> All the steam in the world could not, like the Virgin, build Chartres. . . . Symbol of energy, the Virgin had acted as the greatest force the Western world ever felt, and had drawn man's activities to herself more strongly than any other power, natural or supernatural, had ever done. . ." [25]

There can be no doubt that religious zeal was a factor in mobilizing the work force for the construction of churches. It was the ideological basis for the collection of funds and the drafting of labor. Contemporary records, written by ecclesiastics, tell of the participation of all classes, including members of the nobility, in the work at Chartres, in the middle years of the twelfth century. The labor of persons of the upper class, who are said to "have bowed their haughty necks to the yoke and harnessed themselves to carts like beasts of burden," [26] was of value in setting an example. But all that we know of medieval class relationships makes it unlikely that the huge blocks of stone that formed the base of the *Clocher Vieux* at Chartres, were transported by the hands of gentlefolk.

The work at Chartres was not brought to completion in a spirit of devotion. The twelfth century edifice was largely destroyed by fire in 1194, and a new building was begun on the old foundations. By this time, the alliance between the clergy and the merchants had aroused the opposition of craftsmen and small traders. The canons attempted to extend their ecclesiastical property, claiming jurisdiction over the district in which artisans lived. Work on the cathedral was interrupted by a riot, in which people burst into the cloister and besieged the dean's house. The people procured a heavy wagon, which was used as a battering ram to open the gates and sack the house. Another attack on the clergy occurred five years later.[27]

The relationship between cathedral construction and internal conflict involves many variations and complications. There were differences in each town. In Cologne, the levies imposed for building the cathedral and the profits derived from its construction occasioned a quarrel between the clergy and the dominant mercantile group, the Gild of the Rich. When the structure was still unfinished, in 1259, Archbishop Conrad of Nochstaden made common cause with the artisans, leading a rebellion that drove the merchants into exile. The craftsmen failed to gain the reforms for which they had hoped, and three years later they made a coalition with the merchants, who returned to their former dominant position with some concessions to the craft groups. The interaction between social conflict and cultural expression may be observed in the ornamentation of the Cologne edifice: here, as in many thirteenth century cathedrals, the greater power won by the crafts gives them a freedom and delicacy of sculptured detail, and a bold choice of humanist and anticlerical themes, that would have been inconceivable a century earlier.

Underlying all the local variations, we find a similar pattern of conflict in the life of the town: the growth of industry strengthened the crafts, bringing a struggle "between the Gild Merchant and the rising power of the handicraft organizations."[28] The merchants reinforced their ties with the church in order to maintain their position, while the crafts were in general opposed to ecclesiastical authority. For example, as cloth production developed in England, the textile town of Norwich witnessed a rising of craftsmen in which part of the cathedral was destroyed.[29]

In the industrial cities of Germany and Flanders, the growth of craft production was evidenced in architectural competition with the church. The towers of cloth-halls and gild-halls rose against the sky. The shift from cathedral construction to expenditures for civic or trade purposes left some of the Flemish churches unfinished. In many other cities in central and northern Europe, the merchants continued their successful alliance with the clergy, and mercantile wealth could be estimated by the height of the steeples. "Ulm, for instance, had planned a modest tower, but a sudden boom sent it into a magnificent uprush of lateral line." The churches, like the skyscrapers of an American city, were a visible graph of the town's business activity.[30]

In northern Italy, where economic progress was more rapid than in other areas, the municipal struggle was more intense, and involved the whole balance of European power. The conflict that began with the Milan revolt in 1057 was continued with the active intervention of the empire and the papacy. The tendency of the ruling merchants to form alliances with the clergy was followed on a larger scale in Italy. The Lombard League established economic and political ties with the papacy. In order to counteract the papal influence, the emperor sided with the landholding nobility. The Guelphs became the party of the church and the bourgeoisie, while the Ghibellines represented the aristocracy and the empire.

Guelph successes brought architectural changes. The humbling of the nobility was recorded in the urban skylines. The towers of castles, rising above the cities, constituted a military danger. In leveling down the power of the feudal barons, the towns leveled their dwellings. In Genoa in 1196, all towers were reduced to a maximum height of eighty feet. The massive stumps of towers can still be seen in Siena, Florence and other cities.[31] At the same time, the spires of churches celebrated the alliance—so fateful for Italian history—between the urban rulers and the power of Rome.

The cathedral as a cultural achievement cannot be divorced from the way in which it was built. It transcended the productive capacities of the time, involving a social organization of production and tapping reservoirs of labor-power that overshadowed the meager agrarian and handicraft economy of the age in much the same way that the massive edifice overshadowed the crowded streets around its base. It was not merely the symbol of religious power. It was the functional reality, the price that the population paid—in labor, in tribute, in submission—to the corporate authority of the church.

Sooner or later, the town had to fight back, because ecclesiastical control drained off its resources and obstructed its economic development. The struggle related to class conflicts within the town, and it often led to armed conflict in the market place shadowed by the cathedral's towers. The revolt against clerical domination, which was the first step toward urban independence, became the central factor in the town's later social history.

2 : HERESY

There is an instructive parallel between the beginnings of the Inquisition in the thirteenth century, and the methods employed in our "American century" to restrict the right of association and outlaw dangerous thoughts. Like modern investigating bodies, the Inquisition claimed to seek only information and exposure: men were stretched on the rack and broken on the wheel in order to find out what really went on in their minds.

Our present concern is not so much with similarities in inquisitorial procedures as with the cultural links between the heresies of the medieval period and the thought of our own time. The importance of the heretical sects has been largely unrecognized and their intellectual influence has been almost totally neglected.

We have noted that the opposition to the authoritarian church that appeared in Europe in the eleventh century had its origin in Asia Minor in the first centuries of the Christian era. The diffusion of similar beliefs and methods of organization over a long period of time and over the whole area from the Volga to the Atlantic is eloquent proof of the power of the people to assimilate and transmit ideas. It is also instructive, in analyzing the concept of a unified tradition of "western civilization," to observe that a major factor in releasing European thought from the bondage of ecclesiastical absolutism was the primitive religious communism of the lower classes. The people held to the literal meaning of the Bible statement concerning the followers of Jesus:

> All that believed were together, and had all things in common;

And sold their possessions and goods, and parted them to all men, as every man had need.

. . . . . .

Neither was there any among them that lacked: for as many as were possessors of lands or houses sold them, and brought the prices of the things that were sold. . . .[1]

Modern histories of the early Christian church are far from sympathetic to this simple account. For example, William Scott insists that "it is impossible to find a Christian sanction for Communism" in the biblical description of community of goods. According to Scott, "the believers all felt that the time was short before Christ would return, and, therefore, the practical concerns of life had little value beyond supplying the needs of all."[2]

We cannot guess what the believers may have thought. But eleven centuries later, the practice they had adopted was a powerful social force. The belief that all men have a right to share equally in the fruits of their common labor is the underlying principle that unites all the widely separated heretical sects. We find it carried into Russian by the Stignolniki, Molokani, and Dukhobortsi, and disseminated in Europe by the Patarenes, Cathars, Albigenses, Waldenses, Leonists, Arnoldists, Passangers, Communiati, Beghards, Brethren of the Common Lot, and other groups. Bulgaria was the focal point from which the movements that originated in Asia Minor spread through Russia and Europe. In the eighth century, the Bulgars defeated the Avars who held Hungary, and wrested from them a considerable part of the trade with Constantinople. As always, commerce in goods was accompanied by commerce in ideas. A wealthy mercantile class developed in Bulgaria, and the exploited classes, peasants, artisans and slaves, turned to the doctrine of Christian Brotherhood and of primitive Christian communism which the various monastic and mendicant orders at their inception claimed to be applying. In the middle of the tenth century, the priest Bogomil founded the sect which adopted his name, and the influence of the Bogomils spread rapidly to Serbia and Bosnia.[3] The heresies, which had been preserved in the east, seem to have reached Europe by way of Bulgaria and Dalmatia. The movement spread from Lombardy to the Rhine Valley and Alsace, as well as to southern France. Thirteen heretics were prosecuted at Orleans, in the heart of the Cluniac territory, in 1022. Eleven of them were given to the flames. They were accused of "free love," a frequent accusation against those who insisted on a literal adherence to the Christian ideal of brotherhood. The issue is more clearly defined in the trial of heretics at Arras in 1025: they were accused of asserting that life should be supported by manual labor, that love should be extended to comrades, and that sacraments and ceremonies do not give righteousness. In 1030, heretics who attacked the ecclesiastical mode of life and advocated community of earthly possessions, were investigated at Montforte in northern Italy. In 1052, a number of persons who opposed war were burnt at Goslar in northern Germany.[4]

The connection between these movements and the heresies that developed in Asia Minor in the early Christian era is well established. The rebellion in Milan in 1057 was organized by the Patarenes. The word is supposed to refer to the Pataria, or ragpickers' quarter, which was the center of the revolt, but the name is of eastern origin. Patarenes were found at an earlier date in Bosnia and Dalmatia.[5] The Milan rebels followed a hallowed tradition in denouncing the extravagance and immorality of the clergy, leading crowds to sack the houses of the priests.

The people who faced the rigors of ecclesiastical persecution in Europe were frequently called Bulgars, and were accused of spreading the "Bulgarian heresy." They were regarded as "foreign agents," owing allegiance to a "pope" who was said to reign in Bulgaria.

It is difficult to define the ideological influences in the complex social struggles of the twelfth century. But the demand for the abolition of wealth and the call for community of goods appeared in all the more militant conflicts. It inspired the serf revolts in the Venetian and Lombard plains, and caused frequent outbreaks in the Italian cities. In 1125, the Cathari seized control of Orvieto, and were suppressed by a counterrevolution. There were organizations of the Patarenes in Milan, Ferrar, Verona, Rimini, Florence, Prato, Piacenza, Treviso, Viterbo.[6]

The movement was strong in other parts of Europe, especially in France and Flanders. Theological arguments against heresy reveal its social objectives. The theologian Alanus wrote: "The Cathari say that the marriage tie is against the laws of nature, which ordain that all things should be in common." Everard de Bethune tried to discredit the heretics by a familiar argument: "Your communism is only a superficial one, a matter of words; only as agitators are you communists, for in reality there is no equality amongst you, many are rich, many poor."[7] The popular base of the movement is suggested in the use of the term *Populicani,* apparently from populus or people, which was applied to the heretics in northern France.[8]

While heresy spread among the lower classes, it was also the catalytic agent which changed the intellectual climate and brought new life to the universities. The process is illustrated in the careers of Peter Abelard and Arnold of Brescia. Abelard is better known for his passion for Heloise than for his contribution to rational knowledge. His intellectual courage and his emotional maturity were two aspects of an integrated personality. The "modern" quality of his thought and feeling reflected the environment in which he lived and worked. The crowded streets of Paris were astir with hope and anger. Abelard said of his students that

> They were calling for human and philosophical arguments, and insisting upon something intelligible, rather than mere words, saying that there had been more than enough of talk which the mind could not follow; that it was impossible to believe what was not understood in the first place; and that it was ridiculous for any one to set forth to others what neither he nor they could rationally conceive.[9]

Having written a book based on his lectures, Abelard was charged with heresy in 1121, forced to consign his writing to the flames, and to go into retirement. He remained in comparative obscurity for the next two decades. But Arnold of Brescia, who was probably one of Abelard's pupils and who was certainly influenced by his teachings, returned to Italy to translate theory into practice. We find him in his native city playing an important part in a rebellion against the local bishop. He arrived in Rome in 1145, two years after a popular revolt had driven the pope into exile. He became a leader of the revolutionary party, advocating the principles of the Patarenes, denouncing the clergy and calling for the rights of the poor.

After the pope's return in 1148, Arnold remained in the city, protected by his popularity. The church was not able to proceed against him until the arrival of Frederick Barbarossa in 1155. The German monarch had failed to take the key city of Milan, but he secured the friendship of Pope Hadrian IV by offering to assist him against the recalcitrant Roman populace. Arnold was tried and convicted, hung and then burnt, and his ashes thrown into the Tiber. The execution was a necessary preliminary to the coronation of Barbarossa as Holy

Roman Emperor, which was bitterly resented by the people. The pope performed the ceremony, but the emperor did not have a sufficiently large military force to crush the Italian opposition. He retired in the fall of 1155, to plan another campaign with a stronger army.

Meanwhile, the heresy hunters had brought Abelard to his death by less violent means. He was sixty-two when new and serious charges were brought against him. His relationship with Arnold of Brescia was regarded as proof of criminal intent. Abelard's enemies in France were so strong that his only hope lay in an appeal to Rome. He started on the long journey, but got only as far as Cluny. There, at the great center of the monastic system, the heart of the power that commanded conformity, the nonconformist broke down. He died shortly afterward.

St. Bernard, the embittered defender of orthodoxy, wrote of Abelard: "Nothing may hide from him in the depths of hell or in the heights above! The man is great in his own eyes—this scrutinizer of Majesty and fabricator of heresies." Bernard was even more vitriolic when he described "Arnold of Brescia, whose speech is honey and whose teaching poison, whom Brescia vomited forth, Rome abhorred, France repelled, Germany abominates, Italy will not receive . . ." [10]

Bernard's fury is a fairly reliable barometer of the growing importance of the heretical movement. Italy was in turmoil. In France and England, serfs attacked and sacked the monasteries. Military failures in Palestine emphasized the contrast between the promise of the crusades and their dismal outcome.

The myth that salvation lay in the east died slowly. But it was now so divorced from reality that any attempt to realize the myth resulted in fantastic conduct. Such was the frantic, pathetic hegira of children that began a "crusade" in 1204. Led by a shepherd boy named Stephen, an army of French children that is described by contemporary chronicles as numbering 30,000 reached Marseille. There is no reliable report of their fate. According to a somewhat doubtful version, two merchants offered them transportation without charge to Alexandria, where the youthful crusaders were sold as slaves to the Saracens. The Caliph himself is said to have bought 400 of them. The fate of the German contingent, led by a boy from Cologne named Nicholas, has the same uncertainty and presumption of tragedy. A commentator tells of 7,000 children moving along the Rhine Valley in an attempt to reach Genoa: "Many perished of hardships, hunger and thirst, in the forests and waste places; many were despoiled by the Lombards; many were sold into slavery in divers places." [11]

The children's crusade took place in the same year in which the knighthood of Europe, financed and guided by Venetian merchants, carried the holy war to Constantinople, looting the wealthy city on the Bosphorus in the name of Christ. The agony of the children and the rape of Constantinople were aspects of the moral crisis that gripped Europe. Pope Innocent III tried to meet the crisis by reasserting the imperial supremacy of the church. As in the case of Gregory VII, the actions of the papacy were determined by the actualities of class struggle.

For more than a hundred years, the church had attempted to stop the spread of heresy among the lower classes. But local trials and persecutions had not proved effective. Innocent III was able to force kings to bow before him, because the rising national monarchies needed ecclesiastical assistance in dealing with the classes opposed to the concentration of royal power. But the papacy could not retain the allegiance of kings if it could not maintain its hold on the people. In southern France, the Albigensian movement had attained such strength that it attracted princes and burghers as well as artisans and peasants. Its growth was due to the comparatively high level of economic development in Provence, and the oppressive control which Cluny exercised over the region. The Albigenses constituted an alliance of all the classes which sought freedom from ecclesiastical domination.

In 1207, the pope declared a "crusade" against the people of Provence. The call was answered by land hungry noblemen and adventurers, eager for the plunder of rich cities and the conquest of fertile lands. The liquidation of the Albigenses, and the destruction of the culture of Provence, was accomplished in blood and fire. But the difficulties of the task may be measured by the time it required. After several decades, heretics were still being tried; persons suspected of Albigensian sympathies were still being hunted like animals.

The attack on the Albigenses resulted in the wider diffusion of the outlawed doctrine. There seems to have been contact between the heretical groups in various parts of Europe. For example, eighty Waldenses, who were indicted at Strassburg at the time of the crusade in Provence, were accused of sending money to Pickhard, leader of the heretics in Milan, in order to support the cause there.[12]

The church supplemented the crusade in southern France by similar operations in other areas. In 1234, Hungarian crusaders followed the orders of the Vatican in an invasion of Bosnia to wipe out the heretics. The country was laid waste with fire and sword, and a series of bloody wars followed.[13]

While military measures were locally effective in destroying heresy by destroying people, the church had to find other means of dealing with the continuing opposition. The problem was met by two contradictory and interrelated developments of Catholic polity—the Inquisition and the Mendicant Orders.

The use of the death penalty was customary in dealing with heretics in the eleventh and twelfth centuries. But the legal definition of heresy as high treason against God was provided by Innocent III in order to justify the wholesale executions during the Albigensian campaign. In 1252, the papal bull, *Ad extirpanda,* formally approved the use of torture to obtain confessions.

Of greater cultural interest is the emergence of the mendicant orders. We have stressed the importance of monastic organization in the business activities of the church. But the monastic world had little contact with the people; its scholastic culture was removed from life, and its economic function aroused inevitable hostility. The spread of heresy required the church to find new methods of propaganda and organization to retain some hold on the common people and maintain its vested interests. Throughout history, we find that suppression of dissidence by force is accomplished by propaganda—which frequently includes the adoption, in a modified and "safe" form, of the ideas that are under attack.

The Franciscan order, however, was not organized for this specific purpose and its ideological origins can be traced to the Patarenes and similar sects. The work of St. Dominic, on the other hand, was planned and conducted as counterpropaganda against the heretics. In both cases, the Vatican recognized the value of the itinerant brotherhoods, and utilized them for its own ends.

The Saint of Assisi, exchanging his clothes for the rags of a beggar, ministering to a leper on the road, personified the gospel of love and poverty. Two years after the inauguration of the Albigensian crusade, the Vatican sanctioned the work of St. Francis, and began to guide the newly created fraternity along the lines that were already being followed, with some success, by St. Dominic in France. Operating under instructions from the pope, Dominic spent ten years journeying barefoot through Provence, preaching poverty and obedience. His labors coincided with the military offensive against the Albigenses. In 1215, the Bishop of Toulouse, reporting to the pope on the continuing contumacy of the Provençals, secured permission for the founding of the Dominican order.

Both orders grew rapidly. Among the Franciscans, the contradiction between the teachings of the founder and the purpose which the papacy wanted the movement to serve led to a struggle for control that began in 1220 with the withdrawal of St. Francis. The rule of poverty was relaxed, the so-called "zealots" who believed literally in a life of sacrifice and service were persecuted, and the "moderates" took over the direction of the order.

Both orders were split by ideological conflict—their function as organs of power was at war with the beliefs and services to which they were dedicated. The authoritarian culture was trying to prove its "universality" by adopting the faith of the people. But the popular beliefs, with the sinew and strength derived from their mass support, breached the walls of authority and invaded the citadels of power. The Franciscan and Dominican friars, as well as the white-robed Carmelites, played a vital, and at times revolutionary, role in linking the social thought of the people with the formal learning of monasteries and universities.

The political effects of the Albigensian movement can hardly be overestimated. Refugees scattered through Europe, appearing wherever the brotherhood of destitution rose to fight its oppressors. We shall examine these political consequences in a later chapter. For the present, it will be sufficient to note some of the major cultural influences that stemmed from Provence.

The most immediate result of the heresy hunt was its vitalizing effect on the imperial court of Frederick II in Sicily. The emperor, engaged in a life-and-death struggle with the Vatican, welcomed French poets and philosophers to his Sicilian domain. He was quick to see that he could gain a great political advantage by countering the papacy's fear of intellectual freedom with ostentatious patronage of art and reason. The terror in Provence made Frederick II the leader of European liberalism. Frederick II carried forward in thirteenth century Siciliy the Provençal school of poetry and music which was already important and widely influential.

From the folk ballads of Provençal troubadours came the religious songs or *laude,* and the dialogues in the vernacular, carried through Italy by Franciscan friars, and often sung by organized groups, *compagnie de' laudesi.* In stimulating the beginnings of a vernacular culture, the Provençal-Sicilian influence also invaded the University of Bologna, where a school of poets began to express their opposition to the dogmas of the church in obscure symbolic rhymes.[14] The obscurity, like that of many twentieth century poets, expressed the frustration of the intellectual, his inability to find any meaningful outlet for his social energies, his retreat from external pressures.

From these poetic beginnings, and from France by way of Sicily, came the eagleflight of Dante's mighty line. But before Dante could make the language of the people a more potent instrument than the Latin of the monasteries, the Augustinian church-philosophy had to be replaced by a more rational theory of man's life and destiny. The attack on scholasticism had been begun by Abelard, but the scholastic reasoning was his only weapon. The scholars who came from Provence to Sicily brought with them the advanced scientific knowledge of the Arab world, collated by Jewish scholars, and imported to southern France from Spain. Provence, in the years before the extirpation of the heretics, was a center of Jewish culture which was in close contact with the intellectual life of Spain. The speculations of Greco-Arabic scientists had been generalized and interpreted by Maimonides and other Jewish thinkers. These works, as well as some of the writings of Aristotle, were translated into Hebrew during the period of toleration in Provence.[15]

The cultural debt that Europe owed the Arabs went back over many centuries. The Mohammedan conquests of Spain and Sicily in the early Middle Ages transmitted ideas, inventions, commodities, from Africa and the Orient. Products that were to be carried across the Atlantic to create wealth in North America—rice, sugar, lemons, cotton—made their European debut in this way. The tempo of acculturation was hastened by the crusades. Arabic words, especially terms relating to seafaring, trade, techniques of navigation and warfare, became a part of European speech. Arabic numerals and the decimal system pointed to improved methods of accounting that would come into general use with the rise of capitalism.

While inventions and techniques had been imported from Africa for many centuries, there had been no transmission belt for science and philosophy. The cultural development of Provence gave Greco-Arabic thought a European base, which was now transferred to Sicily. With his northward moving armies, Frederick II carried the ideas that were an essential part of his war against the papacy.

The emperor sent money to the Jewish savant, Jacob Anatoli, and invited him from southern France to settle near the University of Naples in 1224. There he worked on Hebrew versions of the writings of the great Arabian freethinker, Averroes, and other studies of astronomy and logic. Frederick brought the Spanish encyclopedist, Judah ben Solomon Cohen, to Tuscany in 1247.[16] Another member of the imperial circle was Master Theodore, a Greek or Jewish scholar who was probably sent to the emperor by the Sultan of Egypt. Michael Scot, the Scotch mathematician, whose studies in Toledo prepared him for his service to the emperor, was employed in translating Aristotle from Arabic versions, as well as in making Latin transcripts of Averroes' commentaries.

The emperor's interest in science led him to travel around Italy with a menagerie. When the monks of St. Zeno at Verona entertained him in 1245, they had to provide hospitality for an elephant, five leopards, and twenty-four camels. Like other statesmen, Frederick wanted science to bring quick practical results. He demanded that the savants make prophecies concerning the outcome of battles.[17] This the scholars were unable to do, for their learning did not include knowledge of the social forces which shaped both their own speculations and the fate of their patron. The emperor could command the labors of wise men, but he could not command the Lombard communes. He miscalculated the strength of the cities; the defeat of Frederick's army besieging Parma in 1248 was so complete that it broke the imperial power: the crown of empire, captured by the people, was mockingly placed on the head of a hunchbacked beggar.

The humbling of the emperor, which led to his retirement and his death two years later, did not relieve the papacy from the pressure of secular opposition. New forces were stirring the people in the towns, troubling the serfs as they plowed the long furrows. In 1255, the castle of Canossa was stormed and destroyed by a mob. The scene that had occurred in the courtyard seemed like a forgotten myth; the Europe of the thirteenth century was no longer the Europe in which an emperor waited barefoot in the snow for a pope's absolution.

The last half of the century witnessed a decisive ideological battle. The defense of the scholastic dogma was undertaken by Thomas Aquinas. During the period of his most active work, from 1250 to his death in 1274, Aquinas traveled extensively, lecturing at Rome, Bologna, Naples and Paris, with occasional trips to England. Aquinas held that there is only one absolute truth, but he could no longer ignore the impact of Mohammedan science. He argued that the indivisible truth may be derived from two sources: revelation or human reason. The Arab contribution came in the second category, but Aquinas maintained that it must be brought within the range of Christian thought.

Henry Osborn Taylor calls Aquinas "the final exponent of scholasticism . . . The scholastic method was soon to be impugned and the scholastic universality broken." [18] The universality was already breached, as Aquinas admitted, by the knowledge imported from Spain and Africa. The final onslaught on the authoritarian dogma came from England, where the growth of nationalism, with its accompanying distrust of the papacy, provided a favorable political climate for the new philosophy. Greco-Arabic natural science was already established at Oxford in the middle years of the thirteenth century. Roger Bacon took up the tasks that had been indicated by his teacher, Robert Grosseteste. While Aquinas dealt in abstractions, Bacon's interest in experimental science accounts for the legends that linked his name with sorcery and witchcraft. His interest in techniques of warfare, probably stimulated by reports of the fiery missiles used by the Arabs, led to his discovery of a compound of saltpeter, charcoal and sulphur, in 1249.

As explosive as the invention of gunpowder was Bacon's application of his practical research to a general theory of knowledge. In 1271, in the *Compendium of Philosophic Studies,* he proclaimed the rule of reason, blamed the backwardness of science on the limitations of scholasticism, and pointed to the political connection between orthodoxy and the corruption of the clergy. He had moved too far ahead of his time. He was condemned by the Franciscan order, of which he was a member. As far as is known, the last two decades of his life were spent in prison. But the fight was continued by William of Ockham, who extended his influence from Oxford to Paris. The French university, formerly controlled by the Thomists, became another stronghold of the school of rationalism and experimental science.[19]

The way was now prepared for Wycliffe and Huss, and for the revolutionary movements of the next hundred years.

3 : THE PEOPLE AND THE MULTITUDE

IN HIS *History of Florence,* Machiavelli speaks of *the people* in the sense in which the word was always used in the communes: it refers to the small body of citizens who were entitled by birth, gild membership and property qualifications, to exercise the franchise. There is a distinction, therefore, between *il popolo* (the people) and *la plebe* (the multitude). The difference ought to be clear to Americans who are accustomed to reading editorials in which *the people* are identified with members of Chambers of Commerce, while industrial workers, Negroes and other minority groups, are *the multitude* that must be curbed in order to protect the welfare of *the people.*

Machiavelli divides the history of Florence into periods, defined by the nature of the major class conflict. The first era was characterized by the struggle between "factions of the nobility and the people." But in the fourteenth century, the old nobility was defeated and civic strife was motivated by "animosities between the citizens and the plebeians." [1] The epoch in which the change took place was the age of Dante, Boccaccio and Petrarch.

The *Divine Comedy,* Dante's vast critique of the society of his time, opens on Easter Day, 1300. The poet stood at the threshold of a new era, but he could not see the road that lay ahead. Balzac, writing the social history of the nineteenth century, acknowledged his debt to the Florentine poet by calling his work the *Comedie humaine.* The changed title may be regarded as the reflection of a cultural metamorphosis; the nineteenth century no longer regarded the drama of man as divinely ordained. Yet Balzac's view that men make their own history is already implicit in Dante's panorama of the medieval world. The title has a flavor of irony that becomes more disquieting as the poet's journey proceeds. For the regions traversed are the familiar Italian social landscape. The quest is not for other-worldliness, but for worth and honor in the world of men. The orthodox philosophy is tested and found wanting because it does not offer dignity or provide workable values.

There is a resemblance between Dante and Balzac in that both men combined a realistic appraisal of social evils with an acceptance of retrogressive social solutions. Balzac was morally outraged by the corruption of the nineteenth century bourgeoisie. At the dawn of the fourteenth century, Dante saw life degraded by the rising power of industry and finance. He compared the Venice arsenal, the largest industrial enterprise in Europe, then being enlarged with new docks and warehouses, to the fifth chasm of Hell, where public officers who had betrayed their trust lay expiating their sins in a pool of foul pitch.[2] He spoke of the city of Cahors as Sodom because it was the center of Italian banking operations in southern France.[3]

The church was in alliance with these economic interests. Dante, affected by the intellectual ferment of the time and the new interest in science and the humanities, rejected the pope's temporal authority. The poet's support of the empire may be attributed in very large measure to the patronage of art and reason inaugurated by Frederick II, and continued, intermittently and with less discrimination, by his successors.

Dante's anticlericalism, veiled in the *Divine Comedy,* is proclaimed in his most mature political statement, *De monarchia.* His support of the imperial cause, and of the aristocratic Ghibelline party, was based on his belief that the only way to answer the pope's claim to secular power lay in the establishment of a universal empire. His insistence on the pre-eminence of civil power looked forward to monarchial government. But Dante could not completely free his mind from the web of scholastic thought. As we have seen, dualism crept into Catholic doctrine in Thomas Aquinas' admission that the one absolute truth came from two sources—revelation and human reason. Dante carried the Thomist theory into the sphere of practical politics: let the church guard the spirit, while a world-monarchy guards the general welfare. In Dante's mind, the advancement of science was associated with the patronage that the German emperors had given to scholars. The transition from Aquinas to the new rationalism is evident in the poet's formulation of his plan:

> Ineffable Providence has thus designed two ends to be contemplated by man: first, the happiness of this life, which consists in the activity of his natural powers . . . and then the blessedness of life everlasting. . . . Wherefore a twofold directive agent was necessary to man, in accordance with the twofold end: the Supreme Pontiff to lead the human race to life eternal by means of revelation, and the Emperor to guide it to temporal felicity by means of philosophic instruction.[4]

Dante's argument was a defense of imperial intervention in Italian affairs. *De Monarchia* was written to justify the German invasion of Italy from 1310 to 1313. In opposing the Guelphs, Dante opposed the party of industry and commerce. Thus he cut himself off from the most creative social forces in the urban life of his time, and suffered the decree of exile from Florence that darkened his last years. Although he wrote in the common tongue of the people and was largely responsible for making the Florentine speech the national language of Italy, he could not link his dream of a rational society with the popular culture that was in flux and movement around him.

Dante visited Giotto at Padua in 1306, when the painter was preparing the murals for the church there, and the poet may have helped the artist with the masterplan of the work. The contradiction that both men faced as guardians of culture was embodied in the task on which Giotto was engaged. The work was paid for by Enrico Scovegni, son of a wealthy man whom Dante had consigned to the seventh circle of Hell. The panels make the life of Jesus a conflict of social forces: on one side the disciples with their halos, on the other the money-changers, defiling the temple, the time-serving priests, the men of power. The drama reaches a climax in Judas' kiss, with its tumult of soldiers and spears and torches. There was turmoil like this in the streets of Padua, and the hot disorder of the city's life was the reality which the painter and the poet tried to mirror in their art. But they sat in the chapel, precariously separated from the throng by the kindness of princes, by the patronage of money-changers who were now the givers of temples.

Although Giotto and Dante were friends, the artist was more closely bound to the interests and viewpoint of the urban bourgeoisie. The difference was indicative of the dissimilar services rendered by the writer and the painter. The business community had no crying need of literature, but was very much involved in the building of churches. Giotto painted memorial chapels for the Bardi and Peruzzi, and other Florentine bankers. It is probably through these connections that he secured an additional income in the woolen industry. He owned looms which he leased, at exorbitant rates, to poor artisans, getting as much as 100 and 120 percent of the worth of the loom as rent.[5]

Giotto, like Dante, hated the greed and cynicism of the business life in which he participated. He is said to have painted a fresco for the town of Arezzo, showing Florence in the guise of a highway robber, seizing moneybags, and even the clothes, from a shivering old man who personified Arezzo.[6]

Dante expressed the fears of the intellectual, his search for humane values, at a moment of transition, when darkness veiled the medieval social scene and only the first glimmering signs of a new day appeared in the sky. Dante hailed the false dawn of imperial power as the light of the future. He welcomed the separation of church and state as a means of liberating culture from the thralldom of the cloister. But the extent and violence of the social changes that were taking place, without benefit of emperor and pope, were beyond his understanding and alien to his spirit.

Dante died in 1321, two decades before the revolutionary outbreaks that stirred hopes of national unification throughout Italy. Machiavelli describes the shift in class relationships in Florence. The ranks of the plebeians were increased by the expansion of craft production, requiring many subordinate workers. Machiavelli displays a thoroughly "modern" viewpoint toward the plebeians: "It is their nature to delight in evil."[7]

It became increasingly difficult for the leading families to govern in the old way, and in 1342, the Duke of Athens, a demagogue and adventurer, took advantage of popular discontent to seize control of the city with the armed support of the plebeians. He had to conciliate the classes that brought him to power, and (to continue Machiavelli's story) "he began to confer benefits and advantages on the lowest orders," and "the people were filled with indignation."

The Duke tried to establish a military dictatorship, and force the rich to support him by a heavy program of taxation. But "three distinct conspiracies were formed; one of the great; another of the people, and the third of the working classes." On July 26, 1343, the party of the people, forming a temporary alliance with members of the nobility, rebelled, and the Duke found that all were against him except "the butchers, with others, the lowest of the plebeians, who met armed in the piazza in his favor."[8] The Duke was driven from the city, but disorder continued. The plebeians had proved they were a force to be reckoned with, and both the nobility and the bourgeoisie tried to use them for their own purposes. Machiavelli tells how the nobility thought they could overcome the people, "seeing that the lowest of the plebeians were at enmity with them."

In 1347, during a period of famine and semistarvation, the wealthy banker, Andrea Strozzi, bought up a great quantity of grain, and attempted to win the allegiance of the lower classes by selling it to them at cut-rate prices. Machiavelli estimates that four thousand people gathered to buy the grain, but they were not willing to serve Strozzi's political ambitions. A great street demonstration led to attacks on the houses of the rich—especially of the old banking families. Their homes sacked and destroyed, the Bardi and other financiers were forced to flee.[9]

As a result, the leaders of the major gilds found it necessary to grant concessions to the minor crafts. The admission of the less privileged artisans to a share in the government was the only way to wean them away from the mass of unskilled workers. The members of the smaller gilds attained a status that entitled them to be classified as *people*. But it was also necessary to define the class differences among the *people:* a distinction developed between *primo populo* and *secondo populo* (first and second people), *populo grasso* and *populo minuto* (fat people and small people).

The struggle in Florence stimulated a national movement that emerged in its most definitive form in Rome, where Cola di Rienzi proclaimed the republic in 1347, relying on Florentine support, and calling on all the cities of Italy to unite. Attacked by the wealthy patricians and threatened by the pope, Rienzi fled after six months. But *the people,* and especially the *populo minuto* of the minor gilds, secured a larger share in the government. Rienzi tried to cash in on his former popularity in 1354, when he returned to Rome with the blessing of the pope, and endeavored to institute a tyrannical regime. Less than three months later, he was killed by a mob, and the gild organizations, enforcing their will through the *banderesi,* the people's militia, retained control of the city.

The pattern of class conflict in the Italian towns was duplicated in other parts of Europe. The closest approximation to the Italian events is to be found in the cloth-producing cities of Flanders. Appealing to national aspirations and to the discontent of artisans and laborers,

Jacque d'Arteveld led a successful revolution in 1337. D'Arteveld was a member of a rich family of Ghent, and wool was far more important than freedom in his defense of Flemish independence from the feudal domination of France. His mercantile dictatorship, established with English backing, strengthened the wealthy burghers who controlled the textile industry; it increased the exploitation of the lower classes. The betrayal of the national interest, inherent in d'Arteveld's position, was admitted in 1345 when he proposed that the Prince of Wales be acknowledged as master of the Low Countries. He was killed by an angry crowd in the streets of Ghent. The internal struggle in the towns was too sharp to permit effective unity in the fight against feudal control. The Count of Flanders, supported by France, reasserted his lordship.

These disturbances occurred as the Black Death descended upon Europe. The internationalism of disease was an even more compelling cultural force than the spread of commerce. Starting in China in a period of drought and famine in 1333, the plague proved that even in the fourteenth century man's world was one. The plague traveled as slowly as the trade of the time: it spread across Asia and eastward, reaching the island of Cyprus in 1347, then moving over the Mediterranean routes to Southern France and Italy. It came to Florence in the middle of April, 1348. It crossed the Alpine passes to the Rhineland, and traveled to England by sea, appearing at seaport towns in Dorsetshire in August. In 1349, it reached Poland, and then entered Russia. English maritime commerce carried it to Scandinavia, Iceland and Greenland.[10]

The disease, probably a form of bubonic plague, is said to have destroyed a third of the population of Europe. Men cried out, like Job, against God's iron judgment. But the plague was a climax to the long train of epidemics and famines that preceded it; it was transmitted like other commodities, and it flourished on the poverty and malnutrition that made every city a breeding place of infection.

The growing separation between the culture of the bourgeoisie and the common life on which the cultural superstructure rested is illustrated in Boccaccio's *Decameron*. The black plague forms the social framework of the stories. The opening scenes, in which the effects of the disease in Florence are described, introduce a realism that had seldom been achieved in literature. But the realistic framework cannot enter into the content of the tales. It was impossible for Boccaccio to even think of bridging the gap between the terror in Florence and the well-to-do people who took refuge in a country house on the road to Fiesole in order to avoid the pestilence. The use of such a device to bring people together under unusual circumstances is a commonplace of fiction. Its significance lies in the detachment of the internal situation from the larger system of events. There was no escape from the plague for people trapped in Florentine slums. But Boccaccio's storytellers had escaped. The plague was a frame of reference only in the sense that it had been avoided; it was a social issue that had been left behind, and could have no place in the content of the *novelle*.

A generation separated Boccaccio from Dante. Both were members of the upper middle class. But the change that had taken place in Florence is reflected in the moral perspective, and the *schema* of art and ethics, in the younger writer's work. Boccaccio was in Florence during the rule of the Duke of Athens. He was thirty when the Duke was driven from the city. The bourgeoisie emerged from the conflict, shaken by the plebeian opposition, but with a much clearer class viewpoint. The urban life had become urbane, with elements of the aristocratic tradition, but with a marked disrespect for the old scholastic and ecclesiastical values. The *Decameron* is an escape and an affirmation: Boccaccio, like the people who tell the stories, is in flight from the horror, the unbearable social lesson of the disease. But he is realistic in appraising the life that he knows, with its preoccupation with love and money, business fraud and extramarital intrigue.

Boccaccio wrote for an audience that was enlarged by an important contribution to technology. Paper was a gift from China. It was one of the many invaluable offerings to European culture that was transmitted from the Orient by the Arabs, and carried to Spain and Sicily. Paper traveled northward through thirteenth century Italy with rational thought, Greco-Arabian science, songs in the vernacular. The earliest watermarks are to be found on paper manufactured at Fabriano, in the province of Ancona, in 1293. By Boccaccio's time, Italian craftsmen had carried their skill across the Alps, a factory being founded at Mainz in 1320, followed by similar enterprises at Cologne, Nuremberg, Ratisbon, and Augsberg. The substitution of paper for vellum was a mortal blow to the exclusive culture of the monastery, with its laboriously illuminated manuscripts. Boccaccio's stories, deriding the clergy, were copied and bound by hand, and widely circulated throughout Europe.

Painting was also becoming a profitable business. One of the results of the civic reorganization after the grain riots and the Black Death was the separation of the artists from the old gild of architects: the Florentine painters formed their own gild in 1349, and the Siena school followed suit in 1355.

Boccaccio's friend, Petrarch, who was his elder by eleven years, was more deeply involved in politics and more directly concerned with social issues. As poet and philosopher, Petrarch was in a sense Dante's inheritor and executor. But he had discarded Dante's illusions, and stood forth as the champion of the bourgeois culture that had matured in a generation. The shift took place in Petrarch's family. His father, a Florentine notary, shared Dante's enthusiasm for the cause of the empire and the nobility, and was condemned, at the same time as the poet, to lifelong exile. But the son identified himself with the fight for municipal and national independence. He was moved to enthusiasm by the Roman revolution led by Cola di Rienzi in 1347, regarding the Roman Republic as the first step toward the establishment of an Italian nation.

The uncertainties and contradictions in Petrarch's later political views reflected the rapid shifts in power that belied his dream of Italian unity. He was trying to find the path by which the bourgeoisie could create a truly national culture: the search motivated his passionate interest in the Greek and Roman classics; it led to his belief that Italy's economic destiny must be fulfilled in the Mediterranean, didactically expounded in the Latin poem, *Africa.* To Petrarch, the Black Death was primarily a challenge to medical science. The plague, which took his beloved Laura and his son, Giovanni, occasioned his bitter treatise, *Upon his own Ignorance and that of many others.*

Boccaccio expressed the social cynicism of the new urban culture. Petrarch proclaimed its aspirations. The work of each writer compliments and explains the work of the other. Boccaccio's characters, engrossed in the pursuit of money and love, had no answer to Petrarch's indictment of the ignorance that permitted disease to wipe out a large part of the population.

4 : THE FISHMONGER'S CUTLASS

The rise of nationalism in France and England is seldom associated with the Black Death and the great social struggles that arose from it.

It is generally assumed that the English nation, with its unified will and unique liberties, was born with the signing of *Magna Carta* in 1215. The charter myth ignores the fact that the document offered no new rights to the approximately three-quarters of the English people who were serfs or cotters, and that it was in the main a reaffirmation of traditional feudal privileges, which had been recognized in somewhat similar terms in the accession charter of Henry I a century earlier. The settlement of the quarrel between the crown and the barons on terms dictated by the barons was on the whole retrogressive. Charles A. Beard and Mary Beard speak of "the anarchic restraints of Magna Carta in the interest of inherited feudal privileges." [1]

But the charter myth is an important part of our contemporary folklore. In the Freedom Train that toured the United States in 1947, the sacred charter, imported from England for the occasion, lay in a glass case beside the Declaration of Independence. The unseemly association of the two documents suggests the larger meaning of the *Magna Carta* myth. It supports the belief that American culture is exclusively Anglo-Saxon in its origin. The concept links the United States and Britain as the historically sanctioned guardians of "western civilization." *Magna Carta* is treated as the legal statement of a unified system of culture that has been transferred intact across the Atlantic.

English life in the thirteenth and fourteenth century was energized and transformed by European influences. As in Italy and other parts of Europe, the conflict of classes shaped the emergent elements of a national culture, and class relationships determined the course of national development.

Magna Carta registered the fact that, at the beginning of the thirteenth century, the baronial power was strong enough to wring vital concessions from the crown. But by the end of the century, the king had won enough support, and financial aid, from the burghers of the cities, to force baronial recognition of the national state. Parliament was the means by which centralization was accomplished. An assembly in which the burghers played a subordinate, but nonetheless official and recognized role, legalized the collection of the funds needed to administer the state. Parliamentary sessions were regularized in England in the last decade of the thirteenth century, and shortly afterward the Estates General met in France. Taxation was the mother of representation.

Financial necessity also demanded that ecclesiastical power bow to the royal will. The Knights Templars had become a banking monopoly that held all Europe in thrall. In France, Philip the Fair struck the Knights without warning, ordering all representatives of the order arrested on the night of October 13, 1307. The English king followed suit in January, 1308. A royal order stated that "all Temple lands came as escheats into the hands of the king and other lords of whom these lands were held."[2] The profit was a tantalizing preview of the gain that would come from the seizure of all church holdings a little more than a century later.

The dawn of nationalism brought no light of tolerance to the Jewish ghettos. Anti-Semitism had been encouraged, by state and church, for the purpose of offering a "safe" outlet for explosive discontents. At the same time, the crown was able to exact heavy payments from the Jews in return for the partial protection that it gave them. But the impoverishment of the Jews tended to reduce their value as a source of revenue. The king's money needs could be met more satisfactorily by the total seizure of Jewish possessions. The English order of expulsion in 1290 brought all Jewish dwellings as escheats to the crown. But the rentals on this property amounted only to 130 pounds; the Jewish debts collected by the king brought him 9,000 pounds. For this, 16,000 Jews were driven across the channel, robbed by the captains who transported them, drowned in unseaworthy vessels. Those who sought refuge in France found that they must again drink the cup of suffering to the dregs. The edict of expulsion, with the seizure of all property, real and personal, came in 1306. 100,000 Jews were whipped and scourged from the land where many of them had lived for a thousand years.[3]

While all these factors are significant in the rise of nationalism, the mass of the people formed the economic and cultural base on which the nation was built. Like the city, *the nation is the people.* The struggle for subsistence is the driving force of national development.

We have seen how the expansion of craft industry, accompanied by increased exploitation of the lower order of artisans and unskilled laborers, brought misery and revolutionary protest among the lower classes of the Italian cities. A similar process, with a revolutionary ferment, took place in England, but it was accompanied by the more powerful movement of the rural population against feudal exploitation. The peasant movement did not attain as much strength in Italy because the early growth of the towns enabled them to dominate the surrounding countryside and introduce commercial methods in agricultural production.

In England there was a tendency during the first half of the fourteenth century to substitute wages for the old master-and-serf relationship. But the change did not bring any automatic amelioration in the peasant's status. He became a copyholder, occupying the land at the lord's will, "by the custom of the manor." His legal rights were almost nonexistent and the money that was paid him in wages went back to the lord in the form of rent.

The peasant's fight for higher wages created a bond of interest with the poorer classes of the town. Cloth production, with the employment of peasant families in domestic spinning and weaving, increased the mutuality of interest.

The Black Death introduced a wage struggle in England that involved both rural and town labor: the conflict extended over three decades, culminating in the Wat Tyler rebellion in 1381. The period witnessed the beginnings of a national literature in the work of John Wycliffe, Geoffrey Chaucer and William Langland.

Aside from the misery that it caused, the Black Death reduced the population so drastically that it created a labor scarcity. Therefore artisans and laborers were able to get higher pay. In 1349, Edward III issued a proclamation stating that "many seeing the necessity of masters and greater scarcity of servants will not serve until they get excessive wages." Wages were fixed at the rate prevailing in 1347, with severe penalties for giving or receiving higher wages or refusing to work. The effect on the crafts is indicated by the specific inclusion of such trades as saddlers, skinners, tailors, smiths, carpenters and others. The law was strengthened by the Statute of Laborers, adopted by parliament in 1351, embodying the same provisions, with more severe penalties.[4]

The rising of the Jacquerie in France in 1358 was a portent to the rulers of England. The French rebellion was especially frightening, because it involved an alliance between the peasants and the people of Paris. The English lords who were fighting a war against France suspended hostilities in order to join in suppressing the revolt, and the victors revenged themselves in the traditional manner. A minor incident was the burning of 300 peasants trapped in a monastery.

The British government decided to forestall the necessity of such violence by repressive measures which were almost as brutal. In 1360, it was decreed that laborers or artificers who asked wages above the legal minimum were to be imprisoned without bail; those who broke agreements and escaped were to be outlawed, and if caught they were to be branded with F "for their falsity." Towns where runaways were harboured were to be fined ten pounds.[5]

Since it was clearly the purpose of this legislation to reduce the worker to the old bondage, landlords concluded that their most logical course lay in a return to serfdom. The advantages were a matter of simple arithmetic. The Lord of Great Tew, for example, calculated that he had once received 2,000 days of service in winter and 500 days in summer. Commutation had been agreed upon at the rate of a half-penny per day in winter and a penny in summer. His lordship now found that each laborer demanded three pence a day in winter, and more in the busy season.[6]

But neither legal restrictions nor the pressures of the landlords—who were also the Justices of the Peace vested with the power of the law—could break the mass resistance. The militancy of the peasants grew out of their desperate need; but it was given form, a structure of belief and organization, by the experience of the European struggle. The inspiration came from the heretical sects, from Italy and Provence, by way of northern France and Flanders. The Albigensian influence can be traced through more than a century of agitation and armed conflict, from the French Shepherds' Crusade in 1251 (it was really a wage movement and not a crusade at all), through the serf uprisings in

Frisia and Flanders, to the Jacquerie. French shepherds crossed over to England in 1251. English soldiers in France and the Low Countries came in contact with radical activity. Flemish weavers bringing their skills to English cloth production brought their ideas with them. The weavers were accompanied by Lollard priests, the funeral-chanters and itinerant preachers who had been trained in underground work.

The illegal organization known as the Great Society spread from its headquarters in the textile town of Norwich through the eastern and midland counties. The Lollards served as walking delegates from the Great Society. They could travel with comparative freedom, distributing propaganda, holding meetings, collecting funds.

The Great Society's economic program had as its political base the doctrine of equality and Christian brotherhood. The doctrine attacked ecclesiastical authority as the bulwark of entrenched privilege. The church was the peasant's implacable enemy; it pursued him during his life and claimed his dearest possessions after his death. "It was held to be so improbable that a peasant lived without having defrauded the Church of tithe that, at his death, the church felt secure in claiming compensation." The seizure often included the bed and bedclothes of the deceased.[7]

Anger against ecclesiastical authority was shared by the lower clergy. Priests were not exempt from the operation of maximum wage laws, which were applied with bureaucratic severity by their superiors. The majority of priests were somewhat in the position of government employees in our own day, but without even the limited means of protest that government employees are able to utilize. The restrictive measures to which they were subjected account for the participation of so many of them in the Great Society.[8]

In their own way and for their own reasons, wealthy London burghers and an important part of the nobility opposed the church, and the crown was not averse to utilizing their resentment in order to strengthen the monarchial power. Thus the Great Society represented the most radical wing of an anticlerical movement that included a considerable part of the nation and embodied national aspirations. The interplay between the culture of the people and the class interests of privileged groups found its most profound expression in the work of John Wycliffe. The attack on scholasticism begun by Roger Bacon and continued at Oxford was politically useful to the crown in justifying the seizure of the wealth of the Knights Templar. In pressing forward to a more advanced position, Wycliffe had the intellectual support of Oxford University. His political patronage came from John of Gaunt and other influential men who felt that the nation's development—and their own interests—would be served by further seizure of church possessions. In *De Civilio Dominio* in 1376, Wycliffe argued that the clergy had no right to hold property or exert control over civil affairs.

Although he was backed by John of Gaunt, Wycliffe's strongest backing came from a section of the London bourgeoisie. He spoke for the men who controlled the cloth trade and other well-established gilds. These leaders of the wealthy fraternities were traditionally anticlerical. They had fought the church in securing their charters. They were disturbed by the ferment among the lower classes in London, but they believed that discontent could be curbed by rational measures of reform, intelligent leadership and strict discipline. The Presbyterian concept of government as the stewardship of the elect appears in an embryonic form in their political activities.

In spite of their wealth, these men did not enjoy uninterrupted control of the municipal government. But in 1376, they undertook a reform of the civic constitution, establishing a Common Council elected not from the wards but from the companies. There is an evident connection between this change in the city's government and the appearance of Wycliffe's tract in the same year. Wycliffe's declaration that all right to wealth and authority depend on the righteousness of the individual could be interpreted as a mandate to the righteous burghers to pursue their program of reform.

Opposition to the reform party came from a group of equally important and more adventursome capitalists. These were the victualers, whose profit was derived to a considerable extent from long sea voyages. The grocers imported wines from France and spices from the Orient by way of Italy. The fishmongers depended on the fleets that sailed to Iceland. The victualers had profitable dealings with religious establishments. They were astute politicians. They were less concerned about the problem of cheap labor than the old industrial gilds. Although they mulcted the poor by raising food prices, they were able to pose as the "party of the people" fighting for small craftsmen and journeymen against the masters of industry.[9]

The first step taken by the Reform Party when it attained control of the city was to strike at the victualers by revising the ordinances concerning the sale of food. It was at this point that William Walworth, who was to play such a fateful role in the climax of the Wat Tyler rebellion, entered the political arena as the leader of the victualers. Walworth was a dealer in stockfish, the cod taken in the winter in Iceland and hung in the cold air to be cured without the use of salt, forming a hard rod that sold for about half the price of salt fish. The man whose wealth came from selling fish to the poor posed as their champion. The fishmonger's position was no more contradictory than that of Wycliffe, whose revolutionary social convictions became the pawn of party strife in London.

The charge of heresy against Wycliffe was a means of discrediting the reform administration. He was called to trial before the Bishop of London in St. Paul's on February 19, 1377. The affair, as Unwin observes, "was the signal for an outburst of party feeling in the city which had little relation to the religious issue, but was more concerned with the price of fish." As Wycliffe's supporters entered the church, "they had to pass through an angry crowd of orthodox fishmongers." [10] Citizens of both parties stormed the church and prevented the trial from taking place. But the result was favorable to the victualers, who were able to win a sweeping victory in the municipal elections a few weeks later. No less than eight of the new aldermen were fishmongers. Walworth and his friends expelled their opponents from the Common Council. Their popularity did not last, but a loan of £10,000 to the king gave them the royal assistance which enabled them to maintain their power.

The four years of the victualers' London rule were years of increasing corruption in the city and national government. There were higher food prices and oppressive taxation. Wycliffe's abortive trial, which opened the period of revolutionary tension, inaugurated his public role as a popular leader. His social thought continued to exhibit the dualism that was inherent in its class base. His theory was equalitarian: all things must be held in common by the righteous. Yet he could not accept the practical implications of his theory. "The fiend," he wrote, "moveth some men to say that Christian men should not be servants. . . .[11]

It was almost as if he had been caught up in the crowd that interrupted his trial and carried from the ecclesiastical court to a battlefield where the sword of truth was placed in his hand. Enemies converged around him, and he had to strike out with the shining blade. Condemned by a papal bull, deserted by his more timid and highly placed adherents, Wycliffe had to carry his case to the only court where he was sure of a hearing. In 1378, he began to write pamphlets in the vernacular, and to call on his faithful followers to carry his message to the people. The message was eagerly accepted and circulated by the Lollards. Wycliffe's tracts and his translation of the Bible became potent weapons in the Great Society's work of organization.

In his most mature writing, Wycliffe attempts to unite the two currents of culture—the Protestant drive of the bourgeoisie and the revolutionary demands of the people. The 1381 rebellion proved that the two movements were irreconcilable. The divergence was already manifest in creative literature, one tendency being represented by Chaucer and the other by the *Piers Plowman* poems.

Chaucer was a businessman who spent a good deal of time in Europe on mercantile and diplomatic missions. His visits to Italy made him familiar with the work of Dante, Petrarch and Boccaccio. He acknowledged his debt to the first two; his failure to mention the author of the *Decameron* may be due to his use of Italian books which gave no credit to the author. Manuscripts were often circulated anonymously, and even if the first page contained the writer's name, it was frequently lost as the book passed from hand to hand.[12]

Chaucer may or may not have known Boccaccio's name. It is possible that he met him during his visit to Florence in 1572. But there can be no doubt that the *Decameron* was his model; it provided the plots for many of his tales, and he occasionally made verbatim translations of long passages. The culture of the English middle class resembled in many ways the urban culture of Italy. Chaucer caught the color and texture of the changing scene: he spoke with the confidence of national pride. But the integrating and binding element is the viewpoint of the bourgeoisie. Although the people of the *Canterbury Tales* are on a pilgrimage, their anticlericalism is almost as frank as Wycliffe's. They are full of sap and vinegar, greedy, robustly concerned with the things of this world.

Chaucer's compositions cannot be accurately dated, but his most prolific period probably coincided with the decade of the Wat Tyler Rebellion. Yet there is not a trace of the disturbance in his work. His plowman is a pastoral saint, unaware of such problems as wages or taxes:

He'd thresh and dig, with never thought of pelf,
For Christ's own sake, for every poor wight,

All without pay, if it lay in his might.
He paid his taxes, fully, fairly, well,
Both by his own toil and by stuff he'd sell.[13]

One would never guess that this man lived in the land where Piers Plowman also labored, "with his hood full of holes, his mittens made of patches, and his poor wife going barefoot on the ice so that her blood followed."

We know very little about William Langland, and it is not established whether the poems credited to him were written by one, or by several, authors. But *Piers Plowman* reflected the activities of the Great Society. The underground organization circulated Langland's poems along with Wycliffe's tracts. The poems were so widely reproduced that fifty or sixty handwritten manuscripts are still in existence. When the signal for a general uprising was given in May, 1381, the messages sent from place to place used the name of Piers Plowman as a code-word. It was time, said the cryptic announcements, that "Piers Plowman goe to his werke and chastise well Hob the Robber." [14]

The immediate cause of the rebellion was the unbearable taxation, which Chaucer's cheerful plowman paid so "fully, fairly, well." The breaking point was reached with the poll tax of 1380, which imposed a payment of from four pence to one shilling on every working class family.[15] The revolt was well planned and broke out simultaneously in different parts of the eastern counties. The people of Norwich captured the town and stormed the castle. Wat Tyler emerged as the leader of the ragged army that gathered in Kent, and moved to attack the center of ecclesiastical power, Canterbury, where the palace of the archbishop was sacked. At Maidstone, Tyler liberated John Ball, one of the many agitators who had been imprisoned. Ball, who left the Franciscans to become a Lollard, was widely known and respected. The bands converged on London, and Ball preached to the crowd assembled at Mile End. For the first time under an English sky, armed men listened in comradeship, straining to catch the words drifting on the wind, to talk of a primitive communism, the right of all men to equal opportunity, the evil of caste and class. Ball's text was the homely verse—

When Adam delved and Eve span,
Who was then a gentleman?

The story of the quick capture of London is well known—the overwhelming support offered to the rebels by the lower classes, the burning of Savoy palace and the Temple and the prisons of Fleet and Newgate, the establishment of discipline, the trial and execution of lords held responsible for the poll tax, the decision reached in twenty-four hours by the crown's advisers to negotiate with the leaders of the revolt, the meeting between the fourteen-year-old Richard II and Wat Tyler, the granting of radical reforms including the abolition of serfdom and a general amnesty.

The astonishing and apparently assured success of the rising took place on the second day of the occupation of London. Gasping as they breathed the air of freedom, knowing that thirty secretaries were writing releases for all the serfs in the kingdom, naive in their acceptance of the royal promise, the peasants began to disperse.

During these events, the city administration had maintained a friendly attitude toward the rebels. As Mayor of London, Walworth could not have been unaware of the action of two aldermen, John Horn and Walter Sibille, in extending an unofficial welcome to the peasants. Both these men were the mayor's intimate friends and advisers. The victualers were playing their old game, trying to win the adherence of the lower classes. It was a threadbare game, but the revolt gave it a new setting, and the victualers had a gambling chance of snatching greater power from the confusion. Walworth and his associates might have served as mediators, winning concessions for themselves at the expense of the peasants. When the quick royal capitulation made this impossible, Walworth came forward as the hero of the betrayal of Tyler that took place on the third day. At a conference between the rebel leader and the king, Walworth drew his cutlass and killed Tyler. In the disorder that resulted, the peasants were attacked and dispersed: within a few hours, the heads of Tyler and Ball decorated London Bridge, and the royal troops started a bloody progress through the countryside.

In spite of its failure, the revolt marked the beginning of the modern history of England. The fishmonger's cutlass did more than kill a man. It expressed the split between the middle class and the peasantry which was to affect the future course of the nation's life.

The main benefits of Walworth's act accrued to the landed nobility. The crown *seemed* to gain an advantage: the king was able to increase the burden of taxation on the lower classes, but this economic gain was counterbalanced by the loss of popular support. The large landholders were given *carte blanche* to intensify the exploitation of the peasantry, and their improved position encouraged them to take advantage of the royal weakness and press for greater power. Richard II paid for his duplicity at Mile End with the loss of his crown. But his successors were to pay again, in decades of warfare. The weakening of the crown's position led to the Wars of the Roses, in which the Red Rose of Lancaster represented the last attempt of the barons to retain the economic and political advantage they had gained in 1381.

The suppression of the revolt crushed the early promise of a robust national culture. In the following year, the king and the bishops moved to eliminate the heresies that made Oxford one of the most important intellectual centers in Europe. Wycliffe's followers, who were the creative force in the university's life, were driven out or silenced.[16] Wycliffe's attitude toward the uprising was never clearly defined, but he was notably reticent in seeking governmental favor by joining the hue and cry against the rebels. He went into retirement following the witch hunt against his friends at Oxford, and his illness prevented his taking part in political activity in the two years before his death in 1384.

The change in the national culture is illustrated in the different versions of *Piers Plowman,* written before and after the revolution. The changes in the poem are like a barometer of the social climate. The author (whether he was one person or a group of people) exhibited the psychological symptoms of retreat under pressure. The first text, apparently written in the thirteen-sixties, recounts the effects of the plague, but it lacks the sharp sense of class antagonisms and the savage satire that are found in the second version in 1377. The second text is three times as long as the earlier poem. The author's social viewpoint has expanded and matured with the growth of the Great Society. The startling difference in the third version can be attributed to the age and increasing conservatism of the writer. Sometime between 1393 and 1398, Langland, or a younger man who imitated him, attempted to recast the famous work. Serfdom was now re-established, the Great Society was banned, words and thoughts were looked upon with suspicion. The author seems to have lost his vitality. His music is hushed, his theme transmuted: "He is interested in different things—his model man being not the honest labourer like Piers, but the dutiful ecclesiastic."[17]

Fear and suspicion did not provide an atmosphere in which a healthy literature could develop. An England without a Langland had no room for another Chaucer. The demise of *Piers Plowman* ended the salty confidence, the derision of feudal and ecclesiastical repressions, that gave depth and realism to the *Canterbury Tales*. There is an interval of almost two hundred years between the age of Wycliffe and the harvest-time of English culture in the Elizabethan period. Popular ballads form a bridge across the wasteland of the fifteenth century. But the ballad hero is no longer a toiler; he is an outlaw, living in the green forest to rob the rich for the good of the poor. *Piers Plowman* has become *Robin Hood*.

The people who sang of *Robin Hood* had not forgotten the march on London. The Lollard Brotherhood maintained its propaganda in spite of persecution. Remnants of the Great Society continued to function through secret villein unions which fought for higher wages and the abandonment of serfdom. Local uprisings were sometimes successful in forcing reforms. But most important of all, a durable tradition had been created: John Ball's words had not been lost in the wind. They were treasured in the mind, in secret talk, in tales and parables. Over the misery of the eastern counties, the wind whispered, "Promised, promised!"

5 : SACRED AND PROFANE LOVE

THE MEAGER INFORMATION that is available to us concerning the medieval woman is derived from literary sources dealing chiefly with the life of the upper class. Even works which pretend to draw an unbiased picture are heavily weighted with sentiment and perfumed with romance. Yet the element of myth in the medieval viewpoint is in itself an important cultural trait, illuminating the social situation that the myth sought to justify. The structure of ideas that was built around the medieval lady is of special interest, because it has not been wholly abandoned; the modern sex relationship is still dressed in the habiliments of chivalry.

We associate love in the Middle Ages with knightly devotion, tournaments and serenades. Underlying the apparent "unity" of this ideal is the complex of conflicting forces that we have considered in other aspects of medieval life. The over-all struggle between priestly dominance and secular power is reflected, sociologically, in the contrast between the sex-life of the castle and the official asceticism of the monastery. We need not concern ourselves with the violations of the ascetic principle. What is of interest is the gap between two patterns of living. The difference in the moral codes defines opposing material interests.

The celibacy of the clergy was necessary to preserve the wealth of the church. Since feudal marriage was primarily a means of conserving and extending fiefs and jurisdictions, and since the dignitaries of the church were members of aristocratic families, the best way of assuring their loyalty to the corporate institution was to cut them off from family obligations. Having no marital connections or heirs, the custodians of church properties were dedicated solely to the fulfillment of their trust. In a period in which all other property rights were contingent, the church occupied a unique legal position in that its possessions were inalienable and held in perpetuity. A similar advantage was secured by the prohibition of usury, which gave the church a monopoly of banking that enriched the papacy and the monasteries, and brought enormous profits to the Knights Templars.

The prohibition of clerical marriage encouraged illicit alliances on the part of the upper clergy. The economic function of marriage among the nobility had a far more immoral effect in depriving matrimony of any emotional validity. There was no incentive on either side to think of the relationship of the sexes in terms of a holy union. To the church, celibacy was the only spiritual ideal; to the lords of the land, concubinage, including possession of slave or serf women, was a feudal privilege. The love marriage was absolutely outside the ethics and *mores* of the ruling group.

But feudalism was a society in transition and movement. And the woman who managed the manorial estate while her husband followed the trade of war was not a cipher in the process of change. The romantic treatment of chivalrous love was in part an attempt to veil social reality. But the importance of the myth lies in the life force that it only partially concealed. The Provençal poets, the first singers of chivalrous love, did not celebrate conjugal felicity. The *Aubades,* or songs of dawn, tell of the knight stealing from his love's bedside as the first light of dawn brightens the sky. The illicit lover must leave without being observed, and the farewell scene is the climax of the poem.[1]

The lady and the knight came together because one of them had no love and the other had no home. Their relationship was a dynamic reply to a society that frustrated their deepest impulses. Yet this same society gave them enough freedom to provide an emotional outlet for their frustration. Warfare kept the lord of the manor absent for long periods. The necessities that kept the husband away from home created a migratory population of knights, whose social status made them acceptable companions to the lady of the manor and whose profession made it difficult for them to establish permanent ties.

During the lord's absence, his wife had a responsible job in governing the economic life of the manor. Eileen Powell observes:

> When the nobility of Europe went forth upon a crusade it was their wives who managed their affairs at home, superintending the farming, interviewing the tenants, and saved up money for the next assault. When the lord was taken prisoner it was his wife who collected the ransom, squeezing every penny from the estate, bothering bishops for indulgences, selling her jewels and the family plate. . . .[2]

With these responsibilities went a growing psychological maturity. The woman had no release for the emotional needs that were stimulated by the duties she was called upon to perform. The knights compensated for their own insecurity in their idealized contact with the resourceful, emotionally starved women in the castles that they visited. The relationship marked the historically new assertion of love as passion, as personal experience, as an ennobling physical impulse.

For the woman, there was an opposite course which also offered fulfillment, in terms of psychological release on another plane; service to the church was more than a refuge for the unmarried woman. The nunnery offered an active, meaningful life; it combined unusual educational opportunities with rewarding tasks in business management and organization.

The compensations available to the upper-class woman became less attractive as the social system lost its stability. The process was already well advanced in the twelfth century. The manor offered less security. The church had less prestige. As the culture of the town challenged the castle and the monastery, the passion of the dawn song paled. The pleasures of illicit love and the rigors of monastic seclusion no longer met the emotional needs of mature men and women.

Peter Abelard was nearing the age of forty when he was employed to tutor Heloise, the sixteen-year-old niece of the canon Fulbert. The two fell in love, and Heloise found that she was to have a child. Her reaction may not have been typical, but it expressed the upper-class woman's belief, rooted in the thought and literature of the time, that passion has no connection with marriage. Heloise wanted the child; she wrote to Abelard about it "in the greatest exultation";[3] but she was not concerned about marriage.

It is difficult for us to grasp the serious effect which matrimony would have had upon Abelard's career: in a society dominated by the church, the difficulty was self-evident. Abelard could marry if he chose to do so; as a clerk engaged in teaching, he had not taken orders, and there was no ecclesiastical objection to the match. But the alliance would block an otherwise promising career. It would prevent the scholar from securing the ecclesiastical preferment to which his reputation entitled him.

Abelard took Heloise to her sister's house in Brittany, where she gave birth to a son. He returned to Paris and discussed the matter with her uncle. The canon insisted on marriage, but in order to protect the groom's career, it was done secretly, and Heloise continued to live with her uncle. When Fulbert, worried about gossip, told friends that she was married, she denied it, and the situation became so embarrassing that Abelard removed her to a convent at Argenteuil, where she had been educated. Believing that the scholar was trying to get rid of his niece, Fulbert and some of his friends broke into Abelard's home at night and castrated him.

Abelard became a monk at St. Denis, and Heloise took the veil at Argenteuil, where she eventually became the abbess. But the deepest meaning of the story is to be found in the letters that the lovers exchanged for twenty years. A decade after their separation, Heloise addressed her husband in words that might have been written in the twentieth century, assuring him that she "preferred love to wedlock and liberty to a chain."[4] Yet her brooding over the evil that befell them strikes a medieval note:

> "A man taken in adultery would have been amply punished by what came to you. What others deserved for adultery, that you got from the marriage which you thought had made amends for everything."[5]

The abbess felt no shame for the physical passion that was far more consuming than her love of God:

> "Love's pleasures, which we knew together, cannot be made displeasing to me or driven from my memory. Wherever I turn, they press upon me, nor do they spare my dreams. . . . When I should groan for what I have done, I sigh for what I have lost. . . . They call me chaste, who do not know me for a hypocrite."[6]

The unity of intellectual companionship and sensual feeling in the relationship of Abelard and Heloise marks an historical advance which seems to be contradicted in the purely idealized love of Dante for the child-woman, Beatrice. Dante, writing almost two centuries later, was engaged in a vast exploration of the whole system of moral values on which the society of his time rested. It was no longer possible to accept the brief encounter between the knight and the lady as the highest form of emotional expression. Nor was it possible for a man of Dante's learning and wide secular interests to regard religious asceticism as the fulfillment of the human personality. Rejecting the cultural authority of the church and at the same time seeing only the negative aspects of the urban culture that was replacing it, Dante could not envision love in any satisfactory social terms. Yet he was deeply stirred by the potentialities of a pure and enduring man-and-woman relationship. It could be achieved only by taking chivalrous love out of its medieval setting, and intellectualizing it. His feeling for Beatrice is deep and permanent, but it is removed from the hurly-burly of the real world, cut off from the normal problems of social living.

We find a further advance, expressing the emergence of a more confident secular and urban viewpoint, in Petrarch's passion for Laura. The relationship is extramarital and physical. It has the depth of the love between Abelard and Heloise, but the lovers are not doomed and separated. They live in a society in which illicit relationships are taken for granted. The dawn song has been brought down to earth, personalized, given intimacy and subtlety.

However, the seriousness of Petrarch's emotional experience was exceptional. The aristocracy and the upper classes of the towns tended to regard sex with the greedy cynicism and tolerant amusement that we find in Boccaccio's stories. People who were wealthy enough to play at love were not disposed to stake their lives on the game. On the other hand, the artisan class in the towns followed a life-pattern that gave new meaning to marriage. The growth of craft production established a mutuality of interest within the family. The master of a trade performed his tasks at home, assisted by his wife and children. His tools and knowledge were passed on to his sons. The social status of the group hinged on the maintenance of gild membership. When the husband died and there were no male heirs, the family's welfare depended on keeping the shop in operation. Although the English gilds excluded women from many skilled occupations, the gilds made an exception in the case of the master's wife and daughters, who were permitted to learn his trade so that they might maintain the business after his death.

During the fourteenth century, the class struggles in the towns and the differentiation between the masters of industry and the subordinate crafts undermined the unity of the artisan family. Marriage was gravely affected by the industrial expansion that introduced piecework and wage labor and destroyed the independence of the small craftsmen.

An aspect of the change was the increasing employment of women. The multiplicity of new occupations offered opportunities in certain lines of work. In Paris at the beginning of the fourteenth century, five crafts were monopolized by women. Their employment in specialized fields was part of the process of differentiation that substituted piecework or wage labor for the collective work of the family. The household spinning of wool began to command the services of women so exclusively that unmarried females became known as spinsters.

At the same time the urban upper class, reaping the profits of more intensive exploitation, followed the aristocracy's economic use of marriage as a means of combining or strengthening business ventures. Since the union was a contract in which love was a minor consideration, both parties were likely to seek emotional satisfaction elsewhere. Custom granted the husband considerable freedom in the pursuit of extramarital experience. The wife's loyalty was demanded as the guarantee of the legitimacy of the children. But the woman who entered into a lifelong alliance without consulting her personal inclinations was frequently more interested than the husband in finding some emotional fulfillment—because she was deprived of the occupational contacts and activities that her husband enjoyed.

Thus history repeated the experience of the medieval castle. But the amorous adventure had lost its magic: in the restless life of the town, it became a matter of chicanery and deceit. The bedroom farce replaced the dawn song. A money economy reduced all relationships, extramarital as well as marital, to a matter of cash. In the *Canterbury Tales,* the Wife of Bath is proud of her skill in weaving:

> At making cloth she had so great a bent
> She bettered those of Ypres and even of Ghent.[7]

But weaving for a livelihood was an ill-paid occupation in Chaucer's England, and the Wife of Bath would have scorned to depend upon her skill. Her profession was that of a wife, and she did very well in it. Of her five marriages, she explains that the first three were money propositions:

> The three were good men and rich and old,
> They'd given me their gold and treasure more;
> I needed not do longer diligance
> To win their love or show them reverance.[8]

Up to this point, we have dealt with the habits and customs of classes above the level of poverty in which the majority of the people lived. Thus we have relied upon the picture presented in the specialized forms of culture that reflected the interests of these classes—the songs of chivalry, the poems and stories written under the patronage of the court or the wealthy people of the towns, the records of the gilds and the growing middle-class activity in urban centers. But the great stream of the people's culture affected marriage as profoundly as it affected the structure of the town and the nation. The revolutionary drive of the peasantry had its emotional roots in the serf family. The divergence between Chaucer and Langland is most fully expressed in their viewpoint toward human relationships.

The contradictions in the serf's status, his half-freedom and half-slavery, embraced his wife and children. The household was unified by the common labor needed to sustain life. The basic factor in serfdom was the unity and continuity of the servile family. The slave family could be separated at the master's will. Thus each slave was a separate unit of labor. The peasant group had a house and land; since they were working for themselves as well as the lord, their industry was likely to be greater, and the master of the manor could get more return with less supervision.

The minimum of economic security guaranteed to the serf implied an equal marital security, a genuine family life, and the right to raise children who became an additional asset to the lord of the manor. But the personal fealty which was the condition upon which these benefits were enjoyed placed a limitation on the moral freedom of the peasant household as well as upon its economic liberty. Being a transitional stage from slavery to free labor, the right of the peasant and his family to dispose of their own persons was also transitional, and the service and submission that went with the use of the land involved the lord's right to interfere in domestic matters.

Feudalism invaded the sanctity of the home, because the lord of the manor had a legally recognized interest in the peasant's household. The exemplary expression of this interest was the right of the *premier noce*. The sacredness of the peasant marriage was mocked at its most sacred moment by the lord's assertion of his prior right to occupy the marriage bed. The privilege was not a rare and frequently disregarded custom. The prerogative was often insisted upon as a proof of the lord's authority and his claim upon the services of the children of the union. When the custom was not enforced, a money tribute was exacted in exchange for the lord's abstinence.[9]

Vestiges of the *droit de seigneur* may be traced in our contemporary culture: brutality toward women of the lower class, as objects for casual sex use, is expressed in smoking room jokes and stories, and to some extent in the conduct of the American male. The degrading immorality of the plantation in the slave South is continued in a modified form in the treatment of Negro women by their white "superiors." Thomas Wolfe, remembering his boyhood in a Southern town, in a society in which sex had no dignity and grace, recalled that the boy dreamed of the medieval right to possess women without their consent: he imagined himself with the sexual freedom of "a cragged and castled baron, to execute *le droit de seigneur* upon the choicest of the enfeoffed wives and wenches."[10]

The brutality of the fantasy, and its specific historical frame of reference, throws a good deal of light on the sexual immaturity and neurotic compulsions which Wolfe described so frankly in his adult experience. The woman's position in our society is still affected by social attitudes and customs originating in the Middle Ages. The degradation of the woman is based on class distinctions, and is exhibited in the treatment of the upper-class woman as a prized sexual object as well as in the assumption that women of the less privileged classes are available to the conquering male for casual gratification.

In the revolutionary movements that undermined the medieval social structure, the woman's right to protection from physical violation was one of the most powerful motivating factors. The ascetic practices of many of the heretical sects were inspired by the revulsion against the corruption of the sex relationship and the more or less conscious recognition that property rights and class domination were responsible for the defilement of normal human feeling. The charge of "free love" that was so often leveled against the heretics was a derisive comment on the leading role that women often played in their activities and the comradeship between men and women that seems to have characterized some of the communal experiments. There is a revelatory account of the discovery of a band of heretics in Flanders in 1157: suspicion was aroused when a girl refused to submit to a young cleric; her insistence on chastity was considered ominous, and when questioned she admitted that she believed virginity to be obligatory. The authorities then knew that they were dealing with an organized heresy, and through the girl's contacts they were able to trace the other rebels.[11]

The economic oppression that provoked the "green risings" of the thirteenth and fourteenth centuries was directly and degradingly expressed in the customary rape of peasant women. The *droit de seigneur* was the legal aspect of a right which could be exercised without specific legal sanctions; the people of the villages on a lord's land were *serfs of the body* and the women had no protection against violation. The right of *premier noce,* which was exacted by ecclesiastical lords as well as by their secular associates, marked the woman who had been possessed on her marriage night as fair game for the lord or his retainers. Her firstborn was likely to be her master's son. The probability is explicitly noted in the Fors du Bearn: "The peasant's eldest son is always reckoned the Seigneur's child, for he may be of his engendering."[12]

At the same time, women played an important role in the peasant community. They were the midwives, the guardians of medical wisdom knowing the use of herbs and healing drugs. It seems probable that they were also leaders and organizers in the movements of revolt against feudal tyranny. There can be no doubt that the nocturnal assemblies of peasants, which were described by contemporary writers as witches' sabbaths dedicated to the worship of the devil were bitterly anticlerical, and that in some cases the revolutionary purpose was veiled in ritual and ceremony. But the meetings were consecrated to rebellion, and the woman was assigned a special position of honor and creative power.[13] The idea of the woman as a witch—which led to such brutal persecutions over the centuries—is in part a superstitious acknowledgment of her special medical skill. But the more profound reason for accusations of sorcery lay in the fear of the woman's social influence, her role in organizing protest against oppression, and the necessity of *keeping her in her place.*

We find that wholesale trials of witches invariably occur at periods of growing social tension; this was the case in Scotland at the end of the sixteenth century, as well as in New England in the closing years of the seventeenth century.

The peasants and laborers of the Middle Ages looked toward a time when love would no longer be bought and sold, when marriage would become a sacrament, a union of comrades. Their struggles and failures created new cultural values, new approaches to the dignity of love and the sanctity of the family.

6 : THE ASHES OF JOHN HUSS

THE WAT TYLER REBELLION in England was part of a system of events that occurred simultaneously in various parts of Europe—wherever economic development increased the pressure on laborers, serfs and artisans to the breaking point.

The English example inspired the rising of the Flemish cities in the same year. The Flemish movement was predominantly urban; all classes of the cities were prepared to unite, at least temporarily, in the fight against French domination. Philip, son of Jacque d'Arteveld, appealed to the poorer classes; addressing a huge gathering in Ghent, he said, "I am sure there be thirty thousand in this town that did not eat bread this fifteen days past."[1] Within a few months Arteveld was master of the whole country, but class differences and the complete triumph of reaction in England weakened the morale of the Flemish rebels, and the people's army of fifty thousand men was destroyed by French forces in November, 1382.

At the same time, rebellion swept the Italian cities. In Siena, in 1371, the woolcarders, the most exploited of the textile workers, formed the Company of the Worm, seizing the city and sacking the houses of the rich. They were defeated in the civil strife that followed. In Florence the warfare between the city and the pope from 1374 to 1378 was fought over the question of grain, indispensable to the existence of the population. It ended in 1378 with the revolt of the woolcarders, one of the greatest and most profound revolutions Italy experienced during the age of the city-republics.[2] The workers were led by Michele de Lando, described in Machiavelli's history as entering the palace of government "barefoot, with scarcely anything upon him, and the rabble at his heels."[3] Associated with Lando was a member of the major gilds, Salvestro de Medici, who came forward as the champion of the *populo minuto* in order to advance his own political fortunes. The municipal constitution was reorganized; in order to detach the lesser gilds from the proletarians, the *populo minuto* were given greater participation in the government. Four thousand dyers and shirtmakers gained the right to form their own gilds. As a result, the workers were divided. In 1382, the industrial oligarchy, aided by an English adventurer, Sir John Hawkwood, succeeded in reasserting its control, eliminating the democratic reforms. Lando was exiled, but the Medici family emerged from the confusion as a potent force in the city's industrial and political life.[4]

There was no direct connection between the European events and the revolts that occurred in the Russian city of Novgorod in the same years. There were elements of similarity, however. By the diversification of craft production and the impact of urban development on the life of the surrounding countryside, Novgorod is said to have attained a population of 400,000 in the fourteenth century. The industrial growth of Novgorod followed the familiar course—first the fight for municipal freedom against the princes, then the struggle of the lower classes against the major gilds. "In a city of so small a compass and with so large a population, the riots assumed the bitterest character, often ending in murders, looting and burning."[5]

Far away in central Asia, Tamerlane became the master of Samarkand in 1369 as the rescuer of the city from a popular rebellion. Recognizing the importance of craft production, the conqueror chose the ablest artisans in every country he subjugated, assembling 150,000 skilled workers in Samarkand to build palaces and mosques.[6] In China, the fourteenth century revolt against Mongolian domination was led by Chu Yuen-chang, son of a laborer, whose capture of Nanking in 1355 gave him control of the urban centers with their long-established craft gild organizations, and enabled him to become emperor and founder of the Ming dynasty in 1368.

The European disturbances, like those in other parts of the world, did not achieve the goals that the people envisioned. But they had the effect of broadening the current of anticlericalism. Monasteries were burned in Florence as well as in England. The rising tide of protest in Italy was responsible for the decision of Gregory XI to quit Avignon and return to Rome in order to reassert his Italian authority in 1377. The papal attempt to suppress the people's militia in Rome caused a period of riots and disorders, the lower classes in Rome being greatly strengthened by the revolution in Florence. Taking advantage of the papal difficulties in Italy, the French cardinals elected a rival pope: the Great Schism brought the church to its lowest ebb of prestige; in 1409, three popes were hurling anathema at one another; the breach was finally healed at the Council of Constance which met from 1414 to 1417.[7]

The Great Schism reflected the decline of Catholic power. By the time of the Council of Constance, opposition to the church was so widespread that the settlement of internal quarrels was the price of survival. John Wycliffe's pamphlets were circulated throughout Europe. The Englishman's reply to the pope's summons to come to Rome for trial was discussed in gild halls and peasant cottages: advising the pontiff to "leave his worldly lordship to worldly lords," Wycliffe prayed "that the pope's holy intent be not quenched by his enemies. And Christ, that may not lie, says that the enemies of a man been especially his own family."[8]

With Wycliffe's tracts went reports of the three days when the English peasants had mastered London, and stories of the activities of the underground throughout Europe. The movement reached its climax in Bohemia where the growth of an urban economy and the consequent transformation of the labor market was based, not upon wool, but upon metallurgy. The rise of mining in Middle Europe brought the thaler, the ancestor of our own dollar, into prominence as a coin that entered into competition with the florin.

The Bohemian silver mines were at first worked by serfs, but as the industry grew it became more economical to divorce the peasant from the land and employ him as a laborer at starvation wages. The church held no less than a quarter of the whole territory of the kingdom, including the most valuable mines. Other estates and mines were in the hands of Germans. The nation's wealth was systematically siphoned off, to enrich absentee landlords in Germany and Italy. The large production of silver created inflation, adding greatly to the poverty of the people.

In 1413, the butchers of Paris, led by the skinner, Simon Caboche, captured the city, and forced the adoption of the radical reforms known as the *Ordonnance Cabochienne*. The University of Paris, strongly influenced by the ideas of Wycliffe and Huss, assumed the ideological role that was filled by Oxford during the period of radical agitation in England. The university cooperated with the radicals, and drew up the ordinances that embodied their demands. The French reforms were obliterated a few months later, when the party of the nobility, the Armagnacs, captured Paris and instituted a reign of terror.

In 1415, the writing and preaching of John Huss had aroused a national fever of resentment against church and empire. Huss drew his inspiration from Wycliffe, and much of his work was a direct translation of the Englishman's words. The churchmen meeting at Constance recognized that the Hussite movement constituted a danger to their Bohemian properties. But the threat of trouble in Bohemia might well set off a European conflagration. The deliberations at Constance took place against a background of growing unrest in various parts of the continent. There were disorders in Italy, threats of rebellion in Flanders.

A foreboding shadow hung over the Council of Constance. The assembled prelates identified the shadow with John Huss. They called him to appear before them, offering a safe conduct which he was foolish enough to accept. Having seized the menacing shadow, the church had no intention of letting it escape. Huss was condemned for heresy, and burned at the stake on July 6, 1415. The council also decreed that Wycliffe's remains be dug up and burned, and the order was carried out thirteen years later.

The execution of Huss, like so many acts of oppression, added strength to the movement it was intended to suppress. On September 2, the nobles of Bohemia and Moravia, who coveted the estates of the clergy, adopted the *Protestatio,* which in word as well as intention, was a Protestant denial of the authority of the Roman church. For a time the rebellion was a national coalition uniting the barons, the burghers of Prague and other cities, with artisans, peasants and laborers.

But the intensity of the struggle for freedom brought a quick revelation of the conflict of class interests. When the pope's call for a crusade against the heretics in 1420 was answered by a vast army of knights, adventurers and mercenaries, the advancing host was met at the gates of Prague by a force of peasants and laborers gathered from the fields and the mines. The city's defenders had been hastily trained by John Zizka, a blind veteran who had spent most of his life as a mercenary soldier in Poland. History is crowded with proofs of man's creative will. But there are few affirmations of the human spirit more convincing than the story of Zizka and the men who followed him. Blind, at the age of sixty-five, he led 9,000 men to victory over a feudal force said to number 200,000. Then, retiring to the hilltown of Tabor, he developed a people's army, using offensive tactics that were new in warfare and that brought repeated defeats to the huge feudal aggregations that were sent against his troops.[9]

In saving Prague, the peasants and laborers demonstrated a strength that frightened the wealthy burghers of the city and made them reconsider their fervent nationalism. There was a widening rift between the two parties: the Calixtines, or Utraquists, and the Taborites. The former with headquarters in Prague, represented the Bohemian nobility and the urban upper class. The radical party of the Taborites maintained its stronghold at Tabor. After Zizka's death in 1424, there was open conflict between the two parties.

Tabor maintained its invincible military power, and proceeded with a remarkable social experiment. Members of the sects, Waldenses, Beghards, descendants of the persecuted Albigenses, came out of the underground to the freedom of Tabor. A prosperous Communist community was established. The citizens called each other brother and sister, holding that "there should be no kings, no masters, no subjects on earth, and that taxes and duties should be abolished." Public meetings were held which are said to have attracted as many as 42,000 persons.[10] Families engaged in craft production, enjoyed the fruits of their labor and contributed the surplus to a common treasury. A very high level of industrial organization was attained. A great deal of attention was given to education, and service in the citizen's army was compulsory.

The military successes of Tabor were largely due to the employment of new weapons and techniques of fighting. Warfare, like other aspects of culture, is a product of social organization. Military skills, like other skills, serve the classes which are able to master them and apply them to aims that they consider socially desirable. Societies in which dominant groups maintain a rigid caste structure and discourage the advancement of reason and science are invariably backward in their methods of warfare. When people break the bondage of outworn patterns of dominance, they are able to take full advantage of social and technological opportunities. War, like everything else, is revolutionized by popular movements. The lesson is proved through all of history, from Tabor to Stalingrad and Suchow.

The Taborite army, unhampered by tradition and profiting by the experience of miners and ironworkers who were among its best fighters, built wagon-forts. These were armored trucks; one might call them tanks of a primitive sort; they carried a contingent of men protected by metal walls; the soldiers fired through loopholes. Drawn by horses from one point to another, the wagon-forts demonstrated, for the first time in history, the tactical value of fire-power in movement.[11] The system was possible because it was utilized by a people's army with a well-organized productive base. There were no knights or camp followers to encumber the troops of Tabor. There was unified command. Every man was trained to perform his job. Promotion was solely on merit. The town's industrial methods brought efficient and rapid manufacture of firearms.

For a few years, Tabor seemed to be invincible. On August 14, 1431, the people's army met another vast aggregation of knights and adventurers, gathered from all parts of Europe under the leadership of Frederick, Margrave of Brandenburg. The battle of Tauss was more of a rout than a battle. The unwieldy legions of feudalism were helpless before rapidly moving disciplined soldiers, with their wagon-forts and guerrilla tactics.

At the beginning of the same summer, on May 30, Joan of Arc was burned in the streets of Rouen. Joan's visions were undoubtedly heretical, influenced by the ideology of the persecuted sects. She saw a land scourged with suffering and poverty. She dreamed of life, freedom for the peasants. But France was exhausted by civil conflict; all the cities, with the exception of Orleans, were in English hands. Joan's tragedy—the tragedy of France—was the use that was made of her by the party of the nobility, the same Armagnacs who had despoiled Paris in 1413. She accomplished a miracle in bringing honor and national purpose to the corrupt cause of Charles of Orleans. This was her remarkable, but impermanent, achievement.

The anachronistic figure of the girl in armor does an injustice to Joan's military common sense, and the methods by which the English troops were defeated. The lessons of the Taborite victories were known in France. Joan's success was due as much to firearms as to visions. Orleans was able to hold out against the English army because it was protected by seventy mortars, bombards and culverins. The English also had guns drawn by oxen. When the siege was broken, the French army abandoned its traditional feudal methods. The guns that defended the walls were carried forward; and the use of these weapons in the battle of Patay enabled the French to crush five thousand British archers—the same archers who had been so effective against armored knights at Agincourt.[12]

The flame of national spirit burned more brightly at Tabor than at Orleans. But the days of Bohemia's independence were numbered. The nation's freedom depended on Tabor. And Tabor could not remain immune from the class forces that surged around its walls. Individual handicraft production could not form the basis for an equalitarian society. Those who possessed tools and special training dominated the town's economy and demanded a larger share of wealth and power. The conflict inside the city was stimulated by agents of the Calixtine party which in 1433 entered into an alliance with the papacy. The nobles and the rich burghers of Prague made the choice that William Walworth made in England when he stabbed Wat Tyler. Their choice assured the defeat of the national movement. But foreign and clerical domination seemed a small price to pay for the elimination of the dangerous leveling influence that emanated from Tabor.

Treason and desertions weakened Tabor as it prepared to meet the new onslaught. The attack was led by Borek of Miletinek, who had been a general under Zizka, and had adopted many of the novel techniques of warfare perfected by the Taborites.

At Lipan, on May 30, 1434, the people's army of Tabor made its last stand. The men were overpowered, but they did not retreat. They stood their ground and died. Of eighteen thousand, thirteen thousand were killed on the field.

In 1939, as the Nazis prepared to plunge Europe into war, a minor item of news was printed modestly in American newspapers. Czechoslovakia bowed sullenly to the Germans, but the people of a small town in Western Bohemia refused to accept the orders of the conquerors. The resistance was crushed in blood and steel, but it inaugurated the civil struggle that was to spread across Europe during the next six years. The town was Tabor.

The fifteenth century defeat of Tabor was not so much an end as a beginning. When Huss was burned, the charred remains and even the earth contaminated by his touch were removed and scattered over the Rhine. There was no change in the river that received the meager offering of dust. Yet every land that was washed by the Rhine on its way to the sea—Switzerland, Germany, France, the Netherlands—would be kindled into flame by the ashes that had been so carefully quenched.

PART II

The Challenge of Humanism
1450–1600

1 : MONA LISA

Among Leonardo da Vinci's manifold aesthetic and scientific achievements, the work that has evoked the most universal response, as art and as myth, is the portrait of Lisa, wife of Francesco del Giacondo. It is hard to measure fame, and there is no statistical evidence to prove that the *Mona Lisa* is the most famous painting in the world. But there are certainly few pictures that are so specifically associated with a symbol or idea in the popular imagination. Millions who have never seen the painting, knowing it through reproductions or only by reputation, associate Mona Lisa's smile with the "eternal" mystery of woman.

Leonardo was fifty years old when he started the first sketches for the portrait. He worked on it intermittently from 1502 to 1506. As the artist passed his prime, the sun of the Italian Renaissance descended towards its twilight. The painting was done at the climax of a man's career and at a moment of foreboding and foreseen disaster in the life of his time. The picture stands at the end of an epoch of Italian growth, at the beginning of the wider cultural movement that spread across Europe in strife and violence.

The picture exhibits a new approach to portraiture, which is far more than a development of technical virtuosity or psychological subtlety. We can define the change in terms of the artist's growth by comparing *Mona Lisa* with the *Madonna of the Rocks,* painted by Leonardo two decades earlier. Even in the 1480's, Leonardo had begun to humanize the fifteenth century conception of the Virgin: he placed her in an intimate group with two naked children and a youthful angel. But there is a psychological leap from the *Madonna of the Rocks,* with her downcast eyes and her irreproachable innocence, to the Lady Lisa, with her eyes carefully smiling and her irreproachable "mystery."

Lisa was twenty-three, when Leonardo began the painting. She had been married for seven years, coming to Florence from Naples as Giacondo's third wife in 1495. When one looks at the portrait, one is apt to think of Lisa as a mature woman. We know very little about her. But we may suspect that her apparent maturity is related to the circumstances of her life. At all events, Leonardo depicted her with the most perfect physical realism. Working from black-and-white sketches, and using other sitters for the hands and the body, he brought to the task a prodigal concentration of his accumulated knowledge of paint, texture and anatomy.

Lisa is "inscrutable," in the sense that a personality completely seen in its external aspect is not completely known in its inwardness. Lisa's enigma is that of the upper-class woman who has learned to conceal her emotions. She may have depths of character; she may be capable of passion and sacrifice. But the depths are guarded, the passion is stilled. With her eyebrows carefully plucked in the fashion of the time, Lisa has the physical poise of "good breeding," the tranquillity of the flesh richly attired. One may assume that she is following Agnolo Firensuola's advice to the lady of fashion, to open the mouth a little "at the left side, as if you were smiling secretly . . . not in an artificial manner, but as though unconsciously—this is not an affectation, if it is done in moderation and in a restrained and graceful manner and accompanied by innocent coquetry and by certain movements of the eyes . . ." [1]

Lisa is the embodiment of a class. She is the first of a long line of heroines in drama and fiction. She is the archetype of Balzac's and Ibsen's women; of the frustrated, scheming women caught in the net of bourgeois property relationships. There have been many variations in the type, from the simplicity of Eugenie Grandet and the cold anger of Hedda Gabler to the saccharine *women with domestic problems* who parade like models at a fashion show through the pages of American magazines. It is interesting to study Mona Lisa and "cast" her, so to speak, in various roles—but always as a woman with a hidden emotional life, a fire burning under a decorous exterior, with feelings that cannot be fulfilled or expressed in the class milieu from which there is no escape. Lisa is a woman of the bourgeoisie, and cannot play any other part.

Leonardo's concentration on this subject, and his manner of handling it, indicates a turning point in his career, and a crucial change in the political and social climate in which he moved.

The artist's life-span, from 1452 to 1519, covered the period of the breakdown of the medieval structure. He lived in a world that had lost its traditional values. But the forms of organization that would replace the old order had not yet emerged. The uncertainty encouraged the Utopian view that the human energies released from medieval restraints would have a continuing freedom of development. In defying the authoritarian priesthood, the artist and the thinker dreamed that *their* values—the values of a vague but deeply felt humanism—would become the property of the whole society. The illusion was a vital force in a period when the class relationships of the epoch of capitalism had not crystallized. This is the key to the apparent "universality" of Renaissance culture, embodied in its most creative form in the work of Leonardo. The specific circumstances of Leonardo's life were an integral part of the larger pattern of social change. He was the illegitimate son of a prosperous notary. At about the age of eighteen, he was apprenticed to Andrea del Verrocchio. In 1472, when he was twenty, his name was entered in the Red Book of the painters' gild of Florence. Ten years later, he left Florence, established himself in Milan. In order to understand the reasons for his departure, we must turn from art to a more prosaic commodity—alum.

Florence was under the dictatorship of the Medici family. The Medici operated three manufacturing establishments, one making silk and two engaged in the production of woolen cloth. Their financial interests spread across Europe. They had branch banks in Bruges, London, Avignon, Geneva, Venice, Rome and Milan. The economic expansion in the middle of the fifteenth century led the Medici to join with the papacy in one of the earliest cartel arrangements: an attempt to corner the European supply of alum. Alum was indispensable to textile production, since it was used as a mordant in dyeing cloth. Alum was imported from the Levant, but in 1459 rich deposits were discovered in Civitavecchia in the Papal territories. In 1466, the Medici reached an agreement with the papacy for the exploitation of the mines, forming a company which paid a royalty to the Vatican. Thus, the plan envisioned control of the whole European cloth trade.

The projected cartel caused vast political repercussions. In order to enforce the monopoly and raise the price, the pope prohibited the importation of Turkish alum, demanding that laws to this effect be passed in the three great areas of cloth production—England, Flanders and Venice. There was bitter and effective protest, especially in Flanders, where compliance with the pope's demand disrupted the textile industry and brought the cities to open rebellion. Meanwhile, the Medici pushed the monopoly by securing control of other Italian mines, either by agreement (as in the case of the Neapolitan deposits at Tolfa and Ischia), or by military conquest (as in the war against Volterra in 1472). Frightened by the widespread protest, and fearing that the Medici were gaining international power at the expense of the church, Pope Sixtus IV, who received the tiara in 1471, reversed the Vatican's policy, entering into an alliance with the rival Florentine banking house of Pazzi—which, by a not so strange coincidence, was interested in the importation of Turkish alum.

The result was the Pazzi conspiracy, which shook Florence in 1478. The attempt of the Pazzi to seize power failed, but it undermined the position of the Medici. The pope used the occasion to break his contract with the firm; he took over the alum mines in papal territory and excommunicated Lorenzo de Medici. Superficially, the conflict was the sort of thieves' quarrel that is common in the world of high finance. But such quarrels are often symptomatic of deep contradictions, fissures in the structure of power.

The Vatican was desperately seeking to consolidate its hold on the European economy; but it could not control the expanding forces of commerce and craft production. The Medici bank, entangled in the net of ecclesiastical interests, was also unable to maintain its old supremacy.

Thus the quarrel was a sign of weaknesses that were to affect the destiny of Italy. In Florence, the Medici dictatorship could no longer claim even a semblance of popular support. It rested on naked force. The dissatisfaction of the middle class and the increasing exploitation of small craftsmen and laborers pointed to the imminence of a revolutionary outbreak.

The social history of Florence in these years may be traced with painful simplicity in the art of Botticelli. The man who had been engaged in painting the enchanting *Primavera* on the walls of one of the Medici villas was given a sordid propaganda task in 1478; he was ordered to paint the effigies of the Pazzi conspirators, hanging by their necks, on the walls of the Palazzo del Podesta. As the class conflict developed, Botticelli's work moved toward anger and frustration, reaching a climax in the distorted, bent and struggling bodies of his final period.

Leonardo was a greater and more complex figure. Like most thoughtful Italians, he hoped that Italy would unite under a strong national ruler, following the course of development that had already been indicated in England and France. Ludovico Sforza, master of Milan, had the apparent strength and vigor to make him a potential national leader. Leonardo entered Ludovico's service in 1482. One may assume that Leonardo was thinking of Italy's national hopes when he wrote to Ludovico reciting his qualifications as an inventor of instruments of war. He said he could make engines for attack or defense, on land or sea—"armored cars, safe and unassailable . . . cannons mortars and light ordnance . . . catapults, mangonels, trabocchi and other engines of wonderful efficacy . . ." [2]

Leonardo seems to have come to Milan with strong hopes that he would be able to perform important civic services, both in revolutionizing the city's military organization and in developing irrigation projects and improvements in municipal planning which would contribute to the safety and welfare of the people. Leonardo found the protection and encouragement which he required for creative activity and scientific investigation. But Ludovico's patronage did not bring the acceptance of any of the artist's ambitious proposals. The Sforza dictatorship was as oppressive and unpopular as the rule of the Medici in Florence. Ludovico was enormously rich: his gems and gold were piled in the Hall of Treasures, where they could be inspected, and even handled, by important visitors. But the majority of the people of Milan lived in poverty and fear. It was utterly impossible for Ludovico to understand or use the machines of warfare which Leonardo designed, because these engines required qualities of loyalty, skill and initiative which could not be bought with all of the duke's wealth. Like other rulers of the time, Ludovico depended upon mercenary troops, recruited chiefly in Switzerland.

We have discussed the revolutionary changes introduced by the people of Tabor in the art of warfare. The mobility and technical skill demonstrated by the Taborite armies could not be duplicated by other states—because the Taborite methods could be used only by a people's army. As warfare developed in the fifteenth and sixteenth centuries, the wider use of firearms had a twofold effect—it made the knight an easy target, and it increased the casualties in battle. Both difficulties were met by the use of hired mercenaries. Plenty of men could be hired to fight and die for anyone who would pay their wages. Mercenary warfare became a regular profession; Switzerland was noted for the strength and endurance of the peasant soldiers who served any master desiring to buy their services. *Point d'argent, point de Suisse* became a rule of war.

The contemporary methods of war and the social situation in Milan explain the Duke's indifference to Leonardo's military inventions, and the tragic denouement of the artist's long sojourn at the Sforza court.

The intrigue and corruption of Italian politics reached a climax when Rodrigo Borgia secured the papal tiara in 1492. As Pope Alexander VI, Rodrigo's conduct was not much worse than that of some of his predecessors. The passions and crimes that made the Borgia family notorious revealed the moral sickness of the age. It was revealed more strikingly in the political policies of Ludovico; in encouraging a French invasion of Italy, he played a role which was somewhat similar to that of the collaborationists who welcomed the Nazis to Paris in 1940. Instead of uniting Italy, he became his country's executioner, securing temporary immunity for himself and hoping to snatch advantages from the devastation of the land.

The French armies—in which there were almost no Frenchmen, for they were composed of Swiss and other mercenaries—were entertained at Milan when they crossed the Alps in 1494. As they marched south to conquer and loot, the Medici prepared to surrender Florence and pay a large indemnity to protect their property. The threat brought the long-delayed revolution against the dictatorship. The Dominican monk, Savonarola, spoke to multitudes gathered in the cathedral. The ancient cry, *Popolo e Liberta,* rose in the streets. In a few hours, everything that the Medici had built over a century crumbled, and Piero and Giulio de Medici, with a small army of retainers, were in flight.

The period of Savonarola's leadership in Florence is of extraordinary interest, as an example of the changing class relationships at the beginning of the epoch of capitalism; it represents one of the earliest attempts to establish a structure of state-power in the interests of the middle class. Savonarola purported to speak for *everyone,* for the people as a mass, and especially for the exploited journeymen and laborers. Savonarola's preachments against the evils of wealth, his call for simplicity and brotherhood, echoed the unforgotten teachings of the heretical sects. But it soon became apparent that the Popular Party was "popular" only insofar as it sought to rally mass support for the middle group of merchants, enterprisers and skilled craftsmen.

Savonarola opposed the attempts of the wealthy oligarchy to re-establish a dictatorship on the Medici model. But instead of rallying the people to defend the city, he made an agreement with the French invaders on approximately the same sordid terms as those that caused the Medici to be driven from Florence. He insisted on a constitution that followed the Venetian model, vesting all power in a Grand Council that represented only the well-to-do citizens. He stopped a move to exempt the *popolo minuto,* the small people, from taxation. He thundered against *parliamenti,* the assemblies of the population that gathered in the Piazza. His argument against popular assemblies shows the dual role that he was called upon to play, and his method of welding the opposite poles of a contradiction by the heat of his emotion:

> I have been thinking of these parliaments of yours, which are nothing but a means of destruction and must be abolished. Forward, my people! Are you not masters now? . . . Know that *parliament* means robbing the people of their rule. . . . When you hear the bell ringing for parliament, rise and draw your sword and say:—What would you have? Cannot the Council accomplish everything? What law would you make? Can the Council not make it? [3]

The unreality of the argument foreshadowed Savonarola's downfall. His difficulty was also a reflection of the weakness of the class for which he spoke. He was a representative of the rising bourgeoisie —but it was a bourgeoisie corrupted by the instability of the Medicean period, greedy for opportunity but incapable of statesmanship. Savonarola's attack on the pope and the whole church organization prepared the way for the Reformation. But there was none of the stern metal of Calvinism in the men who surrounded him. His emotional religiosity was an attempt to hold the wavering support of the crowd, and at the same time gloss over insoluble contradictions. To the merchants demanding the reconquest of Pisa as the only Florentine outlet to the sea, he announced that he held Pisa in his hand. To the multitude he predicted "the reform of all Italy." And a mocking song echoed in the streets.

> In the pulpit you said, to feed
> Noble and people and patrician.
> "Pisa I hold in my hand." Indeed?
>
> Ask pardon of all men, and mind.
> Feed Florence no longer on wind.[4]

But only the wind of oratory was at his command. As his moderate program met increasing obstructions, as his support melted away, his emotional violence increased. He represented what may be described as the *hysteria of the middle way*—a phenomenon that was to characterize many of the later apostles of bourgeois reform.

The party of the aristocracy seized power in March, 1498. They hesitated to move against Savonarola, in spite of the papal demand for his destruction, for the monk had not completely lost his popularity. But they hit on a grimly appropriate jest: the man who had promised miracles was called to stand before the multitude and perform a miracle. When Savoranola failed to appear for the ordeal, riots and demonstrations led to his arrest. Trial, torture and execution followed.

The contradiction in Savonarola's position extended to his cultural influence. He demanded simplicity and holiness in art, a return to the devout fleshless painting of Fra Angelico, with its carefully draped figures and ascetic visions. Yet artists who did not share Savonarola's primitive theories of art were drawn to his party, the Popular Party, by its patriotic anticlerical aspects. It stirred the discouraged Botticelli and the youthful Michelangelo. The latter, who was nineteen when Savonarola assumed power, was deeply affected by the Florentine events, adopting the Popular Party's program as the guiding principles of his life and art.

While these events were taking place in Florence, Leonardo continued his labors in Milan. We have no record of the full impact of these troubled years on Leonardo's thought. The most profound statement of his intellectual experience at the time may be found in the somber drama of the *Last Supper;* the betrayal of Christ is the betrayal of man; the terrible certainty of the approaching catastrophe is inherent in the mood of the picture; yet it also has a dignity and faith which transcends the tragedy and foretells the ultimate triumph of humanity.

For a time, Leonardo was safe in Milan. But Ludovico's betrayal brought its inevitable reward. The French invaders had caught a glimpse of the Sforza wealth when they visited Milan as friends in 1494. They had not forgotten the Hall of Treasures. When Louis XII came to the throne of France in 1498, he formed an alliance with the Vatican; entering Italy as the pope's ally, he captured Milan. Ludovico fled.

The classic tragicomedy of the collaborationist was played to an appropriate conclusion. Early in 1500, Ludovico purchased an army of Swiss mercenaries, which recaptured Milan. Ludovico's employees faced another Swiss army under the flag of France. The issue was decided, not by force of arms, but by a strike of one body of mercenaries. On the eve of the battle of Novaro, Ludovico's troops refused to fight, not because they had any compunction in regard to killing their compatriots, but because their pay was in arrears. Defeated, Ludovico retired to a French dungeon. This movement of events forms the historical setting for the *Mona Lisa,* and defines its significance as the first and greatest example of the psychological portraiture that was to flower in the art and literature of the epoch of capitalism.

Leonardo had fled from Milan when his patron was driven out in 1498. The artist went to Mantua and Venice, finally returning to his native city. He was fifty years old when he started the picture in 1502. In that year, the last vestiges of free government were eliminated in Florence. The artist painted a woman carefully smiling, against a formal landscape that revealed nothing of the country's agony. The woman revealed nothing of her own experience; she had been only sixteen when she came to Florence, in the first year of Savonarola's rule. She had seen the revolutionary striving of the people, listened to the tumult in the streets, waited with other women of her class to hear the news of the monk's execution and the return to power of the wealthy oligarchy to which she belonged.

There was nothing especially sensational in Mona Lisa's career. She was a year older than Lucrezia Borgia. Lucrezia seems to have been an unexceptional girl. It was not her fault that she was the daughter of a pope, that she was married in the Vatican at the age of thirteen, and then divorced and remarried four times before she was twenty-one, in order to advance the tangled political fortunes of her family. She had even occupied the throne of St. Peter, replacing her father during one of his absences from Rome. One can regret that Leonardo did not paint Lucrezia in her momentary role as the supreme ruler of Christendom—a child-woman hardened to corruption, member of a family that was probably syphilitic—richly attired and smiling with appropriate decorum.[5]

When Lisa sat for her portrait, Lucrezia had retired to lead an exemplary life as Duchess of Ferrara. She left a trail of mystery that was to puzzle future generations. The melodrama of intrigue, murder and possible incest, suggests another aspect of the "eternal mystery" of womanhood—the degradation of woman in the period when the bourgeoisie began to "put an end to all feudal, patriarchal, idyllic relations," resolving "personal worth into exchange value," drowning sentiment "in the icy waters of egotistical calculation."[6]

Leonardo may not have thought of Lucrezia when he painted the imperturbable Lisa, with her plucked eyebrows and her veiled coquetry. But he was unquestionably thinking of the social pressures and dangers of the time. Then as now, the problem of rational social organization was most dramatically expressed in the irrational "inevitability" of slaughter. Leonardo, in 1505, after two decades of devastation in Italy by mercenary armies, now spoke of war as the "most bestial madness." While he painted the portrait of Lisa, he was at work on the mural for the Pallazzo Vecchio, in which he intended to depict the fury of battle with uncompromising realism. His notebooks show his determination to show the true face of war:

> Make the dead, some half-buried in dust, others with the dust all mingled with the oozing blood and changing into crimson mud. . . . Show others in the death agony grinding their teeth and rolling their eyes, with clenched fists grinding against their bodies and with legs distorted.[7]

In planning the mural, Leonardo decided to use a new method of applying the pigment to the wall. The experiment was a failure, and the picture was ruined. We have only the artist's fragmentary sketches of galloping horses, convulsed figures, strained faces, to suggest the impact of the completed work. The mess that might have been Leonardo's greatest painting remained untouched in the Palazza Vecchio for fifty years, the space finally being covered with frescoes by Vasari.

The ruined wall, blotted with paint that had run or scaled, was like a barrier on the road of Leonardo's life—a mess of broken colors where he had tried to see an ordered universe.

There was no abatement in Leonardo's creative energy. He traveled, made sketches, notes, observations on philosophy, anatomy, astronomy, optics, mathematics. But he knew that the hopes of Renaissance humanism had failed. The world was not moving along the road of peace. It was marching to greater wars and more brutal exploitation.

In 1512, a Spanish invasion brought the Medici back to Italy. Giulio de Medici took over the government of Florence, and in 1513 Giovanni de Medici became Pope Leo X. The reversal of fortune for the Medici was the first step toward making the Vatican subservient to Spanish policy. The wealth of the Americas was to form the bulwark that protected the church against the assault of the Reformation. In 1513, as Leo X assumed the tiara in Rome, there were seventeen Spanish settlements in the West Indies, and Balboa was crossing Panama to gaze upon the Pacific.

The new pope undertook to outdo his predecessor in the magnificence of his artistic and architectural projects. The cultural interests of the Renaissance church were motivated by economic and political considerations. The financial factors in ecclesiastical building and decoration were the same as those that lay behind the medieval construction of cathedrals. But in sixteenth century Rome, the process was vastly enlarged: the Vatican collected tribute from every corner of Europe for the building of St. Peter's and other impressive monuments, and the profit—the difference between the collections and the actual cost of construction—was enormous. At the same time, an essential political purpose was served in making Rome, visibly and impressively, the capital of Christendom.

Leonardo was one of the eminent painters who came to Rome under papal patronage in 1513. Other men adjusted themselves to the demands of the Vatican: Raphael became the chief architect of St. Peter's in 1514. Michelangelo, who had been having tragicomic difficulties collecting his pay for the decoration of the Sistine chapel, and who regarded the return of the Medici as a political catastrophe, swallowed his pride and accepted Leo's commissions.

But for Leonardo, with his broad scientific interest, the intellectual atmosphere of Rome was stifling. He was given an apartment in the Vatican, but his experiments and anatomical drawings caused the suspicion that he was meddling with witchcraft. When Francis I invaded Italy in 1515, he invited Leonardo to return to France with him. The artist complied, taking the *Mona Lisa,* which was sold to the French monarch for 12,000 francs.[8]

While Leonardo spent his last years in comfortable exile at a castle in central France, Machiavelli was living in retirement near Florence, writing his views on the dangers that threatened Italy. Machiavelli was an official of the government ousted by the return of the Medici. He was fortunate to escape with a mild punishment—four turns of the rack—and banishment from the city. He expressed with cold logic the position of the class that was represented with such näive emotion by Savonarola. He held that there must be a strong centralized power, but it must be exercised in the interest of "the people" —Machiavelli used the term, as we have noted, to describe the mercantile and industrial leaders who were supposed to possess the franchise. There were about 3,200 persons out of a Florentine population of 90,000 who met these requirements.[9]

Machiavelli spoke with admiration of Venice, where the ruling group's wealth was "founded upon commerce and movable property . . . Venice is divided into gentlemen and commonalty, and the former have all the offices and honors, from which the latter are entirely excluded; and this distribution causes no disorders."[10]

Machiavelli's concern with Italy's national economic development led him to hold the church responsible for Italy's misfortunes:

> We Italians then owe to the Church of Rome and to her priests our having become irreligious and bad; but we owe her a still greater debt, and one that will be the cause of our ruin, namely, that the Church has kept and still keeps our country divided.[11]

He looked for an absolute monarch who would rise as a liberator, a defender of the bourgeoisie:

> I cannot express the love with which he would be received in all those provinces which have suffered under these foreign invasions, with what thirst for vengeance, with what steadfast faith, with what love, with what grateful tears.[12]

Machiavelli's political thought was more intimately related to the Reformation than to the broad humanistic impulses of the Italian Renaissance. His affinity to Luther—and even to Calvin—is obscured by the frankness with which he depicts the state as a class dictatorship.

He stripped the state of the illusion of "moral" or "divine" authority, and foresaw its future development as an organ of power.

For Leonardo, there could be no hope in such a program of class domination. Leonardo's notes are unsystematic, but they reveal the universality of his interests, his faith in man as builder and conqueror. Yet he was a wanderer, a man without an intellectual home. During the last years of da Vinci's voluntary exile in France, Cortes was preparing to conquer Mexico. There was a new world to win. In his *Prophecies,* Leonardo pondered on the new world's promise. He wrote "of the precious metals":

> There shall come forth out of dark and gloomy caves that which shall cause the whole human race to undergo great afflictions, perils, and death. . . . It shall bring to pass an endless number of crimes; it shall prompt and incite wretched men to assassinate, to steal and to enslave. . . .[13]

And "of the cruelty of man":

> Creatures shall be seen upon the earth who will always be fighting one with another, with very great losses and frequent deaths on either side. . . . There shall be nothing remaining on the earth or under the earth or in the waters that shall not be pursued and molested or destroyed, and that which is in one country taken away to another. . . . Earth! What delays thee to open and hurl them headlong into the deep fissures of thy huge abysses and caverns, and no longer to display in the sight of heaven so savage and ruthless a monster? [14]

Was this the answer to the promise of the Renaissance, the revelations of science, the new knowledge of man and nature?

Was this the secret of Mona Lisa's eyes? Was the majority of mankind condemned forever to conflict and toil, while art and truth were dedicated to the texture of rich fabric, the beauty of the flesh, the enigma of a careful smile?

2 : THE UNION SHOE

AMERICAN SCHOOL CHILDREN occasionally sing an old German folk song: "Die gedanken sind frei." The children are not told of the origins of the song: they probably do not know that it was sung defiantly in German concentration camps during the Hitler terror.

"The thoughts are free" was the song of the Union Shoe, the revolutionary organization of German peasants which conducted the struggle for liberation that swept central Europe in 1525. The literature of history pays tribute to Martin Luther as one of the great molders of modern culture. But the key to Luther's career is to be found in the peasant war. It transformed Luther's thought, determined the direction of the movement which he inaugurated. The failure of the revolt delimited the Reformation, defined the irreconcilable split in the forces that opposed Catholic domination, and prepared the way for the Counter Reformation and the continuing strength of the feudal-ecclesiastical structure of power.

The peasants and laborers who sang that "the thoughts are free" inherited a tradition that went back to the Middle Ages, and more particularly to the Bohemian Revolution and the craft communism of Tabor. The growth of metallurgical production at the end of the fourteenth century formed the economic background of the Hussite wars. The further development of mining in central and eastern Europe in the fifteenth century was the basic cause of the second revolutionary upsurge. In order to understand Luther and the peasant war, we must consider the meteoric rise of the Fugger family.

While Tabor was defending itself against crusading armies, the

Fuggers were weaving cloth in Augsberg. The defeat of Tabor assured ecclesiastical and imperial control of the mines. But in most cases the owners were content to receive a profit without taking the risks of capital investment or management. There were merchants in Augsberg, Nuremberg and other German cities who had funds to invest. The exploitation of the mines created a new center of finance, linked closely to the empire and the papacy, in southern Germany.

The Fuggers acquired capital from textile production, and invested it in commerce. From their trade in spices, cloth and miscellaneous merchandise, they became rich enough to loan money to the emperor, receiving valuable mining concessions in return. In 1473, the financial relationship had become so intimate that Frederick III granted the three Fugger brothers, Ulrich, George and Jacob, the right to bear arms. The date is important in the economic history of the Fugger family, but it is also significant in the economic history of Europe. We recall the alum cartel established by the Medici in alliance with the Vatican in 1466, and the subsequent break between the two partners: when Sixtus IV became head of the church in 1471, he began the feud with the Medici which culminated in the Pazzi conspiracy and the excommunication of Lorenzo de Medici in 1478. The papal break with the Medici explains the growing connection between the Hapsburg empire and the Fuggers, and the development of financial interests in southern Germany which rivaled and eventually surpassed the banking power of the Medici. The development of mining in central Europe was responsible for the close cooperation between the empire and the Vatican, and the struggle with the Medici enabled the Fuggers to secure much of the ecclesiastical business formerly controlled by the Florentine firm.

The Fugger fortune grew with the rising graph of iron, copper and silver production in Saxony, Silesia, Bohemia, Hungary and the Tyrol. Other merchants shared in the bonanza.

In inverse ratio to the rise of the Fuggers and their associates was the proletarianization of the peasantry. According to Jacob Strieder, "the term 'laborer,' in its narrower sense, appears for the first time in the sources for the history of mining in the Middle Ages, and has been retained since then as a class designation for the wageworkers of capitalistic industry."[1] Where the peasant remained on the feudal estate, the oppression of serfdom was intensified. But where large-scale mining was introduced, the peasant was evicted in order to provide a reservoir of "free" labor—with the inevitable accompaniment of unemployment, desperate migrations in search of jobs, broken families, people living on the thin edge of starvation.

The first rumblings of peasant discontent that foreshadowed the German peasant war occurred in Eastern Germany and in the Rhine Valley. These activities were influenced by the teachings of Lollards and other propagandists in France and Flanders and were directed against feudal and monastic oppression. Hans Boeheim, known as Hans the Piper, was the leader of a rebellion that mobilized 34,000 armed men in Wurzburg in 1476. The rebels were defeated and dispersed. Insurrections occurred in Holland in 1491, 1492, and 1497. The Union Shoe, or *Bundschuh,* made its first appearance as the emblem of revolt in Alsace in 1493. The banner showed a peasant's shoe with long leather strings: preparations were made for the capture of the city of Schlettstadt. The flag unfurled over the fortress was to be the signal for a revolt throughout Alsace. The plan was discovered, the leaders seized, tortured and killed. As two of the conspirators were led out to be drawn and quartered, they shouted: "The Bundschuh must go forward, be it soon or late."[2]

The words echoed across Europe in the next two decades. In 1513, the Union Shoe was widely organized in the Black Forest and the upper Rhine under the leadership of Joss Fritz, who traveled from place to place holding large meetings at night in the depth of the woods or on lonely mountainsides. The plebeian element in the cities was strongly represented, as well as unemployed knights, priests, and a few members of the lower nobility. Christian fraternity was emphasized. When Fritz called the people to arms at Lehen, he was encouraged by the parish priest, who asserted that "God approved the Bundschuh, as might be shown from the Scriptures; it was therefore, a godly thing."[3]

The program called for confiscation of church estates, abolition of unfair taxes and tolls, freedom of hunting, fishing, pasture and wood cutting, reduction of all interest to five percent. It was a moderate program. The rebels intended to seize a city and then negotiate with the emperor for the acceptance of their demands. But the plan was prematurely betrayed and crushed with the usual ferocity. Fritz escaped to Switzerland, where he maintained contact with his friends across the Rhine and prepared for a new uprising.

The movement led by Joss Fritz was to a very large extent a direct protest against the banking monopoly operated by the Fugger family. The firm had become a financial octopus reaching into every part of the European economy—and into the pocketbook of every family. The close ties between the Augsberg bank and Rome are indicated in the extent and character of its Italian business. The accounts of the Fugger branch office in Venice for the year 1516 showed a turnover of 400,000 ducats, the equivalent of about $4,000,000 in purchasing power today. Most of this business covered credits or exchange transactions linking the firm's Rome office with the headquarters at Augsberg and involving the complicated financial affairs of the papacy.[4]

While Joss Fritz was organizing armed rebellion in the Black Forest, a representative of the Fuggers was negotiating a deal with the papacy which was to arouse an uproar in Germany and lead to Luther's denunciation of the church four years later. The deal, which was concluded in 1514, was a three-cornered arrangement between the Vatican, the Augsberg bankers and Albert, the son of the Elector of Brandenberg. The Fuggers used their influence to secure the archbishopric of Magdeburg for Albert in 1513, when he was twenty-three years old. In the next year, they obtained for him the more valuable see of Mainz. They also gave him a loan of 100,000 gulden. This generosity was not motivated by any special affection for the young man. The loan was secured by authorization from the pope permitting Albert to collect money from the sale of indulgences throughout his diocese. The Fuggers received the right to supervise the collection, and take a substantial fee for their services. The remainder was split half and half between the archbishop and the pope.

Thus the bankers became the guardians of souls; people who paid for the remission of sins won salvation by a gift to God by way of the Fugger family. Since the Fuggers were men of business, they knew how to sell salvation wholesale and with maximum efficiency. The youthful archbishop issued instructions setting a regular schedule of rates in payment for various moral lapses, and stipulating that it was "not necessary to make confession or to visit churches or altars." Cash was all that was wanted. Those who paid need not bother to pray.[5] The Fuggers employed John Tetzel, a famous indulgence preacher, to go from town to town in the manner of a modern revivalist exhorting and collecting.[6]

The arrangement throws a good deal of light on the artistic benefactions of Leo X, the economic background of his dealings with painters, sculptors and architects, and the reasons for the building of St. Peter's. But we are here concerned with its social consequences in Germany—its stimulating effect on the activities of the Union Shoe, and the consequent growth of middle-class discontent culminating in Luther's ninety-five theses.

From 1513 to 1517, rebellions of peasants and laborers spread from Switzerland eastward in a great arc through the mining country. Civil war developed in Austria in 1515. Castles and monasteries were sacked. Captured nobles were tried and executed by popular tribunals. In Hungary a peasant army of 60,000 assembled under the leadership of Gorgy Dozsa and was defeated by government troops in a series of pitched battles. In 1517, Joss Fritz returned to the Black Forest. He still carried under his shirt the flag of the Union Shoe that had been prepared for the rising in 1513. The remnants of the movement that had failed four years earlier were reorganized; Fritz moved from town to town, holding meetings in the woods at night, giving instructions for the day of battle.

On October 31, 1517, Luther nailed the ninety-five theses to the doors of Wittenberg Chapel. There was nothing unusual in posting a "disputation," or challenge to debate a series of propositions. But Luther tackled the most controversial issue of the day: "The treasures of indulgences," he said, "are nets, with which they now fish for the riches of men." Indulgences were supposed to be the greatest graces—"but 'greatest' is to be understood to refer to them as producers of revenue." "Papal pardons cannot take away the least of venial sins." [7]

Luther had probably heard only vaguely about the Union Shoe. Like most of his associates at Wittenburg, Luther came from a middle-class background. His father, Hans Luther, was a Thuringian peasant, who had moved to Mansfield in Saxony in order to work in the iron mines. During Martin's boyhood, his father began to improve his economic position. He leased a small furnace from the Count of Mansfield; acquiring a little capital, he was able to rent another furnace and then a third. Thus money was available to give the son a university education.

Luther's political views were those of his class. His patriotic zeal visioned the free development of the nation's economy and culture. The growth for which he hoped was obstructed by ecclesiastical interference: money that went to the church and the Augsberg bankers was needed for local institutions and for the development of the university.

Luther was swept along by the storm he had unleashed. The ninety-five theses were printed and distributed in large quantities. The professor of theology found himself transmuted into a public leader. Luther accepted the call. The disputation that had been intended for the quiet halls of Wittenberg was conducted in the arena of international politics. Luther was accused of holding the proscribed opinions of Huss; the papal attacks on him and the enormous popular support that he received forced him to adopt an increasingly uncompromising position.

The death of the Emperor Maximilian in 1519 brought a political crisis. Charles, the emperor's grandson, heir to the Hapsburg possessions and already master of Flanders and Spain, had the primary claim to the imperial crown. But the office was not hereditary, and the choice lay with the seven German princes known as electors. The king of France was determined to seize the prize from the Hapsburgs, and even Henry VIII of England announced his candidacy.

The election was a matter of open bribery, the Fuggers spending enormous sums to assure the choice of Charles. The Augsberg bankers were heavily involved in dealings with the Hapsburgs; they controlled extensive properties in Spain—agricultural estates, mercury mines at Almaden, silver mines at Guadalcanal. The Fuggers also hoped to secure concessions in Spanish America. The firm's loans, its existent and prospective investments and monopolies, depended on a Hapsburg victory.

The Fuggers treated the election as "the biggest business deal of the century." They had comparatively little difficulty in buying the support of their friend, the Archbishop of Mainz. But the archbishop's brother, Joachim of Brandenburg, held out for such a large honorarium that the bankers regarded his conduct as unethical. Joachim's vote was finally purchased at a cost of 300,000 gulden and the hand of a Hapsburg princess.[8]

In spite of the Vatican's financial ties with the Fuggers, Pope Leo X feared the growth of Hapsburg power and opposed the election of Charles. There was hope in Germany that the new Emperor would reduce taxes, curb monopoly and favor the development of German trade and industry. Luther reflected these hopes in the pamphlets written in 1520, in which he made his irrevocable break with Rome.

His appeal to German national pride was phrased in much the same terms that Machiavelli used in appealing to the Italians:

> Now that Italy is sucked dry they come to Germany . . . What has brought us Germans to such a pass that we must suffer this robbery and destruction of our property by the Pope.[9]

Luther demanded "some bridle for the Fuggers and similar companies."[10] He accepted, with caution, the heritage of Huss:

> It is not my intention here to judge John Huss's belief and to defend his errors, although my understanding has not been able to find any errors in him.[11]

The pamphlet in which these passages appear is addressed *To the German Nobility*. Machiavelli appealed to a hypothetical prince to save Italy. Luther assumed that the great nobles would lead Germany to salvation. The lords shared his dislike of the church, and were eager to find some pretext for the seizure of ecclesiastical properties. But events were soon to prove that German liberation could not be achieved from above. Luther's national ideal took no account of the forces that composed the German nation.

The political realities that faced Charles V made it impossible for him to pursue a liberal policy. He was financially dependent on the Fuggers and their associates. His ambitious plans for consolidating his European empire required the backing of the church, which had to be won by diplomacy or secured by military force. Charles would eventually take up arms against the papacy in order to make the church subservient to his will. But at the time of his coronation in 1520, he was anxious to secure an accord with Leo X.

The new emperor was frightened by popular disturbances in many parts of his dominions. In Spain, the bloody revolt of the *Communeros* spread through the cities of Castile in 1520. It is not surprising to find the armed uprising at Segovia led by the woolcarders, the traditional rebels in the textile industry. The people of Segovia hanged officers of the crown and took control of the city. In Burgos, a few days later, the people invaded and destroyed the houses of officials; they made a great pile of documents relating to property and taxes and burned them in the square. A contemporary account says that the people did not "attempt to appropriate anything, which is much to be marvelled at, considering the character of base folk."[12] By the end of 1520, the Spanish cities had formed a "union of perpetual brotherhood," pledging every commune to relieve anyone oppressed, and promising never to ask or accept absolution from their oath to do so.[13] At the same time, the peasants of Valencia rebelled.

The seriousness of the Spanish disorders, as a threat to the Hapsburg control of Spain, may be judged by a letter which the viceroy of Castile addressed to Charles on October 25. This was two days after the ceremony at Aix-la-Chapelle in which Charles received the crown of empire. But the viceroy was less concerned with congratulatory messages than with the pressing task of subduing the cities. He wrote the emperor that he was trying "to dissociate Burgos from the Junta people and alienate them from her":

> For that end alone, everything they wanted ought to be granted and conceded; how much more, since upon Burgos depend all the mountain districts and Vizcaya and Guipuzcoa and Alava and vassal villages and other cities and towns, within the province and without, which share her opinion. Were it not done were completely to lose the realm. . . . You Majesty must believe that these your realms are in such state that there is need of pardon and liberties, and a great army in order that the voice of your service may continue in them. . . .[14]

The viceroy's skillful negotiations were of considerable service to the crown. But it was a "great army" led by the nobles, with their mounted retainers and superior equipment, that eventually reduced the cities to obedience.

Charles' coronation was celebrated by popular protest in other parts of his dominions. While the Spanish cities took arms, the German organizations of the Union Shoe were conducting systematic raids on monasteries and churches, and Flanders was seething with discontent. In October, 1520 (the month of the coronation and the solemn league and covenant of the Spanish communes), sullen crowds stood in the public square at Antwerp while a bonfire of Luther's books and pamphlets flamed to the sky. The bookburning, like so many others, was not successful in obliterating the author's influence, for it had to be repeated in the following year.[15]

The social disturbances in central Europe, Spain and Flanders form the background for Luther's appearance before the Diet of Worms in January, 1521. Luther's writings gave ideological support to the rebellions and formed the basis for a potentially broad united front of the dissident classes. The emperor presided over the imperial diet. The most urgent business on the agenda was the condemnation of

Luther. Charles hoped that the matter could be disposed of quietly. But the assembled dignitaries reflected the intense national feeling in Germany. They insisted that Luther be permitted to appear and defend himself. On April 16, disregarding threats, Luther entered the city through cheering crowds. Before the Diet, Luther said:

> I cannot and will not recant anything, for to act against our conscience is neither safe for us, nor open to us.
>
> On this I take my stand. I can do no other. God help me.[16]

In many ways, those words mark the climax of Luther's struggle, the bravest and truest moment of his life. He stood free and sure, but the moment passed. He was never to know the same freedom. His conscience would be divided, torn by the social forces that clashed around him.

A few days after his appearance before the Diet, Luther vanished. The rumor that he had been murdered brought revolutionary warnings from two groups. The word *Bundschuh* appeared on walls and buildings. At the same time, a proclamation announced that four hundred knights would revenge any harm done to Luther. The spokesman for the knights seemed to be confident of peasant support, for he used the peasant slogan: "I mean a great mischief, with 8,000 foot soldiers at my back. Bundschuh, Bundschuh, Bundschuh!"[17]

These warnings came from the two classes that were most anxious for social change. Peasants and laborers had been systematically preparing for an armed uprising. But knighthood had also reached a point at which it had nothing to lose but its practically useless armor. A few knights were lucky enough to hold clerical or administrative jobs. Most of them constituted an anarchic, socially misplaced group, living insecurely on the fringes of the social order. In 1513, Dürer made his engraving of *The Knight and Death:* the melancholy figure on his bony nag is on a pilgrimage that can end only at the grave. Dürer's picture suggests the violent, hopeless role that the knights were to play in the Protestant revolt.

While tension mounted and the mystery of his disappearance deepened, Luther was getting a comfortable lesson in *real politik*. He had been spirited away by his most influential protector, the Elector of Saxony. In the elector's castle, safely divorced from the clamor of the market place, Luther engaged in long conversations with his benefactor. The results of these discussions were soon apparent. The first popular move to establish Protestantism occurred in Luther's own town of Wittenberg. The people invaded the churches, destroyed images and vestments, and forced the city magistrates to adopt the principles of the Reformation. Luther came out of retirement to protest against the Protestants who had followed his teachings.[18]

Luther's appeals for moderation could not stem the tides of discontent. The years from 1516 to 1522 witnessed a rapid rise in food prices, which was largely due to the monopolistic control of imports by the Fuggers and other merchants. Early in 1522, the emperor proposed an ambitious plan for uniform taxes on all imports and exports, to be collected at customhouses that were to be built around his possessions, from Hungary to the Netherlands. The proposal spelled ruin for commerce, and the cities sent a delegation to the imperial court to protest.[19]

The knights, itching for combat and trusting in their military prowess, assembled an army led by Franz von Sickingen, and attacked the city of Treves in August, 1622. Sickingen called on Luther for support, and issued a manifesto to the inhabitants of Treves, promising to "deliver them from the heavy anti-Christian yoke of the priesthood and lead them to evangelical freedom."[20]

The brief, bloody affray proved the isolation of the knights from other classes. It also proved their inability to utilize modern techniques of warfare. Sickingen's final defense of his own castle was a sort of allegory of social and military change. He was sure that the thick walls, standing gray and forbidding on a mountainside, could withstand a three months' siege. As thc guns of the princes smashed the ramparts, he went to a loophole to observe the attack, and another shot crashed through the masonry and pinned him under a falling beam.[21] The defeat of the knights had no effect on the preparations of the Union Shoe, which came to fruition in 1525. Joss Fritz was dead, but his place was taken by able leaders. Among these, the most indefatigable organizer and the most profound thinker was Thomas Muenzer.

Muenzer's itinerary from 1520 to 1525 suggests the methods of the underground and the remarkably wide dissemination of equalitarian ideas. In 1520, at the age of thirty-one, Muenzer went to Zwickau, in Saxony near the Bohemian border, as an evangelical preacher. There were silver mines near Zwickau, and it was a center of cloth production. Here Muenzer came in contact with the sect of Anabaptists, led by a weaver, Nicholas Storch. When the Anabaptists were expelled from the town in 1522, Muenzer crossed to Prague, where he seems to have been in contact with members of the old Taborite sect.[22]

These contacts may have had a profound influence on Muenzer's later activity. Driven from Bohemia, he went to Thuringia in central Germany, preaching sermons at Altstedt which attracted wide popular support. Accused of incendiary doctrines and of organizing miners and peasants, Muenzer went to Muehlhausen, in central Germany, where he issued a pamphlet describing himself as "the man with the hammer," and saying that "A wall of iron against the kings, princes, priests, and for the people, hath been erected. Let them fight, for victory is wonderous, and the strong and godless tyrants will perish."[23]

The pamphlet made it necessary for Muenzer to escape from Muehlhausen, and he undertook a rapid tour of organization. He appeared in Alsace, then in Switzerland. We find him in the Black Forest at the beginning of 1525, aiding in arrangements for the general insurrection that broke out there in February.

Forty thousand armed peasants assembled in the Black Forest. Muenzer returned to Muehlhausen, where his work in the preceding year had laid the groundwork for the revolution that broke out on March 17. The patrician council was overthrown and the people elected an "eternal council" with Muenzer as its president.

Muenzer was both a theorist and a practical organizer. His travels in the mining regions had given him a sense of the injustices suffered by the laborers, and a groping consciousness of their creative power as a class. Some of his statements concerning the role of the workers are years, even centuries, ahead of his time. But he also recognized the necessity of maintaining the democratic coalition that had seized power in Muehlhausen. He faced the task of consolidating his power and using the city as a base for the organization of a national movement. He introduced moderate reforms, conciliated the mercantile and industrial classes, and broadcast messages and appeals to the nation.

The example of Muehlhausen had an electrifying effect. Revolutionary armies were on the march in Thuringia, Saxony, and Franconia. The peasants rose in Alsace in April. The Tyrol and other mining regions in Austria were in arms. Peasants and miners captured the city of Salzburg.

As the rebellion became national in scope, the middle class was swept forward by the revolutionary current and it seemed possible to effect a coalition that would include the bourgeoisie and progressive members of the nobility. An aristocrat, Goetz von Berlichingen, commanded one of the peasant armies. Another division was led by the Franconian knight, Florian Geyer. Wendel Hipler, former chancellor of the Count of Hohenlohe, shared political leadership with the peasant, Jäcklein Rohrbach.

Rohrbach's hatred of the aristocracy is said to have been inspired by the rape of the village girl he intended to marry. However, Rohrbach had wide political contacts and well-organized support when he raised the standard of revolt at the village of Flein, not far from Heilbronn, on April 2. He had been in correspondence with Wendel Hipler, and with representatives of the urban artisans and laborers in Heilbronn. He gathered a force of fifteen hundred partisans, and marched to join the Odenwald peasants assembled under the command of George Metzler. The growing army was called the *Heller Haufen,* or "united contingent"; under Hipler's guidance, the guerrilla bands were welded into an effective military organization.

The rebels moved against the town of Weinsberg, where the castle was held by Count Ludwig von Helfenstein, whose wife was a half sister of the emperor. When a group of peasants came to the gates of the town for a parley, the count made a sortie and massacred them all. On the morning of April 16, the army led by Florian Geyer and Rohrbach stormed the town. The attack was so furious that within a few moments Geyer's banners were waving from the battlements of the castle, and Rohrbach's men were marching through the main street, warning citizens to keep to their houses so that all the nobles and men-at-arms could be put to death. Helfenstein and his wife, with some of their followers, were immediately tried and sentenced to die. The count and the other men were compelled to "run the gauntlet," impaling themselves on the spears of the peasants.

The role of women in the rebellion is suggested in the story of the woman known as the "black Hoffman." Since the descriptions of her are derived from fabricated accounts written by persons hostile to the peasants, it is not surprising to have her portrayed as a witch, taking savage delight in slaughter, and wearing a black cloak and hood with a red girdle. She is said to have stood with outstretched arms on a hill during the assault on Weinsberg, shouting "Down with the dogs; strike them all dead!" We are told that after Count von

Helfenstein's death, she plunged a knife into his body, and smeared the blood on the peasants' shoes and spears.

There are similar tales of alleged cruelty by the men who led the uprising. These fictions occur in all upper-class accounts of revolutionary movements. The evidence, scanty as it is, does not bear out the charge that the peasants engaged in indiscriminate acts of vengeance. For example, the count's wife and child were not killed. She suffered the indignity of being stripped and dressed in the rags of a beggar woman. She was then placed on a dung cart which carried her to Heilbronn.[24]

The capture of Weinsberg and the summary execution of Count von Helfenstein were of great strategic importance. The feudal and ecclesiastical lords in the surrounding country were forced to submit, and the power of the aristocratic burgher party in Heilbronn was broken. The lower and middle classes of the city opened the gates to the peasant army, which entered without resistance, and the city council took the oath of allegiance to the "Evangelical Brotherhood." The agreement with the municipal authorities provided that religious establishments should pay a ransom: the Carmelite monastery was fined 3,000 gulden; the Clara convent paid 5,000 gulden, and smaller religious houses were taxed in proportion. But only the properties of the Knights of the Teutonic Order, the wealthiest and most hated representatives of Catholic power, were given to destruction. Many of the people who sacked and burned the home of the knights were tenants occupying lands belonging to the order.[25]

The capture of Heilbronn marked the high point of the rebellion. Half of Germany was in the hands of the insurgents, and it seemed possible to realize a program of national unity which would grant the most urgent demands of peasants and laborers while protecting the interests of other classes. This was the aim of Wendel Hipler, whose integrity was acknowledged by all the groups in the coalition. Delegates from various peasant organizations assembled at Heilbronn to draw up demands for submission to the emperor. The program under consideration called for a centralized government, removal of commercial restrictions, abolition of internal customs.

It was a moderate, and apparently practical, program of national development. But it could not be achieved because the urban middle and upper classes were frightened by the militant strength displayed by peasants and laborers. While Hipler was drawing up the demands of the coalition, the burghers of Heilbronn were secretly negotiating with the princes, who had mobilized a strong army under the leadership of George Trucksess. Capable and ruthless, Trucksess ravaged the countryside, burning peasant homes and villages. The peasant forces had to leave Heilbronn in order to fight Trucksess. A small garrison was left in the town.

This was what the burghers wanted and planned. They seized the city by a sudden coup, enabling the princes to recapture it. Hipler and the peasant leaders escaped, but the loss of Heilbronn split the coalition, and isolated and demoralized the people who were the backbone of the revolt. A similar pattern of betrayal developed in other cities. Wurzburg was held by the rebels, but the burghers reached an understanding with Trucksess. His troops surrounded the city; on the morning of June 7, the municipal councilors opened the gates. Five thousand peasant soldiers were captured before they could organize resistance. Eighty-one of the prisoners were immediately decapitated.

The intellectual justification for these betrayals was provided by Luther, who reflected the fears of the bourgeoisie in a pamphlet calling for the destruction of the peasants: "They should be knocked to pieces, strangled and stabbed, secretly and openly, by everyone who can do it, just as one must kill a mad dog."[26] This outcry has often been described as an emotional lapse, occasioned by the pressure of events, and unrelated to the main course of Luther's thought. On the contrary, Luther's attitude toward the peasants sprang from his deepest social convictions and expressed the logic of his life and work. One can describe his political conduct in terms that are frequently heard today. He had "repudiated his left wing and was forced to depend on his right."[27] Underlying the political decision was the dilemma that was inherent in Luther's personal history as well as in the history of his time. In an earlier period, when Luther was moving toward the left, he asked a pertinent question about the source of the Fuggers' wealth:

> Is it possible in a single man's lifetime such great wealth should be collected together, if it were done rightly and according to God's will? I am not skilled in accounts, but I do not understand how it is possible for one hundred guilders to gain twenty in a year, or how one guilder can gain another, and that not out of the soil, or by cattle.[28]

The peasant war began to unveil an answer to Luther's rhetorical question. Luther turned from the unbearable truth. The defense of the free conscience did not include the right of workers to determine the conditions of their own existence. Luther called on the bourgeoisie to make a free choice between the peasants and the princes. But the choice was made under the pressure of an inescapable dilemma. In abandoning the peasants, the bourgeoisie sacrificed their interest in national expansion to their fear of democracy: they accepted subservience to the feudal-ecclesiastical structure of power as the only means of curbing the aspirations of peasants and laborers.

The disintegration of the rebel armies was as rapid as their first successes. There was no centralized command, and no time to consolidate gains, or to undertake military and political organization. The cause that looked so bright in April was doomed in May. Among the leaders there were traitors like Goetz von Berlichingen, who joined the peasants only to betray them and was in contact with the princes from the moment that he assumed command of one of the revolutionary armies. In his autobiography, Goetz admits that he never sympathized with the rebellion: "They compelled me to be their fool and leader, and to the end that I might save my body and my life, I must forsooth do as they willed."[29] Berlichingen systematically weakened the morale of the men under his command and kept them out of action. He engaged in futile and wearing maneuvers until he felt that the time was ripe for him to desert to the enemy.

There were other members of the upper class who displayed extraordinary courage and fortitude, standing with the peasants and laborers to the end. Hipler was one of these. Another was Florian Geyer. When his troop was attacked and decimated, the knight reorganized a company of six hundred men. When more than half of these were slaughtered, he continued guerrilla warfare, raising another peasant force and dying in a last battle on June 9.[30]

Meanwhile, late in May, the northern center of the rebellion in Muhlhausen faced a powerful attacking army. There was dissension in the city and Muenzer's men were inadequately armed and poorly trained. Nevertheless, the princes followed their usual tactic of treachery—a false armistice which was violated by a surprise attack. Muenzer held a hill, still known as Battle Mountain, with about eight thousand men entrenched behind a barricade of wagons. A meeting was held. The people were told that the princes offered amnesty if Muenzer were delivered to them alive. A knight and a priest favored capitulation. Muenzer had them brought forward and decapitated.

But Muenzer's determination to fight could not overcome the peasants' lack of guns and ammunition. Without waiting for the conclusion of the armistice, the princes' warriors encircled the mountain, advancing in close columns with their guns pounding the barricade of wagons. The battle was a massacre. 5,000 of the peasants were slaughtered, and Muenzer was captured.[31]

The city of Muhlhausen held out for a few days. When its defense proved hopeless, twelve hundred women streamed out of the gates, barefooted and in tattered clothes, to ask the princes to have mercy on the town. They were told that the men must appear to plead for themselves. Leading citizens came to the camp, bareheaded and barefooted, kneeling three times before the princes and handing over the keys of the city. Muhlhausen paid a heavy penalty. It was deprived of its freedom and given to the Landgrave of Hesse. Many prominent men were executed, including the burgomaster. The town was spared destruction by the payment of a ransom of 40,000 gulden.[32]

The re-establishment of feudal power in Germany had a disastrous effect on trade and industry. The fate of Muhlhausen was duplicated in other cities. Everywhere, the burghers were held responsible for what had happened. Having betrayed the revolution, the burghers had to pay the cost of it in heavy fines and the loss of former privileges. The indemnities paid by the merchants were a foretaste of the tragedy of the German bourgeoisie four centuries later when the military and land-holding class drove the nation to ruin.

Muenzer was condemned to die. Before his execution, he was tortured in the presence of a distinguished group of nobles. The somber scene symbolized the fate of Germany. In the long reach of history, Muenzer on the rack in the circle of princes was the brother and comrade of the men and women tortured by the Nazis.

The Peasant War was fateful for Europe as well as for Germany. Lutheranism as a state religion was adopted by the North German princes, and their example was followed by the Scandinavian countries. The Baltic was a rich commercial region, and its economic ties with Rome were not as close as those that bound southern Europe to the papacy. The break with Catholicism enabled the northern rulers to seize church properties and strengthen their power. Even the Teutonic Knights with their vast grain estates in East Prussia and their lucrative trade in amber and slaves, found that the business advantages of a break with Catholicism outweighed the religious vows embodied in the rituals of the order. The Knights became Lutherans in 1526.

Luther's political views reflected the position of the class which adopted his doctrine. The hatred of the peasantry expressed in the heat of the civil conflict hardened into a fixed mold. When a humane nobleman wrote to Luther that he was worried about the forced labor and heavy dues to which the law entitled him, Luther replied that his conscience need not trouble him, as it was God's will that burdens be imposed on the poor in order to keep them in their place.[33] In a sermon on *Genesis,* Luther appealed to the authority of the Bible as justification of slavery: "Sheep, cattle, menservants and maidservants, they were all possessions, to be sold as it pleased them like other beasts. It were even a good thing were it still so. For else no man may compel nor tame the servile folk."[34]

The identification of Lutheranism with the interests of the landholding aristocracy caused the bourgeoisie to adopt forms of organization which were more in accord with its class ambitions. The movement had its origin in the reforms introduced at Zurich by Huldreich Zwingli. Luther's influence inspired Zwingli to begin his preachments against the authority of Rome in 1519. But the situation in Switzerland made it possible to convert the new doctrine into a militant assertion of the right of the burghers to elect a Presbyterian council, ruling church and municipality in the interest of the bourgeoisie.

The Swiss towns had a long tradition of independence. The peasantry had won concessions in previous rebellions, so that there was far less radical ferment in Switzerland than in the neighboring countries. Furthermore, there was no military force in Switzerland that corresponded to the princely armies mobilized in Germany. While warfare raged on the other side of the Rhine, Zwingli carried through a peaceful reformation in Zurich in 1525, establishing a model which was later amplified in the Calvinist regime in Geneva.

The defeat of the German revolution, and the annihilation of 150,000 German peasants, did not destroy the beliefs for which the rebels died. Armed struggle continued in the mining regions to the east—in Styria, Upper Austria and Carinthia. In the spring of 1526, peasants and miners still held the city of Salzburg against a Bavarian army. One of Muenzer's lieutenants, Geismaier, led a force to relieve Salzburg; after a series of battles, the workers were defeated, and Geismaier escaped to Venice, where he was assassinated in 1527.

The Union Shoe was driven underground. The remnants of the peasant association, proselytizing among the poor and oppressed under various forms and disguises, were generally called Anabaptists. The generic name was derived from the most militant of the radical sects. The practice of adult baptism was associated with the social gospel of the Anabaptists, expressing the right of all men to enter the Christian brotherhood by their own will and choice. The movement was especially strong in eastern Europe, and in the Netherlands.

Workers in Amsterdam and Antwerp were so persistent in their adherence to the illegal cause that the Spanish government resorted to extreme measures in 1529. The death penalty was decreed for any persons meeting together to read the gospel or discuss the articles of faith.[35] The reign of terror failed to deter the heretics whose activities displayed remarkable discipline and wide organizational contacts. Many of the leaders of the underground traveled extensively. Melchior Hoffman, who appeared as an organizer at Amsterdam in 1530, had previously visited Stockholm, Kiel, Livonia, East Friedland and Strasburg. Jan Böckelson, called Jan of Leyden, was a journeyman tailor, who had voyaged as far south as Lisbon and as far north as Lübeck. He went from Leyden to Briel, Rotterdam, Amsterdam, Enkhuysen and Alkmar, baptizing wherever he went and forming groups of ten or twelve persons.[36]

Associated with Böckelson was Jan Matthys, who had also worked with Hoffman. Böckelson and Matthys went to Münster, a German city a few miles from the Dutch border, at the beginning of 1534. They evidently came to give seasoned direction to a movement which already had the support of a large part of the Münster population. On February 21, the Anabaptists secured control of the city council. The experience of the peasant war and the persecution that followed it had steeled the Anabaptists to reject compromise. There was no attempt to form a coalition. No concessions were offered to the wealthy citizens. On February 27, a meeting of the armed people in the city hall called for immediate seizure of property and its conversion to common use. Houses were invaded. Rich men who resisted or concealed their possessions were killed or driven from the city.[37]

The new regime lasted a little more than a year. But the episode is of major historical importance as an indication of the strength of the left in the period after the peasant war and a further link between the Christian communism of the Middle Ages and the political thought of the seventeenth and eighteenth centuries. As in Tabor a century earlier, the people of Münster organized common ownership on the basis of individual craft production. Artisans continued their trade under municipal regulations, each task being regarded as a public charge. The citizens addressed each other as brother and sister. A people's army was quickly and efficiently trained.

The Bishop of Münster moved to recapture the town. The siege began in April. But the people defended themselves with remarkable unity and courage. The bishop called on neighboring princes for aid. The burghers of Cleves and Cologne gave him artillery, infantry and cavalry. But Münster could not be taken. The German princes were haunted by the spectre of another peasant war. They sent assistance to the bishop and asked the emperor to send troops. A powerful army of knights and mercenaries blockaded the city. There was famine inside the walls, but there was no talk of surrender.

The defense of Münster had an explosive effect on the political situation in the Low Countries. Thousands of Anabaptists gathered in Holland, capturing monasteries, marching westward to relieve Münster.[38] The artisans and laborers of Amsterdam rose under Melchior Hoffman and almost mastered the city. The Dutch burghers hated the imperial government, but they cooperated eagerly with the authorities in suppressing the revolt. The defeat of the movement in Amsterdam made it comparatively easy to disperse the poorly armed crowds marching toward Münster. Order was re-established in the Netherlands with the usual reprisals. Men who had taken part in the revolt were burned at the stake; the women were given a more humane death by drowning.[39]

But Münster was undefeated. The capture of the famine-stricken city was finally accomplished by treachery. On St. John's Eve, 1535, a traitor admitted a body of enemy troops to the town. These men had the password of the defenders; they were able to surprise and kill the sentries, and get possession of the gate. A contemporary account tells how the victors "fell with furious rage on the houses, and where they found anyone they dragged him by the head out of the house into the street, hewed him to pieces, or stabbed him dead. Shortly afterward, they slew all around, till there were no more to slay."[40]

The fall of Münster coincided with the establishment of the Anglican church in England and the beginning of persecution of the Huguenots in France. Europe was entering upon a century of bloody religious conflict. The Anabaptists seemed to be submerged in the struggle of more powerful forces. But their strength may be measured by the fear that they inspired: Anabaptism was fantastically misrepresented; it was spoken of as a contagious evil that poisoned the mind and corrupted the spirit. Yet the equalitarian credo continued to exert a profound and complex influence on European culture. It emerged strongly in eastern Europe, spreading from the mining regions of Bohemia to Hungary and Poland. It was carried from Holland to the eastern counties of England, merging with the traditions inherited from Wat Tyler and the Lollards to form the seventeenth century movements of Levellers and Diggers.

3 : THE FEAST OF FOOLS

As AN APPROACH to the sixteenth century origins of nineteenth century thought, it may be useful to select one art form, examining its development under the pressure of competing class interests. Study of the evolution of the drama is especially instructive in this connection. The medieval and Renaissance theatre, as E. K. Chambers observes, "is of the highest interest as an object lesson in literary evolution. The historian is not often privileged to isolate a definite literary form throughout the whole course of its development."[1]

The vast structure of Shakespeare's art finds its origin and explanation in the revelry of the Feast of Fools and the use of the theatre as a weapon in the social conflicts of the sixteenth century. The development leading up to the Feast of Fools can be outlined in four movements: the folk festival, the liturgical drama, the gild plays, the Black Mass. These were theatrical manifestations of four major historical trends: the village community, the power of the church, the rise of craft organization, the spread of heresy.

The folk entertainments, still performed in many parts of Europe, were inherited from the pagan past. Agricultural ceremonies relating to fertilization, spring planting, rain and harvest, retained their hold on rural communities, and were simplified in May-day games, sword dances and morris dances. As the church asserted its authority, these activities were transferred to Christian holidays, keeping much of the vitality, and a good deal of the detailed symbolism, of the pagan celebrations.

The second theatrical period began with the urban growth of the eleventh century. In attempting to make the church the center of the town and the core of its life, the clergy adopted the traditional folk culture, which had already been given a religious form, and brought it into the interior of the cathedral. The celebration of Christmas and Easter became occasions for popular festivals, in which antiphonal chanting developed into recitatives; dialogue and mimetic action were added, and finally actual dramatization of episodes. The liturgical drama reached its highest development in the early part of the thirteenth century.

By this time, the craft gilds were becoming influential in municipal affairs, leading a revolt against ecclesiastical interference in the town's life. As the artisans emerged from the spiritual tutelage of the priesthood, they brought the theatre with them. Entertainment in the market place was popularized by the companies of ballad singers and mimes who carried the Provencal culture out of southern France when the Albigensian heresy was suppressed. The *jongleurs de dieu* performed musical dialogues, "veritable sketches of dramas in the vernacular."[2] The adaptation of the liturgical ceremony to street performance was taken over by the gilds, which recognized the value of drama as an instrument of municipal power, a means of developing an urban culture that would serve their interests. The themes of the gild plays were scripture stories; but they were humanized for holiday amusement.

The processional pageants performed at Chester, Coventry, York and other towns in England were typical of the theatrical activity sponsored by the gilds in every part of Europe. Segments of the biblical story were assigned to various gilds. At Newcastle-upon-Tyne the Shipwrights performed, appropriately, the making of Noah's Ark, while the Bricklayers and Plasterers played the Creation of Adam and the Flight into Egypt. A manuscript dating from the first half of the fifteenth century contains forty-eight York plays, assigned to forty-eight different crafts.[3]

Coinciding with the rise of Gild drama in the fourteenth and fifteenth centuries were the nocturnal gatherings of people in the agricultural districts. The holiday processions in the cities were municipal events that demanded sobriety and a reasonable show of respect for church and state. But the peasants assembled secretly, and their meetings of protest assumed a dramatic ritualistic form. We have mentioned the contemporary accounts of the Black Mass or Witches'

Sabbath, written with such patent prejudice that it is impossible to separate myth from actuality. Jules Michelet stresses the revolutionary temper of the gatherings. To the peasants, says Michelet, "Heaven seemed but the ally of their savage tyrants and oppressors, itself a tyrant as blood-thirsty as any":

> Hence the *Black Mass* and the *Jacquerie.*
>
> The Altar was raised to the Spirit of the revolted serf, *"to Him who had suffered wrong,* the Proscribed of ancient days, unjustly driven out of Heaven, the Great Creator of the earth, the Master that makes the plants germinate from the soil."[4]

What was said and done may have been quite simple, but our knowledge of peasant organization leaves no doubt that the ceremony was anticlerical. It may have returned to pagan beliefs and rituals. From the viewpoint of the lords of the land, any secret meeting of serfs was demonism and madness, worship of anti-Christ. The recitation of inhuman horrors, in upperclass accounts of the Black Mass, was intended to justify brutal punishments and gave a melodramatic zest to the prosaic tasks of the Inquisition. These reports were based on shabby fabrications that had long done service in attacks on Jews and other heretics. The charge of ritual murder repeatedly used against the peasants is still current in the propaganda of anti-Semitism.

We have traced the historical interrelationship between peasant revolts and the discontent of the urban lower and middle classes. The same interaction is to be found in the development of the New Year revel called the Feast of Fools. The feast was celebrated by the inferior clergy in the early Middle Ages; there are records of it in France in the twelfth century. It seems to have been an adaptation of rural observances of the Winter Festival. In the fourteenth century, resentment against the church gave the event an increasingly public and political character. The anticlericalism of the Black Mass was transferred to the streets of cities. The Feast of Fools derided the ceremonies of the church and mocked the authority of the clergy.

John Huss spoke of his participation in the Feast of Fools in Bohemia. A clerk in grotesque costume was dubbed "bishop," set on an ass with his face to the tail, and led to mass in the church, where the clergy danced with their garments inside out.[5] A few years later, the practice was denounced, and vividly described, by the Faculty of Theology of the University of Paris:

> Priests and clerks may be seen wearing masks and monstrous visages at the hours of office. They dance in the choir dressed as women, panders or minstrels. They sing wanton songs. They eat black pudding at the horn of the altar while the celebrant is saying mass. They play at dice there. They cense with stinking smoke from the soles of old shoes. They run and leap through the church without a blush at their own shame. Finally they drive about the town and its theatres in shabby traps and carts; and rouse the laughter of their fellows and the bystanders in infamous performances, with indecent gestures and verses scurrilous and unchaste.[6]

This was written in 1448. The New Year's celebration had reached a halfway point in the evolution from its pagan origins to the tin horns and confetti of our own time. It had gone as far as it could go in public ribaldry and overt criticism of the church. The "joke" had become dangerously serious. Ecclesiastical pressure forced the festival to adopt a more moderate tone, and the holiday merrymaking was gradually divorced from its earlier social meaning. But the social content was not lost: it was transferred from ritual to entertainment. The 1448 description shows the tendency to theatricalization: the participants gathered a crowd and engaged in "infamous performances."

The anticlericalism of the Feast of Fools inspired the secular drama that emerged in the half century before the Reformation. The Feast proved the propaganda effectiveness of allegory spoken and mimed. Groups that had taken part in the festival converted their experience into permanent dramatic organization. The Fools' Companies that arose in France and Flanders were also known as *societes joyeuses,* but their merriment had political implications. Among the earliest of these companies were the *Basoches,* or associations of law clerks, which undertook the performance of short farces or *sotties* in association with the New Year's revel. The Fools' Company known as the *Enfants-sans-Souci* in Paris was related to the *Basoche,* and may have been identical with it. The *societes joyeuses* appeared in many cities; there were the *Connards* at Lyons; *l'infanterie Dijonnaise* at Dijon; the *Suppots du Seigneur de la Coquille,* composed of printers at Lyons.

The savage criticism of the church in these satires is exemplified in the farce of the dying miller, which dates from the last decade of the fifteenth century. The miller's wife is having an affair with the parish priest. The two are waiting for the husband's death while he lies raving and swearing in his bed. The priest takes off his robe and comes to the bedside in the disguise of a relative, then puts on his robe again in order to hear a confession. The change of costume suggests the wearing of garments inside out in the Feast of Fools. The scenes in the miller's house are interspersed with scenes in Hell, in which Lucifer sends an inexperienced devil to get the dying man's soul, and the unfortunate emissary returns with a bag of excrement—which he had mistaken for the soul parting from the body. The play ends with the brutal jest about the soul, which combines mockery of religion with social comment: the spirits of Hell are shocked by the smell of this soul. In a concluding speech, Lucifer tells the devils never to bring a miller's soul to Hell, as "it is nothing but dirt and filth." The millers were hated as profiteers, exploiting the country people and raising the price of bread in the towns.

Plays of this sort had a vital propaganda value in preparing for the Reformation. But the drama also proved to be a valuable asset to the French monarchy at the beginning of the sixteenth century. The theatre's militant anticlericalism was exactly what King Louis XII needed in order to mobilize support for his Italian campaigns and his controversies with the pope. Pierre Gringoir, leader of the *Enfants-sans-Souci,* wrote his most important play, the *Prince of Fools,* as propaganda for the crown. The play was produced at the Halles in Paris on Shrove Tuesday, 1512, while French armies were fighting in Italy. The characters have the conventional names used in the *sottie,* but *Mére Sotte* appears dressed as "holy church," and she is also identified as Pope Julius II. In the end she is stripped of her clothes to prove that the pope is an impostor:

> Let every one take note,
> It is not Mother Holy Church,
> That makes war upon us;
> This is only our Mére Sotte.[7]

Gringoir knew the feeling of his audience. The people had no love for the pope, but the war was unpopular. He made his message more palatable by introducing a character called *La Sotte Commune.* She wants only peace, "for," she says, "it is I who always have to pay the piper."

The drama had come a long way from the simplicities of the medieval mystery. The gild plays were still given; Gringoir wrote for the masons' and carpenters' companies. But the theatre had broken the bonds of gild restrictions. The printing press had revolutionized the communication of ideas. The magic of the word was heightened when it was projected in living speech, swaying crowds to laughter or anger.

While the crown sponsored and utilized the Fools' Companies in France, the German farce developed from similar anticlerical beginnings to satire chiefly directed against the peasantry. The growing rural discontent in Southern Germany was accompanied by mockery of the country people in shows performed in the market squares of Nuremberg and Augsberg. It was obviously of value to the mercantile oligarchy that controlled these cities to divide the urban population from its rural neighbors.

The *Neithart Play,* longest of the German Shrovetide plays, tells of a young knight who finds the first violet of spring; he puts his hat over the flower and goes to find the Duchess and her ladies. In his absence the peasants play a joke on him. They pick the violet, and place excrement in the hat. The knight returns and takes revenge with "comic" brutality. He cuts off a peasant's leg and replaces it with a wooden one. He makes the peasants drunk, dresses them as monks and derides them. Finally Lucifer and a group of devils join the fun, inciting the peasants to quarrel and engage in a fight in which many of them are hurt. At the close of the play, the duke appears and rewards Neithart for his zeal against the peasants.[8]

There could be no clearer comment on the political struggle that was to come to a head in 1525. The propaganda distortion of reality is as blatant as the distortion in some of Hollywood's "pure entertainment" films. The real world is topsy-turvy: the peasants are too stupid and ignorant to have any human feeling; any cruelty against them is justified and applauded. Neithart's torture of the peasants is a popular version of Luther's later demand that they be "knocked to pieces, strangled and stabbed."

In the period following the peasant war, Europe was released from the old pattern of ecclesiastical dominance. The various propertied classes—the upper clergy, the feudal aristocracy, the national monarchies, the masters of industry and trade—were testing their strength, seeking alliances and combinations that would guarantee their economic interests and extend the area of their political power. The dissemination of culture in the sixteenth century seems extremely limited by twentieth century standards. But no earlier age had possessed such facilities for cultural production or such mass participation in the war of ideas. Printing presses poured out books and pamphlets. The stage was in the center of the battle.

In 1541, the *Connards,* a Fool's Company with headquarters at Rouen, presented a play which showed the German emperor, the pope and the king of England playing ball with the globe, "and all of them ill-treated the poor world to such a degree that it had to suffer much at their hands."[9] It is probable that Charles Chaplin had never heard of the farce when he used the same idea in 1940 in Hitler's dance with the globe in *The Great Dictator*.

There is more than an accidental link between Chaplin's art and the comedy acted at Rouen. The rise of capitalism brought culture into the market place as a commodity for sale. The Feast of Fools had performed an historical task in helping to break the spell of religious ritual. The crude pantomime in the streets seemed to belong to the people: it was something they could seize and use for their own ends. But the promise was illusory. As soon as the show demonstrated its value and assumed a definite form, it became something to be bought and sold.

The performance at Rouen was not merely an expression of popular feeling: if it had expressed the deepest feelings of the people, it could not have been performed. The king of France was noticeably absent from the group of rulers who played with the world as if it were a toy. It was therefore, a service to the crown.

In Germany the interests of the bourgeoisie were served by Hans Sachs, who began to write at about the time of the Peasant War. He produced 1,700 tales and fables and 208 dramas in the fifty years that ended with his death in 1574. A note of more militant propaganda was struck by Thomas Kirchmayer, whose extreme views led to a quarrel with Luther and his exile from Germany. Kirchmayer's *Pammachius,* written in 1538, depicted the pope as anti-Christ. The play was dedicated to Archbishop Cranmer of England. It was translated into English by John Bale. For a short time, the drama became a potent weapon in the hands of the radical wing of English Protestantism.

The government of Henry VIII soon discovered that plays were encouraging sedition. In 1537, orders were issued against a "seditious May-game" in Suffolk, which discussed how a king should rule his realm, and in which "one played Husbandry, and said many things against gentlemen more than was in the book of the play." At a later date, the chancellor of Cambridge University declared that a performance by students of Christ College was "too pestiferous as were intolerable"; it was none other than Bale's translation of *Pammachius*.[10]

Bale had to escape from England. But the importance of the theatre as propaganda is illustrated in a remarkable exploit which Bale executed in 1553. Mary's accession to the throne restored Catholicism in England. On the day of the queen's proclamation establishing Catholic sovereignty, Bale appeared in Ireland: with a group of young men, he performed two Protestant plays at the Market Cross in Kilkenny, to the horror "of priests and other papists there." He escaped and took refuge in Switzerland.[11]

Queen Elizabeth understood the value of the theatre and the necessity of keeping it under strict control. The privy council was given the duties of censorship, and a decree passed in 1572 confined the privilege of maintaining minstrels or players to barons or persons of high degree.

The Protestant hatred of the theatre, which was to delay the development of dramatic art in the American colonies for almost two centuries, arose from the English court's control of the stage, and its use, in the period preceding the Cromwellian Revolution, as propaganda for the crown in its struggle against the bourgeoisie.

The conflict was beginning to develop in Shakespeare's time. To the heaven-storming Elizabethans, all the world was a stage. But it was a world shadowed by class conflict, torn by divided loyalties. We shall find that Shakespeare's plays mirrored the forces that surged around the playhouse, entering its doors with the turbulent audience, invading the platform where the actors wore their mimic crowns and parodied the majesty of kings.

4 : THE MORE FAMILY

In 1527, the Flemish artist, Jan Mabuse, painted a picture of Danaë being impregnated by a shower of gold; naked and buxom she lies in ecstasy under the touch of the precious metal. The picture symbolizes the tendency toward sensuality and decadence which began to develop in Italian art after the restoration of the Medici to power by Spain. Since there was a strong rebellious sentiment among the poorer classes of the Low Countries, the defeat of the German revolution was followed by a drive to strengthen Catholic power in Flanders. Mabuse and the artists who followed him enjoyed the patronage of the aristocracy and the church. For almost a century, the distinctive national qualities of Flemish art were overlaid with Italian upper-class mannerisms.

The case of Mabuse illustrates one tendency in a period of shifting class alignments. The pressures on art and thought varied in each locality, depending on the individual's class position, and the forces that were operative in his field of work.

Albrecht Dürer was forty-six years old when Luther posted his theses on the chapel door at Wittenberg. His most mature work had been done in the preceding decade. The engraving, *Melancolia,* completed in 1514, shows a winged figure surrounded by a confusion of scientific instruments. The picture dramatized the doubts that plagued the artist: how was the creative spirit to use the potentialities of science? Dürer's life had been devoted to the exploration of these potentialities. But lucrative commissions for painting were chiefly received from the church or the aristocracy. Dürer went to the coronation of Charles V in 1520 to seek the emperor's patronage. He returned to Nuremberg to devote himself—during the upheavals of the Peasant War—to a series of grandiose and tragically ineffective religious paintings.

Dürer's younger contemporary, Hans Holbein, was eighteen years old in 1515, when he left Augsberg to find employment as an illustrator of books in Basel. His departure from the home of the Fuggers brought him to a bustling center of cultural activity in Switzerland. He worked for the publishing house of Johann Froben. In the religious controversy that raged in the city, Holbein took the Protestant side. The decision did not prove a satisfactory means of earning a livelihood: as the political struggle became more intense, artistic opportunities dwindled. In 1530, Holbein went to England, where the Anglican Reformation welcomed his sober portraits and made him the favored painter of the court and the aristocracy.

Italian art remained dependent on ecclesiastical or aristocratic patronage. In Venice, Titian's work was linked as closely to the empire and the papacy as the business activities of the Fugger's Venetian office: in 1532, Charles V expressed his gratitude for one of Titian's innumerable portraits by making the artist a Knight of the Golden Spur and raising his children to the nobility.

The effect of the Reformation on the life of the Great Dutch scholar, Erasmus, presents a more complicated problem. In the *Moriae encomium,* written while he was visiting Thomas More in England in 1510, Erasmus wrote a declaration of intellectual freedom: the satire on the follies of state and church is like a literary prelude to Luther's attack on clerical authority. The increasing tension that followed the Diet of Worms led Erasmus to leave Louvain, where the university was dominated by the church, for the more congenial atmosphere of Basel. Reaching the Swiss city in the fall of 1521, Erasmus served for eight years as the editor of Froben's press. Erasmus kept aloof from the Protestant cause because he was repelled by the crass ambitions of the bourgeoisie and by the brutality of the conflict. As Luther used religion to heal the divided conscience, so Erasmus retired into the sanctuary of the mind as a refuge for the troubled spirit. He has been called "a liberal adrift in a sea of warring fanatics," [1] but the description hardly suggests the historic scope of the dilemma that he faced. It was the dilemma of the humanist in a society that rejected human values.

The problem is most clearly portrayed in the life of Thomas More and the circle of friends and relatives that gathered around him. The group is a microcosm of the English culture of the period: these were people with the most intense and varied intellectual interests; their practical activities included the publication of books and plays, political service, investment in overseas commerce and American exploration.

More presented his solution for the social ills of the time in *Utopia,* published in 1515. The striking characteristic of the book is the contrast between the realistic frame of reference—the expropriation of the English peasantry—and the Utopian vision that constitutes the body of the work. Serious unemployment and destitution resulted from the conversion of farm lands into sheep pastures. The demand for wool for English cloth manufacturers and for export to Flanders made it profitable to drive tenants from the land. One shepherd could take the place of many laborers engaged in cultivation. More wrote:

> The increase of pasture . . . by which your sheep, which are naturally mild, and easily kept in order, may be said now to devour men, and unpeople, not only villages, but towns . . . the nobility and gentry, and even those holy men the abbots, not content with the old rents their farms yielded, nor thinking it enough that they, living at their ease, do no good to the public, resolve to do it hurt instead of good . . .

Thus miserable people "are all forced to change their seats, not knowing whither to go. . . . What is left for them to do, but either to steal and so be hanged (God knows how justly), or to go about and beg." More attacked monopoly in much the same terms used by Luther in dealing with the Fuggers:

> But suppose the sheep should increase ever so much, their price is not like to fall; since though they cannot be called a monopoly, because they are not engrossed by one person, yet they are in so few hands, and these are so rich, that as they are not pressed to sell them sooner than they have a mind to, so they never do it till they have raised the price as high as possible.[2]

More blamed the nobility and the church for the plight of the peasantry. His Utopia is governed by elected magistrates, who in turn choose the prince to rule for life, "unless he is removed upon suspicion of some design to enslave the people."[3] There is no idleness; women work as well as men. Since all the inhabitants are usefully employed, the working day can be reduced to six hours. Yet More took for granted, almost as a matter of course, that the unskilled and heavy work must be performed by slaves. Forced labor is the base on which the ideal commonwealth is built. Slaves are recruited from persons accused of crimes: "preserving them in a state of servitude is more for the interest of the commonwealth than killing them." No mercy is shown to trouble-makers:

> If their slaves rebel, and will not bear their yoke and submit to the labor enjoined them, they are treated as wild beasts that cannot be kept in order, neither by a prison nor by their chains, and are at last put to death.[4]

More seemed to be unconscious of the conflict between his humane concern for the peasantry and his acceptance of human slavery. Legislation adopted at the time his book was published required the agricultural laborer to work under conditions that were tantamount to bondage. The law placed a ceiling on wages, permitting the employer to exact penalties for laziness, and specified working hours from five in the morning to seven or eight in the evening in summer (with half an hour for breakfast and an hour and a half for dinner and noonday rest), and from dawn to dark in winter.[5]

The lower classes in London were not much better off. The riot that broke out on "Evil May Day" in 1517 was directed against foreigners, who were taking jobs from English workers. A contemporary writer attributes the trouble to the anger of "pore handycraft people" engaged in "makyng pyns, girdells, globes." These people worked in their homes; the gilds, many of which had become associations of employers, did not protect the artisan who sat "in a pore chamber working all the week to sell his ware on the Saturday," only to be told by the merchants that "they had no nede thereof; ther shopps lay storydd full" of imported goods.[6]

More and his friends could not have been unaware of the misery that lived so close to them in London's crowded slums. The contradiction between More's utopian vision and the actualities of his time runs through his life and work. It is even more sharply defined in the career of his brother-in-law, John Rastell, publisher, bookseller, and playwright.

Rastell was born about 1475 in Coventry. His family was well-to-do and played an important part in civic affairs. His lifelong interest in the theatre dates from his youthful participation in gild pageants. He became friendly with the Mores in 1499 and shortly afterward, he married Thomas More's sister, Elizabeth. In 1506, Rastell succeeded his father as coroner of Coventry. He presided over the court of Statute Merchant, and was closely associated with the town's wealthy wool dealers. He established a printing press in London about 1510. *Utopia* was published by him.

Many thoughtful men believed that a Utopia would be created in the newly discovered country across the Atlantic. In 1516, Rastell joined with other businessmen in financing a voyage to Newfoundland. In the following year he embarked on the ship *Barbara*. The vessel was turned back by a mutiny and Rastell sustained a heavy financial loss.

In 1517, Rastell wrote the *Four Elements:* the play is one of the earliest English dramas to attack orthodoxy and proclaim the supremacy of reason. It deals with recent discoveries, asserts that theology must make way for science, and even mentions that the earth is round.

During the years that followed, the news of religious and political changes on the continent stimulated radical thought in England. Rastell's publications, and his own writings, entered boldly into political and social controversies. He built a stage on property that he owned at Finsbury in the suburbs of London, and public performances seem to have been given there.[7] Other members of the family joined in literary and dramatic activities. Rastell's daughter, Joan, married John Heywood in 1522. Another of the three children, William, entered the printing business and became the publisher of Heywood's plays: *Johan Johan* and *The Pardoner and the Frere,* both satires on clerical corruption, appeared in 1533.

More's daughter, Margaret, made a translation of Erasmus' *Treatise on the Paternoster* when she was nineteen years old. The book was printed by John Rastell. Its significance as a scholarly achievement by a woman is enhanced by the introduction, written by Richard Hyrde, the first essay to be published in England on the right of women to enjoy equal educational opportunities.[8]

These happy intellectual adventures were leading to a tragic climax. In spite of their close association, More and Rastell adopted different attitudes toward the Reformation. But More's resistance and Rastell's acceptance were equally dangerous to the program of monarchial absolutism on which Henry VIII embarked in 1534. Like his friend Erasmus, More saw only violence and immorality in the shift from Catholic to Protestant power. The brutality of the king's conduct in his divorce of Catherine of Aragon emphasized the ethical absurdity of converting the corpulent monarch into the spiritual head of the church. More paid the penalty for his refusal to swear the oath of Supremacy. In 1535, his head was displayed on London Bridge.

Thomas Cromwell, the king's adviser, employed a number of writers to popularize Henry's conversion to Protestantism. For a short time, John Rastell was one of these propagandists. Cromwell faced a difficult problem of public relations: he had to encourage the anticlericalism of the lower and middle classes without permitting it to assume radical or militant forms. Rastell's views were too extreme to serve this purpose. In 1535 he was arrested for sedition. The *Four Elements,* which had been published and played for almost twenty years, was the most damning evidence against him. He was accused of opposing the right of the clergy to make their living by tithes and offerings collected from the poor. Rastell admitted the charge. He told the Judge, the Bishop of Winchester, that it was against the laws of God, of nature and of man to oppress the poor. The Bishop replied:

> Mr. Rastell what ye meane by the laws of nature, of man and of God, I can not tell, but of this I am sure that the vilest partes in the creature of nature takes most labours and paynes, and contrary the chefest members whiche are set next to the noble bloud labour least.[9]

Rastell's death was decreed. But before the sentence could be carried out, he died in prison in 1536. His fate was not unrelated to the Anabaptist rising at Münster. The starving English countryside was fertile soil for Anabaptism. The wider circulation of books and the public interest in plays frightened the crown. In 1539, *An Act Abolishing Diversity of Opinion* was passed. Shortly afterward, a priest who had become an interlude player was burned at the stake for taking part in a performance that violated the act. It was at this time that John Bale fled from England. In 1540, Cromwell himself was beheaded.

John Heywood remained a Catholic. In 1544, he was charged with participating in a Catholic conspiracy. He was convicted of treason and condemned to death. But, clad in a white gown, he was permitted to read a humiliating recantation at Paul's Cross and was then pardoned. William Rastell, who also retained his Catholic sympathies, went into exile in 1549, his goods and chattels being forfeited to the crown.[10]

The reign of terror instituted by Mary Tudor when she ascended the throne in 1553 was based on a revival of the old statutes outlawing Lollardry. Lollardry suddenly became one of those all-embracing terms of opprobrium which can be stretched to include any dissident opinion. The first man to be burned at the stake was John Rogers, whose crime was the translation of the Bible into English.

These fiery punishments did not differ from the methods of enforcing uniformity of belief that had been used for several hundred years. The significance of the sixteenth century persecutions lies in their relationship to the Renaissance and the rise of national states. It was a period of intellectual and scientific growth, which stimulated the hope that the life of the mind would be fully released from the shackles of enforced conformity. But the expansion of culture created new problems of cultural control. In those crucial days, "when the solid earth of the State was appearing from among the dividing waters of feudalism," [11] the most creative thinkers found the path to intellectual freedom blocked by the blood and fire of sovereignty, of state power.

5 : SERVETUS AT GENEVA

FOUR NAMES emerge from the turmoil of the middle years of the sixteenth century as great creative thinkers: Servetus, Vesalius, Copernicus and Rabelais. The four were physicians. There was direct contact between three of them, and the fourth was subject to somewhat similar educational and social influences. The Reformation encouraged bold speculation, but medical science was an especially fertile field of inquiry. In following the methodology of Leonardo, medical students made anatomical investigations. The nature of their work linked scientific and social problems; they could not bring order out of the chaos of medieval superstition without examining the social conditions that nourished disease and prevented the advancement of science.

Nicholas Copernicus, member of a Polish mercantile family, went to Italy at the age of twenty-three in 1496, first studying canon law at the university of Bologna, and then entering the medical school at Padua. Both institutions were centers of liberal thought. His nine years in Italy brought Copernicus into contact with Leonardo's work in mathematics, anatomy and astronomy. He was already convinced that the Ptolemaic theory was false when he left Italy in 1505. Copernicus built up a substantial medical practice at Frauenburg in Prussia. His skill was always at the service of the poor, but his major interest was in astronomy.

While Copernicus observed the stars, Michael Servetus and Andreas Vesalius studied anatomy together in Paris under the guidance of Johann Günther. This was the period of Calvin's brief visit to the French capital, and the beginning of wholesale persecution of heretics in France. The motives for the witchhunt were the same as those that actuated Henry VIII on the other side of the channel. Francis I remained a Catholic, but he cooperated with the German Protestant princes in their struggle with the emperor. What he feared was the "radical" Protestantism that questioned the divine right of kings. Calvin was driven from France at the time of Rastell's death in England. Vesalius found it difficult to conduct his anatomical experiments under the conditions of suspicion and surveillance that shadowed scientific work in Paris. He left for the University of Padua, where Copernicus had received his early training.

Servetus replaced Vesalius as Günther's assistant. A few years later, he moved to Vienne, near Lyons, entering the circle of progressive intellectuals that included Rabelais. The first editions of *Gargantua and Pantagruel* had appeared (probably in 1533 and 1535) before the terror began. Rabelais had influential connections. Although his exuberant allegories tore clerical and feudal pretensions to shreds, he published new editions of his books, making only slight deletions to conciliate the authorities. Finally, the increasing pressure of reaction made it unwise for him to remain in France. The death, by strangling and burning, of his former friend and Lyons publisher, Etienne Dolet, in 1546, helped to hasten Rabelais' departure from France.

Meanwhile, in 1543, two epoch-making books appeared. Vesalius published his study of anatomy, *de Fabrica Corporis Humani,* and Copernicus published *de Revolutionibus Orbium Coelestum*. Vesalius' discovery that Galen was wrong about the mechanics of the heart paralleled the discovery that Ptolemy was wrong about the immovable earth. The being who no longer had Galen's mechanical heart, with its invisible "incurruptible bone" [1] walked on a different earth under a different heaven. The medieval regions of Heaven, Purgatory and Hell where Dante had wandered dissolved in infinite space. And in that vast arena, man stood free.

Although they were later to be furiously assailed by the authorities the two books did not provoke an immediate attack. Copernicus was on his deathbed when his book was printed; he never knew that his Nuremberg publisher had included an anonymous preface which stated that the work was purely abstract and hypothetical. Gerardus Mercator, the Flemish map-maker whose approach to cartography was revolutionized by the Copernican theory, was arrested for heresy with a number of other intellectuals in Antwerp in 1544. Many of his companions were burned, beheaded or buried alive. But Charles V needed accurate maps for his military campaigns. He secured Mercator's release, and the cartographer expressed his gratitude by presenting the emperor with an especially designed, and suitably Ptolemaic, map of the universe. Imperial favor also protected Vesalius, who became the emperor's physician, and thus avoided trouble with the Inquisition for another twenty years.

The social problem posed by the sixteenth century advancement of science was an embryonic statement of the twentieth century problem. Modern discoveries open unprecedented possibilities for the use of science to promote human welfare and release human energies. But the control of science for war and profit bars investigation of these possibilities, and the scientist who displays any sense of social responsibility finds his career endangered and his patriotism questioned. In the days of Charles V, the emperor and other potentates valued mathematics and astronomy as aids to war and navigation; they wanted the services of the ablest physicians. But scientists had an almost incurable habit of examining the larger implications of their discoveries. This was an invasion of an area of power in which the scientist had no place, and in which the trespasser was punished by death.

On Sunday, August 12, 1553, Michael Servetus rode on horseback into a village on the French border near Geneva. He sold his horse, walked into the city, and tried to get a boat to cross the lake. Servetus was of Spanish descent; he was a physician, noted in the history of medicine as the originator of a revolutionary hypothesis concerning the circulation of the blood, which was later to be verified and more accurately stated by William Harvey.[2]

Servetus was also a political revolutionist. There was no outward drama in the arrival of a stranger in the quiet Sunday streets of the Swiss city. But Servetus was gambling with his life.

Until six months before his visit to Geneva, Servetus maintained the fiction that he was a conforming Catholic. He could hardly have appeared in any other light, for he served for twelve years as the personal physician of the archbishop of Vienna, and he edited scientific works for the publishing firm of Trechsel at Lyons. He was the author, under an assumed name, of a tract entitled *Christianismi Restitutio:* the restitution of Christianity advocated by Servetus was Unitarian and rational; it placed reason above revelation, and brotherhood above priestly authority. A thousand copies of the book were secretly printed in Austria in January, 1553, and taken to the industrial towns of Lyons and Frankfurt, centers of left wing activity, for distribution.

Servetus had first met Calvin in Paris in 1536. At that time, Servetus was twenty-five years old, and was studying medicine. Calvin, two years older, was escaping from persecution in France to make his home in Geneva. When Servetus completed a first draft of a statement of his views in 1545, he sent a copy of the manuscript to Calvin for criticism and advice, with a note saying he looked forward to visiting him at Geneva. Having met the Geneva leader as a political refugee, Servetus assumed that he could depend on Calvin's friendliness and discretion. He was disabused by an angry reply, and he complained two years later that he could not get his manuscript back. But even these warnings seem to have left him unprepared for the betrayal of his confidence that occurred in 1553.

When the anonymous tract, *Christianismi Restitutio,* came to Calvin's attention, he was inspired by the sacred fury that seems to be one of the psychological characteristics of heresy hunters. He arranged to have a letter sent to Lyons, enclosing a sheet torn from the printed book and revealing its authorship. Servetus was arrested on April 4, and prosecuted by the Inquisitor General, Matthieu Ory, immortalized by Rabelais in the venomous portrait of *Doribus*. Calvin lightened the Inquisitor's tasks by forwarding copies of Servetus' handwriting.

The left was strong in Lyons, and Servetus had many friends. At four o'clock on the morning of April 7, he was removed from the prison. He remained in hiding, somewhere in France, for four months. When he attempted to pass through Geneva, he was apparently attempting to reach safety in Eastern Europe, where the radical sects were strong enough to give him protection. But it was difficult to reach the east through Catholic territory. It seemed wiser to attempt to cross Switzerland than to risk travel in Italy or southern Germany.

Servetus made the mistake of arriving in Geneva on a Sunday. No boat could be hired, and he had to attend church services in the afternoon in order to avoid being noticed and questioned. He was recognized in church, and arrested. Calvin pressed for his conviction as a heretic who was undermining the foundations of Christianity and morality, and approved the imposition of the death penalty. It may be said, in Calvin's defense, that he proposed to mitigate the penalty, by substituting beheading for burning at the stake, but this kindness was not implemented. On October 27, 1553, Servetus was burned at the stake.

The question of power was as pressing at Geneva as in the cloisters of the church or the chancelleries of kings. Calvin knew the background and attainments of the man whom he condemned to death in 1553. He could not have known the value of his victim's medical discoveries, but he knew that he was dealing with one of the most learned and respected men in Europe.

Calvin was afraid of Servetus. His fear, at that particular moment in 1553, reflected the domestic situation in Geneva and the over-all crisis that was developing in Europe.

Cloth was the basis of Geneva's industrial life. The practical effect of Calvinism was to strengthen the political and economic power of the businessmen who controlled textile production. The theocratic principle, giving divine sanction to the rule of the ablest and most prudent citizens, was projected in the language of theology and ethical imperatives. But the simple objective which it accomplished was the cheaper manufacture of cloth. When the people of Geneva were martialled in groups of ten to swear their allegiance to God and his elect, the oath implicitly bound them to make no protest concerning wages or conditions of labor. Calvinism increased the prosperity of Geneva's upper class, and some of the prosperity spilled over to the middle classes of traders, shopkeepers, skilled craftsmen and professionals. But it also increased social pressures and roused deep resentment among the underprivileged workers.

The city's internal difficulties were related to the political and economic changes in Europe. Geneva was the center of a commercial network, and its cloth production was largely for export. Its economy was linked to the continental system. When Servetus rode into the city on that August morning, Europe was moving toward a major crisis, and Geneva was an island surrounded by hostile forces.

Of critical importance from Calvin's point of view was the fact that Servetus was endeavoring to reach eastern Europe. Calvin was aware of the strength of the Moravian Brotherhood in Bohemia, and the existence of similar mass movements with Anabaptist tendencies in Poland and Hungary. Calvinism was also strong in the east, and the first Calvinist synod had been held in Poland in 1550. But it was doubtful whether Calvinism could stem the tide of more radical doctrines. Servetus had wide influence and connections; his arrival in one of the eastern countries might have a considerable political effect, which could bring repercussions of a very dangerous sort in Geneva.

In 1552, the Protestant League of Schmalkalden, which the emperor had crushed a few years earlier, was reorganized. The princes entered into negotiations with Henry II of France, offering him three cities in Lorraine—Metz, Toul and Verdun—in return for his help. Thus the French claim to Lorraine, which was to play such an important part in the warfare of the nineteenth and twentieth centuries, was established as a by-product of the Reformation. In March 1552, Henry II invaded Germany. At the same time, Prince Maurice of Saxony seized the great banking city of Augsberg. Charles V barely escaped capture. He assembled an army, but was defeated again at Metz in January, 1553.

The summer of Servetus' arrest and trial coincided with the Protestant capture of Augsberg and the successful French invasion of Germany. In the conflict between Rome and the Protestant princes, Geneva was regarded as an enemy by both sides. Indeed, the growing power of the German Protestants increased the tensions in Geneva, and made Calvin more uncertain of his position. It is one of the revelatory contradictions of history that Servetus was condemned to die, not because Geneva was disturbed by Protestant defeats, but because the sweep of Protestant victories upset the European balance of power so drastically that the Calvinist burghers could not foresee what the future might hold for them. The old political and economic structure of power seemed to be falling. No one knew what would replace it or what social disorders might result from the crisis.

Calvin was not a man who wastes his energy wrestling with shadows. The spectre that haunted Europe was not a ghostly presence. The anger and bitterness that had arisen out of the Peasant War and the bloody liquidation of the Anabaptists were as real as the disintegration of Catholic power and the increasing instability of the continent's trade and finances.

Calvin was familiar with Anabaptism. He knew its strength and its attraction. He remembered the civil conflict during his first years in Geneva. The Anabaptists had functioned openly, holding public debates which attracted large audiences. The Anabaptist argument was so convincing that the municipal authorities stepped in, announced that the Anabaptist side had lost and that their views would henceforth be outlawed. In the disorders that followed, Calvin was driven from the city; his absence lasted from 1538 to 1541. During that time he married a widow, Idelette de Bur, whom he converted from Anabaptism.

Calvin's emotional bitterness toward Servetus grew out of his personal and political contact with rational thought: his intensity was that of the renegade, who has deliberately turned his back on reason and set his steps on the path to power. Calvin was the master of Geneva; Servetus was a wanderer whose only desire was to leave the city. Yet Calvin so feared the wanderer that he could not tolerate his existence.

Servetus was killed, as so many other men were killed, for writing and publishing unorthodox opinions. The man's political thought cannot be divorced from his life, or from the intellectual movement in which he was a leading figure.

The clash between Calvin and Servetus is one of the most illuminating incidents in the development of the "free" culture of the West. Coleridge looked back upon it as an event that tested the validity of Christian ethics; the ethical failure was, according to Coleridge, not "Calvin's guilt especially, but the common approbrium of all European Christendom."

6 : SHAKESPEARE AND THE FAMINE YEARS

SHAKESPEARE wrote at a moment of transition when the monarchial feudalism that had achieved temporary stability on the ruins of the medieval social system was disintegrating under the pressure of new forces. These were the forces that motivated English colonization in North America and determined the course of colonial civilization. Shakespeare expressed the dominant traits of the society that was emerging from the ruck of feudalism. The whole body of his work is a statement of the conflicts that were to develop with peculiar weight and intensity in the New World.

In the present chapter we shall deal only with the first decade of Shakespeare's creative life, from the production of the second and third parts of *Henry VI* in 1591 to *Hamlet* ten years later.

Shakespeare's appearance in London as an actor and writer at the age of twenty-seven coincided with the political changes that followed the defeat of the Spanish Armada in 1588. It is necessary to deal with these changes in some detail and to establish the historical setting for the individual's creative experience.

The defeat of the Spanish fleet brought relief and exultation. But it often happens that a victory in war sharpens the contradictions that the war was intended to solve. Americans have had occasion to observe this phenomenon twice during the twentieth century. The situation in England in 1588 was somewhat similar: the victory intensified the tensions and animosities that had been held in abeyance while the national energies were engrossed in the struggle with Spain. The smashing of the Armada did not end the war, and its continuance was accompanied by growing dissatisfaction.

Enclosures continued the systematic expropriation of the rural population. The laboring class was controlled by increasingly repressive legislation and summary punishment for minor offenses. The most recent of the perennial rebellions in the industrial eastern counties had occurred in 1549 when 16,000 laborers, led by Kett, captured the cloth-making city of Norfolk, the old center of the Lollard movement. A mercenary army of Germans was imported to crush the rising, and the gentry undertook such a wholesale slaughter of the rebels that the Earl of Warwick warned them against interfering with the normal operation of the labor market: "Will you be ploughmen," he asked, "and harrow your own land?"[1]

The question haunted the Elizabethan landowners. Coming to the throne at the time of the European crisis of 1559, Elizabeth tightened control of the workers by the revision of the Statute of Laborers adopted in 1562. The act introduced more stringent regulation of employment, forebade men to leave a parish without written permission from their employers, made all able-bodied men liable for agricultural service unless they could prove they had other means of subsistence, and classified vagrancy as a crime. The masterless laborer must take any job offered to him and his refusal made him subject to execution as a vagabond. The death penalty was not a legal fiction: in 1575, some men who had been whipped and branded as vagrants in March were rearrested in June and accused "of being over eighteen years old and fit for labour, but masterless and without lawful means of livelihood."[2] They were hanged. Obviously, it was not practical to hang the growing numbers of irregularly or totally unemployed people. But the law was a warning. It deprived the vagrants of legal status, and assured their availability in the "free" market. Since the courts regarded the unemployed as virtually outlaws, it was not difficult to secure their conviction for minor offensives: the theft of anything over the value of a shilling was regarded as a felony, and felonies were punishable by death.[3]

The threat of agrarian rebellion hung like a cloud over the green Elizabethan countryside. The myth of national unity, projected with poetic vigor in the idealization of the Virgin Queen was a propaganda device which had a certain limited validity during the early years of Elizabeth's reign. The myth never pretended to include the mass of the laboring population. But it expressed the aims, and to some extent the actual achievement, of the coalition of classes that supported the absolute monarchy. The major advantages of the coalition accrued to the circle of aristocrats around the queen. Political absolutism included absolute disposal of lucrative economic privileges. The bourgeoisie were by no means satisfied with their role as junior partners in the national enterprise. But decisive sections of the bourgeoisie were willing to participate in the coalition as long as it seemed to offer the only means of assuring stability and promoting expansion. Country gentlemen and owners of industries enjoyed the benefits of cheap labor. London merchants and West Country shipowners shared in the profits of piracy and trade.

For the first twenty-five years of Elizabeth's reign the profits were fabulous. When Francis Drake brought the *Golden Hind* back to England in 1580, he returned a profit of £1,500,000 on an investment of £5,000. The queen received £250,000, while other stockholders, most of them members of the court circle, were paid at the rate of 4,600 percent.[4]

Merchants were bedazzled by such miraculous opportunities for primitive accumulation. They recognized that future opportunities depended on an aggressive foreign policy that would take full advantage of the weakness of Spain and the European disorders that followed the 1559 crisis. Elizabeth and her advisers faced the problem of developing a diplomacy of expansion that would serve the interests of the court and avoid giving more than token aid and comfort to the forces which were fighting absolutism in Europe.

There was one way of extending English power on the continent without strengthening the Protestant bourgeoisie: this was through an alliance with Tsarist Russia, which emerged as a strong national state under Ivan the Terrible. The Tsar's correspondence with Elizabeth hinted that the two powers could divide continental power between them. For a time, the Queen was attracted by the idea. English merchants, while they wanted trade with Russia, also wanted to deal with Russia's enemies, and opposed any political commitments to the Tsar. Ivan wrote an angry letter to Elizabeth, in 1570, saying he had thought she ruled her realm, but "now we perceive that there be other men that doe rule, and not men, but bowers and merchants, the which seeke not the wealth and honour of our Maiesties, but they seeke there owne profitt of marchandize. . . ."[5]

Ivan had trouble enough ruling his own realm: Elizabeth sent him a secret note in the same year, promising to give him and his family shelter in England if political difficulties forced him to go into hasty exile.[6] The Tsar's struggle with the boyars was bloodier than Elizabeth's controversy with the merchants. Yet the English bourgeoisie's opposition to the court was based on an irrepressible conflict of interest. It was held in abeyance while the nation prepared to challenge Spain's mastery of the seas. With the humbling of the Armada, the hopes inspired by the exceptional profits of Drake's voyages became a reality. English ships need no longer content themselves with restricted trade and unrestricted piracy. With the increased opportunities for regular commerce, an appropriate investment promised an incalculable gain. But who was to control the investment? Who was to reap the reward?

In increasing England's national power, the defeat of the Armada intensified the internal struggle for power. It brought a great increase in the organized activities of the Puritans and violent governmental measures for the suppression of the left wing of the Puritan movement. Puritanism is a rather confusing term, being used to describe such different groups as the middle-of-the-road Presbyterians and the more radical Separatists. The vague meaning of Puritanism has been transferred to American cultural history, where it is used with puzzling inconsistency to designate various religious organizations, ethical attitudes, states of mind. The word was employed in sixteenth century England in somewhat the same way in which "progressive" is employed today, as a generic label for a broad opposition movement.

Since Puritanism was strong enough to withstand a frontal attack by the government, it was the main object of Elizabethan policy to conciliate the moderates and isolate the Separatist left wing. The task became urgent in 1688, when the publication of the first of the Marprelate tracts occasioned a furor that revealed the extent of popular dissatisfaction with the ecclesiastical regime. The pamphlet, printed on a secret press, appeared a few months after the defeat of the Armada. The title page stated that it was "Printed oversea, in Europe, within two furlongs of a Bounsing Priest, at the cost and charges of M. Marprelate, gentleman."[7] The government knew that the printing had not been done overseas. There had been many tracts printed by illegal presses, and many arrests had been made. But no previous effort approached the effectiveness or boldness of Marprelate's attack on the church-state which was the legal and moral foundation of Elizabethan absolutism.

The story of the men who issued the pamphlets, and continued to issue them against all odds for ten months, lacks the sweep and color of the fight against the Armada. The work of a few hunted men operating an underground press can hardly be compared to the technicolor pageant of the great galleons fleeing before the English mariners. Yet the two events are complementary and one cannot be fully understood without the other. Having defeated Spain, the crown faced a reckoning with the classes that provided the human and economic resources for the achievement of the victory. The Marprelate tracts were the first step toward the Cromwellian Revolution.

The production of the seven pamphlets was accomplished by an underground organization with members in many places. The first was issued by Robert Waldegrave, a printer whose troubles with the law antedated the Marprelate controversy. His press, publicly engaged in publishing orthodox religious works, was raided in April, 1588. Unable to gain access by the door, the raiders broke through the wall of the shop. Waldegrave managed to escape, but his press was seized along with copies of a seditious pamphlet which he had been secretly engaged in printing. The anonymous author of this document was John Udall, a minister at Kingston-on-Thames. Within less than a fortnight, Waldegrave was operating a secret press at Kingston, where he printed a work by John Penry, a friend of Udall's.

The authorities made a fruitless investigation at Kingston, but Waldegrave and his associates thought it prudent to move the press to the home of Mrs. Nicholas Crane at East Molesey near Kingston. Mrs. Crane's husband, a sixty-six year old minister whose views had occasioned his arrest, died in a London prison in May, at about the time that the press started operating in his widow's home. Works by Udall and Penry were published during the summer, and it was here that the first *Martin,* as the tracts were called, made its appearance in October.

The sensation that resulted made it wise to move the press again. It was carried in a country cart, covered with straw or hay, to the estate of Sir Richard Knightly, where the second *Martin* was printed in November. A great many people, including a number of Sir Richard's servants, were in on the secret. The wide distribution of the tracts required a considerable apparatus: especially efficient service was rendered by Humphrey Newman, a cobbler, who devoted all his time to carrying the dangerous merchandise between the Midlands and London, depositing parcels at various houses and places of call.

The importance of the tracts was recognized by the prelates of the church in January, 1589, when an official answer was provided in *An Admonition to the People of England,* written by Thomas Cooper, Bishop of Winchester. The book made a detailed, and generally apologetic, defence of the ecclesiastical system. Cooper showed how closely the issue was bound up in the rights of property and the control of the poor in his charge that the Puritans advocated the abandonment of the death penalty for theft and "divers other felonies."

The press was moved again, to the house of John Hales in Coventry, and here the third pamphlet, a reply to the *Admonition,* derisively entitled *Hay Any Worke for the Cooper,* appeared in March. 200 copies were sent direct to London, and Newman took 700 for distribution at the usual depots. Ill health and worry caused Waldegrave's retirement from the enterprise. Fearing detection, he crossed the channel in May to the Huguenot city of Rochelle. John Hodgkins was recruited in London to take his place. The press had been carried to Wolston Priory, the home of Roger Wigston, and there the fourth tract, known as *Martin Junior* was completed in July, and Newman trudged away as usual, with "at least 700 or 800 copies." It was followed immediately by another work, familiarly called *Martin Senior.*

The press again started on its journeys under a load of hay. But a fatal accident occurred at Warrington in Lancashire. As the men were unloading the boxes, some type fell out and was seen by passers-by. Frightened but determined to continue, Hodgkins moved on, to Newton Lane, near Manchester, where he and his men were working on the sixth pamphlet when the hue and cry at last caught up with them. As they were being carried to London, Hodgkins whispered to his assistants to remember their oath, to give no names, and promised them their full wages during the period of imprisonment. They were repeatedly put on the rack, but the torture brought no satisfactory information concerning their associates.

The authorities thought they had silenced Martin Marprelate, but Penry and his friends were determined to prove them wrong. The seventh and last *Martin* appeared on September 15, with a defiant title:

THE PROTESTATYON OF MARTIN MARPRELATE

Wherein not withstanding the surprizing of the printer, he maketh it known unto the world that he feareth neither proud priest, Antichristian pope, tiranous prellate nor godlesse catercap: but defieth all the race of them by these presents . . .[8]

Gradually, the ecclesiastical courts pieced the facts together and arrested the leading participants in the campaign. Richard Knightly, John Hales, Roger Wigston and Mrs. Wigston were arrested in 1589 and placed on trial early in 1590. They were let off with heavy fines. The authorship of the tracts has never been established. They were probably the work of several authors. But two of the men who were most seriously suspected were sent to their death. Udall, imprisoned in January, 1590, was condemned to be executed, but died in prison. Penry remained in Scotland for some time; he was finally tried and hanged in 1593.[9]

We have followed the Marprelate struggle in some detail in order to establish the social setting for Shakespeare's first dramatic work. He appeared in the London theatre at the height of the Marprelate controversy. London was the center of Protestant agitation. The sprawling gargantuan city was the key to the nation's economic life, the magnet that drew people from all parts of the realm. The municipal population grew from 93,276 in 1563 to 152,478 in 1595.[10]

The struggle between the nobility and the bourgeoisie was concretized in the conflict between the court and the city. The wealthy burghers who controlled the town government had no sympathy with the aspirations of the artisans, shopkeepers and journeymen who made up the majority of the population. But they sought to use popular discontent as a means of wringing economic concessions from the crown. The queen was also eager to secure the support of her London subjects. Even though most of the people of the city were disfranchised, they represented a concentrated force which would be decisive at a time of crisis.

In attempting to secure the allegiance of the London population, the crown used the stage as a major weapon of propaganda. The political conflict that raged on the boards, and in the audiences of the playhouses, accounts for the extraordinary vitality of the Elizabethan drama. In theory, the crown's control of the theatre was absolute; but plays were of no value as propaganda unless they touched the passions and sensibilities of the audience. On the other hand, if plays spoke the language and thoughts of the people, they ceased to serve the interests of the court. No art form was ever more explosively impregnated with the contradictions between a people's art and art dedicated to the maintenance of power than the theatre which Shakespeare entered in 1591.

The contradiction was embodied in the economic organization of dramatic production. The players were the feudal retainers of the lord who sponsored the company, and their professional existence depended on the favor of their patron. But they were paid by "shares" in the receipts, which in turn came from the money deposited by spectators in the box that gave its name to the later box office. Thus the players were both employees and feudal servants. The managers who employed them were in the same ambivalent position. Philip Henslowe and Richard Burbage were capitalists, building and operating theatres for a profit. Their interests were those of the London burghers. But in order to keep their enterprises open, they had to bow to the will of the court.

Writers and actors were chiefly recruited from the lower middle class. Members of the aristocracy or the upper bourgeoisie could do better for their sons than send them to make a precarious living in the turbulent playhouses. George Peele's father was a salter; Christopher Marlowe's, a cobbler; Anthony Munday's, a draper.[11] Shakespeare's father is supposed to have been a glover. He was a person of some importance in Stratford. But the period of Shakespeare's youth coincided with a general decline of trade in the smaller English cities, and the reduced family fortunes were evidently one of the reasons for William's departure from Stratford.

The conflict between the court and the city was reflected in every phase of the theatre's activity. The artist served the court, but he was bound by personal and class ties to the artisans and journeymen who formed a considerable part of his audience. For twenty years before Shakespeare's debut, the crown and the London corporation conducted a legal fight for control of the stage. The censorship exercised by the Master of the Revels under the supervision of the Privy Council was strengthened in 1572 by a decree confining the privilege of maintaining players to barons or persons of high degree. London replied in 1574 with an ordinance providing that the Lord Mayor and aldermen had jurisdiction over plays and players. The court ignored the city's claims. Puritan hatred of the theatre, which was to play an important part in later history, was a response to the aristocracy's use of the stage for its own purposes. Pamphlets like Stephen Gosson's *Playes Confuted in Five Actions,* which appeared in 1582, thundered in vain against the iniquitous propaganda that was being disseminated in the guise of entertainment.[12]

The agitation around the Marprelate tracts brought a renewed conflict over control of the theatre. The bishops used the playhouses for unbridled attacks on the author of the pamphlets, hiring several writers, including John Lyly and Thomas Nashe, for this purpose. Among the more scurrilous presentations was the portrayal of Martin as a monstrous ape being lanced to let the blood and evil humors out of him.[13]

This was Shakespeare's world, and Shakespeare's theatre. He plunged into the contemporary controversy, his first work seeking to draw an historical parallel between the threatened disorders of his time and the period of civil strife from which Tudor England emerged. In the second part of *Henry VI,* the brutal struggle for power among the nobility demonstrates the necessity of a strongly centralized government. The corruption that surrounds the young Lancastrian king enables the lower classes to rebel; in the speeches of the popular leader, Jack Cade, Shakespeare introduced the satire of socialist ideas which reappeared in his later plays. Cade promises his followers that "There shall be in England seven halfpenny loaves sold for a penny . . . there shall be no money; all shall eat and drink on my score; and I will apparel them all in one livery, that they may agree like brothers, and worship me their lord." Yet there is dignity, or at least a curious irony, in Cade's death. Hunted and without food, he takes refuge in a garden, where he is found and killed. His last words speak of hunger: "I, that never feared any, am vanquished by famine, not by valour."

In the third part of *Henry VI,* the king's weakness and his inability to dominate the ambitions of the barons bring his downfall. The play concludes with the triumph of Edward IV, the "merchant prince." But it is an insubstantial triumph. As Richard of Gloster kisses the king's infant son, he whispers an aside:

> To say the truth, so Judas kiss'd his master,
> And cried, all hail! when as he meant all harm.

The shadow that hung over the ending of *Henry VI* hung over the London in which it was presented. The rebellious temper of Jack Cade was very much in evidence among the "groundlings": in June, 1592, riots broke out in the theatres and caused the closing of the playhouses. Later in the season one of the most devastating of London's periodic plagues, arising from the same social conditions that occasioned the riots, kept the playhouses sealed, except for short intervals at the Christmas season, until April, 1594. It was probably in one of these intervals, in 1593, that *Richard III* was played.

The dark mood of the play reflects the uncertainties of the year. It begins where *Henry VI* left off, the whole play being the dramatization of the "Judas' kiss" mentioned in the last line of the previous work. It is the most compactly constructed of all the chronicles, and presents the simplest social viewpoint. The bloody career of Gloster proves that power divorced from responsibility leads to doom. The play ends with the accession of Henry Tudor to the throne, the beginning of the period that was regarded by Elizabethan historians as the era of "smiling plenty and fair prosperous days." But again there is the shadow, the possibility of future rebellion. The play ends with a sort of prayer:

> Abate the edge of traitors, gracious Lord,
> That would reduce these bloody days again,
> And make poor England weep in streams of blood!
> Let them not live to taste this land's increase
> That would with treason wound this fair land's peace!

Shakespeare had reached the first milestone of his social thought. Relying mainly on Holinshed, and utilizing the writings of Thomas More and the Italian scholar, Polydorus,[14] he had drawn a fairly conventional picture of the origins of the "permanent" prosperity supposedly guaranteed by monarchial absolutism. A more profound influence upon his theory of the state stemmed from Machiavelli. Although the Italian's major works were known only through a garbled adaptation, his ideas were widely discussed in England.

Shakespeare followed the Machiavellian thesis that a "good prince" could not be judged by subjective moral standards; the test of his goodness lay in his ability to unite the nation, which in turn depended upon giving adequate protection to the classes that were essential to the nation's economic welfare. In Florence at the beginning of the sixteenth century, these classes had been clearly defined; when Machiavelli spoke of the *people,* he meant the few thousand enfranchised citizens of the city. The disfranchised majority was regarded with contempt in Elizabethan England, but the lower classes of London had forced recognition of their existence. The recognition is accorded in the use of the term *people* in Elizabethan drama and literature. It is often used ambiguously, but there is no doubt that it included the noisy crowd that crossed the Thames to see Shakespeare's plays.

Shakespeare was aware of the social problem posed by his audience. He could regard its rebellious questionings as a seditious threat to the state, but he had to justify the state to the people who were part of it. He escaped from the problem to the lyricism of the early comedies. The idealized love relationship in the comedies is counterbalanced by the tragic fugue upon the same theme in *Romeo and Juliet.* Young love in London faced dangers as threatening as those that doomed the "world-wearied flesh" of the star-crossed lovers.

Shakespeare's temporary abandonment of historical investigation in 1594 and 1595 coincided with the development of the amusement area in Southwark on the other side of the Thames. The shift relieved the municipal pressure on the theatre and increased its dependence on the court. The court influence is especially evident in *Midsummer Night's Dream,* written in 1595 and apparently designed to celebrate an aristocratic wedding at which Elizabeth herself may have been present.

But the gaieties of the court could not distract attention from the economic plight of the majority of the people. The failure of the wheat crop in 1595 climaxed the rise in the price of food that had been going on for almost a century. In 1530, the average price of a bushel of wheat was 17 cents. It rose to 54 cents in 1550. During the years of the Marprelate publications, it averaged 75 cents a bushel. It jumped to 114 cents in 1595.[15]

Behind the price rise was a political scandal that involved English foreign policy and the continuing war with Spain. Profiteering in grain included the export of large quantities while an artificially maintained price level caused starvation in England. It was no secret that the Spanish Armada had been to some extent provisioned with English wheat, shipped to France and carried across the Pyrenees. In the year after Spain's defeat, when the danger was over and the profit had been made, Elizabeth answered the clamor of protest with a proclamation prohibiting all export of wheat, because "a great part was this last yeere past imploied in the victuallyng of the late Armie and Fleete set foorth to the seas by the King of Spaine, for the invasion of this Realme. . . ."[16] However, the profits of export were so substantial, and the profiteers so highly placed, that the crown modified the ban in 1591; no grain was to be transported to Spanish territory, but it could be sent to other ports under licence. Since the trade had not been conducted directly with Spain, the business continued as before. Monopolistic control, speculative buying, and manipulation of the foreign market brought the country close to disaster in 1595.

Famine conditions continued for several years. This was the period of Shakespeare's second historical cycle. He went back to an earlier epoch of English history, to the origins of monarchial feudalism. The return to the distant past indicates that the "Tudor myth" could no longer be accepted at its face value. The essence of the myth was the theory that royal absolutism promotes mercantile expansion, unites all the propertied classes, and thus promotes the national welfare. In his first cycle of chronicles, the danger of rebellion had been a cloud on the Elizabethan horizon. Now the cloud darkened the sky.

Shakespeare, like all the great humanist thinkers of the sixteenth century, took an ambivalent view of emerging capitalism. He saw the potentialities of economic development, but he also saw the degradation of the human personality in the fever of business competition. He wondered whether the difficulties of the crown might not be due to the pressure of economic forces, the subordination of public policy to considerations of greed and profit. The question is posed in *King John,* written in 1595.

John is portrayed as a weak and inconsistent prince, running the gamut of the problems of statecraft—war with France, trouble with the papacy, aristocratic intrigue, trouble among the people. The strong character in the play is the bastard son of Richard *Cœur de Lion,* who serves as a sort of Greek chorus, contrasting John's vacillations with the virtues of a more heroic age. John's power is undermined because he fails to control the corrupt economic influences that surround him. He is the victim of "Commodity, the bias of the world." The world is "made to run even upon even ground," but it is moved from its course by "this sway of motion, this commodity." The diatribe against commodity, "this bawd, this broker, this all changing word," was a comment on foreign wars that was not too subtly related to the contemporary scandal concerning the export of foodstuffs.

In *King John,* the principle of royal authority rests upon the personality of the ruler:

> Let not the world see fear and sad distrust
> Govern the motion of a kingly eye:
> Be stirring as the time; be fire with fire . . .

Yet the only consistent advocate of the principle is the bastard son of a king. In *Richard II,* in 1596, Shakespeare probed more deeply into the psychological aspect of absolutism. Richard is the prototype of Hamlet. The introspective approach has broad political implications. It makes Richard a symbol of the contradictions inherent in the exercise of absolute power. The king may be God's anointed, but his divine right does not protect him from mortal dangers:

For God's sake let us sit upon the ground,
And tell sad stories of the death of kings:—
How some have been deposed; some slain in war;
Some haunted by the ghosts they have deposed;
Some poisoned by their wives; some sleeping killed;
All murdered;—for within the hollow crown
That rounds the mortal temples of a king
Keeps Death his court . . .

The play points to the growing depth and complexity of Shakespeare's thought, and the tendency to interpret political problems in terms of the destiny of man. The same tendency is to be found in *The Merchant of Venice,* probably completed in the same year. The ambiguities in the play, the mixture of anti-Semitic prejudice and psychological insight, the introduction of valid ethical concepts in false and contrived situations, become somewhat less confusing when we examine the events that form the frame-of-reference for the work. Dr. Roderigo Lopez, a distinguished Portuguese Jew who served as Elizabeth's personal physician, was accused of poisoning the queen, subjected to a vile campaign of propaganda, and executed in 1594. The affair was engineered by the Earl of Essex to strengthen his own position at court and to divert public attention from more pressing political issues.[17]

The political pressures around the Lopez case made it impossible for Shakespeare to challenge the anti-Semitic premise of the trial; a direct demand for justice for a Jew would have been an attack on the government and its methods, and would have been as heretical as the Marprelate tracts. Yet the poet *does* pose the problem in an abstract form, in terms of *justice* and *mercy* as qualities of social order. The play is a preliminary statement of the dilemma of humanism, the conflict between the real and the ideal, that was to be more profoundly formulated in *Hamlet.*

The Merchant of Venice makes the unusual assertion that the Jew has rights. In terms of English experience, the scene in a Venetian law court is pure fantasy: yet the dream world in which the Jew is given full legal equality provides a contrast to the actual procedure in the Lopez case. Behind Shylock demanding his pound of flesh is the very different figure of the Portuguese physician hounded to his death; behind Portia appealing to "the quality of mercy" is the sordid betrayal of Christian morality in Shakespeare's world.

The pressure of events soon forced Shakespeare to reenter the arena of political controversy. 1597 was a year of growing discontent. High prices continued. There was bitter resentment against impressments for military service and the unsatisfactory course of the war against Spain. Unrest invaded the theatre. In July, the city authorities complained that unruly apprentices used the theatres as rendezvous for their "mutinus attemptes."[18] Literature and the drama began to exhibit a pervading mood of pessimism, with savage satire that came close to direct reference to the crown.[19]

The court tightened its control of players by withdrawing the right of Justices of the Peace to licence traveling, and giving noblemen more specific responsibility for the conduct of their servants.[20] The production of *The Isle of Dogs* was found to contain seditious matters; the players and one of the authors, Ben Jonson, were imprisoned, and Jonson's collaborator, Thomas Nashe, fled to Yarmouth.[21]

From 1597 to 1599, Shakespeare wrote the three plays dealing with the youth and royal career of Henry V, which are a last attempt to rationalize the principle of monarchial absolutism. In estimating Shakespeare's social thought, we must consider the improvement in his personal fortunes at the time when famine and high prices impoverished a considerable part of the English population. The dramatist's father applied for a coat of arms on October 20, 1596, and it was granted in 1599.[22]

In the two parts of *Henry IV,* written in 1597 and 1598, the youthful prince is a typical inhabitant of London's Bohemia. In his adventures with Falstaff, he shares the life of the streets and taverns, mocking bourgeois virtue, enjoying cheap pleasures. When he ascends the throne, Henry assumes the divinity that "doth hedge a king" with a suddenness that leaves Falstaff aghast.

The sudden shift is one of the most revealing moments in Shakespeare's work: the ideal sovereign is "one of the people" transformed by the dignity of his office; by the same sleight of hand, his military conquest of France becomes a people's war. In *Henry V,* the king moves through the camp *incognito* on the night before the battle of Agincourt. He talks to the men, knowing their mood, honoring their humble questionings. A soldier talks of the king's responsibility:

> If the cause be not good, the king himself hath a heavy reckoning to make when all those legs and arms and heads, chopped off in a battle, shall join together at the latter day and cry all, We died at such a place . . .

Henry accepts the burden:

> Upon the king!—let us our lives, our souls,
> Our debts, our careful wives, our children, and
> Our sins lay on the king!

The play was produced in 1599, when press gangs roved through streets seizing men and shipping them off for military service on the continent. The theatres were not safe from the recruiting officers. In *Histriomastrix,* the satirical portrayal of the troubles of a group of players ends with the whole company being seized and put in the army. An undated letter by Philip Gawdy, probably written in 1602, reports that "All the playe howses wer besett in one daye and very many pressed from thence, so that in all there were pressed ffowre thowsand besydes fyve hundred voluntaryes, and all for Flanders.[23]

Henry V was propaganda for the crown and the war, and it may not be unrelated to the granting of the coat of arms to Shakespeare's father in the same year. Shakespeare may have *wanted* to avoid coming to grips with the social problems of the time. But he could not avoid feeling the pressure and pulse of the life that surged around him. He could not be content with the facile defence of the *status quo* in *Henry V*. The play is a turning point in the author's search for the principle of state power. The monarchial power was visibly breaking down, and Shakespeare could see no alternative except revolutionary chaos. He examined the alternative in *Julius Caesar,* also written in 1599. In turning from English to Roman history, he was able to present a people's rebellion as a major factor in an historical situation. Caesar is overthrown because he is a tyrant who destroys the people's liberties. But the result is disastrous. Brutus cannot retain the confidence of the fickle populace and Marc Antony precipitates civil war. The people lack the wisdom to use their power intelligently.

The Essex conspiracy in 1601 bore some resemblance to the maneuvers of the Roman politicians in Shakespeare's play. Essex' dispute with the queen involved a number of factors; her displeasure was most sharply indicated in her withdrawal of the monopoly of the trade in sweet wines that Essex had enjoyed for a decade. Elizabeth remarked to Bacon that she had received "some very dutiful letters" from Essex—"but what I took for the abundance of the heart I find to be only a suit for the farm of sweet wines." [24]

There was an element of high comedy in the earl's belief that his loss of one of the monopolies which the people hated qualified him to be the leader of a popular rebellion. There was a less obvious touch of comedy in his use of Shakespeare's play, *Richard II,* as a means of preparing for the uprising. As Elizabeth's popularity waned, it became customary to compare her to Richard II. Essex planned his *coup d'etat* for February 8. The play was presented on the previous evening, and members of the company testified at the trial that the conspirators bribed them "to have the play of the deposing and killing of King Richard" performed on that date.[25]

Essex miscalculated the temper of the people of London. They disliked the queen, but they were aware of the difficulties of revolution and the necessity of reliable leadership. Essex appeared in the streets with a group of followers. But no one rallied to his support. The city was quiet. People peered at the procession anxiously from doors and windows. Neither burghers nor craftsmen—nor the multitudinous poor—wished to join a courtier in a palace revolution. Essex planned like an Elizabethan adventurer in an age that was no longer Elizabethan.

Elizabeth knew it. Essex did not represent the real danger, and his execution did not make the queen a whit more secure. The poverty of the lower classes was less alarming to Elizabeth than the growing resistance of the bourgeoisie to the monopolies which she so lavishly granted to members of the court. These grants were an important part of the apparatus of absolutism, a means of rewarding favorites and consolidating support. But when, shortly after the Essex trial, parliament asked for a reform in the giving of patents, Elizabeth complied with surprising haste. In her grandiose manner, she blamed everything on the holders of patents. "Those varlets, lewd persons, abusers of my bounty, shall know I will not suffer it." [26] Elizabeth was afraid. During the year before her death, she could hardly sleep. She sat night and day with a sword at her side.

Hamlet reflects the prevalent uncertainty, the disintegration of old values. But Shakespeare is no longer primarily concerned with the ethics of absolutism. The old queen dying is like a Shakespearian character, but she is a figure in one of the chronicles that belong to England's, and the author's, past. Elizabeth could cling to the dream that she alone was the state. But beyond the individuals who bowed before her were the shadowy forces that no effort of her will could bring to order and obedience. Shakespeare was not able to see these forces clearly, but he was aware of their presence. From the Marprelate tracts to the Essex conspiracy, he watched the decline of royal power, reflecting each stage of the contemporary crisis in his chronicles of English history, exploring the origins of the monarchial state in order to explain its present instability. The experience of the decade, reinforced by the lessons of the past, proved that the Elizabethan failure was not solely the responsibility of the ruler; absolutism could not answer the needs or unify the conflicting interest of an increasingly complex society.

The discovery destroyed the foundations on which the main development of humanist thought, from Dante to Shakespeare, had rested. Despite the challenge of revolutionary concepts and popular movements, artists and thinkers tended to accept the system of power that controlled their lives and activities. Underlying the concept of sovereignty was the desire for unity and the fear of class conflict; the intellectual transferred his deep desire for justice and cooperation to an individual monarch, whose position placed him above the battle and outside the clash of irreconcilable interests.

The concept was to be revived in many forms in later theories of the state. But *Hamlet* marks Shakespeare's abandonment of the idea of absolutism in its Renaissance form. For Hamlet, everything is relative. Life is a tangle of contradictions. He is divided against himself, because there is no order or unity in the society in which he lives. He is a prince, but he is less interested in achieving power than in finding moral certitude. He cannot accept the old feudal law which commands quick revenge. Yet the only substitute for the feudal code is the ethical confusion of a competitive society. Hamlet is repelled by the corruption of the court at Elsinore, but he can find nothing trustworthy or secure to sustain him in his hour of need. Friendships fail him. The girl he loves serves his enemies. His mother is so entangled in the net of evil that he cannot cut the net without destroying her.

The most striking characteristic of Hamlet is his aloneness. Few figures in the world's literature are so inexorably alone. Yet his isolation is not like that of the English Queen, drunk with the memory of power. Hamlet *does not want power.* He wants social integration, fellowship, the assurance that his conduct serves rational ends.

Hamlet's sickness is the sickness of a society that rewards force and trickery, and thus creates a gap between the necessity of action and man's realization that only antisocial acts are rewarded. The statement of the problem in *Hamlet* influenced the course of bourgeois thought during the next three centuries. Bourgeois philosophy accepted the separation of mind and matter and built intricate structures of theory on the double foundation. The isolation of the individual, lost in an unfriendly world, became a tenet of bourgeois literature and art.

The last period of Shakespeare's creative life coincided with the founding of England's American colonies, and will be discussed in relation to the colonial venture. Hamlet's Denmark was approaching the epoch of maritime expansion that brought the Vikings to England and Ireland across the Western Sea. Shakespeare's England was preparing to complete the Atlantic conquest of which the Vikings dreamed.

PART III

The Colonial Pattern

1492–1600

1 : PARADISE

In examining the cultural forces that shaped the course of Spanish colonization, we are endeavoring to establish the neglected *unity* of *American* history in the true sense of the word American as applying, not exclusively to the United States, but to the whole Western Hemisphere.

There have been occasional attempts, notably in the writings and influence of Herbert Eugene Bolton,[1] to create a concept of Western Hemisphere history. But Bolton's work has had no appreciable effect in enlarging the confines of American historical thought in the United States. We are told, of course, that Spain's sixteenth century empire in the New World included more than 200 communities, in which there were 150,000 Spaniards.[2] Two towns in what is now the United States antedated the English settlement in Jamestown: St. Augustine, Florida, was founded in 1565, and Santa Fe, New Mexico, in 1605.

Hispanic-Indian civilization is acknowledged in the United States, somewhat casually, as a *fringe phenomenon* existing on the edges of the Anglo-Saxon area, and having significance within the bounds of its geographical extension, in Florida, California and the Southwest. But the local culture in the regions in which Spain had priority of settlement has more than local significance: it exhibits the continuing vitality of influences that stem from the first days of colonization; furthermore, it illustrates the complexity of these influences and the unevenness of their regional development, which has proceeded along very different lines in Florida, in Texas, in the Rio Grande Valley, and on the Pacific Coast.

The interaction of European, Indian, and Negro cultures in these regional patterns suggests that a similar, far more intricate, process of contact and differentiation has taken place on a continental and hemispheric scale. The process began in the first years of Spanish settlement. With the revelation that a New World had been discovered, the conquerors sought to link the northern and southern continents in a single commercial and political system, facing problems which were to be key issues of United States policy in the nineteenth and twentieth centuries. The first proposal to build a Panama Canal was made to the Emperor Charles V in 1529. The Philippine Islands were established as a Pacific outpost and a link between the Americas and the Orient before the end of the sixteenth century. The plantation economy of the West Indies became the model for the English plantations on the North American mainland, and the slave markets in the Caribbean provided the laborers for the British colonies.

European concepts of the New World began to crystallize in 1498 when it became apparent that Columbus had discovered an unknown continent. On his third voyage in 1498, Columbus took a somewhat more southerly course, skirting the semi-circle of West Indian islands to reach the coast of Venezuela. The explorer saw the volume of water pouring from the Orinoco drainage and knew that he had found a continental domain. Following the geographical assumptions of his time, he believed that the land was south of Asia, in the location customarily assigned to the Garden of Eden. He wrote in his journal on August 17, 1498, that he had evidently reached "the terrestrial Paradise, because all men say it's at the end of the Orient, and that's where we are. . . ."[3] He referred to the Bible, which tells of a river flowing out of Eden that "was parted and became four."[4] He heard rumors of four great streams pouring into the sea, and he assumed that these were the rivers of Paradise—the Nile, Euphrates, Tigris and Ganges.

Venezuela looked like Eden. But behind the wall of verdure, shimmering in the August haze, were the jungles where generations to come would find the "Green Hell" of malarial swamps. The contrast between the lovely appearance of the land that Columbus called "Paradise" and the labor, poverty, disease and death that would accompany its settlement expressed the social conflicts and contradictions in the movement of colonization. The clash of forces is reflected in the journals and letters of Columbus. But the clearest statement of the

European attitude toward the New World may be found in the writings attributed to Amerigo Vespucci.

The so-called Vespucci letters that deprived Columbus of full credit for the discovery cannot be dismissed as a curious accident. The hoax was perpetrated for specific reasons; it was successful, not only in giving a name to the New World, but in establishing false concepts which have remained intact for 450 years.

Emerson, writing in the middle of the nineteenth century, found it "strange that broad America must wear the name of a thief." He spoke of Vespucci as a man who had been able to "baptize half the earth with his own dishonest name."[5] Recent scholarship enables us to view Vespucci in a somewhat more kindly light. There is not much doubt that the letters attributed to him were forgeries, and that he was not directly responsible for the reports of fictitious voyages which led Europeans to call the Western Hemisphere by its present name.[6] The hoax was perpetrated in two documents—the first, known as *Mundus Novus,* was a short communication purportedly written by Vespucci to Piero di Medici, in 1503; the second was a longer message, the *Four Voyages,* addressed to a prominent citizen of Florence, Piero Soderini, in 1504. Both letters were published in numerous editions, and widely circulated.

Mundus Novus describes an expedition which supposedly left Cadiz on May 10, 1497. There is no record of any such sailing.[7] The story, repeated in the *Four Voyages,* forms the basis for the claim that Vespucci saw the American mainland before it was discovered by Columbus on his third transatlantic journey in 1498.

Vespucci was an inconspicuous merchant, who served as an agent of the Medici banking firm in Spain. He did sail to South America in the expedition commanded by Alonzo de Ojoda in 1499, serving as cartographer. He made another voyage in 1501. These adventures are described in three authentic letters, which were not published for more than two hundred years. Vespucci's style, soberly presenting geographical and astronomical data, differs markedly from the florid prose of the forged letters.

A comedy of errors, as Stefan Zweig observes, gave Vespucci "immortality from 32 pages."[8] But the comedy was not as accidental as it may appear. It is difficult to believe that Vespucci was ignorant of the publication of material which spread his fame throughout Europe before his death in 1512. The false letters were written to men with whom Vespucci had a long association. Piero di Medici was his former patron and employer, and he had gone to school with Soderini in Florence. These bankers were influential in Spain, and Vespucci was an unsuccessful businessman looking for a chance to improve his situation. Columbus, unaware of the titanic joke that had already been perpetrated, wrote of Vespucci in 1505: "He is an honest man. As with many others, fortune has not been kind to him."[9] In 1508, fortune smiled on Vespucci; he secured the office of pilot major, which gave him supervision of pilots in the port of Cadiz. The recognition came when Columbus was dead, when the *Mundus Novus* had appeared in nine editions, when the proposal that the transatlantic continent be called America had appeared in print.

Vespucci's appointment may have had nothing to do with the hoax. But if the pilot major knew of the deception, it would have been highly impolitic for him to do anything about it. It involved his own reputation, but it also involved the eminent men to whom the false letters were addressed. The popularity and repeated publication of the pamphlets demonstrated their value to the interests promoting colonization. The unknown writer who borrowed Vespucci's name wrote with the unfettered imagination of a press agent; unhampered by American experience, he created a fictional America that was to form the basis for many future fictions.

The heart of the fiction, naturally enough, was sex. According to the author, the Indians were "lascivious beyond measure, the women much more than the men." The women were all beautiful; "they are gifted with very handsome and well proportioned bodies, and no part or member is to be seen that is not well-formed." The men hastened to give their wives and daughters to the strangers: "A father or mother considered themselves highly honored when they brought us a daughter, especially if she was a virgin, that we should sleep with her." At another village, "they offered their wives to us, and we were unable to defend ourselves from them."[10]

The description of the docile sensuality of the Indians seems to preclude any conflict. But brutality is necessary in order to complete the conventional picture of the natives. The transition from sex to violence is made with the dreamlike ease of a motion picture dissolve. The explorer seems to be watching the scene in safety through the lens of a camera, as a group of women kill one of the Spaniards. The "women were still tearing the Christian to pieces. At a great fire they had made they roasted him before our eyes, showing us many pieces, and then eating them."[11]

Las Casas, whose knowledge of the American Indians was drawn from long and intimate contact, was the first observer to point out that the narrative attributed to Vespucci "appears to be all fiction."[12] Las Casas could not foresee the influence that the fiction would exert. It introduced the spiced and picaresque treatment of colonization that was to run its course from Captain John Smith to Raphael Sabatini. Underlying the desire to tell a good story was the emphasis on European superiority, and the unpredictable sensuality and fury of the Indians. The use of Vespucci's name is a minor mystery; more important and less mysterious is the role of two prominent bankers, Medici in France and Soderini in Florence, in poularizing the American cliché. There was also interest in the New World among the rising financiers of southern Germany. A printer in Augsberg, city of the great Fugger firm, published *Mundus Novus* in 1504.

The theft of credit from Columbus was a small manifestation of the dynamic drive that would steal two continents from the Indians. The new land was called America instead of Columbia, because the fiction attributed to Vespucci was more serviceable to the bankers than the confused reality reported in the journals of Columbus.

Yet if history (and the bankers) gave Vespucci a distinction that did not belong to him, Columbus has been compensated by the sanctification of his achievement as something unique in the course of human events. The aura of the heroic and the sublime that surrounds the sailing of the *Pinta, Nina* and *Santa Maria* is no more accidental than the naming of America. The idealization of the voyage is another aspect of the cultural process that places the whole movement of colonization in an abstract and unreal setting. The vulgarization of dealings with the Indians in the "Vespucci letters" finds its counterpart in the treatment of the discovery as an individual's personal revelation and creative will. The heroic portrait of Columbus accomplishes a somewhat similar purpose—it glorifies the European conquest, and obscures the brutal exploitation which was the aim of colonization and the fundamental determinant in the development of colonial society.

The writings of Columbus show him as he was: an able navigator, equipped with the best available knowledge of geography, but also a man tortured by ambition, small-minded in his greed, incapable of social vision. These qualities cannot be ignored, for they relate him to the forces of his time, and the role that he played in establishing the essential pattern of colonization.

The voyage undertaken in 1492 was not an isolated occurrence. It was an integral part of the maritime expansion of the latter fifteenth century. However, the specific social situation in Spain deserves some consideration. The unification of the nation was completed by the capitulation of the Moorish citadel of Granada on January 2, 1492.

The essential instrument of unification was the Inquisition. The Dominican priest, Thomas Torquemada, converted the Inquisition from a purely Catholic institution to a department of the state. His purpose was the same as that which motivated the Hitler terror in Germany; he used anti-Semitism as a means of achieving centralized power without the checks and balances that accompanied the development of national organization in other nations. The techniques of the Inquisition included the rack, the hoist, and slow burning of the feet. The most popular punishment was the water torture: the victim's head was placed in an iron clasp, his mouth held open by an iron ring while water dropped slowly on a piece of linen that went down his throat and choked him.

The Jews represented a large and influential merchant class in Spain, and many of them had intermarried with the nobility. The anti-Semitic fury divided the bourgeoisie of the cities and forced the nobility to accept the extension of monarchial authority. Torquemada encountered the most determined opposition in the great mercantile city of Barcelona. Barcelona was forced to submit in 1487.[13] But Torquemada needed a sensational charge to whip up antagonism against the Jews. He resorted to the ancient invention of a ritual murder in 1490. The unknown child who was the supposed victim was made a saint under the name of Cristobal.[14] The holy task was crowned with the edict expelling the Jews from Spain, published on March 31, 1492.

The extensive properties of the Jews were seized by the crown. Even the stones of their cemeteries were used for the erection of buildings.[15] More than 150,000 people trudged along the roads to the seaports, to try to find some means of leaving the country. The four months of grace which the crown gave the refugees expired on the day before Columbus sailed.

The diary of Columbus begins with these words: "—After having driven out all the Jews from your realms and lordships, in the same month of January, your highnesses commanded me that, with a sufficient fleet, I should go to the said parts of India."[16] It has sometimes been claimed, without adequate historical justification, that Columbus himself was a Jew.[17] But there can be no doubt of the economic connection between his expedition and the expulsion. Isabella's jewels had less to do with the enterprise than the substantial loan advanced by Luis de Santangel, chancellor of the royal household, who was of Jewish ancestry, and who paid in this manner for immunity from the fate that befell his people. Among the 120 men who made the voyage, five were of Jewish stock.[18]

The Inquisition became an American institution in the second half of the sixteenth century, but it attained its first triumph as the ships set out for their unknown destination. The forces that were to weaken Spain and restrict Hispanic-American development were already in operation.

Although we can know only fragments of the story of American civilization before the 450 years of European occupation, it is well to remember that 1492 is only one date in the long history of the hemisphere. The first settlement of the continents goes back to the migration of Indians from Asia by way of Bering Straits. The prehistoric travelers moved southward from Alaska; "their journeys and diffusions did not stop until the whole hemisphere had been traversed and occupied."[19] Later arrivals on the west coast of South America may have made the crossing from the Polynesian islands.

European and American thought has placed an absolute value on the conquest. In assuming possession, the Europeans assume that all that went before was without form and void; God's voice separated the light from the darkness, and the history that begins with the conquest is the history of the conquerors. People condemned to servitude or destruction can have no valid past, no culture worth saving, no enduring social achievements.

Columbus himself is the earliest exponent of this view. His writings formulate the pattern of colonization that was to be followed in Spanish America, and with some variations in the French, Dutch and English settlements. The Indian is the key to the pattern; warfare, land distribution, class distinctions among the Europeans, Negro slavery, were necessary parts of the design that was outlined by Columbus in his first contact with the people of the Americas.

The name given to the inhabitants reflected the illusions that motivated the voyage. When the ships moved through the seaweed of the Sargasso Sea and the flight of birds presaged a landfall, Columbus scanned the horizon for the towers of the city with marble bridges described by Marco Polo. Since the *El Dorado* for which he searched was the fabled wealth of the Orient, the people were called Indians. The name was no less a tragic jest than the christening of America. The people had to pay for their name, bearing the burden of the jest on their backs. Their labor was the main resource offered by the West Indies to compensate for the east Indian riches—the spices and silks and jewels—that were conspicuously absent from the Caribbean islands.

But Columbus was not discouraged. There was gold in Hispaniola, and he was sure that the temples of Cathay were just beyond the western horizon. The voyagers left a settlement, and returned to Spain with a few Indians, exhibited as curious prizes along with parrots and gold and animals and plants. The second voyage was prepared speedily, on a scale that contrasted with the meager outlay for the first venture. The extravagant preparations were financed in large part by the money derived from the royal confiscation of Jewish fortunes.[20] Columbus sailed again in September, 1493, with seventeen ships, twelve hundred fighting men, with horses, cows, sheep and goats to provide sustenance for the gold-seekers.

As soon as the expedition reached Hispaniola, the myth of easy wealth met the realities of the colonial labor market. The forty-four Europeans left as masters of the Island had been killed; the Indians did not want masters. Columbus had an army to impose discipline. He planned cities, mines, affluent living. But the rumor of gold was more in evidence than the glittering actuality. Money had to be *made,* if not by alchemy, then by the forced labor of the natives. Columbus approached the problem with naïve directness. Instead of devising productive activity, he ordered the natives to produce gold. Each individual was to bring a pot of precious dust as tribute, receiving in return a tin medal as a certificate of good behavior.[21] The plan proved unworkable, because the Indians had no gold. When the chiefs offered to bring a portion of their crops as a substitute, Columbus accused them of disloyalty. He wrote a letter to Ferdinand and Isabella on January 30, 1494, in which he recommended the enslavement of the Indians. The proposal flowed from the logic of the colonial situation.

When the natives were punished for their failure to make voluntary contributions of gold dust, they rebelled and took up arms—which released the Europeans from any obligations, and excused the enslavement of prisoners of war. Fifteen hundred Indians were captured. Four hundred of these, the most muscular and well-proportioned men and women, were selected for shipment to Europe. It was announced that any Christian might help himself to the left-overs. The people sent to Spain faced the usual risks of the trade. Crowded on the decks, 200 died on the voyage and were thrown into the sea.[22]

Having established forced labor in the colony, Columbus returned to Spain in 1496. He had learned a great deal. He knew the difficulties of colonization. He realized that the profitable occupation of Hispaniola depended on exploitations further West, where he expected to find the rich mainland of Asia. Since reports of sickness and hardship made it difficult to recruit colonists, the third voyage introduced the custom of taking convicts from the prisons for service over seas.

We have mentioned the discovery of the South American mainland in the summer of 1498. The revelation came fourteen months after another Italian navigator's discovery of Newfoundland. John Cabot, sailing under the English flag and financed by Bristol merchants, crossed the North Atlantic in the summer of 1497, believing that he had reached northeastern Asia. The news was conveyed to Italy by the Duke of Milan's representative in London. Raimondo di Soncino wrote on December 18 that Master Zoanne Caboto, "a low-class Venetian," intended to sail again in the spring:

> It is said His Majesty will arm some ships and give him all the criminals so that he may go to that country and plant a colony. . . . In this way, he hopes to make London a greater place for spices than Alexandria, and the principals in the business are citizens of Bristol, great Mariners.

More realistic was Soncino's report of the codfish seen near the Newfoundland coast:

> . . . The sea there is swarming with fish which can be taken not only with the net but in baskets let down with a stone, so that it sinks in the water. . . . They could bring so many fish that this kingdom would have no further need of Iceland, from which place there comes a very great quantity of the fish called stockfish.[23]

Thus basic factors in the economy of the hemisphere began to emerge in the first decade of exploration. The salt cod of the Grand Banks was to be the basic food of the galleons sailing to America and around Africa to the Orient. Its sale in Europe was to convert some of the treasure of the Indies into English capital. The fisheries were to be the foundation of New England's maritime development, linking the British colonies with Spanish America and the slave trade.

When Columbus returned to Hispaniola from his visit to Paradise, he encountered another element in the emergent colonial pattern—an organized revolt of the colonists. The settlers were hungry and disillusioned. In addition, they were plagued by syphilis. There were 160 cases of the disease, representing between 20 and 30 percent of the men who were still alive.[24] Medical opinion is divided as to whether the ailment existed in the Old World before 1492, but there can be no doubt that it spread virulently throughout Europe shortly after Columbus returned from his first voyage. It was known under many names —*English disease, Polish disease, German disease, Neapolitan disease*— but it was most widely recognized as the *disease of Hispaniola,* or the new disease.[25]

In the Spanish colony, the settlers suffered the social effects of the subjection of Indian women, while they were deprived of a satisfactory share in the economic exploitation of their victims. Sexual privileges—and syphilis—were a poor substitute for the profits that went to the crown and the few men who controlled the colonial economy. The first American revolution conducted by Europeans was organized by less privileged members of the bourgeoisie.

Columbus had to meet the demand. He no longer had the military power to fight the insurgents. Another imperative reason for settling the dispute was the danger of an Indian uprising. This agreement with the insurgents inaugurated the system of land and labor that was to become official and general in the Spanish colonies. The settlers received grants of land. The grants included the right to use the forced labor of the Indians in the designated area. The larger and more fertile tracts went to the leaders of the revolt. Therefore, the distribution divided the opposition and created more discontent, which led to the introduction of another feature of overseas administration—brutal punishment for insubordination. Columbus and his two brothers, who shared the tasks of government with him, erected gallows at both ends of the town of San Domingo.

The Spanish court was disturbed by reports of disorders in Hispaniola, and even more disturbed by the inadequate income from the venture. In June, 1500, Francisco Bobadilla sailed with orders to replace Columbus as governor. When Bobadilla arrived on August 23, he saw seven corpses hanging from gallows and was told that five more persons were to be executed the next day. The new governor listened to complaints and charges; Columbus was sent to Spain in irons.

The chained mariner looked back upon the events of the third voyage. The experience was as violent and elliptical as the trailers that advertise future attractions in motion picture theatres. It was an impassioned and inexpert preview of what lay ahead—Indian war and revolt of European settlers, land distribution and private exploitation of forced labor, violent punishments, quick reversals of fortune. Columbus wrote a letter while he was still in irons, on shipboard: "The gate to gold and pearls is now open, and plenty of everything—precious stones, spices and a thousand other things." [26]

In a sense, of course, he was right. The pearls he had found on his journey among the islands near Venezuela and the deposits of gold in Hispaniola were a modest advance payment on the treasures that were in store for the conquerors. As the ship carried Columbus back to Spain, Peralonso Nino visited the pearl fisheries behind Margharita Island on the Venezuelan coast, and gathered a fabulous cargo of gems.

Alonzo de Ojeda gave Venezuela its name of "Little Venice," and explored the coast as far as Panama. At the same time, several expeditions reached Brazil. Vicente Yanez Pinzon saw the mouth of the Amazon and returned to Spain with a cargo of dye-producing brazilwood. The Portuguese commander, Pedro Alvares Cabral, blown off his course on a voyage around the Cape of Good Hope to India, touched South America at Porto Seguro, taking possession in the name of Portugal.

Reports of these mainland explorations made it unwise to keep Columbus in chains. He was welcomed again at court as one of the men who held the keys of "the gate to gold and pearls." The charges against him were dismissed, he was promised full compensation, and Bobadilla was to be impeached and sent home. The experience of these few years had made it distressingly obvious that some change was required in the method of colonial administration. It was decided to limit and define the governor's powers, to emphasize his direct responsibility to the crown, and to encourage emigration by giving the colonists the opportunity to become self-supporting. The last point was the heart of the matter; the distribution of land and workers improvised by Columbus under the pressure of armed rebellion was officially sanctioned. The system, which became known as the *encomienda,* "commended" Indians to landholders, who were their protectors or *encomenderos.*

The distinction between commendation and slavery was important. The system purported to protect and civilize the natives, as well as to exploit them. It was designed in part to cloak the nature of the exploitation and allay the discontent of the Indians by assuring them that they were technically "free." However, the architects of Spanish policy were probably less concerned about the attitude of the Indians than about the Spanish settlers. While it was necessary to give the colonists enough incentive to undertake the transatlantic voyage, the crown had no intention of giving them absolute property rights in land or absolute control of the labor force. The key to the purpose of the *encomienda,* which was to cause sharp conflict in later years, was its limited character. The land was occupied at the discretion of the crown. The landholder did not own the Indians. He merely had the use of their labor.

Under the *encomienda,* the Indian's "freedom," supposedly proved by the miserable sum he received as wages, did not prevent his being worked to death. The instructions given to Governor Nicholas de Ovando when he sailed with 2,500 colonists in 1502 made a pious combination of compulsion and payment: "You are to compel them to work in our service, paying them the wages you think it just they should have." The unity of opposites was reiterated in the revised instructions sent to Hispaniola in December, 1603: "You will compel and force the said Indians . . . This the Indians will perform as a free people." [27]

Ovando's regime was intended to introduce an era of colonial stability. Agriculture and cattle-raising were to be encouraged. A board of trade, the *Casa de Contratacion,* was established to supervise commerce and immigration. Settlers who could afford slaves were permitted to import them, but only "Negro and other slaves born among Christians." [28]

Columbus had done his part in establishing the colonial social order. But he obviously lacked the qualities of an efficient administrator. In view of his reputation, and his determination to find the mainland of Asia, he was permitted to sail again. The last voyage was an

Odyssey of storms and shipwreck and heartbreak. Columbus weathered the tempest that destroyed the homeward-bound fleet, the richest ever sent from Hispaniola. His enemy, Bobadilla, on his way home for trial, perished in the storm. Columbus reached Panama, and again the realm of gold was just over the horizon. Near Porto Bello, Indians conducted the explorers "to a lofty mountain, and thence showed them the country all around, as far as the eye could reach, told them there was gold in every part."[29]

Columbus did not have enough men or supplies to continue the search. On the return journey, he ran his leaky ships aground at Jamaica. He and his men lived there with the natives for a year, until help arrived from Hispaniola.

When the tired mariner came back to Spain, sick and exhausted, in 1504, he was no longer an important figure. The letters attributed to Vespucci were already in circulation. Columbus had outlived his usefulness. His passionate and bitter reports of his exploits were less serviceable to the group controlling colonization than the smooth fictions that were to give the new continents a name. The idealization of Columbus could wait. He received minor gratifications from the Spanish government, including a license to ride on mule-back. He died on May 20, 1506.

The introduction of slavery in America was dictated by the conditions of production relationships in the colony. It was the only means of extracting a high, quick profit from native or imported labor. But when Columbus became the instrument for imposing slavery and the *Encomienda,* he made the Vespucci hopes inevitable. Forced labor demanded the stereotype of the lazy, sexually potent, vicious "native." It is also one of history's ironies that the new continent should bear the name of the man whose signature was placed on the first documents utilizing the stereotype in a description of the American social scene.

Europeans began to speak of "America," and to think of it as the curious landscape depicted in the Vespucci letters. The truth was permanently corrupted. The savagery of the conquest was veiled. Attention was diverted to the "savagery" of the natives, to their wanton sexuality, their primitive rites, their inability to learn the ways of their "masters."

Across the sea, the people, Indian and European, labored to obtain the means of subsistence. The Indians were worked, literally, to death.

The *encomienda* was administered in a way that encouraged absentee ownership; courtiers and prelates, and the king himself, owned large estates operated by workers, duly paid according to the letter of the law. The mortality among the Indians was proceeding at a rate that would almost wipe out the native population in a few decades. And the death rate was dangerously high among the Europeans. Of the 2,500 people who came out with Ovando, 1,000 died within two years.

The people in Paradise had tasted the forbidden fruit, and it was bitter unto death.

2 : THE FIRST UTOPIA

THE ANNALS of the Spanish conquest are crowded with the names of doughty adventurers and sanguinary heroes. But one man stands alone above the throng as the creative thinker of the formative years.

Historical figures are all too frequently removed from their place in history by clothing them in a mantle of virtue that makes them well-nigh invisible. Bartolomé de Las Casas has been praised as an idealist, whose devotion to the welfare of the Indians was incompatible with the practical politics of colonization. The view misrepresents his personality and belittles his achievement. His ideas were welded in the heat of controversy; his recommendations were translated into governmental and ecclesiastical decrees that changed the course of colonial history.

Las Casas, like many other profound thinkers, could not bridge the chasm between theory and practice, between the rational will and the apparently unpredictable movement of social forces. But he was one of the first Europeans to attempt a realistic appraisal of the problems of colonization. He stands at the dawn of the great day of imperialism, boldly demanding an accounting of its social cost. He faced the impossible task of combining the benefits of an advanced culture with the labor productivity that was essential for profitable operation of overseas settlements. The results of his endeavors contradicted all that he willed and hoped: he helped to bring Negro slavery to America, and he prepared the way for the missions that built an ecclesiastical empire on the backs of Indian workers.

Las Casas settled in Hispaniola in 1502, when the *encomienda* system, informally introduced by Columbus, was given official sanction. He came out with Governor Ovando, with the 2,500 colonists who were to prosper under the new dispensation, receiving temporary grants of land and a portion of Indian labor. Las Casas was 28 years old, and it was not his first trip to the New World. His father had accompanied Columbus on the first voyage, in 1492. On the third expedition, in 1498, Bartolomé went with his father. He saw the breakers where the waters of the Orinoco meet the sea; he saw the green jungles that Columbus called Paradise.

The senior Las Casas was rewarded for his services with an *encomienda*. The son went out in 1502 to manage the estate. In 1510, Bartolomé joined the Dominican Brotherhood. The inner conviction that led him to the church was the fruit of the social situation in which he found himself.

Governor Ovando addressed a petition to the king in 1507. The document is a succinct preview of the difficulties that were to plague the West Indies for centuries. The governor's complaint listed four major problems: an increasing shortage of Indian labor, the dangers of Negro slavery, absentee ownership, ecclesiastical control of property and labor. On the first point, Ovando pointed out that the Indian population was disappearing. Negro slavery was increasing, and he mentioned the fear of slave revolts. He objected to the practice of giving grants of land and Indians to persons at the Spanish Court. At the time, the king himself owned the labor (voluntarily given, as the law provided) of 1,430 Indians. Various courtiers had the services of 3,720 Indians. Ovando also objected to giving Indians to prelates and priests on the island.[1]

As an economic footnote to the governor's petition, we may take cognizance of the fact that the cultivation of sugar had begun to attract the interest of colonial landholders. Ovando and his friends grew worried about absentee ownership and the diminishing labor supply when the possibilities of sugar production became apparent to them. They were less concerned about the plight of the small farmer than about the protection and extension of their own properties.

The crown was chiefly interested in maintaining the profits from the royal lands and mines; it also wished to stabilize the social situation by making concessions to the less privileged colonists. These aims were furthered by the instructions given to Diego Columbus, the explorer's son, who went out to replace Ovando in 1509. He was ordered to equalize the distribution of native labor: royal officers were to have 100 Indians; married hidalgos, 80; squires, 60; farmers, 30. The class distinctions were clear enough. But from the viewpoint of the owners of large plantations, the change was "revolutionary" and confiscatory. The standardized distribution threatened their control of the lion's share of the available labor supply. The king also emphasized the temporary character of the *encomienda:* he pointed out that the laborers were assigned only for a period of two or three years.[2]

The king was worried by reports of a labor shortage, and he wanted to guarantee enough workers to keep his mines in operation. But the leading colonists made such an outcry against the redistribution that Ferdinand cancelled his instructions.

The economic pressure in Hispaniola stimulated the geographical extension of the Spanish possessions. Adventurers seeking wider opportunities occupied Puerto Rico in 1503, Jamaica in 1509, Cuba in 1511. But the new possessions duplicated the experience in Hispaniola. The Indians escaped from the settled areas and organized resistance. The majority of the Europeans were destitute, sick, rebellious. In 1511, the labor shortage became so acute that the crown gave general permission to settlers to hunt and capture Indians on the unoccupied islands. Ferdinand went so far as to agree to sacrifice his own share, the royal fifth, in the profits of the manhunt.[3]

These were the circumstances that motivated Las Casas' decision to join the Dominican Order. It grew out of his unsatisfactory experience, the social desolation that he saw around him, the belief that religious organization offered the best hope of creating a workable colonial system. Las Casas had not as yet reached the conclusion that the *encomienda* must be abolished. But life was soon to demonstrate to him the futility of halfway measures. His reputation as a reformer who "understood" the Indians led to his being called to Cuba early in 1512. Diego Velasquez, who began the conquest of the island in 1511, was having trouble, and he wanted Las Casas to assist in the task of "pacification."

Meanwhile, in Spain, the government was endeavoring to formulate a practical labor policy for the colonies. The Laws of Burgos, adopted December 27, 1512, and supplemented by additional regulations the following July, were little more than a codification of the existent system, demonstrating the crown's continued preoccupation with the maintenance of forced labor in the royal mines. Article 1 provided that the Indians should be brought together in villages under European supervision. Article 13 ordered that men engaged in mining gold should work for five months and then have 40 days of rest. Article 20 set their pay at one gold peso a year, which, as Las Casas later observed, was enough to buy combs, a mirror, a kerchief and a red cape. Article 25 decreed that one-third of all the Indians should work in the mines.[4]

In Cuba, Las Casas witnessed the methods by which the system was introduced in virgin territory. He saw the two years of warfare and massacres that prepared the Indians for the blessings of civilization. He protested against the excesses of the conquerors, but he was interested in developing the country, and wanted to combine the humane employment of the Indians with profitable use of the land. He formed a partnership with a close friend, Pedro de la Renteria; the two men received an apportionment of land, with its complement of inhabitants, on the banks of the Arimao River, in the town of Xagua, where gold had been discovered.[5]

Las Casas began farming in Cuba as Spain began the conquest of the American mainland. In 1513, Ponce de Leon reached Florida and Vasco Nunez de Balboa saw the Pacific. There is a connection between the two events. Florida was a gateway to the North American continental domain. Panama linked the two parts of the hemisphere, and the crossing of the isthmus opened the way to Pacific commerce and settlement on the west coast. The ultimate potentialities of the crossing were to be realized four hundred years later when the United States completed the canal that joined the oceans and the continents in an economic network under the aegis of the dollar and the eagle.

It is not our purpose to expatiate on the picaresque and better known aspects of the conquest. But the Panama adventure so clearly indicated the future pattern of mainland expansion and had such an immediate effect on Spanish policy, that it requires brief consideration.

The wind brought only a wild surmise to the sixty-seven men who cut a bloody path across the isthmus to see the surf breaking on the shores of an unknown ocean. Among those who sang a *Te Deum* was Francisco Pizarro, who was to seize the wealth of the Incas twenty years later. Balboa and Pizarro looked upon the Pacific primarily as a highway to *El Dorado*. The Indians told of a rich civilization somewhere to the south, cities and temples, gold and jewels. Land exploration was almost impossible. But materials could be transported across the isthmus to build ships for voyages along the South American coast. Balboa, fired with enthusiasm, returned to Darien to prepare for the treasure hunt.

However, the promise of *El Dorado* had also fired the imagination of the king and his councilors. Ever since the prophecy of Columbus, written as he returned to Spain in irons in 1500, that "the gate to gold and pearl is now open," reports of the riches in the interior of the continent poured into the Spanish court. Balboa had written to the king before starting across the isthmus, promising that he would find gold so plentiful in the streams that it could be collected "without any labor" in enormous nuggets: "The Indians indicate they are of the size of oranges and like the fist." [6]

So the crown decided to send an expedition to Panama that would have the authority and military strength to conduct the search and organize its results. The mission, the first sponsored by the *Casa de Contratacion* was placed under the leadership of an important personage, Pedrarias Davila. He was seventy years old, and was known in Spain as *el Galan,* the Gallant; he was to earn a more impressive sobriquet in the New World—*Furor Domini,* the Wrath of God. Pedrarias sailed in suitable splendor, with brocaded robes and a train of servants and courtiers, and twenty-two ships carrying 2,000 men. The baggage included 200 troughs for washing gold. Among the passengers was an expert appraiser of gems. There was a notary to take charge of smelting gold and branding slaves.

Pedrarias reached Darien, renamed *Castilla del Oro, Golden Castile,* in honor of the occasion, on June 29, 1514. Balboa, at the head of the town council, received him on bended knee. But Balboa's obedience did not profit the new governor or relieve his doomed followers. Within a month, 700 of the gay company were dead, most of them from yellow fever. The rest were starving. Brocade was exchanged for corn. While people died in the streets crying for bread, the governor spent his time at games. One night at chess, he lost 100 slaves.[7]

The situation at Panama duplicated, in a swifter and more melodramatic form, the social disintegration that afflicted the older settlements. Hispaniola in 1514 had a population of 29,000 Indians. This was the first generation after the arrival of Columbus, all that was left of the several hundred thousand whose representatives waited on the shores to greet their visitors with courtesy and gifts in 1492. The

Europeans had not fared much better. Only 1,000 Spanish settlers remained alive in 1514.[8]

Las Casas' sense of personal failure in Cuba was related to his observation of the scope of the colonial catastrophe. The state of the whole overseas enterprise motivated his journey to Spain in 1515 and assured the sympathetic hearing that he received from the government and the church.

Las Casas went to Spain with the blessing of the Dominican Order. The Dominican interest in a drastic change in the *encomienda* system was the outgrowth of economic rivalry between the Dominicans and the Franciscans. The conflict between the two groups, which had been conducted for some years with a good deal of noise and invective, related to the more advantageous position that the Franciscans had acquired in the politics and business life of the island. The disciples of the gentle St. Francis, holding properties operated by Indian workers, were associated with the colonial administration in opposing any readjustment of the organization of land and labor. In attacking the *encomienda* and demanding more charitable use of the Indians, the Dominicans intended to weaken their rivals and increase their own power.

In the larger arena of Spanish politics, the support for Las Casas' proposals was guided more by expediency than by ethical imperatives. The history of the Dominican Order hardly qualified it to appear as the defender of the oppressed and disinherited. Under Torquemada's leadership, it had used the Inquisition as the means of establishing Catholic absolutism in Spain. We have noted the connection between the sailing of Columbus and the expulsion of the Jews. After Torquemada's death in 1498, a Franciscan statesman, Ximenes de Cisneros inherited his power, becoming Grand Inquisitor General in 1507.

Las Casas came to Spain at a moment of political crisis. The death of Ferdinand on January 28, 1516, made Ximenes the regent of Spain. The sixteen-year old Charles, who was to inherit the throne, was in Flanders. The eighty-year old cardinal faced the opposition of the nobility, and the urban discontent that was to erupt a few years later in the revolt of the Communeros. The structure of absolutism was gravely threatened. It was essential for Ximenes to conciliate the Dominicans in order to unite his religious support. He could not afford to have a scandal about the conduct of colonial affairs. The reports from America left little doubt that a major scandal was brewing.

Therefore, Ximenes took prompt action on the basis of Las Casas' representations. In order to maintain the appearance of impartiality as between Dominicans and Franciscans, three Jeronymite friars were appointed to go to Hispaniola and make an investigation. But the scales of authority were weighted in favor of Las Casas. He was officially designated "Protector of the Indians" and the commissioners were told to cooperate closely with him.

Las Casas discovered that the title conferred in Spain was not honored in the West Indies. The political forces that made his suit effective in the homeland were not operative on the other side of the Atlantic. The Jeronymite friars reached the colony in December, 1516, and began the collection of testimony in public and secret hearings. Las Casas arrived soon afterward. The commissioners were already under the influence of the local landholders and the Franciscans. When Las Casas protested that the inquiry was not being fairly conducted, he was threatened with arrest. He hurried back to Spain, arriving in July, 1517.[9]

Ximenes died in November, 1517, and Charles assumed the reins of government. The unsettled state of affairs delayed action on colonial policy. But Las Casas was indefatigable and skillful in the presentation of his case. The political factors that worked in his favor were those that had swayed Ximenes. The youthful king, with his eyes fixed on the imperial crown, had to assure the stability of his American possessions and the safety of his own income from overseas. The plight of Hispaniola and the neighboring islands pointed to the need of drastic remedial measures.

The most alarming news came from Panama. Pedrarias was doing his best to earn the title of *Furor Domini*. The governor's wrath was especially directed against Balboa, who was engaged in transporting supplies across the isthmus in order to begin the search for *El Dorado* on the other side. With thirty Negro slaves and a prodigal expenditure of the labor and lives of Indians, Balboa succeeded in hauling the necessary equipment through the forests and across the cordillera.

Balboa built two brigantines on the Pacific side and made a trial voyage south of the Pearl Islands. When he returned, he learned that a new governor, Lope de Sosa, would soon arrive to suceed Pedrarias. Balboa's success, in contrast to the governor's failure, was the explorer's death warrant. Pedrarias knew that he would be under fire when he returned to Spain and that Balboa would offer the strongest evidence against him. If the explorer acquired the prestige of rich discoveries in South America, Pedrarias would be doomed.

The governor sent a friendly letter to Balboa, asking him to come to Acla to discuss supplies for the ships. Balboa started the journey. On the way, he was met by his friend and lieutenant, Pizarro, who placed him under arrest. The disloyal act was Pizarro's passport to Peru, preparation for the pilgrimage that would end in the halls of the Incas. As is usual in such cases, the charge against Balboa was treason, and the judge was the prosecutor. The trial was smooth, short and secret. The sentence of death was carried out in twenty-four hours.

The date of Balboa's death is unknown; it was between 1517 and 1519. The incident was an appropriate introduction to the great period of the conquistadors, which was to be characterized by frantic, and frequently, murderous, competition among the conquerors. The news of the execution must have had an effect on the negotiations being conducted by Las Casas in Spain. The European reaction is suggested in Peter Martyr's comment in a letter to the pope: "There has been nothing but killing and being killed, massacring and being massacred." [10]

Peter Martyr's correspondence during this period reflects the growing ecclesiastical concern over the conduct of American affairs. There is an instructive contrast between the letters attributed to Vespucci and Martyr's careful reports to this superiors in Rome. The tall stories to which Vespucci's name was appended were intended to amuse and intrigue the public. Martyr owed his position at the Spanish court to his usefulness as a contact between the crown and the papacy. His letters were based on interviews with captains and pilots, data concerning the financing of expeditions and the value of incoming cargoes. This information was invaluable to the Vatican in formulating colonial policy. Martyr had written at length concerning the wealth that might be found in the interior of South America.[11] The church was anxious to protect its own stake in the American enterprise and to prevent the maladministration that reduced profits and delayed colonial expansion.

It should be noted that the treatment of the Indians did not relate solely to the settled areas. It affected the rate of progress in occupying new territory on the mainland. The experience in Cuba and Panama proved that enslavement required long, costly warfare. Las Casas offered a plan for avoiding conflict with the native population, supplying an alternate source of cheap labor, and encouraging emigration. The abandonment of the *encomienda* would equalize the opportunities of European settlers. The Indians were to be released from bondage; they were to be taught European methods of raising crops and to occupy villages under the supervision of priests. The need of cheap labor was to be supplied by Negro slaves. Each Spanish resident was to have the privilege of importing twelve Negroes.

Tentative approaches toward a new policy were made in December, 1518. The Jeronymite Friars, who were stalling for time with endless questionnaires and interviews, were recalled to Spain with the bulky and inconclusive proofs of their industry. The new governor of Hispaniola, Rodrigo Figueroa, was ordered to deprive officials and persons living in Spain of their *encomiendas,* to grant liberty to Indians who seemed capable of enjoying it, and to make further investigations. Charles left Spain in May, 1520, to begin his career as ruler of the Holy Roman empire. The problem of Indian labor was considered so important that, as Las Casas tells us, the week before the king's departure was devoted solely to the discussion.[12]

Las Casas won the argument. Orders were sent to Hispaniola to hasten the release of the Indians. Those employed by nonresidents were to be freed immediately, and others were to gain their freedom on the death of their *encomendero.* They were to be assembled in villages as free vassals. Similar orders were dispatched to Puerto Rico in July. Las Casas was given a grant of land on the coast of Venezuela, where he was to have the authority to build a colony which might serve as a model for other enterprises.

The least controversial part of the program related to the slave trade. Charles awarded a contract for the annual transportation of 4,000 Negroes from Africa to the Indies to Lorenzo de Gomenot, who resold the privilege to a Genoese syndicate for 25,000 ducats.[13]

Ironically and inevitably, the weightiest result of the reforms proposed by Las Casas was the introduction of Negro slavery as a profitable business. It seems curious that a reasonable man could couple the demand for Indian freedom with the proposal to enslave other human beings who happened to be of African descent. His thought was a clouded mirror of colonial realities, an attempt to create a blueprint for an ordered society to replace the chaos of the treasure hunt.

He had seen with his own eyes that the *encomienda* was wasteful. He had seen the burdened laborer die at his work. He had watched the massacres that destroyed the labor reserves in Cuba before the plantations were distributed. However, humanist doctrine did not condemn slavery. Thomas More's *Utopia* was published in 1515, the year in which Las Casas made his first journey to Spain to demand the protection of the Indians. More's ideal commonwealth throws a good deal of light on the hopes that motivated Las Casas' American plans. The good society of his vision *needed* slave labor in order to ensure its development; but the slaves were to be treated as family servants, guarded and protected by their masters.

Especially noteworthy in Las Casas' thought is his emphasis on the rights of small landholders. *El Dorado* was to be a middle-class paradise, each farmer commanding his own acres and exercising patriarchal guardianship over his twelve Negro slaves. The idyl, absurd as it seems in restrospect, expressed the deepest meaning—and the deepest contradiction—in Las Casas' philosophy. In his later years, he regretted his error and denounced Negro slavery. His recognition of its moral indefensibility coincided with his observation of its economic effect, in further undermining the security of the independent farmer.

In the case of the Indians in the Caribbean islands, the deprivation of the "normal, moral and physical conditions of development" shortened the life-span so drastically that the population was destroyed in an incredibly short period. Las Casas was soon to find out that no Utopian blueprint could arrest the process. He received permission in 1520 to establish a colony in the image of his dream on the pearl coast of Venezuela.

The generous treatment of Las Casas must be understood in relation to two essential factors: the cities of Castile were in revolt; and Spain's colonial empire was being enlarged by spectacular discoveries. We have noted the seriousness of the rebellion of the Communes at the time of the emperor's coronation in October. Peter Martyr's voluminous correspondence with Rome bore testimony to the urgency of the Castilian events. He gave less attention to discoveries in America, and wrote lengthy descriptions of the progress of the uprising.[14]

In assuring continued Hapsburg control of Spain, it was also essential to guarantee the better administration of the expanding colonial domain. In the fall of 1520, Hernando Cortes was marching into the heart of Mexico, and had fought the crucial battle which assured his mastery of the Aztec domain. Fernando Magellan, seeking a passage around South America in order to circle the globe, had entered the straits that bear his name.

Las Casas went to Venezuela with a party of peasants and Dominican Brothers. The latter were to educate the Indians. The agricultural skill of the former was to guarantee the peaceful development of a farm community. The brief experiment was the first in the long history of American Utopias. The unrealistic nature of the plan was emphasized by the choice of a location close to the pearl fisheries. The gathering of pearls was conducted with the most wanton disregard of the rights of the native population.

Las Casas arrived at a time when the despoiled and enslaved tribes were preparing to rebel and drive out their oppressors. He attempted to convince the Indians that his ideal community had no connection with the other Europeans. The argument was palpably false: the settlement could not exist economically or politically in isolation from the European activity in its neighborhood. Las Casas was called on to mediate with the Indians, to prevent trouble and protect the pearl fisheries. He found himself on the brink of the terrible chasm that separated his theory from the practice of slavery. He had to take sides, with the Europeans or with the Indians, and there was no middle ground. Within a year, Las Casas turned, defeated, from the intolerable reality. As the ship that carried him away set sail, bloody warfare flared along the coast.[15]

3 : ANATHEMA

THE CLIMAX of Las Casas' career came thirty years after his misadventure in Venezuela. These were the years in which the colonial tragedy assumed its greatest scope and meaning.

The events that took place from 1522 to 1550 did not establish a new social pattern; the continental conquest was a repetition of the Caribbean occupation. The techniques employed in Cuba were utilized in Mexico, Guatemala and Peru. The strife among the conquistadors that began in Panama culminated in the civil war that disrupted Spanish control of the Inca empire. The failure of the Utopia on the Pearl Coast prefigured the holy rage with which Las Casas would shout malediction on colonization and all its works. His mission was not that of an apostle bringing grace; he spoke at last as a prophet crying havoc in the wilderness.

When Las Casas sailed away from Venezuela, it must have seemed as if he had lived the fullness of his life. He was forty-eight years old; he wanted to analyze what had occurred, to see it in historical perspective. He retired to a Dominican monastery in Hispaniola, where he spent most of the next decade in solitude. Here he began writing the *General History of the Indies,* which was to occupy him intermittently during the rest of his life.

The movement of forces that was to bring him out of the monastery was proceeding at an accelerated pace as the monastery doors closed on him. Cortes had wiped out the last organized Aztec opposition. Magellan had died in the Philippines. When the *Vittoria,* the only one of Magellan's ships to complete the circumnavigation of the globe, entered the harbor of Seville with its thirty-one surviving sailors in December, 1521, European concepts of geography were revolutionized. America, looming vast in the vastness of the seas, assumed its true importance in schemes of trade and conquest.

Magellan's voyage had been undertaken in order to find a western route to the Moluccas, the spice islands which supplied Europe with cloves, nutmegs and mace. The Moluccas lay far to the east of the Indian ocean ports reached by Portuguese traders, who obtained the spices from Oriental merchants. The De Haro banking firm of Antwerp, which backed Magellan's expedition, believed that a narrow sea separated America and Asia. Since the Moluccas lay beyond the Indian ocean, it was not unreasonable to suppose that they were just over the horizon that Balboa scanned from a hill in Darien.[1]

The return of the battered *Vittoria* dissipated these illusions, and proved that the Pacific was too wide and dangerous for easy conquest. Interest in a western passage to the Orient was to be revived later in the century, when European capitalists had become more heavily involved in Far Eastern commerce. In 1521, the new geographical knowledge, coinciding with the revelation of the wealth of Mexico, made America a primary object of European interest.

Fishermen of various nations were already frequenting Newfoundland harbors. The English "Company Adventurers to the New Found Lands," chartered in 1502, ran into difficulties which were the result of its overambitious plans. But French and Portuguese ships seem to have reached the Grand Banks as early as 1504. "Newland" fish were being sold in Rouen in 1510. English fishermen made annual voyages across the Atlantic; in 1522, when England went to war with France, there was a request for the dispatch of a convoy to guard the "commyng home of the New Found Isle landes flete."[2]

The era of official piracy was introduced by Giovanni Verrazano, with his capture of the galleons carrying the treasures of the Aztec capital back to Spain. The hijacking of the loot that had just been stolen from Montezuma occurred in the summer of 1522. It was a spectacular coup for the Italian navigator and his French backers. The treasure was calculated at 100,000 ducats, and the pearls alone weighed 680 pounds.[3] In 1524, Verrazano, still sailing under the French flag and financed by Lyons bankers, explored the American coast from Newfoundland to South Carolina, visiting New York harbor.

The course of Verrazano's voyage may have been duplicated by an English expedition which left Plymouth in July, 1527. John Rut, on board the *Mary of Guilford,* wrote from St. John's Harbor, Newfoundland, on August 3, that they "found eleven saile of Normans, and one Brittaine, two Portugall Barkes, and all a-fishing."[4] There is no definite information concerning the later adventures of the *Mary of Guilford,* but it is probable that she sailed south along the coast; she may have been the English ship which appeared at Santo Domingo on November 25; the visit occasioned a governmental inquiry and a sharp reprimand from Spain because the English sailors "landed and visited the city" without interference.[5]

Occasional French and English voyages did not constitute a threat to the Spanish-Hapsburg empire in the New World. But it was already apparent that the defense of the center of Spanish power in the Caribbean and the Gulf of Mexico required mastery of Florida and the coast line north of it. The emperor commissioned a Portuguese navigator, Estaban Gomez, in 1524-1525, to explore the Atlantic seaboard as far as Nova Scotia. Strategic considerations, as well as the hope of finding golden cities in the wilderness, motivated Spanish attempts to establish settlements on the shores of North America.

There were also voyages along the South American coast, the most impressive being the expedition that left Spain in 1526 under the command of Sebastian Cabot. The backing of the venture by an international consortium reflected the growing European interest in colonization. Spanish merchants joined with Genoese bankers in financing the voyage, in which Robert Thorne of Bristol was also interested. Cabot was accompanied by a German merchant and Roger Barlow of Bristol, who was associated with Thorne.

Cabot reached the Rio de la Plata, where he heard tales of a rich Indian civilization somewhere to the West and North. In 1528, Cabot ascended the Parana River as far as the present city of Asuncion in Paraguay. But his backers were disappointed by the unsatisfactory returns of the long exploration, and Cabot could not get support for his plan to go westward over the mountains—which might have brought him to Peru before the arrival of Pizarro.

Spanish attention was focused on the riches of New Spain. Cortes dreamed of extending his conquests to the South Pacific. Ships built in Mexico made the first crossing to the Philippines and the spice islands in 1527 under the command of Alvaro de Saavedra. But a series of calamities—storms, sickness, contrary winds and Saavedra's death—prevented the expedition's return to Mexico, and the passage was not attempted again for thirty-eight years.[6] Cortes and his lieutenants found that they had their hands full in Mexico. Although it had been comparatively easy to crush the Aztec state, it was more difficult to break the will of the people.

When Pedro de Alvarado marched into Guatemala in 1524, he secured order and cooperation by the usual methods. An Indian account tells of Alvarado's constant demand for gold: "He wished that they should give him jars full of precious metals." He told the chiefs: "If you do not bring me the precious metal in all your towns, choose then, for I shall burn you alive and hang you."[7] Alvarado's report to Cortes tells the same story: "seeing that by fire and sword I might bring these people to the service of His Majesty, I determined to burn the chiefs. . . ."

Warfare excused the enslavement of the inhabitants that were left alive. Alvarado was careful to note that the emperor's share was properly safeguarded:

> All the prisoners of war were branded and made slaves, of whom I gave His Majesty's fifth part to the treasurer, Baltasar de Mendoza, which he sold at public auction, so that the payment to His Majesty should be secure.[8]

The fire and sword technique of colonization was costly to the conquerors as well as to the conquered. The Europeans lived in fear of their lives, and the fear could only be appeased by the total extermination or enslavement of the local population. This was a large undertaking, but Alvarado approached it with exemplary vigor. The social consequences were ignored, as long as the loot was big enough to justify the means used in obtaining it: this was true in Mexico and to some extent in Guatemala. But in the West Indies, the first fever of the treasure hunt was followed by a creeping paralysis of the economy.

The orders issued at the suggestion of Las Casas in 1520 for the reform of the *encomienda* system were not obeyed. Although the enslavement of the Indians continued, the population had been so drastically reduced that native labor could not supply the needs of the plantations. The islands depended increasingly on the importation of Negro slaves. The beginnings of the slave trade in its social and cultural aspects will be discussed in a subsequent chapter. It is sufficient for our present purpose to note that the decade of the 1520's was a period of painful transition and disorganization in the Caribbean settlements.

German bankers attempted to bring a more "practical" approach to colonization in 1528, when the Welser firm of Augsberg received Venezuela as a hereditary fief. The bankers agreed to build two cities and three forts, and to transport 350 Spanish colonists. The Welsers hoped to find *El Dorado* in Venezuela, but they protected their investment by securing the right to sell the Indians as slaves. Ambrose Alfinger was sent out to administer the territory. He was killed in an Indian rising in 1531, and the country was in continuous turmoil during the next decade.

Agents of German bankers began to appear in America in increasing numbers, buying and selling everything they could get their hands on, presenting glowing prospectuses based on real and imaginary values.

The emperor's dealings with the Welsers and the Fuggers did not help him solve the problem of securing the political stability of his overseas possessions. Discouraging reports from the West Indies were responsible for the new plan adopted in 1529: feudal lordship over an area of approximately sixty square miles was offered to anyone who would bring over 25 freemen and an equal number of Negro slaves. The proprietor was to be raised to the nobility and given a coat of arms.[9] A similar form of tenure was adopted by Portugal in the settlement of Brazil. Martin Alfonso de Souza, who founded a colony at Sao Paulo in 1532, was ordered to divide the land into *capitaneas,* each having 150 miles of shore line, held in fief to the crown. The proprietor paid a tribute to the king, but his power within his domain was almost limitless, including the sole right to coin money and impose the death penalty.[10]

Questions of land tenure and labor were temporarily overshadowed in 1532 by the news of the conquest of Peru. Francisco Pizarro, assisted by his three brothers, reached the goal for which he had been striving for nearly two decades. His betrayal of Balboa was finally rewarded with interest—not thirty pieces of silver, but a kingdom that was unmistakably *El Dorado*. When Pizarro entered the city of Cajamarca and seized the Inca, Atalhualpa, he offered to release his captive for a ransom equivalent to $15,000,000. The offer was accepted. As the gold and silver and precious stones were carried into the city by the Inca's people, Pizarro realized that he had no further use for Atalhualpa, and put him to death.

The act of blood inaugurated a frenzied fight for gold and power among the European conquerors. The execution of Balboa and the murder of the Inca were preliminary steps in the furious competition that revealed the deepest logic of the treasure hunt.

However, the success of the treasure hunt forced its European sponsors to deal with its antisocial consequences. Disorders which had caused concern in Spain in the second decade of the century were intolerable in the fourth decade, when the wealth of Mexico and Peru was at stake. The Vatican and the empire were determined to put a stop to the confusion which threatened to reduce the income from America. Many thoughtful men were convinced that the main source of corruption in the colonies was the mistreatment of the Indians. Father Francisco de Victoria, who returned to Spain in 1524 after eighteen years in the more liberal intellectual climate of Paris, argued learnedly and boldly for the rights of the Indians.

But Las Casas had the advantage of practical experience in the colonies. He was called from his monastery early in the 1530's to consult with the authorities in Spain. The mystery that surrounds this visit may be explained by the nature of the services that Las Casas was asked to perform. He spent the next seven years traveling in Mexico, Central America and Peru. In view of the detailed reports of his observations that were published later, it seems reasonable to suppose that there was a connection between his journeys and official changes in colonial policy.

Las Casas was in Guatemala in 1532. He then went to Peru to witness the beginnings of the Pizarro regime, and returned to Guatemala in 1534. His later account of his findings, submitted to the Emperor in 1540 and published as the *Brevisima Relacion de la Destruccion de las Indias* twelve years later, contains a bitter denunciation of Pedro de Alvarado's conduct as ruler of Guatemala. Alvarado was in Peru in 1533, and was engaged in some questionable transactions with Pizarro's lieutenants. We can only surmise that Las Casas sent information to Spain which resulted in the order issued in 1535 to deprive Alvarado of his office and send him home under guard.

Pope Paul III entered the colonial controversy in 1537 with a forthright condemnation of Indian slavery. The papal bull proclaimed that the Indians "are truly men," and that they "are by no means to be deprived of their liberty or the possession of their property . . . nor should they be in any way enslaved."[11] Again, we can assume that reports supplied by Las Casas influenced the Vatican's action. The church, fighting to stem the tide of the Reformation, was stung by criticisms of its participation in the profits of slavery. Questions of moral prestige were related to the actualities of colonial power. The church was seeking to strengthen its position in the Spanish dependencies. Its most indispensable function was its ability to establish order and Christian discipline among the Indians.

The pope's bull was issued at a time when the situation in Peru had gotten completely out of hand. Diego de Almagro, who had been in conflict with Pizarro for several years, returned from a disappointing expedition to Chile in 1536 to launch a civil war against the governor. Almagro seized Cuzco in 1537, but he was defeated and executed in 1538. Hernando Pizarro left for Spain to explain what had happened; he was thrown into a dungeon, where he remained for twenty years. Meanwhile, the strife in Peru continued. In 1541, the twenty-two year old son of Almagro captured Lima by a *coup d'etat,* killing the governor. Another of the Pizarro brothers, Gonzalo, was absent on an expedition in search of *El Dorado* on the other side of the Andes. Gonzalo returned to plunge into warfare with the Almagristas. A royal commissioner, Vaca de Castro, arrived in 1542, organized an army and defeated the rebels in the battle of Chupas. Young Almagro was executed.

These events, and the progress of exploration and settlement in other parts of the hemisphere, increased the necessity of formulating a new colonial policy. Las Casas returned to Europe in 1539. He made a full report to Charles V, and consulted with the Council of the Indies. As a result, laws were promulgated in 1542 that abolished the *encomienda,* prohibited forced labor of the Indians, provided that the natives pay a fixed sum as tribute and that all grants of land revert to the crown on the death of the proprietor.

Again Las Casas had won a victory which was really a defeat for his social aims. The legislation was designed to protect the authority of the emperor, and to prevent his subjects from amassing large profits and estates which enabled them to defy the royal will. The Indians were to receive nominal freedom, as an excuse for the transfer of land and labor from private owners to the crown. The laws were obviously aimed at the trouble-makers in Peru. The impermanence of their possessions was intended to guarantee their loyalty.

The plan was unworkable. Instead of bringing peace, it led to a renewal of the Peruvian civil war. When the news reached the colonists that their land grants were temporary and their Indian slaves were to be freed, they rallied around Gonzalo Pizarro in open rebellion. The new viceroy, Nunez de Vela, reached Lima in 1544, and made a public proclamation concerning the enforcement of the laws. The leading citizens, wrote Pedro Ciezo de Leon, "lost all feeling, and from that time looked upon themselves as bereft of Indians, and of all property." [12]

A series of intrigues, arrests and murders followed. The viceroy was seized and put on a ship to be taken back to Spain. Gonzalo Pizarro entered Lima at the head of an army and proclaimed himself governor and captain general. The viceroy escaped from the ship, and organized a large military force in Ecuador. For a year the two armies marched and countermarched. Then they fought near Quito. Pizarro was victorious and the viceroy was killed.

Pizarro's supporters urged him to become king of Peru, to divide vacant lands among his followers as perpetual tenures, with titles of Dukes, Marquises and Counts; he was also advised to secure the devotion of the natives by taking an Inca princess as queen. [13] The proposal was made more attractive by the discovery of the enormously rich silver mines on the Bolivian plateau. The mines were found in 1545 on the Cerro de Potosi, the mountain that rises massively above the plains to a height of 17,006 feet above sea level.

Peru with all its treasure had no value if it were cut off from contact with Europe. And the only communication was by way of Panama and the Spanish galleons. When Pedro de Gasca came out to deal with the rebellion, he had the advantage of carrying the repeal of the objectionable laws. He gained an even more decisive advantage when he secured the submission of Peru's fleet. Pizarro's kingdom was cut off and his doom sealed. He was defeated and put to death in 1548, but the internecine strife continued for six more years.

The disorder did not prevent the feverish exploitation of the Potosi mines, where the royal fifth soon reached the sum of a million and a half pesos yearly. [14] There was also a boom in silver production in Mexico, where the rush to the Zacatecas mines began in 1548. [15]

Thus a spectacular expansion of colonial income took place without any parallel stabilization of the administrative apparatus. The only power that seemed capable of bringing order out of the American chaos was the church.

This was the setting for the mid-century debate in which Las Casas presented his case in its boldest outline. He had accepted the bishopric of Chiapa in Mexico in 1544, but the abandonment of the New Laws and the impossibility of securing any serious reforms caused him to resign in 1547. On his return to Spain, he found that there had been a change in the ideological climate. He was rebuked by the Council of the Indies for his extreme views on Indian freedom. The attack was formalized in two works written by the eminent historian Gines de Sepulveda. As the royal historiographer to Charles V, Sepulveda's views carried weight. He had a European reputation as a Latin stylist, and Erasmus once described him as the Spanish Livy. The Vatican may have had a hand in the formulation of Sepulveda's position. He was in Rome when he wrote the first polemic, entitled *Democrates;* he returned to Spain in 1550, and there elaborated his argument in *Democrates II.* Sepulveda held that it was necessary and just to wage war on the Indians in order to compel them to do the bidding of their European masters.

Sepulveda's learning reflected influential opinion in Italy and Spain. Behind the writer and his political advisers loomed the Cerro de Potosi, with its fabulous mines and its ant-heap of forced laborers. The silver of Potosi outweighed the evils of colonial administration; it paid for all the losses incurred in the years of civil warfare in Peru.

The rich mountain towering above the windswept plateau cast a shadow that reached Europe. Bolivia was to be the historical embodiment of the controversy concerning colonial labor held in Spain in 1550. The third largest country in South America was like a map of the social contradictions that would remain unsolved in the twentieth century. Walled off from the Pacific by the western cordillera of the Andes, Bolivia combines mineral wealth with the unfertile land that supports three-quarters of its population. Tin has replaced silver as Bolivia's most coveted treasure, and its oil reserves have begun to attract foreign attention. But the people, Indian and mestizo, grub out a miserable agricultural subsistence from the bleak uplands.[16]

The extraordinary significance of the debate between Las Casas and Sepulveda may be judged in part by its political effect. Las Casas' indictment of Spanish policy came on the eve of the crisis that was to force the resignation of Charles V, the panic of 1559, and the rapid growth of the Reformation. His denunciation was to serve as one of the major instruments of Protestant propaganda in the global struggle against Spain and Catholicism. It was ironic that the Protestants, imitating the methods that Las Casas exposed, should point to his exposé as proof of their superior morality. Yet it was a minor irony, an aspect of the historical contradiction that Las Casas proclaimed. His criticism foreshadowed the coming centuries of imperial polity.

Las Casas no longer advocated Negro slavery. But he still dealt with the problem in terms of the moral responsibility of the dominant group. The debate revolved around the ethics of warfare; this was the ground chosen by his opponent, and Las Casas accepted it, because it was the only ground on which he was able to stand. The general indictment of war and destruction shrouded the riddle of exploitation and profit.

Sepulveda advanced four reasons for using military power against the Indians. The four points were fundamentally the same: first, the gravity of their sins, particularly the practice of idolatry; second, the rudeness of their heathen and barbarous natures; third, the necessity of spreading the faith; fourth, the harm done by the Indians in making human sacrifices and even practicing cannibalism.[17]

Sepulveda, like later apologists for the necessities of imperialism, simply assumed that the Christian morality was so superior that its imposition by force was self-evidently justified. Las Casas replied with the catalogue of European crimes. The evils were so heinous and the facts so indisputable that there could be no answer to his charges. By the same token, there could be no settlement of the debate. The church and the empire could neither abandon world conquest nor endorse the methods necessary for its accomplishment.

The political considerations that dictated the holding of the dispute assured its uncertain outcome. Las Casas' position was not accepted, but he was not muzzled. Two years later, he published the *Brevisima Relacion*. The book was translated into many languages and circulated throughout Europe. Its effect was so devastating that his masterwork, the *Apologetica Historia de las Indias,* was suppressed for more than three centuries. The complete book, in its 900 folio pages, did not see the light until 1909.

The *Brevisima Relacion* gives an account of the destruction in each of the colonies. There had been more than half a million Indians in

Cuba, and their extermination was virtually complete. In Guatemala, the regime had "killed more than four of five million people in fifteen or sixteen years, from the years 1524 to 1540, and they continue to kill and destroy those who are still left." In all the American possessions, "more than twelve million persons, men, and women and children, have perished unjustly and through tyranny." He touched the economic factor in a phrase: "The reason why the Christians have killed and destroyed such infinite numbers of souls, is solely because they have made gold their ultimate aim, seeking to load themselves with riches in the shortest possible time." [18]

In the debate with Sepulveda, Las Casas spoke with Biblical fury of the guilt of the Spaniards: the "Tyranny wrought by their devastations, massacres and slaughters is so monstrous, that the blind may see it, the deaf hear it, and the dumb recount it . . . God will punish Spain and all her people with inevitable severity." [19]

The anathema pronounced at the dawn of the epoch of colonial expansion reechoes as imperialism approaches the last term of its destruction.

4 : THE PLUMED SERPENT

Among the most significant traits of the dispute between Las Casas and Sepulveda was its purely European approach. It staked off the intellectual boundaries which were to be accepted as the permanent limits of controversy by scholars in Europe and the Americas. Las Casas spoke of the destruction of the Indians; but in spite of the physical extermination of a large part of the population, the people were not erased, wiped from the slate of history. In masking the role of labor, Las Casas necessarily ignored its cultural creativity. He saw the Indian and Negro workers as unhappy robots or unsuccessful rebels; he failed to see them as carriers and builders of culture.

While few historians have spoken with the passion that animated Las Casas, many have verified his denunciation of the methods of conquest. But the indictment has seldom gone beyond the negative recognition of the failure of Christian morality, the breakdown of prescribed values.

The main continuum of historical thought has followed the lines indicated by Sepulveda. The Protestant dialectic, seeing the course of civilization as a beautifully balanced compromise between what is good and what is necessary, translated Sepulveda's raw theology into a pious "philosophy of progress." But modern historiography exhibits a tendency to abandon rationalistic formulations and return to the unabashed defense of conquest as a Christian prerogative. Salvador Madariaga dismisses the whole body of historical evidence with the assertion that "Spanish colonization was singularly free from self-seeking. . . . Much bitter ink has been spent in denouncing Spanish conduct toward the Indians. In actual fact, both in theory and practice, Spain was in advance of the times."[1]

Similar statements appear frequently in the writings of scholars in the United States. Charles Edward Chapman speaks of "the legend of Spanish cruelty toward the Indians." He admits that "there was a great deal of cruelty. . . . On the whole, however, the treatment of the Indians was humane, or at least, not excessively harsh, if only because their lives were valuable to those who were virtually their masters."[2] A more extreme view is adopted by Lewis Hanke. Writing in 1935, Hanke makes the following comment on the *Apologetica Historia de las Indias:* "The history of human aberrations shows few more interesting exhibits than this little known work wherein Las Casas advanced the idea that the American Indians compared very favorably with the peoples of ancient times, were eminently rational beings, and in fact fulfilled every one of Aristotle's requisites for the good life."[3]

Hanke's comment illustrates the gap between historiography and the social sciences among which it is presumed to have a place. Anthropology, having made enlightening comparisons between Indian civilization and ancient cultures at similar levels of development, leaves no room for archaic prejudices that exclude the people of the Americas from the family of "rational beings." The bourgeois historian's neglect of related disciplines is not willful or haphazard; it stems from modes of thought that are almost mandatory in his field. Theories that go back to Plato and St. Augustine in order to justify the rule of "creative minorities" find their ultimate *raison d'etre* in the defense of imperialism.

We are indebted to Toynbee for a comprehensive modern presentation of the philosophy of the defense of imperialism. The philosophy is inherent in the Spenglerian view, elaborated by Toynbee, that history is a series of *waves of power;* separate civilizations rise through their internal unity and strength and disintegrate through inner weakness or external pressures. The expanding influence of each ascendant civilization is accomplished through what Toynbee calls mimesis, which simply means mimicry or imitation; it is, he admits, "one of the less exulted faculties of human nature, which has more in it of drill than of inspiration."[4] However, Toynbee distinguishes drill from the arbitrary use of force; the distinction is mysteriously embodied in the word *mimesis;* the drill is a willing mimicry, a cultural acceptance of the more advanced society's values:

> Wherever a growing civilization is in contact with primitive societies, its creative minority attracts their mimesis as well as the mimesis of the uncreative majority in its midst. But, if this is the normal relation between a civilization and the primitive societies round about so long as the civilization is in growth, a profound change sets in if and when the civilization breaks down and goes into disintegration. The creative minorities which have won a voluntary allegiance by the charm which their creativity exerts are replaced by a dominant minority which, lacking charm, relies on force. The surrounding primitive peoples are no longer charmed but are repelled; these humble disciples of the growing civilization then renounce their discipleship and become what we have called an external proletariat.[5]

The passage is so like Rabelais in its agglomeration of topsy-turvy words and impossible meanings that one hopes, for a mad moment, that the author is indulging in a witty parody of historical obscurantism. But anyone familiar with Toynbee's writings knows that he can be described in the words that Ortega y Gasset applies to Guizot: "Like Buster Keaton," he is "the man who never laughs."[6]

Human history in all its variety is singularly lacking in any quality that can properly be called "charm" in the dealings between dominant societies and less privileged or more primitive groups. One can search in vain for a single instance of "voluntary allegiance" on the part of subject peoples to "creative minorities." The evolution and interaction of cultures has proceeded through migrations, wars, conquests, commercial intercourse, social clash and fusion. All peoples have contributed to the process. To reduce the human processional to a drawing room drama, in which exceptional individuals hold the spotlight while the mass in outer darkness mimics and imitates, is a denial of humanity, an insult to the spirit of man.

The uniqueness of American experience, as distinguished from previous migrations or conquests, lies in the sheer size of the great currents of culture, Indian, European and African, that met and intermingled in the Western Hemisphere. To those who think of culture as the property of an elite, the large number of people involved in the process is of minor interest. The servitude of the majority is treated as *prima facie* evidence that they were *mimetically* controlled and made no contribution to the ideas and customs of the dominant group. The culture of the people engaged in productive activity, their mode of subsistence, their precarious living and obscure dying, is the leaven of change and growth in the historical process.

The gifts contributed by the Indians to the world's agriculture are too well-known to require more than cursory mention. The gold and silver of the New World had less effect on history than the products of American fields and forests. Corn, the most highly domesticated of all grains, leads the list of Indian products. The whole list constitutes about half of mankind's agricultural wealth: the potato and sweet potato, pineapple, avocado, artichoke, peanut, cultivated strawberry, lima and frijole and kidney and tonka beans, squash and pumpkin, chocolate, rubber, quinine, cocaine, tobacco, maple sugar, pecan, brazil nut, sarsaparilla.[7]

Civilization's debt to Africa appears less spectacular, because it accrued over centuries of contact with Asia and Europe by way of Arabia, Egypt and the Mediterranean. The Indian gifts came to the world more or less suddenly, as an extravagant present, a huge package bulging with foods, medicines and narcotics.

Although many American products were known, utilized and transferred to Europe, before the end of the sixteenth century, the temper of the treasure hunt during the first half of the century was not conducive to the constructive adaptation of Indian skills and resources. One cannot say that the lust for gold blinded the conquerors to other values; Spanish colonial records are full of references to the various commodities produced in the New World and the potentialities of diversified agriculture and industry. Blueprints of economic organization were drawn up in Spain, but these proposals were as impossible to realize as the reforms advocated by Las Casas. The economic and social difficulties were identical: the productive relationships established by the colonists were socially destructive, and could not be maintained without systematic and wasteful cruelty. The brutality was systematic, in the sense that it was planned and necessary from the viewpoint of the conquerors, as the only way to obtain the forced labor of the Indians. It was wasteful in that it destroyed the productive capacities of millions of people.

The Spaniards first encountered the isolated and primitive tribes of the Antilles. Then they drove toward the centers of Indian civilization in Mexico and Peru. By the middle of the sixteenth century, they had come in contact with many of the North and South American groupings; they had met the nut-gathering Indians of California and the buffalo-hunting tribes of the plains, the Creek Federation in Florida and the Auracanian Federation in Chile.

The distribution of Indian population is an essential part of the cultural picture. The centers of wealth and civilization were the heavily populated areas. There are various estimates of the number of people in the hemisphere at the time of the conquest. There may have been as many as 10,000,000 in Mexico, another 10,000,000 in Central America, and a somewhat larger number in Peru. There were probably about 3,000,000 Chibchahs in Colombia and Panama.[8] One may assume that the population south of the Rio Grande was between 25,000,000 and 40,000,000. But north of the Rio Grande, in the territory that is now the United States, it is estimated that the total population was 846,000.[9]

The figures pose a social riddle: the thickly populated areas were conquered fairly quickly, while the Indians in the thinly settled regions conducted a successful fight against European conquest for centuries. The riddle relates to the hemispheric pattern of assimilation and conflict. The pattern is similar in the northern and southern continents: the large populations were slaughtered or reduced to peonage, while the primitive tribes erected barriers to further expansion.

The Indian societies of North America—with which the present study is primarily concerned—represent a bewildering profusion of cultures which are nonetheless interrelated, forming the scattered elements of a great movement of civilization. The productive base of the movement is the cultivation of maize, and its most potent symbol is the plumed serpent, known to the Aztecs as Quetzalcoatl. Like all mythological figures, the bird-snake has an historical and economic origin. The real Quetzalcoatl was a Toltec King, priest and astronomer, whose greatest achievement was the reorganization of the Mayan calendar for the use of the Toltecs. He died on April 5, 1208.[10] As the story developed into legend, Quetzalcoatl was said to have been the God of the Air, who descended from heaven to teach wisdom and art. But he incurred the wrath of a greater god, who brought war and misery, and forced the hero to flee; in due time he would return to liberate the people.

The actual history that is recounted in mythical terms is the Toltec conquest of the more mature Mayan civilization, and the later defeat of the Toltecs by the invading Chichimec, Acolhua and Aztec tribes. In taking over the calendar, the Toltecs adopted the knowledge and customs of the Maya. But they were overwhelmed, the treasure of wisdom that they had captured was in turn torn from them.

The feathered serpent was one of the greatest of the Mayan divinities, honored long before the Toltec conquest. Although the detailed meaning of the myth cannot be deciphered from its pictorial representation in the decorations of Mayan temples, the attributes of the deity indicate his connection with the early organization of production and the social changes that accompanied it. He was associated with science, technology, the mastery of nature. As in all the myths of this type, the advancement of culture is identified with violence and conflict—the beginnings of priestly domination and the loss of the old communal spirit. The god with the body of a serpent, the plumes of a bird, and the teeth of a jaguar, had a human head placed in his distended jaws.

In the later interpretations embroidered upon the old myth, the ancient dualism is transferred to the historical conflicts that took place in the Valley of Mexico. In Aztec mythology, Quetzalcoatl's defeat and exile symbolized the degradation of the old culture by the Aztecs themselves. For a century before the arrival of the Spaniards, Aztec society developed an increasingly oppressive caste system; military prowess was encouraged by the awarding of lands and slaves to warriors; private ownership encroached on the communal lands of the clans. The legend of Quetzalcoatl's return embodied the hope that the social conflict would be solved and productive energies released for the general welfare.

The figure of the plumed snake appears in the art and mythology of all the Indian tribes that made the cultivation of corn the basis of their culture: Paul Radin writes that "the trail of the feathered-serpent with outstretched wings is found everywhere and, in a manner, it represents the symbol of the Mayan conquest of the rest of the continent." Northward beyond the Rio Grande, eastward across the Gulf of Mexico to the Mississippi, rites and techniques derived from the Mayas were conserved. "Where the cultivation of maize stopped, civilization stopped." [11]

The myths associated with agricultural production reflect the beginnings of class organization, which are found as far east as the southern Atlantic coast as well as in the lower Mississippi Valley.[12] The presence of the plumed serpent was proof of these beginnings. But the myths built around the culture god were of a much more primitive character. The uncertainties of agriculture were symbolized in an indecisive struggle, in which the god was alternately victorious and defeated. Where agriculture was difficult and the people longed to return to a simpler nomadic existence, the god was portrayed as a thing of evil.[13]

The distribution of the myth is evidence of the great migrations and movements that constitute the clouded history of the pre-Columbian period. The main culture area lay in the heart of the Americas, in the region extending from the Valley of Mexico in the North to Peru and Bolivia in the south. There were two ancient centers of civilization: the Andean culture proliferated from Tiahuanaco, the mighty city on the shores of Lake Titicaca in Bolivia, known to the Incas as the City of the Dead. The nucleus of the Mayan movement, at least in its last splendor, was the temple of Palenque in the jungles of southern Mexico. These societies flowered and extended their influence from the second to the seventh century A.D. There was unquestionably contact between the Pan-Peruvian and the Central American communities. In recent years, as Paul Radin observes, "it has been abundantly proved that the interchange of cultural goods was fairly extensive."[14]

The dissemination of domestic plants affords an insight into the interwoven movement of the culture of the mind and the culture of the earth, the development of social forms and the productive activity on which life and thought are based. Reconstruction of the geographical dispersal of plants is necessarily hypothetical. But it seems probable that "two waves of corn reached the Southwest around the time of Christ." One wave came up the western coast of Mexico. "The other wave came up the east side of Mexico and entered the Southwest only after crossing the plains."[15] Some scientists have argued that Central American corn reached the eastern United States by way of the West Indies and Florida, but A. L. Kroeber believes that there was either a land connection by way of the Gulf of Mexico or a direct sea route.[16] George F. Carter offers evidence that cultural intercourse between Mexico and the eastern United States existed "over a long period of time," and that crops carried to the east were brought back across the plains to enrich the agriculture of the Pueblo and neighboring Indians.[17]

There are detailed studies of the historical distribution of other plants. The use of the lima bean can be traced from its origin in Guatemala to Peru, while it seems to have moved north along three separate lines of dispersal: to Mexico and along the western slope of the Sierras to the Hopi Indians; to the Caribbean Islands; and to the eastern United States.[18]

The domestication of crops in the New World suggests the antiquity of American civilization. The multiplicity of species and the complicated process of adaptation under various climatic conditions indicate that at least 5,000 or 10,000 years were required to bring agriculture to the level it had reached at the time of Christ.

A sense of the background, the travail and achievement of life in the Western Hemisphere, enriches our understanding of the meeting of the Old World and New World peoples. In terms of what we may call recent American history (from 1492 to the present), the age of the Indian culture is less important than its hemispheric interdependence and diffusion. The treatment of European expansion as the conquest of scattered units, most of them barbarous and without cultural contacts and interests, may be justified as a superficial account of *the way it happened,* the appearance of the events to the persons who took part in them. But it gives a false picture of the historical movement, the strength of the opposing forces, the effect of the struggle upon colonial development. From the moment of discovery, the Spaniards approached the task of conquest as a hemispheric undertaking; every fragmentary gain was a step toward empire over the two continents. The Indian counterattack was sufficiently strong to frustrate the plan of empire.

Cortes' successful invasion of Mexico at the head of a small body of troops was not so much due to the resolution of the invaders as to the social situation in the realm of the Aztecs. Having conquered the valley of Mexico about 200 years before Cortes landed at Vera Cruz, the Aztecs had inherited a culture which they were unable to consolidate and enlarge. The exile of Quetzalcoatl expressed the abridgment crisis which could be met only by continuous warfare. The concentration of wealth and power in the hands of the small priestly and warrior castes demanded a surplus of income which the system of agricultural production was incapable of supplying. Intensive exploitation and the reduction of the majority of the people to a semi-slave status increased internal tensions and deepened the necessity of territorial expansion.

The Aztecs inherited the network of commerce developed by their predecessors. Trade by barter extended through Yucatan and Central America; merchants had a special status as "Men who exchange one thing for another," or "Men who take more than they give."[19] The growth of a written language may be attributed to the beginnings of mercantile organization. But money had not as yet come into use. The main accumulation of wealth was for prestige and display, reflecting the control of the state by a privileged class which was too jealous of its power to permit the employment of art or craftsmanship for any purpose other than its own exclusive use. Therefore, while trade continued, the Aztec rulers made it a subsidiary factor in war expeditions, designed to secure booty or slaves.

Military victories could not stabilize the system. Captured enemies created a surplus of laborers for whom there was neither employment nor food. Priestly logic, representing the culture of the dominant class, solved the problem of too many people by proclaiming the sacred value of human sacrifice. By the end of the fifteenth century, the pressure of population and the reduction of natural resources brought ceremonial killings on a mass scale. When a raid into the Oaxaca region resulted in the capture of 20,000 people, the chiefs tore out the hearts of the first ones, and the remaining thousands were turned over to the priests for immolation.[20] Frazer notes the connection between the blood sacrifice and the need of a larger food supply. The maize wanted victims to strengthen its growth, so human beings were killed "at all the various stages in the growth of the maize, the age of the victim corresponding to the age of the corn." [21]

The Aztec priests were early and devout believers in the Malthusian theory that the cultivation of crops cannot keep pace with the troublesome increase in human beings. They redressed the balance by means which may shock the twentieth century followers of Malthus, but their practice accorded with the principle proclaimed by the modern philosophers of scarcity, that war, disease and malnutrition are unavoidable ways of counteracting the fecundity of the earth's millions.

The social decline, of which human sacrifice was a primary cultural manifestation, prepared the way for the European attack. The destruction of lives that was to be conducted ruthlessly by the conquerors, had been begun by the Aztec rulers themselves. It has been said that the Spaniards reached the coast of Mexico at about the time of the predicted return of Quetzalcoatl, and that Montezuma's indecision was due to his belief that the white men were the emissaries of the culture god. It seems probable that Montezuma and his advisers were less concerned about mythology than about saving their own necks. They behaved like any governing caste which maintains its power by force and fear. Faced with the choice between a deal with the enemy and a desperate appeal to the population to rally to the country's defense, the calculated risks of the former course were as attractive to Montezuma as to the government of France at the time of the Nazi invasion in 1939.

The Quetzalcoatl myth was close to the people, a folk memory respected by the reigning priesthood as a concession to popular sentiment. He was a subordinate god, representative of the old civilization. From his temple in Cholula, he protested in vain against the blood sacrifice, asking only offerings from the goodness of the earth, fruits and flowers.[22]

The cult of Quetzalcoatl made the city of Cholula a center of mercantile activity and craft production. Its inhabitants excelled in the manufacture of cotton, metal work and pottery. In an inverted and tragic sense, the arrival of the Europeans was the fulfillment of the myth, the end of a cycle of social evolution. The home of the culture god was the scene of the first revelation of the import of the invasion to the people of the valley of Mexico. Stopping at Cholula on his march to the capital, Cortes accused the municipal leaders of plotting against him, murdered them in cold blood and sacked the city. A new culture had come. But it had come to destroy. The plumed serpent bared his jaguar claws, and in his mouth was a human head.

We have become so accustomed to viewing the conquest solely from the European viewpoint that it is difficult to visualize it as the social catastrophe that overwhelmed the inhabitants of Mexico. The classic account by William H. Prescott is a melodrama of intrigues and hair breadth escapes woven around the figure of Cortes. Underlying the literary vigor of the narrative is an historical principle that is not unrelated to Toynbee's theory of *mimesis*. Cortes' method of subjugating the Indians may have "more in it of drill than of inspiration," but Prescott casts him in an heroic mold, the representative of a higher civilization dealing with treacherous savages: "His manners, frank and soldierlike, concealed a most cool and calculating spirit." His humor and resolution "infused something like awe into the attachment of his most devoted followers," whose "love was tempered by authority."[23] Cortes wanted to "reclaim the natives from their gross idolatry and to substitute a purer form of worship."[24]

The element of mimesis, conversion through charm, is personalized in the love story of Cortes and Marina. The role played by Marina is so appropriate, so necessary to the accepted view of the conquest, that it seems to blend myth and actuality in perfect unity. If there had been no Marina, the Aztec girl of noble birth sold into slavery as a child,[25] it would have been necessary to invent her. But Marina was very real, and performed very real services for Cortes. She acted as a spy, securing information about the Aztec plans that was invaluable to the Spaniards.

A report by Marina was responsible for the massacre at Cholula. The incident illustrates her historical and cultural function. Cortes followed the immemorial custom of conquerors in selecting one of his most attractive captives as his mistress. The story, unexceptional in itself, is utilized to mask the social conflict. Marina is the heroine at Cholula. Prescott tells how she visited the wife of one of the chiefs, "gradually insinuating herself into her confidence," learning that an attack on the invaders was planned. In reporting to Cortes, she proved that she was "the good angel of the expedition."[26] The emotional relationship is in the foreground. In the background are the Indian emissaries hacked to pieces in the temple courtyard, the burned buildings, the people murdered and enslaved.

The historical interest of the conquest of Mexico lies in the clash of forces and values. The treatment of Marina's betrayal of her own people as a categorical imperative blurs the conflict, assumes the exclusive rightness of European values, and idealizes Indian subservience. Prescott's portrayal of Marina is derived from early Spanish sources. He tells the romantic tale of her noble birth as related by Bernal Diaz, and quotes Camargo's description of her as "beautiful as a Goddess."[27]

The story has become a part of the Hispanic-Indian folklore of Mexico. Known familiarly as *Malinche,* Marina has been adopted in literature, and to some extent in popular thought, as the symbol of the fusion of the two cultures. Yet the legend has not altogether lost its bitter meaning; the affectionate and ironic memory of *Malinche* is an acceptance of the European version of the conquest; it is an aspect of the dominant Spanish influence in the life, language and thought of the people. The hemispheric significance of the story is indicated in the appearance of similar myths in all parts of the Americas. Marina is the progenitor of many real and imaginary Indian heroines, of whom the most famous is Pocahontas.

Underlying the romantic unity of the myth as a love story is the social conflict that becomes apparent as soon as we place the legend in its historical setting. The service rendered by Marina at Cholula was continued by her son, Don Martin Cortes, *commendador* of the Military Order of St. James. Don Martin repeated, under different historical conditions, the role played by Montezuma in the conquest. A generation later, when Indian rebellions forced the colonial administration to restrict the misuse of native labor, the landholders began a revolution of their own, choosing Cortes' son as their leader and promising him the crown of an independent kingdom if the movement was successful. The rising, like a similar landholders' revolt in Peru, was a failure, because there was no economic base for colonial independence.

The social struggles that were to shape the structure of Hispanic-Indian society began shortly after Montezuma's surrender to Cortes. The popular resistance that Montezuma had been unable or unwilling to organize rose spontaneously; the Aztec chieftain played the collaborator's role to its classic conclusion; he was killed addressing a great concourse of his subjects, attempting to convince them to accept the rule of the Spaniards. The revolt temporarily drove the invaders from the capital, which was retaken a year later (in August, 1521) after a long siege.[28]

The difficulties encountered by the Spaniards in introducing the *encomienda* led to prolonged conflict. The misuse of labor was responsible for many deaths, but the drive for profits was related to the problem of establishing the authority of a small group in a hostile and heavily populated country. The apparently wanton cruelty that maimed and destroyed lives beyond the requirements of work in the mines and fields arose from the insecurity of the Europeans. It was intended to frighten the people into submission, but it had the opposite effect: it increased resistance and reduced the productivity of labor.

The necessities of the conflict were responsible for the decision to root out every vestige of the native culture. The first bishop of Mexico, Juan de Zumarraga, made a bonfire of the exquisite manuscripts of the Aztecs, and ordered that similar bookburnings be conducted through the length and breadth of the land.[29] The annihilation of these records was an irreparable loss, but it could not obliterate beliefs and folk-memories which were as indestructible as the people who nourished them. The cult of the plumed serpent was locked in struggle with the cult of the Virgin, and new customs and forms of thought were born of the encounter.

The attempt to force the Indians into the prescribed pattern of conformity and servitude was responsible for the political and economic instability of the colony. Brutal punishments, wasteful exploitation and costly rebellions soon created a labor shortage. The silk industry is an example of the problem. Cortes initiated silk production on his estates in the Cuernavaca Valley; it was so profitable that other colonists followed his example, and the industry rose to boom proportions in the 1540's. But its development was disrupted by a critical shortage of Indian workers.[30]

A solution to the labor problem was sought in the introduction of Negro slaves. When the influx of slaves began, the social pattern had been modified by the intermarriage of Europeans and Indians. The extent of intermarriage reflected the intermingling of the two cultures, which was in turn determined by the relationships of production. The system of exploitation impoverished the majority of the Europeans and reduced them to a level that was close to the Indians.

The social structure was finally stabilized as a complicated hierarchy of castes, which crystallized the double process of combination and differentiation that was taking place. The common misery of Indians, Negroes and Europeans brought them together. The leveling tendency was recognized, and to some extent encouraged, by the ruling class. But there were marked differences in the social status and economic exploitation of the less privileged groups. Therefore, these groups were divided, and law and custom sought to deepen their feelings of separateness, insecurity and prejudice. There were seven principal classes: Spaniards born in Spain were at the top of the social ladder, occupying all the important administrative posts. The creoles, native-born whites, were a subordinate aristocracy: landholders, merchants, officials of church and state. The distinction between these two groups was sharply observed. Spanish control of the apparatus of power was assured by the exclusion of the creoles from key positions: only twelve of the first 369 colonial bishops were creoles, and there were only four creoles among 160 viceroys.

The working class was divided into five groups: *mestizos,* mixed Indian and white; *mulattoes,* of Negro and white descent; *zambas,* mixed Indian and Negro; *Indians,* technically free but subjected to forced labor or tribute; and *Negro slaves.*[31]

The hierarchical organization was to some extent an adaptation of feudal social categories, and accorded with Catholic concepts of a stratified class society. But it also reflected the pattern of Indian and Negro resistance, the refusal to accept servitude, the blending of people and cultures.

The conquest of Peru was accomplished as easily as the victory over the Aztecs, but the downfall of the Inca civilization was due to somewhat different reasons. The terraced fields of the Incas, supported by careful masonry and irrigated by water flowing from mountain reservoirs, represented a remarkably efficient organization of agricultural production. The potato was as important as maize in their economy. They possessed a domesticated animal, the llama, and the care and breeding of the flocks received minute attention.

The land in Peru was cultivated under conditions which approximated forced labor. There was no private ownership; land was assigned in small temporary allotments, reapportioned each year, and every worker paid a tribute to the state. A third part of the revenues of the empire went to the priesthood, a third to the caste of nobles who were all related to the Inca and controlled the government, a third to the people. Conquered peoples played an important part in the Inca economy; they were transferred to regions far from their original homes, some of them being given land while others were assigned to labor for the profit of the church or the government.

There were certain similarities between the Inca and Aztec civilizations. Both had reached a similar level of technological development: the wheel had not yet been invented; the use of smelted iron for tools was not yet known. Trade was conducted solely on the basis of barter. But there were marked differences in the productive forces and relationships.

In Peru, the area under cultivation was sufficiently large to support the population. When the Spaniards arrived, it embraced a territory of 380,000 square miles.[32] The whole surplus was siphoned off by rigid control of production and the concentration of power in the hands of nobles and priests. The profits of the rulers were so satisfactory that there was no extensive development of trade. Without commerce, there was no stimulus to build a written language. On the other hand, the method of accounting necessary for management of the land and crops was perfected in the use of the *quipu,* a complicated arrangement of cords and knots.

Disintegrative influences were at work in the Andean society when Pizarro reached Peru. The civil war that was in progress at the time of the invasion facilitated the conquest; the struggle for power between the rival Incas broke through the formal perfection of the state apparatus and revealed its essential weakness. The structure of power had grown out of all proportion to the social benefits it gave. The folk culture had atrophied. The religion that had once been vital had become an authoritarian ritual deprived of contact with the people.

The social organization of the Incas had greater stability than that of the Aztecs. Its ruling class had greater competence and closer contact with the people. Therefore, the Peruvian leaders were not as pusillanimous as the Aztec rulers in dealing with the invaders. The struggle conducted by the heirs of the empire after Atahualpa's death is shrouded in myth. The legend and secrecy that conceal the activities of the last four Incas are sufficient indication that they had popular support. Their center of resistance in the isolated Urubamba Valley was well protected, and their operations were woven into folk fantasies. It is probable that the lost city of Machu Picchu, the ruins of which were discovered in 1911, was the last stronghold of the Incas, the hidden sanctuary that was called Vilcapampa.[33]

Having occupied the two centers of civilization in Mexico and Peru, the Spaniards tried to extend their northern and southern empires. The opposition encountered on the periphery of settlement was far more effective than the struggle in the heavily populated regions. The less advanced tribes, engaged in hunting or subsistence agriculture, with only the beginnings of class organization, had the advantage of mobility, experience in guerrilla warfare, the communal spirit of people inured to hardship and bound together by simple loyalties. In certain areas, the epic defense conducted by Indian societies barred European advance for centuries. This was notably the case in Chile, where the Auracanian Federation maintained a measure of independence until the end of the eighteenth century; and in the southwestern plains of the United States, where the horses acquired from the Spaniards enabled the Indians to resist Spanish expansion.[34]

We are here concerned with the initial stages of the hemispheric struggle, and its effect, especially in North America, on the Hapsburg-Catholic colonial plan. The church and the empire envisioned control of the whole Western Hemisphere. Their failure was to a large extent due to Indian and Negro resistance. The struggle against forced labor that began in Hispaniola and Cuba was carried with the expeditions that attempted to secure a foothold on the North American coast and created the conditions for their failure.

When Ponce de Leon went to Florida, he was looking for slaves as well as for the Fountain of Youth. He had already achieved a reputation for exceptional brutality in the "pacification" of Puerto Rico. The use of dogs for the killing of Indians was an accepted custom among the Spaniards. Ponce de Leon had a dog, Bezerillo, trained to tear Indians to pieces with remarkable skill and ferocity.[35] Having diminished the labor resources of Puerto Rico catastrophically in a few years, the ambitious conquistador set sail for Florida. The reconnoitering expedition in 1513 was followed by an attempt to establish a colony in 1521. Ponce de Leon promised his followers that they would receive generous *encomiendas* and an ample supply of slaves. But the Indians in Florida had learned about the Spaniards. The native bowmen met the invaders with arrows that could pierce a sheet of armor. The Spaniards retreated to their ships. Ponce de Leon himself was wounded, and died soon after his return to the West Indies.[36]

In the year of Ponce de Leon's death, Lucas Vasquez de Ayllon raided the shores of Chicora (Georgia and South Carolina) and kidnapped 150 natives.[37] One shipload was wrecked and drowned on the return voyage and the rest perished in the mines.[38] Thus Ayllon warned the Indians that their only safety lay in resistance. They were ready for him when he returned in 1526 to plant a colony in South Carolina, probably at the mouth of the Pedee River. The expedition reflected the changes in the use of labor that were taking place in the Caribbean islands. Knowing the difficulty of securing the forced labor of the Indians, the 500 colonists brought 100 Negro slaves. The enterprise is historically important as the first attempt to transfer the plantation economy from the West Indies to the Atlantic Coast. The success of the Spanish attempt might have had a very material effect on the later English movement of colonization.

Illness and internal dissension disrupted the settlement, but these disturbances were related to the hostility of the Indians and the breakdown of the organization of labor. In November, a group of slaves rebelled and fled to the Indians. The next month the remnant of the colony—only 150 persons were still alive—departed, leaving the Negro rebels as the first immigrants from other lands to remain permanently in the territory that was to become the United States.[39]

The abortive conquest of Florida undertaken by Panfilo de Narvaez in 1528 assumed a martial character which was intended to frighten the Indians into submission. Narvaez landed with 600 men and marched boldly into the wilderness. His hope of duplicating the triumph of Cortes in Mexico was fed by the Creek Indians, who pointed north saying "Apalachen . . . Apalachen. . . ." The Indians may or may not have intentionally tricked the adventurers, but Narvaez pursued *El Dorado* until he was completely lost in the forests and swamps. When the disillusioned army returned to the coast, the ships could not be found. The men managed to build five makeshift boats. Only 250 of the 600 members of the expedition were alive when they set sail in these vessels, in September, 1528, skirting the coast of the Gulf in the hope of reaching Vera Cruz. There were a few Negro slaves among them. At what was probably Mobile Bay, a Greek and a Negro deserted to the Indians.[40]

The voyagers passed the mouth of a great river, the Mississippi. Finally a storm separated and destroyed the boats. A small group was cast ashore on an island off the coast of Texas. One of the four survivors was Cabeza de Vaca, who wrote an account of the years of captivity among the Indians. Among his three companions was the slave, Estavanico. Like many of the human chattels imported to America, Estavanico was an Arab Moor from the Atlantic coast of Morocco. For six years, until September, 1534, the men lived and traded among the Indians. Then they escaped, and started on a heartbreaking Odyssey that lasted two more years; they traversed Texas and crossed the Rio Grande, where they found people living in permanent houses and eating beans and squash as well as maize.[41] Climbing the mountains of northern Mexico, they reached the Spanish settlements on the Pacific coast in 1538.

The journey of the lost men was a preview of the slow march of the pioneers across the United States. The four packed the experience of the coming centuries into their eight years—they saw the Mississippi where it met the gulf, they traded and lived with the Indians, they knew the greatness of the plains and the heat of the desert, the culture of the Pueblo civilization in the Rio Grande Valley and the towering Sierras.

Our impression of Estavanico's personality is fragmentary and unclear. De Vaca's account suggests that he contributed sound judgment and endurance to the transcontinental trek. But most of the infrequent references to him in the literature of history are tinged with prejudice. Morris Bishop, for example, describes him as a man who delighted in tawdry ornaments and wandered about with a harem of Indian women.[42] To any student of the Indian societies in the southwestern United States and northern Mexico, the statement is as fantastic as the sex stories in the forged Vespucci letters.

The legend of Estavanico's fondness for women serves to conceal the significance of his death, which occurred in an attempt to escape from slavery. Because of his knowledge of the unexplored region beyond the Rio Grande, he was employed in 1539 to guide a group of Franciscan missionaries on an exploring expedition. He went ahead of the party to find the best route. He never returned. Fray Marcos, leader of the friars, pursued the slave as far as he dared and then turned back. Morris Bishop vulgarizes the escape as a rake's progress that ended when Estavanico was killed outside a Zuni village near Gallup, New Mexico. There is no doubt that Estavanico was killed by Indian arrows. But it seems probable that the tribes in New Mexico had heard of the struggle that was being waged against the Spaniards in northern Mexico, and they mistook the slave for his oppressors.

Estavanico's death came at a time when Spain was intensifying its efforts to secure a continental empire in North America. In 1540 Francisco Coronado started north from Mexico with 250 mounted *hidalgos,* 80 foot soldiers, 300 Indians who were classified as "allies," 1,000 Indian and Negro slaves, 500 cattle, and 5,000 sheep. For two years, Coronado explored the states of Arizona, New Mexico, Colorado, Oklahoma, Kansas and possibly Nebraska.

At the same time, Hernando de Soto searched for *El Dorado* in Georgia, North and South Carolina, Alabama and Tennessee. De Soto's men moved through a wilderness of rivers, the network of streams leading to the Mississippi; they called them the River of Peace, River of Snow, River of Flowers, River of the Fishermen; finally they came to the great river, and crossed over to Arkansas and Oklahoma.

At one time, there was only a short distance between Coronado's men and De Soto's band. Between them, they had covered almost the whole area that delimited the influence of the plumed serpent. They were temporary intruders in the land. Castaneda observed that it was strange that Coronado with his troops and camp followers and live stock "would leave no more trace where they had passed than if nothing had been there—nothing."

Occasionally, the Indians gave battle, but more often they were sullen and watchful, avoiding the intruders, waiting for the vastness of the land to swallow the men with the dangerous weapons. When De Soto entered new territory, he made it a custom to capture the local chieftain, holding him as a hostage and compelling him to provide food and carriers. 100 Indians, men and women, accompanied De Soto's march, "in chaines with yron collars about their neckes." [43]

In the spring of 1542, Coronado led his bedraggled army back toward the Rio Grande, leaving two Franciscan friars to christianize the natives. In the same spring, de Soto floated down the Mississippi; having failed to find *El Dorado,* he was not interested in the well-kept fields of golden corn that lined the river. He died, probably in June, and his body was lowered into the water. In November, the Franciscans were killed by the Indians.

1542 was also the year in which Mexico reached out toward the Philippines. Ruy Lopez de Villabos made an unsuccessful attempt to conquer the islands, and named them after the emperor's son, Philip. In the summer and fall of the same eventful year, Spanish ships made their way slowly along the coast of California. Rodriguez Cabrillo's story of the voyage uses strange names for familiar places. At the beginning of October, they reached an island which they called San Salvador, and which is now Catalina. On Sunday, October 8, they skirted the Bay that they called Los Fumos or the smoke; even in 1542, fires ringed the sandy shores of the Santa Monica beaches. On October 17, the ships came to Gaviota Pass, where the present coastal highway running north from Santa Barbara dips back into the hills.[44]

The Spaniards saw the spacious fertility of the northern continent. Here were natural resources that could produce incalculable wealth and support millions of people. But 1542 was the year of the New Laws, the desperate attempt to reorganize the use of Indian labor, the complete breakdown of colonial adminstration in Peru. It was also a period of Indian rebellions in New Spain.

The Mixton War raged in Jalisco from 1540 to 1542. The Indians killed their *encomenderos,* abandoned the towns and took refuge in fortified cliffs. Alvarado, who was accused by Las Casas of murdering millions of Indians, and who had returned to New Spain after his removal from Guatemala in 1535, marched against the rebels, and was defeated and killed. The revolt spread so rapidly that the whole system of Spanish power in Mexico was threatened. A difficult military campaign reduced the Indian strongholds; thousands of the rebels were killed; many more threw themselves from the cliffs and perished, and a large number were sold into slavery.[45] At the same time, unrest was growing among the Indians in Yucatan, where the great revolt of the Mayas came a few years later, in 1546.

A parallel movement developed in South America: the town of Santiago in Chile, founded in 1541, was burned by the Indians, inaugurating the Auracanian Federation's long battle for independence.

Indian resistance must be considered as one of the complex of social forces that delayed and disorganized the American conquest until the mid-century crisis shook the Hapsburg-Catholic structure of power and brought the Protestant bourgeoisie into the race for overseas possessions.

As the Spanish-American social system became stratified, the lower classes, of mixed Indian, European and Negro descent, became tied to the land as sharecroppers, migrant laborers, serfs working on large estates—the *peons* of Mexico, the *plebe* of Peru, the *rotos* (literally the broken people) of Chile. They are the Americans, the bearers of an emergent New World culture.

On June 14, 1867, shortly after the defeat of the slaveholders in the southern United States, a man stood before a firing squad in Mexico. The man called himself an emperor; he was a direct descendant of the Hapsburg masters of sixteenth century America. The squad was made up of soldiers of mixed Indian, Negro and Spanish stock. They obeyed the orders of a man who stands with Bolivar and Lincoln as one of the three greatest figures in the history of the New World. The order to execute Maximilian was given by a descendant of the people enslaved and murdered by Cortes, the Zapotec Indian, Benito Juarez.

5 : SLAVE MARKET

SONG AND STORY have celebrated the romance of the Sea of the Caribe. The concept of the history of the region as a cloak-and-dagger extravaganza is one of the stereotypes of our culture. Like all such stereotypes, it is a fragment of the historical picture seen in false perspective: it is as if the cutthroats and adventurers were observed under a strong magnifying glass while the social background is viewed dimsightedly from a distance. We are familiar with the personalization of history as the work of a few gifted individuals; the Caribbean stereotype is unusual in the selection of the persons upon whom the spotlight is focused.

The emphasis on lawless conduct as the creative element in the life of the West Indies is indicative of the perversion of moral values in the literature of history. The perversion goes deep: the apparently careless acceptance of the antisocial activity of individuals divorces the activity from its roots and causes. The connection between the international struggle for colonial power and the wretched corruption in the West Indies is cut by the sword of the swashbuckling hero, who interposes his own enterprise and will as the center of interest.

The Spanish Main was the focal point of European rivalry for two centuries. Its importance in naval strategy was related to its economic role as the first decisive area of sugar production, and the market for the training and distribution of African slaves. The Negro, in chains and in rebellion, laboring in the fields and fighting guerrilla battles in the mountains, is the heroic and creative figure, the defender of moral values, in the complex of Caribbean social relationships.

In bringing his unwilling labor to the Western Hemisphere, the Negro brought a cultural experience that was interwoven with the growth of civilization in the Old World. The men and women in the slave ships were torn from their background, severed from the context of their traditions. Yet we cannot understand their problem, either in terms of psychological adjustment or as a collective battle for survival, without some knowledge of the heritage from which they were severed and which they tried to preserve in the new environment.

The culture that we call European owes as much to Africa as to Asia. Mennon, king of Ethiopia, led one of the armies that besieged Troy. Two of the greatest figures of Greek literature, Aesop and Sappho, were described as Negroes.[1]

The importance of Ethiopia in the ancient network of eastern Mediterranean trade is indicated in the Bible references to the Negro kingdom: "Ethiopia and Egypt were her strength, and it was infinite."[2] The name is used repeatedly as a symbol of power.[3] The visit of the Queen of Sheba to King Solomon is a more or less legendary account of the intercourse, political and commercial, between the two countries at the time of Israel's greatest prosperity. The profit that Solomon obtained "of the merchantmen, and of the traffick of the spice merchants,"[4] came in part from Abyssinia, and the gold of Ophir that enriched the king's treasury may have come from the east coast of Africa.

About two centuries after Solomon's time, when the power of Israel was waning and Ethiopia had conquered Egypt (in 710 B.C.), Isaiah prophesied the coming decline of "the labour of Egypt, and merchandise of Ethiopia."[5] Ezekiel thundered that "the sword shall come upon Egypt, and great pain shall be in Ethiopia." He spoke of the doom that awaited "Ethiopia, and Lybia and Lydia, and all the mingled peoples."[6]

There is an interesting concurrence of dates between the introduction of Christianity in Abyssinia and the decision to transfer the capital of the Roman empire to the eastern Mediterranean. Constantinople became the seat of imperial government in 330 A.D., and the first Christian bishop of Ethiopia was consecrated in the same year. The event demonstrates the importance of the Abyssinian ports in the trade of the Red Sea and Asia Minor. The Christian discipline was coextensive with the network of industry and commerce under imperial control. Abyssinia was sufficiently involved in the economic system to feel the influence of its religious culture. The adoption of Christianity in Ethiopia inaugurated a period of expansion and the flowering of artistic and intellectual activity. In the sixth century, Ethiopian armies crossed the Red Sea to conquer the richest regions of Arabia, using these territories as a base for the extension of trade with the Orient and Constantinople. Fifty years later, they were driven out of Arabia, and the sweep of Mohammedan power across northern Africa severed communication between Abyssinia and the Mediterranean.

In the twelfth century, when the European attempt to conquer the Middle East was threatened with failure, medieval thought combined vague rumors of Abyssinia with *El Dorado* fantasies to build the myth of the Christian empire of Prester John. About 1165, shortly after the collapse of the second crusade, a letter purportedly written by Prester John to the Byzantine emperor, Manuel Commenus, was widely circulated. Prester John wrote magniloquently of his wealth and devout Catholicism. The obvious purpose of the invention was to revive the prestige of the Eastern adventure, stimulating the hope that a great power would come to the aid of the Europeans and convert the struggle with the Arabs into a two-front war.

The myth had a cultural value that went far beyond its immediate political aims. It appealed to the popular and mercantile interests in the Far East; it was a dreamlike distortion of the reality that existed, an easy vision of the contact that would be established in the fullness of time. The interaction of myth and reality is particularly significant in the transfer of Prester John's Christian kingdom from its real location in Ethiopia to a fabulous place in the Orient. Since Europe had obtained luxury goods from India ever since the days of the Roman empire, it was natural to associate wealth with the Far East. But Africa had also been a part of the Roman trading area, and had established connections with Asia that were never completely severed. During the Middle Ages, Ethiopian commerce was restricted by Mohammedan pressure in the north. But intercourse between the Orient and the East Coast of Africa was maintained throughout the medieval period. Asian traders settled in African ports. Gold from the mines of northern Rhodesia was carried to India, contributing in no small degree to the enormous riches accumulated by the Hindu kings.[7] Along with the gold went Negro slaves who were sold to Indian potentates.

The importance of slavery in developing cultural ties between Asia and Africa is indicated in events that took place in the Indian kingdom of Gaur. In 1486, the 8,000 African slaves in Gaur rebelled and placed their own leader on the throne. The Negro regime lasted for seven years, ending with the defeat of the Negro forces and their exile from the kingdom in the year of Columbus' return from his first voyage to the West Indies.[8]

The special conditions that made the West Coast of Africa the main source of supply for the American market were in part geographical: it was accessible to European ships and was nearer to the West Indies and Brazil than any other parts of the continent. However, the concentration of the trade in this area was also due to historical causes which related to the general development of Africa. The West Coast was neither wholly isolated from the rest of the country, nor was it backward in cultural development. The civilization of the West did not have the advantage of the intercourse with Asia Minor and the Orient that contributed to the mercantile growth of the East Coast. West Africa had communication by sea with Europe in the days of the Phoenicians and Carthaginians; but maritime contact was cut off from that time until the fifteenth century arrival of the Portuguese. The Gold Coast and Nigeria engaged in overland commerce across the Sahara, receiving silk cloths from Tunis and Morocco.[9] There was trade, and warfare, with the interior regions of the Great Lakes, the Congo Valley and the Sudan.[10]

Under these circumstances, the pattern of culture in West Africa was predominantly devoted to agriculture and handicraft production, without the emphasis on mercantile activity that characterized the societies of the East Coast. Cultivation of the land was in part conducted cooperatively, and in part on estates worked by serf or slave labor. Craft industry organized on a gild basis. With the expert making of cloth and the welding of iron, there was an impressive development of plastic and decorative arts. Social organization gradually moved toward industrial and urban forms, but the process was delayed by the lack of extensive commerce and the comparatively limited accumulation of wealth. It is absurd to suppose that the people of the West Coast lived like savages in forest villages. There were a number of great cities. Ibadan in Nigeria, for example, had some 325,000 inhabitants.[11]

The intercourse with Portugal that began in the fifteenth century was at first profitable to the West Africans, who exchanged gold, ivory and pepper for European goods. But in the early sixteenth century, West Africa felt the pressure of world events. The maritime expansion of Europe was met by a powerful Mohammedan counterattack: the discovery of a sea route to the Orient threatened the strategic control of world trade that the Ottoman Empire had achieved through the capture of Constantinople. The Turkish campaigns against Hungary and Austria were accompanied by military drives in Africa and Asia, and the extension of Turkish sea power into the Arabian Sea and the Indian Ocean.

Northeastern Africa, which had already been reached by Portuguese navigators, was an important factor in the Mohammedan plan to maintain control of the whole area from the Mediterranean to the Orient. The Mohammedan invasion of Abyssinia and the Nile Valley caused a vast migration of people into central Africa, pressing westward toward the fertile lands of the Atlantic coast. The migrants met resistance; they destroyed villages and massacred the inhabitants. In the disorder and warfare that followed, the cheap labor of people captured in battle became available on the West Coast—at the historic moment when it was needed for the fields and mines of the New World.[12]

Thus the establishment of the slave trade in Africa was part of a world clash of forces; it represented a European triumph over the Mohammedans, whose invasion of Africa brought additional profits to their enemies. The men who carried the first slaves to Spanish America were not particular about the source of their supply. When the Portuguese captured Zafi in Morocco in 1507, they began a brisk commerce in captive Moors, Berbers, and Jews. These people were often called "white slaves," and a great many of them were women.[13]

While the Spanish government opposed the transportation of "infidels," there was no objection to the use of Christians as slaves. Indeed, in 1512, King Ferdinand ordered the *Casa de Contratacion* to send white Christian slave women to the Indies in order to prevent alliances between the settlers and Indian women.[14] It is probable that most of the women were dedicated to prostitution.

The traffic in Moorish and Berber slaves, as well as in persons bought in the eastern Mediterranean, continued through the sixteenth century, and those who had dark skins were not distinguished from the Negroes. Slaves from Asia Minor and from Greece were sold in America. At a later date, trans-Pacific commerce brought slaves seized in India, Indonesia and the Philippines, and even a few from China, to Mexico.[15]

The international complaisance of the trade made no distinctions of race, color, or "previous condition of servitude": from the viewpoint of the slave dealer, Greeks and Arabs were as "savage" as the inhabitants of Africa. In the early days of settlement, the special exploitation of the Negro had not as yet developed its special brand of prejudice. In those first days, black men earned distinction as leaders. A Negro, Nuflo de Olana, stood with Balboa, as one of his trusted lieutenants, on the hill above the Pacific. A Negro, Juan Garrido, endeavored to solve the food shortage in Mexico, planting the first wheat produced in the New World.[16]

Opportunities for individual accomplishment diminished rapidly as slavery became institutionalized. The pattern began to crystallize shortly after the conquest of Puerto Rico and Cuba, when the labor crisis brought Las Casas to Spain to argue for a new policy toward the Indians and the substitution of Africa workers. In examining the events that attended the influx of Negroes, we find that the violence of the proceedings seem to preclude any normal cultural contact. Scholars have recently begun to appraise the extent of African survivals in the New World. These studies tend to emphasize the more or less passive or defensive preservation of old life ways, and to underestimate the values recreated and transformed in the course of conflict.[17]

The essential characteristic of the first decades of slavery is the intensity of the struggle initiated by the Negroes. It was a far more unequal struggle than that conducted by the Indians; since the slave was a commodity, wholly owned by his master, it involved a more irreconcilable clash of interests, and more intimate relationships of persons and property. The violence of the initial clash, and the very considerable successes achieved by the Negroes, gave the system its historical direction.

The notorious savagery of the slave ships was in part a matter of economy; the cargo was starved, manacled, crowded below decks because it was the easiest and cheapest method of transporting a large number of people. But the cruelty was also systematized in order to break the spirit of the Negroes; it was the first step in the "education" of the unwilling slaves.

We have discussed the circumstances that motivated Las Casas' representations to the crown in 1516 and 1517. The first large-scale importation of Negroes (there were already a good many African and European slaves in the West Indies, introduced under the legal provision that they had been born in slavery) coincided with the growing effectiveness of Indian resistance to servitude. In 1516, while Las Casas was in Spain securing the appointment of an investigating committee, Indian slaves seized the ship from which they were about to be unloaded at Havana. They killed the Spanish crew, and sailed away.[18]

Thus the people who were brought to replace the dwindling Indian reserves of labor found themselves in the presence of an existent conflict. They also found the islands in a depressed economic situation, which their cheap services were intended to remedy. The small number of Europeans and the class divisions among them were factors that favored the organization of resistance. The attempt of the Negroes to secure their freedom must be considered as an integral part of the economic and social picture.

The imported slaves lacked cultural unity. They came from different areas, and spoke various languages. In spite of these disabilities, they were able to organize a large-scale rebellion in Hispaniola as early as 1522.[19] This was the beginning of a movement that spread to the other islands and to the mainland. The cooperation, and in some cases the fusion, of Negro and Indian resistance, could not usually defeat the Europeans with their obvious superiority in arms and the constant availability of reinforcements and supplies. But the opposition disrupted the colonial system, terrorized the colonists, and established the outlaw communities of Cimarrons and Maroons that were to continue their independent existence until modern times.

While the slaves undertook the tasks of underground communication and organization under the most difficult conditions, the colonists faced the deepening contradictions that were inherent in the use of forced labor. Sugar production brought profits to a few merchants and landowners in Hispaniola and Puerto Rico, but the majority of the settlers complained of the scarcity of slaves and the cost of their purchase. There were angry objections to the crown's tax of 30 ducats *per capita* for a special license to import Negroes, and Portuguese captains conducted a brisk illicit trade, offering slaves in exchange for sugar and hides.[20] The frustrations of the small planter, living in constant fear of outbreaks on the part of workers whose services were outside his reach, became a permanent part of the cultural pattern. As the conflict developed and the terror of insurrections increased, the small planter's bitterness all too often found an outlet in pathological hatred of the Negro.

The birth pangs of a plantation economy can be observed most clearly in Cuba, where the social disorganization was more serious than in the other islands. The possibilities of sugar cultivation were recognized as early as 1523, but nothing was done to bring the plans into operation. The shortage of labor was as acute as in the neighboring colonies, but there was greater dissatisfaction among the white settlers, who tried to save themselves by placing heavier burdens on Indian workers and clamoring for additional Negro slaves. The island was controlled by a few wealthy men in Santiago. The governor, Gonzalo de Guzman, and his brother-in-law, Nunez de Guzman, dealt in land, gold, cattle, hogs and crops, while the majority of their compatriots starved.[21]

Although there had been no attempt to enforce the instructions issued in 1520 concerning the protection of the Indians, the Spanish authorities received such alarming reports from Cuba that special measures were taken in 1526 to save the remaining Indian population of the island, where "there is greater need for remedy than in other places." Pedro Mexia, the Franciscan provincial in Espanola, was sent to Cuba with orders to release all Indians then without *encomenderos,* as well as those whose *encomenderos* might die in the following six months. Governor Guzman sent heated protests to Spain, declaring that if the order were not suspended, there would not be one peaceful Indian in the island within a month.[22]

Guzman was right about the danger of Indian revolt. But his failure to act on the home government's instructions brought the incipient rebellion to a head. In 1528, there was an uprising. When it failed, the Indians retired to the mountains, forming guerrilla bands that made effective sorties and won additional recruits during the following years.[23] The establishment of these centers of resistance in the back country had a twofold effect; it brought halfhearted efforts to conciliate the Indians and increased the demand for Negro slaves.

In 1531, the governor made a minor experiment in line with the orders that had been conveyed to him five years before: he assembled 100 Indians, lectured them on the advantages of liberty, and offered them a village where they were to raise their own crops. The Indians were placed under a Spanish administrator, Francisco Guerrero, who commandeered their services for his own use, and treated them as if they were in an *encomienda*.[24]

In the same year, the imperial government responded to appeals for assistance in obtaining African slaves: the crown promised to use its Cuban revenues for the purchase of Negroes, to be distributed among responsible settlers, who had two years in which to repay the loan. The failure to fulfill the promise may have been due to the lack of available revenues.[25] But the deeper reason lay in its Utopian character; it was a dim echo of Las Casas' suggestion, made a decade earlier, that each European receive twelve slaves.

The crown could not afford to finance the purchase of laborers by small or middle landowners; ordinary agricultural production did not yield enough profit to justify the investment. Slaves could only be employed profitably in large enterprises. They were used in Cuba in the Jobabo mines, and it was there that the first Negro revolt on the island occurred in 1533.[26] It was accompanied by renewed and broader Indian rebellion under the chieftain, Enrique. Negroes joined the guerrilla bands, and the struggle began to assume a more organized revolutionary character.

The main base of the slave system in Mexico was the sugar plantation. By the beginning of the fourth decade, sugar had become almost as important as gold in the colonial economy. When Charles V made Madrid his residence in 1532 (a move that was motivated by recognition of the growing importance of his American empire), taxes on Caribbean sugar paid for the architectural improvements of the imperial palace. Sugar financed the enlargement of the alcazar at Toledo and the later building program undertaken by Philip II.

Hispaniola, being most heavily engaged in the production of sugar, acquired the largest slave population, developed the most rigid methods of oppression, and experienced the most violent revolts. There was an uprising in 1533, another in 1537, and a third in 1548. The trouble was not restricted to Hispaniola: there are records of at least eleven slave rebellions in the Spanish possessions between 1522 and 1553.[27]

It seems evident that Negro thought and life must have been concentrated on the preparation and execution of these revolutionary plans. Other aspects of daily life were so negative that, where rebellion was impossible, suicide was a usual form of protest. The custom was so widespread among the Ibo people coming from the Niger Delta that there was a motto in Haiti: "Ibos pend' cor' a you—The Ibo hang themselves." [28]

There were many skills, beliefs and customs that were maintained under the abnormal pressures of slavery. For example, the marked ability which the Negroes exhibited as artisans whenever there was an opportunity to test their skill may be attributed to the emphasis on craft industry in the societies of West Africa. But the emotion and talent of the slaves were channelized almost exclusively in the fight for freedom. The conservation of the African culture and its adaptation to new conditions must have been determined by the necessities of the struggle.

While the lack of historical records excludes any detailed knowledge of the cultural life of the Negroes in the sixteenth and seventeenth centuries, there are certain assumptions which seem to fit the conditions of the conflict and its known consequences: where the struggle was conducted successfully, it prevented or deferred the assimulation of the European culture, and preserved elements derived from Africa. It also brought a fusion of Negro and Indian characteristics, which was most pronounced in the areas of most consistent resistance to servitude.

Wilbur Zelinski suggests that "it would be interesting to compile a map of the New World showing the relative degree of African survival for the various Negro communities." His tentative findings show that the integrity of the African culture is most fully retained "in Haiti, the Bush Negro areas of the Guianas, and scattered localities in the Antilles and Brazil." These are the regions in which revolutionary activity was maintained for centuries. Where the struggle had less continuity and independence, the African elements were diluted: this was the case in northeastern Brazil, the Lesser Antilles, Cuba, coastal Guiana, and part of Colombia.[29]

While the African heritage was defended as an instrument in the fight for survival, it was adapted to a novel situation. The communities of Cimarrons and Maroons had to learn new methods of subsistence and of warfare. The cultural interchange between the Indians and the Negroes was a dynamic factor in these societies. In the centers of Indian population in Mexico and Peru, the confluence of the two cultures tended to create a predominantly Indian pattern. But where the plantation system made the Negroes the basic labor force, they assumed the leadership in the struggle against servitude, and played the most creative role in the process of acculturation.

The fraudulent arguments concerning the Negro's ability to do heavy work in the heat of the tropics and his docility under the yoke embellished the real reasons for the substitution of African slaves for Indian workers. Plantation labor was less destructive than toil in the mines, and the use of the Negroes in the production of sugar was one of the reasons for their survival.[30] There was a more fundamental social factor: it was obviously easier to subjugate men and women imported in chains from distant lands than to enforce discipline over people fighting for their own soil, with bases in the back country to which they could retire.

When the Negroes discovered these bases and allied themselves with the native rebels, their masters became victims of the psychopathic hatred that was to degrade the life of the plantations. The whole culture was infected by the fear of the slaves. Modern thought is still so enthralled in white supremacy myths that it remains blind to the social effects of slavery on the class enjoying its economic benefits. The historiography of the United States, committed to a theory of national development that is largely an *apologia* for the slave system, excludes any objective analysis of the moral and psychological deterioration that accompanies the ownership of human chattels.

The consequences were already apparent in the West Indies in the first half of the sixteenth century. Charles Edward Chapman's statement, cited above, that the Indians were not harshly treated, "if only because their lives were valuable to those who were virtually their masters," is untrue either of Indian or Negro slavery.

Las Casas' charge that the Spaniards "tamed and trained the strongest and most ferocious dogs to kill and tear the Indians to pieces" [31] is borne out by irrefutable supporting testimony, which describes similar, and even more refined, methods in dealing with the Negroes. The dogs were trained to attack a figure resembling a Negro, in which the blood and entrails of beasts were placed. The figure was shown to them temptingly, brought close to the cage so that they could smell the food. Meanwhile, they were kept hungry, until they were finally allowed to devour the bloody meal. When the dogs pursued a runaway Negro, they tore him to pieces instantly.

The fear of the slaves was so great that brutality became a dominant trait of the ruling class culture. Since the system of power depended on keeping the Negroes under control, the punishments which were regarded as socially necessary were given prestige. Cruelty was an end in itself, proof of superiority, a demonstration that the slave was a commodity and could be expended if the owner wished to accept the loss. The *sportive* torture or destruction of life, was most common in the first wasteful days of Indian exploitation, but it continued throughout the plantation period. The mistreatment of slaves as a matter of emulation and display expressed the sickness of the mind and the social organism; the same compulsive malady is observable today in the approach to lynching as a pastime.

The planter, the colonial *Faustian man,* paid a high price for his devil's contract. In return for the right to whip and chain his fellow man, he gave up the most precious human possession, the love of man, the recognition of human worth and dignity. He received the treasure of the earth, the fruit of the Negro's labor; he had to accept the psychological disabilities and irrational prejudices that accompanied the gift.

The women of the plantation had their part in the Faustian agreement. It included the landowner's pledge to destroy the Negro family, to breed slaves like cattle for the profits of the trade, to tear children from their mothers and wives from their husbands. The use of Negro women for the pleasure of the masters was not merely a matter of inclination. Like sportive cruelty, it was an essential element in the slaveholding culture, a necessary demonstration of the slave's subordinate status. The upper-class woman could not avoid the Mephistophelean bargain, which degraded her own family and stultified her emotional life. The agreement gave the defense of all that is most sacred in human relationships—the love of man and woman, the comradeship of the family, the search for probity and freedom—to the despised slaves.

The psychological and social aspects of the slave structure were not unrelated to its economic character. Although it brought a huge profit to large plantation owners, as well as to shippers and traders, it wasted land as well as labor, and paralyzed productive growth.

Wilbur Zelinsky summarizes a verdict which is based on convincing evidence:

> Rather than any genuine development of the region, the prodigal use of slave labor seems to be tied in with an utterly destructive exploitation of the land, which is well known in the Southeastern United States and the Lesser Antilles, and is an apparently irreversible process of economic disaster.[32]

The process, with all its waste and suffering, was historically necessary. It provided the base upon which the structure of capitalism was built. The discovery of gold and silver in America, the destruction of the native population, the commercial exploitation of the African slave depots and the unpaid labor of the Negroes, signalized, as Marx observes, "the rosy dawn of capitalist production," [33] preparing the way for the technological and industrial developments of the eighteenth and nineteenth centuries. W. E. B. Du Bois writes:

> We cannot forget that America was built on Africa. From being a mere stopping place between Europe and Asia or a chance treasure house of gold, America became through African labor the center of the sugar empire and the cotton kingdom and an integral part of that world industry which caused the industrial revolution and the reign of capitalism.[34]

The plantation economy established in the West Indies was duplicated a few decades later in Brazil, when the development of the sugar industry brought the large-scale importation of slaves. For a time, it seemed as if the sugar boom would provide a Utopia for the small farmer in Brazil.

Pero de Maghalhaes wrote in 1576 that the first thing the settlers "try to obtain is slaves to work the farms; and any one who succeeds in obtaining two pairs or a half-dozen of them . . . has the means to sustain his family in a respectable way." [35] But the hope that Brazil would realize Las Casas' dream of a landholding bourgeoisie supported by small groups of slaves was shattered in the seventeenth century. Even when Maghalhaes visited Brazil, he observed that many estates had two or three hundred slaves.

The disaster in the sugar provinces of Brazil came in the middle of the seventeenth century, when the small planters were hopelessly saddled with debts, sugar was rotting in the warehouses, and the civil war between Dutch and Portuguese settlers was accompanied by Negro and Indian revolts, and the founding of the Negro republic of Palmares which maintained an organized state in the forests of Pernambuco for fifty years.[36]

It is estimated that the number of Negroes in the New World at the end of the sixteenth century was nearly 900,000. This scattered but cohesive group, whose ranks were to be augmented during the next century by the arrival of approximately 2,750,000 people from Africa, represented one of the greatest migrations in the course of history.

The Negro's cultural influence, manifested largely through his organized and armed resistance to slavery, was an integral part of his masked, but nonetheless decisive, role in economic and political events. The Cimarrons and Maroons rendered assistance to Drake and other English freebooters in their Caribbean raids, and so played an important part in weakening Spain's colonial position and aiding the rise of England's maritime power.

The long-range objective of the rebels, the destruction of the slave system, was evident in the decade of colonial crisis that preceded the debate between Las Casas and Sepulveda. Girolomo Benzoni, who was in Santo Domingo in 1545, wrote of reports that the Cimarrons "had joined in general rebellion, were scouring out every part of the island, and doing all the mischief they could." These were preparations for the revolt that took place in 1548. Europeans who talked with Benzoni were pessimistic about their future: "Many prophesy for certain that the islands in a short time will fall entirely into the hands of the blacks."[37]

The victory was deferred for 150 years. But when the white inhabitants of the United States won their freedom, the national revolutions that swept the Western Hemisphere began with the Haitian uprising led by the Negro slave, Toussaint L'Ouverture. General LeClerc, sent by Napoleon to reconquer the island, reported "that these people may be killed, but will not surrender. They laugh at death—and it is the same with the women."[38] LeClerc's failure to suppress the rebellion helped make it impossible for Napoleon to proceed with his plans to occupy Louisiana, which led to his decision to sell the Mississippi region to the United States.

Thus the Negro resistance that began in Hispaniola in the first years of the sixteenth century enabled the United States to occupy the rich central valleys of the Northern continent three hundred years later. The struggle in Latin America is part of a heritage that has its origin in Africa. The national consciousness that stirs and unites the Negro people of the United States is rooted in their past, in their unique contribution to civilization in the Americas. Their contribution to the world's culture will be completely recognized, and fulfilled, when they complete their historic task, breaking the chains that still bind them in the United States, in the Western Hemisphere, and in Africa.

6 : THE TWILIGHT OF THE CONQUISTADORS

In 1552, Rabelais published the fourth book of the adventures of Pantagruel and Panurge. The book describes their long voyages and explorations. One day they "sighted nine vessels, filled with monks of all sorts—Dominicans, Jesuits, Capuchins, Hermits, Augustins, Bernardins, Celestins, Theatins, Egnatins, Amadeans, Cordeliers, Carmelites, Minims and other like holy saints." Panurge was delighted, and secured the benediction of the monks by giving them "seventy-eight dozen hams, caviar—six pots at a time, Bologna sausages by the tens, botargos and other relishes of fish-roe by the hundred containers," as well as 2,000 gold coins.[1]

The passage is a happy amalgam of myth and reality. In paying his unflattering respects to the clergy, Rabelais noted the change in Spanish America that resulted from the breakdown of civil governments in the colonies and the concurrent economic and social crisis in Europe. The determination of the church to take over the administration of the overseas territories, lay behind both the debate between Las Casas and Sepulveda, and the permission granted to Las Casas to publish his indictments of the conquistadors. These appeared at exactly the same time as the fourth Rabelaisian fantasy.

In the following pages, we shall consider the cultural and social significance of the mid-century shift in colonial policy, and its long-term effect on the life of the Americas. The change covered the period of European tension leading up to the panic of 1559 and the Protestant resurgence that followed it.

As Rabelais wrote, the clerical deputies were on their way to all parts of the colonial world. Their interest in the good things of life, in food and gold, reflected the material and aggressive character of the Christian crusade which they served. Rabelais knew that the plans for a world Catholic empire would not have smooth sailing. He wrote that the holy men were on their way to "the council of Chesil. (As to this name, it is derived from one of two Hebrew words: *kessil* or madman; *cesil* or star of tempests.)" Thus the symbolism of the encounter is defined. "Seeing these priest-ridden ships, Panurge was jubilant; he vowed he would have good luck that day, and many more to follow." While Panurge is loading the monks with gifts, Pantagruel is watching the sky. "Suddenly the sea swelled, roared, rose mountain-high from the depths of an abyss."[2]

The Pantagruelian storm, which lasts for five chapters of exclamatory and philosophical conversation, includes a dissertation "on the making of Wills at Sea": Panurge is advised that the making of a will is a waste of time: "If we survive, our wills are useless . . . if we drown, surely our wills will go down with us." But Panurge delivers a masterly discourse on the mythology of the ancients to prove that his will would drift ashore, and "Some king's daughter, playing on the beach, would find it and execute it." He mentions some fourteen mythological and historical instances to prove that this eventuality is inherently probable.[3]

The theme of myth and money, which runs through all the work of Rabelais, is interwoven with the fury of the elements. The storm, like Shakespeare's *Tempest* or the terror of the whale in *Moby Dick*, is both reality and symbol. Hurricanes were the bane of transatlantic voyages; but the destruction wrought by winds and waves was an allegory of man's struggle with nature, which was in turn conditioned by his social environment and the organization of his skills and powers.

Rabelais used the storm for a serio-comic discussion of ethics and property. But it had a larger meaning in its juxtaposition to the passing shiploads of monks. The political skies were dark with the signs and portents of the tempest that would shake the thrones of Europe and change the course of colonization, placing the Protestant bourgeoisie in a position to share in the Catholic exploitation of the world and thus limiting the areas in which the Catholic missionaries could operate without interference.

The rise of Protestantism in France accounts for the publication of the book, with its conspicuous mockery of the clergy. The pressures that forced the author's exile in 1546 were lifted in 1550. He was able to return to his native land because France was at war with the Hapsburgs in alliance with the German Protestant princes. The timeliness of the appearance of the fourth book becomes apparent when we consider that Henry II invaded Germany with a French army in March 1552, and that the Emperor Charles V barely escaped capture during the following months and experienced a serious defeat at Metz in January, 1553. These political events explain the official protection of the book in France. It was censored by the Sorbonne and its sale temporarily suspended, but the ban was quickly lifted.

The Hapsburg weakness, accentuated by the emperor's money difficulties, made it imperative that the church take a firm hand in the muddled affairs of the American colonies. The disciplined cadres of the Jesuits had already become a factor in European expansion in the Orient: Francis Xavier, having visited Malacca and Japan, died of fever on the island of St. John, off the coast of China, late in 1552. But the Jesuits were not as yet available for service in the Spanish possessions in the Western Hemisphere. The decline in Charles' fortunes created friction between the empire and the Vatican, and Rome felt that the Spanish Jesuits were too close to the imperial government to serve its interests in the New World.

The earliest activities of the Society of Jesus were restricted to Portuguese Brazil. Manoel de Nobrega reached Bahia in 1549, inaugurating the system of missions supported by the "voluntary" labor of the Indians which was to be introduced later in Paraguay and Lower California. Nobrega was successful in utilizing the Indians for sugar cultivation and craft production. He recognized the importance of education in developing a Catholic culture, starting the first Latin class in 1553, and establishing a college three years later. Nobrega visited Sao Paulo, a thousand miles south of Bahia in 1553, and the college of Sao Paulo was organized in the following year.[4]

The tasks undertaken by the Jesuits in Brazil were entrusted to the Dominicans and Franciscans in the Spanish dependencies. In Mexico, the active discontent of the Indian population stimulated educational work among them. The Franciscans took the lead in teaching Christian principles and European manual arts to the natives. The Academy of Santa Cruz de Tlaltolco, exclusively for Indians, was founded in 1536.[5] The University of Mexico was chartered by royal decree in 1551, and in the same year the Dominican University of San Marcos de Lima was founded in Peru.

In the foregoing pages, we have placed such repeated emphasis on the significance of the debate on Indian rights in 1550, that it is unnecessary to reiterate its connection with the beginnings of Catholic education in the New World. The founding of universities was a sign of cultural stabilization. Civil order was at last established in Peru. The first European roses bloomed in Lima in 1552.[6] Four years later, the frontier town of Potosi expended 8 million pesos on the four-day celebration of the coronation of Philip II. The notorious courtesan, Doña Clara, was said to spend 2,000 pesos a day on jewels, clothes and entertainment.[7] Potosi remained the symbol of the New World's economic sickness. Inflated prices increased the gap between the few people who reveled in mining profits and the Indian workers dying in the mines.

In seeking to establish a workable structure of power in the Western Hemisphere, the church was motivated by the increasing threat of Protestant intervention. The holding of an *Auto da Fe* in Lima in 1548, was a sign of ecclesiastical nervousness; Jan Millar, a Fleming, was burned for Protestantism,[8] as a warning against the infiltration of French or Flemish merchants.

The French publication of the Fourth book of *The Deeds and Heroic Sayings of Good Pantagruel* was an augury that the Huguenots were about to undertake transatlantic adventures. Henry II was a Catholic, but his successful alliance with the German Lutheran princes added greatly to the prestige and influence of the French Protestants. The defeats of Charles V and the confusion of papal policy wavering between France and the empire, offered unusual opportunities for the invasion of the Catholic overseas domain.

Protestantism was closely associated with maritime activity; its most militant stronghold in France was the great seaport of La Rochelle, which sent a large fleet each year to the Newfoundland fisheries. The voyages to the Grand Banks were profitable. But the merchants of the French channel ports and the bankers of Lyons were as world-minded as their Catholic and English competitors. They wanted maritime control of the whole Atlantic area, as the key to American wealth and the global system of trade.

The genius of French colonization was Admiral Gaspard de Coligny, national leader of the Huguenots. When Charles V signed the

Peace of Augsberg in 1555, Coligny prepared for the first attempt to plant a Protestant settlement in America. Coligny and his friends were aware of the strategic importance of Brazil: it provided a base for territorial expansion in South America, and for naval operations in the South Atlantic. It was also wise to avoid a direct clash with Spain, and the distant coast of Portuguese Brazil was more difficult to defend from intruders of other nations than the shores of Spain's American possessions.

The French colony at Rio de Janeiro was founded in 1558. But the ambitions that inspired the Huguenot plan were in unhappy contrast to the physical and political limitations imposed on the undertaking. Coligny had to conceal the Protestant aims of the venture; he entrusted leadership to Nicolas Durand de Villegagnon, a Catholic, who seems to have given assurance to both Coligny and Calvin that he was secretly in sympathy with their cause. However, at Rio de Janeiro, Villegagnon rallied the Catholic members of the expedition around him, and initiated a local conflict which mirrored the European struggle on which the fate of the colony depended.

The hopes of the Huguenots in France were frustrated by the collapse of the *Grand Parti,* financed to a considerable extent with Protestant funds and the economic disorder that followed. Coligny was unable to send help to his friends in Brazil.

At the same time, England's temporary return to the Catholic fold occasioned English participation, at least in name, in the settlement of the most remote regions of the South American frontier. In honor of the marriage of Philip II and Queen Mary, a province in the interior of Chile, in what is now western Argentina, was called *Nueva Inglaterra,* and one of its towns was christened London.[9] It is fascinating to speculate on the possibility that the continuance of Britain's Catholic and Spanish affiliation might have placed New England in such an unlikely location, under such unpromising auspices.

However, England's historical development decreed the quick dissolution of the Catholic alliance, while the relationship of forces in France led to civil strife and the decline of Huguenot power. European politics were related, in the sixteenth century as in the later history of the Americas, to the Indian's attempt to maintain his freedom. The Auracanian Federation, which renewed its warfare against the Spaniards in 1553, wiped out the South American New England in 1560.

On the other side of the continent, the French settlers, weakened by internal dissension and driven from Rio de Janeiro by a Portuguese attack, made the first of the Indian alliances which were to characterize the whole course of French colonial policy. Retreating to the interior and joining the native enemies of the Portuguese, they were able to organize a counteroffensive and reoccupy Rio de Janeiro. Nobrego and his Jesuit followers did effective work in preventing a general Indian uprising and persuading many of the natives to fight on the Portuguese side.[10]

The decision in Southern Brazil depended on the European balance of power. France and Spain, weakened by the panic of 1559, entered into an alliance. Philip II, feeling that his marriage to Elizabeth of Valois protected him from French interference and eager to prevent English colonization in North America, took a personal interest in the expedition that carried 1,500 Spanish colonists to Florida in 1559. The settlement was located at Pensacola, on the Gulf of Mexico. The hostility of the Indians forced the abandonment of the plan; the ships moved north to Port Royal Sound in South Carolina, but it was feared that this location was too isolated, and the project was abandoned in 1561.

In France, the Huguenots were temporarily strengthened by the weakness of the monarchy and the unpopularity of the Spanish alliance. Therefore, Coligny was able to send an expedition to Port Royal Sound a year after its abandonment by the Spaniards. But a major political upset occurred just three weeks after the two ships departed. They sailed on February 18, and on March 1 the massacre of Protestants at Vassy launched a civil war.

On May 1, Jean Ribaut, commanding the Huguenot venture, reached South Carolina. On his return to France, Ribaut left thirty men at Charlesfort, named hopefully in honor of the thirteen-year-old king, Charles IX. But neither the king nor his mother, Catherine de Medici, had any desire to assist their subjects on the inhospitable North American coast. The deserted settlers, waiting in vain for the sight of a French ship on the horizon, embarked in a small boat and were picked up, half dead from hunger and exposure, by an English vessel.

The peace of Amboise, concluded in 1563, gave the Huguenots a breathing spell. Coligny, still sure that successful colonization in America would strengthen his party in France and force the abandonment of the Spanish alliance, equipped another expedition, which sailed in 1564 to found Fort Carolina on the St. John's River in northern Florida. There was sporadic conflict with the Indians, but the arrival of Ribaut with seven ships and 600 men gave promise that the settlement could be maintained.

The Florida colonists were soon to be the victims of another shift in European politics. Catherine de Medici entered into secret negotiations with Philip II, making commitments which guaranteed the renewal of the civil war in France. In submitting to the Hapsburg-Catholic demands, Catherine sealed the doom of the Huguenots in Florida. Philip, knowing that the French government would not and could not make any serious protest, was able to order the annihilation of the settlement.

The attack on Fort Carolina, led by Pedro Menendez de Aviles, was as much a part of the Catholic counteroffensive as the Council of Trent or the work of the Council of Blood in the Netherlands. The capture of the colony in 1565 was climaxed by the slaughter of all the male inhabitants. Following the same policy, Portugal, closely allied with Spain, proceeded with new vigor against the French colony in Brazil: a Portuguese fleet landed forces at Rio in 1565; it took two years to conquer the French colonists, who were captured and put to the sword in 1567.

The massacres in Carolina and Brazil were the prelude to the massacre of St. Bartholomew, in which Coligny was murdered in 1572. St. Bartholomew may be regarded as a turning point in the history of the Americas. It stopped French maritime and commercial expansion in the crucial years of the emergence of English and Dutch sea power, and prepared the way for the eighteenth century defeat of France in North America.

The decision to utilize the Society of Jesus as an instrument of Spanish colonization was made in 1565, and was part of the same movement of historical forces. Having eliminated the French threat in America, it was essential to complete the task of founding Spanish bases on the Atlantic coast of North America. Settlements could not be maintained without securing some cooperation from the Indians. The Jesuits were assigned to this delicate undertaking. There were probably many Indians in Florida and Carolina who knew of De Soto's march through the country with his hostages and chained slaves. De Soto's visit was only a generation away, and it had been followed by other unsatisfactory experiences with European settlers. Within a few years, the Indians killed seven Jesuits and three postulants. The martyrdom of Juan Bautista Segura, who attempted in 1570 to carry Spanish colonization as far north as Virginia, marked the failure of the Jesuit effort.

But, in spite of Segura's failure, the Jesuits proved indispensable to the clerical authorities in the New World, establishing educational and propaganda institutions in the centers of population and performing their missionary tasks with indefatigable zeal. Shortly after Segura's death, the archbishop of Mexico wrote to Philip asking for more Jesuits: "Send another group of them at once, and see that they continue to come in each fleet."[11] The archbishop was searching desperately for an answer to the economic and social ills that continued to plague the colony.

As a tested and persuasive answer, the church transplanted the Inquisition to the New World. Miles Philips, one of the English sailors captured in Hawkins' defeat at Vera Cruz in 1568, spent years as a prisoner in Mexico. He wrote: "In the yeere of our Lord one thousand fiue hundred suenty foure, the Inquisition began to be established in the Indies, very much against the mindes of many of the Spaniards themselues."[12]

The Inquisition was actually brought to New Spain in 1570. But Philips referred to the spectacular *auto da fe* organized in 1574, which was the first colonial event to mimic the splendor of similar punishments in Spain. The show was announced through the city for a fortnight by drums and trumpets. The victims were compelled to rehearse the whole night before the performance, being carefully drilled in their unhappy parts. There were 74 participants, of whom 36 were Lutherans. Only two of these were burned. The most common punishment for the rest was a wholesale scourging through the streets. The development of the *auto da fe* as a publicized circus made it a part of the dominant culture, and delivered its warning against nonconformity in a manner that was intended to amuse the populace and attract general attention. From 1574 to 1600, the Inquisition in New Spain handled 879 cases, an average of 34 each year.[13]

We have mentioned the earlier use of the *auto da fe* in Peru. The right of inquiry and punishment was taken away from the bishops and assigned to a separate tribunal with broad independent powers in 1570. It developed in much the same way as in Mexico. In both provinces, it was an instrument for the accumulation of huge wealth. The income from fines and penances led to ownership of extensive lands and *encomiendas*. The magnificent eighteenth century palace of the tribunal in Mexico City was a monument to the civilizing influence of the fire and the whip.[14]

The system of power was maintained by the repression of all art or thought which might challenge the dominant pattern. Few civilizations have suffered such a total eclipse of cultural life as that which was imposed on Latin America from the arrival of the Inquisition to the nineteenth century revolutions. Higher education was intended primarily for the training of priests, and secondary schools were devoted to religious indoctrination or manual training. "The sum total of education," says Chapman, "was very slight."[15]

The printing presses were in the hands of the priests, and there was very little printing of any kind. When the wife of Charles V learned that works of fiction in the vernacular were being sent to America, she issued a royal edict, stating that "This is a very bad thing for the Indians, and a thing which they should not know of or read. I order, consequently, that henceforth no one shall be allowed to take works of fiction or of secular subject matter to those territories."[16]

It goes without saying that the smuggling of books could not be stopped. But the facts concerning presses and publications are dismal proof of the level of literary activity. A press was operated in Mexico as early as 1532, and there are extant copies of religious books published there in 1544. But publication was restricted almost exclusively to religious tracts, and the only significant writing was devotional mysticism or theological speculation.[18] There was even less secular publication in Peru, where a printing office was established in 1584.

Outside of these two centers, there was virtually no printing at all until the eighteenth century. The first book manufactured in the West Indies appeared at Havana in 1707. There is no record of publication in Colombia until 1738. There seems to have been a press in Chile in 1748, but there is no indication that books or pamphlets appeared until 1776. A book was published in Venezuela in 1764.[19] Brazil, with its wealthy plantations and sugar production, was similarly backward in literary development. Gilberto Freyre speaks of the destructive influence of the Jesuits on the Brazilian Indians; theirs was "the first culture to be subtly and systematically degraded."[20] The degradation of the Negro culture, which followed, debased the masters as well as the slaves. In 1706, an attempt to establish a printing press at Recife was met with peremptory suppression, and in 1747 an order was issued for the arrest of persons who brought a printing outfit to Pernambuco.[21]

There is one literary achievement of sixteenth century Latin America that deserves mention: the various versions of the Chilean epic, *La Araucana,* suggest the emotional impact of European contact with the Indian culture of the frontier, and the stifling of what might have been a fresh creative impulse. The poem was written by Alonso de Ercilla, a young conquistador who took part in the fighting against the Araucanian Federation. His first version, completed in 1569, combines the glorification of Spain's world mission with recognition of the courage and sincerity of the Indian defense. A second version, written in 1578 after Ercilla's return to Spain, abandons simplicity to toy with visions, fates and prognostications. The Spain to which Ercilla returned had lost confidence in its own power. The third form of the poem, finished in 1590 after the defeat of the Armada, is extremely complex, arid and formal.[22]

The final draft was carried back to South America in the epic on the same theme composed by Pedro de Ona, a Chilean Creole, early in the seventeenth century. The author spent his early life in a frontier fort under the constant threat of Indian warfare, but he wrote *Arauco Domado* in a baroque style, which is as unrealistic as the title's assumption that the Araucanians had been tamed.[23]

The Araucanian epics stand like ornate towers, without much human warmth or usefulness, in the desert of early Hispanic-American culture. Their history reflects the increasing intellectual sterility of the colonial upper class, which could draw no satisfactory cultural sustenance from Spain and had no roots among the alien people whom it exploited. Thought and creativity were officially consigned to the care of the priesthood.

The last act in the drama of the conquistadors took place in 1560 and 1561. An expedition led by Don Pedro de Ursua crossed the continental divide in northeastern Peru to search for *El Dorado* in the Amazon drainage. The second in command was Lope de Aguirre. There were a few women in the party, including Doña Inez de Atienza, a widow whose love for Don Pedro caused her to sell all her possessions in order to follow him. With her were Aguirre's daughter and a few waiting women. There was plotting and bickering from the start of the trip. Aguirre organized a group of malcontents who murdered Don Pedro on the night of January 1, 1561.

Having found no gold, Aguirre decided to set up an independent kingdom in the jungle. He chose one of his followers, Fernando de Gusman, as the puppet ruler who was crowned "Lord and Prince of Peru." When the king tried to assert his power, he was slain; Doña Inez was raped and then murdered. Fighting among themselves and with Indian tribes along the route, the blood-stained Argonauts reached the Atlantic in July, 1561. They built ships, and sailed along the coast on a piratical voyage that ended in Venezuela, where Aguirre killed his daughter as he was about to be captured. He was executed.[24]

The episode suggests the last decadence of the Spanish treasure hunt; in a more profound sense, it is a typical American gangster story. The struggle for money and power, sanctioned by the *El Dorado* myth and by the *mores* of the conquest, had become pathologically violent. Like the modern gangster's use of the machine gun as a business argument, Aguirre's frenzy was an extension, under unfortunate pressures, of contemporary business practice. He was a Pizarro without a kingdom. He enacted a realistic sequel to the Amerigo Vespucci letters, translating the romantic picture of sex and war among the natives into its tainted actuality, revealing its antisocial content in terms of European conduct.

Early in the nineteenth century Robert Southey wrote the story of Aguirre in the manner of the Gothic novels that were popular at the time.[25] Like the Gothic tales or the scenes of horror preserved in wax in Madame Tussaud's museum, it expressed the psychological stress, the sense of social evil and moral insecurity, that haunted the British middle class in the epoch of imperial expansion. But Aguirre was not a fiction. Nor was he an isolated case of antisocial conduct. He was the prototype of men and women who were to play their parts in the history of the Americas.

Violence and fraud, justified in the name of free competition and personal advancement, and often carried to pathological extremes, were to find a permanent place in the American cultural pattern. A complex process of psychological development links the conquistadors with the pirates of the Spanish Main, the bandits of the Western plains, and the men who make murder a profitable business in our own time.

7 : THE PROTESTANT PIRATES

In the year after Aguirre's death, John Hawkins made his first voyage to the shores of Africa for a cargo of slaves. Hawkins was a militant Protestant, a pious man who was as shocked as his nineteenth century descendants by the iniquities of men like Aguirre. Yet his business ethics, to which he adhered with evident feeling and conviction, exhibited blind spots which had more than a casual connection with Aguirre's crimes.

The necessities of the treasure hunt, which drove the Spaniard to a doomed and unbusinesslike venture in piracy, were translated into a divinely sanctioned code of conduct by the Protestant adventurers. The hunting and killing of Negroes were included in the code, as well as scrupulous regard for economic obligations. On one occasion, when Hawkins had sold 200 Negroes at Santo Domingo, he left 125 slaves in trust to cover any charges that might be outstanding against him.

His first voyage to the Guinea Coast was motivated by the change in the European balance of power following the panic of 1559. There is a more important causal link between the beginning of the English slave trade and the adoption of the Elizabethan Statute of Laborers in the same year.

The embryonic capitalism which found it wise to hang "masterless men" in order to keep a fluid supply of workers in England was ready to make its contribution to the fluidity of the American labor market. The creativity of labor, which appeared to Las Casas as a moral dilemma and which would be recognized by Marx two centuries later as the key to man's freedom, offered no difficulties to the

Puritan conscience, which accepted the servitude of the underprivileged as proof of God's grace. When Hawkins' ship was becalmed and its living cargo was dying, the captain consoled himself for the loss with the reflection that God would not suffer his Elect to perish.

The Statute of Laborers and the opening of the slave trade established the two cornerstones of England's industrial and imperial power. Anglo-American thought developed various rationalizations in defense of slavery, but its fundamental justification was to be found in the theory and practice of British industrial production, with its discriminatory laws and its pitiless use of the labor of women and children.[1] The reasons for slavery, wrote E. G. Wakefield in the nineteenth century, "are not moral, but economic circumstances; they relate not to vice and virtue, but to production."[2]

In the West Indies, the Spanish producers of sugar were clamoring for Negro slaves. When Hawkins reached Hispaniola in March, 1563, he had no difficulty in getting rid of his cargo of 105 Negroes, and returned to England with ginger, sugar and pearls.[3]

In the same year, the French explorer, Jean Ribaut, was in England. He had just returned from South Carolina, to find that the difficulties of the Huguenots in France discouraged colonial enterprise. His journey across the channel was symptomatic of the shift in transatlantic activity from France to England. During his visit, he published a pamphlet, *The True and Last Discoverie of Florida,* inaugurating the literature of colonization that was to play such an important part in the Elizabethan and Stuart culture.

Hawkins immediately undertook a second voyage, in which he again received the cooperation of Spanish colonial officials. From Santo Domingo, he proceeded to Rio de la Hacha, a small port on the Venezuelan coast. Here he obtained official documents from the authorities permitting him to deal in "slaves, cloths, linens, wines, arms and other merchandise," with a proviso that a customs duty of seven and one-half percent be paid on all goods sold. The servants of Philip II had no legal right to make such an agreement; they were motivated in part by personal greed, but a more decisive factor was the desperate desire of the settlers to get out of the economic straitjacket in which governmental restrictions encased them. Hawkins took orders at Rio de la Hacha for future deliveries.[4]

On his return, Hawkins was given a coat of arms, with "a demi-Moor, proper, in chains" as his crest. The orders from Rio de la

Hacha were filled by Hawkins' ships, sent out this time under the command of John Lovell. But when the fleet reached Venezuela early in 1567, it was not greeted with the friendly enthusiasm that characterized previous visits. The angry orders transmitted from Spain were not merely routine objections to contraband trade: Philip's dealings with Catherine de Medici enabled him to adopt a stronger colonial policy. Having eliminated the French settlement in Florida, Philip could not tolerate English traders in the Indies. The Spanish governor shut off all supplies to the ships, and Lovell had to leave ninety slaves in order to prevent their dying of thirst.[5]

The change in political climate brought a corresponding change in Hawkins' methods and plans. He set sail in October, 1567, with eight or nine ships. The two largest were the property of the queen: the flagship, the *Jesus of Lubeck,* drew 700 tons, carrying 180 men, 22 guns and 42 secondary pieces of armament. The *Minion* was a vessel of between 300 and 350 tons.[6] Obviously, Hawkins was prepared to use more than moral suasion in establishing his right to trade in the West Indies.

His business difficulties began on the Guinea coast. Robert Barrett, a member of the expedition who signed a deposition after his capture in Mexico, said that the fleet first visited Cabo Verde, where they "had an encounter with certain Negroes." Seven or eight were captured, and others killed: "Deponent does not know how many, and they burned most of the Negroes' houses. The Negroes wounded and killed more than twenty-five Englishmen." They were more successful at Sierra Leona, where "certain Negro kings were at war with certain others." Participating in the battle, Hawkins secured 220 prisoners, and "they bartered on the said river and coast for one hundred more Negroes." [7]

At Rio de la Hacha, Hawkins demanded commercial privileges. When the authorities refused, he captured the town. A slave belonging to one of the officials told him where "chests of clothing and valuables were hidden." However, Hawkins maintained his conscientious interest in a fair bargain.

> The General ordered many Negoes, much linen and cloth, to be set ashore and did business with the burghers and sold them as many as one hundred and fifty Negroes and cloth and linens in exchange for gold and some pearls and some silver.[8]

Hawkins started for home in August, 1568. He ran into a tempest in the Florida channel. Scudding before the wind, the badly battered ships reached the island of San Juan de Ulua, opposite the port of Vera Cruz, in mid-September. An impressive Spanish fleet, carrying the new viceroy of Mexico, Don Martin Enriquez de Almansa arrived soon afterward. Hawkins, holding the entrance to the harbor, entered into negotiations with the viceroy concerning the admission of the galleons. An agreement was reached. But when the galleons entered the port, it was found that the English had seized the fortress of San Juan de Ulua. Enriquez ordered an attack, which resulted in a bad defeat for Hawkins. Most of his men and ships were captured. Only the *Minion* and the *Judith* got away; Hawkins was in command of the former; the captain of the *Judith* was Hawkins' cousin, Francis Drake.

Earlier in the same year, on June 6, an unusually impressive execution took place at Brussels. Count Edmont and Count Horn were beheaded by the order of the Council of Blood. The third leader of the independence movement in the Low Countries, William of Orange, had escaped and was gathering an army for the struggle against Spanish control. A *Fugger News-Letter* tells of the event: "When both gentlemen had been executed, their heads were placed on two iron spikes, where they remained till the afternoon at three." A few months later, a Fugger correspondent in Seville gave a rather garbled account of Hawkins' defeat.[9] The two events inaugurated the Anglo-Dutch offensive that was to deprive Spain of maritime supremacy.

Drake was probably not more than twenty-four years old at the time of the Vera Cruz battle. He had seen the wealth of Spain's American ports. He knew the strength of the Spanish galleons, but he also knew that the colonial towns were badly defended. It is possible that Drake spent some time in the Caribbean Sea in 1569 and 1570, operating with the French pirates who traded and fought in the Indies. In those years he may have learned another lesson which was to prove invaluable to him—that the organized bands of Maroons and Cimarrons were dependable allies in fighting the Spaniards.[10]

Drake left England in May, 1572, with the purpose of capturing the annual shipment of silver from Peru, which was carried across the Isthmus of Panama and loaded on galleons for the Atlantic voyage. He had two small ships, manned by 73 men and boys. On the night of July 28, this miniature army stormed the town of Nombre de Dios, escaping at dawn with a good deal of booty. For the next six months, Drake cruised and looted on the coast, carefully cementing his relationships with the Maroons and Cimarrons. In January, 1573, the Spanish fleet which was to receive the silver of the Potosi mines arrived at Nombre de Dios, to wait for the mule train which would bring the silver from the Pacific side of the Isthmus. Drake was also waiting for the mule train. He plunged into the jungle, his small force assisted by Indian and Negro allies.

Drake's men had to spend five months in the interior. But their carefully laid plans brought them ultimate success. The pack train traveled at night to avoid the heat of the day. There were two hundred mules, and their approach was heralded by the tinkling of the tiny bells worn on their collars. The English adventurers captured the whole treasure—the richest spoils of the era of piracy—and escaped in safety.

The feat would have been impossible without the aid of the Maroons, who received no satisfactory recompense for their assistance.

During the months of waiting and guerrilla fighting in the jungle, Drake saw the Pacific and—if we are to believe the familiar story—resolved to sail a ship on those forbidden seas. Whatever he may have said or thought on that occasion, he stood at the strategic center of the Americas—and he knew what that meant in terms of world trade and conquest. When Balboa gazed on the Pacific half a century earlier, he had a reasonably accurate vision of the riches of Peru and a considerably less accurate notion of trans-Pacific commerce with the Orient. Drake's geographical knowledge was greater. And the world which he wanted to conquer for England was different, politically and economically, from the world of fifty years ago.

What was the world scene that lay beyond the lazy breakers of the Gulf of Panama? Spain had just succeeded in linking Mexico with the Orient by way of the Philippines. Control of the islands was part of the Catholic world-plan. In November, 1564, Miguel Lopes de Legazpi left Mexico in command of four ships: he was under orders to colonize the Philippines and to investigate contact with Japan. He established a colony at Cebu and returned with a cargo of cinnamon. In 1571, the capital was moved from Cebu to Manila, and in the following year the Manila galleons began their annual voyages.

The Philippines were important as a base for trade with China and Japan, and because of their proximity to the Spice Islands. Commerce with the Far East had become a dominant factor in European affairs—so important that it was one of the principal points at issue in Holland's war of independence. Italian and German bankers financed Spanish and Portuguese overseas trade. But the ports of the Netherlands were the great European mart for Oriental goods, and especially for spices. In 1570, a German banker, Hermann Rott of Leipzig, made a contract with the Portuguese government which gave him control of the pepper imported from the Far East.[11] The cartel agreement interfered with the profits of Antwerp merchants at a time when the town's business was injured by the Duke of Alva's depredations and wholesale arrests. Dutch businessmen became less cautious in their covert financial aid to the struggle against Spain.

The future of Oriental trade was involved in the successes of the Dutch Sea Beggars, who captured Brill and Flushing in 1572. Since Flushing commanded the approach by sea to Antwerp, its possession affected the world system of commerce, of which Antwerp was the focal point.

Another link in the global network was the slave trade between Africa and America: 1570 is the date that marks the beginning of the heavy traffic in slaves to Brazil. The comparatively short distance between the Brazilian bulge and the African coast at Sierra Leone—1807 statute miles—was almost as important for the slave trade, with its perishable goods, as it became for airplane transport during the second world war. Brazil was also a factor in control of the South Atlantic and the routes to the Orient.

These commercial developments increased the interdependence of the two Catholic maritime powers, Spain and Portugal, who shared the colonial world between them by papal decree. They were mutually involved in the Orient, in America, and in the slave trade. Both countries were weakened by internal pressures and conflicts. The social deterioration in Portugal was to a large extent the penalty that the nation paid for its early mastery of the slave trade. Negro and other slaves were substituted for serfs or tenants on the estates of the Portuguese nobility. The result was widespread unemployment, the drift of the dispossessed people of the countryside to the cities where hunger and poverty caused frequent plagues. In the summer of 1569, 500 people a day died on the crowded streets of Lisbon, and the death rate was almost as high in the following years.

Slave labor was also used, although less disastrously, in Spain. The money troubles that afflicted Philip II weighed far more heavily upon his subjects; the pressure of the Inquisition was economic as well as cultural; it implemented the constant demands of church and state on the trading and industrial classes, and stifled protest against unemployment and industrial stagnation. While the unrest throughout the country was kept under control, a revolt of Moriscoes in 1568 desolated the province of Granada for two years.

One cannot tell whether young Francis Drake reviewed the world situation as he looked at the Pacific in 1573. But he knew Spain's weakness, for he was standing in the heart of her empire. He may have heard, from the French mariners with whom he was in contact, that during the previous summer the massacre of St. Bartholomew had marked the triumph of Catholic policy in France and ended any possibility of French colonial expansion for several decades. It is said that when Philip II heard the news that 2,000 Protestants had been murdered in Paris, he laughed for the first time in his gloomy life. The massacre was Philip's largest and most pleasurable *auto-da-fe.*

When Drake returned to England, the popular acclaim which greeted him and the personal welcome which he received from the queen were determined by changes in the world situation as well as by the extravagant profits of the voyage. With the Low Countries in revolt and France weakened by civil war, England could undertake maritime conquest on a global scale. Drake's dream of carrying English power into the Pacific was based on commercial realities: the development of European trade with the Orient and the recently established intercourse between Mexico and the Philippines seemed to suggest that trans-Pacific shipping might be a factor in commerce with Japan, China and the Spice Islands.

Drake sailed again in 1577. Going through the Straits of Magellan, he ravaged the coasts of Chile and Peru. Moving north, he landed in June, 1579, at a point which is probably Drake's Bay, a few miles above San Francisco. He named the country New Albion, exchanged gifts with the Indians, and went through a coronation ceremony in which the natives placed a feathered crown on his head.[12]

Having circumnavigated the globe, Drake reached England in the fall of 1580. The voyage had a far-reaching effect on English policy and culture. It was the modern equivalent of the Argonaut myth, the symbol of Britain's imperial hopes. Wood from the *Golden Hind,* Drake's ship, is still preserved as a holy relic at Oxford University.[13]

The enormous loot that Drake captured was less important than the political impact of his achievement: even though only one English expedition had embraced the world, it constituted a challenge to the Spanish-Catholic power that pointed to an imminent showdown. It hastened Spain's determination to seize Portugal, which was done in 1581 at the behest of the Vatican and the German bankers. A Fugger correspondent, in the Far East on pepper business, wrote from Cochin China in 1580:

> The King of Portugal despite all his power is too weak for this vast country. The King of Spain, if he but took possession of Portugal, would be the right King for these lands. He should take over the whole of India, all the kingdoms and provinces right into China, where it adjoins Tartary, and unite under his rule his Spanish India with the Portuguese municipalities.[14]

The writer was predicting an event which he knew was about to take place. The merger of Spain and Portugal satisfied Rome and reassured the nervous German financier. It promised unified Catholic control of the all-important Oriental trade, and eliminated wasteful competition in two essential products of Africa and America—slaves and sugar.

There was another lesson that England learned from Drake's voyage. It exploded the idea that the Pacific was an easy road to *El Dorado*. While there was wealth to be obtained in raids on the west coast of America, it was clear that the main battle with Spain would be fought in the Atlantic. A preliminary skirmish took place in Ireland, where Spanish troops landed to aid the Irish rebels in 1579.

The transatlantic struggle developed as a two-pronged English drive to colonize the North American mainland and to secure a base in the West Indies, with subordinate attacks—hit-and-run raids not intended to have any permanent effect—on Brazil and the Pacific American coast. In 1583, Humphrey Gilbert sailed to Newfoundland to make the first attempt at English settlement in the New World. Gilbert's death on the return voyage resulted in the transfer of his patent to Sir Walter Raleigh in 1584.

Raleigh sent out an expedition to find a suitable site for a plantation. The ships visited Roanoke Island and Pamlico Sound in North Carolina, bringing home glowing accounts of the climate and the fertility of the country: "We brought home also two of the Sauages being lustie men."[15] On the basis of these reports, Raleigh organized an ambitious colonizing venture, to the land which was now called

Virginia. The ships left, under the command of Sir Richard Grenville, in April, 1585.

The expected and carefully prepared break with Spain came in the summer, while the English colonists were building the first huts on Roanoke Island. In July, Philip seized all the English ships in Spanish ports. In August, Elizabeth entered into a formal alliance with the rebellious Netherlands. In September, Drake sailed for the West Indies with thirty vessels and 2,300 men.

The settlement sponsored by Raleigh and the armada led by Drake were parts of a coordinated American design. A base north of Florida was a means of safeguarding a stronghold in the West Indies. Recently discovered notes relating to the preparations for the Virginia voyage show that its sponsors were aware of the difficulties of the undertaking. There was careful consideration of the military problems, requiring that the colonists "haue furnytur to preuent the Inuasion of the Spanyardes." It was suggested that 800 soldiers would be needed, and that 100 men should stand guard day and night. A geographer, a chemist and a lapidary were required, as well as carpenters, masons, "sum of your myners of Cornwell," and "Sume exilent husband men, with all things appertayninge to husbandry." The necessity of conciliating the Indians was stressed: the colonists were "to use the naturall people there with all humanitie, curtesie, and freedom."[16]

The expedition to Virginia was not on the scale indicated in the notes, but it was based on the principles that had been outlined. It was predominantly military: there were between 400 and 600 soldiers, and few men of other trades. The mystery of the project is Grenville's decision to leave only 100 soldiers at Roanoke Island when he returned to England: this seems to have been an abandonment of the plan to establish a strong military base. The main factor, as in previous Spanish attempts to colonize on the Carolina coast, was the hostility of the Indians. The soldiers were not able to organize agricultural production quickly enough to provide a winter supply of food; hundreds of men could not live through the winter without the corn which the Indians were unwilling to provide.

Those who were left had trouble with the Indians, probably as a result of their desperate efforts to secure corn, and the next spring found them on the edge of starvation. Meanwhile, Drake had been successful in his raid on the West Indies. The help of the Cimarrons in Hispaniola enabled him to capture Santo Domingo. He held the city for a month, leaving only on the payment of a ransom of 25,000 ducats. He then proceeded to Cartagena, one of the richest ports on the Spanish Main, hoping to hold it as a permanent base for English operations. But his forces were insufficient; he contented himself with a ransom of 110,000 ducats, and then sailed north, pillaging St. Augustine, Florida, on his way to Roanoke Island.[17]

The English offensive was conducted on a world front in 1586. An expedition plundered the coast of Brazil. Thomas Cavendish started on the Pacific voyage which led to the capture of nineteen Spanish vessels, including the heavily loaded Manila galleon. The only British failure was in North Carolina. It is possible that Drake, being familiar with the plans of Raleigh and his associates, expected to find a strongly fortified military post when he reached Roanoke.[18] He found a few beleaguered and emaciated men, asking for passage to England. Drake carried them home. He may have pondered on the difficulties of North American settlement, illustrated in the contrast between the ragged survivors and the two million dollar booty of the West Indies that he carried with him.

Raleigh had learned that a North American settlement could not exist unless it was self-supporting. He tried to realize this objective in his third venture, sent out under the leadership of John White in July, 1587, 150 emigrants, including 17 women, made the trip. Raleigh advised White to settle on the shores of Chesapeake Bay, as a more sheltered location which was more suitable for agricultural pursuits. White made the mistake of returning to Roanoke instead of following Raleigh's instructions. But the location was not the only reason for the failure of the venture. It reached its destination too late to plant crops for use in the fall and winter. White seems to have realized, much too late, that the food situation was serious. After only a month, he hurried back to England for supplies.

But England was preparing for the Spanish invasion. White managed to equip two ships and set out in April, 1588, but the vessels were attacked by Spanish warships and had to return to port. It was two years after the defeat of the Armada before White could secure any attention or assistance. When he finally reached Roanoke in 1591, the settlement had vanished.

A great deal has been written about the mystery of the "Lost Colony." The colonists were the victims of the Spanish Armada, which cut off their supplies for four years. They might have existed for this time, if they had secured corn from the Indians and if they had received instruction in Indian methods of cultivating the land. It is probable that they made vain demands on the Indians for food, and that their attempts to take it by force led to reprisals and the destruction of the settlement.

The fate of Virginia Dare has enriched our folklore. The child, born soon after the colonists arrived at Roanoke, was the granddaughter of John White, whose daughter was married to one of his assistants, Ananias Dare. As the first English child born in the New World, Virginia Dare has become a symbol of the colonizing spirit. The treatment of the "Lost Colony" as a tragic enigma serves to conceal the simple reasons for its failure, and makes it a useful starting point for the mythology of Anglo-Saxon conquest. The newborn child and the presence of women seem to prove that the settlers had no aggressive intentions, and that the unknown horror of their deaths was due solely to the unreasoning cruelty of the Indians. But the problem of the colony's existence was a food problem. It was also a problem for the Indians, whose subsistence economy was often inadequate to supply their own needs. If the Indians did not have enough corn for themselves, they would be obliged to resist efforts to requisition their reserves. But if the colonists were starving, they would have been obliged to secure food from the natives by negotiation or force. A clash was unavoidable.

While Virginia Dare and her elders were dying in Carolina, the smashing of the Armada opened a new phase of England's world mission. The plan of conquest was popularized in a stream of books and pamphlets. The works of Richard Hakluyt and other writers were not merely factual records of voyages of discovery. The literature of exploration performed an ideological function; it developed a theory of history which is fully represented in Hakluyt's *Principall Navigations, Voyages and Discoveries of the English Nation,* first published in 1589, and enlarged to three volumes in 1600.

Hakluyt begins with King Arthur:

> In the yere of Christ 517, king Arthur in the second yeere of his reigne, having subdued all parts of Ireland, sailed with his fleet into Island (Iceland), and brought it and the people thereof under his subjection.[19]

Hakluyt's pageant of history is weighted heavily on the side of English achievement. We are surprised to learn that Constantine the

Great was born in England of an English mother. An Englishman discovered the island of Madeira in 1344. Of more immediate propaganda value is the statement that the first European voyage to the West Indies was made by Mado, son of Owen Gwyneth, Prince of North Wales:

> This Mado arriving in that Westerne country, unto which he came in the yere 1170, left most of his people there, and returning back for more of his owne nation, acquaintance and friends to inhabit that faire and large countrey, went thither againe with ten sailes . . .[20]

Thus England had a prior claim to possession of the Caribbean islands. When we smile at Hakluyt's errors, it is well to remember that the contemporary historical mythology accepted in the United States is only slightly less naïve, and that it still serves the grand design of Anglo-Saxon power which emerged in the English culture of the late sixteenth century.

8 : THE POTATO

Although the tree is proud
He only gives us wood,
But from the poor patat,
We get our daily food.[1]

THE SONG is sung by Dutch settlers in South Africa. One can undoubtedly find similar folk tributes to the potato in many corners of the world. The potato has traveled far from its Peruvian home, and its migrations have influenced social and cultural history.

The story that the edible roots were brought back to England by the refugees from Roanoke Island who returned with Drake in 1586 is probably a myth. But it is a suggestive myth, with historical implications that deserve consideration. It has gained sufficient credence to find its way into the *Encyclopedia Britannica:* in 1585 or 1586, according to the Eleventh Edition, tubers of the potato "were brought from what is now North Carolina to Ireland on the return of the colonists sent out by Sir Walter Raleigh, and were first cultivated on Sir Walter's estate near Cork."[2]

The literary origin of the story is to be found in Thomas Harriot's *Briefe and True Report of the new found Land of Virginia,* published in 1588, which describes a Virginia potato, "with roots as large as a walnut and others much larger . . . they are good food either boiled or roasted."[3] John Gerard published a woodcut of a potato in his *Herball or generall historie of Plantes* in 1597. Gerard called it "Battata virginian sive Virginianorum, et Pappus, Potatoes of Virginia."[4]

Gerard made a distinction between the Virginia vegetable and the "common potato." The common variety was the sweet potato, which he speaks of buying on "the Exchange in London."[5] The reference to the sweet potato as the common kind is confusing, but more perplexing is the suggestion that the ordinary potato came from North

America. The Indians in what is now Virginia did not cultivate potatoes at all, and the potato which is at present called "Irish" came from the Andean region of South America. The sweet potato has a rather obscure history. It may have been cultivated in southern China in the fourth and third centuries B.C. It was in use by the natives of the West Indies when the Spaniards arrived, and it is said to have been grown in Florida.[6] There is a possibility that the colony at Roanoke Island obtained sweet potatoes from some other part of the coast. But if the potatoes which later became known as "Irish" were brought back to England and planted in Ireland in 1586, they must have been obtained from some trading vessel or gathered by Drake and his men as part of the booty of the Spanish Main.[7]

Whatever the facts may be, there can be no doubt that the description of the potato as a typical product of Virginia was inaccurate, and that this fanciful identification performed a cultural function. In spite of the failure of Raleigh's colonizing ventures, it was recognized that the North American mainland offered the best opportunities for securing large and presumably rich territories in the New World. In asserting that Englishmen had brought the potato directly from Virginia, Harriot and Gerard adhered to the general principle that England was first in all matters of colonial discovery. Since the potato was already known in England, it was useful to associate it with the land named in honor of the queen.

In *The Merry Wives of Windsor,* Falstaff climaxes his love-making to Mistress Ford with the exclamation: "Let the sky rain potatoes."[8] The play was written in 1600, an outburst of harsh ribaldry that came just before the Essex conspiracy and the dark questioning of *Hamlet.* It is said that *The Merry Wives* was written at Elizabeth's request, as she wanted to see Falstaff in love. In obeying the royal command, Shakespeare made the fat knight a mirror of the times; his speech is full of classical allusions and genuine learning, but all the resources of the imagination are turned to ignoble uses, to lechery and greed. When Falstaff writes to Mistress Page, he says: "She is a region in Guiana, all gold and bounty." He is going to have both the wives: "They shall be my East and West Indies, and I will trade to them both."[9]

When Falstaff spoke of potatoes raining from the sky, he touched the feeling of the miraculous that still surrounded the humble vegetable. It was both a marvelous novelty and a lowly root that was

America's gift to the undernourished peoples of the world. There is a curious appropriateness in the legend that makes the potato a link between Virginia and Ireland. The myth pointed to a later stage of history, when failures of the potato crops were to be a driving force in Irish emigration to America. The connection between the country across the Irish Sea and the continent on the other side of the Atlantic was already established in the English thought of the later sixteenth century. Hakluyt made Ireland the starting point of British expansion, beginning with King Arthur and continuing with King John, who "conducted a fleet of 500 ships into Ireland, and subdued it unto himselfe."[10]

It needed no historical justification to prove to the Elizabethan mind that Ireland was England's first "plantation," the initial experiment in the exploitation of foreign land and labor. The all-out battle with Spain for control of the Atlantic area began in Ireland in 1579. Having expelled the Spanish soldiers and suppressed the rebellion, the English pacification of Ireland was almost as furious as the Spanish conquest of the West Indies—with the same economic incentives. People and cattle were indiscriminately killed. Crops were burned to starve the inhabitants into submission. Edmund Spenser, secretary to the Lord Deputy during the campaign, wrote that the rebels "looked like anatomies of death; they spoke like ghosts crying out of their graves; they did eat the dead carrions, happy where they could find them."[11]

The author of the *Faery Queen* was not stirred to compassion by the Irish tragedy. Since famine and sword had not crushed the rebels, he recommended that strong military reinforcements be sent over, that the people be given a fixed period of twenty days in which to render obeisance to the English authority; those who failed to submit were to be hunted like wild beasts in the winter when food was scarce: "If they be well followed one winter, ye shall have little work to do with them the next summer." The plan must be followed relentlessly—"no remorse or drawing back for the sight of any such rueful object as must thereupon follow, nor for compassion of their calamities."[12]

This was an English poet, speaking with a high consciousness of his nation's destiny. Spenser shared in the profits of the campaign of 1580. 500,000 acres were seized and distributed to servants of the queen. The poet secured 3,000 acres and a fine house.[13] Raleigh was another beneficiary of the war, receiving the estate near Cork on which he is supposed to have planted Virginia potatoes in 1586.

The general use of the potato in Ireland came at a later date, and it probably arrived by a more circuitous route. The Peruvian vegetable is mentioned by Pedro Cieca in his *Cronica de Peru,* published in Spain in 1553. Cieca called it by its Indian name, *battata* or *papa.* It was introduced in Europe at about that time, being carried from Spain to Italy, then to Central Europe and Flanders, and thence across the English channel.[14]

Its wide acceptance as a staple diet was deferred until the pressure of poverty and hunger forced its adoption as a crop that could be grown more cheaply than wheat, with a larger yield per acre. The movement of potato production is like a barometer recording the course of class conflict. It became important in England shortly after the Restoration, when the lower classes paid heavily, in reduced wages and limited rights, for the failure of the Cromwellian Revolution.[15] In 1663, the Royal Society recommended the planting of potatoes in all parts of the kingdom to prevent famine.[16] The advice was not followed with any enthusiasm in England, but the Irish peasantry became increasingly dependent on the half-acre or acre of "potato ground" which provided the laborer and his family with their means of subsistence.[17]

The potato was carried back to America from Ireland in the early years of the eighteenth century. It is said to have been introduced at Londonderry, New Hampshire, by the Scotch Presbyterians who came from Ulster to settle in New England in 1719.[18] But it was not popular: in Europe and America, people associated it with extreme poverty, and were unwilling to concede that it was a satisfactory substitute for wheat or corn. As late as 1740, apprentices asked masters to stipulate that their service should not include a compulsory diet of potatoes.[19]

In Europe, the potato was introduced in the period of social tension that preceded the American and French Revolutions. The people opposed its use. Frederick the Great sent soldiers to force his Prussian subjects to plant the tubers. In France in 1771, the Academy of Besancon offered a prize for a crop that would take the place of cereals in case of famine. Parmentier exhibited potatoes, and received an award of over 100 acres of land from Louis XV. The king told Parmentier that he had "found bread for the poor," and Marie Antoinette, who was sixteen years old and had just married the Dauphin, wore potato flowers in her hair.[20]

History was soon to prove that the king was a little oversanguine about the benefits that the people would derive from the potato. We may wonder whether Marie Antoinette remembered the flowers when she made her ill-advised suggestion some two decades later that the people eat cake.

Irish experience in the eighteenth century proved that the use of the potato in the manner that was planned by the rulers of Germany and France, as a means of keeping the rural laborers alive without the expense of bread or cereals, brought social disaster. The monoculture of the potato was the mark of Ireland's degradation. But it was also a creative factor in the culture of the people. Personal and family relations were built around its cultivation. When the crop failed, families were broken, death shadowed the land. But out of the tragedy of recurrent failures, came the great movements of people across the Atlantic, and the rebirth of freedom in Ireland.

The seeds of these future developments were sown in the last years of the sixteenth century. The experience of Raleigh's Virginia expeditions proved the difficulty of developing self-sustaining agricultural communities on the North American coast. There was hunger in Ireland, and in England, as well as in Virginia. In spite of the increasing social tensions in Great Britain, English adventurers continued the search for *El Dorado.*

In 1595, as the failure of the wheat crop brought a dangerous rise in English food prices, two expeditions set out for Spanish America. Twenty-seven vessels, commanded jointly by Francis Drake and John Hawkins, son of the slave trader, sailed for the West Indies. But Spain had strengthened her defenses. Hawkins died during an unsuccessful attack on San Juan de Puerto Rico. Defeated again near Havana, Drake retreated to Nicaragua, where malaria and dysentery swept through the fleet. The plague killed Drake in January, 1596.

Raleigh also sailed in 1595. His voyage was literally a trip to *El Dorado.* Raleigh had a map and detailed directions for reaching the golden city. The documents had been stolen from a Spanish ship. A certain Juan Martin, who had spent ten years with the Indians in the interior of Venezuela, came out of the jungle in 1592. Since there was still intense interest in *El Dorado,* Martin obtained brief notoriety by giving the Spanish colonial authorities a vivid description of the kingdom. He said it was located near the headwaters of the Caroni River, a tributary of the Orinoco, and that the chief city, called *Manoa,* was so vast that he had walked through the golden streets for two days to reach the palace in the center of the town. He prepared a notarial paper reciting his findings. It was drawn up in duplicate and sent to Spain in different ships. One of these vessels was captured, and the papers fell into Raleigh's hands.[21]

Raleigh's quest for *Manoa* was conducted on an extremely modest scale: for various political and personal reasons, he had incurred the queen's disfavor. He was able to equip only four ships, with 100 soldiers. He reached the Orinoco, and went up the river as far as the junction with the Caroni. But his force was too small to risk further exploration. He heard reports of a gold mine somewhere in the neighborhood, and returned to England without booty. He tried to appease the queen's anger by writing an imaginative, discursive account of "the large, rich and beautiful Empyre of Guiana," peppered with learned references to the wealth of the Incas and the probability that some of it was preserved in the city of *Manoa.*[22]

Elizabeth was not disposed to accept gems of literature as a satisfactory alternative to tangible properties. Raleigh's book was a success; it was a colorful addition to the mythology of empire, and was to have a considerable later influence on British policy. But Raleigh's suggestions for South American conquest had no practical value in 1596. His description of "the great and golden Citie of Manoa" was a curious commentary on the hunger that haunted London's streets.

Hunger was everywhere. The pursuit of *El Dorado,* ranging from Greenland to the Straits of Magellan, proved again the old truth that the treasure of the world is the food that sustains life. Human beings starved in the Caribbean Paradise, in the terraced highlands of Peru, in Europe and Asia.

The hunger that created social conflict in the last decade of the sixteenth century was, to a considerable extent, man-made. The *real* quest for *El Dorado* was not an adventure in the wilderness: it was "the restless never-ending process of profit-making" [23] which accompanied the rise of capitalism, and which brought increasing misery to the mass of the population and an irrepressible conflict between the old feudal rulers and the new bourgeoisie for the division of the spoils. The heart of the struggle was in Europe, but there were interrelated disturbances in other lands.

The Fugger *News-Letters,* being written by money men whose business depended on accurate information, especially about disorders that threatened industry or trade, placed an emphasis on social conditions that is not found in conventional historiography. A tour of Europe with the Fugger correspondents portrays the realities of the time. In 1590, Paris was under siege by a French army: the city was held by Spanish troops, sent to France to support the Catholic cause, and it was surrounded by the soldiers of Henry IV. A Fugger *News-Letter* written in August reported "great hunger in Paris; a pound of white bread costs half a crown. . . . Rumour has it that people are eating mice, cats and dogs." [24]

In the same summer, Rome and other Italian cities were devastated by the plague. A letter in August tells of eight thousand deaths in Rome, and terrible mortality in Leghorn and Pisa. There was civil strife in Spain, where the Inquisition terrorized the people of the cities. A letter from Saragossa in May, 1591, tells how "the population of the whole town rose in arms with shouts of 'Liberty'" to protest the activities of the Inquisition. "More than six thousand men foregathered," and "two servants of the tribunal were killed before order could be restored." [25]

In Germany, popular anger was directed against the Protestant merchants, who were held responsible for high prices and low wages. A letter in February, 1592, reports a riot in Leipzig, where a "common mob of artisans and shop-apprentices" gathered to protest against their destitution and the recent dismissal of "near on seventeen hundred persons." [26]

There was a more serious outbreak a few years later in Austria, where the empire and the church exerted unbearable pressure on the lower classes. The rebellion lasted two years and was virtually a renewal of the German peasant war. A Fugger report on November 13, 1595, tells of a pitched battle at Linz:

> Six hundred men on both sides are said to have fallen, but victory remained with the peasants, who pursued the lansquenets as far as Freistadt. . . .
>
> There be posted up everywhere notices for the levying of troops, for the peasants are waxing ever stronger. They are said to be encamped not far from here, forty thousand strong, near the Danube. . . .
>
> They have most stately and experienced leaders who keep strict discipline, so that much might be learned by us from them.[27]

A letter from Vienna quoting market prices for foodstuffs in the city throws some light on the rural disorders. Bread, meat and wine were plentiful, and the bread was large and white, but "everything costs a pretty penny." [28] In April, 1596, the peasant war shifted to lower Austria: the peasants could not be subdued, although "many of them are being killed, hanged and made prisoners by the cavalry." Vintagers in different localities struck simultaneously, refusing "to work any longer for their old wages." They gathered in arms, but a strong force of soldiers and landowners fell upon them "before daybreak and immediately hanged a drummer and six ringleaders." At the same time, the trouble in Upper Austria continued:

> They seem bewitched, for as soon as the word is given, even in this cold, they leave their wives and children, hasten from their houses and farms, yet attacking neither towns, castles, nor even villages.

The movement was broken in the summer of 1597. A letter from Vienna tells of the punishment of some of the leaders:

> Yesterday the chief ringleaders of the rebellious peasants, the cooper and the tailor, together with two others, a provost and a commander, were executed. . . . The cooper was quartered alive, and the two others beheaded. . . . The cooper died unrepentant in his Lutheran heresy.[29]

The Austrian rebellion is of great historical importance as the prelude to the Thirty Years' War and the revelation of its social origins. The connection is evident if we turn to Bohemia: just two weeks after the Vienna executions (on September 8), a letter reports a rising of the "Bohemian rabble" in Neustadt near Prague; a few thousand people, "with firearms, iron tools, flails and other murderous weapons" attacked the Walloon mercenaries employed by the emperor to keep order in Bohemia; more than fifty of the soldiers were killed, their horses and weapons were stolen, and the emperor himself was aroused at ten o'clock at night to take measures for the suppression of the rebellion.[30]

Bohemia had been the scene of the first great movement of peasants and laborers at the time of the Hussite wars; the disturbances in Eastern Europe at the end of the sixteenth century connected the earlier rebellions with the approaching continental conflict between the Catholics and Protestants that was to begin as a national revolt of the Bohemian people.

1597 was also the year of renewed civil war in Ireland. Among the

Irish casualties was the fine house received by Edmund Spenser for his services against the previous rebellion. The poet's dwelling was burned to the ground, but he escaped and returned to England to demand sterner measures against the rebels.

The decade was not altogether peaceful in the Western Hemisphere. In Mexico, the Jesuits were slowly and painfully extending the colony's northern boundaries. Gonzalo de Tapia began the organization of the Sinaloa area on the Pacific coast in 1591. In 1594, he was beaten to death in an Indian uprising. A Fugger letter written from Venice in August, 1597, reported a rebellion in Peru, in which 15,000 Indians were joined by 500 Spaniards: "This is bad news not only for Spain but for the merchants, as gold and silver arrives from Peru, conveyed hither by the fleet, and this will now be prevented by this rising." [31]

The letter points to the obvious connection between the disorders in America and European events. Occurrences in other parts of the globe were not so closely related to the beginnings of capitalism in Europe; nevertheless, similar tendencies, proceeding in part from local causes and in part from pressures exerted by the world competition of the more advanced nations, were evident in other areas.

In Russia, the conflict between the centralized national power and the landholding nobility placed added burdens on the peasantry. Ivan IV was known as "the dread" because of his uncompromising methods of securing the submission of the boyars. The big landlords protected their economic position by increasing the exploitation of the serfs. After Ivan's death in 1584, Boris Godunov tried to conciliate the boyars by regularizing the conditions of serfdom: in 1592 and 1593, there was a census of land and population, and all peasants registered as belonging to a certain landholder were henceforth considered his adscripts or serfs. In 1597, a ukase was issued, establishing a five-year period in which runaway peasants were subject to seizure and return to their owners.[32] The pressure on the peasants prepared for the revolutionary struggles that were to bring Russia's "time of troubles" early in the seventeenth century.

In India, the concentration of governmental power during the reign of Akbar the Great led to a detailed survey of agricultural resources: the yield of every acre was estimated, and the peasants were forced to pay one-third of the gross produce that their fields were supposed to yield. Akbar's levies brought a revenue of £16,500,000.

In Japan, Toyotomi Hideyoshi completed the subjugation of the feudal barons in 1587, and invaded Korea in 1592; the attempt to establish an Asiatic "co-prosperity sphere," like the similar plan in the twentieth century, was designed to solve internal contradictions by external conquest. The disastrous six-year campaign in Korea and China is said to have cost the lives of 260,000 soldiers. But its cost to the Japanese peasants, whose labor was the main source of the wealth that financed the enterprise, is beyond calculation.

The social consequences of these political and economic movements, in their relationship to the rise of capitalism in Europe, will be discussed in later chapters. For the present, it is enough to note that the revelation of the riches of the Western Hemisphere—gold and silver and agricultural products—had the effect of increasing, rather than alleviating, the world's hunger.

The history of the potato, its gradual dissemination, its service to humanity, the retribution it claimed from those who were solely dependent on its use, the influence it exerted on conflicts and migrations of people, suggest the interaction of hunger and politics, poverty and power, on a world scale. As Hamlet posed a moral problem, the problem of Man's destiny, millions of people faced the ultimate question—

> Whether 'tis nobler in the mind to suffer
> The slings and arrows of outrageous fortune,
> Or to take arms against a sea of troubles. . . .[33]

Many labored and suffered. And many took arms.

PART IV

The European Background of English Colonization

1593–1607

1 : PROLOGUE IN VENICE

THE RISE of the bourgeoisie is generally described by historians as a movement covering a period of approximately three hundred years, from 1450 to 1750.

These years witnessed the end of the Elizabethan period and the developing conflict between the crown and the bourgeoisie in England, the re-establishment of Catholic power after decades of civil strife in France, the deterioration of Spain's European and world position, the rise of the Dutch Republic, the founding of the first permanent English colonies in North America.

The cultural history of these pivotal years may properly begin with the intellectual experience of an Englishman who traveled in Europe during the last years of the sixteenth century. Edwin Sandys was thirty-two years old, and had spent his young manhood in leisurely study, when he began the six years of his continental sojourn in 1593. As the second son of the Archbishop of York, Sandys' contact with human misery was probably limited to intellectual awareness of the problem and occasional observation of the way in which the poor lived. His continental tour could hardly have brought him closer to the sight, sound and smell of poverty than hasty passage through urban slums, and discussion, among people of his own kind, of the dangerous discontents among the lower classes. However, the moral and political questions that preoccupied Sandys were related to the deep sickness of European society—a sickness that endangered the whole structure of power. In the background of legal and diplomatic conflicts were the millions whose productive labor was the prize for which the privileged classes were fighting.

Three major political events provide a key to the European situation in 1593: Dutch armies were driving Spanish troops from the soil of the northern provinces. In France, Henry IV, who had been educated as a Protestant and had fought for the Huguenot cause, announced his conversion to Catholicism. In Italy, the exiled Italian philosopher, Giordano Bruno, was unwise enough to visit Venice, where he was arrested by the Inquisition and carried to a Roman dungeon.

The last incident is of the clearest cultural significance. Yet it can be understood only in connection with the Dutch and French situations. The victory of Catholicism in France strengthened the papacy and intensified the activities of the Inquisition, resulting in Bruno's arrest. But the Dutch successes made it inadvisable to execute Bruno, and his fate remained in suspension for seven years. The principles of rational thought also remained in suspension; it seemed as if the creative life of man was being weighed in the scales that might tip toward Calvinism or Catholicism.

Although Giordano Bruno was not a Protestant, he achieved a philosophic synthesis of the Protestant ideology. He reduced the humanist aspirations of the Renaissance to an organic system of thought, crystallizing the viewpoint of the class which intended to profit by the limited, and carefully controlled, application of the law of reason—not to man and the universe, but to the advancement of its class interest.

Bruno left Italy in 1576, when the afterglow of the Renaissance was fading to dusk. The Catholic Counter Reformation, recognizing the weakness of Spain, and the growing strength of Holland and England, could no longer afford to make even superficial concessions to humanism. It relied increasingly on the Inquisition, the Index, and the questionable methods of the Jesuits, to enforce cultural uniformity. Bruno was twenty-eight when he escaped from Rome in order to avoid persecution for his unorthodox opinions. He traveled widely, but his definitive works were written in England in the years just before the defeat of the Armada, when the approaching showdown with Spain encouraged anticlericalism.

Bruno took the astronomical science of Copernicus as the basis for his system of philosophy. He held that society is governed by laws which are as reasonable and knowable as the laws governing the universe, but he defines social laws in terms of moral virtues and wise leadership—the qualities on which the Calvinist bourgeoisie based its claim to a divinely ordained authority over less privileged classes. Especially characteristic of Bruno's class viewpoint is his treatment of *prudence* and *providence* as two aspects of the same thing: the careful man can take advantage of the tricks of fate, turning chance happenings to his advantage. *Wisdom* is thus related to the ability of the businessman to accumulate capital and master the uncertainties of fortune.

The whole course of modern philosophy as a generalized defense of property rights is foreshadowed in Bruno. His work reveals the origin of the Protestant emphasis on the rights of the individual: it prefigures the concept of all social organization as based upon property rights—which therefore determine the individual's place in society and substitute a money stratification for the hierarchies of feudalism.

While Bruno was delimiting the realm of reason as the fenced and guarded property of the bourgeoisie, a hysterical mysticism swept Spain. A sense of unreality and mystic compulsion was nurtured, and strictly supervised, by the church. Religious ecstasy could, if not controlled, achieve a personal intensity which was too emotional and rebellious to fit the authoritarian pattern. Even Luis Ponce de Leon, greatest of the devotional writers, was reported to the Inquisition in the fifteen-seventies, and spent four years in prison. Like Dostoyevsky in the nineteenth century, Ponce de Leon learned the harsh lesson of the dungeon.

The structure of Catholic power, which had never fully recovered from the effects of the panic of 1559, received another blow in the defeat of the Spanish armada in 1588. The Vatican relied increasingly on the Inquisition and the Jesuits in order to meet the threat. In 1591, the pope reaffirmed the extraordinary powers of the Society of Jesus, including the right to excommunicate anyone except the pope himself or one of his legates. At the same time, the general of the order, Claude Aquaviva, secured papal endorsement of the system of education outlined in the *Ratio atque institutio studiorum,* still obligatory in Jesuit colleges, which provided that no novel opinions could be discussed, no debate could be tolerated; the eternal rightness of what is taught must be taken for granted.

Jesuit rules and regulations could not arrest the progress of Holland's armies. But the Jesuits had a hand in the French king's sudden conversion to Catholicism in July, 1593. Henry IV had fought for the Huguenot cause with Coligny and had barely escaped death in the massacre of St. Bartholomew's Eve. His conversion has been ascribed to his desire to end internecine strife and restore order in the kingdom. This interpretation ignores the class interests which were at stake in the civil war. Henry deliberately abandoned his alliance with the bourgeoisie and turned to collaboration with Rome and the Jesuits. The move was affected, not only by the internal situation in France, but by the growing strength of the bourgeoisie in Holland and other parts of Europe. Henry feared, not without reason, that the Huguenots might follow the Dutch example, and dispense altogether with the expensive apparatus of royal absolutism.

The shift to Catholicism in France had the effect on the European balance of power which Henry must have foreseen and intended. It gave the church another sphere of influence in the west in the strategic area between Spain and the Netherlands. France, with its seaports on the channel as well as on the Mediterranean, its Newfoundland fishing fleets, its colonial ambitions, its thriving centers of finance and industry, had almost been won by the bourgeoisie. In restoring the ecclesiastical influence, Henry acted in accordance with his fundamental class interest. Monarchial feudalism could no longer be maintained in France without clerical support.

This was the moment at which Sandys began his European sojourn. It was also the moment of Bruno's visit to Venice. There was strong opposition to the papacy in the Italian cities, and the opposition was especially outspoken in the great seaport on the Adriatic. It was for this reason that Bruno dared to visit the city. But his arrival coincided with the unexpected Catholic coup in France. If it had not been for this event, the Inquisition might have hesitated to act against him and the city administration might have been able to protect him. He was taken to Rome, but his fate was a matter of high policy. It remained in the balance for seven years, while the Vatican weighed the rapid shifts in the European situation, the strength of Holland, the economic difficulties of the Spanish crown, the disturbances in the Hapsburg dominions, the vacillations of French and English diplomacy.

During this period Sandys spent a good deal of time in Venice, where he enjoyed the friendship of Paolo Sarpi, the Venetian scholar and publicist. As the intellectual leader of the anticlerical party in Venice, Sarpi adapted Bruno's philosophy to the specific interests of the Republic. The link between Bruno's speculations and the views of

John Locke is provided by Sarpi, whose political writings, translated and published in England in the years preceding the Cromwellian Revolution, were part of the ideological preparation for the English bourgeoisie's seizure of power.

There is reason to suppose that Sarpi anticipated the sensationalism of Locke, but his treatises on science and philosophy have been lost, and can be judged only by the reports of his contemporaries. Sarpi's political views are vigorously defined in his historical and polemical works. The *History of the Council of Trent,* published in London in 1619, is an analysis of the aims and policies of the Counter Reformation, a notable advance in the development of historiography as an interpretation of social forces. In his *History of the Quarrels of Pope Paul V with the State of Venice,* published in England in 1626, Sarpi dealt with current history, describing the successful Venetian defiance of the papal authority which he led in 1607. Sarpi showed little respect for the divine right of kings: he spoke of the tendency of princes "to write God himselfe the Author of all their usurpations." He was bitter against the Jesuits, describing them as "Janizaries" of the Spanish crown. He held Spain chiefly responsible for the "present miserable Face of Europe"; he repeated the famous Las Casas denunciation of Hapsburg colonial policy. He wrote that Spain, "under shadow of Converting the *West Indies* hath depopulated them, baptized these poor *Paynims* in their owne bloud, and to make them *Christians,* hath made them no men."[1]

In championing the rights of Venice, Sarpi proclaimed the separation of church and state: "As it appertaineth not to the *Venetians,* to Governe the *State* of the *Church,* no more doth it appertaine to *Ecclesiastiques* to governe the *State* of *Venice.*"[2]

These words, published in England in the second year of the reign of Charles I, were heady wine to the Commons in its struggle against a monarchial power which used ecclesiastical sanctions and ecclesiastical courts to enforce its will.

Sandys wrote his *Europae Speculum, or A View or Survey of the State of Religion in the Westerne parts of the world,* during his Venetian visit, with Sarpi's advice and guidance. The book contained such inflammable material that it was inadvisable to publish it, and it was circulated in manuscript form. When an edition printed from a stolen manuscript appeared in 1605, at the moment when Sandys was assuming leadership in the parliamentary attack on the crown, the author managed to secure the suppression of the book. It was not published until 1629, the year of Sandys' death, when the pirated edition was reprinted at the Hague. The English edition which came out on the eve of the Revolution in 1638, described the previous publication as "most shamefully falsified and false Printed." [3]

The work could have caused trouble for Sandys, because his attack on the Catholic structure of power touched fundamental questions relating to the nature of the state, pointing to the misuse of power under monarchial feudalism, questioning the divine right of kings and suggesting, at least by implication, that Calvinism offered a more rational system of power. Although the book's title proposed a survey of the whole religious field, Sandys dealt only with Catholicism; at the end, he notes that he had intended to "proceede to the CHURCHES REFORMED," but had decided to "deferre the rest till some other occasion." [4] The decision was politically expedient, for he had already made his views on monarchial power dangerously clear.

Sandys' recognition that kings needed the church in order to support their claim to absolute authority was aptly illustrated. His observation was to find confirmation in England a few years later when James Stuart countered the demands of the bourgeoisie with attempts to conciliate Spain and the Vatican. There is a note of prophecy in Sandys' charge that the papacy had "so deepely engaged and interested from time to time the greatest MONARCHS of Christendome, in the upholding of that state, that without the Papacy sundry of them have no hope, and some no title, to continue in their own dominions." [5]

Sandys spoke of the Jesuits as "that super-politick and irrefragable order." [6] He wrote of the decline of Spain: "their Cities remain wholly peopled with women, having some old men among them, and many young children, whereof the grave attends the one, and forraigne service the other." [7] These opinions were similar to those expressed by Sarpi; they were also the common coin of Protestant argumentation.

Sandys reflected the feeling of many Protestants that the Vatican would resort to wholesale violence in order to protect its interests. The fear seemed to be justified by the situation in France, where the civil strife that had raged for decades threatened to erupt again at any moment. Sandys wrote that priests in Paris were asking Catholics to be prepared to die for their faith "if neede should require," and that Paris was troubled by "a general rumour and terrour of new Massacres." He saw a danger in the multitude of priests and friars—

"if the Papacy being reduced to any termes of extremity, should resolve to PUT THEM IN ARMES for his final refuge and succour."[8]

Sandys made these observations when he was in a Catholic country, and while he was under the influence of a scholar who was noted for the sobriety of his judgment and who was himself a member of a religious order. The fears which he expressed show the degree of tension that existed in Europe, and the attitudes that molded his later career and the conduct of the class he represented.

Sandys devoted the main body of his book to an analysis of the deteriorating social and economic situation in Italy. The country was still the richest in the West:

> Yet considering that the wealth there is so ill digested, and unequally divided in the body thereof, "the infinite and ever-sucking veines of their taxes and imposts carrying all the bloud to the higher parts, and leaving the lower readie to fainte, to starve and whither" that it may be truly said, the rich men in ITALY are the richest, and the poore the poorest things that any one Countrie can yeeld againe.[9]

Sandys held that the corrupt structure of ecclesiastical power was directly responsible. The popes tended to "fall into ryot able to ruine any Prince."[10] Religious houses function "as very spunges to drinke what juyce they can from the people."[11] Sandys emphasized the restrictions placed on culture: "Neither is it lawfull in Italy to carrie bookes about from one place to another, without allowance of them from the Inquisitors."[12]

Sandys showed a judicious understanding of the connection between the corruption of the church and the sterile censorship which it attempted to enforce. He spoke for a young class which was grappling boldly with the problem of power. Many of the passages in his book are a prophetic forecast of the future course of Catholic policy: the church had already embarked on the drive for the total control of culture, which is historically noteworthy in two respects: no state or institution has ever attempted to control thought and communication on such a scale over such an extended period of time; no campaign for the suppression of ideas has ever been a more signal failure.

The Index of prohibited books, which was already extensive in Sandys' time, was to encompass the whole intellectual and creative life of the modern world; among the 7,000 to 8,000 titles which were contained in the 1930 edition of the Index we find the works of Luther, Rabelais, Erasmus, Bacon, Milton, Hobbes, Descartes, Leibnitz, Dumas, Flaubert, Locke, Pascal, Voltaire, Rousseau, Spinoza, Defoe, Kant, Heine, Taine, Bergson.[13]

It is difficult to imagine what the culture of our time would be like if the prohibition of these books had been even partially effective in preventing their circulation and use. Sandys noted the ineffectiveness of censorship, even in the places where the Inquisition functioned with prodigal energy: . . . "This too rigorous cutting of all Authors tongues, leaving nothing which may savour any freedome of spirit, or give any satisfaction for understanding of times past" tended to "raise such a longing for the right Authours in the mindes of all men" as to encourage illegal publication.[14] Sandys observed that there was a strong Protestant movement in Italy: "Some of that sort there are scattered in all places: especially in the State of VENICE." [15]

While suppressing books that were deemed subversive, the church encouraged literary propaganda ("yea some of their bookes or passages illustrated also with picture") [16] which portrayed the Protestants as "Church-robbing Politicians and Church-razing souldiers . . . innovators of orders, underminers of Government, troublers of states, overturners of Christendome." [17]

Propaganda against innovators follows a depressingly familiar pattern. It is discomforting to find that all the things which are said about Communists today were said about the Protestants three and a half centuries ago. The Italian public was told that Lutherans and Calvinists "vilifie our Lady, saying plainely shee was no better than one of their owne wives. . . . Where-ever they come, they either raze or robbe Churches, and make stables of them . . . that in ENGLAND they have neither Churches nor forme of Religion, nor serve God in any way . . . that their Souldiers are very Canniballs." [18]

Ever since the days of Petrarch, national unity had been a central theme of Italian thought. And now the national hopes were blighted; the bourgeoisie had not been able to break the stranglehold of the church. The arrest of Bruno was more than the persecution of an individual; it was the suppression of the creative force that had made Italy the most productive and technologically advanced nation in Europe. While Bruno waited and Sandys labored on his manuscript, the Vatican succeeded in annexing the city of Ferrara to the papal states. This occurred in 1598; the result was an object lesson in the blessings of ecclesiastical control. Ferrara lost its former prosperity;

trade and industry were discouraged by prohibitive taxes; within a short time, the city lost two-thirds of its population.

In 1598, the murder of Francesco Cenci by his children placed a spotlight on the corruption in the inner circle of the Vatican. Cenci was an Italian nobleman who had intimate and questionable economic dealings with Pope Clement VIII. The scandal which the case occasioned reflected the uneasiness of the time. The moral climate in Rome was no worse than it had been in the days of the Borgias. But Cenci's career was drab and sordid; it had none of the color of Renaissance crimes; he had operated in the manner of a modern gangster, receiving the protection of the papacy in return for services rendered. The sordid economic background of the crime was more significant than its sensational sex aspect. The case was more disturbing to the prestige of the church than earlier scandals, in which the popes had been more directly involved, because the church was on the defensive. The morality, as well as the money of the bourgeoisie, had become a force to be reckoned with.

In the same year, 1598, Philip II of Spain died, leaving the Spanish crown's finances in an incredibly bad condition. In the years preceding his death, Philip had resorted to desperate expedients to get money. He had followed the usual procedure of cancelling debts to the Fuggers and other bankers; the Fuggers took a loss of 2,300,000 ducats, while Italian financiers lost 6,500,000 ducats.[19] But the cancellations did not remedy the situation. Philip tried to get a large loan from Portuguese merchants, but they were understandably worried about adequate security. The king then resorted to inflation, raising the value of the *real* from thirty maravedi to forty maravedi.[20]

All these efforts were in vain. A Fugger *News-Letter* written two months after Philip's death reported that he left his son facing "great penury," and that the new king was trying to borrow enough cash to cover his expenses until the arrival of the silver fleet—which was due in January, 1599.[21]

The Spanish monetary situation was so desperate that it enabled the merchants of Amsterdam to move boldly against Spain's global power. Early in 1598, fourteen ships left Holland for India. A Fugger communication from Amsterdam on July 24, 1599, told of the return of four of the vessels, laden with pepper, cloves, nutmeg, and cinnamon: "They will make yearly a great trade in spices and cause many others to alter their course." [22]

The Dutch achievement was indeed destined to affect the polity and culture of Europe. East Indian pepper had been a major factor in the beginning of the Dutch war of independence; it had started when a German monopoly, organized in 1570, threatened to exclude the merchants of the Netherlands from the profits of the trade. This was virtually at an end when Holland was able to establish its own monopoly, raising the price of pepper from three shillings to six and eight shillings per pound, and forcing the formation of the English East India Company in 1600.[23]

The papacy, disappointed in Spain, still had its hold on France. Henry's conversion was not convincing enough to satisfy the Jesuits. The order's dissatisfaction was expressed in the attempt of a Jesuit pupil to assassinate the king in 1594. However, Italian bankers were more persuasive than Jesuit intrigue. Henry's financial connections with the Medici linked Paris and Rome. His marriage to Marie de Medici in 1600 formalized his ties with the Vatican, and pointed to the further subordination of French national interest to Catholic policy. The marriage was an answer to Holland's Oriental voyages and the Dutch pepper cartel.

One of the results of this victory for Catholic diplomacy was the death of Giordano Bruno. The church acted against Bruno at the moment when the Medici alliance with France strengthened the papacy and distracted attention from the trial. The progenitor of the empirical philosophy of capitalism faced his accusers in February, 1600, when the arrangements for the coming alliance were completed. Having waited for seven years, the Inquisition proceeded with indecent haste. Bruno was excommunicated on the ninth of the month, burned at the stake on the seventeenth.

Science, providing the technological base for economic development, was the handmaiden of the bourgeoisie. It was therefore the enemy of the church. The church knew, from hard experience, that knowledge is a communicable disease, and that scientific progress has unavoidable political consequences. In the period of Sandys' Venetian visit, Galileo was a young scientist—he was three years younger than Sandys—who had attained a considerable reputation. He already faced the decisions concerning the freedom of science which were to bring him before the Inquisition in his old age. Galileo had a filial relationship with Sarpi, of whom he spoke as "my Father my master."[24]

Galileo came to the University of Pisa as a lecturer on mathematics in 1591. During his two years there he conducted experiments to determine the velocity of falling bodies by dropping objects from the leaning tower of Pisa. His interest in the theory of dynamics embarrassed the university. In the year of Bruno's arrest, Galileo was forced to resign.

But Venice took a more liberal view. Sarpi may have been influential in securing a post for Galileo at the University of Padua, which was in Venetian territory. Sandys commented on the liberalism of Padua: he said it was the only place in Italy which permitted serious debate on some of the points of difference between the Catholics and the Protestants. Galileo remained at Padua for sixteen years. He soon proved that his research had commercial value. In 1597, he invented the thermometer, utilizing a bulb and tube filled with air and water. His discovery of the proportional compass dates from the same year.

Galileo had already adopted the Copernican theory of a universe in flux and movement. A letter written to the German astronomer, Johann Kepler, on August 4, 1597, mentions his advanced opinions—and the unhappy necessity of keeping them secret. His friend's reticence could not have surprised Kepler, who was also secretly committed to the Copernican doctrine. Kepler was uneasily occupying the chair of science at Gratz in Styria. The labor troubles in Austria led to a purge of all persons on the staffs of schools or universities who were suspected of Protestant sympathies. Kepler fled to the Hungarian frontier in 1598. However, Kepler had influential friends. In the year before his difficulties at the university, he had married Barbara Muller von Muleckh, member of a noble and wealthy Styrian family. Through his wife's connections, he was permitted to return to his post.

But he found the school deserted. Thought control was so rigid that pupils were afraid to attend classes. The disconsolate professor was forced to leave Gratz again in 1600, but he was fortunate enough to secure a position as assistant to the liberal astronomer, Tycho Brahe, in his observatory near Prague. Although Bohemia was part of the empire, the strength of the Protestant movement and the commercial importance of Prague created a more favorable climate for scientific research. On Tycho's death in 1601, Kepler inherited his observatory. By concealing his real opinions and devoting a good deal of time to astrology, drawing flattering horoscopes of the emperor and members of the court, the astronomer was able to retain the imperial favor and pursue his investigations.

Sandys' friendship with Sarpi may have brought him into contact with Galileo. It is possible that the young scientist discussed the Copernican theory with the Englishman. At all events, Sandys returned to England in 1599 with the deep conviction that reason could conquer the world, harnessing the forces of society and nature to the chariot of bourgeois progress. He was less concerned with the mystery of man's place in the universe than with the subordination of every scrap of knowledge to the service of his class.

Sandys' interest in practical politics was determined by the changed relationship of forces in England. The bourgeoisie had attained a strength which enabled it to play *practical* politics. But there was also a general change in the climate of European culture, which marked the end of the Renaissance and the beginning of a new period of class struggle. The old humanist faith was replaced by a professional and businesslike approach to science as a service to the class in power. As might be expected, the change was most clearly defined in Holland. The requirements of the prosperous Dutch optical industry were responsible for the research that led to the invention of the compound microscope by Zacharias Jannsen in 1590.

But more significant as a premature, and well-nigh perfect, model of the bourgeois scientist, was the personality and work of Simon Stevinus. In a sense, the Dutch mathematician's experiments were as varied as those of Leonardo, but Stevinus had no passion for the arts, no concern with social or philosophic questions. He maintained his political neutrality so carefully that he left no definite clue as to his religious beliefs. In a period of violent change, he could boast that he had always been in full harmony with the executive power. He was a man of science, serving the business interests and the state with tireless zeal. His most important achievement was the invention of the decimal system; he foresaw that a decimal coinage, and decimal weights and measures, were destined to revolutionize commercial intercourse. He persuaded Prince Maurice to utilize double entry bookkeeping for the national accounts. He explained the tides by the attraction of the moon, analyzed the science of fortifications and the effective use of artillery, invented a system of sluices which was valuable in the defense of the Netherlands.

In 1600, Prince Maurice and other notables assembled on the beach at Schveningen to witness a curious spectacle. Stevinus had constructed a carriage with sails; it moved along the sands faster than horses could gallop.

The horseless carriage was a scientific oddity. The winds that propelled it were less powerful than the winds of change that were sweeping Europe. Yet the experiment with a winddriven vehicle was a foretaste of the discovery of new forces—steam, oil, electricity and atomic energy—which would carry men faster than the wind, revolutionizing commerce and communication, and thus intensify the contradiction between the private ownership of these forces and their use for human welfare.

2 : A LETTER TO THE POPE

In the summer of 1601, Anne, the wife of James Stuart, King of Scotland, wrote a letter to the pope, in which she told of her conversion to Catholicism, assuring his Holiness that she held firmly to the true faith. The pope replied in July, 1602; he "expressed pleasure at her conversion, and urged once more the conversion of her husband." [1]

The correspondence is one of the threads in the skein of intrigue which enabled James to secure the throne of England in 1603. Only the most naïve student of politics would venture to assert that Anne's conversion was a matter of private conviction. Rome and its Jesuit emissaries had been endeavoring for years to bring England back into the orbit of Catholic power. For several decades, sons of English Catholic families had been sent to the continent to be trained in the tasks of propaganda and organization that they were to undertake in England. The college for English Catholics at Douai was moved to Rheims when the warfare in the Low Countries endangered its safety. Pope Gregory XIII, who supported the Douai school with a monthly subsidy, founded a seminary at Rome for the conversion of England.[2]

The attraction of a powerful section of the English nobility to Catholicism is a basic factor in the political and cultural development of the Stuart period. The upper-class appeal of the Catholic world-view was as potent in the early seventeenth century as it is in the twentieth. It forms one of the essential cultural links between the two periods. The sacerdotal continuity of Roman elements in the ritual of the Church of England is an expression of ideological influences which go back to the Elizabethan era, and which were revitalized by

Cardinal Newman in the nineteenth century, to be given a modern and more openly reactionary form in the writings of T. S. Eliot and his associates.

The class struggle which was ideologically reflected in the opposition between the feudal Catholic culture and the emergent culture of the bourgeoisie was conducted on a European scale; the fears which Sandys expressed in his study of Catholic power were motivated by the actual difficulties that faced his class in England.

It would be an oversimplification to say that James followed a consistently pro-Catholic policy. Consistency was not a trait of the king's character, and his personal vacillations are of interest mainly as an expression of the contradictory forces which compelled him to vacillate. James had no attachment to his mother's creed, and he treated her death callously, as a means of strengthening his own ties with Elizabeth. His experience in Scotland was a dour apprenticeship for the business of governing England. The son of Mary, Queen of Scots, had reason enough to know the uncertainties of royal power. He was kidnapped at the age of sixteen by a group of nobles and held prisoner for a year. He was twenty-one when his mother was executed in 1587. During the next fifteen years, he reigned by doing a sort of sword dance among the weapons of the Highland Lords and the sharp sophistries of Presbyterian ministers.

James' personal philosophy—if the frantic pragmatism of a beleaguered politician can be called a philosophy—was based on the divine right of kings. Other rights, human or divine, were recognized by James only if they contributed to the glory of the crown. Since royal absolutism clashed with Catholic absolutism, James had no desire to accept the authority of the pope. Included in his preparations for his English reign was a book which he wrote in 1598, *The True Lawe of Free Monarchies,* in which he argued that the proper freedom of monarchies demanded independence both from the importunities of the people and the interference of the church.

The irony of James' position when he finally fulfilled his ambition and secured the English throne lay in the fact that he had *less* power than he had wielded in Scotland—simply because the country was more advanced economically, and its progress placed inescapable restrictions on the authority which the king claimed. The relationship of forces in England, as in France, made it impossible to maintain the divine right of kings without the support which only the church could provide. James' position as head of the Anglican establishment was a political fiction which added little of value to his monarchial function. He stood in need of a higher priestly sanction, backed by Rome's efficient techniques of organization and tested methods of propaganda. But Rome's support could not be cheaply purchased.

Queen Anne's letter to the pope in 1601 may not have been decisive as a commitment; James' path to the throne of Britain was strewn with secret negotiations and contradictory promises. But the letter is in a somewhat different category. Related to the whole system of European events, it was a reversal of Elizabethan policy, affecting the relationship of forces in every part of the continent.

At the time it was written, English Catholics, including such rich and powerful families as the Treshams and Catesbys of Northamptonshire, were actively assisting Spain's attempt to subdue the Netherlands. Interest in the Dutch fight for independence was as intense, and as sharply divided along class lines, as the international interest in the anti-fascist struggle in Spain from 1936 to 1939. An English regiment of some 1,600 men was recruited to serve with the Spanish forces in the Netherlands; all the chaplains were Jesuit priests, and Guy Fawkes was one of its officers.[3]

There is a correlation of dates between the Queen's letter and the course of European events which cannot be accidental. The Vatican, having consolidated its position in France by the Medici marriage in 1600, could again hope to crush the Dutch bourgeoisie. France had been neutralized, but the poverty of the Spanish government made it unlikely that a successful offensive in the Low Countries could be undertaken unless England's aid—or at least her passivity and tacit encouragement—could be guaranteed. The difficulties were overcome in the summer in which Anne wrote to the pope. Her pious assurance to his Holiness had an immediate effect on the campaign in the Netherlands: Spain received new loans from the Genoese banking firm of Spinola and was thus able to prosecute the war with renewed vigor.

Ostend was Holland's only remaining seaport in Flanders. Being a short distance across the channel from Dover and the mouth of the Thames, it was a strategically important link between England and the united provinces. For the same reason, it was invaluable to Spain, and the siege, begun in 1601 at the time of Queen Anne's letter to the Vatican and prosecuted for three years with a prodigal expenditure of men and money, assumes its real political significance when it is considered as an aspect of the Catholic plan that unfolded after the coronation of James. He reversed Elizabethan foreign policy, abandoning hostilities with Spain at a moment when it would have its maximum effect as a betrayal of the Dutch cause. The impact of the English withdrawal from the alliance was immediately felt by the hard-pressed defenders of Ostend.

James was crowned on March 24, 1603. In September, Ambrosio de Spinola took personal command of the Spanish forces investing Ostend. In these days of banker-generals, it is not surprising to find that military and economic interests required a unified and foreign command of the Spanish troops. The Spinola family had invested a fortune in loans to Spain: the accession of James brought the hour of decision which would determine the value of the investment.

James' *rapprochement* with Spain was a warning to the English bourgeoisie that their interests, closely linked to those of their class in Holland, were endangered. The treaty with Spain, signed in 1604, affected important sectors of the English economy. The surrender of England's right to trade in the West Indies was more than a blow to national pride; it struck at vital interests engaged in transatlantic trade. The scale on which clandestine commerce with Spanish America was conducted is indicated by the number of vessels, English and Dutch, that came to Punta Araya on the coast of Venezuela to dispose of contraband goods and take on cargoes of salt in the year before James' accession to the throne. From June, 1602, to May, 1603, 172 salt ships and 30 barter vessels of large size visited the Venezuelan port. In January, 1603, there were sixty salt ships and four merchantmen in the port at one time.[4]

The cutting off of this trade had a disastrous effect, not only on the persons directly engaged in it, but on a network of British interests. For example, the West Country fishermen who made yearly voyages to Newfoundland used Venezuelan salt, and the cod fisheries faced the necessity of securing supplies from other sources. Wealthy Elizabethan shipowners like Lord Robert Rich, who had made fortunes in privateering in American waters, were forced to transfer their vessels to Middleburg or Flushing, sailing under the Dutch flag and depriving English seaports of all the business connected with repairing and supplying their fleets.[5]

In order to stifle opposition and prepare the public for the signing of the Spanish treaty, James ordered the arrest of Sir Walter Raleigh on a charge of treason. The man who had pioneered in North American settlement was placed on trial in November, 1603. But the trial, like all political trials, had a double effect. It silenced Raleigh, but it placed the new government's aims under a dramatic spotlight. James had to have Raleigh convicted, in order to prove (especially abroad) that England accepted Spain's mastery of the Western Hemisphere and was sincerely supporting the aims of the Hapsburg-Catholic coalition. But the guilty verdict aroused such opposition that it was unwise to carry out the sentence of death, and Raleigh remained in the Tower, waiting, as Bruno had waited in an Italian prison, until the political barometer pointed to his execution or his release.

The domestic barometer prophesied imminent storms. The early months of 1604 crystallized impressive opposition to the crown: first, at the Hampton Court Conference in January, and then at the parliament which began its sessions on March 23. But James proceeded with his secret negotiations with Philip III, which had as their aim nothing less than the destruction of the Dutch Republic. England and Spain were to join in an invasion of the Low Countries, and in return England was to receive a large portion of the Spanish Netherlands.[6] The plan was facilitated by the Fall of Ostend, which capitulated to Spinola in September, 1604.

The deal with Spain failed—for the reason that all of James' diplomatic schemes were destined to fail. It in no way corresponded to the relationship of forces in England. James could put Raleigh in the Tower, but he could not persuade his subjects to join a Catholic crusade against Dutch independence. By the time that the fall of Ostend offered a real military basis for the plan, its political basis had evaporated in England. Like many diplomatic conversations, the arrangements for the dismemberment of the Netherlands were conducted on a plane of pure fantasy.

The Hampton Court Conference, which brought the king into direct conflict with an important part of the bourgeoisie, was called as a result of the millenary petition, signed by one thousand ministers who demanded changes in the Prayer Book to satisfy Puritan objections. The fact that the Puritans, whose activities had been so rigorously suppressed during most of Elizabeth's reign, were able to make this public demonstration, indicated the growing strength of the people for whom they spoke. James presided in person at the gathering, convened in the wake of the excitement occasioned by Raleigh's trial and conviction. If there were any doubts concerning the political character of the debate, the king dispelled them. He gave the recalcitrant divines a royal scolding, telling them that "A Scottish presbytery agreeth as well with a monarchy as God with the devil. Then Jack and Tom and Will and Dick shall meet, and at their pleasure censure me and my council." [7]

The conference ended in an impasse. The king followed it with a purge of the church; 300 members of the clergy were deprived of their livings. But the purge was ineffective; it widened the gap between the crown and the classes which provided the mass support for the ministers who had signed the millenary petition. There were 1,500 Puritan clergymen in England at the time of Elizabeth's death.[8] A few years later, the Spanish ambassador estimated their following at 600,000.[9]

Puritanism embraced a variety of trends, but the political weight of the movement was provided by the middle section of the bourgeoisie, which had sufficient social status and economic power to demand political recognition—London tradesmen and leaders of craft industry who resented the monopolies granted by the crown; provincial businessmen and shipowners who objected to the special privileges enjoyed by a few powerful London merchants; country gentlemen who had accumulated wealth in capitalist farming and wanted larger investment opportunities.

In opposition to this coalition was the small but enormously powerful group that surrounded the king and drew heavy dividends from the centralized power of the crown. Monarchial absolutism served the interests of the upper nobility, the great London merchants, and the Anglican hierarchy. The nobility and the privileged group of London merchants shared monopolies and privileges which hampered normal business activity and obstructed the nation's economic development.

The London magnates whose control of industry and trade was protected by royal favor were in competition with Holland for the riches of the Orient: the first voyage of the East India Company in 1601 represented an investment of £68,373, and returned a profit of ninety-five percent.[10] This promising result explains the fact that the great merchants were not unduly alarmed by the abandonment of the alliance with the Dutch bourgeoisie; they were more interested in the pepper market than in the dangers and uncertain profits of a continuing struggle with Spain for colonial power in the Western Hemisphere.

The Church of England, with its extensive and bureaucratic apparatus, formed an important part of the crown's support. While there was a good deal of disaffection in the lower ranks of the clergy, the ecclesiastical aristocracy looked to the king, oddly enough, as their spiritual leader—and the source of their benefices and emoluments.

The interests of the court circle were in conflict with the aims of the bourgeoisie as a whole—and especially with the ambitions of the numerically large and heterogeneous group which was in the *middle* of the middle class, occupying a crowded area of uncertain competition, slow accumulation of capital and bitter struggle for survival. These people were politically conscious and they were beginning to have political influence. Their differences with the crown crystallized around the question of foreign policy.

Class interests are more clearly exhibited in diplomacy than in any other phase of history. Perhaps "exhibited" is the wrong word; statesmen are careful to veil their real aims in patriotic phrases, and historical scholarship has tended to accept the illusions propagated by the professional diplomats, taking their patriotic intentions for granted and ignoring the material interests advanced under the guise of the national welfare. The obfuscation is assisted by the fiction that all fundamental class differences stop at the nation's boundaries: the "patriotism" which governs foreign policy is too sacred to permit investigation; we are told that diplomacy is a mysterious art, following rules and laws of its own, beyond the comprehension of the layman.

However, the struggle of classes in Stuart England developed so rapidly that it left the ruling group without adequate ideological defenses. The assumption that the king was divinely right tended to negate the necessity of propaganda devices to win popular approval of the government's course. James' rash reversal of foreign policy in 1603 placed him in an exposed and untenable position. Although the Commons dealt mainly with domestic issues when it met in 1604, it opposed the crown with a boldness which was without precedent in English history.

Edwin Sandys, sitting as a member for Stockbridge, came forward as one of the strongest leaders of the opposition party. It could hardly be called a party in the modern sense, for the crown controlled the administrative and judiciary branches of the government; the veto exercised by the House of Lords, as well as the direct intervention of the king, reduced the power of the lower house, making its debates more effective as propaganda than as decisions concerning national issues.

The bourgeois coalition—for it represented a number of conflicting interests—could not as yet build a legal party apparatus. But it could establish an informal association and fight for a program. There was a four-pronged attack on royal power: the assertion of the rights of legislative bodies, the assault on the king's feudal prerogatives, the denunciation of monopolies, and the refusal to permit taxation without parliamentary approval.

The House was sensitive about its privileges. One of its members, Sir Thomas Shirley, was arrested for debt, and the Commons demanded possession of the body of the delinquent knight. As a result of the controversy, the principle was established that members of parliament were exempt from arrest for debt during the sessions, and for forty days before the assembly met and a similar period after it adjourned.[11]

There was also a formal protest against a book recently written by a bishop, which tended "to the derogation and scandal of the proceedings of the House." The matter was brought to the attention of the House of Lords, and the bishop was reprimanded and forced to apologize.[12]

The king met unexpected difficulties in regard to the union of Scotland and England. The trouble lay in the clauses of the Act of Union which guaranteed the crown's control of wardships, purveyances and other feudal privileges. The king would not abandon these prerogatives, and the Commons would not accept them. James sent a sad message to the House, regretting that its deliberations resulted in "so few matters of weight passed, and that matter of Privilege had taken so much time . . . he was moved with jealousy that there was not such proceeding as, in love, he expected."[13]

James was annoyed by the clamor against monopolies. He had proclaimed that grants and licences would be allowed only after examination by himself and his council, and the assurance that they were "fit to be put into execution without any prejudice to his loving subjects."[14] The royal promise meant nothing to merchants and craftsmen whose business ambitions were blocked at every turn by existent monopolies.

The most vigorous parliamentary fight developed around control of foreign trade. The attack on the exclusive control of maritime commerce by London companies came from West Country fishing and shipping interests. The merchants of Bristol and other seaports sent their fleets to Newfoundland for cod, and the fish was carried to Europe for sale. Free access to European markets was essential for this commerce. The end of the Spanish war brought a renewal of the exclusive charter for trade with Spain originally granted in 1577. Since the fisheries intended to sell a large part of their product in Spanish and Mediterranean ports, the charter deprived them of the one advantage they could gain from the conclusion of peace. The fish merchants were allied with the West Country cloth industry, which wished to break the hold of the Merchant Adventurers Company on the textile trade with Europe.[15]

Sandys and his associates proposed the abolition of all privileges in foreign trade, and the opening of membership in companies engaged in overseas commerce to anyone paying a moderate entrance fee. Sandys declared that, since merchandise is "the chiefest and richest" of the nation's interests, it is "against the natural right and liberty of the subjects of England to restrain it into the hands of some few." He charged that two hundred families had a stranglehold on the country's economic life: "The whole trade of the realm is in the hands of some 200 persons at the most, the rest serving for a show and reaping a small benefit." [16]

The bill for free trade failed to pass; it was introduced again, unsuccessfully, in 1605.[17] The issue was closely related to the question of transatlantic colonization. The demand for the organization of companies for American settlement came primarily from the underprivileged capitalists who were seeking wider commercial and investment opportunities. Associated with Sandys in the struggle against monopoly was George Somers; both men were to be active in the Virginia Company, and Somers was to give his name to the Bermudas, called the Somers Isles in his honor.

Questions of monopoly and foreign trade were bound up in the larger issues of foreign policy. Until the Commons received some satisfaction on these questions, it was unwilling to vote sufficient funds to satisfy the crown's extravagant needs. The attitude of the Commons in 1604 and 1605 proved that James could not carry through his secret plans for an alliance with Spain and a joint invasion of the Netherlands.

The crowded events of 1605 brought a crucial turn in English and

European politics. Without the English support for which Philip III was negotiating, Spain lacked the financial or military strength to follow up the capture of Ostend with a crushing blow against Holland. The failure of the deal with England was apparent at the moment when the death of Pope Clement VIII, which occurred on March 6, 1605, created a break in Vatican policy.

The weakness of Spain seemed to offer the French king an opportunity to cash in on his conversion to Catholicism. Henry bought the Holy Office, at a reputed cost of 300,000 ducats, for a member of the Borghesi family, who received the tiara as Leo XI. The investment became a total loss when Leo died twenty-seven days later. He was followed, on May 16, by Paul V, the candidate favored by the Jesuits as a man who would take the strongest measures to re-establish the "universality" of Catholic power. The Jesuits distrusted Henry IV, and were alarmed by the failure of the English negotiations and the unsettled situation in western Europe.

Holland was the key to the whole system of European events. Since it was impossible to crush the Dutch bourgeoisie without English aid, the church had to resort to any means, however desperate, to secure the help which James proved unable to deliver.

The result was the Gunpowder Plot. The plot originated early in 1604: it matured as it became apparent that it was impossible for James to follow the course on which he embarked at the beginning of his reign. The probability of a serious English alliance with Spain against the Netherlands could be gauged by the degree of toleration which Catholics enjoyed in England. During 1603, the Elizabethan fines and penalties were abandoned, and Catholics were able to practice their religion without interference. But in 1604, the Hampton Court Conference and the king's difficulties with the Commons forced a reversal of the government's policy. On February 22 (in preparation for the opening of parliament), a proclamation was issued banishing priests; in November, recusancy fines were exacted from 13 wealthy Catholics. On February 10, 1605, the penal laws were re-established.

It was plain, by this time, that the money, supplies and men needed to turn the tide of battle in favor of Spain in the Low Countries would not be available. A *coup d'etat* in England was the only solution. The plot bore less relation to the internal situation in England than to the necessity of bringing help to the Spanish cause in the Netherlands. The English Catholics with the Spanish troops knew that official and large-scale assistance was required in order to solve the military problem. After consultations in England and Flanders, Guy Fawkes was sent back to England to do the most dangerous work in connection with building the tunnel under the House of Lords and planting the explosives there. When Paul V became pope on May 16, there was no longer any doubt that the plan accorded with the wishes of the Vatican. Fawkes made a trip to Flanders, to inform his English and Spanish associates and to assure proper contact with the papacy; for this latter purpose, Sir Edmund Baynham was sent to Rome.

The dramatic last-minute revelation of the plot is a familiar story. The discovery of the gunpowder and the arrest of Fawkes took place on the night of November 4, a few hours before the time of the explosion, which was designed to blow up the building at the opening of parliament, when the king and prince of Wales were in attendance. The men who were most directly implicated in the conspiracy fled; they were tracked down; some of them were killed on the spot; others were tried and executed. Anger and horror swept England. Anti-Catholic feeling reached a new pitch of intensity.

One cannot guess what disorders might have occurred if the explosion had taken place. But it could not have changed the basic relationship of forces in England. The miscalculation of these forces by the conspirators makes the venture seem like a chimera of diseased minds. Yet the treatment of it as a criminal fantasy places it in a false perspective, isolated from the system of international pressures and irreconcilable class interests which gives the event its significance and explains the motives of the participants.

The mistake which the conspirators made was not the error of a misguided group of individuals. It reflected the viewpoint of their class, which was cut off from the creative forces in English life, and unable to appreciate the strength of these forces. The king himself shared this astigmatism; his conduct during the first two years of his reign was preparation for the plot which was aimed at his life. The king had appeased and strengthened the Catholics; then his vacillations convinced them that he was unable to cope with the bourgeoisie, and that they could do the job better by smashing the limited political rights which the bourgeoisie enjoyed.

Although the gunpowder failed to explode, the discovery had an explosive effect on English thought. It revealed the chasm that existed between the class in control of the state and the class which was attaining sufficient economic strength to bid for a share in the state power. The conflict had been concealed during the Elizabethan period: it had been like a pit covered over with green boughs and leaves—the camouflage that had hidden the dangerous crevice was the myth of a unified national interest. Long before the death of Elizabeth, the myth had worn threadbare, but the middle and upper classes continued to pay lip-service to it as a tradition that must somehow be restored and preserved. The revelation that there could be no compromise came, as is usual in such cases, from the right. The fact that the attack was directed against the king himself—the symbol of monarchial absolutism—was a demonstration of the insignificance of the symbol. The plot sprang from the fury of the aristocracy, revealing its inability to solve the dilemma of power. But the king was also proving himself utterly unable to solve the dilemma—his concessions to the bourgeoisie were as distasteful to James as they were to the conspirators.

The Catholic appeal was as fundamental to the aristocracy of England and Europe as the attraction of fascism to the financiers and statesmen of our own day. James' attitude toward Protestantism was as ambivalent as the attitude of American politicians to what they call "democracy." The king made a discreet obeisance to Protestantism as the "English way of life." He endorsed sporadically, and under pressure, the popular view that England's national destiny depended on cooperation with the Protestant forces on the continent. James regretted that the Protestant "ideal" was all too frequently pushed to immoderate extremes.

James was as unable to abandon his Catholic sympathies as he was impotent to realize them in governmental policy. The failure of the Gunpowder Plot was utilized in order to strengthen the crown's position. But the punishment of persons caught red-handed, and the seizure of Catholic estates in England and Ireland, had no more effect on the class structure of English society than the occasional antitrust suits against monopolies or indictments of corrupt congressmen have on the class structure in today's United States.

In the king's immediate circle, as in the nation generally, the period following the discovery of the plot was one of increasing tension and uncertainty. But the Catholic influence at the court was not appreciably diminished. A minor, but dramatic, touchstone of the politics of the period is provided by the activities of Luisa de Carvajal. The middle-aged Spanish woman, sent to London by the Jesuits in 1605, was cheated of the martyrdom she recklessly pursued. She functioned openly, operating from the Spanish embassy, conspicuously ministering to the Catholics arrested for complicity in the Gunpowder plot. Luisa, like her less demonstrative Jesuit colleagues, was protected by persons close to the king.

The propaganda activities of Luisa de Carvajal cannot be isolated from the general cultural picture. Catholic influence was permitted, and encouraged, in many areas of cultural activity, and its presence was neither accidental nor without official endorsement. William Byrd, the most eminent master of church music in the Elizabethan period, was a practicing Catholic. The toleration accorded to him, at a time when many of his coreligionists were persecuted, was not due to Elizabeth's respect for artistic accomplishment. The queen was not hesitant in dealing with artists whose views or activities offended her. Byrd was honored because his influence on the ceremonies of the Church of England was of political value to the court; he counteracted the attraction of Protestant musical culture and gave a formal and mystical quality to the music of the established church.

Byrd was sixty years old when James came to England and he was to enjoy another twenty years of fruitful labor. The value which the crown set upon his services was demonstrated in 1604, when his right to continue in possession of a country estate was affirmed by the king. The complicated legal dispute regarding the property stemmed from its having been confiscated from a recusant before Byrd obtained control of it. Byrd was himself an acknowledged recusant, but the royal favor protected him both in the enjoyment of the property and in his professional career: he took part in the coronation of James as a member of the Chapel Royal.

The penetration of Catholic thought in the most popular area of art and propaganda—the theatre—is indicated in the case of Ben Jonson, whose acceptance of Catholicism dated from 1598. We cannot pause to examine the psychological motivations for the poet's conversion, but the social setting has been sketched: as the famine years brought growing discontents and the storm clouds gathered on the Elizabethan horizon, Jonson turned from the uncertainties that plagued Shakespeare to reaction and the church. Jonson's views commended him to the court, and led to his employment in preparing the masques which became an increasingly extravagant form of court entertainment in the Stuart period. In 1605, Jonson wrote two plays which were a reflection of the crown's attitude toward the bourgeoisie, and a substantial service to the Catholic cause.

Volpone lampooned the upstart merchants who "possess wealth, as sick men possess fevers." It is a brilliant, and still valid, affirmation of the older humanist tradition against the vulgarities of the cash nexus. The attack on the corrupting power of money had a genuine appeal to the journeymen and artisans in the London audience. But *Volpone* utilized the appeal in a period of parliamentary struggle, a few months before the Gunpowder Plot. It cannot be divorced from the political climate of the crucial year, when the Catholics were preparing to destroy all the gains made by the bourgeoisie.

Volpone is an amalgam of inconsistent elements. It jumps from lines that breathe the fire of humanism to cheap propaganda, from human insights to inhuman vulgarities. The play is like a bridge across the arena of class struggle, linking the upper-class derision of the bourgeoisie with the lower-class hatred of exploitation. In *The Puritan,* Jonson crossed the bridge. Here he is no longer deriding the corruption of money; his attack is leveled against the creative idealism and moral vigor of the lower middle class. The crude caricature of the rebellious Puritans is a dramatization of the position taken by the king at the Hampton Court Conference. As such, it conformed with Jonson's desire to please the crown. But *The Puritan,* even more than *Volpone,* tended to provide an ideological base for the Gunpowder Plot.

Jonson was under suspicion of being involved in the conspiracy, but his participation was never proved. If he did not know of the plot, he unwittingly used his pen to prepare for it. His double-barrelled indictment of businessmen and Puritans was calculated—either by the writer or by persons who advised and influenced him—to neutralize the anger of the London crowds when the *coup d'etat* took place. Catholic proselytism thrived on the charge that the king conciliated the *Volpones* of business and was inadequately severe in dealing with the "subversive" Puritan opposition.

While Ben Jonson utilized his theatrical talents to serve reaction, Shakespeare's work mirrored the stress and uncertainty of a period of social disorganization and deepening conflict. The three great tragedies of the diseased will—of the corruption of power—were written in 1604 and 1605. In *Measure for Measure,* probably produced late in 1604, the moral climate in which the characters move is electric with unresolved tensions. Angelo's hypocritical insistence on ethical absolutes may be regarded as a jibe at Puritanism. But the attack on Puritan ethics is converted into its opposite—a picture of the degradation of a society which has no standards—

> Where I have seen corruption boil and bubble
> Till it o'errun the stew.

Isabella's fight for her personal integrity is set against a pageant of the city's life that is almost like a *montage* in a motion picture. Can we doubt the significance to a London audience of the Bawd's lament? "What with the war, what with the sweat, what with the gallows, and what with poverty, I am custom-shrunk." There is Hogarthian passion in the dialogue that follows the clown's announcement that a proclamation has been issued to destroy all the houses of ill-fame in the suburbs:

> Bawd: And what shall become of those in the city?
> Clown: They shall stand for seed: they had gone down too, but that a wise burgher put in for them.
> Bawd: But shall all our houses of resort in suburbs be pulled down?
> Clown: To the ground, mistress.
> Bawd: Why, here's a change indeed in the commonwealth! What shall become of me?
> Clown: Come; fear not you; good counsellors lack no clients: though you change your place you need not change your trade . . . you that have worn your eyes almost out in the service, you will be considered.

Everyone who was familiar with the Stuart court had seen "corruption boil and bubble" in the intimate group around the king. The uncertainty and confusion among the aristocracy in the months following the Gunpowder Plot brought a further decline in the morality of the royal circle. Sir John Harrington wrote of the Danish King's visit in July, 1606: "The ladies abandon their sobriety and are seen to roll about in intoxication." Harrington told of a masque that ended disastrously because both the performers and the royal spectators were incapacitated by liquor.[18]

The drunkenness and promiscuity of the court reflected the political degeneration of the class in power.

3 : A SHIPMENT OF CURRANTS

THE FRUSTRATIONS that plagued the court, finding an outlet in the breaking of moral barriers, were in direct ratio to the militant sobriety of the bourgeoisie in the year following the discovery of the Gunpowder plot. The revelation, identifying Catholicism with treason, proved that a foreign policy of alliance with Spain and appeasement of the Vatican betrayed the national interest. In abandoning the alliance with Spain, James moved reluctantly, retreating only when the pressure was more than he could withstand. The pressure was at the boiling point in 1606. If the policy that dictated Raleigh's trial and the Spanish treaty had remained intact, English transatlantic settlement might have been delayed until other powers had gained a foothold in North America. The two American continents were claimed *in toto* by Spain under papal authority, and continued control, either by Spain or by a reliable Catholic power, was obviously part of the global strategy of the church.

The charter for American colonization granted in 1606 was a reversal of the previous foreign policy. The significance of the charter becomes clear if it is placed in the setting of parliamentary conflict from which it was born. The debates which had stirred the Commons in 1604 and 1605, were conducted with a very different temper and assurance in 1606. Sandys and his associates undertook the preparation of a Bill of Grievances, enumerating their complaints against the crown. The issues were familiar—the abuse of monopoly privileges, the feudal prerogatives of the crown, the funds demanded for support of the government. But the question of taxation tended to assume increasing importance, because it involved the function—and even the existence—of the monarchial state. Royal feudalism made no distinction between the government and the king. James' demands for his personal expenses included the vast waste and display connected with the court; but lumped with these outlays for the royal prestige and pleasure were the costs of maintaining the whole apparatus of the state, including the army and the navy.

When the Commons refused to grant adequate subsidies for the king's needs, James asserted the right to levy import duties without parliamentary consent. By imposing taxes at his own discretion, James took the matter out of the arena of parliamentary debate. But he also posed the problem of the rights of the Commons—and the rights of the classes which had majority representation there—in a new and clear light. The dispute was transferred to the law courts. John Bates, a merchant of the Levant Company, refused to pay a tax of five shillings per hundred-weight on a consignment of currants.

The Bates case seemed to have more far-reaching implications than any other issue before the Commons in 1606. Its portentious connection with the plan to colonize Virginia could not have been fully realized. Yet the two issues were complimentary aspects of the campaign conducted by the bourgeoisie for political recognition and wider economic opportunity.

Sandys had risen repeatedly in the Commons to denounce monopolies of foreign trade. He spoke for the West country cloth and fishing interests in demanding liberty of trade with Europe. But the West Country's interest in Europe was linked to its profits from the transatlantic fisheries, its desire to extend its activities in American coastal waters and to protect its investment by control of bases on the American mainland.

Early in 1606, parliament passed a bill similar to those which had been defeated at earlier sessions, eliminating monopolistic restrictions on commerce with Spain, Portugal and France.[1] This was an important victory. But the opportunities for the general investor to secure profits from European trade were limited. The lucrative voyages to the Orient and other distant lands were controlled by the great London Companies. The bourgeoisie looked to America, as a land of economic and political promise.

The strength of the opposition in the Commons made it imperative that the king make concessions in order to counterbalance his unwillingness to compromise on feudal privileges or the right of taxation. The most popular step that he could take, both as proof of the abandonment of the detested Spanish alliance and as an affirmation of the expansionist patriotism of the Elizabethan period, was the approval of transatlantic colonization.

The granting of the charter in April was designed to increase the king's popularity and to relieve the pressure against the crown in the Commons. However, one of the major aims of the crown was to prevent the opposition from gaining any advantage from the move; the document was drawn in a manner which seemed to guarantee control by persons whom the king regarded as reliable, and it was assumed that the dispensation was nonpartisan and unrelated to the debates in the Commons.

In *The Proceedings of the English Colony in Virginia,* a compilation of narratives published under the supervision of John Smith in 1612, Bartholomew Gosnold is described as "the first mover of this plantation"; the account tells how Gosnold involved a few friends, "who depended a yeare upon his projects, but nothing could be effected, till by their great charge and industrie it came to be apprehended by certaine of the nobilitie, Gentrie, and Merchants . . ." [2]

Gosnold is an interesting and somewhat mysterious figure in the Virginia enterprise. He was an experienced navigator. He commanded the ship *Concord,* which crossed the Atlantic in 1602 on an expedition in which Bristol merchants were interested. He cruised from Maine to Martha's Vineyard. He gave its present name to Cape Cod, and gave the name of Martha's Vineyard to the small island now known as No Man's Land. Martha was Gosnold's eldest child.

We know nothing of Gosnold's political views. But his family connections, and the auspices under which he made the 1602 voyage, throw some light on the role that he may have played in the organization of the Virginia Company. He was a member of a wealthy Suffolk family, being intimately connected with the group of landed gentry, residing principally in Suffolk and Essex, who played an important part in colonization and in the struggle against the crown. Gosnold's wife was a cousin of Sir Thomas Smythe, governor of the East India Company and one of the most powerful members of the clique of London financiers which was close to the court.[3]

Thus Gosnold had personal and business ties with three different groups. His American voyage indicated contact with the West Country merchants. His relatives included the most prominent and respected leaders of the parliamentary opposition. Through his wife, he was associated with the mercantile oligarchy in London.

Gosnold had obvious qualifications for the role of "first mover" of the Virginia project. His efforts to secure a patent, probably inspired by his friends among the landed gentry and his Bristol associates, came to nothing until after the discovery of the Gunpowder Plot. Then "certaine of the Nobilitie, Gentrie, and Merchants" appeared publicly as sponsors of the plan, and the king granted their request for a charter.

The patent mirrors the inconclusive political conflict from which it was born. It appears to encourage high enterprise and large achievement. Here is no parsimonious setting of boundaries or limitation of territories. The whole North American coast, from the 34th to the 45th parallels, from Carolina to Nova Scotia, is turned over to two corporations, with "all the Lands, Woods, Soil, Grounds, Havens, Ports, Rivers, Mines, Minerals, Marshes, Waters, Fishings, Commodities, and Hereditaments." [4] However, the generous gift is negated by a form of organization that discouraged investment and reduced the chances of success almost to the vanishing point.

There were many people in England, including Gosnold himself, who knew the difficulties of establishing permanent settlements on the North American coast. The insufficiency of men and supplies which had doomed the colonies sponsored by Raleigh at Roanoke Island was a matter of record; it could not be ignored by men who looked across the Atlantic for a potentially profitable field in which to invest their surplus capital.

The intense interest in colonization indicated that money was available for the purpose. But it could not be obtained for an enterprise which was entirely in the control of the crown and subject to the uncertainties of an indecisive foreign policy. The controversy in the Commons showed that the people who were looking for business opportunities were acutely conscious of the problems arising out of royal interference.

The two companies which were set up under the charter had no corporate existence, in the sense in which corporate organization was understood at the beginning of the seventeenth century. Management of both companies was vested, exclusively and finally, in a council appointed by the crown. Each colony established overseas was to be administered by a local council of thirteen persons, accountable to the parent body in England. The division into two companies had a bearing on the question of power. It had the effect of making doubly sure that the opposition leaders could not gain control of the undertaking. Sir George Somers, who had been prominently identified with the West Country merchants in their fight against trade restrictions, was named in the charter as one of the leaders of the London Company. But the economic power wielded by Sir Thomas Smythe and his London associates gave them a dominant position in the corporation. In addition to his leadership of the East India Company, Smythe was on the interlocking directorates of a dozen corporations. He went to Russia as a special ambassador to the Czar in 1604, and became governor of the Muscovy Company in 1607. He did not become treasurer of the Virginia venture until 1609, but the weight of his influence was felt from the beginning.

When the names of the council appointed by the king were announced, it turned out that it included three relatives of Smythe, and other business leaders whose loyalty to the crown was a matter of primary economic necessity. The interests of these men were directly opposed to the interests of the West Country merchants. Not only did the Londoners seek to monopolize trade with Europe, but they sent their ships to Newfoundland to buy fish and transport it to Europe in competition with the smaller vessels of Bristol and other West Coast ports.[5]

The establishment of a second company, with rights—which specifically included "fishing"—over the Atlantic seaboard as far north as Nova Scotia, was a further threat to the West Country. The second paragraph of the charter tended to give the impression that it was designed to serve the western seaports; it mentioned "sundry knights, Gentlemen, Merchants, and other Adventurers, of our Cities of Bristol and Exeter, and of our Town of Plimouth, and of other places" as beneficiaries of the patent. But the reference to Bristol was merely complimentary. In the fifth paragraph, where specific individuals are named, there is mention only of "*Thomas Hanham,* and *Raleigh Gilbert, William Parker,* and *George Popham,* and all others of the Town of Plimouth in the County of Devon."[6] These were men who were dependable servants of the crown: Popham was the nephew of Sir John Popham, Lord Chief Justice of England. Raleigh Gilbert had nothing to recommend him except his name, which connected him with the great days of Elizabethan seamanship as Sir Humphrey Gilbert's son and Sir Walter Raleigh's namesake. Control of the Plymouth Company was largely in the hands of Sir Ferdinando Gorges, whose office as captain of the castle and fort at Plymouth made him dependent on the king's favor. Gorges' participation in the Plymouth venture, unprofitable as it seemed at the time, prepared the way for the vast land schemes which he later organized, involving claims to most of New England, causing legal complications and social strife that continued in Maine and New Hampshire for more than a century.

The potentialities of the charter, the imperial ambitions which it inspired and the political storms which it heralded, were swathed in patriotic generalities as the ships prepared for the Virginia voyage. But the modest scale on which the enterprise was planned was due to the limitations imposed by the charter, which were also responsible for the incompetent organization of the Plymouth Company's expedition to Maine undertaken a few months later. The lack of proper supplies and the unrealistic selection of personnel for both ventures have been attributed to ignorance of the problems of colonization and the illusion that gold would be found on the North American beaches.

It is true, of course, that the gold myth permeated the culture of the period. Books and plays tickled the popular imagination with talk of the profusion of riches in North America. "I tell thee," said a character in *Eastward Ho!*, produced in 1605, "golde is more plentifull in Virginia than copper is with us . . . All their dripping pans and chamber potts are pure gold . . . and for rubies and diamonds, they goe forth in holidays and gather them by the seashore to hang on their children's coats."

The happy fantasy performed an important function: it preserved the Elizabethan faith in the wondrous possibilities of maritime conquest. It helped to check popular disapproval of the activities of the great trading companies, suggesting that their sensational profits would eventually bring benefits to the whole people. But the *El Dorado* myth had to be localized in some area which was not fully explored and which was a possible field for English colonization. Virginia provided the right setting for the legend. It was desirable, from the viewpoint of the crown, to weave golden hopes around the Virginia voyage: the myth obscured the political issues and dramatized the venture as a national undertaking for the pride and profit of a united citizenry. A society shadowed by class conflict, embittered by sickness and unemployment and penury, was to be healed by the shining panacea imported from the other side of the Atlantic.

Michael Drayton, whose poetry had not won him the royal favor which he sought, may have felt that his *Ode to the Virginia Voyage,* urging the explorers "To get the pearle and gold," would commend him to the court. But if James or anyone in his entourage had believed that there was a good chance of finding gold, the official attitude toward the venture would have exhibited a good deal more warmth and interest.

There were sober and well-informed men who believed that valuable mines might be found; there was also considerable interest in the possibility of discovering a northwest passage which would provide a shorter water route to the Orient. But the experience proved that the establishment of a permanent settlement to facilitate exploration along these lines required a reasonably strong military force and a body of laborers, with sufficient arms, tools, and foodstuffs to keep the settlement alive until agricultural production could be organized. The failure to meet these requirements was not due to ignorance so much as to lack of funds.

Each of the settlements, in Virgina and Maine, consisted of about 100 people. There was an unnecessarily large number of persons classified as gentlemen—thirty-four of the 104 who remained at Jamestown were listed in this category—[7] because these were adventurers who could pay their own way. Servants or boys could be sent without payment of wages, but it was still necessary to provide their transportation, food and tools. Being understaffed, the expeditions also lacked the minimal necessities for the subsistence of the colonists. For the same reasons, the leadership did not measure up to the national importance of the undertaking. It would have been difficult, in 1606, to find an Englishman of stature and acknowledged ability, who would have accepted the command of such a small group under such unpromising conditions. The prospect of gain was uncertain and the political perspective was even more dubious.

The expedition to Maine suffered under an additional disability. It started so late that it did not reach the mouth of the Sagadahoc River until August 19, when the season was too advanced to permit the planting of crops. The error was not unrelated to the political and economic circumstances: the men who led the expedition, George

Popham and Raleigh Gilbert, had no qualifications for the job. Popham was nearing the age of sixty. The two men quarrelled fatuously, in the manner of Shakespeare's comic knights, while the colony starved. Gilbert bragged that the land really belonged to him, on account of the Elizabethan grant to his father. Popham sent back reports to England that Gilbert was irreligious and "prompte to sensuality."[8] The bickering was cut short by Popham's death.

The tragedy of the first winter in Maine, of isolated men starving in the New England snows, stemmed directly from the charter. It would have been logical to establish a contact between the colony and the Newfoundland bases of the English fishing fleets. But the patent contravened the interests of the West Country fishermen, and no arrangement was made to secure aid or advice from these experienced transatlantic voyagers. Thousands of Englishmen made the North Atlantic crossing every year; hundreds of them stayed each year to face the rigors of the winter; but in Maine, one hundred huddled in an unfinished fort as their food supply dwindled to nothing. The forty-four who survived the winter returned to England in the spring. The Plymouth Company had no more funds for another experiment in colonization.

The Virginia settlers managed to win a victory over disease and death. But the battle was won by the narrowest margin. The trouble in Virginia, as in Maine, stemmed from the unwillingness of the crown to trust the work of colonization to the only class that had the will, the available capital, and the ability to proceed with the work. The king's plan to limit colonization and keep it subservient to the court was as unrealistic as the course that James attempted to follow in foreign affairs.

A brief legal drama took place in November, 1606, while the ships for the Virginia voyage were being outfitted in the Thames. John Bates appeared before the Court of the Exchequer, defending his refusal to pay the duties levied on his shipment of currants. The case illuminated the issues that were to bring revolution in England and in America.

Since the four barons who served as judges were appointed by the king and removed at his will, they delivered their verdict with judicial "impartiality." Chief Baron Fleming expressed their unanimous opinion that "the King's power is double ordinary and absolute," and that "the people is the body and the king the head."[9]

The words were heavenly music to James. Yet the political dangers of the decision were so evident that the king had to exercise extreme caution in using the legal right conferred upon him by his own servants. In turning to the judiciary to affirm the absolutism that was challenged in the Commons, James posed the question of power in the clearest juridical and economic terms. The outcry against taxation without representation—the cry that was to unite the colonies in war with England—echoed through the land as the ships dropped down the Thames. It became the central theme of the Bill of Grievances, the first of the great series of documents proclaiming the rights of the bourgeoisie.

4 : THE CASE OF JOHN SMITH

AT THE THRESHOLD of the history of the English colonies, we meet a figure unadorned with weighty symbolisms. The improbabilities of the Pocahontas story are accepted, or rejected, as an anecdote which adds warmth to the portrait of the doughty captain without affecting his credibility or changing the homespun substance of his career.

However, as we proceed to explore the interaction of myth and reality in the case of Captain Smith, we shall find that the historical assumptions which cluster around his name touch fundamental aspects of our culture and influence our approach to American history.

The tale of the Pocahontas rescue is part of the structure of ideas. The quality of salty realism which seems to remove the portrait of Smith from the realm of myth is itself an essential aspect of the myth.

Smith is the creator of the legend; his writings are still utilized as the main source of our knowledge concerning the founding of Virginia. Historical scholarship continues to endorse the accuracy of his account. His hold on the popular imagination is so great that his name and that of Pocahontas are more widely known than any other names in early colonial history. Few Americans could describe the events of the first grievous year in Virginia, the plague under the summer sun, the strife under the shadow of the winter's hunger. But every schoolchild can tell the story of Pocahontas.

There is a curious anomaly in Smith's achievement: he was a comparatively unknown adventurer when he went to Virginia; he spent only two and a half years there, and for the last half of that time he ruled the settlement under an absolute dictatorship. He was sent back to England under serious charges made by his fellow colonists. Yet the literary labors which he undertook on his return were so convincing that his viewpoint became authoritative, not only as to the controversial events in which he participated in Virginia, but as to the affairs of the colony and the company in the next fifteen years.

The forces that were to catapult Smith into prominence were operative in the formation of the Virginia Company. If the charter had encouraged larger financing or more responsible leadership, a man of Smith's vague background and uncertain qualifications could not have hoped to play an important role in the venture. But the uncertainties of the voyage offered an unusual opportunity to the seasoned fortune hunter. Smith could claim to have tried every turn of fortune, and to be ready for any risks.

He had not yet reached the age of thirty. Son of a well-to-do tenant farmer, apprenticed in his youth to a merchant, he ran away at the age of sixteen. If we are to believe his own story, the adventures of a dozen lives were crowded into the following decade. He was miraculously rescued after being thrown into the sea from a Mediterranean vessel. Serving the emperor in the Turkish campaign, he fought and killed three Turkish warriors in succession in single combat, while both armies watched. This event is not recorded by other chroniclers of the war. Their silence in regard to Smith's amorous adventures is more understandable; he tells of being captured by the Turks, sold as a slave, befriended by the beautiful "Lady Tragabigzanda," sent to the Tartars on the Don River, whence he escaped into Russia, being aided by the generous "Lady Callamata." Later in France, he was saved again by "Lady Madam Chanoyes."[1]

In view of these experiences, Smith can hardly have been surprised when Pocahontas hurried forward, exactly on cue, to repeat a performance which had become a matter of routine.

The pattern of conduct which is somewhat extravagantly portrayed by Smith in his story of his early travels was exhibited on the outward voyage. The conditions under which the trip was undertaken were not conducive to discipline. No one knew who was to have authority when the mainland was reached. Captain Christopher Newport was in command during the journey. He carried sealed orders, to be opened on arrival, containing the names of persons appointed to serve on the governing body in Virginia. The secrecy concerning the identity of the leadership seems to have been intended to prevent discussion of the council's function and to emphasize the failure to place definite responsibility on any individual. It was like an invitation to dissension on the long voyage.

Smith got into trouble during the first weeks. He was accused of participation in what Samuel Purchas describes as "a supposed Mutinie, though never no such matter." [2] Since Purchas wrote this comment at a later date, when he was associated with Smith in an organized literary campaign to depict Smith as the ablest leader of the enterprise, the question as to whether there was a mutiny or "no such matter" is moot. At all events, Smith was put in irons and remained in confinement for four months, including the whole voyage and the beginning of the settlement on the James River.

Quarrels continued to mar the serenity of the long cruise. Purchas observes that "The very Aire of the Indies seems to be of inclination and disposition to contentions, which easily ruine and dissolve the greatest and best enterprises." [3] The infection, which seemed to be in the air, may be attributed in part to the fact that no one knew who was to have authority when the ships reached their destination. The adventurers were conscious that they had no stable backing, that the crown had consented reluctantly to the undertaking, and might withdraw its consent at any moment.

The uncertainty was primarily related to the government's foreign policy. A *rapprochement* with Spain would leave the colonists as defenseless as the French settlers in Florida, who were exterminated in 1565 when Catherine de Medici bowed to Spanish pressure. The men who started to build the stockade on the James River in May, 1607, knew that their lives depended on the European balance of power, on decisions made in London, Madrid and Paris.

The world situation was responsible for the choice of a location which had obvious disadvantages. The narrow neck of land between the James and the York rivers was unfavorable for agriculture and dangerous to health. There were other places which, as George Percy observed, offered "many great and large Medowes." [4] But the settlers chose a heavily wooded area near swamps. The ground that could be placed under quick cultivation was restricted. The forest facilitated the approach of hostile Indians. The marshes constituted a health hazard which was to prove serious. But all these considerations were subordinated to the necessity of protecting the fort from European attack by land or sea. The narrow space between the two rivers provided a barrier to the approach of a considerable body of European troops, and the narrow entrance to the river guarded by Point Comfort gave greater assurance against maritime assault than a more exposed and healthier position on the shores of the bay.

Fear of Spanish attack was one of the more obvious links between the people in the lonely fort and the political situation in their homeland. The bickering on shipboard was not altogether due to strained tempers; personal disagreements had social roots in the various class interests that were represented in the enterprise. When Newport opened his sealed orders, it was found that the persons appointed to the council were Bartholomew Gosnold, Edward Maria Wingfield, John Ratcliffe, John Martin, George Kendall, and John Smith. We have discussed Gosnold's background. There was an intimate connection between Gosnold and Wingfield; their families were neighbors in Suffolk, and had intermarried for generations.[5] Also close to Gosnold was Gabriel Archer, who had been his companion on the voyage to New England in 1602. Although Archer was not included in the council, he was to play a significant role in the political struggle that was soon to develop.

Gosnold's influence, which seems to have carried a good deal of weight, secured Wingfield's election as president of the council. Smith took no part in the choice; he was not released from confinement until shortly before Newport's departure late in June. He took his seat on the council at a time when the colony's affairs were approaching a crisis. Kendall was removed from the ruling body and imprisoned, on the charge that "he did practice to sowe discord" between the president and the other members.[6]

The settlement was "verie bare and scantie of victualls." Lack of food lowered resistance to disease. The plague made its appearance in August, when John Asbie died "of the bloudie flux." "Our men," wrote George Percy, "were destroyed with cruell diseases, as Swellings, Flixes, Burning Fevers."[7] The epidemic that caused forty-six deaths in a month has often been described as malaria. But recent studies suggest that "the causes of death were starvation, scurvy, dysentery, and possibly typhoid."[8]

The medical causes of the plague have been no less obscured than its political components. Lack of food and failure to take the most elementary health precautions were in themselves political matters, growing out of the limitations imposed by the charter. As death swept the settlement, the struggle for survival merged in a struggle for power—for control of the dwindling store of supplies which were the only defense against the plague.

Gosnold's death, on August 22, led to the removal of Wingfield from the presidency. Wingfield wrote that during Gosnold's sickness, he "did easily foretell his own deposing from his Commaund: so much differed the President and the other Councellors in mannaging the government of the Collonye." The *coup d'etat* took place on September 10. As Wingfield described it, "Master Ratcliff, Master Smyth, and Master Martynn, came to the Presidentes Tennt with a warrant, subscribed under their hands, to depose the President."[9]

There was no question that the desperately needed supplies were at stake in the dispute. Wingfield was charged with malfeasance in handling the common store. The starkly simple economic issue—possession of the means of subsistence, and especially the precious stock of things that had some medicinal value, such as oil, vinegar, sherry and brandy—evoked social attitudes which reproduced, in intensely concentrated and personal terms, the great conflict that was developing in England. Wingfield held that he was responsible to the community for the protection of the common store. When other members of the council demanded articles, he insisted on legal procedure, demanding the submission of vouchers and asking that the council vote on any proposal for an increase in the distribution of supplies.[10] Although the evidence is far from conclusive, there seems no reason to doubt Wingfield's assertion that "I had never bestowed the valew of three penny whitles to my own use, nor to the private use of any other."[11]

The controversy is of historical interest, for it was not restricted to the little group of men exchanging charges and countercharges in the wilderness; it was to be carried to England, to be thrown back into the arena of class conflict from which it originated. For this reason, the interpretation of the events in the fever-ridden stockade affected the parliamentary struggle and the determination of colonial policy.

Interpretation is still obscured by the bias of the various personal narratives, and the weight has been given to Smith's version. Even though only a small number of people were involved, the drama was not a simple conflict of two fixed viewpoints. Like all factional struggles, it proceeded by way of temporary alliances, compromises, intrigues. Wingfield was tried, found guilty, and heavily fined. The former president was indignant that Archer deserted him, and secured the office of recorder or magistrate, participating in that capacity at Wingfield's trial. Archer seems to have had no hesitation in using Wingfield's downfall for his own advancement. He may also have hoped that his position as magistrate would enable him to enforce order and discipline.

However, the dynamics of the situation led to increasing disorders. The men who had seized power in order to have easier access to the common store could not enjoy the fruits of their victory without coming into collision with the majority of the colonists. They had to resort to violence to maintain their power. John Ratcliffe, who replaced Wingfield as president, formed a triumvirate with John Martin and John Smith. According to Wingfield's account, Ratcliffe and his associates "beate men at their pleasures. One lyeth sick till death, another walketh lame, the third cryeth out in all his boanes." [12]

Among those who were beaten was a blacksmith, James Read, who struck back at the president. For this, he was sentenced to be hanged. He saved himself by confessing a "conspiracy," in which he implicated George Kendall, a deposed councilman. On the basis of Read's charges, Kendall was tried, found guilty, and condemned to death. The first man in the English colonies to pay the supreme penalty for "sedition" against the established order—a "state" which had just been improvised by methods of doubtful legality—was shot on December 1.

The discontent of the colonists, unrelieved by the execution of Kendall, weakened the little settlement at a time when its prospects were beginning to improve. The fall weather abated the plague. The neighboring tribes of Indians were willing to supply corn in exchange for European goods. In November, the surplus of corn having been exhausted in the villages near the settlement, Smith undertook a longer expedition, to the river called Chickahominy, whose inhabitants were known by the type of food prepared there as "the coarse-pounded corn people," or "hominy people."

The voyage was successful. Smith returned again a few weeks later to explore the upper river, and on this occasion he had trouble with the "hominy people." Having reached a point at which the stream was too narrow and swift to permit his barge to proceed,

Smith assigned seven men to guard the vessel, and continued in a canoe with two Englishmen and two Indian guides. Twenty miles further, Smith and one of the guides left the canoe to reconnoiter. During their absence, the two Englishmen, Robinson and Emry, were killed. Shortly afterward, Smith was surrounded by about two hundred Indians and taken prisoner.

The capture took place on December 10. Smith was taken by a circuitous route to a village on the York River, only twelve miles from Jamestown. There he was led before Powhatan, chief of the confederation of Algonquin tribes inhabiting the coastal area from the Roanoke River to the head of Chesapeake Bay.

According to the *True Relation,* written by Smith and sent back to England shortly after the event, Smith spent a good part of the three weeks of his captivity in edifying conversation with the chieftain. Powhatan described the geography and customs of "his great and spacious dominions," and Smith "requited his discourse" with an account of "the territories of Europe," the greatness of the English king, "the innumerable multitude of his ships." The Englishman astonished his host by giving "him to understand the noyse of Trumpets, and terrible manner of fighting" to which Europeans were accustomed.[13]

The rescue by Pocahontas, which seems so strangely at variance with this cordial interchange, made its first appearance in Smith's writings some fifteen years later. In the earlier narrative, Smith gives no hint that his life was in danger. Powhatan was consistently friendly:

> Having with all the kindness he could devise sought to content me, he sent me home with four men; one that usually carried my Gowne and Knapsacke after me, two others loaded with bread, and one to accompany me.[14]

We can defer further discussion of the Pocahontas legend and the social and political forces that determined its invention at a moment of crisis in the struggle between the bourgeoisie and the crown for control of the Virginia colony. The local beginnings of the conflict, fought out among the less than two score individuals who remained alive, took a sharp turn while Smith was visiting Powhatan. Smith and Archer had emerged as the representatives of two irreconcilable points of view concerning the administration of the settlement. Archer took advantage of his rival's absence to secure the upper hand and gain a seat on the council. When Smith returned, no joyous welcome greeted him. He was arrested, charged with responsibility for the death of his two companions who had been killed by the Indians, and condemned to die. He was saved by a last minute rescue which was almost as dramatic as the Pocahontas story—and much better authenticated. Just as the hanging was about to take place, Captain Newport returned from England. Newport, with the authority of the crown behind him, took Smith's side and ordered his release.

We need not sympathize with Archer's arbitrary procedure in order to recognize the political tendencies that lay behind the personal clash of wills. Archer, like the Calvinists of New England, used the Bible as the supreme legal authority, justifying the death sentence by specific reference to the Levitical law which demands "breach for breach, eye for eye, tooth for tooth." [15] Wingfield tells us that Newport's arrival "prevented a parliament," which Archer "intended thear to summon." [16] It seems probable that Archer wanted to set up an acceptable governing body elected by the freemen of the community. The proposed elimination of Smith reduced the council to three members—Ratcliffe, Martin and Archer—and Archer's appointment did not accord with the terms of the charter. There was nothing in the charter to legalize a "parliament," but the suggestion indicates that Archer represented other settlers beside himself.

On April 10, Newport sailed for England, taking Wingfield and Archer with him. Smith was jubilant:

> Wee not having any use for Parliaments, plaies, petitions, admirals, recorders, interpreters, chronologers, courts of plea, nor Justices of peace, sent M. Wingfield and Captain Archer with him, for England, to seeke some place of better imploiement.[17]

The colony was strengthened by the arrival of the *Phoenix,* which reached Jamestown ten days after Newport sailed, with additional settlers and supplies. Medical problems, which should have been of primary concern when the first journey was planned, were at last given attention. Among the one hundred and twenty people joining the thirty-eight survivors of the original voyage were two apothecaries and a surgeon. Three councilors presided over the settlement. Newport had brought a new member of the council, Matthew Scrivener, but Martin left on the *Phoenix*. Smith removed Ratcliffe from the presidency in the summer of 1608, and replaced him with Scrivener. Two months later Smith took the presidency himself, eliminating the council.

Meanwhile, the issue had been transferred to England where men who were deeply interested in colonization did not share Smith's contempt for parliaments, petitions, courts of plea, and other devices for the protection of personal and property rights. Wingfield was old and tired, and understandably angry at Archer. He seems to have withdrawn from the controversy. But Archer made his report to Sandys and other opposition leaders, and it convinced them that colonization could not succeed without a change in methods of administration and control. While Smith ruled without interference in Virginia, the drive for the reorganization of the enterprise gathered strength in England. When the reorganization was accomplished through the charter of 1609, Smith was removed. He returned to England, bitter against the people who had ended his short reign. The crown was also bitter against these people, and Smith found that his version of the conflict in Virginia was an effective weapon in the English conflict. He was employed to write the "authentic history" of the first years of colonization for a specific political purpose—to prove that "politics," and more particularly the politics of the dissident bourgeoisie, interfered with colonial enterprise, and that colonies prospered better under direct royal control than under corporate management.

We have dealt only with the origins of Smith's fame—of his rise from obscurity to power in the disorders of the first year. His removal from authority in Virginia, and the extraordinary influence of his propaganda writings, will be dealt with below.

5 : JAMESTOWN AND MOSCOW

We are not accustomed to think of any connection between the settlement of Virginia and eastern Europe or Russia. But if we are to link the formal aspects of culture with the life force of the people, we must also link the first summer on the James River with the parallel events taking place halfway around the globe.

While plague and social conflict threatened the Virginia colony, Russia was in the midst of "the time of troubles." During the summer, a pretender to the throne, the second false Dmitry, besieged Moscow. A little more than a hundred miles south of Moscow, an army of peasants and cossacks led by the serf, Ivan Bolotnikov, held the city of Tula against a superior enemy force. Hunger and disease were as merciless in Tula as among the dwindling population of Jamestown. In both cases, the problem of hunger was a problem of power; in both cases, the conflict was interwoven with the movement of European and global forces; in both cases, the issues are linked across the centuries.

The disorders in Russia were part of a social ferment that extended through all of eastern Europe. The struggle for power among various competing interests, the constant warfare, shifting boundaries, destructive conquests and broken treaties, seem to have no recognizable pattern. But the basic factor in the political and military strife was the Baltic wheat which formed a very essential part of the European food supply. The northern voyages of Dutch merchants were possibly more prosaic than Jason's journey to the Black Sea. But a considerable part of Europe was as dependent on imports of grain as Greece had been at the dawn of Mediterranean civilization.

We have said that pepper was the most important factor in the Dutch war of independence. But spices were luxuries. Bread, as the saying goes, is the staff of life. Holland's ability to challenge Spain's control of the luxury commerce with the Orient was made possible by the Dutch conquest of the northern grain trade at the beginning of the fifteenth century. In seizing the initiative from the Hansa towns, the Dutch merchants secured command of the wheat which was indispensable to the population of southern Europe, and thus laid the foundations of Holland's maritime supremacy. The Elizabethan corn laws, relaxing the limitations on export, were designed to meet Dutch competition and give English merchants a share in the profitable continental trade.[1] The English merchants profited; the price rose and there was a scarcity in the domestic market, resulting in the famines of the fifteen-nineties.

There were also famines, for interrelated reasons, in northeastern Europe. The Dutch demand for wheat, accompanied by continually rising prices, brought wealth to the great landholders of East Prussia, Lithuania and Livonia, whose estates were cultivated by serfs or itinerant laborers. These lands were part of the kingdom of Poland, which underwent a rapid national development as a result of the commercial intercourse with Holland. The process was similar to that which took place in England and other nations: the crown tried to take advantage of the conflict between the nobility and the rising bourgeoisie by granting concessions to trade and industry, and moving toward tighter monarchial control of the economy.

But the large-scale production of wheat gave a special character to the Polish conflict: it gave greater economic power to the landed aristocracy. At the same time it united the opposition against the nobles, forcing craftsmen and merchants to join with peasants and laborers against their common enemy. This accounts for the rapid spread of religious radicalism in Poland, and for the vacillating policies of the Polish kings, who were caught between the demands of the nobles and a popular movement which was too strong—and too valuable as a curb on the nobility—to be summarily crushed.

Thus there was unusual religious toleration and a rich development of social ideas and organization in Poland during the last half of the sixteenth century. The main intellectual trend in Poland may be traced to Michael Servetus and the liberal, humanist philosophy which denied the Trinity and attacked the authoritarian dogma of Calvinism. Modern Unitarianism regards Servetus as one of its founders, and attributes the first organization of a church to the labors of Giorgio Biandrata, an Italian physician, who came to Poland in 1558. In 1568, a ten-day debate was held at the royal court: six Calvinists disputed with five representatives of the so-called "Minor Reformed Church," which held an anti-Trinitarian position and demanded full religious toleration. Biandrata and a Transylvanian bishop, Francis David, led the assault on the Calvinists.

That such an argument should be held at the court of a Catholic sovereign is sufficiently indicative of the intellectual climate in Poland. Although it was held in Latin, the obscurity of the language did not prevent a popular demonstration in favor of the "Unitarians." David was carried through the streets in triumph at the end of the discussion.[2]

The great period of the Polish movement opens with the arrival of Faustus Socinus at Cracow in 1579. Socinus, born in Siena, Italy, in 1539, fled from Italy in 1559, when the instability resulting from the financial crisis occasioned feverish activity on the part of the Inquisition. Socinus was probably influenced by the doctrines of Servetus before he left Italy. From the first publication of Servetus' anti-Trinitarian opinions in 1531, there had been private associations of Unitarians in Italy.[3] Faustus' uncle, Laelius Socinus, and other members of the family, were in contact with followers of Servetus. Faustus pursued these contacts when he visited Lyons during his Italian exile. At the age of twenty-three, the young scholar questioned the actual divinity of God, and shortly afterward denied the natural immortality of man.[4] However, he concealed his views, and returned to Italy for twelve years, serving Isabella de Medici.

We find him in Basle in 1575. Socinus came in contact with Biandrata and David, and was involved in a complicated theological dispute which led to David's imprisonment in Transylvania in 1579. The Jesuits were exerting great pressure on the Transylvanian government to curb the anti-Trinitarians. David seems to have placed himself in a dangerously exposed position by a sermon denouncing the worship of Christ as a divine being. At Biandrata's request, Socinus tried to persuade David to take a more moderate public position. But the bishop refused; he was sixty-nine years old; he died after a few months in confinement.

Socinus, impressed with the extent of Unitarian activity in eastern Europe, went to Poland where he established a university at Cracow. During the later years of the century, the school was attended by 1,000 students. Books and pamphlets from the printing presses at Cracow were circulated in every part of Europe. Socinians were active at all the Protestant universities of Holland and Germany.[5]

In denying mystic concepts of immortality and divinity, Socinus asserted the dignity of man and his ability to control his own destiny. His beliefs had their origin in the Arian heresies of the fourth century, preserved through the Middle Ages by the equalitarian sects and the secret organizations of peasants and laborers. However, the doctrine preached at Cracow was modified, and divorced to a considerable extent from its revolutionary past. He attacked war, capital punishment, and serfdom. Although Socinus avoided the leveling tendencies of Anabaptism, the leaven of Anabaptism was at work among his followers. The mass base of the movement was largely in the country districts,[6] and the churches in the villages attracted the poorest and most militant part of the rural population.

Although King Sigismund III tolerated the Socinians, his attitude toward them varied with the pressures of the internal situation and the demands of foreign policy. The growth of the wheat trade made control of the Baltic the *sine qua non* of Poland's economic expansion. In order to defeat Sweden and Russia, Sigismund needed the support of the predominantly Catholic upper nobility and the predominantly Calvinist lower nobility and upper middle class. He also felt that he needed the support of the empire and the papacy. For these reasons, the government became increasingly unsympathetic to the Socinians in the last years of the century. In 1598, Sigismund made an unsuccessful invasion of Sweden. In the same year, Socinus' home was attacked by a crowd of students. He was ill, and was forced into the streets half naked. His books and manuscripts were burned, and it was only by the intercession of two Catholic professors that he was saved from being thrown into the Vistula.[7]

The riot, like similar disorders in our own day, was symptomatic of official attitudes which permitted such outbreaks and prevented prosecution of the guilty persons. Socinus spent the last years of his life in retirement, but the Socinian influence continued to spread.

In 1598, Boris Godunov became Tsar of Russia. A few years previously the Russian defeat of Sweden had won back the territories on the Gulf of Finland which gave Russia access to the Baltic. Godunov wished to build up commerce with the West. But his plans were obstructed by the great famine that swept the land in 1601 and lasted for three years. The famine was the result of the backward organization of Russian agriculture, the hoarding of grain at high prices, and the lack of an adequate labor force.

The conditions on the landed estates were so intolerable that there had been an exodus of peasants as serious in its economic implications as the escape of Negro slaves from the South in the days of the Underground Railroad. Even the intolerable conditions of migratory labor in East Prussia or Poland seemed to offer more hope than the hungry toil of the serf under the boyar's whip. But the main movement of peasants was toward the eastern frontiers, where the serfs and laborers joined the Cossacks on the upper reaches of the Oka, in the Bryansk forests and along the Don.

The famine caused wholesale starvation. Villages died *en masse;* people lived on weeds and birch bark. The Moscow streets were littered with corpses. There was the usual profiteering, and the Tsar averted trouble by inadequate distributions from the state granaries. These measures could not avert the coming storm. In 1603, peasants and serfs formed detachments, gathering together in an army that was defeated at the gates of Moscow.

Sigismund III, whose interest in control of the Baltic coincided with his desire for the fertile lands to the east—which would provide additional wheat for the Dutch market—attempted to take advantage of the Russian disorders to make an easy conquest. Since it was desirable to cloak the aggression in a show of legality, the first of the false Dmitrys was invented. He was supposed to be the brother of the former Tsar; the real Dmitry had died at the age of nine.

The false Dmitry, backed by the land-hungry Polish magnates, invaded Russia in 1604. Cossacks, peasants and fugitive serfs flocked to his support, believing his claim that he had come to free them from oppression. Boris Godunov died in 1605; the boyars, whose class interest made them prefer Polish occupation to further concessions to the peasants, opened the gates of Moscow to the false Dmitry.

It was soon apparent that the new Tsar's promises were as fictitious as his name. The peasants were reduced to more merciless servitude;

Polish exploiters were even greedier than the Russians whom they replaced. In May, 1606, Moscow rose in rebellion. The false Tsar was killed, his body burned, his ashes stuffed in a cannon and fired in the direction from which he had come. The Polish gentry, barricaded in their houses, were besieged by people with knives and stones, who killed about 2,000 of them.[8]

The boyars hastened to elect Prince Shuiski as Tsar, hoping that a strong government could deal with the peasant discontent. But the fall of 1606 witnessed sporadic outbreaks in many parts of the country: on the Don, on the middle Volga, in Astrakhan, and northwest of Moscow at Tver, Pskov and Novgorod. The movements coalesced under the leadership of Ivan Bolotnikov. As Bolotnikov marched toward Moscow his forces were augmented by miscellaneous recruits, including some discontented nobles and landlords as well as craftsmen and peasants. In October, the people's army laid siege to Moscow, and Bolotnikov wrote appeals to the population to rise against the nobles. However, his position was weakened by the betrayal and desertion of some of the nobles who had joined him. In a battle with the Tsar's troops early in December, a body of nobles went over to the enemy. The shattered peasant army retreated to Kaluga, where they received heavy reinforcements, which enabled them to defeat the Tsar's army and move to Tula.

In May, 1607, the Tsar appeared at the walls of Tula, taking personal command of an army of 100,000 men. The city held out for four months. In spite of hunger and lack of arms, the besieged men made sorties almost daily, inflicting heavy damage and weakening the morale of the attacking force. Finally, a dam was built to stop the flow of the Upa River, which flooded the town and necessitated surrender. Bolotnikov, having been captured, was blinded and drowned.

It was obvious, from the Polish point of view, that the situation was ripe for another false Dmitry. The second pretender, supported by a strong Polish army, appeared on the frontier of Muscovy in the fall of 1607, and approached Moscow in 1608. Meanwhile, other peasant rebellions had broken out. A serf attack on Nizhni Novgorod was beaten back, but in the fall of 1608, the Middle Volga was in the throes of a general uprising.[9] The Tsar, unable to cope with his foreign or domestic enemies, called on Sweden for aid, offering cession of the province of Karelia in return for assistance. The entry of Sweden into the war forced Poland to make a formal declaration of hostilities. The conflict moved toward the climax which, in 1613, brought the Romanov family to the throne of Russia.

The class warfare in Russia intensified the ideological and social differences in Poland. Intrigue among the nobles, dissatisfied with the progress of the Russian campaign and with the concessions the king felt compelled to make to the bourgeoisie, caused a series of plots and insurrections. The country was in an anarchical condition from 1606 to 1610.

The weakness of the Polish crown favored the further growth of the Socinian movement. Socinus died in 1604. But the college at Cracow prospered. The number of congregations in Poland grew to three hundred.[10] The leaders tried to strengthen their position by proposing a fraternal alliance with the Moravian Brethren.[11] No formal unity was established, but the Socinians were sufficiently powerful to stage public debates with the Jesuits. These discussions, which occurred frequently from 1603 to 1610, were printed and circulated throughout Protestant Europe.[12]

The social conflicts in eastern Europe indicate a wider dissemination of revolutionary ideas and forces than has generally been realized. One cannot follow the underground movement that carried the news of the peasant war and the work of the Anabaptist underground to the rebellious serfs and Cossacks marching against Moscow. But it is likely that there was commerce of ideas from the mining regions of Central Europe across the Carpathian ranges to the Baltic wheat fields. Migratory laborers moved across the whole area. Maritime intercourse provided a cultural contact between Holland and the Baltic seaports.

The Socinians were tolerated as long as they reflected, at least to a limited extent, the revolutionary ferment among peasants and laborers. Their following in Russia in the first years of the seventeenth century was sufficiently substantial to cause the first false Dmitry to announce that he was a follower of Socinus when he was trying to ingratiate himself with the lower classes of Moscow.[13]

The Socinians could win intellectual victories in their debates with the Jesuits. But the freedom of speech which they enjoyed was maintained only while they were backed by a mass movement. When the popular forces were split and broken, the Socinians faced defeat. This happened in a few decades, in the course of the Thirty Years' War. In 1638, the Socinians were banished from Cracow. With their departure, intellectual liberty died in Poland. A Unitarian writer of a later period was to look back upon their fall as a national tragedy: "The very eye of Poland was plucked out, the sanctuary and refuge of exiles, the shrine of religion and the muses." [14]

We know the tragic fate that awaited Poland. But the work of Socinus was not lost. His beliefs were carried to England, to be revitalized in the doctrines of the Separatists and Seekers, as well as in the personalized religion of the Quakers and in the later growth of Unitarianism. The Socinian influence is evident in the life and thought of Roger Williams; it illuminates the writings of John Woolman; and finds expression in Paine and Whitman as well as in Channing and Parker.

6 : MALTHUS AND THE MIDLAND RIOTS

WHILE AN ARMY of Russian peasants defended Tula, and the little band of colonists built their fort on a marshy neck of ground in Virginia, riots swept the Midland Counties of England.

The 1607 disturbances in the central counties were not fundamentally different from the outbreaks that had occurred at intervals from the days of Wat Tyler. However, the outbreak in 1607 came at a time when the social situation in England was undergoing far-reaching changes. The significance of the riots lies less in their direct political impact—for the impact was slight—than in the shadow of coming events that was cast across the green land. The shadow did not attract great attention. Yet it darkened the mood and temper of the time.

A new word was used for the first time in connection with the trouble in the Midlands. The people were called *Levellers;* [1] the word was to ripple like a banner over the heads of marching men in the Cromwellian Revolution. The word was also to appear in the American colonies in the agrarian conflicts that led to the Revolution.

The 1607 protest was occasioned by the policy of the crown and the specific situation resulting from the Gunpowder Plot. In terms of general policy, the Stuart regime increased the severity of the long rural depression. Since James favored the nobility as against the bourgeoisie, he favored the maximum exploitation of the agricultural population in the interest of the great landholders. The discovery of the Gunpowder Plot gave the king a special opportunity to confer favors on his friends at the expense of the rural poor, in England as well as in Ireland. The seizure of the vast properties of the Earls of Tyrconnel and Tyrone in Ireland was accompanied by the confiscation of English estates belonging to persons implicated in the plot. The new owners were anxious to get a quick return by enclosing the common lands, dispossessing tenants, and converting the properties to sheep-farming, cattle-raising or dairying.

This renewal of the enclosure movement worked hardships on the people of Warwick, Leceister and Northampton. These regions had not been seriously affected by the sixteenth century enclosures, which had been concentrated largely in the more industrialized eastern counties.

The rebellion was brief; it involved the usual spontaneous assembling of people driven by despair; the tragedy of inadequate preparation and purely local organization; the wonderful strength of people, the moment of hope and the quick crumbling of the enterprise. There seem to have been about 8,000 rebels. Soldiers called to suppress the rising refused to attack, and the manor lords assembled their personal retainers in order to defeat and disarm the yeomen and peasants. Little is known of the man called Captain Pouch who led the revolt. He was hanged, drawn and quartered, while his associates, treated with greater leniency by a legal system that employed careful distinctions in administering justice, were only hanged.[2]

An official view of the riots is contained in a paper dated July 5, 1607, and entitled *A consideration of the Cause in question before the Lords touchinge depopulation*. It was apparently drawn up for the consideration of the royal council. It begins with the warning that concessions to the peasantry would be dangerous, for "suche encouragement may move the people to seeke redresse, by the like outrage." It recalls that, in case of Ket's revolt in 1549, "the remedie was not pursued until twoe Yeares after the rebellion."

The document defends enclosures, on the ground that common lands are "Nurseries of Beggers," and that enclosures are a defence against foreign invaders, "who cannot soe easelie marche spoile and forraye in an enclosed Countrie." The argument shows that the king's advisers were as cynical as modern propagandists in using the fear of war to divert attention from economic issues. The suggestion that England was to be protected by fences erected in the middle of the island gave a patriotic flavor to the new wave of enclosures.

There were plenty of laws against enclosures on the statute books.

But the report gave notice that there would no longer be any pretense of enforcing the laws. It compared two counties—Northampton, where the people still held the common lands, and Somerset where the land was "all enclosed but inferior in *quantitie and qualitie.*" A detailed summary of tax payments showed that the supposedly inferior Somerset lands paid four times as much as the more fertile Northampton area. The statistics proved, therefore, that enclosures were profitable and necessary.

Since the expropriation of the poorer farmers created a surplus population, the report proposed a "Malthusian" remedy:

> Soe must the state either by transferinge to the Warres or reduceinge of *Colonies* vent the daylie encrease that ells will surcharge the State: for if in London a place more contagious than the Countrye the nomber of Christenings doth weekely by 40 exceede the burialls, and that Countries proportionally doth equall if not outgoe that rate, it cannot be but that in this State, as in a full bodie theare must breake out Yearely tumors and Impostures as did of late.[3]

The appearance of "Malthusianism" in an English document in 1607 does not mark the first formulation of the doctrine. The idea that people must be eliminated in order to provide adequate food for the living is the *rationale* of the blood sacrifices practiced by many primitive peoples. We have noted its development in the religion of the Aztecs as the pressure of population increased in the Valley of Mexico in the period before the Spanish conquest. While civil war was raging in sixteenth century France, Montaigne compared the diseases of society to the ailments of the body, suggesting that "purges and bleedings" are occasionally necessary. States, according to Montaigne, "resort to diverse methods of purging. Sometimes they expel a great multitude of families to relieve the country of them . . . Sometimes, too, they purposely fostered wars . . . to serve as blood-letting for their commonwealth." [4]

One finds the theory in an English document published in 1581: *The radicall cause of sondry offences that are happened withyn our state,* which complains of the increase of population and mentions the infrequency of war as one of its main causes.

The doctrine that was to become world-famous when it was enunciated by an English parson at the end of the eighteenth century is as old as the class organization of society. The specific statement of the theory at the moment of English settlement in North America is of interest in its bearing on the role that rural unemployment was to play in the English transatlantic migration. Colonization, especially in the form of a lucrative traffic in convicts, children and indentured servants, was encouraged as a way to relieve the "tumors and impostures" of the countryside. The surplus of dispossessed people was dangerous, because it was far in excess of the need for a reservoir of cheap labor to maintain the "fluidity" of the labor market.

Theories of population took a different turn in the middle of the eighteenth century, when the beginnings of the industrial revolution occasioned a wider demand for labor. English population theory at that time was largely concerned with the maintenance of an adequate supply of workers to keep wages at the lowest level.

The view that people are the riches of a nation is expressed in Robert Wallace's treatise *On the Numbers of Man,* published in 1753. The impact of growing industrialization is evident in Wallace's argument that overproduction of luxury goods is undesirable because it diverts capital and workmen from the manufacture of basic commodities.[5] Wallace echoed Montesquieu's view that the population of the ancient Greek and Roman world was larger than the eighteenth century population of Europe.[6] Montesquieu's argument was motivated by his recognition of the waste of human life caused by the continuance of feudal oppression in France. Montesquieu occupied a "centrist" political position. He could not share the revolutionary materialism of the Encyclopedists. Neither could he ignore the suffering that he saw around him. He clothed his contemporary criticism in historical analogies; he did not approve of slavery, but he pointed out that the human chattel was treated less destructively than the serfs and wage slaves of his own time.[7]

David Hume disagreed with Montesquieu. Hume's well-known disbelief in miracles included his disbelief in the possibility or desirability of improving the lot of the laborer. As the ablest ideologist of the Tory oligarchy, he held that the poor of England were blessed beyond their deserts, and he resented the suggestion that the contemporary population had less advantages in the fight for survival than the slaves of Greece and Rome.[8]

Benjamin Franklin's *Observations Concerning the Increase of Mankind,* printed in 1755, was like a lightning flash among these murky speculations. Although Franklin has been inaccurately described as a forerunner of Malthus,[9] his work was a declaration of faith in human progress through rapid increase of population. Attacking the concept of "inevitable" poverty and limited growth, Franklin expressed confidence that the number of people in the American colonies would double every twenty or twenty-five years.[10]

This was like a preliminary declaration of American independence —and it was recognized as such by English publicists. Oliver Goldsmith was one of the writers who warned against "peopling the desarts of America" with "laborious and enterprising" people, who "can be serviceable to their country at home . . . men who ought to be regarded as the sinews of the people." [11] The proposals to limit the expansion of colonial territories or populations were answered heatedly by Franklin in 1760; since England seemed so anxious to check normal growth, he suggested that parliament might order American midwives to stifle every third or fourth child at birth.[12]

Franklin had exposed the political issues underlying English population theories.[13] While the American lands promised sustenance to unborn millions, England continued to drive the population from the land in order to force children and women, as well as men, to accept employment in mines and industries at starvation wages. Goldsmith gave a moving portrayal of the tragedy of the English countryside in *The Deserted Village,* written in 1770.

When Thomas R. Malthus published an *Essay on the Principles of Population* in 1798, he responded to an historic change in the relationship of social and economic forces. By the end of the century, the demand for industrial labor lagged behind the growth of a dispossessed and unemployed population. Under these circumstances, it was necessary to take the most brutal measures to prevent popular organization and compel the acceptance of starvation. The trial of Tom Paine in absentia was part of a series of prosecutions designed to outlaw freedom of speech and assembly, and to illegalize the mildest protest.

Furthermore, the distress of the lower classes crystallized in powerful movements of protest inspired by the American and French Revolutions. The charges in most of these cases related to attempts at political organization. In Scotland, the men who had planned a conference to discuss universal suffrage and annual parliaments were arrested and given savage sentences. The use of government spies was revealed in the case of Robert Watt. He was accused of preparing an armed conspiracy to seize Edinburgh Castle. It turned out that

Watt had been a police spy, that the whole plot was stimulated, and perhaps invented, by the government in order to justify its charges of sedition. Unfortunately for Watt, he had outlived his usefulness to his employers. The state had to have a conviction in order to protect itself. Watt, like worthier martyrs, was honored with the extreme penalty, being hanged, drawn and quartered on October 15, 1794.[14]

The scandal around the Watt case was in part responsible for the failure of the attempts to convict the English radicals who were also accused of "seditiously" calling a convention under the sponsorship of the London Corresponding Society which derived its name and program from the colonial Committees of Correspondence which organized the movement for independence. William Pitt followed the course adopted by American statesmen 150 years later in seeking to make political capital out of anti-Communist hysteria. Pitt appeared before the House of Commons to speak vaguely but fervently of a shocking conspiracy, demanding emergency powers and a special commission to try the offenders.[15]

London juries retained their common sense, the defendants were acquitted, and the government found it necessary to abandon its plans for a wholesale witch hunt. Eight hundred warrants which had been prepared for immediate use were torn up.

The acquittals reflected the deep currents of protest stirring the English people. There were hunger riots in 1795; soldiers and militia helped workers plunder food stores. The King's carriage was surrounded in the streets of London by a crowd estimated at 200,000, shouting "Peace" and "Bread" and throwing stones at the royal coach. In 1797, the English fleet mutinied. In 1798, the people of Ireland rose in insurrection.[16] A factor in the shortage of food in England was the cutting off of imports from the Baltic, still the main source of the nation's wheat supply. Prices of wheat rose sharply when France conquered Holland in 1795, breaking the trade connections between England and northern Europe.[17]

This was the setting for Malthus' *Essay on the Principles of Population*. As Marx points out:

> The great sensation this pamphlet caused was due solely to party interest . . . The "principle of population," slowly worked out in the eighteenth century, and then, in the midst of a great social crisis, proclaimed with drums and trumpets . . . was greeted with jubilance by the English oligarchy as the great destroyer of all hankerings after human development.[18]

The argument embodied, in the simplest and most effective form, the theory that the exploiting classes had no responsibility for the suffering of those whom they employed—and consigned to total starvation when there was not enough work to go round. The responsibility, said the pious parson, rested with God. Malthus rejoiced that the population is reduced by poverty and hunger, which demonstrate that it is against God's will for the lower classes to multiply so incontinently. The fear that the meek may inherit the earth made it desirable that a considerable number of them be removed from it. In answer to Paine's *Rights of Man,* Malthus said: "there is one right which man had generally been thought to possess, which I am confident he neither does nor can possess—a right to subsistence when his labour will not fairly purchase it." [19] He proposed that the people be told that, in marrying and having children whom they cannot support, "they are plunging themselves into distress, and that they are acting directly contrary to the will of God, and bringing down upon themselves various diseases." [20]

Malthusian theory was linked to the treason trials and to the philosophy on which the trials were based. If people have no right to subsistence, attempts to assert their right violate divine law and social order. Two books appeared at almost the same moment as Malthus' work. One of these was written by John Robinson and published at Edinburgh—where the sedition trials had started—in 1597. Its title describes its contents: *Proofs of a Conspiracy Against All the Religions and Governments of Europe, carried on in the Secret Meetings of the Free Masons, Illuminati, and Reading Societies.* The second work, Augustin Barruel's *Memoirs of Jacobinism,* printed in London in 1798, contained similar proofs of a world-wide "conspiracy."

These volumes occupy an unrecognized, but by no means inconsiderable, place in the history of American thought. They were exported to the United States to give ideological justification to the Alien and Sedition Laws. Malthus' theory was not particularly applicable to the American situation; the vast reaches of land beyond the Appalachian barrier made it evident that the country could support a growing population. But "proof" that organization for democracy and human welfare was the result of an international conspiracy was seized with indecent haste by the Federalists. Robinson's book was printed simultaneously in New York and Philadelphia, the Philadelphia edition being rushed to completion in three weeks.[21]

In addition to the New York publication of Barruel's *Memoirs,* editions appeared almost simultaneously at Hartford, Connecticut and Elizabethtown, New Jersey.

It is easy to look back across the years, and smile at the aberrations of another age. In *The Growth of American Thought,* Merle Curti makes passing reference to Robinson as an "unbalanced professor at Edinburgh." [22] But Robinson was a man of scholarly attainments, having been secretary of the Royal Society of Edinburgh and Professor of Natural History at the university there.[23] It is unwise, especially in view of our twentieth century experience, to underestimate Robinson's American influence. Such distinguished figures in the academic world as Timothy Dwight, president of Yale University, accepted the "diabolical conspiracy" as an established historical fact. In a sermon which he delivered on July 4, 1798, Dwight traced the spread of "every novel, licentious and alarming opinion" to the French Encyclopedists and other thinkers who had abandoned "reverence for everything heretofore esteemed sacred":

> Minds already tinged with philosophism were here speedily blackened with a deep and deadly die; and those which came fresh and innocent to the scene of contamination became early and irremediably corrupted . . . In these hot beds were sown the seeds of that astonishing Revolution, and all its dreadful appendages, which now spreads dismay and horror throughout half the globe.[24]

These fantasies were promulgated because they met a political need. As Vernon Stauffer observes, the charges invented by Robinson and Barruel were "framed to meet the necessities of a case which in the judgment of dilettante historians positively *required* the hypothesis of a diabolical conspiracy against thrones and altars." [25]

The warnings of catastrophe did not convince the American people: Jefferson became president in 1801, and the Federalists were driven from the political scene. Alexander Hamilton drank the cup of defeat to the dregs. He wrote to Gouverneur Morris: "What can I do better than withdraw from the scene? Every day proves to me more and more that this American world was not made for me." [26] Hamilton's program aimed at a higher rate of exploitation and lower standard of living, causing malnutrition and death by reducing wages below the subsistence level, and preventing the fulfillment of Franklin's prophecy concerning the growth of the American population. The Jeffersonian victory helped to prove that Franklin was right. The

Malthusian God seems to have had less objections to procreation in the New World than in the old, for the population of the United States continued to double every twenty-five years or less by generation alone from 1790 to 1860.[27]

But the Federalist philosophy did not die with Hamilton. It has been resuscitated, with all its ideological baggage, in the twentieth century. Hamilton's prophecy that "this American world" was not made for him is belied by the triumph of the financial oligarchy which he prematurely attempted to impose on the predominantly agrarian democracy of the early nineteenth century. The contemporary culture of the United States is poisoned by historical misconceptions which repeat the fantasies of Robinson and Barruel concerning a "conspiracy against all religions and governments." Communists and persons suspected of Communist sympathies are substituted for "the Free Masons, Illuminati and reading societies." But not a word of the fantasy has been changed.

The modern campaign is based upon the same imperative need that motivated "the hypothesis of a diabolical conspiracy against thrones and altars" in the last decade of the eighteenth century. The people of the world are again stirred by the old dream of freedom, peace and creative labor for the welfare of the whole society. But today, the dream is realizable. The forces which seek to perpetuate war and misery must call again upon the Malthusian God of wrath, the God of blood and disaster, to justify the continuance of their destructive power. Malthusian theory has the double value of providing both a religious and a "scientific" basis for the eternal necessity of wage-slavery, unemployment and perennial starvation. The United States is no longer an exception to "the law of overpopulation."

So scholars again proclaim the principle of insufficient resources, supplementing the reactionary fears and phobias that were employed a hundred and fifty years ago as propaganda against the French and American Revolutions. The field of the social sciences has been invaded—one might almost say ravaged—by an epidemic of neo-Malthusianism. After a century and a half of scientific progress, utilizing resources that go beyond the most hopeful dreams of eighteenth century science, we return to the eighteenth century belief that poverty and disease and war are a God-given means of getting rid of useless, and potentially dangerous, people.

A recent attempt to dress the theory in up-to-the-minute scientific terminology has been made by William Vogt in *Road to Survival.* But the introduction of terms like "biotic potential" and "environmental resistance," and loose historical references to Babylon, Ur, Assyria and Carthage, do not alter Vogt's pessimistic approach to "the spawning millions," whose "untrammelled copulation" has produced "too many people in the world for its limited resources to provide a high standard of living." [28]

The theory is especially valuable in justifying imperial exploitation and explaining the "inevitable" poverty of colonial areas. "If relief from population pressure is the goal," writes Frank W. Notestein, "it is dangerous to continue frittering away the productive power of modern techniques in a social setting calculated to maintain high fertility. There is urgent need to apply in synchronized fashion every device for the creation of a social setting favorable to reduced fertility." [29]

It seems strange in this era of scientific advance that technology cannot solve the problem of food production to maintain a decent standard of living for the world's population of approximately 2,100,000,000. Many scientists hold that the methods of production which are at present available can provide satisfactorily for at least a billion more than the present population.[30]

Let us turn back to the riots of 1607 and dig a little more deeply into their historical and cultural meaning, especially in relation to the American colonies. We have seen how the leaders of the sick and starving settlement in Virginia quarrelled for control of the diminishing store of food. The struggle between the crown and the bourgeoisie in England was a similar battle for mastery of available and potential resources. The Midland Riots reminded the contending classes that the mass of the people had a stake in the conflict. Both the court and the opposition attempted to utilize the popular discontent in order to advance its own cause. For this reason, the government did not follow the execution of the leaders of the revolt with severe measures. A proclamation in July pardoned those who had taken part in the riots. A commission was appointed to make a further investigation.[31]

While it was impolitic to take steps against the Midland people which might have provoked further disturbances, the trouble gave James an opportunity to move against some of the more radical Puritan groups, whose doctrines were held responsible for the general unrest. Thus a by-product of the Midland Riots was the persecution of a little congregation of Separatists at Scrooby in Nottinghamshire, forcing them to begin the pilgrimage which brought them to Cape Cod twelve years later.

Nottinghamshire, north of the counties where the riots took place, was an early center of woolen production; the textile trade declined in the sixteenth century, but its place was taken by stocking manufacture. The growth of the industry led to William Lee's invention of the stocking frame in 1589. The mechanical method of producing knitted fabrics was the basis for the development of hosiery and lace machines. But Lee could not get capital for the promotion of his device, and he went to France, where he established a factory at Rouen. Two centuries later, Nottinghamshire was to be the scene of the Luddite riots, in which the workers destroyed the stocking and lace frames, which had returned to bring misery and unemployment to the land where they were invented.

Even in the early seventeenth century, industrial uncertainties darkened the lives of the Nottinghamshire people. There were beginnings of coal mining; but weaving or knitting in the home were the means by which the lower classes supplemented the meager returns from agricultural labor. The members of the Scrooby congregation were people of moderate means. But as small farmers or merchants they felt the impact of the prolonged depression, which depopulated the country and wrecked the craft industries in the towns. They were desperately afraid that the wall which separated them from the propertyless mass would crumble. In asserting the right of the independent congregation, they proposed to erect a bulwark against the oppression of the landholding aristocracy, which was driving them toward destitution. The Scrooby congregation was not an isolated group. It was part of a movement which, as William Bradford tells us, functioned in "sundrie townes and villages, some in Nottinghamshire, some of Lincolnshire, and some of Yorkshire, where they border nearest together." [32]

These yeomen and traders eschewed the equalitarian beliefs of the Anabaptists, and there is no reason to suppose that they sympathized with the Midland demonstrations. But the hunters for sedition ignored distinctions between degrees of radicalism. The Puritans had to choose between prison and flight:

Some were taken & clapt up in prison. others had their houses besett & wacht night and day, & hardly escaped their hands, and ye most were faine to flie & leave their houses & habitations, and the means of their livelihood.[33]

The exodus could not take place at once, or in a body. The members of the Scrooby congregation fled singly, or in small groups, during the winter of 1607-1608.

Among the most important cultural achievements of the English revolution were the tracts written by John Lilburne, William Walwyn and Gerrard Winstanley, calling for all men to share equally in the fruits of their common labor.

When the people's revolution was crushed by Cromwell in 1649,[34] the class interests of the bourgeoisie forced it to turn against the genuinely revolutionary classes which had fought and won the battle against feudal power. Being deprived of its mass base, the bourgeois dictatorship could not exist without a compromise with the landholding aristocracy.

Milton, however, blind and defiant, held to his faith in the power of man. But he could think of the individual only as a solitary soul in a hostile universe. The aged poet wrote *Paradise Lost* in 1667. The poem ends as Adam and Eve leave the lost paradise before "the brandished sword of God . . . fierce as a comet." The sense of loss and loneliness is overpowering in the lines that close the poem.

> They, hand in hand, with wandering
> steps and slow,
> Through Eden took their solitary way.

Four years later, Milton wrote his two last poems. *Paradise Regained* is the legend of atonement for man's sins through Christ's vicarious suffering. In *Samson Agonistes,* the protagonist, alone and betrayed, can fulfill himself only by pulling down the temple, "both to destroy and be destroyed." Seventy years later, in the period of England's drive toward world domination, Samson's agony was married to the monumental music of Handel. The baroque style had won another victory.

When Milton wrote his final statement, the agrarian struggle that had failed in England was developing in Virginia. The Negro slaves and white indentured servants who conspired together in Gloucester County, Virginia, in 1663, were inspired by the ideals of the English Levellers. There were exiled Puritans and Oliverians among the servants who joined with the Negroes in planning the uprising.[35]

The conspiracy was betrayed, and several bloody heads were displayed from local chimney tops. The legislature gave appropriate thanks to the God who rejoices in the suffering of the poor. It was voted "that the 13th of September be annually kept holy, being the day those villains intended to put the plot into execution." [36]

The event is important as the beginning of the great sweep of agrarian and slave revolts that created social strife in most of the colonies for more than a hundred years. The movement can be traced from the Midland Riots in 1607, through Bacon's Rebellion, the insurrections in Maryland and Carolina, the Leisler revolution in New York, the slave risings during the early eighteenth century, the organization of farmers in New England, the armed seizure of land by the Elizabethtown Associates in New Jersey, the gathering of the Westchester Levellers in the Hudson Valley in 1766.

The Leveller movement in the Hudson Valley, the last of the colonial agrarian revolts and most directly connected with the Revolution, emphasizes in its name the continuity of the equalitarian tradition. The men, numbering nearly two thousand, who took up arms, were defeated by British troops. Tenants of many of the great estates were driven from their homes. A contemporary account tells how redcoats pillaged and burned the houses of tenants at Philipse' Manor:

> 'Tis beyond the Power of Language to paint in lively images the Horror! the Surprise and Astonishment of this poor distressed People . . . to see them at once, as it had been, in an instant, deprived of all their substance for which they had laboured sweat and fatigued themselves all the Days of their Lives . . .[37]

As these people turned away from their ruined homes, they took the road to Valley Forge and Yorktown. Yet the achievement of independence was not to solve the problem of poverty amidst plenty. The pattern of agrarian conflict continued in Shays' Rebellion in New England, the Whiskey Insurrection on the Pennsylvania frontier.

"The pressure of population," wrote Frederick Engels, "is not upon the means of subsistence but upon the means of employment."

PART V

The European Background of English Colonization

1607–1618

1 : CORIOLANUS

A HISTORY of western civilization widely used in colleges describes the beginning of the epoch of capitalism in the following terms:

> Three threads of progress give us the approach to the modern world: the expanding self-consciousness of the individual; the rise of the middle classes; and the evolution of the modern state . . . One can discover in the study of the Renaissance and the religious wars that ushered in the modern age signs of the eventual triumph of the individual in science, business, politics, and art—a genius that was to have much to do with the making of our twentieth century society . . .

We have considered aspects of this "expanding self-consciousness of the individual," not as an abstract flowering of the human personality, but as an expression of the viewpoint and interests of the classes that sought to establish new structures of power on the ruins of the medieval structure.[1]

In the following pages we shall deal more fully with concepts of human personality in their specific relationship to class conflicts and changes in the organization of the state.

We must turn again to Shakespeare for the most striking statement of the problem of power, as it became more clearly defined in the struggle between the crown and the bourgeoisie at the time of the Virginia voyage and the Midland Riots.

Coriolanus contains one of Shakespeare's most quoted lines: "The city is the people." The phrase is occasionally used, without regard for the context in which it appears, to express a purely democratic content.[2] But scholars have tended to ignore the crystal sound and vitality of the phrase, striking a note that is new in the poet's work. It does not imply that Shakespeare had adopted a democratic viewpoint, or that he had endorsed the program of the bourgeoisie.

The play does reflect, sensitively and profoundly, the social tensions of the time. The Midland Riots evidently aroused considerable interest in London. The degree to which the theatre was affected is suggested in *Coriolanus*: it is also indicated in the reference to enclosures in *Pericles,* and in the sense of frustration and despair that permeates *Timon of Athens.*

The scene which opens the second act of *Pericles* is in a part of the play which may not have been written by Shakespeare; however the speculation regarding the authorship of the scene is based on scanty evidence, and there are critics who feel that the dialogue of the fishermen is Shakespearian in tone and metaphor:[3]

> First Fisherman: The great ones eat up the little ones. I can compare our rich misers to nothing so fitly as to a whale; 'a plays and tumbles, driving the poor fry before him, and at last devours them all in a mouthful: such whales have I heard on the land, who never leave gaping till they've swallowed the whole parish, church, steeple, bells, and all . . .
>
> Third Fisherman: . . . When I had been in his belly I would have kept such a jangling of the bells that he should never have left till he cast bells, steeple, church and parish up again.

The fisherman adds that, if the king were of his mind, "He would purge the land of these drones that rob the bee of her honey."

The passage may not have been an important factor in the success of *Pericles,* but its appearance in one of the most popular dramas of the day suggests that the conglomerate culture of the London streets and theatres was touched by the plight of the dispossessed rural population. Knowledge of the suffering of the countryside is related to the degrading uncertainties of urban life, which are etched in *Pericles* as virulently as in *Measure for Measure.* In the scenes in which Marina is sold to a brothel, the brutal humor rests solely on the fact that money corrupts all values. When she protests to the pander's servant, he replies:

> What would you have me do? go to the wars, would you? where a man may serve seven years for the loss of a leg, and have not money enough in the end to buy himself a wooden one?

It is instructive to contrast the success of *Pericles* with the failure of *The Knight of the Burning Pestle,* probably produced at about the same time. While Shakespeare reflected the popular mood, Beaumont and Fletcher tailored their play to serve the interests of the crown. *The Knight of the Burning Pestle* was plagiarized from *Don Quixote,* but Cervantes' theme was turned upside down. The Spanish author's onslaught on feudalism became a satire on London tradesmen and artisans. The antics of Ralph, the grocer's apprentice, disporting himself as "a brave-spirited knight," were hardly calculated to please an audience drawn very largely from the ranks of apprentices and shopkeepers. The rowdy mockery wore the mask of "pure entertainment," but Londoners who were stirred by the Bates case could not fail to note the connection between the political events of the day and the jibes at the stupidity and arrogance of the mercantile and industrial classes. The city was proud of its militia. It found nothing hilarious in Ralph's story of how one of the men befouled himself because he was frightened by an unexpected noise. The remarkably cold reception of the play was admitted when it was published in 1613: we are told that it was written in eight days and "exposed to the wide world, who . . . utterly rejected it." [4]

Shakespeare was haunted by the money theme. The date of *Timon of Athens* is uncertain, but it may be provisionally assigned to the same season, beginning in the autumn of 1607. *Timon* seems to carry over and extend the disillusionment of *King Lear.* In the earlier play, the conflict between the old absolutism and the new money-power is suspended in the dream world of the king's insanity. In *Timon,* the problem is presented with an incoherent intensity that is like an externalization of Lear's psychological breakdown. The king's eloquent madness, full of "matter and impertinency mix'd," has become so all-inclusive that it dominates and beclouds the action.

Kenneth Muir notes that the bitterness of *Timon* "has been ascribed by some critics to Shakespeare's sympathy with the riots in Warwickshire against the enclosures, and by others to a more personal cause." [5] Whatever Shakespeare's griefs or emotional anxieties may have been, he never wrote in terms of inwardness or avoidance of life. There is unmistakable social passion in Timon's apostrophe to the power of gold:

> Thus much of this will make black, white;
> foul, fair;
> Wrong, right; base, noble; old, young;
> coward, valiant . . .

This yellow slave
Will knit and break religions; bless the
accurs'd;
Make the hoar leprosy ador'd; place thieves,
And give them, title, knee, and approbation,
With senators on the bench.

Shakespeare could not remain enthralled in this somber mood. He could not feel that there is no answer to man's hope, no cure for the corruption of the heart. There was "something rotten" in the state of England—and it related to the state itself, to the nature of sovereignty. In *Coriolanus,* Shakespeare turned again to the question of power, but he saw it in a new light, in terms of a new situation. The king's right to speak in the name of the whole people had been challenged. The representatives of the bourgeoisie in the Commons claimed that *they* defended the people against the greed of the aristocracy. And in the Midlands, the people themselves—the mass without political identity—raised their voices.

Coriolanus may have been written before *Timon,* but it is more probable that it appeared in 1608.[6] It begins without poetic preliminaries; the scene is a street in Rome: "Enter a company of mutinous Citizens, with staves, clubs and other weapons." The complaints of the Roman populace relate both to the Midland Riots and to the anger of London crowds against the skyrocketing price of food. The people want bread:

We are accounted poor citizens; the patricians good. What authority surfeits on would relieve us . . . the gods know I speak this in hunger for bread, not in thirst for revenge.

When it is suggested that this is slander against "the helms of the state, who care for you like fathers," a citizen answers:

They ne'er cared for us yet. Suffer us to famish and their storehouses crammed with grain; make edicts for usury, to support usurers; repeal daily any wholesome act established against the rich; and provide more piercing statutes daily, to chain up and restrain the poor.

When Coriolanus scoffs at the people and denies their demand "for corn at their own rates," the crowd calls for his banishment. He is told that it seems to be his design "to unbuild the city and lay all flat." For "what is the city but the people?" A citizen answers: "True, the people are the city."

Coriolanus refuses to bow to the popular will. Accused of seeking tyrannical power, he is called "a traitor to the people." In a violent scene in the Forum, he defies the multitude, and is condemned to banishment. He accepts the sentence, shouting "You common cry of curs!" He goes into exile, saying "There is a world elsewhere," and again: "The beast with many heads butts me away."

But there is not a world elsewhere. Coriolanus must return to Rome as a conqueror. He joins his old enemy, Tullus Aufidius, leader of the Volscians, whom he has repeatedly defeated. With Aufidius, he brings an army to the gates of Rome. He is no longer faced with a military problem, but with the moral problem of power: his own mother, Volumnia, comes out of the gates as the representative of the people he hates. She tells him he is "tearing his country's bowels out." If he proceeds with his plan to ravage the city, his name will be forever "dogg'd with curses . . . To the ensuing age abhorred." Volumnia's long pleading ends with the terrible words:

I am hush'd until our city be afire,
And then I'll speak a little.

Coriolanus cannot withstand the appeal. He agrees to make peace, although he knows that the decision is dangerous, "if not most mortal to him." The contradiction between patriotism and class interest is insoluble. In the denouement, Coriolanus is trapped and killed by Aufidius. The betrayer is betrayed.

The play is extraordinary in its starkness. The political problem is stripped of all psychological or emotional complications. Coriolanus is a one-dimensional character. He has no passion except his hatred for the common herd. His relationship to the people supersedes all other relationships. It is the motivation of all his actions, the sole cause of his destruction.

Coriolanus marks a turning point in Shakespeare's thought—and in the thought of his time which he so profoundly encompassed and projected—in that it raises the question of power in a dual aspect: as a revolutionary threat from below and as an obligation from above. In a decade, the principle of the king's sole responsibility expressed by Henry V on the eve of the battle of Agincourt—

. . . Let us our lives, our souls,
Our debts, our careful wives, our children, all
Our sins lay on the king!—

has lost its competence. The patriotic impulse can no longer be stated as undivided loyalty to a personal ruler. The division between classes cannot be concealed: before Coriolanus is banished, his friends beg him to make concessions to the people, lest "our good city cleave in the midst, and perish."

The play does not suggest that there is merit on the side of the popular forces; on the contrary, Shakespeare's temperament, background and intellectual development made it impossible for him to accept the right of the people—or a class purporting to speak for the people—to share in the control of the state. Coriolanus is projected as a heroic figure, justified in his hatred of the "subversive" multitude. Yet his hatred brings him to a disaster as irrevocable as Lear's madness or the maze of evil where Timon walked. He asserts the prerogatives to which his class is entitled—and he finds himself allied with Rome's mortal enemies, warned by the voice of his own mother that he will be cursed as a traitor.

It may be said that Coriolanus embodies the qualities of the Renaissance aristocrat. But these virtues have become negative; humanism dissolves in malevolent anger. Hardin Craig observes: "As we contemplate the situation in which Coriolanus stands before Rome, Coriolanus the aristocrat, we realize that he is about to cease to be himself, about to lose his own soul." [7]

The question of patriotism, which is probed like a raw wound in Shakespeare's study of the Roman patrician, was posed as confusingly in Jacobean England as in the United States in the twentieth century. As the parliamentary struggle developed, the opposition became known as the Patriot Party, mobilizing public support as the defender of England's vital interests against the betrayal of the nation's welfare by the Court Party. The issue was to come to a head at the beginning of the Thirty Years' War, when the crown's refusal to aid the Protestant forces in Europe brought vitriolic attacks on the king.

But it was no secret in 1607 that many of James' intimate advisers had close ties with Madrid and Rome, and that the uproar around the Gunpowder Plot had not eliminated the Spanish-Catholic influence in the royal household. Puritan ministers who ventured to make mild criticisms of the church-state could be brought before the Star Chamber on charges of "sedition," but the actuality of treason was much closer to the king's person.

A few years later, at a time when circumstances forced the temporary adoption of an anti-Spanish policy, the English ambassador at Madrid brought James a list of officials who were being regularly paid —for services rendered—by the Spanish government. Among the persons accepting bribes from Philip III was Sir William Mason, admiral in command of the channel fleet. Others on the list included the Earl of Northampton, the Earl of Suffolk, and Mrs. Drummond, first lady of the queen's bedchamber.[8]

The king was not impressed. He probably knew that many other members of his intimate circle, including his youthful favorite, Robert Carr,[9] were so devoted to Spanish interests that they might as well be paid for it. The accused individuals had been wise enough to sell themselves to a cause of which James approved, and which corresponded to the class interests of the aristocracy and the crown.

Shakespeare went to the heart of the problem of patriotism when he showed Coriolanus driven to treason by his hatred of the people. The problem became a burning issue in the years following the French Revolution, when the victory of the French people was transformed into Napoleonic aggression.

European art and thought, stirred by the fall of the French monarchy, went through a difficult crisis in the period of the Napoleonic Wars. Beethoven's musical art was shaken, and to a considerable extent cast in a new pattern, by the European cataclysm. The story of the *Eroica* symphony is too well-known to require extended comment. But it may serve to indicate the impact of the political situation on the composer's life and art: his work on the symphony in 1803 and 1804 paralleled the revelation of Napoleon's imperial design. The majestic passion of the *Eroica* could not be debased to applaud the operatic "heroism" of the man who placed the imperial crown on his own head with his own hands in Notre Dame cathedral on December 2, 1804, repeating the ceremony with the iron crown of Lombardy in Milan cathedral on May 26, 1805.

The symphony, which had its inception in Napoleon's career, was completed in 1804. When a printed edition appeared in 1806, Napoleon's name was omitted from the dedication; it was dedicated simply to the "memory of a great man."[10]

The creative problems which are suggested by the change may be more fully explored in the case of Beethoven's only opera, *Leonore*. The preparation and revision of the work covered the whole decade of Napoleonic triumphs and defeats, and the work was finally performed under a new title, *Fidelio,* in 1814. The fact that Beethoven wrote no other opera is in itself significant. The use of the dramatic form was directly inspired by the musical culture that developed in Paris during the great days of popular triumph in the seventeen-nineties. The opera is especially influenced by Cherubini's revolutionary music-drama, *Les Deux Journeés.*[11]

The first version of the work, as an opera in three acts under the title of *Leonore,* appeared in 1805, shortly after the completion of the *Eroica.* The ensuing changes in the score, and especially in the overture, form an incomparable record of aesthetic response to social events. In technical terms, the problem in the *Leonore* overture related to the symphonic principle requiring a more or less literal recapitulation of the first part of the sonata allegro. The overture written in 1805 is unique in that it dispenses with the recapitulation after the trumpet call announcing the arrival of the liberator. Here Beethoven sacrificed symphonic structure in order to get the full dramatic force of the trumpet call of deliverance. But in the next overture, in 1806, when Napoleon's armies were converting additional countries into vassal states, musical design is substituted for dramatic fervor, and the theme of liberation is followed by an anticlimactic recapitulation. The composer tried another overture in 1807, but the problem seemed insoluble. He turned to instrumental compositions, publishing a pianoforte score of *Leonore* in 1810, and finally rewriting the opera with an entirely different overture for its 1814 production.[12]

During that time, the Napoleonic campaigns had ended in catastrophe. The failure of Bonaparte's plan of world dominance was to a considerable extent due to the semi-spontaneous organization of the people. The rising of the Spanish people in the summer of 1808 upset the whole schedule of conquest. The emperor had planned to use the Spanish dockyards and warships to assure maritime supremacy in the Mediterranean as the first step toward breaking England's commercial power and destroying the Turkish empire. The disaster in Spain was fatal to the whole plan, and Napoleon knew it. "Everything," he wrote, "is connected with this event, Germany, Poland, Italy." [13] He was proved right four years later when his broken army fled through the snow from Moscow, harried by Russian partisans and guerrilla bands.

Beethoven may not have understood the full meaning of Napoleon's failure. But it proved, as it was to prove to Tolstoy later, that history is not made solely by the will of great men. The artist's new consciousness that the people are a latent force in history required a revision of *Leonore* that affected the whole score and libretto as well as the overture. In *Fidelio,* the trumpet call announcing the deliverer has a different relationship to the drama of deliverance. The opera builds with growing unity to the song of the prisoners, swelling as they emerge from prison to an overwhelming hymn of freedom.[14]

An important turning point in this decade of musical development is the *Coriolanus* overture, written in 1808. It reveals the artist's continuing preoccupation with the problem of power, and forms the bridge between the *Eroica* and the completion of *Fidelio* in 1814. Beethoven turned back to Shakespeare's play as a key to the Napoleonic betrayal. Like Coriolanus, the emperor stood at the gates of the city of man, ready to burn and destroy in order to conquer.

The idea projected in *Coriolanus* that the misuse of power is treason to the people enabled Beethoven to see the political cataclysm of his time in a new perspective. The idea is vitally important in the United States today, when our culture is torn by two concepts of loyalty—one imposed by military and financial "heroes" whose ambitions outrun Napoleon's dreams, the other concept being rooted in the life of the people, who hold that the city and the land are theirs and that there can be no loyalty which denies their will or subverts their welfare.

Since government is an instrument of class power, the moral problem of patriotism cannot be divorced from the realities of class conflict. This was obvious to the people of the colonies when they defied the British crown in 1776. The Declaration of Independence was based on the doctrine that the highest patriotism for Americans lay in the defense of their class interests against English power. Many Americans realized that a similar cleavage of classes existed in England, and that the government which oppressed the colonies was guilty of treason to the English people. The point is made with remarkable vigor in a play, *The Fall of British Tyranny,* published in Philadelphia a few months before the signing of the Declaration. The first scenes show Lord Paramount (a satirical portrait of the Earl of Bute) discussing his plans with Mocklaw (who is intended to represent Mansfield); Paramount is conspiring to overthrow the Whig government of England and set up a dictatorship. The plan includes treasonable cooperation with the reactionary governments of France and Spain, which are to send their troops to England to help in establishing a reactionary regime.

The Fall of British Tyranny is uninhibited propaganda for the revolutionary cause. The charge that the Earl of Bute intended to promote civil war in England with the aid of French and Spanish soldiers was based on the attacks on the Tory statesman circulated by his enemies in England. Bute's sympathies with the continental aristocracy were well-known. He had been accused of serious improprieties in negotiating the peace treaty with France during his brief term of office as prime minister, from 1761 to 1763. Popular hatred of Bute, aroused chiefly by the excise taxes which imposed burdens on the English people similar to those against which the colonies rebelled, forced him out of public life.

The significance of *The Fall of British Tyranny* is not to be found in the accuracy of its portrait of Bute. The cruel caricature is of interest, because it links the American rebellion with the class strife in England; the suspicion that Bute and other Tory politicians were trying to make political capital out of the rebellion, and that they were even prepared to call on foreign aid in order to achieve a *coup d'etat* in England, was evidently given enough credence to make it effective in an American play. Lord Paramount's views in the play corresponded with Bute's known opinions. Paramount announces that "Charters, magna chartas, bill of rights, acts of assembly, resolves of congresses, trials by jury (and acts of parliament too) when they make against us, must all be annihilated." In the same scene, he looks out of the window to see a passing procession of the Lord Mayor and aldermen, with the London livery companies. He exclaims: "Ignorant brutes! . . . We despise them and their politics, and it's not unlikely it may end in blood."[15]

It is noteworthy that the first drama to introduce George Washington as a character on the stage linked the American struggle with the aims of the middle and lower classes in England.

The concept of treason as growing out of the corruption of the governing class takes us back from 1776 to 1607, from the crude propaganda play published in Philadelphia to *Coriolanus*. The Tory party's ties with the French and Spanish aristocracy in the second half of the eighteenth century were a continuation of the policies inaugurated by the Stuart monarchy. The belief that the crown was disloyal to the people became current in the first years of James' reign, and was strengthened by the Bates case, the Midland Riots, and the parliamentary quarrels over taxes, monopolies and feudal prerogatives. James' shabby personality was a commentary on the divinity that "doth hedge a king." But his personal weakness was largely determined by the situation in which he found himself. The tangle of contradictions caused him to vacillate in a sort of measured frenzy, with the regularity of a metronome. His absolute power was so relative that it consisted chiefly in his absolute right to accede to contradictory pressures.

James was Coriolanus, stripped of Shakespearean eloquence and without magnanimity of spirit. Like Coriolanus, he held it an indignity that the people should question his motives or demand an accounting of his stewardship. He could not destroy his enemies. He needed no woman's impassioned plea to convince him that he had to compromise, at least with some of the more influential groups which opposed him, and that failure to do so might transform the clamor in the Commons into rebellious charges that he was a traitor to the nation.

Another facet of the problem of power, as it affected one of the ablest thinkers of the time, may be explored in the case of Francis Bacon. We have discussed Bacon's split personality, the dichotomy between his intellectual and political interests. The dilemma which the crown faced in 1607 gave Bacon an opportunity for political advancement and thus deepened the contradiction in his soul.

Bacon was socially connected with many of the more prominent leaders of the opposition. He was a member of the influential middle group of politicians and businessmen who formed a more or less cohesive aggregate of related and intermarried families.[16] For this reason, he was particularly valuable to the crown. The king had come to a point at which a clever "liberal" presentation of his policies, in terms that would appeal to the bourgeoisie, seemed absolutely necessary. Bacon fitted the bill. He was a staunch supporter of absolutism, but he wrote and talked with an intellectual vigor that was rare in court circles. James suffered from his own inability to express himself with grace or subtlety, and the king's arrogance was all too often imitated by his principal counsellors.

Bacon's appointment as crown solicitor in June, 1607, just after the Midland Riots, was intended to bring some much needed style and intelligence into the legal affairs of the crown. The royal solicitor occupied an important position. He handled litigation affecting the king's privileges and touching the most urgent political issues of the day. One of the first proposals made by Bacon was characteristic of his social views and methods. He suggested a change in the jury system, which was designed to make the juries less responsive to popular pressure. The political intent was obvious, but Bacon phrased the proposal with his customary tact. His words, substantially unaltered, soon appeared in a royal proclamation, condemning the tendency of sheriffs to "spare gentlemen of quality in a kind of awe and respect," thus permitting service to rest with the "simple and ignorant." [17] Like so many of Bacon's schemes, the proclamation was in the nature of an intellectual exercise. The king had no adequate means of controlling local juries, and there is no indication that the admonition led to any change in their composition.

Bacon was rewarded with a special gift of £100 from the king. But this was also in the nature of an intellectual exercise; six months later, on Christmas eve, the holiday season seems to have reminded Bacon that the gift had never been received, and he wrote an ill-tempered letter of complaint to an officer of the Exchequer. The delay related to the realities of power: there was no money in the treasury.

Nevertheless, Bacon's personal fortunes were prospering. On July 25, 1608, he sat down at his desk and began to make notes on his financial and social position. It was a Monday morning, and it seemed an appropriate time to take stock of himself and his career. In fourteen months, he had trebled his income. Early in July, 1608, he became clerk of the Star Chamber, which brought in approximately £2,000 a year. With money from his wife's property, Bacon figured that his annual revenue was now £4,975, and that his property, "as *in pretio* to be sold," was worth £24,155. Satisfied with this achievement, he turned his attention to detailed methods of utilizing his friendly relationship with the king, of making himself agreeable to the new treasurer, Lord Salisbury, and other prominent persons, and of measures for the improvement of his lands and leases.[18]

Bacon had not abandoned his scientific pursuits. Satisfied with the security of his position, he turned on the next day, Tuesday, July 26, to the problem of getting advice and assistance in the preparation of the vast survey of human knowledge which he called *The Great Instauration,* and which was never to be completed. The scope and nobility of the plan, with its bold declaration that "an entirely different way from any known to our predecessors must be opened to the human understanding,"[19] emphasizes the split between the philosopher and the politician. Bacon was beginning to feel the psychological effects of the split. He was forty-seven, and he complained of nervous indigestion. He made a minute record of the state of his health, emphasizing its psychological aspects: he was afflicted with "melancholy," "doubt of present peril," "strangeness in beholding and darksomeness," "inclination to superstition," "cloudiness."[20]

There were political reasons for the disturbed condition of the philosopher's soul. The royal government could not be maintained without money. Adequate funds to meet the king's needs could not be obtained without parliamentary consent. But another session of parliament would give the bourgeoisie another field day of demands and grievances. While Bacon suffered fits of melancholia, Sandys was at work on a new Virginia charter, boldly planning to shift control of the colony from the king to the stockholders. Sandys' confidence sprang from the knowledge that James would be forced to reach some agreement with the opposition, and that the liberalization of the Virginia patent could be made part of the general settlement.

Bacon was one of the men on whom the king relied to work out a compromise with the bourgeoisie that would not sacrifice the essential prerogatives of the crown. Bacon knew that this was expected of him, and that he would be highly honored if he succeeded. It is small wonder that the task weighed heavily on his mind during the year in which the usual session of parliament was omitted. He had achieved a respectable income, but wealth and power lay within his grasp. Yet phantoms thronged his quiet study; his eyes were clouded, and "doubt of present peril" afflicted his spirit.

Bacon had made his choice. But in choosing personal advancement and security, he found himself entangled in the uncertainties he was so anxious to avoid. He wanted to bask in the sunlight of royal favor, but power brought no warmth or assurance. It brought only a growing sense of personal and political insecurity.

Shakespeare's social conscience forced him to ask the questions that Bacon dared not ask. But for him there was no answer. There was only the dilemma of power, eating the flesh and soul of man. Shakespeare walked in a strange world. It was the ribald, poverty-stricken London of his youth. But the old political and moral landmarks were dissolving in mist. Out of the street cries and the tavern talk there rose a chant of the murmurous crowd; it was not really words, for no words were spoken; it was the rumble of a muffled oracle. But the poet heard with his heart, and he was afraid, for he knew the sound would grow and shake the earth: "The city is the people . . . the people are the city."

2 : THE BURIED WEAPONS

THE INDIAN SOCIETIES of North America offer a plenitude of materials bearing on political and cultural organization. When the American anthropologist, Lewis Henry Morgan, published *Ancient Society* in 1877, he utilized the study of the Iroquois Confederation as the basis for the formulation of general laws concerning the development of human institutions. Morgan's scientific work led him to the conclusion that man's intellectual and emotional life is shaped by the material conditions of his existence. He believed that "a critical knowledge of the evolution of property would embody, in some respects, the most remarkable portion of the mental history of mankind." [1]

Frederick Engels, relying largely on Morgan's research for his own work on *The Origin of the Family, Private Property and the State,* wrote that "Morgan in his own way had discovered afresh in America the materialistic conception of history discovered by Marx forty years ago, and in his comparison of barbarism and civilization it had led him, in the main points, to the same conclusions as Marx." [2]

Engels' comment may explain the fact that, while Morgan's contribution to anthropology is acknowledged, his theory of history has been conspicuously ignored. Yet *Ancient Society* stands out as one of the great landmarks in the cultural life of the United States: conducting his research at a moment when American capitalism moved toward concentrated control of the economy and the state-organization, the scientist discovered the elements of a science of history, linking the origin of property relationships among the Indians with the society of the nineteenth century. "The passion for the possession of property, as the representative of accumulated subsistence," wrote Morgan, "has now become dominant over the human mind in civilized races."[3]

We cannot attempt detailed consideration of the anthropological data on which Morgan based his findings. But his emphasis on productive organization as the basic factor in social evolution forms an appropriate starting point for an examination of the contact between the Indians and the Europeans in the first years of English colonization.

When the English ships reached the James River in 1607, the Indians with whom they came in contact were members of the Algonkin family. The widely dispersed Algonkin tribes held most of the territory east of the Mississippi, from Tennessee and Virginia in the south to Hudson Bay in the north. This was a domain of forest lands, with many streams and lakes. The Algonkin culture was largely that of a woodland people. They lived by hunting, and the deer was a staple article of food. The skill with which they fashioned birchbark canoes was typical of their genius and way of life. They could travel swiftly over long distances in these light craft, carrying the canoes over portages from one waterway to another. Their homes were also taken from the trees. Wigwam is an Algonkin term for house; the conical structure with a fire in the center was generally made of birchbark. Bark and wood furnished most of their household utensils. They shredded base fibers from the inner bark of trees to make twine for primitive weaving. Metal tools were unknown, but they made black clay pots with pointed bottoms, and stone and bone implements were common.[4]

Members of the same Algonkin family were found in other parts of North America; there were the buffalo hunting Blackfoot tribes of midwestern Canada, the Arapaho and Cheyenne of the plains between the Mississippi and the Rockies, and two small Algonkin tribes lived in northern California.

Among the tribes scattered along the Atlantic seaboard the village was often the unit of organization. But there were loose federations of communities or tribes in certain areas. The tendency to federation occurred wherever agricultural production had been sufficiently stabilized to reduce interest in hunting and create a surplus of corn, bringing a need of stronger organization to protect the fields, and administer the use of the surplus. This was the case in Virginia where the Powhatan confederation controlled the region from the Roanoke River to the head of Chesapeake Bay.

The food problem was fatally urgent to some of the northern tribes where lack of reserves for the long winter occasioned an annual battle with starvation. Champlain told of the arrival of famished Indians at his quarters at Quebec during the winter of 1608-1609. They were half dead as they crossed the icebound river. Squaws carrying their children fell ravenously on the carcass of a dead dog. Champlain was informed that this was a usual occurrence, a normal incident of the "wintry purgatory" of the tribes.[5]

A few centuries before the arrival of the Europeans, the Iroquois tribes entered the far-flung and sparsely settled territories of the Algonkins. The Iroquois originally came from the lower Mississippi delta. It is impossible to fix the date of their departure from their home on the Gulf of Mexico. But when they left, they carried with them vestiges of cultural influences that reached the Mississippi Valley from Mexico. Although customs and ceremonies of the Iroquois are related to Aztec and Toltec sources, there is one difference: the Iroquois reckoned descent in the female line and maintained elements of matriarchal organization which seem to antedate the periods of Mexican and Central American civilization of which we have any knowledge. We may guess that the contact between the Iroquois and the societies in the south was broken at a very early time, or that the matriarchal system was revived in order to prevent social disintegration during the long trek to the east.[6]

The women must have played an indispensable role in maintaining the ancient maize culture during the shifting fortunes of the migration. The role is suggested in the Condolence ceremony, a more or less incidental part of Aztec life, which was transformed into a vital ritual by the Iroquois. The warrior's death is lamented: "He also will in time take with him the whole body of warriors and also the whole body of men, they will go with him. But it is still harder when the woman dies because with her the line is lost."[7] There could be no more poignant illustration of the determination to maintain the tribal organization—and the agriculture which was its heart and sustenance—against death and adversity.

For an indeterminate period, the Iroquois lived in the Lower Appalachians. Here they began to expand and new tribes were formed. The Cherokee split off from the main body and remained in Tennessee. The other tribes pushed northward, probably following the road that was later to be traveled in the opposite direction by European immigrants from Pennsylvania. They came to the fertile valleys of central New York, and it was here that the Federation was formed, probably not more than one hundred years before the English settlers arrived on the Atlantic coast.[8]

The problem of power was a matter of life and death for the Iroquois, for they held their lands in the midst of hostile Algonkin tribes. In the period prior to the founding of the federation the five nations were unable to make a common front against their enemies because they were constantly at war among themselves. They had developed agricultural production to a point which made land and power synonymous. They were not well enough organized to achieve further territorial expansion; therefore, they engaged in fratricidal strife for control of the Mohawk and upper Hudson Valleys which constituted an agricultural base for hunting and military expeditions in the neighboring forests. The struggle was analogous to the conflict that had taken place in the Valley of Mexico in the centuries before the arrival of the Spaniards.

The only alternative to destruction was socially controlled use of the society's available resources. The ancient maize culture, preserved through all the tribal wanderings, offered a basis for peaceful organization. The maintenance of the old culture corresponded to the level of productive forces; the migration had prevented the accretion of surplus stocks of food or commodities, with the accompanying rise of new patterns of dominance and intensified exploitation of labor; but corn cultivation, with its social and cultural base, had continued. In the new home in central New York, the internecine strife was ended by a revival of the cultural heritage in a new and stronger form to meet new productive opportunities.

The founder of the league was Hiawatha. His achievement is so encrusted with legend that one cannot separate the myth from the actuality. But the myth is the significant aspect of the story for it identifies Hiawatha with the ancient hero of the maize culture, the inventor of arts and skills, the apostle of social cooperation. The story, as Paul Radin observes, "fairly bristles with analogies to the Mexican legend."[9]

Like Quetzalcoatl, Hiawatha was plagued by the machinations of a rival, Atortaho, the "Entangled-One." Rejected by his own tribe, the Onandaga, Hiawatha went on a fabulous journey. He plunged through forests, crossed mountains, went by way of lakes and rivers. The quest seems to symbolize the migration of the Iroquois in search of a home. Hiawatha finally found a chieftain, Deganawida, who favored his plans. Deganawida is a more mystical and venerated figure than Hiawatha. He is of virgin birth; his mother, Djigonsasee, "She of the Doubly New Face," guided and assisted him. Thus he embodies the ancient communal spirit; the virgin birth suggests the period that antedated the complex organization of society on the basis of sex and caste; the woman is the transmitter of the old values, but they are transformed and she has a "doubly new face." Hiawatha comes with the arts of life, to realize Deganawida's intuitive vision.

With Deganawida's help, Hiawatha persuaded the five tribes to join together in a federation of delegated and limited powers. It was really an extension of the existent tribal and clan organization, which was rooted in the matriarchal family. "The government of the clan," writes J. N. B. Hewitt, "was a development of that of the several brood families of which it was composed, and the brood family, strictly speaking, was composed of the progeny of a woman and her female descendants, counting through the female line only."[10] Thus the brotherhood of the family was extended in a system of rights and obligations embracing the approximately 20,000 people of the league.[11] The forty-nine chiefs of the federation were selected by the mothers of lines of descent which possessed hereditary chieftainship rights. But "uterine families" not holding the hereditary right were admitted to participation in leadership, either through selection by the council or by choice of "sister families" as their representatives.[12]

The communities were spread out from the Hudson to Lake Ontario. The Mohawks were between Syracuse and Albany. Further west were the Oneidas. The Onondagas, in the center, were the keepers of the council fire, and the guardians of the wampum belts on which treaties were recorded. To the west were the Cayugas and the Senecas; beyond Seneca Lake were the "guardians of the western door."

The aim of the confederacy was universal peace. Through adoption by one of the "uterine families" any Indian could secure the privileges of membership, and many joined, either voluntarily or by capture. The code of the league read:

I, Deganawida, and the Confederated Chiefs, now uproot the tallest pine tree, and into the cavity thereby made we cast all weapons of war. Into the depths of the earth, deep down into the under-earth currents of water flowing to unknown regions, we cast all weapons of strife. We bury them from sight, and we plant again the tree. Thus shall the Great Peace be established.[13]

There was to be no peace. The dream of buried weapons symbolized the hope of orderly and expanding agricultural production. It was an unrealistic hope, because increased production and growing population would require additional territories, which could not be won without aggression and the subjugation of other peoples, which would in turn dislocate the communal organization and introduce exploitation of servile or slave labor.

One cannot say that the coming of the Europeans destroyed the peaceful potentialities of the league of the Iroquois. It is more accurate to say that it greatly intensified the contradictions inherent in the plan, plunging the league and the surrounding tribes into economic and social conflicts that were far more destructive than any wars the Indians had known. However, these pressures strengthened the inner stability of the league. Its power was the central factor in the whole system of Indian and European relationships during the colonial period.

Europeans first entered the territory of the Iroquois in 1609, when Champlain approached it from the north, while at almost the same time the *Half Moon,* the Dutch ship commanded by an English navigator, sailed up the Hudson River to be welcomed by the Mohawk communities near Albany. But a pattern of contact with the Indians had already been established by the French settlers on the St. Lawrence River in Canada, and by the English on the James River in Virginia.

The dealings between the English colonists and the Algonkins during the first two years of Virginia settlement are of sufficient historical interest to merit careful study. The first contact formulated English policies which were to characterize the whole course of colonization. John Smith and the other chroniclers have provided a fairly minute record of the negotiations.

The Powhatan confederation was a loose aggregation of tribes which had only a modicum of the cultural unity of the Iroquois league. But the motives for confederation were the same as those which moved the Iroquois: the Powhatans had begun to accumulate corn beyond their own needs. Since the surplus was very limited, the necessity for social organization was also limited.

The most striking thing about the first contact between the Powhatans and the English settlers is the friendly manner in which the Indians treated the colonists. Their conduct contrasted with the hostility which had caused the failure of previous expeditions to Carolina and Chesapeake Bay. Spanish attempts to settle north of Florida had been defeated; Jesuit missionaries had been killed; there is not much doubt that an Indian attack wiped out the Raleigh settlement at Roanoke Island.

Yet, a generation after Roanoke, at a point which is not far away on the same coast, we find the Indians manifesting an obvious desire for peaceful trade. In the *True Relation,* Smith tells how the food brought by the natives saved the colony when it was threatened with death and famine in the fall of the first year: "it pleased God (in our extremity) to move the Indians to bring us Corne, ere it was halfe ripe, to refresh us, when we rather expected when they would destroy us." Again, "the Indians, thinking us neare famished, with carelesse kindnes, offred us little pieces of bread and small handfulls of beanes or wheate, for a hatchet or a piece of copper . . ." "They were no lesse desirous of our commodities than we of their Corne."[14]

A short time later Smith was attacked and his companions murdered on the Chickahominy River. But the welcome he received when he was brought before Powhatan shows that the incident on the river was due to an error on the part of the tribe in that vicinity and was not approved by the leaders of the federation. In sending Smith back to Jamestown with gifts and four attendants, Powhatan must have followed a policy which had been weighed and agreed upon.

Smith and his companions assumed that the Indians were irrational and treacherous, and that their actions had no continuity or sense. George Percy speaks of their kindness, but attributes it to fear: "If it had not pleased God to have put a terrour in the Savages hearts, we had all perished by those vild and cruell Pagans."[15]

There is nothing in the history of the Indians to suggest that they were afraid of fifty men who were on the verge of death by starvation. Nor need we assume that the tribes on the James River were unaware of the experience of other tribes in dealing with Europeans. It is difficult to form any estimate of the extent of intercourse among the tribes along the seaboard. But there was evidently some contact over considerable distances. When Smith explored the shores of Chesapeake Bay in 1608, he was told by the Indians about the tribes that "inhabit the river of Cannida, and from the French to have their hatchets and such like tooles by trade." [16]

We can only guess at the motives of Powhatan and his councilors. But it seems reasonable to suppose that the existence of a surplus of corn available for trade was a determining factor in their policy. The weakness of the English group may also have tended to make the desire for goods overbalance the fear of conquest. By the beginning of the seventeenth century, the Indians of the Atlantic seaboard were aware of the usefulness of European commodities. People without iron tools were able to make spectacular improvements in their way of life by the use of axes, hatchets and knives. Their methods of warfare were transformed if they could get guns. In seeking these advantages, the Indians found themselves entangled in a net of deception and intrigue, from which their primitive culture gave them no means of extricating themselves.

The conduct of the Europeans was motivated by their desire to secure the land and the products of native labor as cheaply as possible. It would have been suicide for the small band of Englishmen to attempt to reduce the Indians to servitude or slavery. During the first winter, the question of food was too urgent to permit any consideration to interfere with obtaining the reserves which the Indians possessed. Smith's ability to negotiate with the Indians—which was largely due to his capture by Powhatan and the relationship with the chieftain which resulted from it—was a factor in enabling him to seize control of the colony.

Relations with the Indians deteriorated during the summer of 1608. The trouble related to tools. The Indians were accused of trying to steal "Spades, Shovells, swords, or tooles," and Smith alleged that he had discovered a conspiracy "to surprise us at work, to have had our tools." [17] The tools, obviously, were the key to agricultural production. One can understand the feeling of the Indians: corn was life or death; they had saved the colony with their meager surplus, and they wanted assistance in their own agricultural labor in return.

But the tools were *for Europeans only;* they were too precious to give or sell.

The dispute was adjusted. Powhatan demonstrated his good faith by sending his daughter to the stockade. In the *True Relation,* which Smith wrote and sent back to England in 1608, it is quite evident that he had not seen Pocahontas before, although the rescue which he later invented was supposed to have taken place several months earlier. Smith describes her as "a child of tenne yeares old . . . for wit and spirit, the only Nonpariel" of the country.[18]

In October, 1608, Captain Newport returned to Jamestown with colonists, supplies, and a group of skilled craftsmen. Smith had made himself the sole ruler of the colony, but Newport re-established the council. It consisted of Ratcliffe, Scrivener and two new arrivals, Captain Richard Waldo and Captain Peter Wynne. Newport brought instructions from England that he was to secure Powhatan's allegiance by the simple expedient of crowning him "emperor of the Indians." This was in accord with European procedure: having received an "empire" from his English protectors, Powhatan was expected to aid the territorial expansion of the colony and to fight other tribes in order to force their submission.

The coronation was performed. But the chieftain objected to the undignified proceedings; he refused to kneel to receive the crown, and he rejected the proposal which was the real reason for the ceremony: he refused to use his men for an attack on the tribes above the falls of the James.

The whole business of the coronation was calculated to arouse the suspicions of the Indians. And their fears were soon confirmed by the conduct of the Europeans. Newport's departure in November left 200 settlers and a serious problem of obtaining sufficient food to last through the second winter. The colonists had kept their tools, but the arrival of additional people in the fall left a dangerous gap between the results of the summer's labor and the winter's needs. The conditions were quite different from those of the first year. The increased number of Englishmen made them stronger. But it also made it more difficult for the Indians to supply their needs. Therefore, Smith decided to abandon polite negotiations and obtain what he needed by force. The *Proceedings of the English Colony,* written by Smith's friends as a defense of his conduct, speaks of Smith's determination "to surprise Powhatan and al his provision." Some of the other councilors objected, but Smith, "whom no perswasions could perswade to starve," set out with forty-six men to secure the necessary corn. The negotiations that followed were carried on in an atmosphere of unconcealed hostility. Powhatan resented the threatening attitude of the Europeans. He told Smith:

> Some doubt I have of your coming hither, that makes me not so kindly seeke to relieve you as I would; for many inform me, your coming is not for trade, but to invade my people and possesse my country.

On another occasion, Powhatan said:

> Captaine Smith, you may understand that I, having seene the death of all my people thrice, and not one living of those 3 generations but my self, I know the difference of peace and warre better than any in my Countrie.[19]

These speeches, and the story of the negotiations as told from the English viewpoint, seem to refute Smith's charge that "this Salvage but trifled the time, to cut his throat." Powhatan assembled his warriors, but under the circumstances he could not have done anything else. An armed conflict was narrowly averted. The *Proceedings* attributes the submission of the Indians solely to Smith's ability to outwit and frighten them. An agreement was finally reached; in return for copper, iron and beads, a supply of corn was obtained. "Men maie thinke it strange," write the authors of the *Proceedings,* "there should be this stir for a little corne: but had it been gold with more ease wee might have got it."[20] The truth of the matter was that the Indian surplus was not enough for their own needs.

Powhatan's anger at Smith's display of force was increased by his knowledge that the dealings meant life or death to his people as well as to the Europeans. The narrative notes the reluctance with which the Indians gave the maize; in many places, "the people imparted what little they had with such complaints and tears from women and children, as he had bin too cruell to be a Christian that would not have bin satisfied and moved with compassion."

Compassion did not change the pattern of property relationships exposed in the conflict over food. The pattern included the internal life of the settlement as well as its dealings with the Indians. The arbitrary methods employed against the natives were also used to keep servants and laborers at work, on short rations. As a result, the discontent of the underprivileged majority encouraged illegal contact between the settlers and the Indians. There were wholesale thefts of the company's property; the commodities which the Indians coveted, and which were most essential to the life of the European community, disappeared. We are told that, within a few weeks after Newport's departure, about 300 "hatchets, chissels, mattocks, and picaxes" were missing, and "scarce 20 could be found . . . They knew as well (and as secretly) how to convay them to trade with the Salvages, for furres, baskets" and other native goods.[21]

This situation explains Smith's re-establishment of a personal dictatorship. His seizure of power was facilitated by the hardships of the winter and the death of the three remaining councilors. Ratcliffe had gone back to England with Newport. Scrivener and Waldo were drowned on a trip from Jamestown to Hog Island. Wynne's death is not explained, but it occurred at about the same time. The social reason for the dictatorship is revealed by the theft of tools. These were the means of production which could give the Indians an advantage in the struggle for food. While Smith was determined to prevent the natives from gaining this advantage, the increasingly acrimonious class relationships in the English community defeated this purpose. In order to meet the danger, the small group of "gentlemen" who ruled the community were willing to delegate their authority to one individual.

The famous speech in which Smith informed his followers that they "must be more industrious, or starve" has been misunderstood, because its class purpose has been disregarded. Smith was simply telling the workers that they would be kept at forced labor and that any protest or complaint would bring brutal retaliation: "There are now no more Councells to protect you, nor curbe my indeavours. Therefore he that offendeth, let him assuredly expect his due punishment."[22]

The *Proceedings* is frank about the intent of Smith's declaration and the people to whom it was addressed: "Let no man think that the President, or these gentlemen spent their time as common woodhackers at felling trees, or such like other labours, or that they were pressed to anything as hirelings or common slaves." They worked "only as a pleasure and a recreation." Smith took the view that people of the lower class were incurably lazy. We are told that thirty or forty gentlemen could "doe more in a day than 100 of the rest that must bee prest to it by compulsion." There is a note in the margin of the manuscript: "one gentleman better than 20 lubbers."[23]

If the marginal observation is to be believed, the situation in Virginia was unique in the history of colonial enterprise—or, for that matter, in the records of any field of human endeavor. It must have been a very peculiar sort of class relationship in Virginia if the group ranked as gentlemen, having the power to enforce their will and admittedly imposing the most brutal penalties on disobedient laborers, nonetheless did more work themselves, "as a pleasure and a recreation," than the men laboring under their orders. Such an arrangement would make it unnecessay to punish anyone—for it would contradict the end which the punishments were designed to achieve. It seems more reasonable to regard the passage as a typical expression of the upper class viewpoint, invariably heard in similar situations, less valid as a statement of fact than as an indication of the ill-feeling that existed between the controlling group and the majority of the "lubbers."

The animosities in the community seem to have reached a point of explosive tension, when news arrived that the company was to function under a new charter, and that Sir Thomas Gates, with a commission as governor, would arrive with a fleet of ships and colonists. The information was brought by a ship which reached Jamestown on July 13, 1609. The vessel was commanded by Captain Samuel Argall, who was in the service of Lord Robert Rich.

Argall's report must have been a serious shock to Smith. But it had large implications, affecting the destiny of the colony, its relation with the Indians, and the future course of European colonization on the Atlantic Seaboard. The central factor in the system of events which led to the granting of the new charter was the conclusion of the twelve-year truce between Holland and Spain, signed on April 9, 1609. The agreement ended the two years of uncertainty following the 1607 armistice.

Two immediate results of the Dutch peace were the voyage of the *Half Moon* and the revised Virginia charter. Henry Hudson left Holland in his little sixty-ton ship on April 6, three days before the actual signing of the treaty. The English navigator had made two voyages for the Muscovy Company, in search of a northeast passage to the Orient. His failures discouraged his English backers. But the Dutch East India Company, aware of the secret clause in the Spanish treaty which promised that Spain would not interfere with Dutch commerce, was eager to gain a further advantage over its English rivals by the discovery of a shorter route to the Far East. So Hudson started eastward, going north of Scandinavia into Barents Sea. The way was blocked by ice. Unwilling to abandon hope, Hudson turned west, crossing to Newfoundland and sailing south along the American coast looking for a westward passage. What he found was the Hudson River, and the Iroquois Federation.

The new Virginia charter was signed on May 23. Its provisions, and its significance in the English political situation, will be discussed in another chapter. For the present we need only indicate its connection with the settlement of the dispute between Holland and Spain, which strengthened the English bourgeoisie, demonstrated Spain's inability to interfere with transatlantic colonization, and made it imperative that England extend its influence in North America. Argall left England early in May, almost three weeks before the actual signing of the new charter. We may recall that Robert Rich, having made a fortune in semi-piratical trading ventures in American waters, transferred his ships to the Dutch flag in 1603, when James reversed the Elizabethan foreign policy and promised Spain to stop English privateering in the West Indies. Now, six years later, the interest which Rich displayed in Virginia testified to the change that had taken place in international relationships, reviving hopes of profitable transatlantic commerce.

Argall crossed the ocean without cargo or passengers; his sole purpose was to find a more direct route to Virginia than the customary passage by way of the West Indies. He proved that by keeping just south of the Gulf Stream, the time of crossing could be considerably reduced. He made the voyage in sixty-nine days, which was a record.[24]

The voyage of the empty ship betokened the feeling of urgency, of tonic expectation and resolve, which accompanied the formation of the new Virginia Company. There was haste, and there was no longer a shortage of funds. The empty ship was followed by the fleet carrying the governor and his staff. It was essential, an earlier experience had proved, to reach the colony before the summer season was too far advanced. The ships and colonists were ready to sail two weeks after the royal seal was affixed to the patent. Nine vessels transported 500 colonists. On the flagship, the *Sea Venture,* Gates was accompanied by Sir George Somers, with the title of admiral, and Captain Newport as vice-admiral.

One might suppose that the news brought by Argall would have thrilled the colonists; the little settlement was about to receive supplies and reinforcements on a scale that could not have been expected. But for Smith, the news was catastrophic. Smith had been in the habit of reading the patent weekly to the community, to prove that he was acting under royal authority. But the patent provided for government by a council. There was at least considerable doubt concerning the legal sanction for the power which Smith had arrogated to himself. Smith had assumed that the colony would receive little attention in England, and that Captain Newport's return would cause nothing more troublesome than a personal explanation, and possibly a personal reprimand. But he now faced an accounting before a new administration, which would give a real hearing to the charges against him. Smith knew that he was bitterly hated, and that he would face grave accusations.

The weather intervened to give Smith a reprieve. Ten days after Argall's arrival, a hurricane swept the Atlantic in the vicinity of the Bermudas. The approaching fleet was driven before the tempest. On August 11, four bedraggled ships entered the James River. Two more vessels arrived a few days later. They told of having followed a course similar to that taken by Argall, and of having lost contact with the flagship during the storm. The *Sea Venture,* with the governor and his staff and his credentials, was given up for lost.

If Smith had had any doubt concerning the effect which the reorganization would have on his personal fortunes, he was convinced by the return of his three enemies, Ratcliffe, Martin and Archer: "They were formerly deposed and sent for England: yet now returning againe, graced by the title of *Captaines of the passengers.*"[25] Smith refused to relinquish his authority, making the technical claim that the new governor had not appeared and there was no legal proof that the newcomers were empowered to remove him. In the defense of Smith written by his friends, it is claimed that he had no responsibility for the trouble which resulted. "Hee would not suffer those factious spirits to proceed," because "they would rule all or ruine all." He refused to "submit himselfe to theire stoln authorities."

It is difficult to understand how Smith's position could be justified, even on technical grounds. Everyone knew that the company had been reorganized, and that a new administration had been appointed. The men who were officially designated as "captains of the passengers" under the new dispensation, and who were former members of the council, were unquestionably in the right when they insisted on sharing the authority with Smith. The narrative in the *Proceedings* indicates that Smith maneuvered to secure some legal basis for the continuance of his power. "He made Martin President: who knowing his own insufficiencie, and the companies scorne, and conceit of his unworthinesse, within 3 houres, resigned it again to Captane Smith." [26]

The most important aspect of the quarrel was its effect on relations with the Indians. The arrival of such a large number of new settlers required the expansion of the colony. Among the plantations established in outlying areas was a settlement at the Falls of the James, where Francis West planted a community of 120 men. Since this was a frontier outpost, it was necessary that it maintain friendly contact with the Indians. Trouble there might bring fatal results for the whole Virginia project.

Smith went to the Falls. He was dissatisfied with the location that had been selected for the plantation. He negotiated with Powhatan for another site, but the men refused to move. Smith claimed that the men were ill-advised to reject the offer, and he may have been right. The Indians complained to Smith about the conduct of the settlers, who were "stealing their corne, robbing their gardens, beating them, breaking their houses." It seems probable that the Indian complaints were well founded.

But the events that followed throw an interesting light on Smith's character and methods. According to the *Proceedings,* the Indians asked Smith to join them in an attack on the plantation: "They offered, if hee would conduct them, to fight for him against them." Smith refused. But he could not manage the people at the plantation. He tried to imprison "the greatest spirits amongst them, till by their multitude, being 120, they forced him to retire." He managed to seize a boat belonging to the plantation. He started down the river: "No sooner was the ship under saile, but the salvages assaulted these 120 in their fort, finding some stragling abroad in the woods, they slew manie." Smith returned, and found his compatriots "so strangelie amazed with this poore simple assault as they submitted themselves upon anie tearmes to the Presidents mercie." Smith placed "6 or 7 of the chiefe offenders in irons." [27]

Smith met with an accident on the return journey from the Falls. While he was asleep in a small boat, a powder bag exploded, burning him badly. On his arrival at Jamestown, he was charged with a number of offenses. The *Proceedings* asserts that Martin, Ratcliffe and Archer "joined together to usurp the government, and that Smith was too ill to defend himself: Had that unhappy blast not hapned, he would quickly have quallified the heate of those humors and factions." In his weakened condition, Smith was unable to fight the growing opposition:

> Now all those Smith had either whipped, punished, or any way disgraced, had free power and liberty to say or sweare any thing. . . .
> The mutiners at the Falles complained he caused the Salvages assalt them, for that hee would not revenge their losse (they being but 120, and he 5 men and himselfe): and this they proved by the oath of one hee had oft whipped for perjurie and pilfering.[28]

No action was taken on these accusations. But Smith was placed on board a ship, and George Percy was made president of the council. There is a lyrical passage in the *Proceedings* about Smith's departure: "What shall I say? but thus we lost him that, in all his proceedings, made Justice his first guid, and experience his second; ever hating baseness, sloth, pride, and indignitie more than any dangers." [29]

The charge that Smith provoked the assault on the plantation has a direct bearing on the events that followed his departure. The trouble at the Falls was a prelude to the hostilities which broke out immediately after he was sent back to England: "The Salvages no sooner understood of Captaine Smith's losse, but they all revolted, and did murder and spoile all they could incounter." [30] Famine was more devastating than warfare. The Indians kept their corn while 150 colonists died of hunger during the winter. Two of Smith's old enemies succumbed. Ratcliffe, going out to trade for food, was ambushed and killed. The famine killed Archer.

It is one of the curiosities of history that scholars have ignored the question of Smith's responsibility for the starving time, which he was later to describe so cavalierly, and which almost destroyed the colony. The factional struggle in which he engaged weakened morale, wasted the precious fall days, and made it impossible to prepare the newly arrived settlers for the winter. While he may not have been solely to blame for the changed attitude of the Indians, the story as told by his friends gives a good deal of weight to the accusation that he was responsible for the attack on the plantation at the Falls. There is nothing to show that he suggested the Indian raid or was informed of it in advance. But he was aware of the threat against the plantation, and the danger was greatly increased by his quarrel with the people there. There is no evidence that he placed the safety of the plantation above his own interest, or that he made a responsible effort to mollify the Indian resentment and protect the settlement. He used the incident to regain control and punish his adversaries.

The event must have had a considerable effect on the Indian attitude toward the colonists. The statement in the *Proceedings* that the change in Indian policy was motivated solely by their affection for Smith and their anger at his departure does not jibe with the account of his previous dealings with the natives, which had been anything but friendly. He had threatened and tricked them, and taken their corn by force. But he showed them that the white men were not strong and united. The Indians, having killed a number of men at the Falls, saw Smith return to put some of the defenders in irons.

It was a useful lesson in the ways of Europeans. And it came at a time when hundreds of new colonists had arrived, taking the fertile fields along the river. The men with guns were more numerous, but they were disunited and therefore vulnerable. The Indian attempt to establish commercial reciprocity had been a failure. Smith had taught them that the Europeans were arrogant in the use of power, and then he exposed the white man's weakness. The Indians applied the lesson after his departure.

In the same summer, a short time before the strife developed in Virginia, Champlain traveled southward from the French fort at Quebec. He accompanied a war party of Algonkins, following the Richelieu River to the lake which was to be called Champlain. Near Ticonderoga, at the lower end of the lake, the expedition met a detachment of Iroquois. A battle occurred on July 30, and the redoubtable Iroquois warriors were put to flight by the unfamiliar guns of the Frenchmen.

On September 20, the *Half Moon* sailed up the river which was to be called Hudson. The combination of circumstances that almost brought a meeting of the Dutch and French expeditions, defined the conditions for the long European and Indian struggle for control of the fur trade. France held one major waterway, the St. Lawrence, leading to the interior of the continent and the Great Lakes. Holland had accidentally secured command of another major route to the interior, by way of the Hudson and Mohawk Valleys. The Algonkin were committed to the alliance with France. The Iroquois were to be Holland's allies in commerce and war.

On October 4, the *Half Moon* sailed through the Narrows past Staten Island on its return journey to Europe. On the same day, the ship carrying Smith back to England sailed out of Chesapeake Bay.

The struggle for North America had begun. But the heart of the struggle was in northern New York state, where the Iroquois held the gateway to the Great Lakes and the West. Francis Parkman says that the skirmish at Ticonderoga "was the beginning, and in some measure doubtless the cause, of a long suite of murderous conflicts, bearing havoc and flame to generations yet unborn." [31]

3 : MYTH AND MONEY

Myths are to a considerable extent economic allegories, dealing with the accumulation of wealth, the control of the society's surplus and the beginnings of trade. Since the process of emergent civilization has followed a similar course in widely separated areas, one finds similarities in the folklore of many lands. The process is exceptionally clear in ancient Greece, because the early mythology is supplemented by an extensive literature of interpretation.

Gold appears in three forms in the folklore of the Greeks: as an ornament of heaven, as the object of an earthly quest, as a dangerous source of power. The three forms mark three stages in the development of Mediterranean civilization.

In primitive societies, the first recognition of the value of gold is associated with its display as a symbol of authority. The wealth derived from military conquest of slave labor is hoarded in the temple, showing that it is now only *symbolically* the property of the community. The people, being forced to accept the idea that the alienation of the surplus is divinely ordained, invent a mythical land where the gold is so plentiful that the guarded splendor of the temple is everyone's possession.

The legend had many forms. Atlantis, with its towers of gold, was somewhere in the western sea beyond Gibraltar. There were many other lands in the west. Immortality awaited those who reached the Isles of the Blest or the Fortunate Isles.

The mythical country was often a land of women, or a place where women enjoyed exceptional freedom and happiness. Thus the myth related the promise of an after-life with the communal past, when women had enjoyed a privileged social status.

The degradation of women was connected with the alienation of property and the growth of commerce. It was the link between the "pure" myth of a promised land and the complicated legends that related to the expansion of Mediterranean trade. The transition is shown in the story of the garden of the Hesperides: the island was the home of the maidens who guarded the golden apples given to Hera at the time of her marriage to Zeus. We cannot attempt to disentangle the various functions attributed to Hera; all her duties were associated with productivity—marriage, womanhood, the rites of spring, the growth of vegetation. The apple is mentioned in many ancient records, in the Egyptian *Book of the Dead,* in the annals of Babylon and China. In the biblical story of Adam and Eve, it is the symbol of earth's fruitfulness, alienated by man's greed. When Hera married the greatest of the gods, agriculture was wedded to power. It ceased to be the common possession of mankind. The treasure of the earth became gold, and was removed to a land of myth and promise in the West, where women, the ancient guardians of the social order, watched the golden fruit.

As commerce spread across the Mediterranean, the exploits of early maritime trade are projected in the labors of Heracles. He undertook the perilous voyage to the garden of the Hesperides, bringing the apples back to mankind: first he brought them to Argos, the oldest center of Greek trade, and then to Athens, which was destined to rival and surpass Argos. Through mercantile activity, a part of the urban population regained its inheritance, tasted the apple of wealth.

The later expansion of Greek mercantile activity was eastward, to Asia Minor and the Black Sea. In the legend of the Golden Fleece, the story shifts from the fabled west to the area of known historical development. In the course of their voyage, the Argonauts find a land where the women have killed their husbands and re-established their rule. But the goal of the quest is beyond the Dardanelles, on the other side of the Black Sea. The Golden Fleece may have symbolized the grain of the Crimea, or it may have referred to the metal found in the streams tumbling into the sea from the mountains of the Caucausus. But whether the expedition found food or gold, it marked the beginning of the trade between the Aegean and the Black Sea that was to enrich the towns of southern Greece and the Ionian islands.

Homer's *Iliad* recounts the warfare for possession of the strategic Dardanelles (Troy commanded the western entrance to the straits) at a period of prehistory when the people were still organized in tribes led by a chieftain and a council of warriors. Priestly power was just beginning to assert itself, as is evident in the intimate and confused relationship between mortal kings and the gods who participate in their quarrels. But the favor of the gods was already a matter of property relationships, a means of obtaining wealth. The Greek word for the three Fates means share or portion; it originally referred to the division of land and the distribution of booty among the tribes.[1] The terror associated with the Fates reflects the methods by which the rulers enlarged their possessions, calling on the gods to justify their seizure of the common property.

Four or five centuries separate the mysteries of the Homeric age from the clear outlines of urban civilization as it emerged in the seaports on the coast of Asia Minor in the seventh century B.C. The Ionian cities derived their wealth from the movement that is mythologically presented in the voyage of the Argonauts and the Trojan wars. The development of Black Sea trade intensified class distinctions: merchants tried to extend their power over the lower classes of the towns; the owners of landed estates improved their position by heavier exploitation of slave labor and the exaction of tribute from the free peasantry.

From the melee of conflicting interests, new rulers were able to seize power. These men were known by a new name—*tyrants*. They were money kings, and their rise is celebrated in a new type of money-myth, of which the stories of Midas and Gyges are the best known examples.

Midas and Gyges became the masters of neighboring kingdoms, Phrygia and Lydia, where the profits of trade were augmented by the income from the gold and silver mines of Sipylos and Tmolos. Greek tradition holds that coins were first introduced in Lydia; the earliest Lydian money was made of an alloy of gold and silver, and was of comparatively high value.[2] Gold was no longer a temple ornament; it was an instrument of commerce and a source of power. In Phrygia, control of the mines gave Midas the inhuman ability to turn everything he touched into gold. In Lydia, the myth tells of Gyges' possession of a magic golden ring, which made him invisible. By the use of the ring, he was able to enter the palace of the king, seduce the queen and secure her help in murdering her husband.

The bitterness of the myths leaves no doubt that the tyranny of the money kings rested on an insecure foundation. They rose to power because they held the key to increased metallurgical production. They performed a progressive historical function in breaking the power of the landed nobility and stimulating the development of an urban economy, commercial interchange, mercantile wealth—with an accompanying growth of art and thought. The tyranny of Pittacus over the rich island of Lesbos at the end of the seventh century B.C. coincided with the rise of the dithyramb and the poetry of Sappho.

But this economic and cultural expansion brought more violent clashes of conflicting interests. Rural poverty increased; in the cities, the exploitation of slaves and the poorer classes of laborers and artisans created a class of rich merchants and traders who challenged the centralized authority of the tyrant; at the same time, the discontent of the poor became dangerously explosive.

During the sixth century, the Ionian cities were weakened by internal conflicts and were thus unable to withstand the expanding power of Persia. Athens, having imported the art and science of the eastern towns, entered on a similar cycle of social change. The age of Athenian tyranny, under Pisistratus, lasted for half a century, from 561 to 511 B.C. It was followed by the century of intensive commercial and industrial expansion and increasingly violent class conflict that culminated in the brief splendor of the Periclean age; during those golden years, it seemed as if the apples of the Hesperides, which (according to the legend) had been brought to Athens by Heracles, had been planted in an inexhaustibly fertile soil. But the social structure, with its towering superstructure of art and thought, rested on slave labor. In 431 B.C. there were 172,000 citizens in Athens and 115,000 slaves. This was the year in which the Peloponnesian war began. The poverty and malnutrition which afflicted a considerable part of the population were to a considerable extent responsible for the great plague that swept the city in 430. In 413, 20,000 slaves, most of them employed in the mines, deserted to the enemy. The loss of these trained workers was an irreparable blow,[3] guaranteeing the defeat which came a few years later when a Spartan garrison occupied the city.

The Athenian culture in its flowering period was largely devoted to the interpretation of mythology. As the hope of social progress in Aeschylus turned to foreboding in Sophocles and recognition of doom in Euripides, the legends were transformed to provide new meanings. Aeschylus believed that it was feasible to revitalize the old communal organization, so that the free citizens might derive equal benefits from the growth of productive forces. His plays reflect the Pythagorean doctrine of the fusion of opposites—the doctrine which expressed the interests of craftsmen, small traders, free peasants, demanding a satisfactory compromise between the greed of the ruling oligarchies and the controls required for the exploitation of slave labor. There was to be slave labor without *excessive* oppression; there was to be a mercantile state without *excessive* profit for vested interests.

Sophocles lived only a generation later. Commercial expansion had brought a vast increase of wealth and culture—and exposed the contradictions that threatened the social order. To Sophocles, gold—as the symbol of prosperity—was the Midas curse, the root of evil:

> Of all foul growths current in the world,
> The worst is money. Money drives men from home,
> Plunders great cities, perverts the honest mind
> To shameful practices, godlessness and crime.

In Euripides, the corruption is deeper and irrevocable. The Jason of the golden fleece has become a careful politician, discarding Medea so that he can get ahead in the world, explaining to his wife that his betrayal is solely for economic reasons: "that we—and this is most important—may dwell in comfort, instead of suffering want." Medea's answer is a foreboding comment on the moral disintegration of Athenian society: "May that prosperity, whose end is woe, ne'er be mine, nor such wealth as would ever sting the heart."

The bold voyages of Heracles and Jason have brought tragedy. The apples of the Hesperides have become the tree of evil; the golden fruit is like bitter dust in the mouth; it poisons and kills.

We cannot attempt to trace the later and more mature interpretation of mythology in the writings of Plato and Aristotle and other philosophers of the ancient Mediterranean world. With the rediscovery of Greek culture in the later middle ages, the myth of money and power reappeared under various guises, in the service of various class interests. In the fifteenth century, the Duke of Burgundy celebrated his feudal lordship over the rich textile towns of Flanders by creating the knightly Order of the Golden Fleece, which played a leading part in European politics for five centuries. In England, the legend became a symbol of mercantile power, the fleece being an emblem of the wool which was the realm's "sovereign merchandise and jewel."

But a more profound and novel allegory, reflecting the rise of new social forces, is embodied in the Faust legend. The origins of the story may be found in the medieval tales of alchemists who, by magic or a pact with the devil, transmute the baser metals into gold. The relationship to the story of Midas may be noted. But the Greek allegory has lost its simplicity; it has been given scientific implications. The development of chemical experimentation encouraged hopes that it might be possible to change lead into gold. But the church frowned on the advancement of science; the men who dared to trespass beyond the monastic boundaries of knowledge were accused of serving the devil, and the charge became identified with the power that might be achieved by the creator of gold. Thus the myth developed around real persons: the pathfinder in the methodology of science, Roger Bacon, became the Friar Bacon who "dived into hell, and sought the darkest pallaces of fiendes."

The essential content of the myth lay in its ambivalent treatment of gold as an object of desire and a destructive plague. But the ethical dilemma was extended to include the field of science. Wealth can be multiplied by human skill and invention. But the process is demoniac; it is shadowed by the greed of private accumulation. The wisdom that might benefit mankind is subverted by the avarice of the alchemist. The Midas touch becomes the symbol of the divided conscience. The transformation of the legend, from alchemy to the whole arena of human endeavor, is completed in the Faust story.

In order to grasp the far-reaching intellectual significance of the Faustian drama, we must place it in its historical setting—the sweep of the Reformation, the advancement of learning, the impact of the discovery and colonization of the Americas. The gold and silver of the New World disrupted the European economy, changed monetary values, debased living standards, stimulated social conflict.

As there was a real Midas and a real Friar Bacon, so there was a real Faust. He was an obscure scholar caught in the social upheavals of the German peasant war. Melanchthon, one of Luther's principal lieutenants, wrote that Faust studied magic at the University of Cracow, one of the great liberal academies of the time. Then, according to

Melanchthon, he "roamed about, and talked of secret things," becoming "a disgraceful beast and sewer of many devils." The description suggests that Faust held dangerously radical opinions. Melanchthon speaks of him with the anger that was usually reserved for Anabaptists and other preachers of equality who continued their underground activities after the defeat of the peasant rebellion in 1525.

The first statement that Faust possessed supernatural powers secured through a pact with the devil was made by a Protestant pastor, Johann Gast, in a book of sermons published in 1543. The significant date, which, according to Gast, marked the end of Faust's career, was 1525: thus, at exactly the moment when the peasant movement was broken and reaction triumphed, Faust was carried to eternal torment by the devil. The story did not become popular until half a century later, when various versions were published in Germany and translated into other languages.

The alchemy of the Elizabethan imagination added poetic fervor and dramatic scope. Marlowe's Faust is an intellectual Tamerlaine, gratifying his antic imagination, playing practical jokes on the pope, calling Helen of Troy to be his paramour. The metamorphosis of the real Faust, the wanderer lost in the anonymity of the Underground, into the mighty sorcerer of the Elizabethan play, has a poetic completeness that seems to sever all contact between reality and myth. Yet the connection is there; it is veiled because it involves social issues that cannot be exposed. The real Faust was called a "sewer of many devils" because he served, however humbly, the cause of reason and science, preaching the forbidden creed that men should share equally in the fruits of their knowledge. An alchemy as potent as any magic formula makes him the symbol of selfishness, of the misuse of power for inconsequential and extravagant ends.

The trick is played with monotonous regularity upon persons who advocate social justice. We see it in the mass propaganda currently directed against Communists, whose moral passion is described as "contempt for morality." But the trick was peculiarly effective in the case of Faust. It worked, because the shabby scholar became identified with the evils of primitive accumulation. In Marlowe's play, he wants only personal gratification; he dedicates his will to what Thorstein Veblen calls "pecuniary emulation" or "conspicuous waste." He utilizes his pact with Mephistopheles in a way that fits Veblen's description of the typical member of the leisure class, who "consumes freely and of the best, in food, drink, narcotics, shelter, services, ornaments, apparel, weapons and accoutrements, amusements, amulets, and idols or divinities." Marlowe depicts Faust as "glutted with conceit" of spirits that will bring him riches from every land:

> I'll have them fly to India for gold,
> Ransack the ocean for orient pearl,
> And search all corners of the new-found world
> For pleasant fruits and princely delicates.

The moral lesson that Marlowe draws from the story is the warning "only to wonder at unlawful things." The play was probably written in the year after the defeat of the Armada: England was about to secure a goodly share of the riches of "the new-found world," but it was not wise to probe too deeply into the magic of primitive accumulation.

The riches imported from America had whetted the appetite of the capitalists, who were looking for quicker and surer methods of making money. They still believed that it might be made, literally, by a chemical formula. The Fugger *Newsletters* tell of the alchemist, Marco Antonio Bragadini, who convinced the cautious merchants of Venice that he could manufacture gold. The Fugger correspondent wrote on December 16, 1589: "The alchemist is said to be at work now in making five thousand sequins per month at the request of our rulers. Thereafter he will make fifteen or sixteen millions more." Bragadini enjoyed a meteoric success; he lived with Faustian largesse, holding daily banquets for five hundred people. But his time was short; his private contract with the devil ran out in 1590, and he was hanged on a gilded gallows, in a garment of imitation gold spangles.

The philosophic implications of the contract with the devil, the degradation of the human personality in utilizing rational knowledge for irrational and antisocial ends, were explored by Goethe, and re-examined as a twentieth century dilemma by Thomas Mann. In Mann's novel, *Dr. Faustus,* the musician Adrian Leverkühn sells his soul and body in return for twenty-four years of creative activity; the period coincides with the rise and disintegration of Nazi power in Germany; the artist can win his freedom only by the sacrifice of his humanity; the climax of Leverkühn's tragedy, as his time grows short and syphilis eats his brain, coincides with the tragedy of the German spirit, seeking "freedom" by a blood-pact that leads to destruction.

A long historical process separates Marlowe's greedy extrovert from Mann's doomed musician. But the movement of ideas and forces over the centuries forms a discernible pattern. The devil in Mann's parable has a sense of history. He explains that he is "German to the core, yet even so in an older, better way, to wit cosmopolitan from my heart." The contract with the artist is countersigned by the long agony of the German people, including children's crusades, famine and the Peasant's League—and the arrival of the busy germs of syphilis, "the loving guests from the West Indies into the German lands."

The devil exclaims that "it is such a snug, familiar world wherein we are together." The seeds of the disaster were sown when the real Faustus wandered the German roads. Unconscious of the future, the eager scholar talked of "secret things"—rational thought and the dignity of man—while ships circled the globe, and the compass and the gun gave European adventurers mastery of the seven seas. The real man may have marched with the peasants under the banner of the Union Shoe. But the myth converted him to capitalism, gave him a contract written in blood, made him the symbol of the tortured intellectual, the modern Prometheus selling the holy fire for a few feverish untrammelled years.

Thus it is possible to trace the historical evolution of the money myth from the primitive tales of golden cities, found in a hundred different forms in early societies, to the broodings of a twentieth century Faust selling his soul for a brief glimpse of the lost Atlantis. The myth, like all other modes of art or thought, has been a reflection of embittered class conflict. It has expressed the dynamic content of the struggle, its historic forward drive. The myth has often served as an instrument of class domination. But in its most profound and creative forms, it has embodied the recognition that wealth is achieved through inhuman exploitation, corrupting man's essential humanity, depriving the people of the fruits of their toil.

The far towers of Atlantis may serve as a priestly deception, a dream that dulls the sense of present struggle. But Atlantis may also symbolize the classless future, the fulfillment of social potentialities, the free city of man.

4 : THE OPERA

THE YEAR of Jamestown's settlement and the failure of the French project at Port Royal witnessed an important musical event in Italy. At the court of Mantua, Claudio Monteverde produced his first opera. The work, *Ariana,* honored the marriage of the Duke of Mantua's son to Margherita, Infanta of Savoy.[1]

The development of the opera was part of a revolution in musical thought that began in the last years of the sixteenth century. The connection between musical theory and the rationalism of Bruno and Sarpi is personalized in the family of Galileo. The scientist's father, Vincenzio Galilei, was a leader of the musical revolt. As a member of the circle of Florentine intellectuals known as the *Camerata,* Galileo wrote one of the earliest manifestoes of the new school—the *Dialogo della musica antica e della moderna,* which appeared in 1581. Galileo called for realism and emotional vitality in music. This was to be achieved by a more direct correspondence between the instrumental composition and the words which it accompanied, so that the words could be given intelligible meaning. The *dialogue* caused a violent debate, heated approbation and angry ridicule.[2]

The heat was generated by the political importance of the conflict. It was a struggle between ecclesiastical control of music and its secular use.

Music is often regarded as one of the most abstract of the arts. But the history of music from its primitive origins proves it is a concrete expression of class forces. The quality of music which supposedly removes it from the arena of social struggle—its emotional appeal--makes it a peculiarly effective and sensitive instrument in the service of classes competing for power.

The mood and spirit of sixteenth century Catholicism found massive realization in the compositions of Giovanni Pierluigi da Palestrina. Palestrina's service was not performed accidentally or without political direction. It was the outgrowth of the deliberations of the Council of Trent, which recognized that music was indispensable to the church in the effort to regain popular support. In 1564, the pope appointed a commission of eight cardinals to investigate the problem and recommend musical styles that would meet the needs of the Counter Reformation. Palestrina was invited to assist the commission. He submitted three masses, and the cardinals selected one which was given their approval.

The decisions reached at Rome, and the appointment of Palestrina as composer of the Sistine Chapel, were followed by provincial synods which adopted similar rules concerning the reform of ecclesiastical music—Milan and Cambrai in 1565; Constance and Augsberg in 1567; Namur and Mechlin in 1570.[3]

Palestrina softened and stylized his art, giving a feeling of hypnotic awe, even of sensuality, to his spiritual exercises. However, the structural simplicity of Palestrina's work was not effective in meeting the challenge of secular music. The "modernists" of the Florentine *Camerata* utilized forms which had their origin in the creative life of the people: the adaptation of the minstrelsy of the city streets to the tastes of the upper class was accomplished through the madrigal, which may be traced back over centuries of Italian development to its beginnings in Provence in the twelfth century.[4]

The transformation of the madrigal in the second half of the sixteenth century was largely the work of Luca Marenzio, "the first modern composer in the fullest sense of the word." Seeking the presentation of psychological moods and attitudes, Marenzio treated the madrigal as a lyrico-dramatic composition: "Finding the old choral idiom insufficient to paint such pictures, Marenzio abandoned it to enter into the field of modern tonality."[5]

The church did not restrict itself solely to the defense of the *musica antica*. It undertook a militant offensive in the activities of the *Congregazione dell'Oratorio* founded at Rome in 1575 by Philip Neri. For about a decade before the establishment of the society at Rome, Neri supervised a group in Florence which performed musical pieces called *oratorios.* These were settings of scenes from sacred history which were originally of an extremely simple devotional character, drawing their inspiration from the *laudi,* the religious poems that had been chanted for generations in the Tuscan countryside. But the oratorios were also affected by the lyrico-dramatic development of the madrigal, adapting the intense personal lyricism of the secular form to religious themes.

Although Neri was responsible for the founding of the congregation in Rome, he remained in Florence until 1583, when he was ordered by the pope to take personal charge of the Roman society. The date is significant; it was two years after the storm of controversy that greeted Galileo's *Dialogo della musica antica e della moderna.* The "Palestrina" style had become outmoded, and Neri was called upon to meet the "modernists" on their own ground. The mystical intensity which began to characterize the compositions performed by the congregation was an imitation of the *form* of the madrigal; the *content* was derived from Jesuit and Spanish influences. In his younger days, Neri had been intimate with the Jesuit leader, Loyola, and the Jesuits maintained close contact with the work of the oratory. The Spanish music of this period was almost exclusively ecclesiastical, shadowed by a dark strain of mysticism. Many of Neri's musical collections bore the imprint of the Society of Jesus, some being published in the Spanish language.[6]

Palestrina died in 1594; and Neri's death came at the age of eighty in the following year. The musical conflict moved toward a climax. In *Il Conte Ugolino,* Galileo made an original experiment, exploring the possibilities of a cantata for solo voice which would combine dramatic and musical qualities along the lines indicated in his *dialogue.*[7] But a solo could not achieve the emotional scope and clash of human wills for which the composer was seeking.

The obscure sixteenth century origins of the opera have been explored by Romaine Rolland and other critics.[8] The madrigal was the immediate forerunner, for musical thought was more concerned with the potentialities of the madrigal than with other artistic traditions. But the madrigal could not fulfill its destiny until it merged with forms which were more theatrical than musical—the aristocratic masque and the popular drama. These elements were fused in a single presentation, and the opera was born.

The earliest work that can be called an opera, *Dafne,* with libretto by Ottavio Rinuccini and music by Jacopo Peri, seems to have been staged at Florence in 1597.[9] But most of the music has been lost. The first complete opera which survives is *Euridice,* prepared by the same authors for Florentine presentation in honor of the marriage of Henry IV and Marie de Medici in 1600.

In the same year, the Jesuits tried to capture the new form and adapt it to their uses. *Anima e Corpo,* a "sacred representation" by Emilio de Cavalieri, was performed in the Oratorio at Rome. Bukofzer observes that it was "created for the Jesuits," being "one of the many attempts of the counter-reformation to salvage from secular art forms all those features that lent themselves to the promotion of the *ecclesia militans.*"

The composer asserted that he intended to prove that the modern style "can also move to pious affections."[10]

The work could hardly be called an oratorio, for it had scenery, costumes, dances, and all the accoutrements of stage production. The author was aware of the contradiction between these unworldly attractions and the supposedly devotional purpose of the entertainment, and utilized it as a dramatic climax. When the characters impersonating the World and Life first appeared on the scene, they were magnificently dressed, but they lost their splendor as the show proceeded, and at the end they were miserable skeletons.[11]

The stilted symbolism of *Anima e Corpo* would seem to suggest that religious mysticism was losing the musical battle. The baroque music of the seventeenth century was not built around skeletons; it was music of the flesh, of earthly passion, presented in ornate settings and rich costumes. But the opera was itself a combination of discordant aesthetic tendencies, reflecting the movement of political forces from which it was born. It is significant that the opera emerged as an art form in celebration of the marriage of the "bourgeois king" of France and his Catholic bride. The compromise which allied the French king with the Vatican was to cast a long shadow over European culture. The opera, throughout its history, was to bear the impress of the compromise.

The opera was distinguished from the usual court entertainment, the masque, by the continuity of the music, the weight given to the recitative, the emphasis on dramatic values, and the attempt to weld music and speech in a new unity of meaning. Peri wrote in his preface to *Euridice* that he had listened to the conversation of people, and attempted to render it realistically in music.[12]

Yet the realistic aim was belied by the nature of the presentation and the audience to which it was addressed. The work was privately performed, for the pleasure of a group of aristocrats and their dependents. The Medici marriage weakened the bourgeoisie in Italy as well as in France; it strengthened the alliance between the French and Italian nobility and the church. It brought the aristocratic tendencies in the development of the madrigal to full fruition. The revolutionary musical ideas of the Florentine *Camerata,* which were in part a reflection of the aspirations of the bourgeoisie, became the property of the class which could afford lyrico-dramatic presentations for its private diversion.

It is important today, when the assumption that music is an abstract art is so widely accepted, to note that the early creators of opera thought in terms of realism. But concepts of reality are determined by class attitudes. The tendency toward realism of the opera, as it developed in the work of Monteverdi, was checked by the aristocratic audience who were the composer's patrons.

Monteverdi was conscious of the conflict in the musical field. He wrote in 1605 that he had abandoned the precepts of the old school and followed what he called the *seconda prattica.*[13] The innovations which he introduced in his first opera prepared for the deeper realization of his aims in *Orfeo,* produced at the court of Mantua in 1608. Monteverdi's search for emotional values led him to utilize the human voice in new ways and to extend the range and individual qualities of various instruments. His disregard of the strict rules of the *prima prattica* was most dramatically indicated in the use of unprepared discords. It has been said that without these discords, "passionate utterance in music would be impossible." [14]

Monteverdi, like many of his contemporaries in music and the other arts, looked for "passionate utterance" in terms of the social environment in which he lived and worked. The society which he mirrored found emotional fulfillment chiefly in erotic experience and conspicuous display. It would have been impossible to please this society by portraying it realistically on the stage. The composer tried to idealize its virtues by the use of the allegory of Orpheus and Euridice. The same theme had served Peri in 1600, and was to be a perennial subject of operatic treatment for the next three hundred years.

As always with myths, there is a connection between the primitive social meaning of the Orphic legend and its more or less ornamental use in European entertainment. Orpheus was one of the gods of progress and civilization, the inventor of the lyre, of medicine, of writing and architecture. We recognize the typical attributes of the culture hero, which are always associated with the rise of arts and crafts in primitive societies. The Orphic rites practiced in Greece in the sixth century B.C. were a popular revival of the ancient cult, which developed among the peasantry and spread to the cities as a movement of protest against exploitation. The connection between the cult of Orpheus and the Pythagorean doctrine is mentioned by Herodotus. In assuming an urban form, the cult led to the theatrical festivals which arose in Athens toward the close of the sixth century B.C.[15]

Euridice, the wife of Orpheus, symbolized the early role of women as bearers of culture and organizers of the community. As the serpent destroyed the innocence of human fellowship in the Garden of Eden, so the serpent must destroy Euridice. Her death and descent into Hell suggest the change in the woman's position in the period of the alienation of property and the rise of priestly power. The contributions that women like Sappho made to the beginnings of urban civilization were no longer possible as society developed, converting the gifts of the culture god to formal "mysteries" and stage presentations, and depriving the woman of her share in the common culture. Orpheus descended into Hell to find Euridice; his lyre softened the hearts of Pluto and Persephone, whose deathly kingdom was also the region of the riches of the earth. The gods who controlled wealth decreed that Euridice might return to earth, provided Orpheus walked in front of her and did not look back. But he failed; his love was too strong and defeated itself; Euridice was lost to him forever; woman's function as man's equal and comrade was destroyed.

In losing Euridice, Orpheus becomes a transitional figure, halfway between the old communal culture and the specialized culture of the cities. The social implications of the legend were still understood in Plato's time. Plato objected to the treatment of Euridice as a real person. He insisted that she had no corporeal existence; the infernal gods deceived Orpheus, and "presented an apparition" to him in the guise of a woman.

The Platonic approach suggests the meaning which the tale assumed as an upper-class allegory in the early seventeenth century.

Orpheus, the culture-hero, pursues the idea of love in unreal and idealized surroundings, ringing all the changes on the tender passion, from the pastoral charm of the first scenes to melodramatic lamentation amid the fires of Hell.

But Monteverdi had difficulties with the libretto. Alessandro Striggio, who wrote it, reached a climax in stark tragedy, following the version of the classic myth which showed Orpheus killed by raving bacchantes. Monteverdi rejected this ending, and provided a more fitting conclusion, with the protagonist ascending to heaven.

The legend went through many metamorphoses in its later development. In 1762, Gluck used it as a symbol of bourgeois virtues, "a beautiful and noble epic of conjugal fidelity."[16] A hundred years later, in a period of cynicism and disillusionment, Offenbach turned the myth into a satirical *opera bouffe*.

It is not without reason that Orpheus has been called the first professional musician. He could serve many masters and express many viewpoints. It may be that the poet, Striggio, sensed the tragedy of the artist, and felt that it was necessary that he should meet his doom among the bacchantes. But Monteverdi was wise enough to know that the artist who serves the upper class is not torn to pieces by the Furies; he is rewarded with limited but exciting participation in the pleasures of his masters.

The baroque style, which Monteverdi perfected, and which was to play a dominant role in literature and the arts as well as in music, is most clearly defined in its attitude toward the human personality. The Renaissance pride in all that is human, in the dignity of the body and the integrity of emotional experience, becomes erotic sentiment or exaggerated melodrama. Love could be converted into a "spiritual" allegory, as in the case of the Orpheus story. But the search for dramatic values tended to depict love in terms of crises of jealousy, betrayal, momentary sensation, hysterical passion. This corresponded to the way in which the pursuit of love was conducted by the people who attended the operas. Their sense of life was "operatic": it was based on feeling for its own sake, on the momentary gratification of desire.

Art was accepted as a special and highly desirable aspect of life. But it required an emotional sensibility which they believed was as much the property of a privileged class as the money and leisure which permitted the enjoyment of art or the pursuit of emotion for its own sake. Ideas of psychology—insofar as these ideas were formulated in the seventeenth and eighteenth centuries—tended to accept the "operatic" view of personality as a bundle of separate moods or emotional states loosely tied together by religious or ethical rules imposed on the individual in order to maintain social discipline.

The tendency in music was paralleled in other creative fields. In the year in which Monteverdi's first opera was produced at Mantua, Federico Zuccari published a book on the philosophy of art. Zuccari, in his sixty-fourth year, was still the most popular painter of the time. He wrote that "the art of painting does not draw her principles from the mathematical science." Attacking da Vinci and Dürer, he asserted that Leonardo was wrong in laying down "mathematical precepts for drawing the movements and attitudes of figures by means of perpendicular lines, the square and the compass."[17]

There were many schools of painting in Italy, but a basic tendency was expressed in the sumptuous and facile canvasses which Guido Reni produced with inexhaustible devotion to a profitable market. The transition from humanism to the baroque may be estimated by a comparison of Leonardo's painstaking study of man with Caravaggio's *Love as Conqueror,* depicting a fleshly adolescent wearing wings and standing among musical instruments.

The connection between baroque music and baroque painting has been recognized. A recent history of music notes the similar tendencies:

> The Baroque painters tried to move their disillusioned spectators in much the same way, by filling their works with sentimental appeal, gorgeous color, over theatrical form, and dramatic intensity.[18]

The baroque movement emanating from Italy represented a powerful political and social force, which extended into the Protestant countries as well as into areas under Catholic domination.

English music of the early seventeenth century was largely dominated by the Catholic ideology of Byrd and other masters of the old choral style. Indeed, "the influence of the style of the experimenters in the 'Nuove Musiche' is hardly to be found in any of the Virginial and Organ music of the time" in England.[19] Baroque architecture and stage design reached England sometime before the influence was felt in music.

The first public opera house was opened in Venice in 1637. The experiment proved so popular that by the end of the century, Venice had eleven opera houses. The vogue spread through Europe in the eighteenth century.

In Handel's impressive contribution to the Anglican musical culture in England, the baroque style provided the basic structure for the Protestant cantatas and oratorios. Baroque composers had never ignored the necessity of design. Monteverdi was a master of complex forms. But the form was superimposed on the personal and unruly passions that gave the work its psychological effect. It was an abstract pattern, reflecting the authoritarian power which was superimposed on the casual and undisciplined emotional life of the aristocracy. In Bach and Handel, the structure of religious feelings is imposed in somewhat the same way on the disorder of mundane emotions; it is *only* in religion that man can find order and reason. These musical compositions were the artistic forerunners of the "transcendental idealism" formulated by Immanuel Kant in the *Critique of Pure Reason*. The religious mysticism of the first oratorio won a belated victory in the eighteenth century compositions which adopted the same name.

Music was one of the most important factors in the culture of the English colonies on the Atlantic seaboard during the eighteenth century. This was especially true of the southern colonies, where the wealthy planters found what was probably their most satisfying cultural experience in musical evenings at which amateur performers, members of the family and their friends, displayed their virtuosity in performing songs and instrumental pieces. This music was largely of Italian origin, derived directly from Italian sources or from English imitators of the Italian style.

The inventory of the library of Cuthbert Ogle, a Virginia music teacher who died in 1755, included a large amount of English music, but it was mainly work that followed the prevalent baroque pattern. Ogle had an extensive collection of Italian composers, including works by Corelli, Alberti, Giardini, Pasquali, and Palma, and "an unbound book of Italian songs." [20]

The Beggar's Opera, which appeared in England in 1718, introduced a novel realism in musical stage presentation. John Gay's work became popular in the American colonies, and exerted an influence which may have somewhat counteracted the "polite" vogue of musical emotion. Yet Gay's answer to the artifice of the baroque was to transfer the pursuit of sensation from the upper-class world to a mocking

Bohemia, where thieves and prostitutes defied conventional morality. It is said that Gay intended to satirize the loose morals of the English upper classes; but the realism of *The Beggar's Opera* continued the fragmentation of personality, the denial of integrated will or purpose, which was also to be found in the picaresque novels of Sterne and Smollett.

A more profound drive toward musical realism arose in France, reflecting the social forces that were preparing for the French revolution. Diderot, Rousseau and D'Alembert were the leaders of the movement to abandon the classical art of Lully and develop a human and meaningful music drama. The result was the presentation of two works written by Beaumarchais: *The Barber of Seville,* with music by Rossini, and *The Marriage of Figaro,* with music by Mozart.

The musical warfare in France had no effect on the American musical scene. *The Barber of Seville,* the first of the Beaumarchais operas, was staged in 1775, when the colonies were on the verge of revolution, and there is no indication that the earlier attack on formalism was known or discussed in America.

In the period from 1750 to the Revolution, musical entertainments were increasingly popular in New York, Philadelphia, Williamsburg and Charlestown. *The Beggar's Opera* appears frequently in the old playbills, along with other ballad operas, classical allegories and pantomimes.[21]

The stage appealed to a restricted middle-class audience, and it had little of the vitality of the folk music which was to assume distinctive American forms in the course of the Revolution. Elements of popular balladry entered the theatres, especially in the miscellaneous entertainment which often accompanied the formal presentation. But in general, music was a concern of the upper class, and retained its aristocratic character.

Jefferson wrote that music "is the favorite passion of my soul." Even in the midst of the war in 1778, Jefferson was thinking of importing some domestic servants from France who could, literally, double in brass, by playing "on the French horn, clarinet, or hautboy, and bassoon." He wrote to France about the possibility of hiring such persons.[22] It was not until he went to Paris after the war that Jefferson came in contact with the new forces in music. In the years that he spent in France, from 1784 to 1789, the growing tensions leading to the outbreak of revolution sharpened the conflict in the musical world.

The informal popular opera which outraged the classicists had its headquarters at the Opera Buffon. The majority of the Encyclopedists, with whom Jefferson was intimate in Paris, were interested in the Opera Buffon, and he wrote of its opening with approval: "A new theatre is established, that of the Opera Buffons, where Italian operas are given, and good music." [23]

The Fall of the Bastille was followed by an extraordinary flowering of musical art in the great popular pageants and mass chants composed by Gossec, Mehul, Lesueur and Cherubini; "given an entirely new function, music took on new forms, structures, orchestration." [24] The creativity of the revolutionary years was brief, but it exerted a potent influence on Beethoven, Verdi, and Chopin, and affected the whole course of nineteenth century music.

The formal musical culture of the United States as distinguished from the popular and folk musical culture during the nineteenth century was largely derivative, reflecting European tendencies and failing to develop a distinctive national style. We cannot attempt to analyze the social and economic factors which have delimited the development of American music. But it may be germane to the general consideration of the opera to note the degree to which the theatre of the nineteenth century was affected by psychological approaches to character which stem from the baroque influence . . . The connection can be made clear by study of the acting and staging of Shakespeare's plays.

The stage of the Elizabethan period, with the actors appearing on a platform in a circular arena under the open sky, demanded shouting delivery and sweeping gesticulation. Yet Shakespeare saw the absurdity of tearing "a passion to tatters." The later style of English acting, which irreverently changed Shakespeare's lines to fustian rhetoric, was the product of the Restoration, when the baroque influence was restored by the royalists, who returned from their French exile "with their pockets full of tragedies." The Restoration transformed the tragic beauty of *Romeo and Juliet* into the wooden formalism of Thomas Otway's *Caius Marius,* which stole most of Shakespeare's lines, Marius the Younger taking Romeo's place, while Juliet became Lavinia. *Romeo and Juliet* remained in abeyance for more than sixty years, while *Caius Marius* held the stage.

Similar violence was done to other Shakespearean dramas. Although the original texts were restored in the eighteenth century, baroque methods of staging and acting were retained. When Fanny Kemble made her first appearance as Juliet in 1829, she wore a plain white satin gown, with a low bodice, short sleeves, and a long train, the costume being ornamented with a belt of fine paste diamonds.[25]

Underlying the interpretation of Shakespeare, which was imported from England to the United States, was the conception of character as a bundle of psychological moods—pity, fear, jealousy, love, hate. The actor was judged by his ability to express these fragmentary emotions, without reference to integrated personality or sustained will. Walt Whitman judged by what he heard and saw in the theatre when he complained that there was "certainly some terrific mouthing in Shakespeare." Whitman wrote in 1846 that actors "imitate humanity so abominably . . . If they have to enact passion, they do so by all kinds of unnatural and violent jerks, swings, screwing of the nerves, of the face, rolling of the eyes, and so on."[26]

Whitman's complaint touches large social and psychological questions. It is an error to suppose that the culture of the popular stage is unrelated to the main currents of thought and life. The touring companies traveling westward with the advancing frontier provided a vital cultural experience to the frontier communities. Shakespeare, as Constance Rourke observes, was a perennial favorite, and the plays were performed with special emphasis on blood and violence: "*Richard III,* cut to the bone, created a heavy sense of fate." It seemed "as if the violence that had been basic and was still dominant in American frontier experience were transmuted and expressed by these remote situations and alien characters."[27]

The fusion of aristocratic and popular elements in every phase of operatic presentation—the economics of production, the character of the audience, the aesthetic and social interests of composers and performers—reflects the dominant role that the aristocracy and church have played in the culture of Europe. The audience is mainly drawn from the urban middle and lower middle classes. The glittering boxes respond to the exaggerated lyricism of the performance as a reflection of the intrigue and love that occupy the lives of men and women in the best society. The crowded galleries come to satisfy their hunger for genuine aesthetic experience—which they can receive only from a distance, and in terms that are foreign to their own lives.

In Tolstoy's *War and Peace,* the scene at the opera is a key to the social situation in Moscow on the eve of Napoleon's invasion of Russia. Natasha "saw only the painted cardboard and the queerly dressed men and women who loved, spoke, and sang so strangely in the brilliant light. She knew what it was all meant to represent, but it was so pretentiously false and unnatural that she felt ashamed for the actors and then amused at them." Yet Natasha was hypnotized by the false passion. She "began to pass into a state of intoxication," and the experience led to her frenzied and nearly disastrous affair with Anatole Kuragin. [28]

The approach to personality as dominated by erotic motives and personal gratification was revitalized by Wagner with a new emphasis on the will to power and the Nietzschian superman. The "Dionysiac man," as Nietzsche and Wagner conceived him, is a pitifully limited individual, emotionally unstable and intellectually underprivileged—a German burgher released from his class status, inviting his soul in a *papier-mâché* wonderland, drenched in myth and ecstasy. Yet the genuine artistic power of Wagner's operas lay in his ability to give the "operatic" psychology a new social meaning. The sexual impulse became an ocean that engulfs humanity in the sweep of *Tristan and Isolde*. The opera was the prelude to the political development of Bismarckian Germany, which in turn found its sublimitation, its authoritarian and mystical justification, in *Parsifal*.

Although Wagner claimed to have created a new cult of nationalism, his mode of thought may be traced chiefly to non-German origins —to the birth of the baroque style in Italy, and its development in France and Flanders. Many of Rubens' paintings have the structure, and even the *dramatis personae* of Wagnerian opera. Wagner's world is Rubens' feudal world of knights and priests, armored heroes mingling with naked women.

The attempt to revitalize and extend the power of Rome in the second half of the nineteenth century, carried forward in the series of encyclicals condemning the secular state and excoriating rationalism and socialism promulgated by Pope Leo XIII during his long pontificate, involved a return to the principles of musical culture proposed by the Council of Trent in the sixteenth century. The archaic simplicity of the Palestrina style was revived. In 1868, the pope reestablished the *schola cantorum* at the Lateran, and institutions for the teaching of church music were founded in Milan, Rome and Venice. In 1884, Leo XIII issued a decree restricting the use of instruments and of the organ. In 1903, one of the first acts of Pius X after receiving the papal tiara was the publication of the *Motu Proprio,* banning the use of women in the choir or diversification of instruments, and canonizing the Palestrina style as the official music of the church.

As in the days of the Counter Reformation, the drive toward ecclesiastical absolutism in the twentieth century was implemented by compromises with the secular power whenever these compromises seemed to advance the interests of the church. While Italian and Spanish ecclesiastical music held to the rigorous simplicity of Palestrina, the sensual splendor of Wagner's art helped to prepare the way for the Nazi conquest of Germany. There is a nineteenth century picture which shows Emperor William I standing with a Lohengrin helmet beside a swan. The operatic portrait suggests the political debt which the government owed to the composer. The temple of all the arts which Wagner hoped to build at Bayreuth may have been designed to revive the cult of Orpheus. But it was an Orpheus who had lost his contact with love or life, destined only to serve the bloody purposes of the furies.

We know what happened to the "Dionysiac man" in the middle years of the twentieth century. The Kaiser-Lohengrin became the Parsifal of the gas chambers, and German financiers directed the re-enactment of the Nibelungen myth, beginning with the gold of the Rhine and ending with the *"Gotterdammerung"* before Stalingrad.

5 : THE BEGINNINGS OF THE NOVEL

RALPH FOX, the brilliant English critic who was killed fighting fascism in Spain, observes that "Rabelais and Cervantes, the real founders of the novel, were more fortunate than their successors in that they did not live in the new society of which they were the heralds." [1]

When Cervantes wrote *Don Quixote,* the transition from the old to the new had reached a point of tension that made his life, as well as his immortal book, an expression of forces which were to mold the future development of the novel.

When we speak of the aristocratic sentimentalization of human feelings in the first decade of the seventeenth century, we must remember that it was also an age of creative titans—Shakespeare, Bacon, Cervantes, El Greco, Lope de Vega—and that these men accomplished some of their most epoch-making work at the moment of Holland's victory over Spain and the beginning of American colonization. 1604 to 1606 were the years of Shakespeare's three tragedies of the diseased will—Hamlet, Macbeth and King Lear. Bacon's *Advancement of Learning* appeared in 1605, and the first part of *Don Quixote* was published in the same year. In a sense, *Don Quixote* is an allegory of the clash of ideas and forces which shaped these various cultural achievements. But the social meaning of *Don Quixote* cannot be understood without reference to the life of the author.

Cervantes was sixty when his book appeared. His life was an epitome of his country's social and psychological experience. His early years were spent in military service. The young poet—some of his verses were printed in 1569, when he was twenty-two—savored the excitement, but more particularly experienced the horror and disillusionment, of the army life. He was wounded at the battle of Lepanto in 1571, captured by Barbary Corsairs in 1575, carried to slavery in Algiers. He spent the five years of his captivity writing sonnets and weaving plots to escape from captivity. He was caught in repeated attempts to win freedom, threatened with torture and death and spared by the intervention of Hassan Pasha, Bey of Algiers. He wrote versified letters to the Spanish secretary of state suggesting plans for an invasion of North Africa. The climax of the drama was as improbable as the incidents that led up to it: in 1580, Cervantes was placed on a galley to be shipped in chains to Constantinople. He was saved by the last minute payment of his ransom when the galley was about to sail.[2]

From the dismal romance of Algerian captivity, Cervantes returned to the more prosaic servitude of genteel poverty: he wrote romances and plays; he pawned five rolls of taffeta on behalf of his sister Magdalene in 1583; in the next year he married a woman eighteen years younger than himself from whom he received a modest dowry; in 1587, he was employed as a commissioner to requisition wheat and oil for the provisioning of the Armada.

His zeal got him into trouble; he was incautious enough to take supplies from the ecclesiastical authorities at Seville, and was excommunicated. However, the difficulty was settled, and he kept his government job after the defeat of the Armada. The work was badly paid and the salary was in arrears.

His only hope of a more satisfactory job lay in America, and in 1590 he petitioned the king for appointment to a position in the New World. The request was refused, with a note that he had better look for something nearer home. Since there was nothing else, he continued what he had been doing; he tried to collect the large sum of 110,400 maravedis which was due him in back pay; he was answered, in 1592, by a cut in salary, from twelve to ten reales a day, which was followed by an investigation of his accounts and the discovery of a deficit of 27,046 maravedis. He got out of this scrape, and continued his work.

On May 7, 1595, Cervantes won a prize in a poetical joust organized by the Dominicans of Saragossa. The award consisted of three silver spoons. But two years later, he was imprisoned at Seville, on charges growing out of the supposed irregularities in his former government service. After twelve weeks in prison, he entered on a period of obscure poverty. In 1601, the Treasury auditors were still trying to collect 79,804 maravedis from him, and it is probable that his inability to pay led to his imprisonment again in 1602.[3]

The poet's financial miseries are a social portrait of the time. In the prologue to *Don Quixote,* Cervantes says the book is "just what might be begotten in prison." There is the somber anger of an imprisoned lifetime in the story.

The elderly public official, stung by petty grievances, rose to deliver a funeral oration over the grave of feudalism—a cautiously allegorical discourse upon a social order that refused to die decently.

The irony of the work was echoed in the circumstances of its publication. It brought no economic comfort to its creator. It was sold outright to a publisher, Francisco de Robles, who did not think highly of its prospects. He was wrong, for it was so successful that it was immediately pirated by two printers in Portugal. Robles took legal action, and Cervantes, who had nothing to gain from the suit, had to sign a paper authorizing Robles to take action.

The fame of his book did not prevent Cervantes from getting into prison again; this time, the misadventure was like something he might have invented for *Don Quixote:* a knight was fatally wounded in the street outside the house where Cervantes lived in Valladolid. The wounded man was taken into the house and nursed by members of the family. Since the street was poor and not of good repute, the women of the household were suspected of some intrigue which led to the knight's death. Cervantes' wife was away, but he was carted off to jail with his sister, his daughter and his niece, along with seven other persons.[4]

It was the crowning jest of Cervantes' life: the man who exposed the false morality of his time was accused of being connected with a bawdy house in which the women of his own family were involved. There was a complicated trial; the case was dismissed; the defendants returned to the doleful street. And they took the only course which seemed to offer any dignity or solace to the wounded heart. In 1609, Cervantes sought refuge in the church: he joined the Confraternity of Slaves of the Most Blessed Sacrament. Two months later, his wife and his sister, Andrea, received the habit of the Third Order of Saint

Francis, of which his other sister, Magdalena, was already a member.[5]

The deterioration of Spanish society, which caused members of the middle class, and especially intellectuals, to turn to the church, was related to the whole movement of European politics. The armistice between Holland and Spain in 1607 was converted into a twelve-year truce by the treaty signed two years later. Cervantes' personal decision, so at variance with the philosophy of his book, coincided with the Spanish acceptance of the treaty that was public acknowledgment of the empire's defeat. The author joined the religious fraternity on April 17, 1609, exactly eight days after the Dutch peace was signed.

Cervantes continued his work on the second part of *Don Quixote;* the manuscript was unfinished when a forgery that purported to be the completed work appeared in 1613. In the same year, and perhaps as a further expression of his literary disillusionment, Cervantes took another step in his religious career: at the age of sixty-six, he donned the habit of the Franciscan Tertiaries.[6]

The contrast between the personal degradation which Cervantes suffered during most of his life and the personal reputation which he achieved reflected the conflict between the aspirations of the Spanish middle class and its fate under the Hapsburg regime. A vivid and embittered urban culture—the product of the century of colonial exploitation—found itself inhibited and deprived of further development. The issue was so intense, and so personal as it affected the individual, that it found expression in disordered fantasy, combining realistic and subjective elements in a manner that is unique in the development of modern art.

The individual who had acquired education and a sense of the potentialities of his class, moving through the poverty and wealth of the cities, restrained in every move by the Inquisition and the power of corrupt officials, could find peace only in the subjective side of the *Hamlet dilemma.* An escape from the slings and arrows of outrageous fortune was offered, along with very real protection from the caprice of the law, by the church.

Cervantes, entangled in bureaucratic red tape, caught in the reasoned madness of accounts that would not balance, was able to depict the absurdity of feudal "ideals" without encumbering his work with the "idealism" of the bourgeoisie. It is said that *Don Quixote* was accepted in Spain "as the quintessance of the cynical disillusionment that had fallen upon the nation."[7] The disillusionment was rooted in economic and social realities. Cervantes' trouble with his accounts reflected the difficulties of the state. It was a time of wild currency disorders. Having debased the coinage in 1599, Philip III cut living standards still further three years later, when he decreed that the face value of every coin be doubled. The government imposed sales taxes which at times ran as high as fifteen or twenty percent. The economy fluctuated between dizzy inflation and severe deflation.[8]

Since the "national spirit" of Spain was the product of environmental factors, it is not surprising that the most powerful pictorial representation of the Spanish "soul" was the work of a Cretan artist, El Greco. His tragic figures wander through a passionately unreal landscape, distorted to fit the mood of encompassing despair. *Toledo in Storm* was painted at about the time of the publication of *Don Quixote*.[9] The cathedral is strangely displaced from the center of the town to the hillside below the Alcazar, the walls and bridges are like memories of a dead medieval town. The doom upon the city suggests the agony that awaited Spain in the coming centuries. Yet El Greco's most profound social message lies in his study of the human personality. He painted few women, for the humanity of sex is absent from his world. His men are weary with the agony of living. The carefully studied skulls hold thoughts that cannot escape through the smoldering eyes.

After 1606, there is a markedly increased brutality and distortion in El Greco's work. The lighting becomes more artificial; there is a quality of melodrama in the use of light solely for emotional effects. Although El Greco's art was far from the "operatic" artifice of the Italian mannerists, he shared the Italian view of the scientific techniques of the previous century. One of his fellow artists, Francisco Pacheco de Rio, wrote that El Greco felt that coloring is more difficult than drawing, and that he had little esteem for Michelangelo, saying "he was a good man but did not know how to paint." [10]

A link between the subjective bitterness of the middle class and the disorder of the poverty stricken cities is to be found in Lope de Vega's torrential output of dramas and farces. The bewildering variety of Lope's styles indicates the breakdown of old cultural values, the attempt to please the church with religious allegories while appealing to the people with plays that touch social reality. In general, Lope tried to compromise with commercial and political pressures by the use of vulgar humor, sentimentality, and bombast. But there is one exception. *Fuente Ovejuna,* or *The Sheep Well,* written between 1606 and 1610, is an astonishing social document.

While it is utterly unlike *Don Quixote,* the play expresses the same contempt for feudal *mores.* The three hundred inhabitants of a village, infuriated by the exactions of the lord of the manor, force their way into the castle and kill him. When judges arrive from the royal court to punish the ringleaders, they find that they cannot break the unity of the community. When the people are tortured on the rack to give the names of the guilty persons, they reply only with the name of the village, *Fuente Ovejuna.* The fact that a play with such a theme was permitted is due to the climax, which shows the king generously pardoning the rebels, and taking them under his protection. The crown may have felt that there was something to be gained by diverting the attention of the discontented urban population to a rural situation, in which a representative of the troublesome nobility is the villain.

Nevertheless, the appearance of such a play reflected the temper of the submerged masses in city and country; it appealed to an audience which could identify its own grievances with those of the peasants. Out of the night that closed around Spain came the collective voice of the people of *Fuente Ovejuna;* it was a voice that could not be stilled, that would be heard again in eighteenth and nineteenth century rebellions, and in the singing columns that marched against Franco in the nineteen-thirties.

Lope de Vega heard the mighty voice, and wrote with a fire that his previous plays had never known. The fire died. No more could be said, for there was no more that he dared to say. He turned to the church in 1614, taking minor orders and becoming a "familiar" of the Inquisition. The step did not interrupt his Bohemian literary career or his innumerable love affairs. Yet it is also said that he was in the habit of scourging himself till the walls of his room were flecked with blood.[11]

While Lope was a neurotic personality in the modern sense of the term, he created the only work of art of his time which may be said to project a genuinely heroic personality—in the sense of the will directed with consistent fortitude to recognizable social objectives. But the heroism in *Fuente Ovejuna* is collective: the individual finds his strength in conscious identification with the group. The name of the community gives courage to each man and woman and child.

The contrast between *Don Quixote's* heroic madness and the communal heroism of *Fuente Ovejuna* poses a question that affects the whole future development of the novel. Can man rise to heroic stature, if he is detached from other men, aloof from the social environment? If the will is directed solely to personal ends, can heroism achieve anything more valid than the pathos of Don Quixote's imaginary triumphs?

The need of identification, of shared experience, drove Spanish intellectuals to the church. But the frustration that plagued the cultural life of Spain was not a local phenomenon. It was a heightened expression of social contradictions which were present in every country.

Shakespeare's answer to the question regarding the potentialities of the will was written in the three plays that appeared in 1604 and 1605, in the shadowed years between the death of Elizabeth and the Gunpowder Plot. Here the human will is strong and, up to a point, "free." But it is a corrosive, anti-social force, a cancer that corrupts and destroys. The dynamic factor in human relationships is not the erotic impulse, the seeking after illusion or ecstacy. It is the drive for power, exercised without restraint or conscience. While Spanish thought was preoccupied with the threat of clerical feudalism, and the art of France and Italy celebrated the more mundane and hopeful viewpoint of a secular aristocracy, Shakespeare explored the psychological premises on which England's power-drive was based.

He could see no moral conviction or social purpose that gave the individual integration and a sense of group solidarity. Macbeth and his wife are enthralled by their "infected minds." Iago is bent solely upon wrecking the love that binds Othello and Desdemona. There is a hero in *Othello*. But his heroism leads to his being enmeshed and deceived. And he is a black man. While there was a distinction, not too carefully observed in the practice of the slave marts, between Moors and Negroes of the African east coast, a black skin meant Africa and slavery, and England had tasted the profits of the slave trade; had a deep interest both in the African continent and in the lucrative traffic in human beings. The dominant cultural attitude may be found in Ben Jonson's *The Masque of Blackness,* produced at court a short time after the appearance of *Othello*. The ballet is performed by twelve Ethiopian maidens, who have come to Britain in order to get white complexions—a miracle to be accomplished by the benevolent English sun,

Whose beams shine day and night, and are of force
To blanche an Aethiop and revive a corse.[12]

The connection between dark skins and colonial expansion, ornately dramatized by Jonson could hardly have been ignored at a time when English ships were making yearly sailings to the Orient, and when there was much discussion of African and American conquest. Shakespeare could not have made his hero a Negro without being conscious of the contrast between his passionate rectitude and the ignoble conduct of most of the other characters.

The importance which Shakespeare attached to the black hero is clarified by consideration of the play which probably followed it, *King Lear,* in which the dramatist explicitly related the problem of the will to the social conflicts of the time. In *Lear,* the will is caught, as Othello was caught in the wiles of Iago, in the clash of two hostile forces; the patriarchal authority of feudalism opposes the power-drive of the bourgeoisie.

The problem is posed with schematic simplicity in the first scene: Lear insists on unquestioning obedience, not only from his daughters, but from everyone around him. When the Earl of Kent dares to question his decision, Lear addresses him as "vassal! miscreant!" and decrees his banishment. Opposition to the feudal law has two aspects the businesslike hypocrisy of Goneril and Regan, and the youngest girl's insistence on personal rights and obligations. When Lear demands that the three swear their eternal allegiance to him, Cordelia refuses on the ground that marriage will require that she love and honor her husband. For this assertion of a "modern" viewpoint, Cordelia is disinherited. But her sisters are also "modern" in their cold appraisal of their father's weakness:

Regan: 'Tis the infirmity of his age: yet he hath ever but slenderly known himself.
Goneril: The best and soundest of his time hath been but rash.

The theme develops in a framework of social disorder and moral breakdown:

Love cools, friendship falls off, brothers divide; in cities, mutinies; in countries, discord; in palaces, treason; and the bond cracked between son and father.

Disaster forces Lear to realize that he has lived by false values. As he wanders in the storm, he thinks of the "poor naked wretches," whose "houseless heads and unfed sides" give them no defense against the pitiless elements. The only solution that Lear can find is in the subjective world of madness. It is only in the sanctuary of the mind that he can be reunited with the daughter who loves him. He tells Cordelia:

> We two alone will sing like birds i' the
> cage;
> When thou dost ask me blessing I'll kneel down
> And ask of thee forgiveness: so we'll live,
> And pray, and sing, and tell old tales, and
> laugh . . .
> And take upon's the mystery of things
> As if we were God's spies . . .

The concept that man can only be free in the subjective prison of the mind, where he can preserve the purity of feeling which society violates, moves far beyond the dilemma posed in *Hamlet.*

The Dane's madness is feigned in order to achieve an objective solution, to break from the subjective prison; but *Lear* can find no solution except in total escape.

However, another solution was offered at the moment when Lear's tragic lament was first heard. In the same year, Francis Bacon published *The Advancement of Learning.* Here was a manifesto of intellectual progress, answering Lear's madness with the verities of science. Yet Bacon's insistence on objective truth was combined with a retrogressive political viewpoint. He called for the advancement of science, but he gave unqualified support to monarchial absolutism. Like the Dutch scientist, Stevinus, Bacon assumed that science could pursue its own ends, untroubled by class conflict. This was the view which was to dominate the history of science under capitalism, which would demand that research serve business and the state without looking toward wider social horizons.

Bacon looked forward to the freedom of inquiry that would be made possible, within prescribed limits, by the rise of the bourgeoisie. But he wanted to eat his cake and have it too. He wanted the protection of science in absolute terms, and accepted royal absolutism as the only means of attaining that end. *The Advancement of Learning* denied social advancement. It combined a philosophy of intellectual change with a philosophy of political permanence. Bacon wrote that Great Britain had passed through "a full period of all instability and peregrinations." But the Stuart monarchy promised an end to "these prelusive changes and varieties." [13] The statement may be dismissed as a bit of harmless flattery to the king. But it expresses the faith in the *status quo* that was to be the guiding star of Bacon's life.

Bacon's personality was split between the past and the future. He was a man of the Renaissance in the sense that his interests were both cultural and political; but the two interests had become irreconcilable. The statesman and the scientist spoke different languages. Bacon has been charged with insincerity in his political career. But his belief in the royal power was his Renaissance inheritance; it was as deep in his soul as his faith in science.

Bacon devoted himself to politics, because it gave him the sense of personal fulfillment, of accomplishment and mastery, which could not be found in the field of science. Yet his political aims were as unrealistic, as fully committed to *unscientific* values, as his belief in 1605 that the reign of James brought permanent stability. The ambivalence was to wreck Bacon's career, to deprive him of the fulfillment which he craved. Although he did not reach the subjective *impasse* dramatized in Lear's fury, he was at last alone, pursuing "the mystery of things," like one of "God's spies," in a vacuum.

We shall deal with Bacon's career in greater detail as we proceed. It is useful to our study of the various types of individuality that emerged in the culture of the early seventeenth century, as a commentary on the treatment of character in *Don Quixote*. The protagonist of the novel lives in an unreal world, and his contact with reality is either pure fantasy or hopeless frustration. Despite his wanderings, his mind is as imprisoned as Lear's. In Bacon, we have the noblest scientific spirit of the age. In the long reach of history, his work was enormously productive, pointing the road that generations of scientists would travel. But as a person he was less than heroic, unable to achieve integration of his scientific and political life, torn by irreconcilable conflicts. Alexander Pope was devastatingly accurate when he called him the "wisest, wittiest, meanest of mankind."

The culture-hero, the man following a socially motivated and conscious vision was to play very little part in the future development of the modern novel. The culture-hero must have his roots among the people, and serve the large needs and hopes of the people. Bacon typified the scientific and creative personality of the epoch of capitalism. The philosophers and artists who followed him were to achieve miracles of research and reasoning. But the world of action in which they moved condemned them to pay a price for their intellectual attainments. They were cut off from the totality of human experience. They could neither be heroes nor create them.

6 : THE CORPORATION

Corporate organization goes back to the Middle Ages. Medieval charters of incorporation, granted to religious and educational institutions, as well as to towns and gilds, provided a legal precedent for the charters of the mercantile and industrial companies of the sixteenth century. The Scotch immigrants who settled in Ireland after the crown's seizure of Ulster properties were not unfamiliar with corporate power: some of them held their Irish lands as tenants of the London municipal corporation, and all of them felt the effects of the London merchants' control of the trade that passed through the port of Londonderry.

Edward P. Cheyney observes that "the whole advance of English discovery, commerce, and colonization in the sixteenth and early seventeenth centuries was due not to individuals, but to the efforts of corporate bodies." [1] The fact that colonial charters were given to corporations is, of course, common knowledge. But historiography has not stressed the connection between these associations and the system of state power that developed in the United States. Everyone knows that the transfer of the Massachusetts Bay charter from Britain to New England in 1630 changed a corporation into a state. But this remarkable transfiguration has not been related to the twentieth century growth of big business combinations, which have reversed the process and changed the state into a political arm of the corporation.

The men who assembled at Philadelphia in 1787 to write a Constitution which would serve to protect their various interests were familiar with colonial forms of governmental organization originating in the corporate charters won by the English bourgeoisie in its struggle against Stuart absolutism at the beginning of the seventeenth century. American thinkers might quote Locke's generalizations about freedom and property. But the rights and institutions which came within the orbit of their experience, and which they had sought to defend and extend by the revolutionary break with England, grew out of an earlier period when the bourgeoisie had not attained the luxury of abstract speculation.

The constitutional history of the United States begins with the Virginia charters of 1609 and 1612. Detailed study of the charters, and of the battle between the crown and the bourgeoisie from which they were born, provides promising clues to the later development of law and custom in the United States.

During 1608 and 1609, there were no sessions of parliament. The crown and the opposition were maneuvering, martialling forces and preparing reserves, for the battle which would take place when the Commons met. The decision could not be long deferred, for James was in serious financial straits. Since monarchial feudalism identified the king and the state, there was no distinction between the personal expenses of the royal household and the maintenance of the government—the army, the navy, the host of officials from clerks to privy councilors. The king's ability to raise funds without the consent of the Commons was limited—and its extension, as the Bates' case had proved, involved grave dangers to the royal popularity and prestige.

We have described Bacon's cogitations on July 25, 1608. His personal finances, as we have seen, were in a healthy condition. But his physical health was unsatisfactory. His accounts and his psychology were determined by political considerations. His further advancement depended on the favor of his sovereign, and James' accounts showed a catastrophic deficit. On July 28, the Treasurer, Lord Salisbury, issued a new Book of Rates, a tariff schedule: the higher duties increased the revenue from tonnage and poundage by about £70,000 annually. The decision against Bates had given the government the legal right to take this step. But a year and a half had intervened; James' advisers, weighing the anger aroused by the judicial ruling, knew that it was politically inadvisable to make use of the power that had been won. The increase in rates in 1608 was too moderate to meet the crown's necessities; it was imposed on certain luxuries. It is amusing, but of major significance as a gauge of the crown's embarrassment, that currants—which were at stake in the Bates' case—were given a lower import duty.[2]

During 1608, Sandys was at work on the draft of the new Virginia charter. The reports of mismanagement brought back by Archer and others pointed to the need of drastic reorganization. The first condition of any reorganization was the money to carry it out; the class which had money to invest, and which Sandys represented, would not put up the financing unless it was assured of reasonable control of the undertaking. As in the case of the national government, money was power. The national and colonial problems were two sides of the same coin—and it was good, negotiable coin of the realm. Arbitrary royal taxes struck at the same interests which opposed arbitrary royal control of the Virginia Company.

The crown's decision to give a more liberal charter was motivated by the considerations which had occasioned the granting of the first charter in 1606. But in 1609, the bourgeoisie had acquired greater strength; the king's financial position had deteriorated, and the international situation favored the bourgeoisie's demands. Therefore, the concessions wrung from the crown went far beyond the gains won in the earlier grant.

The settlement of the twelve-year truce between the Netherlands and Spain made it imperative to carry through the reorganization of the transatlantic enterprise. But the specific terms of the patent reflected the domestic political situation. James was looking forward to the approaching showdown with the Commons. The charter was part of the price which he was reluctantly compelled to pay for the money he hoped to receive.

However, the patent, like everything James did, expressed the ambivalence of his position: he gave only what he was forced to give, hedging the granted privileges with the ambiguities and double-meanings which are used in decrees and laws as well as in diplomacy, to insure that the future interpretation of the words will depend on power rather than on reason. Bacon was a master in devising these subtleties. There is no question as to what Sandys and his friends wanted: they proposed that authority be transferred from the crown to the corporation, so that the investors could manage their own affairs. Bacon's duty as the king's solicitor was equally clear; the transfer of authority was to be made as indeterminate as possible, so that it could be subject to later contradictory interpretations.

The charter provided for regular meetings of the corporation, being the stockholders "or the major part of them." But control of the company did not rest in this body; it rested in a council, which acquired the control formerly vested in the king. The council was described as a continuation of the royal council created in 1606: it was "perpetually one Council here resident, according to the Tenour of our former Letters-Patent." The stockholders had the important right of filling vacancies in the council, but it was by no means clear whether the councilors were responsible to the stockholders or to the crown.

The company was given wide governmental powers; it was authorized "to make, ordain, and establish all Manner of Orders, Laws, Directions, Instructions, Forms, and Ceremonies of Government and Magistracy . . . not only within the Precincts of the said Colony, but also upon the Seas in going and coming . . ." It had "full and absolute Power and Authority, to correct, punish, pardon, govern, and rule . . ." However, this extensive control was not vested in the stockholders. The right to appoint governors, as well as make laws, was assigned to the council. The right of admitting members to the corporation was given to the "Treasurer and Council . . . or any four of them." The importance of the treasurer was stressed in the name under which the company was incorporated, as "The Treasurer and Company of Adventurers and Planters of the City of London." [3]

Sir Thomas Smythe became the treasurer. Since he was a leader of the clique of merchants enjoying the favor of the crown, his appointment seemed to guarantee that the council would be subservient to the royal will. However, the popular response to the patent was so overwhelming that James must have had some qualms concerning the sagacity of his legal adviser. The safeguards erected by Bacon did not prevent Sandys' followers from treating the charter as a political demonstration of the strength of their class. The majority of the bourgeoisie which considered itself underprivileged saw its aims realized in the green wilderness across the Atlantic. Although its rights in the corporation were undefined, it had secured a foothold in a company which had territorial and governmental powers of a very substantial kind. With economic opportunity went the chance to seize and develop these powers.

The historical significance of the event was indicated in the rush to subscribe to the stock and in the social status of the persons who sought participation. There were 659 subscribers. Fifty were currently members of parliament, and fifty more had served in that capacity at other times. The social composition of the group, so far as it is known, was as follows: 21 peers, 96 knights, 11 members of the learned professions, 53 captains, 58 gentlemen, 110 merchants, 282 citizens. The others were not classified.[4]

There was official participation by the fifty-six London companies. The records of the Grocers' Company include a receipt showing that £69 was placed with the warden by members to be invested for their private benefit in the Virginia undertaking. The Mercers' Company gave £200. The Clothworkers subscribed both as a body and as individuals. The Fishmongers gave active support.[5]

The twelve great livery companies represented big capital, which was more sympathetic to the crown than to the opposition. Some of the other companies were controlled by wealthy men, but there were many in which artisans, shopkeepers and tradesmen were fighting to maintain their status. In voting subscriptions and passing resolutions directing their members to subscribe, these groups were acting with a conscious political purpose.

William Strachey, the London Company's secretary, describes the public excitement:

> "Not a yeare of romain-jubilie, noe nor the Ethnick-Queene of Ephesus, can be said to have bene followed with more heate and zeale; the discourse and visitation of it took up all meetings, times, termes, all degress, all purses, and such throngs and concourse of personal undertakers, as the aire seemed not to have more lights than that holie cause inflamed spirits to partake with it." [6]

In order to understand the significance of the "Holie cause," we must appreciate the function of the corporation in the life of the period. Economic activity was conducted almost exclusively through gilds or various types of association. The increasing monopoly control of these organizations, either by rich merchants or by royal favorites receiving special privileges from the crown, was a deadly threat to middle and small business interests.

At the time of the granting of the Virginia charter, the corporation was a battleground of conflicting classes. For example, the Pewterers' Company had conducted a long and bitter fight to secure tin without paying tribute to monopolists; it is curious, but characteristic of the business methods of the time, that the tin market was conrolled by the all-powerful Haberdashers' Company. The Pewterers attempted to raise a fund of three or four thousand pounds, in order to buy tin independently, but they lacked the collective capital to raise this sum; a few wealthy members undertook to purchase the necessary supplies of tin—securing the permission of the gild's executive committee—and obtained a substantial profit on the transaction.

The Feltmakers, also seeking to escape from the burdensome jurisdiction of the Haberdashers, issued an interesting prospectus for a new corporation:

> The Company of Feltmakers of London thereunto moved by sundry mischiefs and miseries they have endured by the Company of Haberdashers of London have resolved for remedie thereof and for Government of the poore of their trade and profytt of such as will come with them therein to buy a Stock or bank of money for the takeing in and buying up of all the wares they make into their own handes which Stocke is projected to be £15,000 to be raised by themselves and such as will adventure with them.[7]

The plan failed. It was to be revived, as we shall see, a few years later. It suggests the feeling that must have stirred the members of many London companies when they voted to buy stock, and voting rights, in the government of Virginia.

The crown's misuse of monopolistic grants may be illustrated in the case of the Yorkshire alum works. We may remember that the attempt of the Vatican and the Medici to secure control of the European alum market was one of the great political issues of the fifteenth century. Alum was a no less vital factor in the economy of Stuart England. In 1607, valuable deposits were discovered in Yorkshire. The king gave an exclusive patent to a group of his friends, who secured capital from London merchants to erect buildings and import experienced workmen. The project was protected by prohibition of imports and suppression of other domestic manufacture. But it could not be protected from the stubborn resistance of clothworkers, who resented paying more than they had paid for foreign alum. They engaged in smuggling successfully and on a large scale. The Yorkshire Works, facing increasing opposition and saddled with incompetent management, was in trouble in 1609. The crown took over the monopoly. The merchants who had provided the original capital resigned their interest in return for an annuity of £6,044 for 26 years. The holders of the patent were also guaranteed an annual income.[8]

The alum arrangement, which was to prove disastrously unprofitable, is an amusing commentary on the contradictions in James' position and policy. When the courtiers and merchants whom James had favored found that the enterprise did not pay, they took advantage of his necessitous finances to hand it back to him, along with all the headaches which went with it. His absolutism was as unsound economically as it was politically unstable. He was at the mercy of the people on whom he conferred benefits.

We can imagine the king's annoyance as he received reports of the huge profits of the East India Company, while he struggled to meet a growing deficit. James could not make heavy economic demands on people like Sir Thomas Smythe, because he needed them even more than they needed him. Smythe's participation in the Virginia Company was invaluable to the crown as a barrier to the Sandys forces.

The gift of Ulster Plantation to the twelve London livery companies was intended to counterbalance the "democratic" charter of the Virginia Company, and to tie the London financiers more closely to the crown. For the same reason, James conferred a new charter on the East India Company in 1609. The patent granted by Elizabeth in 1600 had given a monopoly of trade for 15 years. The new instrument, which made the monopoly perpetual, protected the company against interlopers by a provision that unlicensed persons venturing to "visit, haunt, frequent or trade" within the corporation's jurisdiction would forfeit their ships and goods, half to go to the company and half to the crown. The merchants celebrated their enlarged powers by building a ship of 1,100 tons, the *Trade's Increase*. When the vessel was launched, a banquet was held on board. His Majesty attended; the food was served on the strange dishes called china in honor of the country of their origin. James placed a chain of gold and a medal around Sir Thomas Smythe's neck.[9]

The ceremony symbolized their mutual interdependence. James may have thought that a gift of gold from the merchant would be more appropriate under the circumstances. But Smythe's humility was no doubt genuine, for his political power was indirect and limited; he could hardly have guessed that in less than a century men like himself would hold the nation's purse-strings and manipulate its finances through their mastery of a corporation—the Bank of England.

When parliament met on February 9, 1610, the party of the bourgeoisie was in undisputed control of the Commons. It was strong and confident, prepared to make a money settlement with the crown, but only on terms that would give adequate guarantees for the protection of its class interests. James' advisers, among whom Bacon occupied a prominent place, offered a permanent agreement, known as the *Great Contract.* In the form in which it was first presented, James was to get a lump sum of £600,000, and a guaranteed annual income of £200,000. In return, he promised "a general redress of grievances."

During the first weeks of negotiation, the House received a complaint that a law dictionary published in 1608 contained opinions derogatory of the rights of parliament. The action taken by the House, following the precedent established in the case of the bishop's uncomplimentary writings in 1604, shows the importance which the bourgeoisie attached to the political prestige of the Commons. All business was suspended; nothing more could be done until the king issued a proclamation condemning the dictionary. The royal ukase was prepared and brought to the Commons on March 27; it prohibited "the buying, uttering or reading" of the book.[10]

We have stressed the impact of the Dutch peace on England's internal politics. The fact that the signing of the treaty strengthened the opposition was evidenced on April 19, ten days later, when the crown made the first definite commitment to give up some of the more oppressive feudal privileges: these related to "wardships, marriages, Premier Seizin, relief, respect of homage, and the like." These royal prerogatives, which brought considerable sums to the crown, were extremely burdensome to the propertied classes. The king imposed exorbitant fees for the transfer of property; he interfered in marriage contracts and other family affairs, and he obtained profit for himself and his friends through control of the estates of minors. The Commons replied to the crown's proposal with an offer of £100,000 per annum. James answered, through the Lord Treasurer, that he could not part with his feudal rights unless he received the whole sum for which he had asked—£600,000 cash, and £200,000 per year.[11]

The Commons had the advantage of the king in a number of ways: the haggling over money hurt his prestige, and his need of money was so pressing that it weakened his bargaining power. He met the emergency by borrowing £100,000 from the City of London. The merchants could not do less, after the banquet at the launching of the *Trade's Increase,* the expanded privileges conferred on the East India Company, the gift of Ulster Plantation. However, Smythe and his associates were not deeply interested in the political conflict, nor were they willing to make any real sacrifice to improve the government's finances. They were intent on the advancement of their own affairs, which were chiefly concerned with meeting Dutch competition in the Orient. Success in the Far East depended on their own initiative; they could get little assistance, naval or diplomatic, from the government. If there was any fighting to be done, it must be carried on by their ships, with men, guns and equipment furnished by their own resources.[12]

These years show a rapid increase in the profits of the East India Company; the voyage in 1609 involved an investment of only £13,700, and brought a return of 234 percent. In 1610, three ships sailed, representing the much larger investment of £82,000, of which £21,300 covered commodities exported to the Far East. The profit on this venture was to amount to 121¾ percent.[13]

The London group, like its Dutch competitors, was eager to find a shorter route to the Oriental markets. In April, while the parliamentary battle raged, Henry Hudson sailed from England in search of a northwest passage. This time, he was employed by a syndicate headed by Smythe. Having secured the Hudson River for Holland, the navigator was about to bring the English flag to Hudson Bay, where rivers draining half of Canada enter the sea. The discovery was in part responsible for England's later control of central and western Canada, and British mastery of the world's fur trade in the nineteenth century.

There was no reason to attach any special importance to Hudson's departure in the spring of 1610. Political interest in America was divided between the Virginia Company and the Newfoundland fisheries. Although the two enterprises were geographically separated, they involved interlocking political and economic interests. We have mentioned that the men who controlled England's West Country fishing industry were influential in the parliamentary opposition, and that Sandys spoke for them in the first sessions of the Stuart parliament.

There was increasing friction between the West Country and the London capitalists: the latter sent their large ships to Newfoundland to buy cod there; these so-called "sack ships" were interested in getting fish as cheaply as possible for sale on the European market. They would buy from English fishermen or those of other nationalities. The West Country resented this interference, which deprived it of the profits of the carrying trade. The struggle became acute when the king granted a charter to the London and Bristol Company on May 2, 1610. The move grew out of James' dissatisfaction with the Commons' attitude toward his demands. He struck back at the opposition at a critical point in the negotiations by granting a patent which was strongly resented both by the West Country fishing industry and by the Virginia Company. The new syndicate was given control of the Newfoundland coast, so that it could charge the fishermen for the use of landing platforms, as well as for salt and other essential supplies. While the charter spoke consolingly of the protection of persons engaged in trade or fishing, it was obvious that the new corporation could, and would, exact tribute from the fishermen. To the Virginia stockholders, the London and Bristol Company represented a grave threat to their plans for fishing and trade in American coastal waters.

The stockholders were not aware of the straits to which the colony on the James River had been reduced. While the debate raged in the Commons, the settlement was on the verge of destruction. The winter of the starving time left only about sixty people alive. On May 23, they were joined by 140 survivors of the wreck of the *Sea Venture*. The ship had gone to pieces on one of the Bermuda islands. The passengers spent the winter building two pinnaces from the wreckage, and in these makeshift vessels they managed to reach the James River.

At last, the colony had a governor. But Sir Thomas Gates found the surviving inhabitants so weak that they could hardly stand. Jamestown was in ruins. The new arrivals complicated the food situation. It looked as if the Indians had won their war of attrition against the invaders. Gates decided that the only possible course was to admit defeat. There were two small boats at Jamestown in addition to the two pinnaces. On June 7, the four vessels, carrying all the people and their belongings, dropped down the river. But as they approached the mouth of the James, they met a long boat coming from a fleet that lay off Point Comfort. The three ships brought a new Governor, Lord Delaware, with 150 colonists and ample supplies.

The refugees turned back to the desolate town. The tall ships followed. The colony was saved.

Meanwhile, the gap between the king and the Commons became

wider. In May, the opposition got down to fundamentals, raising the old question of the crown's right to impose taxes without parliamentary consent. Bacon, the most skillful spokesman for the crown in the House, fought to prevent any action on the part of the Commons that might lead to a definitive break. He was worried, not so much about offending James, as about statements concerning sovereignty which would endanger the principle of monarchial power. He advised that an angry message to the king be modified; the notes reporting his speech contain this revelatory comment: "Sovereignty and Liberty to pass in silence: not to be textual." [14]

The news of the assassination of Henry IV frightened the Commons and strengthened the crown. Although the fundamental interests of the court were benefited, James must have been frightened by the event in France. Regicide was a constant danger to the monarch's person as well as a challenge to the divine right of kings. But, however much James might condemn the means which the pupil of the Jesuits had adopted, the end achieved was all that he could wish: the European bourgeoisie was weakened, and Catholic-feudal power was increased everywhere, especially in Spain. The extension of Spanish influence was gratifying to James and the aristocracy, making it easier to move toward the alliance with Philip II which was the sometimes invisible, but never forgotten, guiding star of Stuart foreign policy.

The assassination had a direct effect on the negotiations for the *Great Contract*. The Commons, troubled by the situation abroad, was ready to effect a compromise. On July 13, it voted to give the king the largest annual stipend it had yet suggested, £180,000, in return for a satisfactory adjustment of the grievances that remained unresolved. But James, seeing the gaudy regency established across the channel, was less anxious to settle. On July 23, he categorically refused the Commons' offer.

Since it was impossible to reach a quick agreement, parliament recessed for the summer. The interval gave the members of the House a chance to sound out the feeling of their constituents. Of major political significance was the news of the miraculous survival of the passengers of the *Sea Venture,* and the tragic condition in which they found the colony on their arrival. Sylvester Jourdain told the story in his *Discovery of the Bermudas;* the book was probably published in October, at about the time of the reconvening of parliament on

October 18. It stirred the popular imagination. But to Sandys and other stockholders, it raised several practical questions: they wanted to include the Bermudas in the patent; they were aware of the urgent need of raising additional funds in order to get the colony on its feet; and they knew that more funds could not be raised without remedying the defects in the second charter and assuring more effective control by the stockholders. Sandys was already at work on a revised charter in the fall of 1610, and was discussing its acceptance with the government. The proposed changes in the Virginia Company were tied in with the negotiations for settlement of the *Great Contract.*

The tone of the fall debate in the Commons exhibited the growing intransigeance of both parties. The question of funds had become merged in the larger question of state-power. A memorandum of a speech delivered by Sir Roger Owen in November urged that "no gap be left open for the King to impose on his subjects." Owen exposed the real issue when he insisted on the need of having "parliaments hereafter though the king's wants be fully supplied."[15] This was exactly what James did not want: the *Great Contract* was designed to dispose of the Commons and its debates once and for all. James, goaded by resentment, showed the impossibility of compromise when he said that "Kings are not only God's lieutenants upon earth and sit upon God's throne, but even by God himself they are called Gods . . ."[16]

In one respect, at least, James was not like a God. He had to pay his bills. His position was so ungodlike that he could not control the price of alum, for fear that his enemies would make political capital out of it. The managers of the Yorkshire alum works complained that they were compelled to sell their product at a loss as long as parliament was in session, in order to avoid complaints from the Commons about high prices.[17]

James, as usual, was caught in a net of contradictions. He could not submit to the pretensions of the bourgeoisie, but he was too weak to risk a violent break. He sent a message to the House on November 5th in which he presented what he called "the clear mirror of his heart."[18] The mirror reflected such a desperate need of money that it must have given great comfort to the king's enemies. Bacon and other political realists were now mainly concerned with ending the conflict as gracefully as possible. James saw the need of conciliatory tactics. He wrote on November 25th that he hoped "the Parliament may end quietly, and he and his subjects part with the fairest show." [19] The session dragged on aimlessly into the new year. It was dissolved on February 29, 1611, and James faced the task of securing funds without parliamentary sanction.

The task was not one whit easier in 1611 than it had been in 1608. James sold titles and obtained forced loans. One of his money-raising schemes was connected with the recently established plantations in the north of Ireland: a new order of baronets was founded; persons paying £1,000 had the privilege of having the "bloody hand of Ulster" on their coat of arms.[20]

The alum works in Yorkshire were moving toward bankruptcy, but this did not prevent the king from trying a similar experiment, involving similar political repercussions, in another field. He gave four favorites a monopoly of the manufacture of gold and silver thread, made by winding gilded silver around a core of silk thread. The business was one of the most important luxury trades in the kingdom. The word *royalty* as applied to patents or copyrights is, of course, derived from these practices. James' royalty from the gilded thread amounted to £10,000 per year. But he had made his customary miscalculation of the strength and resourcefulness of the interests injured by the patent. Goldsmiths and silkmen refused to bow to the monopoly, manufacturing thread in defiance of the law. A large quantity of thread was smuggled into the country. The whole industry was disrupted, and James lost immeasurably in popularity and prestige.[21]

Anti-monopoly sentiment became stronger and better organized in 1611. The defensive measures taken by small craftsmen may again be illustrated in the case of the pewterers and the feltmakers. A body of workmen pewterers, led by a former beadle of the Pewterers' Company, presented a petition to the crown demanding that the men who controlled the tin market "should deliver forth four-score thousand weight of tynne to be wrought into pewter by the workmen of the company." The petition was refused, but it led the government to set a fixed price on tin, and to assure a supply to "shop-keepers and those which worked it either themselves or by their servants and workmen."

The feltmakers, whose plans for raising a capital of £15,000 for the purchase of materials had failed a few years earlier, carried through a less ambitious project in 1611. They formed a corporation with a capital of £5,000, separate from the Feltmakers' Company, but using its hall and allowing the company a penny on each pound of profit. The scheme was intended to circumvent the Haberdashers' Company, and to secure supplies for the small masters at reasonable prices.[22]

The royal monopolies and the attempts of artisans to secure capital marked two extremes of the complicated struggle for corporate power. The two extremes met in the Virginia Company, where control of an overseas empire was at stake. In the 1606 charter, the king had exercised full control through his right to appoint a council; in 1609, the power of the council was limited by the formation of the general assembly of stockholders, a heterogeneous group with a large representation of small investors. In 1611, Sandys and his associates demanded full power for the stockholders.

Early in the year, the company started a campaign to raise £30,000 to pay for three cargoes, to be sent out during the next three years. In February, at the time of the dissolution of parliament, £18,000 had been raised.[23] This was sufficiently encouraging to justify the dispatch of the largest contingent of colonists that had ever crossed to the English settlement. Six hundred were sent in two expeditions: the first fleet of three vessels, leaving early in 1611, was under the command of Sir Thomas Dale, appointed as deputy governor to replace Lord Delaware, who had returned to England. Shortly afterward, Sir Thomas Gates left with three ships and three caravels, with ample provisions.

While the new colonists were finding homes in Virginia, Henry Hudson was engaged in a life and death struggle for power with a mutinous crew on the shores of Hudson Bay. The ship had been frozen in the ice during the long winter months; shortage of provisions made the men discontented; when the vessel broke out of the ice, a mutiny was organized. On June 22, 1611, Hudson and eight companions were put ashore to die in the wilderness, and the ship sailed away without them.

More than half a century was to pass before the practical value of Hudson's explorations would be realized. But the fate of Virginia hung in the balance in 1611, and the decision could not be deferred. The company's resources were exhausted by the expenditures for the expeditions commanded by Dale and Gates. The political uncertainty of the period following the close of parliament made it impossible to collect more funds until the government's attitude toward the company was clarified. The charter written by Sandys was ready; but James delayed and hesitated. Every day made it more evident that his position was economically and politically untenable. He did not have the resources or the popular support to risk an attempt to rule by force. And there seemed to be no other way of ruling without calling another parliament and again attempting a settlement with the opposition.

The royal dilemma was expressed in cultural terms in the publication of the King James' version of the Bible in 1611. There are few statements in literature that has as fine a flavor of irony as the dedication in which the translators offer James the fruit of their labors, "not only as to our King and Sovereign, but as to the principal Mover and Author of the work."

The proposal to undertake a new translation of the Bible was made by a Puritan clergyman at the Hampton Court Conference in 1604. James was not unaware of the propaganda value of the Bible, and the bitter class struggles that had been waged over its interpretation and use. During Elizabeth's reign, ninety versions of the Geneva Bible had been published, and forty editions of other versions.[24] James seemed to believe that a new translation, prepared under ecclesiastical supervision, might avoid some of the tendencies which seemed to him dangerous in the Bibles in common use. He was particularly anxious that there should be no notes or comments in the margin: he observed that some of those in the Geneva version were "very partial, untrue, seditious, and savouring too much of dangerous and traitorous conceits."[25]

Like everything James did, the result was the opposite of what he anticipated. It did not occur to him that the sedition was not in the margins. Nothing that happened at Hampton Court was half so dangerous for the future of monarchial absolutism as the Bible decision. The anger generated at the conference was ephemeral. But the King James version opened the floodgates of wrath. It provided the stuff of sermons and hymns. The low thunder that began in the churches came out into the highways. It became the thunder of armies marching to the biblical cadences.

The book is so woven into our common speech that we take the enrichment it has brought to our culture for granted. The phrases are heard everywhere—"apple of his eye," "army with banners," "fat of the land," "handwriting on the wall," "powers that be," "pride of life," "salt of the earth," "still small voice," "thorn in the flesh," "whited sepulchres," "wings of the morning."

The seven years during which fifty-four learned men worked on the translation coincided with the maturing strength of the bourgeoisie. Although the Bible was humbly dedicated to James, it appeared at a moment when the king was bereft of dignity. Under the pressure of events, the psychological split in his character was beginning to show. He was becoming a peevish Hamlet, combining two irreconcilable personalities—thundering Jove and royal zany.

The man who was hailed as "the principal Mover and Author" of one of the world's greatest literary achievements was heaping extravagant honors on his twenty-one year old favorite, Robert Carr, who was one of the most active members of the Spanish cabal at court. Carr had intrigued throughout the parliamentary session to prevent an agreement, and he regarded the dissolution as a personal triumph. He was rewarded, on March 25, 1611, with the title of Viscount Rochester, and soon afterward was made a privy councilor.

While James shared the viewpoint of the extremists who rejoiced at the break with the Commons, he was astute enough to listen to the more sober opinions of men like Bacon. Bacon was devoted to the principle of monarchial absolutism, but he differed from many of the crown's advisers in the quality of his intelligence as well as in his class interests. These were the factors which made Bacon invaluable to the government.

Since he did not suffer from the aristocratic astigmatism which afflicted most of the court circle, Bacon could see the problem of power as a national question rather than as a matter of arbitrary class domination. He wanted the king to assert his absolute authority, but he saw the royal will as a means of overcoming class antagonisms and forcing the propertied classes to work together for their mutual advantage. This is the classic theory of the state, which can be traced from Machiavelli and other Renaissance thinkers to the twentieth century. The bourgeoisie was to take over the theory along with the apparatus of state power, fervently proclaiming the principle that government is above classes and serves only the national interest. But the question of power appeared in a very different light when the state was controlled by the crown and the court. The opposition party could not be convinced that monarchial feudalism was above classes.

Bacon thought he could convince them. The sweeping changes in English governmental policy in 1612 and 1613 were an attempt to carry out Bacon's plan. He had disapproved of the vulgar bargaining over the *Great Contract,* because it exacerbated class differences and exposed the king's selfish aims. As an intellectual structure, Bacon's idea was impressive: James was to reassert his national leadership, balancing the interests of various propertied groups with such open-handed majesty that no one would dare to question his motives or oppose the subsidies which were necessary to maintain the state apparatus.

James, who thought only in terms of personal and class objectives, may not have grasped the intellectual scope of the plan. He accepted it because it appeared, in a narrow practical sense, as a continuation of the double-dealing, the giving with one hand and taking away with the other, which he had practiced ever since he ascended the throne. But the grandeur of Bacon's plan—which doomed it to failure—lay in its abandonment of petty compromises, its large and unwarranted assumption that a unified national policy could be accepted and consistently followed.

One could formulate a policy for the advancement of industry, foreign commerce, territorial expansion and colonial aggrandizement. But such a policy demanded the elimination of monopolistic practices and feudal privileges; it required an extension of English power in the Western Hemisphere, which would involve a clash with France in Maine and Canada, and trouble with Spain in the West Indies and South America; it required the strengthening of England's economic and political influence in Europe, which could only be accomplished through opposition to the Hapsburgs and the papacy and an alliance with the Protestant forces on the continent.

All these things constituted the program of the bourgeoisie—which contravened the class interests of the crown and the court. Bacon's reconciliation of classes was an abstraction: it meant that absolutism would take over the program of the bourgeoisie and make it its own. This was a neat trick, and it seemed rational in the philosopher's mind.

The first step in inaugurating the new policy was the third Virginia charter, granted in March, 1612. It would be a mistake to oversimplify the character of the charter, or the degree to which it represented a victory for the party of the bourgeoisie. The Baconian scheme did not intend to strengthen the opposition, but to weaken it by stealing its program and adapting it to the interests of the crown. The Virginia Company was still controlled by Sir Thomas Smythe and his friends. The ostensible purpose of the new patent was to provide the corporation with additional sources of revenue. It was given the Bermudas, which were soon sold to a separate, but interlocking, group of promoters for £2,000. The company was also authorized to conduct lotteries, which for a time proved a popular and painless method of securing funds.

But the charter established the form of organization which Sandys wanted. In contrast to Bacon's belief in a single supreme head of the state, Sandys based his theory of power on the example of Geneva. The Calvinist principle was fully realized in the third charter; it completed the transfer of authority from the crown to the whole membership of the corporation, which was to meet four times a year in "one great, general, and solemn assembly." The quarter-court had full power "to elect and chuse discreet Persons, to be of our said Council for the said first Colony in *Virginia,* and to nominate and appoint such Officers, as they shall think fit and requisite, for the Government, Managing, Ordering, and Dispatching of the Affairs of the said Company . . ." The assembly also had power to make laws and ordinances.[26]

Thus political power over an extensive territory and its inhabitants was collectively vested in the persons who were able to pay £12 10*s* for a share of stock. Each individual had one vote, regardless of the number of stock certificates which might be in his possession. This was extremely important for the Sandys' group in the struggle for control that culminated in Sandys' election as treasurer seven years later. If money had voted instead of persons, Smythe and the London merchants could never have been ousted.

Although the decisive struggle for control developed slowly, it was no secret in 1612 that the majority of the stockholders were dissatisfied with the administration of the project. But Smythe was strongly entrenched. For the time-being, dissatisfaction with the administration took a negative form: the meetings of the corporation were not well attended. It was impossible to sell more stock, and many persons who had signed promises to buy shares refused to fulfill their commitments; attempts to collect from the delinquents led to a tangle of lawsuits in the court of chancery.[27]

It was absolutely essential, to the crown and the London merchants, that the discontent among the stockholders should be held in check, and countered as far as possible by propaganda defending the Smythe administration. Knowing that he would soon have to call another parliament, James could not afford to let the opposition make capital out of the situation in the Virginia Company. John Smith was the ideal candidate for the propaganda job. He could speak authoritatively as a leader of the settlement during its first difficult years. His personal experience coincided with the interests of the Court Party; the second charter had led to his downfall in Virginia; from his point of view, the liberalization of the patent was a catastrophe for the colony, and proved the desirability of autocratic control on both sides of the Atlantic.

This was the partisan aim of the *Oxford Tract,* which appeared in two parts, bound together in a single volume, in 1612. The first part, entitled *A Map of Virginia,* was signed by Smith. The other, *The Proceedings of the English Colony in America,* was written by six of Smith's friends. The political background of the work is suggested in the dedication to Edward Seymour, Earl of Hertford, an aged member of the most reactionary circle of the upper nobility. The words addressed to the earl appear only in one copy of the *Map of Virginia,* bound in vellum, with the arms of Lord Hertford on both sides in gold.[28] It would have hurt the popular appeal of the book to print the author's thanks to his powerful patron. In his private address to the earl, Smith wrote: "It is the best gift I can give to the best friend I have." [29]

The gift was much more than a literary offering. It was an effective, popularly written refutation of the claims and aims of the Sandys group. It derided the program that had evoked such public support and such unprecedented participation on the part of the middle and lower bourgeoisie. It blamed all the difficulties in Virginia on the stupidity and laziness of the colonists, abetted by trouble-makers and unprincipled politicians. "Thus from the clamors and the ignorance of false informers are sprung those disasters that spring in Virginia, and our ingenious verbalists were no lesse plague to us in Virginia, then the Locusts to the Egyptians." [30] In case anyone should miss the not-too-subtle sneer at "ingenious verbalists," they were identified as advocates of "parliaments" and "petitions."

The narrative glorified autocracy, derided people, depicted ordinary human begins as lacking in dignity or sense, needing the whip of authority to keep them from engaging in "disgustful brawls." Smith was so successful in establishing his interpretation of Virginia history, with himself occupying the center of the stage as the homespun hero, that it has remained virtually unchallenged for more than three centuries.

His success has been due, in no small degree, to the reluctance of historians to examine the class struggles from which the Virginia colony was born. Scholars are especially loath to admit any connection between the problem of corporate organization and the problem of state sovereignty; their reluctance is understandable, for the corporate origins of the bourgeois state reveal its class character and function.

Bacon's great design, for a reconciliation of the propertied classes under a revitalized and benignant absolutism, crystallized slowly. James found no relief from his money troubles. There was danger of a serious scandal around the insolvency of the Yorkshire alum works. Early in May, 1612, the chancellor of the Exchequer received a frantic letter from the management, demanding immediate help: "Unless you take some present course, it is utterly overthrown . . . There is no other way to preserve the king's honor and profit but to give all the grace and assistance to it you can . . ." The appeal went unanswered, and the company failed on May 20. Although James had no money to assist the company, he could not afford to let the matter take its normal legal course. He issued a general "protection" against bankruptcy proceedings. After complicated negotiations, the concern was taken over by Robert Johnson and two partners.[31] Johnson, whom we shall meet frequently in the affairs of the Virginia Company, was Sir Thomas Smythe's son-in-law and business associate. The transaction is illuminating: a group of London capitalists had abandoned the enterprise to the king when it failed to yield a profit. Now a more select group bought it back at a reduced price.

Bacon wrote to the king on September 12, noting the rather obvious fact that the improvement of his finances would be a slow process: "As your Majesty's growing behind hath been a work of time; so must likewise be your Majesty's coming forth and making even."[32] A long step toward the expected solution was taken on February 14, 1613, when the nuptials of the Princess Elizabeth and Frederick V, Elector Palatine, were celebrated. The occasion was a spectacular declaration of a new foreign policy. The elector was the acknowledged leader of the German Protestant princes. Bacon wrote a masque for the occasion, which he staged as a wedding present, at at cost of £2,000, paid out of his own pocket. It was entitled "The Marriage of the Thames and the Rhine." [33] The alliance between the rivers was advanced two months later, when the United Netherlands, acting on James' request, signed a treaty of mutual aid with the Union of Protestant Princes.[34]

In turning toward the Rhine, the crown caused a flurry of activity across the Atlantic. The abandonment of the vacillating attempts to conciliate Spain and the Vatican meant that traders could again undertake piratical or smuggling expeditions in the Spanish Main, and that the French colonies in the north could be attacked without risking the king's displeasure. Even while the marriage was being solemnized, Robert Rich sent Captain Argall across the sea with a ship of 130 tons, manned by 60 men and carrying 14 guns. Argall visited Jamestown, then sailed for Maine, where he destroyed the Jesuit colony on Mount Desert Island. He carried fifteen prisoners, including two priests, to Virginia. He made a second trip a few weeks later, taking the unwilling priests along as guides, plundering and destroying the French settlement at Port Royal.

In England, preparations for the approaching session of parliament proceeded in the fall of 1613. The king's debts continued to mount catastrophically. He was over £680,000 in arrears. Ambassadors were not receiving their salaries; sailors in the navy were far behind in their pay.[35] But Bacon held to his theory that the king's majesty must be absolute and unruffled. He wrote to James advising against any effort to make a bargain. He urged "that your Majesty do for this Parliament put off the person of a merchant and contractor, and rest upon the person of a King." He suggested that the assembly "be a little reduced to the more ancient form (for I account it but a form) which was to voice the Parliament to be for some other business of estate, and not merely for money." [36]

In spite of this soothing advice, James was now so entangled in the net of contradictions that there seemed to be some danger of its choking him. Although he was publicly committed to the Protestant Alliance, he was privately surrounded by Spanish intrigue. His favorite, Robert Carr, had been having an affair for several years with Frances Howard, wife of the Earl of Essex. In September, 1613, her marriage was annulled, on the ground that her husband, to whom she had been married for seven years, was impotent. In November, Carr was made Earl of Somerset, and in December his marriage to the former Lady Essex was solemnized. She was the daughter of the Earl of Suffolk, and the great-niece of the Earl of Northampton.

There was a good deal of scandal around the marriage,[37] but the sensational revelation was delayed for two years; it was then charged that Sir Thomas Overbury, who was poisoned in the Tower of London ten days before Lady Essex received the annulment, had been murdered by the lovers. Northampton was also involved in the plot. Overbury had information which might have caused legal complications in the suit for annulment. The case had startling political ramifications, because it involved the king's most intimate associates and the leading advocates of an alliance with Spain. The significance of the wedding was apparent in 1613. Coming less than a year after the marriage of the Thames and the Rhine, it was proof of the continuing influence of the Spanish faction at Court.

James was not unaware of the ties between his closest companions and a foreign power. Early in 1614, the English ambassador at Madrid, believing that the king was no longer friendly to Spain, brought James a list of English officials who were in the pay of Philip III. The Earl of Northampton and the Duke of Suffolk headed the list. There was treason in the Navy, for the commander of the Channel fleet received money from the Spanish king. And there was treason in the Queen's bedroom, where Mrs. Drummond, first lady of the bedchamber, acted under Spanish instructions.[38]

James did nothing about the information. On the contrary, Suffolk was rewarded with the post of Lord High Treasurer. (It may be noted, in passing, that the former treasurer, Lord Salisbury, who died in 1612, was also on the Spanish payroll.) [39] Northampton died in 1614, and his will showed that he was a Roman Catholic.

There were other indications that the bonds of class interest which bound the court to Madrid and Rome had not been severed. Luisa de Carvajal, continuing her activities on behalf of the Jesuits, was arrested in 1613, when the Protestant alliance indicated a change in government policy. But the Spanish ambassador protested to the king, and she was released, dying at the ambassador's home on January 2, 1614.[40]

Bacon, who knew everything that happened at court and who observed political tendencies with the meticulous zeal of a trained scientist, realized that the task of reconciling the crown and the Commons was becoming more difficult with each passing day. But he was also aware that the tense political situation made the king dependent on him. James demonstrated his confidence by giving him the post of attorney general. In planning the coming meeting of parliament, the crown's advisers realized that there was little chance of a successful session unless the Commons would agree to unity on the king's terms. This was unlikely, unless the government could command a majority in the house. For the first time in English history, there was an election campaign. In spite of the narrowly restricted franchise, the public manifested lively interest in the outcome. The crown made scandalous efforts to influence the vote, but the victory for the party of the bourgeoisie was overwhelming. A feature of the election was the appearance of a new, and somewhat more popular, type of candidate. Of the nearly 500 members of the Commons, some 300 were newcomers.[41]

James addressed the opening session on April 5, 1614. He made another speech on April 8, announcing his conviction that it would "be a parliament of love." [42] At least, Bacon had been right when he suggested that the Commons might deal with other business, and "not merely with money." The House showed no intention of worrying about money. It ignored the king's request for funds, and proceeded to take the offensive against monopolies and abuses of the royal prerogative. With frightening speed, the "parliament of love" turned into what courtiers called the "addled parliament."

The boldness with which Sandys led the attack on the crown may be judged from the brief notes of a speech of which the text has not been preserved:

> No successive King, but first elected. Election double, of person and care; but both come in by consent of people, and with reciprocal conditions between King and people. That a king by conquest may also (when power) be expelled.[43]

The passage might have been written by Thomas Jefferson when he was jotting down ideas for the Declaration of Independence. The introduction of the question of sovereignty in such unequivocal terms explains the haste with which James moved to get rid of the recalcitrant assembly. His action was hastened by the pressure of the

Spanish cabal, led by Northampton, Suffolk and Somerset, who were determined to prevent an agreement with the Commons. Their wish was granted on June 7, when the dissolution took place amid uproar and denunciation. James sent four members of the house to the Tower. Four others, including Sandys, were ordered not to leave London. But the king's fury was circumscribed by the thought which Sandys had placed in a parenthesis in his notes—*when power* . . . James lacked the power to proceed against the opposition. The prisoners were soon released; Sandys and the others were permitted to return to their homes.

However, the wider split between the king and the bourgeoisie brought another turn in foreign policy. James again sought *a rapprochement* with Spain and the papacy.

A similar defeat of the bourgeoisie occurred in France at the same time. Dissatisfaction with the regency's pro-Spanish policy was militantly voiced at the meeting of the Estates General in 1614. Robert Miron, representing the Paris merchants, spoke in language that deserves comparison with Sandys' notes:

> If royal government fails in justice, despair will inform the people that a soldier is merely a peasant who bears arms, and when the wine-dresser has assumed the musket, that which is today the anvil will become the hammer.[44]

The threatening emphasis which Miron placed on the might of the people is understandable when we consider that civil war had been intermittently conducted in France for more than half a century. Sandys' statement looked forward to the Cromwellian Revolution and the compromises that followed it. Miron's words foreshadowed the French Revolution. He was speaking before a body which was never to be permitted to meet again until the fall of the Bastille. He spoke violently, but without power. On February 24, 1615, the representatives of the estates found their meeting place locked. There was an appropriate pretext: they were told that it was *needed for a ballet.*[45] Marie de Medici was at last free to follow the advice of the Jesuits without interference: she carried through the two marriages which were designed to guarantee a permanent alliance with Spain: Louis XIII, the boy king, married the daughter of Philip III, and Philip's son married Louis' sister.

When Sandys spoke of "the people," he referred to the people who were represented in the Commons and for whom he spoke. Sandys' theory of government was essentially economic. He was concerned, more frankly if not more intensely than later political thinkers, with the protection of property rights in land, trade and industry. He made no sharp distinction between the corporation and the state, because he could not conceive of any function of the state which went beyond the purpose of the corporation in organizing the transatlantic domain for the profit of persons whose purchase of stock entitled them to all the prerogatives of government.

The conception of power as the shared and collective authority of a class may be clarified if we examine the double meaning of the word *election*. We identify the word with the power which supposedly resides in the people to choose their leaders. But an apparently different meaning was more common in the early seventeenth century: election referred to God's choice of persons who were especially blessed with divine favor. Richard Hooker spoke of "the elect Angels," who "are without possibilities of falling."[46] In *The Advancement of Learning,* Bacon referred to "the favour and election of God."[47] A little later, in the early days of the Cromwellian Revolution, James Ussher wrote in defense of Calvinism and its political methods that "Election . . . is the everlasting predestination, or foreappointing of certain Angels and Men unto everlasting life."[48] Appointment to the life everlasting included the preliminary right to exercise the franchise in political elections.

We cannot separate the democratic connotation of the word from its Calvinist and anti-democratic usage. The meanings are inseparable. The corporate charter, conferring rights which were transferred across the Atlantic and developed in colonial struggle against imperial domination, created a privileged group which was, literally, *a company of the elect.* In the records of the Virginia Company, there are frequent references to the combined economic and political functions of the association. For example, it is called a "body politic . . . with divers grants liberties franchises preeminences privileges profits and commodities . . ."[49]

In his attack on the New England theocracy, Roger Williams pointed to the distinction between the corporation and the whole body of the people. Writing in England in 1644, when the Cromwellian Revolution permitted the publication of unorthodox opinions, Williams wrote:

The Church or company of worshippers (whether true or false) is like unto a Body or College of Physicians in a Citie; like unto a Corporation, Society, or company of East-Indie or Turkie Merchants, or any other Societie or Company in London: which Companies may hold their Courts, keep their Records, hold disputations; and in matters concerning their societie, may dissent, divide, break into Schismes and Factions, sue and implead each other at the Lawe, yea wholly break up into pieces and nothing, and yet the peace of the Citie not be in the measure impaired or disturbed; because the essence of being of the Citie, and so the well-being and peace thereof is essentially distinct from those particular Societies; the Citie-Courts, Citie-Lawes, Citie-punishments distinct from theirs. The Citie was before them, and stands absolute and intire, when such a Corporation or Society is taken down.[50]

In the convention that framed the Constitution of the United States, the distinction made by Williams was accepted as a general principle. The government of the Republic was not a corporation, although "preeminences privileges profits and commodities" were well represented in the convention and well protected in the fundamental law. The existence of class interests was recognized by the founding fathers. James Madison wrote in the famous tenth number of *The Federalist* that "a landed interest, a manufacturing interest, a mercantile interest, a moneyed interest, with many lesser interests, grow up of necessity in civilized nations, and divide them into different classes, actuated by different sentiments and views." Madison held that the main function of government is "the regulation of these various and interfering interests." [51]

Soon after the adoption of the Constitution, it became apparent that there was danger of the seizure of the apparatus of government by a dominant class, thus destroying its intended operation as the regulator and conciliator of conflicting classes. The corporation was a means of accomplishing this purpose. George Logan, a wealthy Pennsylvania farmer who believed that the only legitimate function of the state is protection of the "sacred law of property," [52] was nevertheless frightened by Alexander Hamilton's schemes for corporate organization. He denounced the *Society for Establishing Useful Manufactures* as a dangerous use of "the principle of partial association," by which rich individuals could pool their power and gain control of the state.[53]

Logan's fears, which were shared by Jefferson, were confirmed in 1819, when the Supreme Court enlarged the powers to the corporation in the Dartmouth College Case. Jefferson saw the shadow darkening the land. In attacking the decision, he pointed out that:

> The idea that institutions established for the use of the nation cannot be touched nor modified, even to make them answer their end, because of rights gratuitously supposed in those employed to manage them in trust for the public, may, perhaps, be a salutary provision against the abuses of a monarch, but it is most absurd against the nation itself.[54]

Chief Justice Marshall justified the decision by the so-called "fiction theory," which regarded the corporation as an imaginary individual:

> A corporation is an artificial being, invisible, intangible, and existing only in contemplation of law. Being the mere creature of law, it possesses only those properties which the charter of its creation confers upon it, either expressly or as incidental to its very existence . . . Among the most important are immortality, and, if the expression may be allowed, individuality; properties by which a perpetual succession of many persons are considered as the same and may act as a single individual.[55]

No poet or seer has ever created a more potent myth. By its magic, the humanist hopes of the Renaissance are transferred to the corporation; the genius of the individual, which was a creative force in the early struggles of the bourgeoisie for personal and property rights, has taken its appointed course from the tortured Faust and the hourglass hero to the sawdust Caesars of fascism, to end in corporate anonymity; the government is staffed by the dapper, corrupt and soulless representatives of the trusts, for man's aspiring spirit has been exchanged for a stock certificate, and the cartel stands supreme, as the church stood in the Middle Ages, the symbol of the soul.

7 : BRAVE NEW WORLD

MOST SHAKESPEAREAN SCHOLARS believe that *The Tempest* was written in 1611, but there are some critics who maintain that it was first performed at the wedding of Princess Elizabeth and the Elector Palatine in February, 1613. The nuptial masque in Act IV may have been written for the ceremony.

At all events, the masque seems to foreshadow the failure of the political hopes that were inspired by the Protestant alliance. It is in the form of a courtly harvest festival beginning with an appeal to Ceres, guardian of "wheat, rye, barley, vetches, oats, and peas." Ceres sings of the bounteous future:

> Earth's increase, and foison plenty,
> Barns and garners never empty;
> Vines, with clust'ring bunches growing;
> Plants, with goodly burden bowing . . .

There is a dance of reapers, "sun-burn'd sicklemen, of August weary," and nymphs. But the hopes of a rich harvest are only a vision. Suddenly the spell is broken: "To a strange, hollow and confused noise, they heavily vanish." The sound is like the broken chord in *The Cherry Orchard,* and has the same social implications. Man's will is frustrated; a sense of doom pervades and conditions the action.

There is no mystery about the doom that shadows the masque of plenty in *The Tempest.* The vision is created by Prospero, and it is dispelled when Prospero remembers "that foul conspiracy of the beast Caliban and his confederates." Prospero speaks with a philosopher's resignation:

Our revells now are ended: these our actors,
As I foretold you, were all spirits, and
Are melted into air, into thin air:
And, like the baseless fabric of this vision
The cloud-capp'd towers, the gorgeous palaces,
The solemn temples, the great globe itself,
Yes, all which it inherit, shall dissolve,
And like this insubstantial pageant faded,
Leave not a rack behind: We are such stuff
As dreams are made of, and our little life
Is rounded with a sleep.

Could Shakespeare have thought of the royal marriage as an insubstantial pageant? And would he have dared to express the thought? There must have been many people who watched the fine show, with Bacon's allegory of *The Marriage of the Thames and the Rhine,* knowing that the political promise was a "baseless fabric." Shakespeare may not have written his dreamlike pastoral for the specific occasion, but the masque, and the play of which it is a part, reflect the cultural crisis that led Shakespeare to abandon the London theatre.

The Tempest is a symbolic account of the wreck of the *Sea Venture,* which was more prosaically recorded in Sylvester Jourdain's *Discovery of the Bermudas,* published in the fall of 1610. The play contains a number of verbal parallels to Jourdain's book as well as to other accounts of the ill-fated Virginia voyage.[1] It is probable that it appeared in 1611, and there is some evidence that it was produced at court on November 1 of that year.

The two plays which precede *The Tempest* are *Cymbeline* and *A Winter's Tale*: they were written between 1609 and 1611, during the parliamentary conflict over the Great Contract. After the painful confusion of *Timon of Athens* and the bitter analysis of the problem of power in *Coriolanus,* there seems to be a break in the poet's creative activity. Then, as the political tension increased, he turned to themes which may be described as escapist. In *Cymbeline* and *A Winter's Tale,* we move in a fantasy realm of courtly love. Yet even here, the dream world is invaded by a sense of frustration and doom, expressed in the irrational jealousy which motivates the plot of both plays. There are also occasional barbed comments on living issues.

It is an heretic that makes the fire,
Not she which burns in't—

These lines about heresy in *A Winter's Tale* must have evoked a nervous response from audiences witnessing the play in 1611, at a time when the failure of the crown's negotiations with the Commons caused two hapless Puritans to be burned at the stake.

If, as seems likely, *The Tempest* was first produced in November, 1611, the mood of the play may be related to the dissolution of parliament and the growing sense of impending class conflict that would culminate in civil war. The Elizabethan hopes were fading like an "insubstantial pageant." But Shakespeare showed his grasp of social realities in relating the crisis in England to the colonizing efforts of the Virginia Company.

The loss of the *Sea Venture* and the eventual reappearance of its passengers seemed to symbolize the potentialities and uncertainties that lay across the Atlantic. In a sense, *The Tempest* is the first statement of "the American dream." Shakespeare had reached the *Ultima Thule* of his social thought. He had written of the divided conscience, of crowds demanding bread, of the corrupting lust for gold. He observed the enthusiasm, the "throngs and concourse of personal undertakers," that greeted the reorganization of the Virginia Company. Yet the bright hope was darkened by the old evils—there was no peace for the unquiet conscience, no answer to the hungry crowds. Was the answer hidden in the Atlantic fog?

Across the western sea there was a myth and a reality. Both related to money. The myth visioned gold and silver and precious stones. The reality could be purchased for £12 10*s*, for each "bill of adventure" or stock certificate.

The *Sea Venture* symbolized a social experiment. Yet the ship was freighted with all the ills of the society that built and equipped her. The vessel foundered. Yet somehow the people lived, built other ships with the splintered timbers, reached their destination. The storm seemed to conquer man. But man persevered, conquered the storm.

In *The Tempest,* the storm is man-made. Prospero, who by magic can make the elements do his bidding, creates "the direful spectacle of the wreck" in order to remedy the injustice done him in the old world. The theme of the play, embodied in Prospero's relationship to Ariel, is man's potential mastery over nature.

The potentialities of science, so confidently proclaimed by Bacon in *The Advancement of Learning,* stirred and troubled Shakespeare. His preoccupation with the problem is suggested in the increasing use of the words *nature* and *natural* in his plays. The words are employed only 71 times in the eleven plays written in the sixteenth century. In the same number of plays written in the seventeenth century (omitting the doubtful *Pericles* and *Henry VIII*) the words appear 300 times, including 40 times in *King Lear*—which was written at about the time of the publication of Bacon's book.[2]

Shakespeare saw the mastery of nature as an enlargement of the human spirit. But in seeing it in these terms, he related it to Hamlet's dilemma. What would it profit a man to master nature if he could not master himself and the conditions of his social being? Would the advancement of learning cure the sick conscience, rouse the paralyzed will?

In *The Tempest,* Prospero's control of natural forces is related to two fundamental social concepts—human equality and human labor. The equalitarian principle is dismissed. Gonzalo speaks of a land where there will be

> No use of service,
> Of riches, or of poverty; no contracts,
> Successions; bound of land, tilth, vineyard, none
> All things in common nature should produce
> Without sweat or endeavor; treason, felony,
> Sword, pike, knife, gun, or need of any engine,
> Would I not have; but nature would bring forth
> Of its own kind, all foison, all abundance,
> To feed my innocent people.

This was the doctrine of the Anabaptists and the Levellers. Shakespeare portrays Gonzalo as an honest man, but his Utopian vision cannot solve the problem of labor. Nature will not give her riches without man's "sweat or endeavor." With all his magic, Prospero needs the services of the degraded, rebellious Caliban.

Caliban is the original owner of the island. He showed Prospero "all the qualities of the Isle." Prospero cannot exist without him:

> We cannot miss him: he does make our fire,
> Fetch in our wood; and serves in other offices
> That profit us.

In his song of revolt, Caliban rejects these necessary tasks:

> No more dams I'll make for fish;
> Nor fetch in firing
> At requiring,
> Nor scrape trencher, nor wash dish.

Caliban, plotting with his drunken accomplices, knows that their first task is to seize Prospero's books—"for without them he's but a sot, as I am."

Caliban's demand for equality is legally based on his mother's possession of the land. It is rationally motivated by the assertion that Prospero's power lies in his "brave utensils," his books. But Shakespeare presents Caliban's arguments only to denounce them as monstrous and unnatural. Caliban has no use for the books except to burn them. His claim to equality endangers the social order, and all the knowledge in the books must be used to keep him in chains.

The allegory unites three conflicting principles—human knowledge, human welfare, human labor. The advancement of science created new values and intensified the struggle for control of the means by which these values were produced. The equalitarian current was deep and strong, rising from Tabor and the German Peasant War and Münster and the long history of agrarian revolt in England. In his presentation of Caliban, Shakespeare reflected the fear that gripped the middle and upper classes as they heard the rumors of rural discontent and skirted the poverty of the city slums. Under the compulsion of their fear, the representatives of the rising bourgeoisie tempered their opposition to the crown with the sobering knowledge that the royal power guaranteed discipline and order.

The phrase, the *rascal people,* which Shakespeare used in the Jack Cade scenes in *Henry VI,* was a common way of describing the lower classes. A sixteenth century writer said that England is a commonwealth "governed, administered and manured by three sorts of persons." There were gentlemen, who were subdivided into two groups—"the barony or estate of lords containing barons and that be above the degree of a baron," and "those which be no lords, as knights, esquires and simple gentlemen." Then there were the citizens or burgesses. The third class was composed of yeomen, freemen owning land or serving as "farmers to gentlemen." But there was a fourth class which constituted the majority of the population, having "no voice or authority in our commonwealth, and no account is made of them but only to be ruled." These were laborers, husbandmen and artisans. The yeomen were drawn from this class; they were people who had managed to raise their heads above the anonymous mass: "Amongst the husbandmen, labourers, lowest and rascal sort of the people, such as be exempted out of the number of the rascality of the popular be called and written yeomen," with the honor of placing goodman before their names.[3]

The Midland Riots and the disturbed political situation in the years following the death of Queen Elizabeth forced Shakespeare to doubt the permanence of monarchial power. But as the shadow of future strife darkened the land, the subjugation of labor seemed more pressing than all other problems. All the potentialities of science, symbolized in Prospero's magic, cannot maintain an ordered and disciplined society unless Caliban is kept enchained. The conflict between the propertied classes—the court and the bourgeoisie—has no place in the play. Yet the action grows out of the earlier struggle for power which drove Prospero from Milan and led to his exile on the island. The storm is invented by Prospero so that the shipwreck will enable him to confound the usurper and regain his throne. But his plan is endangered by Caliban's rebellion.

The controversy between the king and the Commons tended to feed the discontent of the lower classes. It created opportunities for rebellion, and suggested possible alliances, just as the arrival of Prospero's enemies brought Caliban the chance, and the allies, that inspired his revolt. The happy denouement is achieved when Caliban is outwitted and his continued enslavement is guaranteed.

The allegory was to be repeated on the stage of English history—in the defeat of the popular forces in the Cromwellian Revolution, the savage laws against labor organization in the eighteenth century, the massacre of workers at Peterloo in 1819, the profits wrung from children employed in mills and mines, the twentieth century betrayals of the workers.

In the middle years of the nineteenth century, Sir John Tenniel made a drawing of the scene in which Caliban plots with Trinculo and Stephano for the conquest of the island: Caliban has a deformed body and the face of an ape, and he carries an object that looks like a bomb in his left hand. The figure is somewhat similar to the cartoons of "communists" and "agitators" that appear in the American press, and it is not surprising that the Tenniel painting was reproduced in newspapers owned by William Randolph Hearst in 1949.[4]

The Tempest illuminates certain aspects of American social development. When Governor Gates sailed on the *Sea Venture,* he carried instructions for the rigid discipline of the colony's labor force. The political struggle concerning the rights of the stockholders did not involve any disagreement concerning the rights of the servants who were transported to Virginia. Shortly before the granting of the second charter in 1609, the company addressed a communication to the mayor, aldermen, and companies of London. The letter adheres to the "Malthusian" principle embodied in the government's report on the Midland Riots. It was known, the company said, that the municipal authorities were "desirous to ease the city and suburbs of a swarme of unnecessary inmates, as a contynual cause of dearth and famine, and the very originall cause of the Plagues." The city was therefore urged to "make some voluntary contribution for their remove to this Plantation in Virginia."[5]

Every book that deals with early American history describes the colonial labor system. But it is treated very much as Shakespeare treats Caliban: the servant is a necessary evil; "he does make our fire, fetch in our wood." We may be sorry for him as a human being, but he performs "offices that profit us," and that are essential for gracious living. The life of the servant is no part of the society he serves; he walks a secret path, his ways and thought excluded from the social fabric, as Caliban's hatred is excluded from the world in which Miranda and Ferdinand laugh and love.

In the early days of settlement, the company was the only employer, or master, of the laborers and boys sent to the colony. Their seven-year term of servitude combined three forms of labor—apprenticeship, serfdom and slavery. The seven-year term was borrowed from apprenticeship, but the servant did unskilled work on the land, and there was no obligation to teach him a trade. The overseas settlement was like a feudal manor, operated by absentee landlords, the stockholders. But the servant did not have the partial freedom that the peasant derived from the cultivation of his own land and the performance of specific services. His contract was a total assignment of his labor, and he tended to sink to the status of a slave, his lot differing only in the expectation of freedom, and in certain cases, land, at the end of his term of employment.

In liberalizing the rights accorded to the stockholders, the 1609 charter restricted the rights of the workers. This was logical and inevitable, for the right most urgently demanded by the stockholders was the right to get a maximum profit from their investment. The people who adventured £12 10*s* in Virginia Company stock knew that the American land and climate would not increase their capital by magic. Profit had to be sweated out of the soil by obedient Calibans.

The transfer of powers from the crown to the company in 1609 gave the corporation virtually unlimited authority over its servants. The instructions given to Governor Gates included the following passage:

> You shall for capitall and Criminal justice in Case of Rebellion and mutiny and in all such cases of urgent necessity, proceede by Martiall lawe accordinge to your commission as of most dispatch and terror and fittest for this government and in all other causes of that nature as also in all matters of Civill Justice you shall finde it properest and usefullest for your government to proceede rather as a Chauncelor than as a Judge rather uppon the naturall right and Equity then uppon the niceness and lettere of the lawe which perlexeth in this tender body rather then dispatcheth all Causes so that a Sumary and arbitrary way of Justice discreetely mingled with those gravities and fournes of magistracy as shall in your discrecon seeme aptest for you and that place . . .[6]

The enforcement of martial law through "a summary and arbitrary way of justice" was delayed by the tempest which shattered the *Sea Venture*. The system came into full force with the arrival of Deputy Governor Thomas Dale in 1611. Dale's code, known as the *Lawes Divine, Morall and Martiall,* was drawn from the regulations governing English troops in the Netherlands. The combination of three apparently uncongenial words pointed to the nature of the law: it was proclaimed as a moral imperative; it was enforced with military precision; it was divinely ordained. Harsh penalties were imposed for minor offenses. More than twenty crimes were punishable by death. The beating of a drum called the men to their work in the fields, and they were marched out in gangs under the supervision of officers, who gave them their tools during the day and replaced the tools in the storehouse at night.[7]

The complaints which had been brought back to England concerning Captain Smith's conduct did not relate to his severity in dealing with labor. Men like Gabriel Archer and John Martin would never have objected on this score. Smith's personal dictatorship was resented because he was willful, quarrelsome, and unable to maintain effective discipline. Smith also lacked the family and social background which would have qualified him for the role he attempted to play. He was not a Prospero, to command by the nobility of word and posture.

There was not much of Prospero in Sir Thomas Dale. But he was a knight, and a military martinet with twenty years experience in European campaigns. However, Dale's martial administration required the use of the company's legal authority to prevent servants from escaping and to assure their arrest and punishment if they managed to return to England.

The more "democratic" charter of 1612 provided a necessary extension of the corporation's police power in dealing with recalcitrant laborers. The patent noted that many persons, "having contracted and agreed with the said Company . . . have afterwards, either withdrawn, hid, or concealed themselves." Specific authority was given to pursue and arrest these persons in England. The treasurer and one other member of the council were authorized to issue a "Warrant under their Hands, to send for, or cause to be apprehended, all and every such Person or Persons, who shall be noted, or accused, or found, at any time or times hereafter, to offend, or misbehave themselves, in any of the Offences before mentioned or expressed."

The company's council was the judge and jury, with authority to exact special penalties for "any insolent, and contemptuous, or indecent Carriage and Misbehavior, to or against our said Council, shewed or used by any such Person or Persons, so called, convented, and appearing before them." The company had the further right "to remand and send back, the said Offenders, or any of them, unto the said Colony in *Virginia,* there to be proceeded against and punished . . ." [8]

Prospero's magic, with Ariel's swift obedience, never devised a means of subduing Caliban as potent as the words written by Sandys to insure the property rights of the class he represented. Although the charter was forfeited to the crown in 1624, the powers conveyed to the company were transferred across the Atlantic to form the basis of colonial labor legislation, giving the master of servants and slaves an authority over his human chattels which was almost as sweeping as the rights originally conferred on the company.

The Tempest was not Shakespeare's last play. *Henry VIII,* produced in 1613, is stilted and episodic. But it returns to the historical problems from which the poet could not escape. It goes back to the beginnings of English Protestantism to pay a suitable tribute to the birth of Queen Elizabeth. Yet there it the inescapable ethical dilemma posed by the king's actions. The only moment of compelling passion is Katherine's bitter outcry—

Would I had never trod this English earth,
Or felt the flatteries that grow upon it!

It was grimly appropriate that *Henry VIII* was being performed at the Globe Theatre on June 29, 1613, when the playhouse burned to the ground. Shakespeare owned an interest in the building, and many of his plays had been produced there. *Henry VIII* was presented with unusually elaborate settings and costumes. Henry Wotton described the performance as "set forth with many extraordinary circumstances of pomp and majesty, even to the matting of the stage, the Knights of the Order with their Georges and garters, the Guards with their embroidered coats, and the like: sufficient in truth within a while to make greatness very familiar, if not ridiculous." [9]

The actors fled and the rich trappings went up in smoke. A ballad commemorated the occasion:

Out runne the knightes, out runne the lordes,
And there was great adoe;
Some lost their hattes, and some their swordes;
Then out runne Burbidge too . . .[10]

The old order had passed. It seemed as if the poetry of the Elizabethan age had burned to ashes with the theatre. Shakespeare was only forty-nine. But his life moved to its close. Other men would battle tempests to seek a brave new world. Shakespeare turned to the nearer refuge of a Stratford fireside.

In April, 1616, when Shakespeare died, the *Lawes Divine, Morall and Martiall* had failed to produce a profit for the Viriginia Company. But they had brought suffering and death to the people of the settlement. Out of more than 1,000 persons who had been in the colony in 1610, only 351 survived in the spring of 1616.[11]

Nevertheless, the code instituted by Dale established the system of indentured servitude, stripping it of patriarchal illusions, and pointed toward the later organization of servile and slave labor.

In February, 1849, a man stopped at a bookstore in the city of Boston and bought a copy of Shakespeare's plays. Herman Melville had never read Shakespeare before, and he began to "exult over it, page after page."

Melville was trying to write a novel about a whaling ship, using the ship and its crew and the pursuit of the whale as a symbol of dark forces and conflicts in American life. Shakespeare seemed to offer a clue, "short, quick probings at the very axis of reality." Melville marked passages and wrote notes in the margin. After Miranda's lines—

> How beauteous mankind is! O brave new world
> That hath such people in't—

Melville encircled Prospero's answer: "T'is new to thee," and wrote at the bottom of the page: "Consider the character of the persons concerning whom Miranda says this—then Prospero's quiet words in comment—how terrible! In *Timon* itself there is nothing like it." [12]

Melville found Prospero's comment more meaningful than Miranda's exclamation, shadowing her naïve faith with realistic foreboding. Melville did not define the connection between *Timon* and *The Tempest,* but it is in the inwardness and heart of the two plays. Shakespeare turned from the corrupting power of money, "the common whore of mankind," to an island Utopia. But the corruption is there. The life of plentitude and beauty is built on human degradation.

In *Moby Dick,* Melville endeavored to probe "at the very axis of reality" in his study of the workers gathered in the forecastle of the whaling ship. The voyage was a treasure hunt; the men were serving one of the greatest capitalist industries of the first half of the nineteenth century. Melville knew the scope and importance of the industry. He wrote in *Moby Dick*:

> We whalemen of America now outnumber all the rest of the banded whalemen in the world; sail a navy of upward of seven hundred vessels; manned by eighteen thousand men; yearly consuming 4,000,000 dollars; the ships' worth, at the time of sailing, $20,000,000; and every year reporting into our harbours a well-reaped harvest of $7,000,000.[13]

The workers were so intensively exploited that only inexperienced men could be persuaded to ship on the long voyages. Of the 18,000 mentioned by Melville, one-half were green hands, and more than two-thirds deserted every voyage.[14]

Melville knew these things. And he wrote of the men with extraordinary understanding. Yet their lives are dominated by the demoniac personality of Captain Ahab. There are moments when he seems to be a combination of Mephistopheles and Faust. He has sold his soul to conquer the whale. His will is satanic: "In his fiery eyes of scorn and triumph, you then saw Ahab in all his fatal pride." [15] But early in the story, Peleg reveals that the fury in the captain's soul has not deprived him of his share in the tragedy of Faustian man: "Stricken, blasted, if he be, Ahab has his humanities!" [16]

The central and dominant figure of Ahab is the key to the author's feeling about human aspiration and achievement: the spirit is crushed and frustrated, deprived of normal social growth, finding fulfillment only in a half mad conflict with secret and unconquerable forces of nature—the sea, the fate darkening the waters, the white whale. Ahab is defiant in his last agony, shouting:

> Oh, lonely death on lonely life! . . . Towards thee I roll, thou all-destroying but unconquering whale; to the last I grapple with thee; from hell's heart I stab thee! for hate's sake I spit my last breath at thee.[17]

There is a final symbolism in the sky-hawk which becomes entangled in the flag as the ship sinks:

> . . . So the bird of heaven, with archangelic shrieks, and his imperial beak thrust upwards, and his whole captive body folded in the flag of Ahab, went down with his ship, which, like Satan, would not sink to hell till she had dragged a living part of heaven along with her, and helmeted herself with it.[18]

Melville himself was like an eagle caught in the flag of defeat. But the doom that engulfed him was without splendor, a slow death-in-life, the monotony of drab employments. His fate seemed to him mysterious and predetermined—like the battle with the white whale —because he could not come to grips with the thing that strangled his heart. He thought that it was somehow ordained and written—perhaps in the fundamental law, in the Constitution, in the social order from which he had attempted to escape by long sea voyages. But the social order reclaimed him and consigned him to servitude. And he could not strike back, because he did not know that his own drab doom lay in the servitude of millions of people, Negro and white.

His intuitive insight had seen a frightening message in *The Tempest.* But he missed the heart of the play, the enslavement of Caliban. He saw evil in the world, but he could not trace it to its origin in the treatment of Caliban as an inhuman and dangerous monster.

Melville's tragedy is the perennial tragedy of the intellectual: unable to achieve an integrated life devoted to rational social aims, he decided that social integration is neither possible nor desirable. But his despair made him a victim of the power he hated. The society that called him back from his wanderings to earn his bread in bitterness wanted to enslave the mind as well as the body. *Moby Dick* was virtually the end of his creative life; he was thirty-two when the book appeared. But he continued to write; and no word could be written in the decade before the Civil War which did not serve one side or the other in the preparation for the impending conflict.

"How many," Melville had written in *Moby Dick* of Tashtego's fall into the whale's head, "have likewise fallen into Plato's honey head, and sweetly perished there?"[19] The strain of mysticism and transcendental philosophy that was strong in the author's thought was like a retreat to "Platonic" seclusion. But the escape was illusory; there was no safety, no sweet death for the living, in Plato or in transcendentalism.

In 1855, Melville wrote a short novel which exhibits the tragic decline of his talent: the tragedy is all the more poignant because the author is unconscious of the servitude to which he has submitted. *Benito Cereno,* published serially in *Putnam's Magazine,* is not an original creation; it is adapted from a book of voyages by Captain Amasa Delano. But Melville changed Delano's tale in order to make it more effective—as propaganda for slavery. The story tells of a revolt of slaves at sea, in which the Negroes commit wanton cruelties—"in the various acts of murder, they sang songs and danced." The Negro Babo, is the devil incarnate, guilty of the most subtle perfidy toward the captain of the slave ship, the sensitive aristocrat, Don Benito.

The characterization of the captain is Melville's most significant deviation from Delano's narrative. In the original story, he is treated realistically as a man who is more brutal and unprincipled than the forces pitted against him. Thus there is a genuine conflict. This would have invalidated Melville's purpose; it would have given some justification to the revolt of the slaves. In making Don Benito a sympathetic figure, Melville draws a moral which is explicitly stated at the end of the novel. Benito is asked: "What has cast such a shadow upon you?" and the Spaniard answers, "The Negro."[20] Even when Babo is executed, his body burned to ashes, he is still a symbol of evil: "The head that hive of subtlety, fixed on a pole in the Plaza, met, unabashed, the gaze of the whites."[21]

One wonders if Melville remembered the line about falling into "Plato's honey head" when he used a somewhat similar metaphor in regard to the dead leader of the Negro revolt. Melville's retreat to "Platonic" solitude had led him straight into the camp of the slaveholders. Lewis Mumford, with the disregard of social issues and the special callousness toward Negro slavery which characterizes American criticism, says that *Benito Cereno* "marked the culmination of Melville's power as a short-story writer."[22] From an aesthetic point of view, the story is cheap melodrama, a distortion of human and moral values; few heroes in literature are as absurd as the delicate Don Benito, retiring to a monastery to die of grief over the "inhumanity" of the Negro. The portrait is a pitiful attempt to accomplish the task which Shelley rejected—to reconcile "the Champion with the Oppressor of mankind."

One can say of Melville that he was only seeking to taste a little of the wine of literary success. There was a ready commercial market for proslavery material. But the ignoble motive must be weighed in the scales of political reality: the story made its contribution to the southern campaign in the crucial election of 1856. It appeared at a moment when even such temperate liberals as George William Curtis were calling on Americans to decide "whether their government shall be administered solely in the interest of three hundred and fifty thousand slave-holders."[23]

The corruption of Melville's talent was part of the social corruption that Whitman observed in Washington, where the nation's destiny was in the hands of "deformed, mediocre, sniveling, unreliable, false-hearted men."[24] These men were leading the nation to the edge of destruction, to four years of agony. But even that bloody penance could not exorcise the "spell" with which Prospero had bound Caliban. After the Civil War, the people of the south, Negro and white, sought to master education, to possess the books that were Prospero's "brave utensile." But thousands of fleshly Ariels, brutal and grotesque in their sheets and hoods, rode to sustain the "charm" of mastery, burning school houses and flogging teachers to guard the secret of the books—the secret of man's freedom.

Today, in the middle of the Twentieth Century, the Klan still rides. The *Caliban complex* is strong in our culture. Writers and scholars endorse the legend that Negroes and foreign-born workers are brutish Calibans. Underlying the prejudice against these groups, is the contempt for all those who toil.

Man, the master of the earth, has been deprived of his heritage. As Caliban said of Prospero:

> I say, by sorcery he got this isle:
> From me he got it.

But Prospero's magic is not eternal. Shakespeare's vision of bounteous crops and merry harvesters will become reality, and the cloud-capped towers and solemn temples of privilege will melt away like an "insubstantial pageant," to "leave not a wrack behind."

8 : LAND OF COCKAIGNE

THE MYTH of the realm of Cockaigne is of ancient origin. But it is, at least to some extent, a popular satire on the many-faceted legends of a land where the streets are paved with gold. In Cockaigne—so the story goes—the houses are built of pastry; geese and fowl already roasted wander about asking to be eaten in the manner of Al Capp's shmoo.[1] It has been claimed that the word *cockney* is derived from the name of the gourmet's paradise, and it is not unusual to refer to London as Cockaigne.

When Pocahontas crossed the ocean in 1616, London, and all of England, must have seemed like Cockaigne. There was prodigal wealth, a civilization that lived up to the boastful descriptions of homesick colonists. But it was a civilization in turmoil, turned topsy-turvy by the winds of change. And the word on everybody's lips was Cockaigne. The Cockayne patent, a monopolistic grant on a scale far beyond anything the crown had previously attempted, established a company which was given exclusive control of the English cloth industry. The patent was named in honor of Sir William Cockayne, an alderman of the city of London, who originated the plan and headed the new company. It dislocated the English economy to such an extent that the effects were felt in Holland and throughout Europe, and as far away as the Orient. Before we discuss the Cockayne patent, let us go back to the day in June, 1614, when the king dissolved parliament, in order to get a somewhat clearer picture of the consequences of the dissolution.

Following Bacon's advice, James had gambled on unity on his own terms. Having failed, he turned sharply, undisguisedly, to the right.

The urbane and skillful Spanish ambassador, Count Gondomar, became the king's confidant in domestic as well as in foreign affairs.

As always, the first, most pressing and most insoluble problem, was money. Soon after the dismissal of parliament, bishops and lords were called upon to make a "voluntary" gift to the king. This appeal was followed by a general request for donations to the crown—as if it were a popular charity. In July, James asked the city of London for a loan of £100,000. He was no longer a good risk; the cautious burghers replied that they would rather make a gift of £10,000 than a loan of ten times that amount. Every county and borough was ordered to raise funds, but the drive aroused no interest, and the receipts for a nine months' period amounted to only £23,000.[2]

The unsatisfactory response was a warning to the government that the opposition was strong and that the people were discontented with the policies that led to the break with the Commons. Since the Puritans were the most militant representatives of the opposition, they were subjected to a renewal of the persecution that had flared up at the time of the Midland Riots and again in 1611.

The stage, being dependent on court patronage, reflected the royal viewpoint in plays denouncing and ridiculing the Puritans. On June 30, 1614, just three weeks after the closing of parliament, the elaborate new Globe Theatre, built to replace the building destroyed by fire, opened its doors. In view of the king's financial difficulties, it may seem odd that the new playhouse was built "at the great charge of King James and many Noble men and others."[3] The court knew what it was paying for. Ben Jonson was at work on a play, and it was said that "King James made him write against the Puritans, who began to be troublesome at the time."[4]

Bartholomew Fair was the answer to the royal request. There were anti-Semitic overtones, as the name suggests, in the portrait of a religious zealot, Rabbi Zeal-of-the-Land-Busy. In linking the Puritan to the Jew, Jonson's caricature performed the function that is fulfilled by the caricature of the Communist—often with anti-Semitic overtones—in our own times. It justified persecution of any citizen suspected of being zeal-of-the-land-busy about matters that should be left to the judgment of wiser men.

Jonson's satire amused the court when it was acted there on November 1, 1614. There may have been people in the audience whose laughter was shadowed by the thought that the portrait of the absurd "rabbi" was a libel on the brave men and women who faced persecution for following the dictates of their conscience. However, the courtiers would probably have derided such solemn thoughts as a "Puritanical" attempt to impose significance on a work of art.

Among their other objectionable habits, the Puritans took the theatre seriously, insisting that such innocent merriment as the antics of the "rabbi" had social implications. This was one of the traits that Jonson satirized in the play: the "rabbi," getting drunk at the fair, pulling down a pile of gingerbread cakes because it looks "idolatrous," is especially angry at a puppet, "Goldylocks, the purple strumpet"; the doll, he says, is "a beame in the eye of the brethren; a very great beame, an exceeding great beame; such as are your *Stageplayers, Rimers* and *Morrisdancers,* who have walked hand in hand, in contempt of the *Brethren,* and the *Cause*."

Jonson's jokes about the *cause* merited a government reward, which he received two years later in the form of a royal pension.[5] Meanwhile, the play performed the service for which it was intended. It helped to justify the trial and torture of the Puritan minister, Edward Peacham, which took place a few months after the court presentation of *Bartholomew Fair*. Audiences laughing at the funny "rabbi" were less inclined to be disturbed by reports of the doings of the Star Chamber. Another case was that of Oliver St. John, a gentleman of Marlborough who was brought to trial in April, 1615, on the charge that he had written a letter suggesting that the king had broken his coronation oath.

These proceedings involved the growing conflict between Bacon, the king's attorney and defender of monarchial supremacy, and Edward Coke, creator of the first systematic study of the Common Law. Coke, as Chief Justice of the King's Bench, opposed the trial of Peacham, arguing that no mere declaration of the king's unworthiness could constitute treason. Bacon, in his capacity as attorney general, was present when Peacham was tortured in the Tower of London. The Secretary of State and the Chancellor of the Exchequer also watched the aged minister writhe in pain. Bacon joined the other observers in certifying that the torture had been conducted with all due regard for legal forms and the rights of the defendant.[6]

Peacham, who admitted he had criticized the crown and questioned the authority of ecclesiastical courts, was condemned to death in August, 1615. He was over sixty, and he died in prison before the sentence was carried out. St. John was condemned to imprisonment for life and a fine of £5,000, but he was released, and the fine was remitted, after he made a full apology and submission.

Coke was interested in keeping a record of the proceedings of the Star Chamber. He was assisted by a boy who was only twelve or thirteen years of age; the youngster had become adept at shorthand, and his skill in reporting made him invaluable to the jurist. The boy's name was Roger Williams. Coke's daughter wrote long afterward: "This Roger Williams when he was a youth would, in shorthand, take sermons and speeches in the Star Chamber and present them to my dear father." Coke, "seeing so hopeful a youth, took such a liking to him" that he sent him to the Charter House school.[7]

The boy, Williams, could learn from the incorruptible example of his patron. Coke was in an anomalous position as Chief Justice of the King's Bench. The class conflict, temporarily removed from the arena of parliamentary debate, was transferred to the field of law. Having dispensed with the troublesome advice of the Commons, James could not permit a leading member of the opposition party to preside over the court which was historically the king's own and proper court, his "royal hall" where matters pertaining to his interests were decided.[8]

The inevitable collision occurred in a case which appeared to involve a legal technicality. But it touched the most sensitive aspect of the royal authority—the feudal prerogatives which had been under fire in the Commons. A suit was brought which questioned the validity of a grant made by the king to the bishop of Lichfield of a benefice to be held *in commendam*. The Latin term meant that the income from the living was conferred on a person who was not the incumbent. In terms of contemporary American practice, the grant *in commendam* would be something like giving a government official a number of fictitious appointments from which he would derive additional salary. This would be regarded as a corrupt practice, although the privilege assumed by certain congressmen of putting their friends or relatives on the payroll is not altogether dissimilar. The custom was a valuable form of political patronage in Stuart England, and it often brought a substantial money return to the crown.

Bacon, as the attorney general, was entrusted with his usual unhappy responsibilities: he had to find some way of preventing the judges from rendering a decision which would displease the crown.

With Coke presiding on the bench, this was not an easy task. After the case had been heard, Bacon consulted with James; then he went to the chief justice and suggested that no decision be rendered until James himself could discuss the matter with the judges. Coke was wise enough to propose that the royal command be conveyed in writing to each of the three judges, and Bacon was foolish enough to comply. Coke then persuaded his two colleagues to sign a letter to the king, stating that the attorney general's request was illegal, and that they would not comply.

James summoned the judges to a council meeting on June 6, 1616. Bacon presented the point of law, holding that the king had the right to consult the court on any matter that concerned him. More effective than the legal arguments was James' anger. He had a sharp tongue, and when he finished speaking all the judges, including Coke, fell on their knees and asked the royal pardon for the improper form of their letter. However, Coke refused to join the other judges in their promise to consult the king in the future on questions affecting his "power and profit." Coke's insistence on the freedom of judicial action insured his immediate dismissal. He was accused of various past and present errors; the most substantial charge against him related to his disrespect of the crown in the matter of *commendams*.

While Coke went into retirement, Bacon received his reward. Three days after the council meeting, he was made a privy councilor, and a little more than a year later, he became lord chancellor.

The various tendencies and tensions which we have discussed—the *rapprochement* with Spain, the frantic appeals for funds, the persecution of Puritans, the dismissal of Coke—were peripheral squalls moving around the storm center, the Cockayne patent. The crown could not assert effective political authority unless it controlled the nation's economy. All the difficulties of James' reign had their origin in the king's lack of genuine economic power. The patents of monopoly which had been granted were piecemeal, and manifestly ineffective, attempts to dominate profitable areas of trade or production. But the cloth industry was the citadel of Britain's productive strength. If cloth could be conquered and coordinated under royal supervision, the financial problem would be solved. The move against the textile industry followed immediately on the dissolution of parliament.

In July, 1614, a proclamation was issued prohibiting the export of unfinished cloth. This was a preliminary, and carefully camouflaged step toward the predetermined objective. The edict was publicized as an effort to protect English production at the expense of the merchants engaged in the export trade. It was a blow at the powerful Merchant Adventurers' Company, which derived a good part of its income from the shipment of the unfinished product of English looms to be dyed and dressed in Holland. The Adventurers were unpopular because of their monopoly of foreign trade.[9] The proclamation was demagogically presented as an attack on big business, and a boon to the numberless "little capitalists," industrial entrepreneurs, and master craftsmen engaged in the manufacture of textiles.

It received a good deal of support from these classes, and thus prepared the groundwork for the creation of the new monopoly, granted in February, 1615, to a company which acquired the sole right of dyeing and dressing cloth under what was supposed to be an improved process. The patent allowed the company to export specified quantities of dyed and finished cloth, from which the crown expected to derive a profit.[10]

With breath-taking abruptness, the control of the manufacture, distribution and export of textiles passed out of the hands of the merchants and artisans who had engaged in the business for generations, and became subject to the will of the new syndicate. Since wool was purchased either for English manufacture or for export, the wool producers were also brought under monopolistic domination, and no wool could be sold without a special license.

The most sweeping effect of the patent, which was undoubtedly foreseen and desired by the king's advisers, was the disruption of England's commercial ties with Holland. The key industry in the Netherlands was the dyeing and dressing of so-called "white" unfinished textiles imported from England. Deprived of these raw materials, Holland retaliated by closing its ports to all English cloth, finished or unfinished. England answered by prohibiting the export of raw wool to the Netherlands. It was then proposed to exclude all Dutch imports, unless every Dutch ship agreed to take away manufactured cloth to the extent of one-fourth of its cargo.

The dispute was not limited to Anglo-Dutch trade. "The Low Countries," says William Hyde Price, "were in a position to disorganize seriously the trade of England with a large part of Europe."[11] The breaking of England's ties with the Protestant mercantile interests on the continent was a great victory for the advocates of a Spanish-Catholic alliance. It was a disaster for the mass of the people in England and Holland. The latter country made hasty efforts to develop a weaving industry, but meanwhile the dyers and finishers were thrown out of work, and there was desperate unemployment. In England, the cutting off of the market for wool intensified the crisis in agriculture, and deprived weavers, along with craftsmen in dozens of allied trades, of their occupation.

A little more than a year after the granting of the Cockayne patent, in the spring of 1616, its devastating impact on the nation's business was unmistakably apparent. The party of the bourgeoisie was strengthened by the growing anger of the people, and the king's advisers were searching frantically for some way of remedying the damage without further injury to the royal prestige.

While these events were taking place in England, the introduction of tobacco caused a more hopeful dislocation of the Virginia economy. In September, 1615, the *Flying Horse of Flushing* reached England with "one great roll containing 105 lbs. of Middling Tobacco." [12] In 1616, 2,500 pounds were shipped out of the colony. The inhabitants were so enthralled by the possibility of profit that food crops were neglected, and the tobacco fever threatened to bring another starving time. Before returning to England in 1616, Dale promulgated a law that each landholder must plant two acres of corn for himself and for each male servant as a condition for raising tobacco.

Virginia had found a substitute for the gold and silver that lured the first settlers. The people sweating in the sun felt a cool presence beside them, the visitant described by Shakespeare in *King John*—

> That smooth-fac'd gentleman, tickling commodity—
> Commodity, the bias of the world . . .
>
> This sway of motion, this commodity,
> Makes it take head from all indifferency,
> From all direction, purpose, course, intent:
> And this same bias, this commodity,
> This bawd, this broker, this all-changing word——

Tobacco was an all-changing word in Virginia. The discovery of a commercial crop that could be transported in bulk without prohibitive cost concretized the illusive question of profits and affected everything relating to the colonial experiment—the colony, the company, the crown, the domestic and foreign policy of the English government.

The possibilities of tobacco were revealed at a moment when the Virginia Company was on the edge of bankruptcy and its management discredited, when reports of the severity of the Dale regime made it impossible to recruit settlers. From the viewpoint of Sandys and the small stockholders, the arrival of marketable tobacco in England revitalized the hopes that made the purchase of shares a "Holy cause" in 1609. It was a call to action, to fight for the economic and political rights promised in the 1609 and 1612 charters. And the call came at the moment when the popular anger aroused by the Cockayne patent was at fever heat.

In addition to his other troubles, James faced the danger that the voices which had been silenced in the Commons would speak out boldly in the assembly of the Virginia Company. Tobacco was far less important economically than cloth. Nonetheless, it played a part in foreign policy. The Virginia product competed with the Spanish leaf, the main source of English supply and a commercial link between the two countries. James had used cloth to effect a diplomatic break with Holland; now tobacco threatened to cut one of the few mercantile ties with Spain.

It was therefore essential for the government to keep the Virginia situation well in hand, to regulate tobacco imports in accordance with the crown's political aims, and to prevent the party of the bourgeoisie from utilizing the renewed interest in the colony for its own advantage.

These were the considerations underlying the recall of Deputy Governor Dale in 1616. He was accompanied by Rolfe, his wife, Pocahontas, and their baby son, with ten or twelve Indians "to be educated in England."[13] Having served the colonists in their dealings with the Indians, Pocahontas was now to be a pawn in a more complicated political game. A savage princess and at the same time an English lady of quality, she had a publicity value that could be turned to the advantage of the crown and the controlling group in the Virginia company.

Pocahontas reached England on June 12, six days after the scene in which James forced the judges of the king's bench to their knees. As in so many of his regal acts, James had won a Pyrrhic victory. The cloth industry in the country districts was at a standstill. The breakdown affected the whole population: "Country gentlemen were being dealt with in the Star Chamber on the charge of buying and selling wool." [14]

In August, the government tried to conciliate Gloucestershire craftsmen who complained that they had woven cloth which they were not permitted to sell: the Cockayne Company was pre-emptorily ordered to buy an unlimited quantity of the Gloucestershire cloth, although the company protested that the work and material were bad. But the syndicate was not properly organized to dye and dress the cloth it acquired. Cockayne was summoned before the king's council, and was told that he and his associates must dispose of their cloth, "whereof it behooved them to have a care at their uttermost peril." They were ordered "to resolve among themselves whether they would go forward in the work of dyeing and dressing." [15]

Bacon wrote to the king in September: "I perceive the cloth goeth not off as it should and that Wiltshire is now come in with complaints as well as Gloucestershire and Worcestershire; so that this gangrene creepeth on." [16]

The gangrene was in the body politic as well as in the cloth industry. It affected the moral climate of the nation, and the private conduct of the class in power. We may turn again to the London theatre as an index of the cultural life of the time. John Webster's *Duchess of Malfi* may have been produced as early as 1613, but it contains many contemporary allusions which show that it was revised and frequently performed in 1616 and 1617.[17]

Few Elizabethan dramas achieve such a concentrated mood of despair. The duchess, condemned to torture and death by her own brother, waits for the horror to engulf her. When she is told that her brother has sent a "wild consort of madmen" to frighten her, she says:

> Indeed, I thank him. Nothing but noise and folly
> Can keep me in my right wits; whereas reason
> And silence make me stark mad.

She watches the executioners enter with her coffin. She is strangled slowly, deliberately. And her brother's words, as he looks down at what he has done, are passionless.

> Cover her face; mine eyes dazzle; she died young.

The refinement of horror replaced the hopeful poetry of a happier day. To Shakespeare, the lust for money was the root of evil. To Webster, in a darker period, corruption was man's life, evil was purposeless and all-consuming.

Pocahontas may have known little about the woman question. But she cannot have avoided hearing the gossip and controversy around the trial of the Earl and Duchess of Somerset for the murder of Sir Francis Overbury. She must have been utterly bewildered by the topsy-turvy ethics and fantastic customs, so unlike anything in the life of her own people, that were exposed to public scrutiny in the case.

It was a *cause célèbre* for political as well as for moral reasons. It seems probable that political pressure caused the belated revelation of the crime. The apothecary's apprentice who prepared the poison went to Flanders; he talked indiscreetly;[18] but it is a reasonable guess that his indiscretion was encouraged by Protestant sympathizers, who saw an opportunity to discredit the most blatant supporters of Spain in the king's intimate circle.

The evidence presented at the trial was so damning that both the Earl and the Duchess were found guilty. But there was undoubtedly damning information about the king which James' former favorite could have brought into open court. It was a foregone conclusion that the defendants would not suffer the extreme penalty. They retired to the Tower to await a favorable moment for their release.

The people were passionately interested in the case. It involved morals, politics, and foreign policy. An extensive pamphlet literature dealt with the crime as a horror story; but it also emphasized the woman question and the sanctity of the family. It happened that Overbury himself had written a poem describing an ideal wife. Published under the title, *A Wife now the Widdow of Sir Thomas Overburye, Being A most exquisite and singular Poem of the choice of a Wife,* it appeared in innumerable editions. Many pamphlets placed responsibility for the crime on the incontinence of women. A general statement of this view was provided in Joseph Swetnam's *Araignment of Lewd, Idle, Forward and unconstant women,* first published in 1615 and so popular that it ran through at least ten printings in the next twenty years. Swetnam derided the women who spend "the most part of the forenoone painting themselves, and frizzling their haires, and prying in their glasses like Apes . . ."

There were many works along the same lines. Barnabe Rich, who had been indicting the conduct of women for a decade, wrote *My Ladies Looking Glasse* in 1616: he said that women no longer ostracized harlots: "The worse a woman lives, the better shee is thought on." [19]

But the striking thing about the attack is the fact that it did not go unanswered. The political ferment and the breakdown of the authoritarian state encouraged independent thinking. The first stirrings of a movement of middle-class women to defend their integrity and rights are to be found in the pamphlet controversy inspired by the Somerset trial. Rachel Speght was under twenty when she wrote a reply to Swetnam, whom she described as *"The Cynicall Bayter of, and foule mouthed Barker against Evahs Sex."* In the same year, 1617, a woman writing under the psuedonym of Esther Sowerman published *Ester hath hang'd Haman: Or An Answere To a lewd Pamphlet, entituled, The Arraignment of Women.* It is politically significant that she addressed her appeal to "the best disposed and worthy Apprentises of London . . . I know that you the Apprentises of this Citie are as forward to maintaine the good, as you are vehement to put downe the bad." Another woman, using the name of Constantia Munda, wrote *The Worming of a Mad Dogge* in 1617. The extent of the debate is suggested in her reference to the "many sottish and illiterate Libels . . . when every foule-mouthed male-content may disgorge his *Licambaean* poyson in the face of the world." [20]

Both sides of the argument appealed to a predominantly middle-class audience. The "cynicall bayters" like Swetnam reflected the Puritan's hatred of the court, and the fear that the bourgeoisie was being affected by the manners of the aristocracy. But the women who wrote their spirited answers expressed the more affirmative and aggressive viewpoint of the Puritans, and especially those of the lower middle class, fighting to maintain the sanctity of the home against the disintegrating effects of poverty and unemployment.

The woman question was bound up in the fight against the Cockayne patent. The militant tone of the defense conducted by women like Constantia Munda and Esther Sowerman in 1617 was inspired by the growing confidence of the middle and lower middle classes in asserting their rights against the crown. It was apparent in the fall of 1616 that the oppressive monopoly of the textile trade could not be maintained.

The king's council had reached such an impasse that it was ready to entertain the most feeble-minded proposals. Among the suggestions for the forced sale of cloth, a memorandum by Sir Julius Caesar deserves honorable mention. In order to meet "so desperate and dangerous a case," Sir Julius proposed that everyone in the city of London worth more than £10,000 be forced to buy at least £1,000 of cloth. Woolen drapers who were worth £5,000 or more were to undertake a similar obligation. The court was asked to share, somewhat more modestly, in creating an artificial market—"the King's Counsellors and Courtiers and all their servants to wear nothing but broad cloth in their gownes, clokes, girthes, robes or breeches." [21]

The fantastic character of this plan explains the government's reluctant acceptance of a more realistic solution in January, 1617. The Cockayne Company admitted what everyone already knew, that it was dead. The patent was abandoned and the cloth trade returned to its former method of operation—but not to normalcy: it took more than a decade to overcome the economic effects of the breakdown.[22]

Meanwhile Pocahontas was one of the celebrities of the London season. She was presented at court by Lady Delaware. Her portrait was engraved by Simon de Passe. She was entertained with unusual splendor by the Bishop of London. On January 28, 1617, she attended *Christmas His Mask,* written by Ben Jonson. On the same evening, John Chamberlain wrote to Sir Dudley Carleton at the Hague: "The Virginia woman Pocahontas, with her father's counsaillor, had been with the king and graciously used." [23]

The honors accorded Pocahontas served the general purpose for which they were intended: the king and the court received useful publicity. But the more specific aim, of regaining public confidence in the administration of the Virginia Company and proving the crown's benevolent interest in the enterprise, could not succeed. It was doomed to failure by the demise of the cloth monopoly, which weakened the crown's prestige and encouraged a revolt of the Virginia stockholders. The issues were interwoven. The Virginia investors belonged to the same classes—and were in many cases the same persons—involved in the fight against the Cockayne patent.

Early in 1617, a group of dissident stockholders, called together by Sandys and some of his friends, started holding "sundry private meetings among themselves." [24] The plans were being laid for the campaign that would give the Sandys group control of the corporation.

In spite of the effective progaganda use of Pocahontas, it was well known that there was sickness, misery and mismanagement in Virginia. While Pocahontas fulfilled her social obligations, her husband was called upon to defend the colonial administration. During the last months of their English visit, Rolfe wrote his *Relation of the State of Virginia.* The pamphlet defended "this cause, so much despised and disgraced." Rolfe described the supposedly idyllic life of the settlers, every man sitting "under his fig tree in safety, gathering and reaping the fruits of their labours with much joy and comfort." [25]

To back up Rolfe's happy description, so at variance with the reports of the *Divine, Morall and Martiall laws* and the available information concerning the high death rate in Virginia, the company issued a proclamation announcing that the plantation needed nothing "but more hands to gather and return those commodities which may bring profit to the Adventurers," and that henceforth "wee have resolved to give free leave and licence to any who are now remaining in *Virginia,* at his will and pleasure to returne home into England, which liberty wee doe likewise grant and confirme unto all those which hereafter from time to time shall go thither in person." [26]

The proclamation and Rolfe's pamphlet indicate that there was a labor crisis in the colony. The harsh provisions of the 1612 charter, permitting the company to pursue and punish persons who escaped from its jurisdiction, had not provided a stable and efficient work force. Laborers could not be pursued beyond the grave. People who had come out for seven-year terms with the first large contingent in 1609 had completed their period of service, and were now occupying land on a rental basis.[27] The company was in urgent need of men to cultivate its tobacco fields, and it had to promise better conditions in order to obtain recruits.

As Rolfe and his wife prepared to return to Virginia with the new deputy governor, Samuel Argall, another colonial expedition was in preparation. After nearly thirteen years as a prisoner in the tower, Sir Walter Raleigh was to sail again in search of the golden city of Manoa, which he had so eloquently described in 1596.

The political situation, and the king's prodigious need of money, procured Raleigh's release. In 1616, Raleigh was sixty-four years old.

He had spent his years in the Tower writing a *History of the World.* In the preface, he spoke of the inconstancy of kings:

> Oh, by what plots, by what forswearings, betrayings, oppressions, imprisonments, tortures, poysonings, and under what reasons of state and politic subtlety have these forenamed Kings, both strangers and of our owne Nation, pulled the vengeance of God upon themselves, upon theirs and upon their prudent ministers!

The contemporary significance of these remarks was obvious. But Raleigh was careful to note that he avoided the history of his own time: for "whosoever in writing a Modern History shall follow truth too near the heeles, it may haply strike out his teeth." [28]

Raleigh was aware of the crown's economic difficulties and the disorder created by the Cockayne patent. Although James was intent on seeking an alliance with Spain, Raleigh knew that the king could not resist the lure of gold. He sent word to James that he had secret information about a gold mine in Guiana on the banks of the Orinoco River. The secret was a little stale: it was contained in the memorandum stolen from a Spanish ship in 1595, and it had been described by Raleigh in the book published in the following year.

But James was desperate. He was willing to place his pro-Spanish foreign policy in the scales to be weighed against a gold mine. Raleigh's life was also thrown into the scales: he was warned that he would pay for failure to find the mine with his head.

Raleigh was not a fool. He knew the risk he was taking. He was old, tired of prison, anxious to taste the Atlantic wind before he died. Yet he was following the logic of his life. It was the logic of English expansion, which pointed to the Caribbean and South America.

Raleigh's fleet consisted of ten ships equipped at a cost of £30,000. His flagship was the 500-ton *Destinye.*[29] Raleigh's fleet weighed anchor on March 17, 1617. Four days later, as Argall and his friends prepared to sail for Virginia, Pocahontas died suddenly at Gravesend.

Political tension increased in England in the following months. In August, the privy council issued a belated proclamation announcing the abandonment of the Cockayne patent. Since the company had ceased to exist in January, the delay indicated the embarrassment of the government, and the search for a satisfactory formula to explain the debacle. The August statement was lame enough to have been written in ten minutes: "Finding that time discovereth many inhabilities which cannot at first be seen . . . we intend not to insiste and stay longer upon specious and faire showes which produce not the frut our actions do aim at . . ."[30] We can hardly believe that Bacon had a hand in this sorry confession.

The struggle for control of the Virginia company entered the stage of open conflict, sharpened by the rapid rise in tobacco shipments. The 2,500 pounds of colonial tobacco imported into England in 1616 jumped to 18,839 pounds in 1617, and 49,518 pounds in 1618.[31]

The seven-year period established by the charter of 1609, in which all corporate profits would be kept in a common fund, had ended. But there were no profits to be distributed. Since Smythe and the group that controlled the company had been in charge of the purchase and transportation of supplies, they had made a profit on these operations while the corporation functioned at a loss. But now that the seven years had come to an end, and the company's funds were exhausted, the insiders, led by Smythe, looked for a new method of securing private gain at the expense of the other stockholders. They formed a separate corporation, "The Society of Particular Adventurers for Traffic with the People of Virginia in Joint Stock." The "Particular Adventurers" monopolized purchases in England and sales of goods in the colony, excluding other persons from the trade, and running the "magazine" in Virginia for their private gain. The director of the "magazine" was Robert Johnson, Smythe's son-in-law, whom we have already met in connection with the Yorkshire alum works.

Since supplies purchased in Virginia were paid for in tobacco, and since the tobacco was carried to England in the ships that brought the supplies, the "Particular Adventurers" controlled the tobacco market. Thus the majority of the stockholders were deprived of an adequate share in the profits from the sale of tobacco. At the same time, it was suspected, and later proved, that Johnson juggled the accounts so that money belonging to the corporation was diverted to the "magazine," which was getting an exorbitant profit from its exclusive control of commodities sold to the company or to individual settlers. Johnson was accused of misappropriating £341 13*s* 4*d* belonging to the company in 1617. In the following year, he managed to secure most of the money due to the company from the sale of tobacco grown on its land.[32]

To cope with this situation, Sandys moved at a stockholders' meeting on May 16, 1618, for the appointment of a five-man committee to investigate the treasurer's accounts. The committee included Sandys and one of his close collaborators, Sir John Danvers. The committee's work was opposed and obstructed by Smythe, who refused to turn over papers and information to the investigators. He said, not without reason, that he "believed they ment him noe good by their earnest requires for all old bookes of accounts." [33]

In 1617, the preparations for a general European war proceeded at an accelerated pace. The Cockayne patent was a factor of incalculable importance in reinforcing the Catholic position on the eve of the outbreak. The deterioration of England's relations with Holland, and with the Protestant bourgeoisie in other parts of the continent, was so helpful to the Hapsburgs that it frightened the ruling class in France, and led to a temporary diminution of Jesuit influence. Having reached the age of sixteen, Louis XIII rebelled against his mother, and arranged the assassination of her favorite, the Marshal d'Ancre. However, Marie's exile left France so weak and divided that it could play no effective part in the approaching conflict.

It would be absurd to suppose that Pocahontas had any inkling of the forces that were at work in the strange land in which she spent a few fantastic months. England may have seemed like the Cockaigne of the fable, a pastry-cook's dream. She could not know that the political strife of which she heard only fortuitous rumors would bring a terrible fate to her own people.

She did not return to see the spreading fields of tobacco driving the Indians back to the uplands and the mountains. She did not live to see the beginning of the heroic and hopeless effort of the Indians to stem the tide of conquest. She had learned the ways of the conquerors. She knew a woman's duty as it was understood by the Europeans, and she played her part with decorum. Having accomplished her English mission, she closed her eyes, politely and forever.

There is an entry in the parish register at Gravesend: "Mar. 21, 1617. Rebecca Wrolfe, wyffe to Thomas Wrolfe, gent., a Virginia lady borne was buried in the Chauncell." [34]

9 : THE FISHERMEN

THE HISTORY of the United States is told primarily as a land story, a tale of men and women hungry for the green earth and engaged primarily in agricultural production. But the fortune of the land seekers has been to a considerable extent dependent upon the sea, and upon the labors of the sailors and fishermen who have provided transportation and food—and wealth—for the people on dry land.

On March 17, 1874, the Massachusetts House of Representatives passed the following resolution: "That leave might be given to hang up the representation of a cod-fish in the room where the House sit, as a memorial to the importance of the cod-fishery to the welfare of this Commonwealth." [1] While the legislators recognized the value of the cod as a commodity, they may have been somewhat less cognizant of the contribution made by the men who caught the fish. Since historiography has also ignored the fishermen as a political and social force, it seems proper to conclude our survey of the cultural background of American settlement with consideration of the role played by the toilers of the sea in the movement of colonization. It was a vital, and in some respects decisive, role; it was determined by the economics of the fishing industry. While fishing has developed historically as part of the general organization of production, it has had certain unique characteristics, expressed in unusual productive relationships.

Art and literature have always associated fishing with poverty and wearisome toil. In *Fishing from the Earliest Times,* William Radcliffe writes:

Greek fishermen, whether we read of them in the Epigrams or in the fragments of lost works, all come down to us as old, patient, half-starved, through dint of toil by day and night, sea-worn.[2]

Winslow Homer's pictures, painted on the coast of Maine in the last years of the nineteenth century, show us the faces of old men, worn and patient in their battle with wind and sea. In *The Herring Net,* an old man bends over the net, while a boy labors beside him. The presence of the boy points to the obvious fact that men do not learn to fish when they are gray and wrinkled. Fishing is a skilled trade, which is handed down from father to son. It is possible, as in the case of some of the Portuguese fishermen sailing out of Monterey or San Francisco, to trace the history of a family which has fished for thirty generations.

The essential contradiction in the lives of these families is to be found in the extremely high skill that is required and the extremely low return that the worker receives. The boys gain experience in seamanship on the small boats of the fishing fleet. But this experience makes it possible for them to get more lucrative employment in other maritime pursuits. Their wandering manhood takes them across the world in naval service or on trading voyages. But they come back to the ancestral port when the wandering years are over, to sail the small vessels that are as weatherbeaten as themselves.

The story has many variations: longer voyages, such as the transatlantic journeys to the Grand Banks in the sixteenth and seventeenth centuries, or the South Sea whaling voyages in the nineteenth century, have required larger ships, with a heavier investment of capital and different methods of organization. But the social pattern remains as characteristic of the industry as the clusters of small boats, with tattered sails and nets hung out to dry, that can be seen in any fishing port in the world.

From the days of ancient Greece to the late middle ages, war and commerce were served chiefly by vessels which used oars as the basic means of locomotion. The holds of these ships were like furnaces, burning out the strength and lives of slaves. But galleys were not practical for fishing. Fish is a universal article of food, and the demand for it developed with the first growth of urban civilization on the shores of the Mediterranean. The men who met the demand could not be chained, beaten, or pressured into the position of the slave or the serf, because they had to operate their boats under conditions which required independent responsibility and technical training.

Fishermen did their work in comparative freedom, because it could not be done in any other way. But their freedom ended when their ship touched the land. The law of the market decreed their compensation. The merchant could not supervise them at sea, but he had all the bargaining power that he needed at his disposal when they offered their fish for sale: with a product that was quickly spoiled, the fisherman's pay was limited by the time factor as well as by the more privileged position of the mercantile class with which he was forced to deal. The merchant solved the problem by recognizing the fisherman's independence at sea, and making him a partner—he could take his chance as a free enterpriser, but the extent of his share was dictated by the social situation on land.

The development of larger sailing ships, capable of long ocean voyages, transformed the fishing industry. The decisive technological advance in the use of sails occurred in the fifteenth century. Societies with a plentiful supply of slave labor were more interested in applying technological improvements to the galley, enlarging it to employ three, four, or even five banks of oars, than in solving the problem of applying wind power to large vessels. During the period of Rome's greatest maritime supremacy, the need of greater cargo space inspired the use of sails: the corn ships that carried breadstuffs from Egypt to the capital were three-masters with square rigging. But the more restricted commerce that followed the dissolution of the Roman empire brought new reliance on slave driven ships.

The Vikings combined sails and rowers: the vessels that set out to conquer the world in the ninth and tenth centuries were small, with from ten to sixteen oars on a side, and a single strong square sail on a central mast. These were suitable for marauding expeditions in which maneuverability in battle was essential. The oars gave the necessary speed and flexibility of movement. The rowers were freemen, doubling as warriors. Slaves could not be trusted on ships which could be so easily seized by the crew.

The Vikings operated on the share system. The crew participated in the spoils. One of the reasons for the failure of the Norse wave of conquest was the lack of ships which were large enough to develop organized trade. The question of size was not, of course, an isolated factor: it was determined by the productive forces and relationships in

Scandinavia, as well as by the general level of economic development in the whole area which the Norsemen attempted to conquer.

Galleys operated by slave labor continued to fulfill the requirements of Mediterranean commerce during the Middle Ages. The Venetian galleys made their annual trips through the straits of Gibraltar to English and Flemish ports. But the decline of Viking power enabled the cities of northern Germany to seize the richest prize of northern waters—the herring of the Baltic Sea. The Viking ships, efficient as they were for purposes of war, were not big enough to carry a satisfactory cargo of fish. The more advanced organization of craft production in the Hansa towns was able to meet this need. These towns were nearer to the European market, from which they were therefore able to derive a satisfactory profit. The fishermen built the early prosperity of Lübeck and other cities of the Hanseatic League.

At the beginning of the epoch of capitalism, these northern business centers suffered an apparently mysterious economic catastrophe: by the end of the fourteenth century, it was evident that the herring were deserting the Baltic and migrating to the North Sea. This occurred at the moment when Dutch merchants challenged the commercial power of the Hansa towns. It seemed as if the fish were following the movement of trade toward the west.

The withdrawal of the herring from the Baltic was due to the decreasing amount of salt in the water. It posed a serious problem to the Hansa ports: were their fishing fleets able to follow the herring to the stormy waters of the North Sea? The fishermen possessed the skill to undertake the task, and the Hansa shipbuilders were accustomed to make ships capable of making long commercial voyages. But the social structure of the towns made it impossible to link the fisherman's skill with commercial shipping: The mercantile oligarchy which governed the towns was not able to reorganize the fisheries; the money was available, but the human resources were not at hand; the fishermen could not be transferred to different ships and different methods of work.

The control of the North Sea fisheries passed to the Low Countries, and it has been said that the houses of Flemish burghers were built of the carcasses of herring. The people of the Netherlands were a seafaring people, and their skill in building ocean-going ships was in advance of other countries. The competition of English fishermen was delayed by the backwardness of English shipbuilding. At the end of the fourteenth century, England was importing fish in large quantities. The need of this food supply was so great that special permission was given to foreign fishermen arriving in small boats (the permission did not extend to trading vessels) to sell their catch for gold or silver, provided they did not "meddle in other merchandise." [3]

Many of these foreigners came from the Netherlands. Others sailed from Scotch or Norwegian ports. The welcome that was extended to them, with the unusual privilege of exporting hard money, indicates the primitive level of economic organization in England. But the social conflict that culminated in the Wat Tyler rebellion prepared the way for the rapid expansion of English trade and craft production. We may recall that it was a fishmonger dealing in Iceland cod who betrayed Tyler and thus ended the peasant revolt. Walworth's act was a symbol of the part that the fisheries were to play in the further development of the English economy.

The more adventuresome voyages of fishermen into the open ocean as far as Iceland were due to intensive competition, as well as to improvements in shipbuilding and navigation. Ocean fishing introduced a more diversified product. In leaving the Baltic, the herring entered into competition with the salmon, the eel, the sturgeon and the cod.

Flanders maintained control of the European market for fish. By the beginning of the sixteenth century, the merchants of Antwerp and other Flemish towns were buying all the herring they could get from any source; the cured fish was sold as "Flemish herring," although a great deal of it came from the British Isles.[4]

Salmon and herring played an important part in the growth of Glasgow, Aberdeen and other towns on Scotland's east coast. But Scotland was at a disadvantage in competing with England for the profits of trade with Flanders. England was linked to the Low Countries by the commerce in wool. Fish and wool were intimately connected: in the fourteenth century, the English fishing fleets sailed from east coast ports, which were also the main centers of the trade in wool. As the West Country began to develop a cloth industry, exporting unfinished textiles to be dyed and dressed in the Netherlands, the merchants of Bristol and other west coast ports sought to secure a larger share in the profits of the fisheries.

William Canynge of Bristol owned 2,853 tons of shipping in the middle years of the fifteenth century, and his fortune—which was huge for the time, enabling him to entertain Edward VI with magnificent courtesy when the king visited Bristol in 1461—was derived largely from the Iceland fisheries.[5] The tonnage controlled by Canynges is historically significant: it marks the rise of capitalism in the fishing industry. The fishermen no longer owned the means of production. The little boats that sailed from east coast ports to fish in the North Sea generally belonged to the men who operated them. But larger and stronger ships were needed to make the dangerous voyage from the West Country through the Scottish archipelago to Iceland. The merchant who financed the building of the vessels bargained with the fishermen for their services.

The bargain was governed by the relative strength of the two groups. The fishermen, like other craftsmen, were organized in gilds. This was the normal form of association for skilled workers who owned the means of production. However, there were many fishermen who did not possess boats, nets and tackle. Their dealings with fellow-craftsmen who owned the boat were based on the traditional sharing system; they agreed to participate on a more or less equal basis in the profits or losses of the voyage. As capital entered the industry, the fishermen held stubbornly to their share, as the only defense of their craft status. As the industry developed, the arrangement between the shipowner and the fisherman tended to assume the character of an employer-employee relationship. But the relationship was masked by the distribution of shares, which placed the fisherman in a halfway position between the free artisan and the wage laborer.

The growth and character of England's West Country fishing industry—the beginnings of capitalism and the fishermen's fight for an equitable share in the income of the voyage—formed the basis for the development of England's transatlantic fishing industry during the sixteenth century. However, all of Europe was concerned in the Newfoundland fisheries, and the men tossing in storm and fog on the Grand Banks were not aloof from the political and social struggles that stirred the continent.

No study seems to have been made of the interrelationship of fish and ideology. But there is considerable evidence that the fisherman's work pattern is reflected in the pattern of his culture and political activity. This was notably the case in the sixteenth century.

Portuguese and Basque fishermen were among the most daring seamen of the fourteenth and fifteenth centuries. But the restrictions which Spain and Portugal placed on mercantile activity prevented the growth of their fishing industries in the period of American discovery and colonization. Spain and Portugal, like other Catholic countries, consumed large quantities of fish, and they required additional supplies for provisioning the ships that voyaged to the Western Hemisphere, Africa and the Orient. But all the capital available for shipbuilding was devoted to the great galleons that carried colonial commerce and the vessels of war that protected the galleons. Fish was supplied by imports rather than by the expansion of the local industry.

During the first half of the sixteenth century, the fishermen of the Low Countries were chiefly engaged in catching herring in the North Sea. Herring was still so vital to the economy of the Low Countries that the inventor of a better method of curing the fish was given an unusual tribute by Charles V: the emperor ordered mass to be said at the man's tomb, and personally attended the ceremony.[6]

While the West Country of England manifested an early interest in the Newfoundland fisheries, English investment in voyages to the Grand Banks was for some time limited by the necessity of meeting Dutch and Scandinavian competition in the North Sea and Iceland. The dominant position which English fishermen had achieved in these seas could not be abandoned for the greater risks and as yet uncertain profits of the fisheries on the the other side of the Atlantic.

The fishermen of the channel ports of France were virtually the masters of the Grand Banks from the discovery of Newfoundland to the middle of the sixteenth century. La Rochelle and other French ports were centers of commercial activity, which was held in check by the predominantly feudal character of the French economy. The merchants of these towns had money to invest, and the seamen and fishermen had technical knowledge and experience derived from centuries of maritime activity. French capital and skill, deprived of the larger opportunities that had been won by England and Flanders, were ready to take the risks, and garner the profits, of the overseas fisheries. We have mentioned the fact that "Newland" fish were on sale at Rouen in 1510. A few years later, John Rastell, the English printer who made an unsuccessful attempt to cross the Atlantic in 1517, wrote a rhyme about Newfoundland:

> Nowe frenchemen and other have founden the trade,
> That yerely of fyshe there they lade,
> Above an hundred sayle.[7]

Rastell may have exaggerated when he spoke of one hundred ships making the annual crossing at this early date. But there can be no doubt that there was a large, and steadily increasing, number of French vessels engaged in fishing on the Grand Banks. These ships made two voyages each year, hurrying back to France without going ashore in Newfoundland to dry or cure the fish, which was therefore called wet-fish, and was either cured in France or sold locally for immediate use.

La Rochelle took the lead in organizing and financing the fishing fleets. It was also destined to be the great stronghold of Huguenot power, and the rise and decline of the French fisheries followed the course of the Protestant movement in France.

A list of vessels which are known to have sailed to Newfoundland prior to 1550 includes 71 ships from La Rochelle and 22 from other French ports. There are only 12 Portuguese ships listed, 11 English, and 9 Spanish.[8] But this was on the eve of civil war in France. And the Reformation had come to England, strengthening the bourgeoisie and inaugurating a period of maritime expansion. The abandonment of Lent decreased the English consumption of fish. The problem received governmental attention: in 1549, an English law restored Lenten abstinence from meat to give employment to "Fishers, and men using the trade of living by fishing in the sea." The establishment of political Lent was followed in 1563 by adding Wednesday to the "fish and navy days."[9]

During the Elizabethan period, the considerations of policy which had forced England to give primary attention to the North Sea and Iceland fisheries were no longer operative. Holland's fishing fleets were to a considerable extent diverted to the war with Spain, in which the fishermen played a leading role. England was also engaged in a struggle with Spain, and control of the North Atlantic was of crucial strategic importance.

Spain, forced to recognize the international significance of the Newfoundland fisheries, made a halfhearted attempt to divert some of its warships from the protection of the silver fleet to northern waters. Ten French fishing vessels were attacked by a Spanish squadron in 1554, and in the following year Spanish warships captured 48 French ships and made a raid on St. John's harbor in Newfoundland.[10]

In conjunction with these warlike activities, Spanish fishermen made their appearance in increasing numbers on the Grand Banks, meeting their English and French rivals without hostility. In 1578, Anthony Parkhurst reported "above 100 saile of Spaniards that come to take cod." [11] The same observer noted that the English fleet, "since my first travell being but 4 yeeres, are increased from 30 sayle to 50." [12] There were 150 French ships, but they were considerably smaller than the others, most of them being under 40 tons.

The large number of French ships shows that civil strife and the persecution of Protestants had not caused La Rochelle to abandon its interest in the Newfoundland fisheries. The Huguenot banner still waved proudly over the beleaguered fortress of the Protestant resistance. After the massacre of St. Bartholomew's Eve, La Rochelle held out for more than six months against a Catholic army, which was forced to raise the siege after losing 20,000 men. On June 24, 1573, La Rochelle signed a treaty on behalf of all the French Huguenots which guaranteed freedom of worship in the town and other specified areas.

The seamen of La Rochelle aided the Dutch Sea Beggars and their English allies in the struggle against Spain. And they continued to cross to the Grand Banks. However, the political situation in France was responsible for differences in the size of the French fishing vessels and the organization of the French industry. Bristol and other West Country ports had comparatively large sums of money to invest. They were able to build and equip bigger ships, with provisions for a longer voyage. They found it profitable to secure land bases, where the fishermen could bring the fish to be cured, so that it could be stored economically for the return voyage. The harbors of southern Newfoundland were used for this purpose. The seasonal visits of the English fleets had established *de facto* control of the Avalon Peninsula by the end of the sixteenth century.

The French, on the other hand, had more limited funds and equally limited opportunities for marketing the fish. They continued to follow the old custom of two trips a year to the Grand Banks, bringing back the *wet-fish* for local sale while the English merchants secured the lion's share of the international trade. Much of this trade was actually conducted by way of France. Since England was at war with Spain, the dried cod was brought to France for transshipment to Spain or Italy.[13]

England's fishing fleets participated in the defeat of the Spanish Armada. The economic results of the victory, oddly enough, were an increase in the sale of fish to the defeated enemy. Spain had neglected her fishing industry while she built a navy of castellated galleons. The galleons were no match for the light, mobile craft of Holland and England. But the galleons were the lifeline between Spain and her world empire. Having smashed the Armada in the English channel, the fishermen returned to Newfoundland, to supply the salt cod which had become the staple diet on Spanish vessels traveling to America or the Far East. Through these transactions, some of the gold and silver of the American mines enriched British capitalism. According to Harold A. Innis:

> The growth of the power of Holland after 1581 and her importance in the North Sea fishery accentuated the development of the West Country fishery interests in Newfoundland . . . England was able, in part because of her relatively shorter distance from Newfoundland and in part because of the nature of fish as a foodstuff, to secure a strong and continuous hold on a product by which she obtained a share of Spanish specie and the products of the Mediterranean. Cod from Newfoundland was the lever by which she wrested her share of the riches of the New World from Spain.[14]

This economic process was conditioned by the conflicts that developed in England in the early Stuart period. The class interests of the fishermen were opposed to the interests of the merchants who financed the voyages. At the beginning of the seventeenth century, the share system was organized on the basis of a three-way division: one-third of the gross return went to the captain and crew; one-third went to the owner of the ship; one-third was given to the investor who advanced the money for nine months' supplies, including food, salt, nets and other necessities.

In many cases, the owner of the ship and the backer of the voyage were the same person. The two-thirds profit on a successful voyage was a very substantial return on the investment. Disputes with the fishermen arose chiefly in regard to the provisioning of the ships. Crews complained of the quantity and quality of food, and investors pointed to the rising costs of such essential items as salt, bread and beer. Where a separate investor provided the supplies, he was often able to secure an agreement which gave him half the total income, leaving half to be divided between the crew and the shipowner.

The fishermen's share was reduced by various charges for "extra" victuals, "special" expenses, and damage to the ship's property. The owner of the vessel generally gave a special allowance to the captain, and bonuses to members of the crew who were recommended for efficient work. Since the owner depended on the captain for the success of the voyage, the captain was in a position to exert a good deal of pressure on the men under him. The bonus gave the captain an additional advantage: he could use it as a means of placing a few members of the crew under personal obligations to him and thus breaking the solidarity of the men.

Although the fishermen were at odds with the shipowners and merchants, the West Country was united in its opposition to the mercantile oligarchy in London. We have discussed the leading part played by the West Country in the fight against monopoly in the first years of James' reign. The London financiers interfered with the West Country's European trade. But they also sent their ships across the Atlantic to buy fish in Newfoundland. They could argue that their large ships could handle the transportation of dried fish from America to Europe more efficiently than the boats which actually did the fishing. The growth of the industry and the heavy European demand favored the London argument.

Both the owners of the fishing fleets and the fishermen whom they employed resented the interference of the "sack ships," so-called because they carried the heavy white wine of Spain and the Canaries as a return cargo after the dried fish had been disposed of in the Spanish market.[15] The opposition of the owners was not as intransigeant as that of the fishermen. The owners could make up for their exclusion from European trade by the larger amount of fish which could be caught to fill the sack ships: the fishermen could make two trips between the Grand Banks and the Newfoundland or Nova Scotia harbors where the fish were dried and sold. For the fishermen, this meant double work for a smaller return. Their share was cut, and their labor was subjected to a burdensome speed-up.

The political crisis in 1610, when the king and the Commons were at loggerheads over money, taxes, and feudal prerogatives, brought the formation of the London and Bristol Company, which was bitterly opposed both by the West Country and by the majority of the Virginia stockholders. The royal grant of Newfoundland to the Company meant, in effect, that the sack ships had a base on land, from which they could control the sale of supplies and dictate the conditions under which the fish was cured. The company owned the land on which the drying platforms were erected. They could make rules governing the use of the harbors, sell commodities at their own price, and buy the fish—also at their own price.

The effect of the London and Bristol Company charter may be gauged in terms of a single commodity: salt had been carried across the ocean by the fishing fleets on their outward voyage. Since they crossed the Atlantic without cargo, the transportation of salt involved no added expense. They were now asked to buy salt in America, at a price that included carrying charges and a profit for the carrier, and refusal could be punished by exclusion from the harbors where the fish was cured and dried.

In this case, the struggle against the monopoly was not conducted chiefly by the representatives of the bourgeoisie in the Commons, but by the fishermen on the rocky shores of Newfoundland. It was a campaign of passive resistance and sabotage that continued for a decade, paralleling the struggle in England for control of the Virginia Company, and exerting an even greater influence on the whole course of English colonial development.

The opposition in the Commons contained the seeds of the role that the bourgeoisie would play in the American Revolution. But the conflict in Newfoundland planted the seeds of popular resistance to English domination, and created the preconditions for the removal of the fishermen and a substantial part of the industry, from England to Massachusetts.

John Guy was sent out by the new company in 1610. He was ordered to export "twelve months victualles with munition, nets and with all manner of tooles and implements." It was planned to sell pine boards for the mending of fishing boats. Guy's instructions spoke specifically of salt, "which you shall unloade and lay it in your warehouses to be readie there for our use to be used in fishing or to be sold to ye fishermen." But the most interesting part of Guy's instructions relates to his handling of the fishermen:

> Upon your first arrival there the sooner to operate our patent and to prevent ye murmuring of suspicious and jealous persons that perhaps will not (fail) to spread abroad that this enterprize will be to the prejudice of the fishermen as well of our nation as others, we do hould it expedient that you call an assembly of all the fishermen that shall be nere thereabouts . . .

The assembly was to hear the patent read, "that by the tenour of it they may be satisfied that there is no intent of depriving them of their former right of fishing." [16]

The fishermen listened and were unimpressed. The first indication that there was organized resistance to the company is to be found in an order issued on August 13, 1611. The fishermen were warned that further damage to the company's property would be punished severely. Detailed regulations covered everything from throwing ballast in the harbors to failing to leave drying stages in good condition, and penalties were set for every violation of the rules.[17]

Faced with a shrewd and consistent campaign of sabotage, the company made no progress in its efforts to establish profitable supervision of the labors of the fishermen. It was evident that this could not be accomplished without the founding of strong colonies, with enough police power to back up the legal authority of the royal charter. But the unruly opposition of the fishermen made it difficult, and expensive, to colonize in the area which they had pre-empted for their seasonal activities. Therefore, attention was directed to New England as a base for control of the fisheries and the exploitation of the comparatively unused fishing banks off Cape Cod and Nantucket.

The prelude to the drama of New England settlement took place in 1614, and arose from the shift in the crown's policy in that year. The king's break with the Commons encouraged the king's friends to hope that they could secure advantageous grants at the expense of the West Country. James was veering toward a pro-Spanish policy, which meant that adventures in the area of Spanish power in the New World would be discouraged. This might have an adverse effect on the Virginia settlement, but English interest in the fisheries was too well established to be called in question. And it was politically useful to the crown to curtail the power of the West Country and of the Sandys group in the Virginia Company. Since the attempt to impose direct control on the fishermen had failed, the way was open to other schemes.

Sir Ferdinando Gorges, the ambitious royalist who commanded the fortress at Plymouth, watched ships sail out each spring to return in the fall with Newfoundland cod or Spanish gold. After the failure of the Popham colony in Maine in 1608, Gorges had participated cautiously in transatlantic fishing and trading voyages, studying reports of American conditions, waiting for a favorable moment to make use of the patent rights derived from the 1606 charter. The situation seemed promising in the spring of 1614. John Smith, who was exiled from Virginia and whose loyalty to the court had been demonstrated in his writings, was eager to serve Gorges. The events that preceded the meeting of parliament early in April guaranteed that the session would deepen the rift between the king and the opposition. The festivities attending the scandalous marriage of the Earl of Somerset and Frances Howard left no doubt of the continuing influence of the Spanish clique. And the parliamentary elections left no doubt of the opposition's strength.

In April, as the "parliament of love" deteriorated into the "addled parliament," Smith sailed with two ships, the second vessel being under the command of Captain Thomas Hunt. Smith explored the coast and was struck by the advantages of a place called Accomack on the west side of Cape Cod Bay, which he described as "an excellent good harbor, good land, and no want of anything but industrious people." [18] The comment is noteworthy, for Accomack was Plymouth, where the Pilgrims settled a few years later.

One of the results of Smith's voyage was the substitution of English names for the Indian place-names. Smith claimed that the names he adopted were supplied by Prince Charles, who was then fifteen years old. In addition to Plymouth, the Charles River and Cape Ann owe their present nomenclature to the expedition in 1614. Smith's interest in names was largely motivated by the necessity of separating the region from its former association with Virginia: it had been called Northern Virginia, and Smith was thinking about politics and public relations in changing it to New England.

Smith returned with a cargo of furs and fish. But Captain Hunt, who remained at Cape Cod after Smith's departure to dry fish for the Spanish market, came back with another commodity—Indian slaves. Hunt had erected drying stages on the shores of Cape Cod Bay. Friendly Indians gathered to watch, and possibly to assist, the operation. As he was about to leave, Hunt persuaded twenty-four of the natives to come on board the ship. Courteously, he led them below decks, then clamped down the hatches and carried them to Spain, where a number of them were sold as slaves. A few of them reached England. One of these was Squanto, who was later sent back to America in a fishing boat, possessing a knowledge of English which was to prove invaluable to the voyager on the Mayflower.

There is a fascinating mystery concerning Squanto: he seems to have been employed by Gorges who spoke of him as "one of my Indians," and there is ground for suspicion that his chance appearance at Plymouth to aid the harassed settlement was not by chance at all, but was arranged by Gorges in order to utilize the Pilgrims for his own colonizing schemes.[19]

That is another story, and it belongs to a later time. There is no mystery about the plans that Gorges began to formulate in 1615. When Smith returned in August, he gave Gorges a careful account of his voyage. The "addled parliament" was over. James was preparing to grant the Cockayne Patent in an all-out drive to divert the profits of English trade and industry into his own hands. Gorges was also ready, on the basis of the information conveyed by Smith, to begin the drive to secure control of New England and its fisheries. The drive was to last until his death in 1647, and it was to leave a residue of territorial claims and privileges that were to cause strife throughout the colonial period and to be among the causes of the Revolution.

Gorges may be regarded as the leading architect of feudal proprietary rights in English America. The Baltimore family and many others secured far more extensive privileges and territories. But Gorges was one of the earliest and most energetic advocates of feudal prerogatives in the colonies; his proposals were made at a time when the king's difficulties with the opposition made him eager to find some method of colonization which would not give the bourgeoisie the advantages it had found in the Virginia Company.

Gorges' plan matured slowly. It was to be realized in the charter granted to the Council for New England in 1620. Gorges was playing for high stakes: the political uncertainties of the period from 1614 to 1618 made it inadvisable to show his hand. Gorges and his associates were operating under the old 1606 patent, which was wholly unsuited to their plans for securing monopolistic privileges on land and sea. The sea was of special importance on account of the fishing rights. The agitation against the Cockayne patent and its withdrawal early in 1617 made it impossible for James to convey the sweeping privileges that Gorges was angling to obtain.

As preparation for his ambitious scheme, Gorges aimed at establishing a small colony on the New England coast in the vicinity of Cape Cod, operating drying stages and sending fish to Spain: the accomplished fact would give some color of reason and necessity to the appeal to the crown for a new and all-inclusive patent. In line with this purpose, Smith sailed with two ships in 1615, with orders to leave a permanent settlement. But Smith's vessel was disabled, and returned to England for repairs. It set out again, but was captured by a French cruiser, Smith being taken to France as a prisoner. Gorges dispatched another ship in 1616, but it proved unseaworthy, and returned to England. In the spring of 1617, Smith came back from his French captivity. He had a brief meeting with Pocahontas and John Rolfe on their arrival from Virginia and then sailed with three small vessels. He was becalmed and returned to the home port.

These repeated attempts show that Gorges was exceedingly anxious to establish a settlement. But the repeated failures were not altogether accidental. Ships were crossing the ocean in increasing numbers, and it is hardly reasonable to suppose that it proved impossible, year after year, to transport enough people and supplies to Cape Cod for a settlement. The difficulty was in part due to Smith's incompetence; his career gives ample evidence that he was much more capable as a propagandist than as an organizer or explorer. But a deeper cause of the trouble lay in the inadequate preparation and limited financing of all the ventures. Gorges was operating very cautiously; he was apparently afraid to call public attention to his plans. The conflict in the Virginia Company and the growing strength of the Sandys forces, made it wise to avoid any move which would inevitably arouse the opposition of both the West Country and the Virginia stockholders.

Virginia was increasingly interested in the fisheries, and there was a good deal of contact between Jamestown and Newfoundland. Historiography has adopted an unsatisfactorily fragmentary approach to colonization, treating the various settlements as separate entities. This was not the contemporary viewpoint in England or in the colonies: it was evident that the Atlantic seaboard constituted an interdependent commercial area, which had its strongest economic base in the northern harbors, where hundreds of ships and thousands of people gathered every summer. During its seasonal activity, Newfoundland witnessed a lively exchange of goods and a Babel of languages that resembled the busiest marts of European trade. During the first lean years in Virginia, the fishermen frequently carried goods or settlers to Virginia, earning an extra income by calling at Jamestown before proceeding to the Grand Banks.[20]

When Richard Whitbourne visited Newfoundland in 1615, he noted that "three ships returning from the West Indies did arrive there . . . and so have divers others done at other times to my knowledge." He proposed opening Newfoundland to settlement in order to make it an important halfway station to New England, Virginia, Bermuda and the Caribbean Sea.[21]

In 1619, Rolfe reported to Sandys that the *George* had been sent to "New-found-land to trade and buy fishe for the better relief of the Colony and to make triall of that passage." She returned in about two months, with "so much fishe as will make a saving voyadge, which, beside the great relief, giveth much content to the wholl Colony."[22] Sandys endorsed the letter with a notation: "Cape Cod-fish larger than that of Nue-found-land,"[23] expressing a confidence in the superiority of the fish along the middle Atlantic coast that appears frequently in the records of the Virginia Company.

In December, 1618, as Sandys moved toward control of the Virginia corporation, the West Country launched a concurrent drive against the London and Bristol Company. The company's failure was evident. John Mason, who was later to form a partnership with Gorges, was sent out to replace Guy as the company's overseas representative in 1615, but he was as helpless as his predecessor in handling the rebellious fishermen. The West Country merchants wanted legal protection from further interference. They charged that the settlers sent out by the company usurped "the chiefest places of ffishinge there," that they stole goods belonging to the fishermen, and that they summoned a court of admiralty "in the chiefest tyme of ffishinge," and "exacted ffess of trayne and ffishe for not apperinge."[24]

The West Country interests were not strong enough to force the withdrawal of the charter. But the fishermen had proved strong enough to make the charter valueless: the company's settlements dwindled, its commerce collapsed, its fees could not be collected. By 1620, the accomplishments of the fishermen were listed as follows:

> Eight stages in several harbours worth at least in labour and cost £180 maliciously burned by certain English fishers . . . Great damage done by certain English fishers to a saw mill and a grist mill built by the plantacion . . . 5000 acres of wood burned maliciously by the fishers in the bay of Conception anno 1619 with many more thousands of acres burned and destroyed by them within these twenty years.[25]

The fishermen had won their fight. Having defeated the monopoly, they had prepared the way for the intimate contact they were soon to establish with Plymouth, and later with Massachusetts: their independent trade with these colonies led to New England's control of the sale of fish to the West Indies and South America and the rapid development of New England's shipbuilding industry. The fishermen moved from the West Country to Cape Ann, and the fishing fleets sailing out of Salem and Gloucester provided the cargoes for the tall ships that traversed all the oceans of the world.

We know little of the part that was played by the toilers of the sea in the development of the English colonies. There are reports of occasional economic disputes in which sailors and fishermen were engaged. The fishermen enjoyed certain benefits in the colonies: there was greater assurance of regular employment, a shorter voyage to the fishing grounds, and winter fishing kept them busy throughout the year. But the New England merchants were more brutal in driving a bargain than their colleagues in England, and they had greater political power. The fishermen continued to fish on shares. But the third which was customary for annual voyages from England was reduced to a portion varying from one-sixth to one-tenth in seventeenth century New England.[26] The reduction in living standards may not have been as severe as this figure would indicate: "References to the earnings of men engaged in the industry are so rare as to be practically nonexistent."[27]

Massachusetts legislation indicates that the fishermen were not satisfied with their lot. A law adopted in 1668, provided penalties for any member of a boat's crew who shall "refuse or neglect to obey the Order of the Master of the Vessel to which they belong, for the times and seasons of Fishing."[28] The following law was passed in 1679:

> It is Ordered by this Court & the Authority thereof, that all fishermen that are shipt upon a winter & spring voyage, shall duely attend the same, according to custome or agreement, with respect to time. And all Fishermen that are shipt upon a Fishing voyage for the whole Summer, shall not presume to break off their Voyage, before the last of October . . .[29]

A case tried in the Massachusetts courts in 1720 charged that a man named Holmes, who had bound himself to sail to Cape Sable on the schooner *King Fisher* as a fisherman on shares, had deserted and "was Instrumental to Cause others of the Crew to relinquish the Vessel." Holmes and another seaman were fined £250 and costs.[30]

A long historical process separates these colonial incidents from the trial of a fisherman's union in the United States District Court in Los Angeles in 1947. The government charged that Local 36 of the International Fishermen and Allied Workers of America, C.I.O., was guilty of a "wrongful and unlawful combination and conspiracy" to violate the law against monopolies which restrain trade or prevent competition.[31] It may seem strange that antitrust legislation which has proved ineffective in dealing with the giant corporations that control steel, copper, aluminum or oil, is applied with uncompromising severity against an association of fishermen seeking to get an equitable return for their hazardous and uncertain labor.

PART VI

The English Colonies

1618–1628

1 : THE FIRST SLAVE SHIP

On July 30, 1619, the House of Burgesses, the first representative assembly to meet in North America, was called to order in the church at Jamestown. American historiography has tended to treat the House of Burgesses as the beginning of "pure democracy" in the English colonies. Scholars have ignored the actual purpose and function of the Virginia assembly, and have failed to note any connection between the legislative gathering and another event that took place three weeks later—the arrival of a ship in the James River with twenty Negroes for sale.

The meeting of the House of Burgesses and the introduction of Negro labor were aspects of a single social-economic movement. In order to define this movement, we must examine the specific economic aims and interests which motivated the election of Sandys to the leadership of the Virginia Company.

We have described the choice of Sandys as treasurer on April 28, 1619, as a victory for the bourgeoisie. What did the bourgeoisie intend to accomplish through its control of the company? Its larger political aims were related to the European conflict, and the struggle between the crown and the commons in England. But the stockholders were immediately concerned with securing a profit from their overseas investment. Tobacco had made the land in Virginia valuable, but profit depended on efficient organization, cheap labor, and control of the tobacco market in England.

Captain Samuel Argall, who became governor in 1617, had been even more corrupt than previous governors. He may have realized when he left England with Rolfe that the reorganization of the company could not be long deferred. He used his position to get the largest gain in the shortest time. He stole the stores of grain that were given to the company as rental payments. He made private deals with ship captains for the disposal of tobacco and furs. He forced the company's servants, as well as many of the "ancient colony men" who were entitled to their freedom, to work for his personal advantage.

Sandys, reviewing Argall's conduct after his removal from the governorship, pointed out that at the time of his arrival, the portion of public land called the company's garden was yielding a profit of about £300 per year. Fifty-four servants were employed in the garden and the salt-works. The corn received from tenants and as tribute from the Indians amounted to over 1,200 bushels per year. The company also had 80 kine and 88 goats. When Argall left, escaping just before Yeardley's arrival early in 1619, the "whole estate of the public was gone and consumed, there being not left at that time to the Company either the land aforesaid or any tenant, servant, rent or tribute corn, cow or salt-work, and but six goats only, without one penny yielded to the Company for their so great loss in way of account or restitution to this very day."[1]

Smythe and other officials winked at Argall's peculations. They were not interested in the governor's corrupt practices, as long as their own source of income was guaranteed: their easiest profit came from the separate corporation transporting the colony's supplies. Smythe's son-in-law, Robert Johnson, was director of the magazine. When Sandys and his associates secured control of the company, they charged that Johnson had juggled the accounts so that money belonging to the company found its way into the magazine's funds. Johnson was accused of diverting £341 13*s* 4*d* in this way in 1617; in the following year, he appropriated most of the money due the company from the sale of tobacco grown on its land.[2]

Underlying the miscellaneous graft that characterized the Argall regime was a fundamental purpose: the manipulation of land titles in order to divert the profits of increasing tobacco production from the majority of the stockholders to a few privileged individuals. Argall, governing without any constitutional limitations on his authority, exercised life and death power, not only over servants and laborers, but over the land which they cultivated. His regime introduced feverish land speculation. Argall gave grants of land recklessly—but for substantial considerations—to individuals and groups. It was questionable whether the governor had legal authority to make these grants, but men who wished to secure valuable properties were not worried about legal niceties.

The Sandys group was determined to gain control of the land. Its plans for the distribution and ownership of property were embodied in the instructions given to Sir George Yeardley when he was sent out to replace Argall late in 1618. The instructions are so comprehensive that they are sometimes described as a new "charter" of colonial rights.

The instructions accused Argall and the clique that worked with him of securing land by illegal grants:

> We understand that certain persons having procured such Grants in general Words to themselves and their Associates or to like Effect have corruptly of late endeavoring for gain and Worse respects to draw many of the ancient Planters . . . to take grants also of them and thereby to become associated unto them with intent also by such means to overstrengthen their party. And thereupon have adventured on divers Enormous Courses tending to the great hurt and hindrance of the Colony Yea and have also made Grants of like Association to Masters of Ships and Mariners never intending there to inhabit . . .[3]

Yeardley was ordered to cancel "a charter of Land granted to Captain Samuel Argal and his Associates . . . forasmuch as the same was obtained by slight and cunning."[4]

The instructions to Yeardley dealt with three forms of tenure: (1) land held by the company or its officials; (2) grants of 50 or 100 acres to individuals who had completed their term of service or had come to the colony at their own expense; (3) grants of extensive areas to subsidiary companies or associations.

Under the first heading, the stockholders were concerned with the general welfare of the company and the necessity of providing for the support of the governor, the clergy and local magistrates. The settled part of Virginia was divided into "four Cities or Burroughs," to be known as Jamestown, Charles City, Henrice and Kecoughtan. In each of these, 3,000 acres was reserved for the company's use, to be farmed by tenants sent out at the company's expense. The tenants were to receive half the profits of their labor, the other half going to the company.

At Jamestown, 3,000 acres was given for the support of the governor and his successors. At Henrice, 10,000 acres was granted for building and endowing a "College for the Children of the Infidels."

Under the second heading were the provisions dealing with the rights of old settlers or persons who paid their own transportation to Virginia. "The ancient Adventurers and Planters," who had come to the colony at their own expense prior to the departure of Governor Dale, were given one hundred acres of land, and if they were shareholders in the company they received an additional grant of equal size for each share. Those who had come to the colony before 1616 at the company's charge were to receive one hundred acres after their term of service on the public land had expired. Persons who came to the colony at their own expense after the date of Dale's departure were to receive fifty acres. There was no specific provision for a distribution of land to the tenants transported by the company in the period after 1616.

Of far greater importance to the stockholders was the third form of tenure. Argall's operations in juggling land grants proved that "associations," often formed with visiting sea captains as dummy directors, were a means of securing valuable plantations and defrauding the company. The first patent of this kind was probably the one held by Argall to which special and unflattering reference is made in the instructions.[5]

The core of the stockholders' plan was the regularization of these grants so that they could be controlled by the stockholders—"That no patents or Indentures of Grants of Land in Virginia be made and sealed but in a full General and Quarter Court the same having been first thoroughly perused and Approved *under* hands of A Select Committee for that purpose."[6]

Thus the subsidiary corporation, chartered and protected by the main body in much the same way that the modern state charters and protects corporations, was the means by which the English bourgeoisie hoped to assure its profit from its Virginia lands. Since the land had to be cultivated in order to bring a return and aid the colony's commercial growth, land ownership and the availability of labor were linked together in the head-right system: a bonus of fifty acres, with a promise of fifty more at the time of the second division, was given for every person transported to Virginia, "if he continue there three years or dye in the mean time after he is Shiped."[7]

The subsidiary corporations were to prove unsuccessful, and were to give way, after a few years, to individual holdings. But the head-right system prepared the way for the development of large plantations, obtained by the simple multiplication of acreage in terms of the number of servants imported from England.

The political change in the administration of the colony instituted by the meeting of the House of Burgesses was designed to reinforce the new system of land tenure. There is no mention of an assembly in the instructions given to Yeardley; the authorization was contained in a separate document delivered to the governor before he left for Virginia; but the original paper is not preserved, and we know it only by a transcript which is supposedly a true copy of the original, dated July 23, 1621.

Since the stockholders, acting through subsidiary corporations, were securing land in the colony, they wanted local representation for themselves or their representatives. The House of Burgesses was composed, to a considerable extent, of delegates from the corporate plantations. It was constituted as an embryonic parliament, consisting of a council of state (the governor and his council) and two burgesses chosen by the inhabitants of each town, hundred or "particular plantation." Of the twenty representatives attending the first meeting, eight came from the four boroughs, and the other twelve came from six joint-stock plantations. Thus the majority of the body spoke for the absentee owners of these estates. The voiceless population of the plantations was made up almost entirely of servile labor. The records of Berkeley Hundred, for example, show that all the residents with the exception of the governor were under indentures for three to eight years.[8]

With the transfer of land from the company to the private plantation, owned by a group or by an individual, the control of labor became a matter of special concern to the landholders. The colonial assembly was chiefly interested, not in "democratic" rights, but in guaranteeing the master's unrestricted use of the servant's labor power. The House of Burgesses passed the first of the long series of colonial laws designed to reduce the servant to virtual slavery. Punishment was prescribed for anyone guilty of "inticing awaye the Tenants or Servants of any particular plantation." [9] A "maide or woman servant" could not marry without permission.[10] Severe penalties were imposed on a servant who escaped from his master:

> Be it enacted by this present assembly that whatsoever servant hath heretofore or shall heretoafter contracte himself in England, either by way of Indenture or otherwise, to serve any Master here in Virginia and shall afterward, against his said former contracte depart from his Mr. without

leave, or, being once imbarked shall abandon the ship he is appointed to come in, and so, being lefte behinde, shall putt himselfe into the service of any other man that will bring him hither, that then at the same servant's arrival here, he shall first serve out his time with Mr. that brought him hither and afterward also shall serve out his time with his former Mr. according to his convenant.[11]

The provision for serving extra time in case of a dispute left the servant with no legal protection against anyone who claimed him. According to the rule adopted by the House of Burgesses, the servant could be bound "by way of indenture or otherwise"; he could be committed by a verbal agreement, and proof rested solely on the master's word.

The interest displayed by the House of Burgesses in the problem of servile labor explains the welcome which was accorded to the slave ship when it entered the river with its cargo. In most histories of the United States, the arrival of the Dutch vessel is treated as a matter of chance. Oliver Perry Chitwood informs us that the slaves "were huddled together in close quarters, and the settlers bought them largely out of kindness." [12]

The settlers obviously had other motives than kindness, and the Dutch ship did not arrive altogether by chance. It is not altogether certain that the Dutch captain sold the Negroes: he was accompanied by an English vessel, and it is not improbable that the Englishmen carried and sold the slaves, and falsified the record in order to conceal the transaction.

The case was a *cause célèbre* in England during the following year, involving the Virginia Company, the European war and momentous issues of English foreign policy. The problem did not arise because the Negroes were *slaves;* it related solely to the fact that they were contraband property, seized, probably by force, from their Spanish owners. Therefore, the crown's negotiations with Spain were affected, and the king could use the case as a means of proving that the Virginia Company was engaged in illegal activities which endangered the government's foreign policy.

The English ship that arrived in the James River with a Dutch consort in August, 1619, was the *Treasurer*. She was the same vessel that had captured Pocahontas in 1613 and conducted the raids against French settlements in the north in that year. The *Treasurer* was still owned by Lord Robert Rich, who had recently become the Earl of

Warwick by making the customary payment of £10,000 to the king.

Warwick sent the ship across the Atlantic in 1618, when his protégé, Argall, was still governor of Virginia. At that time, there was no difficulty in providing the ship with supplies, and recruiting additional personnel, at Jamestown. The *Treasurer* then proceeded to the Spanish Main, where it fell into the company of a Dutch man-of-war. Having taken some prizes, and secured some Negro slaves by unknown means, the two ships returned to Jamestown. But the situation there was changed. Argall had fled. Governor Yeardley, knowing that the crown was seeking any excuse to attack the new administration of the company, could not afford to welcome the visitors.

The two ships were greeted with a marked lack of hospitality. The *Treasurer* was in urgent need of water and supplies. But she was not permitted to remain long enough to meet these necessities. The transaction concerning the Negroes is obscure. Rolfe tells us that the governor and the Cape merchant bought the twenty Negroes from the Dutch captain in exchange for food, "at the best and easyest rate they could." [13] But both ships carried slaves, and Rolfe may have been anxious to protect the *Treasurer* from the charge of engaging in contraband trade.[14]

The *Treasurer* still carried fourteen Negroes when it reached Bermuda, "so weather beaten and torn as never like to put to sea again." [15] She was safe in Bermuda, which was still governed by a representative of the Earl of Warwick. The governor, Nathaniel Butler, wrote prudently to his patron that he thought it best, "for fear of prejudicing your lordship," to put the Negroes to work on the company's lands, promising to "quietly turn them over to your lordship" at a later date. The last sentence of the governor's letter is eloquent in its simplicity: "I humbly thank your lordship for my two." [16]

We need not follow the course of the later complications that developed around the case of the *Treasurer* in England. It led to an angry controversy between Warwick and Sandys, and caused Warwick to align himself with Smythe in opposition to the Sandys group. We are here concerned with the sale of the Negroes in its relation to the labor system in Virginia. Superficially, the introduction of Negro workers made little difference in the colony's work pattern. These workers were indentured servants, for slavery did not exist in Virginia until about 1650, and was not legalized until about 1660. Negroes were listed as servants in the census enumerations in 1623 and 1624.[17]

The failure to distinguish between the slave and the servant is proof of the rigors of the indenture system. The subordination of the white servant was so complete that it was not necessary to place the Negro in a separate category. Some idea of what the system meant in terms of human degradation and suffering may be obtained by an examination of the lists of persons transported to Virginia, and the death rate among them.

As soon as Sandys and his friends took control of the company, they began the organization of subsidiary corporations. Six patents had been granted before Sandys' election. Forty-four were issued during the next four years. Each of the patents covered an extensive area, and involved a promise "to transport one hundred men att the least." [18]

The company and the various subsidiaries began to send large numbers of workers to the colony. Eleven ships sailed in 1619, bringing 1,261 persons to Virginia. Some of these came as tenants, but the majority were indentured servants. The tenants had only slight advantages over the servants; they were under similar controls, and the demands upon their time and labor were only slightly less burdensome.

Ninety women were sent over in 1619, the first of a series of shipments of prospective wives, to be sold for 120 pounds of tobacco to cover the cost of their transportation. The ninety maids, like the fifty *Danae* in the Greek myth, were the victims of fate—and the laws of commerce. It was difficult to prevent the girls from exercising some freedom of choice: their tendency to marry servants was deplored by the company in a letter sent to the colony with a later shipment:

> Though we are desirous that marriage be free according to the law of nature, yett would we not have these maids deceived and married to servants, but only to such freemen or tenants as have means to mainteine them.[19]

The moral problem of freedom of marital choice was bound up in the system of indenture, which also degraded the family and inflicted special penalties on the woman. Servants were not allowed to marry without the master's consent. Permission was often withheld, because marriage might make the servant less tractable or efficient. A woman was useless during part of the period of pregnancy and for a time after the birth of the child. The master had the right to exact an additional term of service to compensate him for the loss of time. This rule tended to increase the sexual use of indentured women by the master or members of his family. The woman could be penalized with extra labor for her "sin," and her period of service could be extended to cover the time "wasted" in bearing children.

Another aspect of the moral problem was the transportation of teen-age boys. One hundred of these "apprentices" were sent out in 1619 by the City of London, which provided the sum of £5 for each boy's clothing and shipment. The money was collected from various parishes, and from private donations. Sandys found the plan satisfactory, and tried to extend it to other parts of England, asking justices of the peace to send boys over fifteen years of age who were a burden to the community.[20] The suggestion was not carried out, possibly because the boys sent from London put up such determined resistance. They were confined at Bridewell while awaiting shipment. The second contingent in 1620 refused to leave, and it was necessary to procure a warrant from the Privy Council to take them to the vessels by force.[21]

The mortality among the workers sent to Virginia was so great that the labor force was continually depleted. Since it was necessary to make a profit on the transportation of servants and tenants, as well as on their labor in Virginia, they were given inadequate food on shipboard; they were weakened even before their arrival in the colony by living in crowded cabins, on a dangerously insufficient diet. The same unhealthy conditions obtained in the colony. The food for workers toiling from daylight to dusk was often reduced to a pint and a half of "musty meal for a man a day." [22]

There was nothing mysterious, or unavoidable, about the appalling death rate that resulted. Shortly after the Indian massacre in 1622, John Wroth compiled figures on the mortality during the previous years. There had been about 700 people in the colony when the Sandys group took control. From 1619 to 1622, Wroth calculated that 3,560 or 3,570 persons were transported to Virginia, so that there should have been about 4,270 people in the settlements at the time of the Indian attack. But there were only about 1,240. "It Consequentlie followes, that wee had then lost 3000 persons within those 3 yeares." [23]

This represented, of course, a very serious loss of manpower to the colony. But the stockholders would not consider providing better food or medical care for the workers, or modifying the relentless exploitation of the diminishing work force. The pressure on the stockholders to obtain a quick return was increased by the political difficulties which they faced in England.

The company's conflict with the king involved the competition between Virginia tobacco and the Spanish product. The Spanish leaf was considered superior; it sold at a slightly higher price, and appealed to a more aristocratic clientele. Therefore, class relationships in England, as well as foreign policy, were affected by the struggle to establish an English market for Virginia tobacco. During the period from 1619 to 1622, the volume of import from the American colonies (Virginia and Bermuda) amounted to a total of 238,562 pounds. However (and this reveals the seriousness of the political and economic issue) imports from Spain for the same period totalled 411,917 pounds.[24]

As soon as Sandys became treasurer of the company, the crown showed its displeasure by doubling the tax on Virginia tobacco. Spanish imports had paid a duty of 2*s* per pound, while Virginia had paid only 6*d*. The amount for Virginia was suddenly raised 1*s*. The company protested that the increase was contrary to the provisions of the royal charter, but the government disregarded the protest.

As James proceeded with his plans for the Spanish alliance, he increased the pressure on the Virginia Company. Early in 1621, the king gave an exclusive monopoly of tobacco importation, tax collection and distribution, for one year, to a syndicate headed by Sir Thomas Roe. Roe, a prominent London financier and diplomat, proceeded to give marked preference to Spanish tobacco.[25]

James also interfered directly in the affairs of the Virginia company. On May 17, 1620, he sent a message to the stockholders recommending that they select another treasurer to replace Sandys. This unprecedented violation of the corporate rights guaranteed by the charter was accompanied by a list of four persons who were satisfactory to the crown: Sir Thomas Smythe, Sir Thomas Roe, Alderman Johnson, and Morris Abbott.[26]

The names speak for themselves. They must have spoken eloquently to the embattled stockholders. Smythe had just been ousted. Roe was the owner of the obnoxious patent giving him a monopoly of tobacco. Johnson was Smythe's son-in-law. Abbott was the brother-in-law of the archbishop of Canterbury. The election of any one of these men would have destroyed all that Sandys had tried to accomplish.

The company refused to obey the royal request. It deferred the election, and sent a committee to confer with the king. James had evidently thought that his letter would frighten enough of the stockholders to assure the election of one of his candidates. But he could not afford to risk an open fight, which might expose his weakness and defeat his delicate dealings with Spain. He followed his usual habit of planned indecision. He said that the names he had proposed were merely suggestions; he would not tolerate the election of Sandys, but would not interfere with any other choice. If James supposed that this concession would be reciprocated by the election of someone opposed to Sandys, he was badly mistaken. The company met on June 28, and elected the Earl of Southampton, one of Sandys' closest co-workers, who was sure to work under his direction.

A few days later, the company made a strong protest against the monopoly granted to the Roe syndicate, which was limiting combined imports from Virginia and Bermuda to 55,000 pounds, considerably less than the amount imported in the previous year. When the protest was rejected, the company decided to sell the year's crop in the Netherlands: the English quota of 55,000 pounds was given to Bermuda, which had sufficient production to supply the whole amount. The Virginia crop went to Holland, where the town of Middleburg agreed to admit it at a tariff of only a halfpenny per pound.[27]

The company's assertion of its right to trade where it pleased was almost as significant as the struggle waged in the Commons against taxation without representation, and was as portentious for the future course of colonial development. The arrangement was made in August, 1620, at a time when the fate of the Bohemian revolution was still undecided. The crop was duly shipped to Middleburg in the fall. The power of the bourgeoisie and the court was so delicately balanced in England, that the government did not think it wise to interfere with the shipment.

However, the crown continued, and increased, the economic pressure on the company during 1621. This pressure, combined with the depletion of the labor force, was to a considerable extent responsible for the weakness of the colony, which made it possible for the Indians to undertake a general attack in 1622.

The area of tobacco production had been extended. But the colonial administration did not have the resources to take the most elementary steps for the protection of its territory. Rolfe wrote to Sandys in 1620 that the colony was defenseless and that something must be done about it quickly. It was decided to send an experienced military officer to organize fortifications and train soldiers. But the lack of money and difficulties with the government prevented this decision from being carried out. Captain William Nuce, selected for the job, was still in England in 1622, as letters from the colony assumed a tone of desperate pleading.

In spite of the lack of sufficient workers, the desire for profit led to the growth of straggling estates along the rivers. The attempt to make these lands productive placed heavier burdens on the available servants, and added to the toll of sickness. Many plantations were "reduced to a small band, weak in numbers and in provisions for defense. To add to their difficulties, there was an astonishing shortage of arms and munition." [28]

These circumstances account for the Indian attack in 1622. The social development of the colony from the time of the first meeting of the House of Burgesses and the arrival of the slave ship made a clash with the Indians increasingly inevitable. It is a general law of colonial history that Indian warfare occurs at periods of maximum internal tension in the colonial society; this is true of the whole series of bloody conflicts with the Indians in which the English settlements were engaged during the seventeenth and eighteenth centuries, since the Indians were in commercial contact with the Europeans, chiefly through the fur trade, but also through the exchange of Indian handicrafts and food for manufactured goods and occasional day-labor, the natives were affected by economic pressures in the European community.

From 1619 to 1622, the Indians saw the English fields expanding on the fertile banks of the river. At the same time, they were tricked and cheated in the sale of furs and other mercantile transactions. They were engaged in illegal dealings with the disaffected servants and tenants. They knew the colony's weakness, and the discontent among the lower classes.

Their experiences taught them that they could not hope for any honest agreement with the settlers. They chose the best time for an attempt to wipe out the colony. The attack was carefully prepared. All the outlying plantations were assaulted simultaneously on March 22, 1622. The attack caused the death of 347 persons. In terms of loss of life, the destruction that had systematically resulted, year in and year out, from fever, overwork and malnutrition was ten times as great as the more dramatic damage wrought by the tomahawks of the Indians.

It was only by desperate efforts that the colony was able to survive the blow. The people who were able to escape tried to reach Jamestown. The defense of the town was organized in time to prevent its capture, but it was crowded with refugees, for whom there was no accommodations or provisions. It was impossible to plant the spring crop. After fifteen years, Virginia was in a plight that was almost as desperate as the first season of plague and hunger.

The colonists managed to resist the Indian attack, and they took bloody vengeance on the natives. They utilized the massacre as "proof" that the Indians were inhumanly cruel, and that any brutality was justified in dealing with them. This concept, which was already part of the pattern of colonial thought, provided an ethical argument for the seizure of the Indian's land without compensation. There is almost a note of triumph in Edward Waterhouse's comment on the event:

> Because our hands which before were tied by gentleness and fair usage, are now set at liberty by the treacherous violence of the Savages, not untying the Knot, but cutting it. So that we, who hitherto have had possession of no more ground than their waste, and our purchase at a valuable consideration to their own contentment gained; may now by right of War, and law of Nations, invade the Country, and destroy those who sought to destroy us.[29]

Waterhouse describes the comparative ease with which the war can be conducted.

> Victorie of them may bee gained many waies; by force, by surprize, by famine in burning their Corne, by breaking their fishing Weares . . . by pursuing and chasing them with our horses, and blood-Hounds to draw after them, and Mastives to tear them . . .[30]

These methods are described in the earliest known piece of American verse to be printed, a ballad sent to England and published as a broadside. George Sandys, Sir Edwin's brother, is singled out for praise:

> Stout Master George Sandys upon a night,
> did bravely venture forth;
> And mong'st the savage murtherers,
> did forme a deed of worth,

For finding many by a fire,
to death their lives they pay:
Set fire of a Towne of theires,
And brevely came away.[31]

George Sandys, who was treasurer and director of industry at Jamestown from 1621 to 1625, was engaged in a significant cultural undertaking at the time of the massacre. He was completing a translation of the fifteen books of Ovid's *Metamorphoses.* Although this work was done on American soil and contains many references to the American environment, there is some doubt as to whether it can properly be said to "belong to American literature." [32]

Sandys' translation was one of the most influential books written during the seventeenth century. It was this translation "bred in the New-World," that brought Ovid to Milton and Keats.[33] It has been called "the greatest repository of allegorized myth in English." [34]

There is a suggestive contrast between Sandys' scholarly Latin studies and the fury which he displayed in setting fire to an Indian village. But the choice of Ovid as the subject of translation provides a link between the life of the sedentary scholar and his attack on the Indians. Ovid was the poet of Rome's Augustan age, reflecting a society drunk with power, decadent and amoral, sensitive to every nuance of sensual experience and contemptuous of ethical values. The *Metamorphoses* have none of the dignity of Aesop's *Fables.* Ovid compares animals to people in order to deride humanity, to mock human infirmities and suggest the lust and corruption of all mankind. The mythology of the barnyard replaced the social allegories of the older myths.

Ovid's influence on the culture of the English upper class increased during the seventeenth century. After the Cromwellian Revolution, Ovid was a sanctuary for the demoralized intellectual, a means of converting disillusionment with the revolution into a sort of aristocratic nihilism.

It is noteworthy that Sandys was engrossed in Ovid at a time when the system of plantation labor—and the concurrent brutal mistreatment of the Indian population—was assuming its distinctive historical character. Sandys filled his notes and comments on Ovid with allusions to the flora and fauna of the New World. But this attitude toward the social organization of the colony is suggested in a passage concerning the yokels metamorphosed into frogs: Sandys observed that the frogs in Virginia were called "Powhatan's hounds" by the English:

> . . . They croake and ride one another in shallow plashes; so Pesants baule and gamball at their meetings; soused in liquor, so frogs in the water. It is worth the observation, that a frog, though she have her heart and liver puld out, will skip up and down notwithstanding.[35]

Sandys heard the sounds of the swamp and forest. But for him the poorer classes were no more important than frogs. And it was a happy deed of courage to burn women and children in an Indian village.

In England, John Donne preached a sermon to the Virginia Company, which embodied an official government viewpoint toward the massacre. In his earlier years, Donne had been a poet, speaking of love's delight—

> Love's mysteries in souls do grow
> But yet the body is his book.

As the political skies darkened, Donne turned from the body to the soul, from poetry to the more profitable composition of clerical prose. In 1615, the year of the Cockayne patent, he entered the service of the church. His advancement was rapid. His cadenced sermons were highly praised. In 1621, the king made him dean of St. Paul's.

Donne addressed a meeting of the Virginia stockholders:

> Be not you discouraged, if the promises you have made to yourselves, or to others, be not so soon discharged; though you see not your money, though you see not your men, though a flood, a flood of blood, have broken in upon them, be not discouraged . . . Only let your principal end be the propagation of the Glorious Gospel.

Donne pointed out that, although the plantation was not as yet profitable, it had served great purposes, redeeming many from the hands of the executioner, taking idle persons and their children from the streets: "It is already, not only a spleen, to drain ill humours of the body, but a liver, to breed good blood." Donne pointed to the essential connection between religion and profits, assuring his hearers that they "may well consist together."[36]

Under Donne's pious phraseology was an explicit message: he was telling the stockholders to regard the massacre as a divine judgment for their sins. The grace of God, and much profit, would be theirs if they turned from their evil ways and bowed to the king as the representative of the divine will.

The stockholders did not heed Donne's advice. They continued their struggle to maintain their rights against the arbitrary power of the crown. Included in the "freedom" for which they fought was the merciless exploitation of slaves and laborers, the theft of Indian lands, and the subjugation or extermination of Indians who rejected the "blessings of civilization."

The ship that arrived in 1619 had brought only a few dark-skinned laborers to dig in the tobacco fields. Yet it also brought an unwritten indenture, a contract that promised sweat and toil, and unimaginable suffering, to unborn generations.

2 : THE ACCIDENT OF THE WIND

IT IS OFTEN assumed that it was an accident, caused by unfavorable winds and tides, that brought the *Mayflower* to the wintry shores of Cape Cod when the ship had intended to land in northern Virginia.

Whatever the truth of the matter—and the whole truth may never be known—the obscure intrigue surrounding the voyage presents a fascinating problem, not merely as a historical detective story (with a question mark for its conclusion), but as a revelation of the forces and interests that shaped the early development of Plymouth.

We have told how the patent was granted hastily by the Virginia Company to John Wynkoop in May, 1619. The patent was not used, because the uncertainties of the English and European situation made the London merchants who were asked to finance the venture exceedingly chary concerning the safety of their investment. The merchants were good Puritans; by the same token, they were good businessmen. The terms upon which they insisted were dictated, to a considerable extent, by their knowledge of the uncertain fortunes of the Virginia Company and the fact that the crown would not look with favor on a Puritan colony in the territories controlled by the company.

The arrangement under which the Plymouth settlers pooled their labor has been inaccurately described as a "communist" experiment. It was, on the contrary, a contract which subjected the colonists to harsh exploitation. It may best be described as a group indenture, assigning the collective labor of the whole community to the financiers who backed the enterprise. In return for the cost of transporation, the voyagers had to invest the only thing they had, their labor-power, which they assigned *in toto* for the usual period of individual identure, seven years. The assignment entitled the individual to one share of stock, at a par value of £10. The merchants who financed the company would buy as much stock as they wished at the same price. The money went into a central treasury, from which all expenses were met, including the food and clothing and tools of the colonists. At the end of seven years, the assets were to be divided among all the holders of shares—investors in England and colonists in America.

This was the offer that was made by the London group, and the negotiations dragged on into the spring of 1620. The members of the Leyden Congregation had no objection to assigning part of their labor-power. The rub came in the demand that they give up *all of it*. They insisted that they be allowed to work for themselves two days each week, and that each individual retain permanent ownership of houses and improvements built by his labor.

Since the controversy seemed to have reached an *impasse* in the middle of 1620, and the time for making a transatlantic passage in the summer of that year was rapidly passing, the congregation split into two groups: the majority voted to stay in Holland. A small number led by Carver, Brewster and Bradford, decided to proceed with the undertaking. Arriving at Southampton, England, late in July, they were met by Thomas Weston, representing the London financiers. Weston had obtained a new patent from the Virginia Company to replace the Wynkoop patent.

Weston demanded that the Pilgrims sign the agreement he had prepared—embodying the terms to which they had all along objected. The Pilgrims refused to sign unless the document was changed to conform to their wishes. Since Weston would not help them discharge their financial obligations until he had their signatures, they were forced to sell thirty or forty tubs of butter that had been brought from Holland in order to pay bills they incurred during the delay in England. However, Weston and his friends were still paying for the ship and its supplies, evidently feeling sure that the Puritans would be compelled to meet their terms. The transatlantic colony could not exist without getting goods from England, and no one was likely to supply goods on credit. So Weston watched the ship sail, and put the unsigned contract in his pocket.

The fact that the vessel sailed without the Pilgrims having signed the contract is a further indication of the political and economic uncertainties that surrounded the expedition. The leaders of the voyage undoubtedly hoped that they could avoid accepting the obligations that Weston sought to impose on them, and this hope may have been in some degree related to the ship's arrival at a place outside the jurisdiction of the Virginia Company, and not included in Weston's patent.

There are two widely accepted myths concerning the *Mayflower:* there is the legend that the motivation for the voyage was predominantly religious, and the related assumption that the passengers constituted a cohesive and democratic group. Both myths dissolve when we examine the social composition of the passengers. Of the 102 colonists on the *Mayflower,* only 35 were members of the Leyden congregation. The other 67 persons were recruited, without any great selectivity, in London; they had no religious or social ties with the Puritans.

There were class differences among the passengers. As far as the Leyden group was concerned these distinctions had existed in Holland, where a few members of the congregation were comfortably above the dead level of poverty on which the majority lived. Bradford, for example, was a member of a well-to-do family in Yorkshire. When he went into exile in Holland, he still owned property in Yorkshire, and the sale of his English holdings enabled him to set up a modest silk business in Leyden. William Brewster, who was to be closely associated with Bradford in the leadership of the Plymouth colony, had supported himself in Holland by teaching English. He had also owned a printing press in partnership with Thomas Brewer, publishing books that were banned in England.

The class distinctions among the people on the *Mayflower* are most clearly indicated in the presence of servants. Bradford's list of the passengers includes 24 family groups, and ten single men. Eight of the families had from one to three servants. Each servant was worth a single share of stock to his master, or a double share if the master paid for his equipment and transportation. Children over sixteen years of age were counted in the same way, and those between ten and sixteen rated half a share.

It may seem strange that the Puritans, who had been impelled to leave Holland in order to protect their children from the corrupting effects of child labor, did not object to the transportation of children as servants. Charles Edward Banks observes that "a number of the passengers on the *Mayflower,* particularly among the London contingent, brought over minors classed as 'servants' or 'boys' of no known kinship to their masters, and it may be supposed they were picked up in London with the consent of the authorities." [1] The number of these persons is not known, nor is there any record of the way in which they were "picked up."

Banks notes that three children, Richard, Jasper and Elinor More (she is called Ellen in Bradford's list) were assigned to three different families. Jasper and the girl died soon after their arrival, but Richard lived in Plymouth for more than sixty years. He made a deposition in 1684, saying that prior to the voyage he had been a member of the household of Thomas Weston, ironmonger, in London, and "was thense transported to New Plymouth in New England." [2]

These young people were the forerunners of hundreds of children, seized on the streets of London, or sold or transferred from homes where they had been placed at service, and carried across the Atlantic to labor in "free" New England.

The *Mayflower Compact* has been given even more significance than the first meeting of the Virginia House of Burgesses, as a pioneering step toward "pure democracy." The document signed on shipboard by the heads of families, agreeing to form themselves into a "body politic" is important as the first of the "plantation agreements" which were later utilized to establish local governments in Rhode Island and Connecticut. The passengers on the *Mayflower* found it necessary to make a compact, because they were about to settle in a region that was outside the jurisdiction of existent charters. In drawing the document, they followed the conventional language, used in contemporary charters or articles of association. The agreement was daring, only in the sense that it lacked governmental authorization.

The essential interest of the *Mayflower Compact* lies in the movement of political and economic forces that seems to have carried the ship off its intended course.

In his history *Of Plimouth Plantation,* Bradford tells us that after a stormy passage, the *Mayflower* chanced to reach Cape Cod; consultation among the passengers and with the master of the ship led to the decision to sail southward, "to finde some place aboute Hudsons river for their habitation." But the ship "fell amongst dangerous soulds and roring breakers," and it seemed wise to return to the cape and remain there.[3] Apparently, it was "God's will" that led to the settlement in New England, far from the northern Virginia land to which the patent secured by the Pilgrims entitled them.

It was also "God's will" that occasioned another historical "accident" in the spring of 1621. At a moment when the colony faced extinction, it was saved by the arrival of two friendly Indians, Samoset and Squanto, who spoke English and secured the aid and friendship of the neighboring tribes for the desperate settlers. Bradford speaks of Squanto as "a septiall instrument sent of God for their good beyond their expectation."[4]

The drama underlying the *Mayflower's* voyage has none of the classic unity of time and place: it covers years of explorations and political maneuvers, unclearly motivated, involving an ill-assorted cast of characters—the familiar figure of John Smith appears prominently among the *dramatis personae;* the royalist politician, Sir Ferdinando Gorges, and the Indian, Squanto, play vital roles; subordinate characters include the sea captains, Thomas Hunt and Thomas Dermer; a puzzling part is assigned to Christopher Jones, commander of the *Mayflower,* who apparently held the secret of the plot and never revealed it.

A commonly accepted theory concerning the *Mayflower's* chance arrival at Cape Cod is derived from Nathaniel Morton's *New-Englands Memoriall.* Morton, clerk and secretary of the Plymouth colony for fifty years after his arrival in 1623, asserted as a fact, of which he had personal knowledge, that Captain Jones was bribed by the Dutch to prevent the Pilgrims from carrying out their intention of landing in the vicinity of the Hudson River. Morton wrote:

> Nevertheless, it is to be observed, that their putting into this place was partly by reason of a storm, by which they were forced in, but more especially by the fraudulency and contrivance of the aforesaid Mr. *Jones,* the Master of the Ship; for, their Intention, as is before-noted, and Engagement, was to *Hudsons River,* but some of the *Dutch* having notice of their intentions, and having thoughts about the same time of erecting a Plantation there likewise, they fraudulently hired the said *Jones* by delayes while they were in *England,* and now under pretence of the danger of the Sholes, *etc.* to disappoint them in their going thither.[5]

Morton wrote some forty years after the event, and he gave no clue to the source of what he called the "late and certain intelligence" on which he based his statement. It is not improbable that representatives of Holland exerted some influence on Captain Jones. The expedition started from the Netherlands, and the Dutch must have taken more than a desultory interest in an attempt to colonize territories in which they had already established trading posts and to which they claimed prior ownership.

But whether or not Holland bribed the *Mayflower's* commander to keep away from the Hudson, there were certainly people in England who were interested in the destination of the voyage. Sir Ferdinando Gorges and a group of court favorites associated with him had been attempting to secure a foothold in New England for many years. We have discussed the voyages sponsored by Gorges and commanded by John Smith and other adventurers, which explored the New England coast from 1614 to 1619.

We have mentioned that Smith, visiting Plymouth in 1614, commented on the excellence of the harbor; Captain Thomas Hunt, who visited Cape Cod with Smith, captured a number of Indians; one of these was Squanto, who was taken to England. He was evidently given to Gorges, who referred to him as "one of my Indians." In the next year, Smith attempted to across the Atlantic again. One of the two ships that sailed under his command was in charge of Captain Thomas Dermer. Smith's vessel was disabled and he returned to England; but Dermer continued to Newfoundland. Little is known of his activity during the next two years, but he seems to have remained in Newfoundland. At some time during this period, Squanto, for unexplained reasons, was sent to Newfoundland in a fishing boat.

In the latter part of 1618, Dermer and Squanto returned to England. Dermer was closeted with Gorges; the conversation, according to Gorges, involved "particulars of highest consequences and best consideration." [6]

That conversation introduced a far more active phase of Gorges' New England plans. We do not know what was said, but we know that the situation in England made it possible, and imperative, that Gorges proceed more vigorously with his American project. Sandys was moving to full control of the Virginia Company. The king was moving toward a *rapprochement* with Spain. James wanted men whom he could trust in charge of the further development of transatlantic colonies.

The news that Dermer brought from Newfoundland may have related to the failures of the London and Bristol Company, the stubborn resistance of the West Country fishermen, and the consequent uncertainty and tension in the northern fisheries.

One of Gorges' own ships was placed at Dermer's service, and he was sent back to America, taking Squanto with him. This was early in 1619. Dermer was instructed to go to Plymouth, to explore the surrounding region more thoroughly than had been possible on previous occasions and to make friendly contact with the Indians through Squanto. Dermer performed his assignment. He was guided by Squanto in examining the surroundings of Plymouth. The area was unoccupied, for a plague had wiped out the entire Patuxet Tribe, of which Squanto had been a member. But two days' journey into the interior enabled Dermer to meet two Indian chiefs, who were probably Massasoit and his brother, Quadaquina.

This brings us to the nub of the mystery. Were Bradford and other leaders of the voyage in contact with Gorges and had they agreed on a plan to meet Dermer and Squanto at Cape Cod, in order to receive assistance in founding a settlement at Plymouth? There are two clues to the answer. One is the circumstantial evidence derived from the record of Dermer's activity during 1619 and 1620. The other is the inconclusive, but nonetheless suggestive, indication that Bradford had some contact with Gorges and some information concerning Dermer's movements, before the *Mayflower* sailed.

Dermer kept a journal, recounting his experiences, which he forwarded to Gorges. After his visit to Plymouth in 1619, Dermer went around Cape Cod to Martha's Vineyard, then cruised northeastward to the island of Monhegan. He went to Virginia (where he may have received dispatches from Gorges) late in 1619, returning to Plymouth early in 1620. Apparently Squanto joined him there in June.

Dermer sailed from Plymouth to Monhegan, but he returned to Cape Cod in July or August. Squanto was with him. Assuming that the Pilgrims had left England in July as they originally planned, they would have reached their destination late in August or September. But their departure was delayed. Meanwhile, Dermer went around the Cape to Martha's Vineyard, still accompanied by Squanto. He went ashore to trade with Indians, but was, according to Bradford's account, "betrayed & asaulted by them, & *all his men slaine, but one that* kept the boat."[7] Badly wounded, Dermer managed to regain his ship, and he was taken to Virginia, where he died.

Lincoln N. Kinnicutt thinks it probable that Dermer was at

Martha's Vineyard to await news of the *Mayflower's* coming: "It would have been almost impossible for a ship to approach Cape Cod from any direction without it being known, at least by the Indians, and Squanto was with Dermer as an interpreter." [8] But the plot—if any plot existed—took another turn with Dermer's death. When the ship made its belated arrival, Gorges' trusted emissary was being rushed to Virginia to receive medical care. Squanto left alone, had obvious reasons for being cautious about approaching the people who landed from the *Mayflower,* shortly after the neighboring Indians had shown such marked hostility toward English visitors.

Now let us turn to the other clue to the mystery—Bradford's possible knowledge of Dermer's plans. Bradford refers to a letter written by Dermer from Plymouth on June 30, and apparently addressed to Gorges. Bradford comments on the fact that "ther was but 4 months difference" between Dermer's sojourn at Plymouth and the arrival of the *Mayflower*.

In the letter, as quoted by Bradford, Dermer mentioned Squanto's service in protecting him from hostile Indians. Dermer wrote concerning Plymouth: "I wish that the first plantation might hear be seated, if there come to the number of 50, persons or upward . . ." (He feared that if there were less than fifty, the Indians would cause trouble). "The soyle of ye borders of this great bay, may be compared to most ye plantations which I have seene in Virginia . . . In ye botome of ye great bay is store of Codd & basse, or mulett, etc." [9]

Bradford does not tell us where and when this letter came into his possession. Was it received by Gorges before the *Mayflower* sailed in September, and was it shown to Bradford as proof of Gorges' good faith and the desirability of diverting the expedition to Plymouth? Bradford and his associates may have felt that they could not afford to depend solely on the friendship of Sandys; they were caught in dangerous cross-currents.

As for Gorges, he had plenty of reason for wanting the Pilgrims to settle in the region which he intended to control. When the Pilgrims sailed, his ambitious colonial plans were about to come to fruition.

While the *Mayflower* approached the sand dunes of Cape Cod, the royal seal was placed on the charter of the Council of New England. The patent, granted on November 3, gave Gorges and his friends title to the land between the fortieth and forty-eighth parallels, from Philadelphia to the Gulf of St. Lawrence. There was no nonsense about voting rights in the council. It was a limited body of forty members, drawn almost exclusively from the nobility.

The members of the Council knew that the unrestricted feudal privileges which they received, together with a monopoly of fishing rights, would arouse a storm of protest. In protecting themselves against attack, it was of the utmost importance to have a colony—and especially a colony of humble Puritans—established in their territory. From the viewpoint of the Pilgrims, it was equally important to have the protection of such powerful persons as the members of the council.

The circumstances of the *Mayflower's* arrival at Cape Cod suggest a plan that had gone awry. The ship sighted land on November 9. The decision to turn southward to the Hudson was so halfhearted that it was abandoned after half a day's sailing. Bradford does not mention a storm; he speaks only of shoals and breakers. Captain Jones must have been sadly deficient in knowledge of the American coast if he did not know that he could circumvent the obstruction and proceed by the open sea to the mouth of the Hudson.

On November 11, the ship was at anchor in Provincetown Bay, and the decision to remain in New England was formalized by the *Mayflower Compact.* At the same time, John Carver was chosen governor.

Yet an entire month was spent in slow painful exploration of the cape, seeking out a satisfactory place of habitation. That month is as much of a mystery as the letter from Dermer quoted by Bradford. Thirty precious days, with the gray skies and threatening winds heralding the approach of winter, were passed in what appears to be the aimless wandering of small groups, instead of in the work of building shelters that would provide protection against the coming snows. The delay is inexplicable unless we assume that some of the leaders of the expedition were awaiting help or guidance that failed to arrive. The searching parties may have been seeking for some sign of Dermer and his men, to assist in planting the colony and negotiating a peaceful arrangement with the Indians. They can hardly have been looking for Plymouth harbor, for when they sent the shallop on December 6 to explore the other side of the bay, it was piloted by "Mr. Coppin who had bine in ye countrie before"; he knew Plymouth, which he "did assure them was a good harbor, which he had been in, and they might fetch it before night." The shallop ran into heavy rain and wind, and the mast broke as night came on. They finally got under the lee of an island, and entered the harbor on the following morning, sounding it and finding it "fit for shipping." [10] A week later, the *Mayflower* crossed the bay, and the building of the community began.

Squanto made his belated appearance in the spring. Meanwhile, in England, the Council of New England was one of the most explosive subjects of debate in the parliament that met early in 1621. Gorges was summoned, not once, but three times, to appear before the bar of the Commons in person, to answer charges that he was using the pretense of planning a colony to secure a monopoly of land and fishing rights. Gorges' lame defense might have brought his plans to disaster, if the king had not intervened to prevent further action by the House. But Gorges could point to the fact that Englishmen were actually living in New England; it added a spice of humor to the argument that the settlers were Puritans, sponsored by Sandys, financed by Puritan merchants.

The Council of New England hastened to strengthen its position by granting a subsidiary patent to Weston and his London associates. (Neither the Council, nor Weston's own partners, knew that the contract with the settlers had not been signed.) The patent, dated June 1, provided one hundred acres for each colonist, fifteen hundred acres for the support of a church, hospital and other public needs, with the privilege of trading with the Indians and fishing.

Gorges had taken the first step, with the conscious or unconscious help of the Pilgrim fathers, toward feudal control of New England and its fisheries. But he miscalculated the strength and determination of the fishermen, as well as of the Plymouth settlers. When the two joined forces, the Council of New England faced sure defeat.

3 : THOMAS WESTON'S PILGRIMAGE

THE STORY of Thomas Weston's dealings with the Plymouth Colony illuminates the problems that the colony faced in the first years of its existence. It may be said to have a large significance, as a segment of economic history, throwing some light on the habits and aims of a more or less typical businessman, with moderate capital and large ideas, in the early seventeenth century.

The assignment of children from his household was a minor contribution made by Thomas Weston to the success of the colony. Since it is improbable that Weston would part with the children without recompense, we may assume that he received some remuneration, in cash or shares of stock, for the services of the young people. However, Weston's interest in the enterprise seems to have sprung from a compelling faith in its possibilities. His unsatisfactory negotiations with the Puritans were the beginning of a high adventure, which carried him overseas and involved him in unexpected risks and dangers.

The sickness and hunger that plagued the Plymouth settlers during the first winter made it impossible for them to secure furs or other commodities for the *Mayflower's* return voyage to England. In March, Squanto arranged a peaceful meeting between the English leaders and the sachem, Massasoit. Having given the colonists safety from attack, Squanto taught them the secret of Indian agriculture, showing them how to plant corn in hills, fertilizing it with fish. On April 5, Governor Carver was taken ill. On the same day, the *Mayflower,* without a cargo, sailed for England. Carver died a few days later, Bradford, thirty-one years old and already respected as a leader, was chosen governor.

When the empty *Mayflower* reached its home port in May, 1621, Weston's frugal soul was wounded. He wrote a letter to Plymouth, expressing his astonishment "that you sent no lading in the ship . . . I know your weakness was the cause of it, and I beleeve more weakness of Judgmente, then weakness of hands. A quarter of ye time you spente in discoursing, arguing, & consulting, would have done much more." [1]

Weston was not altogether unjust in noting the argumentative habits of the Puritans. But his harsh words took no account of the suffering of the winter that had killed half the colonists and left the others ill and half-starved. As a businessman, Weston had no sentiment to waste on hardships that failed to yield a cash return. Yet he was to have his own share of suffering in the competition for the profits of colonization. The people, through their sweat and labor, on the fishing banks and the rocky shore, could defeat the crown's plans for feudal fiefs and monopolies. But Weston, the bourgeois gentleman dreaming that he could embrace the cash nexus like a yielding woman, was to meet many troubles in the course of his romance with primitive accumulation.

Weston's angry letter in May seems to have been chiefly intended to make the colonists feel their dependence on him, and thus force them to sign the contract which guaranteed their services for seven years. Weston had misled his London partners into believing that the agreement was already signed, sealed and delivered. He had to clear himself with these men, and it was important to do it quickly. Weston's dealings with Gorges had convinced him that a fortune could be made in New England. He was now anxious to use his connection with Gorges for his own benefit without bothering about Plymouth. The Plymouth people had served their purpose in giving the Council of New England a colony. Now Gorges was in the midst of larger plans, and Weston hoped to get at least some of the crumbs from the approaching feast.

Weston could not free himself from the Plymouth venture until he secured the contract about which he had lied. If he failed to get it, he would be subject to legal reprisals, and his financial position would be endangered. In the summer of 1621, Weston outfitted the *Fortune* and sent the ship across the ocean. On board was Robert

Cushman, with instructions to get the agreement signed, and bring it back speedily with a saleable cargo. The letter, carried by Cushman, was urgent:

> If you mean, bona fide, to performe the conditions agreed upon, doe us ye favors to coppy them out faire, and subscribe them with ye principall of your names. And likewise give us accounte as perticularly as you can how our moneys were laid out . . . And consider that ye life of the bussiness depends on ye lading of this ship, which, if you doe to any good purpose, that I may be freed from ye great sums I have disbursed for ye former, and must doe for the later, *I promise you I will never quit ye bussiness, though all the other adventures should.*[2]

In italicising the last sentence, Weston followed a custom which is not unusual in business or other correspondence: he gave special emphasis to something he knew to be untrue. As Bradford observed, in looking back at the incident after its outcome was known, Weston had deserted the business "before he so much as heard of ye returns of this ship, or knew what was done."[3] Weston's conduct was logical. He wrote the letter to get the document signed. He did not have to wait for the result, for he knew well enough that the colonists had no choice.

The *Fortune* reached Cape Cod early in November. She carried 35 settlers, but utterly inadequate supplies. Weston's London partners, knowing of the depleted labor force in the colony, may have insisted on sending additional people. But Weston spent as little as possible on food and clothing. The 35 new arrivals were in a sad condition: "neither had they any beding, but some sory things they had in their cabins, nor pot, nor pan, to dress any meate in; nor overmany cloaths . . ."[4]

The Plymouth people shared their meager rations with the newcomers. Bradford and his advisers, realizing that they could not exist without supplies from England, and that the cargo which they sent back would simply be confiscated if they failed to sign the paper sent by Weston, affixed their names to the document. The *Fortune* was loaded in two weeks, and sent off with a cargo of furs and clapboards. However, the fortune which Weston may have associated with the name of the ship failed to smile upon him: the vessel was captured and plundered by a French privateer.

Meanwhile, in England, James got rid of parliament in December. Disregarding the popular outcry and the warnings of *Tom Tell-*

Troath, the crown continued negotiations for an alliance with Spain. Gorges went ahead with his plans to control the New England fisheries and divide the land into princely estates for himself and his associates. The king, smiling upon the Council's activities, requested in return for his favor that the land which the French called Acadie be given to his Scottish friend, Sir William Alexander. The Council complied, and on September 10, 1621, Alexander became the owner of the territory between the present northern border of Maine and the St. Lawrence River. Alexander issued a proclamation in Edinburgh appealing to younger sons of wealthy and noble families: a payment of £100 would give these men, who might otherwise be troublesome to their families and friends, land grants in New Scotland and the title of baronet. Thus the colony was designed to serve as a refuge for "all such younger bretheren and meane gentlemen whose moyens ar short of their birth, worth or myndis." [5]

The patent given to Alexander did not interfere with Lord Calvert's control of part of the Avalon Peninsula. This estate had originally been purchased by Sir William Vaughn from the London and Bristol Company, and Calvert bought it from Vaughn early in 1620. Calvert was a royalist politician, a devout Catholic, who had fought against Sandys in the General Court of the Virginia Company. He resigned from the Virginia corporation when Sandys secured control. Calvert's advocacy of the Spanish alliance, as well as his Catholic connections, placed him high in the king's favor, and his purchase of Avalon was connected with the general political situation in 1620. The adjustment of the differences between the aristocratic party of Prince Maurice and the financers of Amsterdam was signalized in 1621 by the formation of the Dutch West India Company, with a twenty-four year monopoly of trade in Western Africa, and North and South America, and the right to erect feudal principalities.

The cod was the major inspiration for the English activities on the northeastern American coast. Gorges and his associates in the Council of New England were especially interested in the potentialities of the fisheries on the New England coast. The reports which Gorges had received from Captain Dermer and others may have convinced him that Alexander and Calvert were destined to have serious difficulties with the West Country fishermen in Newfoundland. The men from the West Country had begun to visit the coastal waters from Maine to Cape Cod, but they had not yet pre-empted the harbors for drying platforms and winter settlements.

The New England fisheries promised golden profits. In 1619, a 200-ton ship left Plymouth, England, and earned for each member of the crew £16 10*s* for their share in the season's catch. In the following year, three ships reported even higher returns. "Some sailors that had but a single share had twenty pounds and at home again in seven months, which was more than such a one would have got in twenty months had he gone for wages anywhere." In 1621, the number of vessels sailing for New England increased to 10, and in 1622, 37 ships made the crossing.[6]

The unusual income received by humble fishermen explains the haste with which both Gorges and Weston acted to secure what they believed to be their rightful participation in the fisherman's share. Early in 1622, Gorges formed the association with John Mason which was to be so fateful for the history of New England. Mason, having served six years in Newfoundland as the representative of the London and Bristol Company, had firsthand experience of the difficulty of forcing the fishermen to accept monopolistic regulation. The only way to control the fishermen was through the establishment of a colony which would sell supplies and shore facilities, and organize its own fishing expeditions. On March 9, 1622, Mason obtained a patent from the Council of New England, giving him the land between Salem in Massachusetts and the Merrimac River. A few months later, the two men secured a joint patent for the region from the Merrimac to the Kennebec River in Maine. Between them, they now held 125 miles of coastline.

Weston's plans were on a more modest scale. But he acted with dispatch. He formed a partnership with another London merchant, John Beauchamp, early in 1622.

The two men dispatched a ship, the *Sparrow,* to fish off the Maine coast and to leave a few men for the purpose of founding a separate plantation adjacent to Plymouth. The *Sparrow* remained with other fishing vessels at Damariscove, near Monhegan Island, but she sent a shallop commanded by Master Mate Gibbs, to Plymouth. The ship brought seven men to establish a plantation and to prepare for the arrival of additional colonies.

The shallop brought a letter from Weston which was a masterpiece of business double talk. He was sorry to report the "parsemonie" of the other investors. He had begged them to send men and supplies: "They all answer they will doe great maters, when they hear good news." Meanwhile, Weston and Beauchamp "have sent *this ship* and these passengers on our owne accounte: whom we desire you will frendly entertaine & supply with such necessaries as you can spare . . . we purpose *to send more people on our owne account,* and *to take a patente.*"

As usual, Weston's heart, if not exactly on his sleeve, was in the passages he underlined. Bradford's comment on the letter is a quotation from Psalm 146, with an appropriate aside: *Put not your trust in princes* (much less in ye merchants) *nor in ye sone of man, for ther is no help in them.*

Despite their suspicion of Weston's motives, the Plymouth people could not refuse food and shelter to the seven men, who "might have starved if ye plantation had not succoured them."[7] However, in return for their aid, they persuaded Gibbs to take Edward Winslow to Monhegan to purchase fish from the fleet anchored there. Going northward in the shallop, Winslow found thirty vessels. Among them was the *Bona Vista,* licensed by the Virginia Company and fishing off the Maine coast in open defiance of the Council of New England's authority. Captain Hudlston of the *Bona Vista* received Winslow with great friendliness; he was anxious, as were many of the other fishermen who were at Monhegan without legal permission, to win allies in the fight against the Council. He "not only spared what he could, but writ to others to doe ye like." The plantation, observes Bradford was doubly benefited—"first, a present refreshing by ye food brought, and secondly, they knew ye was to those parts for their benifite hereafter."[8]

The full significance of Weston's plans was evident later in the summer, when another ship belonging to him, the *Charity,* reached Plymouth. It brought sixty men for Weston's private plantation. It carried contradictory letters, one from Weston and the other from two other members of the company, Edward Pickering and William Greene. The note from Pickering and Greene, carried by one of the passengers, warned Bradford that Weston had broken with the company, and that he was sending his brother to America to defraud the colonists: "we are informed his purpose is to come to your colonie, pretending he comes for and from ye adventurers, and will seeks to gett what you have in readyness into *his ships,* as if they came from ye company, & possessing all, will be so much profite to himselfe."

The message from Weston said that he had discovered that one of the passengers was carrying a secret letter and he had persuaded the passenger to let him see it: he "found this treacherous letter . . . Wich letter had it come to your hands without answer, might have caused ye hurt, if not ye ruin of us all." He denied he had any ill-intentions toward the colonists: he merely wished to leave in the country *"a little ship* (if God send her safe thither) with mariners and fishermen to stay there, who shall coast, & trad with ye savages, & ye old plantation. It may be we shall be as helpfull to you, as you will be to us."

Bradford was not impressed by Weston's protestation. But the *Charity* had a number of passengers who had paid for their transportation to Virginia. Weston's servants were to be left at Plymouth, and the *Charity* left them there—"60 lusty men," says Bradford, who were given "housing for them and their goods; and many being sicke, they had ye best means ye place could aford them." [9]

In England things were going badly for Weston. The New England Council had been willing to deal with the ironmonger as a representative of the Plymouth colony. But Gorges and his friends had no intention of letting this comparatively insignificant merchant become a power in New England. The minutes of the meeting of the Council on the last Saturday in May begin with an item about Weston: "First it is ordered that concerning the Complaint made of Mr. Weston, petition shall bee made to his Majestie for ye forfeiture of his shipp and goods to ye president and Councells use." [10]

Late in the summer of 1622, Weston's servants departed for their own plantation at Wessagusset, on the south side of Massachusetts Bay. As the cold weather approached, the people at Plymouth faced a more serious shortage of food than at any time since the dismal winter of their arrival. This was partly due to an unsatisfactory harvest, and partly to the fact that the hospitality accorded to Weston's men put a strain on the colony's food resources. Bradford's comments on the theft of corn before it was ripe shows the discontent among the settlers and the harsh punishments meted out to offenders: "Though many were well whipt (when they were taken) for a few ears of corne, yet hunger made others (whom conscience did not restaine) to venture." [11] It must be noted that many of the colonists, including Weston's men, were servants who had no rights either in protecting themselves from whipping or in securing an equal share of the available food.

The colony had received nothing. The London merchants were sticking to their decision to send nothing until they received saleable goods. It was impossible to get corn from the Indians, because the colonists "had no trading commodities." Everything they had in the way of European goods had been given to the Indians in exchange for beaver, which was stored at Plymouth for transmission to England when a ship arrived.

Starving people could not eat furs. But fortunately, a vessel arrived from Virginia late in August. It was the *Discovery* commanded by Captain Thomas Jones, on its way to the fishing banks for illegal fishing. "This ship had store of English-beads (which were then good trade) and some knives, but would sell none but at dear rates." The colonists were "faine to buy at any rate," giving coat-beaver at one-sixth of its value in order to get the goods that would save them from starvation.

With these commodities, Plymouth organized a joint trading expedition with the Wessagusset colony. Weston's men had a small ship; they promised to pay for their share of the goods "when Mr. Weston, or their supply, should come." The expedition went around Cape Cod to the south. During the trip, Squanto, performing his usual task as guide and interpreter, was taken ill and died. The voyage resulted in procuring "26 or 28 hogsheads of corne & beans, which was more than ye Indians could well spare in these parts."

It seems probable that there was some sharp bargaining and some friction in the dealing with the Indians at this time. There was also some ill-feeling between the Plymouth people and Weston's men concerning the disposal of the food. In New England, as in Virginia, the struggle for the means of subsistence produced social tensions which affected both the European and their Indian neighbors, leading to brutal conflict with the Indians. The report of the massacre in Virginia, brought to Plymouth by ships coming north to trade and fish, was directly responsible for the decision of the Plymouth authorities to teach the neighboring tribes a murderous lesson. However, the action taken in the spring of 1623 was also motivated by the friction between the Cape Cod colony and the Weston plantation at Wessagusset.

Bradford criticizes Weston's men for "their great disorder," their intimacy with the Indians and their improvidence in dealing with the natives. He says that some of the Wessagusset people even "became servants to ye Indieans." Since the men at Wessagusset had no food, it is reasonable to suppose that they were willing to work for the Indians in order to obtain corn. But this situation violated the cardinal principle of colonization—that the Indians must be treated as inferiors and kept at a distance.

Bradford gives a cautious and misleading account of the expedition sent to Wessagusset under the command of Captain Miles Standish. Bradford tells us that Standish "found them in miserable condition, out of which he rescued them, and helped them to some releef." Bradford also speaks of an Indian conspiracy against the English, and reports that Standish "cut of some few of ye cheefe conspirators." [12]

What Standish actually did, on his arrival at Wessagusset, was to lure four unarmed Indians into a room, lock the door, hack three of them to pieces, and hang the fourth, a boy of eighteen. He then killed some more Indians, and the rest made their escape. He thus accomplished a double purpose; he took vengeance on the Indians (although it is not clear that there was anything that needed to be revenged); and he made Wessagusset uninhabitable for Weston's men. Surrounded by hostile natives, they no longer had any chance of trading or getting food. Standish offered to bring them back to Plymouth, but they preferred "to goe with their smale ship to ye easteard, where hapily they might here of Mr. Weston, or some supply from him, seeing ye time of ye year was for fishing ships to be in ye land."

Weston was in fact on his way to Maine. But he did not come with ships or supplies. Being in trouble with the powerful leaders of the New England Council and uncertain concerning the fate of his plantation, he "came over with some of ye fishermen, under another name, and ye disguise of a blacksmith." He secured a boat, with one or two men to handle it, and started down the coast to Massachusetts, but he was shipwrecked, and "afterwards fell into the hands of ye Indeans, who pillaged him of all he saved from the sea, & striped him out of all his cloaths to his shirte." Finally he reached the Piscataqua River, where a small English colony had just been founded. Here he borrowed some clothing and a boat to take him to Plymouth.

Bradford observes that "A strang alteration there was in him to such had seen & known him in his former florishing condition; so uncertaine are ye mutable things of this unstable world." It was indeed an unstable world for the aspiring small capitalist.

The "strange alteration" in Weston does not seem to have made him less adept at a bargain. There is satisfactory explanation of the transaction by which he secured 100 beaver skins from Bradford. The Plymouth governor says that he protested that such a gift "were enoughe to make a mutinie among ye people." Nonetheless, it was given. Weston still had a valid claim against the colony, and it may have seemed wise to conciliate him by a partial payment of the debt. The beaver skins gave Weston enough capital to return north, salvage his wrecked ship, and reassemble some of his men.

In the same spring of 1623, Bradford and his associates took the first steps toward freeing themselves from the unprofitable connection with their London backers. They abandoned the system of group indenture, which forced the whole colony to labor for the corporate treasury, and corn fields were allotted to each family with the provision that they could use what they raised for their own needs. The change, which "made all hands very industrious" did not give permanent possession of the land; it was assigned "only for present use." Bradford, being an intense believer in the blessings of private property, took the colony's experience as proof of "the vanitie of that conceite of Platos & other ancients, applauded by some of later times;—that ye taking away of propertie, and bringing in communitie into a comone wealth, would make them happy and florishing."[13] Later historians have echoed Bradford's view.

But the Plymouth colony in its first years may properly be compared to a company town rather than to an experiment in communal labor. People cannot pool their labor unless it belongs to them. The labor of the Plymouth colonists belonged to a company in England, and their share in the corporate undertaking was by no means equal. Edward Winslow, with nine shares, was not pooling his labor with the indentured servant who represented a stock certificate belonging to his master. Winslow, Bradford and other men of substance were in America to make money. Their abandonment of the group of indenture gave them a tighter hold on the colony's trade and resources, and prepared the way for their private negotiations to obtain a release from the corporation and to obtain all its potential profits and privileges for themselves.

The action taken by the Plymouth leaders was motivated by their knowledge that they were on the edge of a projected business empire. Trading posts were being established along the coast, and illegal fishing expeditions, ignoring the claims of the New England Council, were doing a flourishing business.

In England, the Council passed angry resolutions against unlicensed activities in the lands and seas under its jurisdiction:

> It is thought fitt that there shall bee an order procured from ye Lords of his Majestie's Councell for sending for such as have in contempt of authority gone for New England this last yeare, As also to procure a further warning to bee given to them from further attempting . . .[14]

Six weeks later, the minutes contain another reference to illegal fishing. It is decided "to sollicite ye Lords for procurcing from his Majestie a proclamation concerning ye fishermen of ye Westerne parts. Likewise to procure some course for punishing their contempt of authority." [15]

In order to protect its interests overseas, the Council appointed Robert Gorges as governor of New England, and Captain Francis West was given the title of admiral. West was instructed to restrain interlopers and punish fishermen who visited Maine without licenses. West arrived in June. But, as Bradford observed, West's title did not impress the fishermen: "He could doe no good of them, for they were to stronge for him, and he found ye fisher men to be stuberne fellow." [16]

The summer of 1623 witnessed increasing activity along the whole coast. In order to encourage licensed fishing, it was desirable to have a trading post on Monhegan Island. Since no one on the Council was prepared to handle the business, the exclusive patent was given to Abraham Jennings of Plymouth, England, in return for a fee of £110. A temporary license was given to Richard Bushrode and a group of associates in the town of Dorchester "to send forthe a Shippe for Discovery and other Imployments in New England." [17] The Bushrode Company set up drying stages at Cape Ann. Christopher Levett received a patent for a plantation at Casco Bay in May. David Thomson was already established at Piscataqua, on the present site of Portsmouth, New Hampshire.

Lord Calvert reinforced his claim to the Avalon peninsula in April 1623 by a royal charter which gave him the whole province as a feudal barony. Calvert could make laws and appoint judges, grant pardons, impose martial law, confer titles, convey estates and incorporate towns.

However, since the licensing of fishing caused such determined opposition, the patent specifically reserved the freedom of fishing, and of drying and salting fish, both in the sea and in the ports of the province.[18] The arrangement was in accord with Calvert's purpose: since he wished to develop a private fishing industry, he intended to avoid as far as possible any direct conflict with the English transatlantic fleets. There were soon thirty-two vessels in his employ, operating from the settlement at Ferryland.[19]

These activities explain both the determination of the Plymouth leaders to escape from their obligations to the London merchants, and the decision of the London merchants to take a more friendly interest in the enterprise. In midsummer, 1623, a ship and a pinnace reached the colony with the first contingent of people and supplies sent over by the company. The ship was the *Anne,* with sixty persons transported at the company's expense, and a number of persons who paid their own passage. The pinnace was to remain at Plymouth for fishing and trading.

The arrival of the *Anne* led to disputes over food. The people who had been planting their own fields "were afraid that their corne, when it was ripe, should be imparted to ye newcomers." However, the arriving settlers, and especially some of those who had paid their own way, were well supplied with food, and were "as much afraid that ye hungrie planters would have eat up ye provisions brought." The authorities decreed that all provisions were privately owned, and could be secured only "by bargaine or exchainge."

The *Anne,* loaded with clapboard and furs, sailed on her return voyage on September 10, carrying Edward Winslow to arrange for additional supplies and to negotiate with the London merchants. Bradford wanted to use the pinnace that had been sent over with the *Anne* for coastal commerce, but the plan was delayed by the first strike of seamen in New England. The men had shipped out on shares, but they were not satisfied with the probable income that they would receive from local voyages:

> They would neither trade nor fish, excepte they had wages; in fine, they would obey no command of the maisters.

The strike was won. The governor was persuaded "to chaing their condition and give them wages." The pinnace sailed around Cape Cod to trade with the Indians.

In the fall of 1623, Governor Gorges, possessing authority over the whole New England area, reached Plymouth. Thomas Weston was unlucky enough to enter Plymouth Harbor at about the same time, with the ship he had salvaged and reconditioned.

A year earlier, the Council of New England had decreed the forfeiture of Weston's ship and goods. Gorges pressed various charges against the merchant, and was annoyed by his presumptuous answers, which included "provocking & cutting speeches." The matter was temporarily smoothed over; the governor was mollified by the use of the buildings erected by Weston's men at Wessagusset.

Gorges departed for the plantation. But he was evidently dissatisfied. He sent a warrant to Plymouth to order Weston's arrest and the confiscation of his ship. Weston was not altogether unwilling to give up the vessel, for the sailors on it were becoming troublesome and Weston "was deeply ingaged to them for wages." The governor commandeered the ship, and sailed north in it to visit Piscataqua. Weston waited patiently until the spring, when the governor returned and gave the ship back to its owner. Gorges was no longer interested in Weston or his vessel. One winter had been enough to discourage him with the wonders of New England. He embarked for home, and Weston proceeded to Virginia.

Winslow returned early in 1624. He brought back a minister, the Reverend John Lyford; "3. heifers & a bull, the first beginning of any catle of that kind in the land." Winslow also brought a ship's carpenter and a salt-maker. The London merchants wrote encouragingly that the carpenter should immediately build "2 catches, a lighter, and some 6 or 7 shalops . . . The saltman is a skilfull & industrious man." Thus the Londoners were sure that three essential problems would be solved, "viz. fishing, salt making and boat making."

The tasks did not prove as simple as the merchants supposed. The carpenter died of fever during the first summer. The salt-maker "was an ignorante, foolish, self-wild fellow . . . he could not doe any thing but boyle salt in pans." But the greatest difficulties revolved around the Reverend Lyford; it is hard to determine whether Lyford was actually sent out by the merchants to give them secret reports on the situation in the colony. But Lyford soon entered into an alliance with a group of dissatisfied settlers led by John Oldham. Oldham was one of the men who had come over at his own expense, and he resented the economic power of the Bradford group. Bradford stole some letters which Lyford and Oldham attempted to send to England. The two men were placed on trial, the letters were exhibited, and the offenders were exiled. Oldham, taking Roger Conant and some others with him, went to Nantasket on the south shore of Massachusetts Bay. Lyford was given six months' grace.

Whatever Lyford's connections with the London stockholders may have been, his conduct exhibited the typical duplicity of the paid informer. He made an hysterical confession, weeping that "he had don very evill, and slanderously abused them . . . if God should make him a vagabun in the earth, as was Caine, it was but just . . ." At the same time, he wrote another secret letter to England saying that his intercepted letters contained "nothing but what is certainly true, and I could make so appeare plainly to any indifferent men, whatsoever colours be cast to darken the truth, and some ther are very audatious this way."

Bradford says that Lyford's conduct "made them all stand amased." The minister was sent to join Oldham on the bay. The episode indicated that Bradford and his friends would not have an easy time winning the economic freedom that they sought. When the news of the trial and banishment reached England, the merchants cut off all credit to the colony. The next supplies sent over were available only to individuals who paid cash or beaver skins. The goods were valued at a 40 percent advance for the cost of sending them over, and the beaver skins were accepted at a 30 percent discount for the risk of carrying them back.[20]

Plymouth had embarked on the course that was to lead to the future development of New England. But the independent growth of the colony was obstructed by lack of capital, and the even more desperate lack of skilled workmen for shipbuilding, salt-making and fishing. The colony's welfare, and even its survival, was also bound up in the intricate and rapidly changing situation in England.

Meanwhile, Thomas Weston had settled in Virginia. His New England pilgrimage had impaired his capital and taught him not to rush in where wealthier men feared to tread. But he had enough money and servants to secure land under the headright system. He became a member of the House of Burgesses, and turned up twenty years later as lord of the manor of Westbury in Maryland. Lord Calvert was also to undergo vicissitudes and changes of fortune before he turned from the northern fisheries to a feudal dominion on Chesapeake Bay.

It is instructive that the old Puritan finally fulfilled his ambition by securing a baronial-fief from the Catholic lord of Maryland. Weston died, on the eve of the English revolution, in 1644.

4 : THE MAYPOLE ON BOSTON BAY

MILES STANDISH was sent to London by the leaders of the Plymouth colony in the summer of 1625. He was to buy supplies and to attempt to negotiate some sort of settlement with the merchants who still held a stranglehold of the colony's economic life. When Standish reached London, he found the city suffering from one of the recurrent plagues that rose out of the disease-breeding slums. As Bradford wrote, "ther dyed such multitude weekly of the plague, as all trade was dead, and little money stirring."

As troubling to the city's business as the plague were the uncertainties of foreign policy. To the difficulties inherited from his father, Charles soon added difficulties of his own making. The vacillating course which he followed was basically a duplication of James' contradictory actions, and arose from the same contradictory pressures. Charles soon made it clear that, rather than make a choice between two opposing policies, he intended to move as rapidly as possible in two directions at once.

European diplomacy reached the nadir of confusion in 1625. England was at war with Spain and had concluded an alliance with France. English troops had been sent to the Netherlands to aid in the defense of the Low Countries. But the English expeditionary force was left without reinforcements or funds; they were starving and demoralized in the spring of 1625, and most of them deserted or found their way home.

The Commons that met in 1624 had demanded, and received, solemn assurances from the crown that, in case Charles married a Catholic, there would be no toleration of Catholic activity in England. But the contract for the marriage of the Prince to Henrietta Maria, sister of Louis XIII, signed in December, 1624, contained a secret clause directly violating the royal pledge to the Commons.

Prince Maurice, the ruler of the Netherlands, died on April 4. His death is said to have been hastened by despair over his inability to relieve Breda. The pastor of the little congregation of English Puritans remaining at Leyden died at about the same time.

When Governor Bradford of Plymouth heard the news of John Robinson's death, he observed: "Thus, these two great princes, and their paster, left this world near aboute one time. Death makes no difference."

But death showed a decided preference for the poorer classes, who died on the battlefields, and whose homes and fields were devastated by marching armies. Having displayed indifference to the fate of the English soldiers who were supposed to be aiding in the defense of Holland, Charles undertook two naval actions which cancelled each other. He sent an expedition against the Spanish port of Cadiz, and at the same time he loaned English ships to aid Catholic France in attacking the rebellious Huguenot fortress of La Rochelle. The Cadiz expedition was hastily assembled and badly equipped. It was hoped that the English warships would capture Spain's American treasure galleons. But after landing near Cadiz, it was decided that the town was too strong to be taken. Abruptly lifting the siege, the fleet sailed away, just two days before the galleons weighted with gold and silver entered Cadiz Bay.

While English ships joined in the attack on the Protestants at La Rochelle, Charles sent Buckingham to Holland to negotiate an alliance with Christian IV of Denmark for the defense of European Protestantism. Although the English soldiers on the continent were unpaid, Buckingham offered the Danish king a monthly gift of £30,000 for his expenses in prosecuting the war.

This was the background of the first parliament summoned by Charles I. Soon after his marriage to Henrietta Maria, the young king found it necessary to call parliament in order to secure funds. He asked for £1,000,000 to carry on the war. The Commons asked, in effect, "What war?"—and revived all the issues of foreign and domestic policy that had been raised in previous sessions. The whole question of the Virginia Company was reopened, and a petition was given to the king to restore the charter that had been revoked. Charles refused, but the continuing, and growing, strength of the opposition forced him to give a conciliatory answer.

Coke thundered against the Council of England:

> Your patent contains many particulars contrary to law and the liberty of the subject; it is a monopoly and the ends of private gain are concealed under color of planting a colony; to prevent fishermen from visiting the sea coast for fishing is to make a monopoly upon the seas which are wont to be free; if you alone are to pack and dry fish you attempt a monopoly of the wind and sun.

The Commons passed a bill for the complete freedom of fishing, but it was defeated in the House of Lords. The parliamentary debate was possibly less decisive than the struggles conducted by fishermen on the American coast, in preventing the New England council from carrying out its plans. It was symptomatic of the general situation that Lord Calvert, who had intended to cross the Atlantic to take personal charge of his Newfoundland properties, decided to delay the voyage. In the last months of James' reign, Calvert had officially acknowledged that he was a Catholic—which James and everyone else at court knew all along—and was rewarded by his elevation to the Irish peerage as Baron Baltimore. Shortly afterwards, Lord Baltimore decided to retire, temporarily, to his Irish estate.

The contradictions that plagued English policy were operative in somewhat the same manner in Holland. In spite of the nation's military weakness, the great merchants of Amsterdam retained their financial power, and their far-flung fleets continued to reap profits from world-wide commerce. The Dutch West India Company began to take an increasing interest in the fur trade of the Hudson River Valley in 1624; the interest was signalized by Peter Minuit's famous purchase of Manhattan Island for goods valued at $24.

The Dutch bankers wished to reap the largest possible profit from the European war. Although there were still close economic ties between Holland and England, the friendship of the two countries had been weakened by the Cockayne patent, the intense competition for control of Oriental trade, and the pro-Spanish policies of the English crown. The financiers of Amsterdam had extensive interests in the Baltic, and had a great deal of influence on the Scandinavian countries. They had also entered into increasingly close relationships with France.

Holland, having no confidence in the strength or consistency of English policy, gave only halfhearted support to the alliance that England had concluded with Christian IV of Denmark. The English bourgeoisie had a similar lack of confidence in the crown. In 1625, the Commons voted only £140,000 in response to Charles' request for £1,000,000. Thus it was impossible to fulfill the extravagant commitments which Buckingham had made to the Danish King. Christian, deceived by the English promises, marched against the imperial army led by Wallenstein. Lack of money was largely responsible for the disastrous defeat which Christian suffered in 1626.

The Danish defeat increased the danger to both Holland and England. Prince Frederick Henry, who had succeeded his brother as stadholder and virtual military dictator of Holland, was more convinced than ever that it was useless to look to England for serious help. Facing marauding armies on his frontiers, Frederick Henry turned to France for assistance. Richelieu, who had negotiated the marriage between Charles and the French princess and who had risen to power as a result, was one of the first European statesmen to employ "modern" techniques in the use of war and diplomacy as instruments of state power. Richelieu was engaged in civil war with the French Protestants, but he had no objection to an alliance with the Protestant bankers of Holland. Knowing that the Netherlands was in a dangerously exposed position as a result of the Protestant victories in central Europe, Richelieu was able to make harsh conditions as the price of an alliance. He demanded that the Dutch navy assist in reducing the Huguenot stronghold of La Rochelle. Prince Frederick Henry agreed.

The English parliament that met early in 1626 found a new dynamic leader of the party of the bourgeoisie in Sir John Eliot. Eliot charged the king's intimate friend, Buckingham, with responsibility for the debacle of English foreign policy. Buckingham was impeached as a traitor, being held responsible for the abortive expedition against Madrid and the deceptive promises made to Denmark. In order to save Buckingham, or—to put the matter more accurately—to save the crown and the aristocracy from the effects of a full investigation of the charges against Buckingham, Charles dissolved parliament. The action was taken so hastily that no deal was made in regard to money, and not one penny was voted for the royal subsidy. In order to repair the shattered prestige of the crown, Charles had to make a frantic shift in foreign policy. He declared war on France.

Miles Standish remained in London until the spring of 1626. He was unable to reach a final agreement with the London backers of the colony. He had to pay fifty percent interest for the small sum of £150, which was all he was able to raise. He invested this amount "in trading goods & such other most needfull commodities as he knew requisit for their use." He carried these supplies as extra cargo on one of the fishing ships crossing to the Maine coast.

When Standish reported the European situation to his colleagues at Plymouth, they were shocked and disturbed. Bradford wrote: "Being well weigheed and laied togither, it could not but strick them with great perplexitie; and to look humanly on the state of things as they presented themselves at this time, it is a marvell it did not whole discourage, and sinck them." [1]

It was unquestionably perplexing when one looked "humanly on the state of things." The people of La Rochelle, fishermen and sailors, merchants and craftsmen, were faithful to the Huguenot cause. The ships of Holland, which had won its independence with the help of Huguenot seamen, joined Richelieu's armies in the attack on the town. And Buckingham, the English aristocrat who had gone to Spain on an appeasement mission in 1623, led an English fleet and army to the defense of the beleaguered port.

In 1626, St. Peter's in Rome, the great symbol of Catholic supremacy which had been begun in the days of Michelangelo and Raphael, was completed.

In London, the climate of theatrical culture was indicated in the production of John Ford's *T'is Pity She's a Whore,* the story of an illicit love between brother and sister. Their tortured passion is attributed to fate. Giovanni exclaims: "I'll swear my fate's my God." The climax brings death, not as a tragic end to man's striving, but as a welcome release—"Death, thou'rt a guest long look'd for."

Death came to the badly equipped and incompetently led British army attempting to relieve La Rochelle. In October, 1627, Buckingham was in desperate need of men and reinforcements. But the government's funds had given out. Disease and malnutrition had weakened the army. When the order to retreat was given, French soldiers fell upon the English troops as they tried to regain their ships. Out of

6,800 men, only 3,000, hungry and ill, made the return voyage to England.

The explanation for the debacle is not difficult to find: the class conflict in England made it impossible for the government to conduct an efficient or properly financed campaign, even when its purpose was approved by the bourgeoisie. On the other hand, Prince Frederick Henry and the Dutch bankers had reached agreement on policy, and money was available for the forces which Richelieu sent against La Rochelle.

When parliament met again in 1628, the Commons, led by Eliot and Thomas Wentworth, demanded that Charles sign the Petition of Right, circumscribing the king's authority to collect forced loans, to execute martial law in time of peace, or to imprison people by royal command without showing cause for their arrest.

The Petition of Right reveals the abuses of authority which made it impossible for the crown to mobilize popular support, even for a war that promised aid to the French Huguenots. Persons were seized and imprisoned for the crime of "contempt," or for undefined "subversive" activity.

Charles and his advisers had probably received secret information that Richelieu was negotiating with Spain for a joint attack on England. The Netherlands could hardly have permitted the conquest of England by the two Catholic powers. But there was no doubt that Britain was isolated. Charles could not refuse the Petition of Right. In the form in which it became law on June 6, 1628, it was a very moderate document.

In October, 1628, La Rochelle capitulated, having lost 16,000 inhabitants by hunger and pestilence during the siege. Its fall signalized the decline of the French fishing industry. Many of the people of the channel port were to emigrate to Nova Scotia, and eventually to find their way to a little community at the western end of Long Island Sound, named after the beloved city—New Rochelle.

Holland's betrayal of the Huguenots did not interfere with the profits of Dutch businessmen. While La Rochelle was in its last agony, the Dutch admiral, Piet Heyn, captured Spain's whole fleet of treasure galleons returning from Panama. The Dutch West India Company added 15 million guilders to its treasury, enabling it to decline a fifty percent dividend and to undertake more ambitious plans for North American colonization.

In spite of the discouragement that affected Bradford and his friends when they heard Standish's report from London, the European situation was really favorable to their economic plans. The strength displayed by the English bourgeoisie, the long resistance maintained by La Rochelle before its final capitulation, and the activities of Protestants in other parts of Europe, were of the utmost importance in preventing the Vatican from consolidating its gains, and making it impossible to adjust the conflict between France and the Hapsburgs. The internal struggle in France, Spain, and the empire, made establishment of an accord among the Catholic powers impossible.

The weakness of the Court party in England made the crown unable to follow the autocratic colonial policies which had been envisioned by the king's advisers at the time of the abrogation of the Virginia charter. Although Charles ignored requests to renew the patent, he was unable to interfere in the colony's affairs, and permitted the House of Burgesses to function without interference. The war with Spain did not keep Charles from attempting to grant special favors to importers of Spanish tobacco; in 1626, he gave permission to two men to import 50,000 pounds free from all customs duty. This gave a great advantage over the Virginia crop, which paid the regular duties. But in 1627, the necessity of conciliating the bourgeoisie made it impossible to renew the Spanish contract. In August of that year, the crown decreed that no tobacco except that from Virginia and Bermuda could be imported into England without a royal license.[2]

The cutting off of Spanish imports at a time when tobacco was increasingly popular in England created a boom in Virginia. There were 3,000 people there, and "the spirit of the colony resembled that of a mining camp in the feverish desire of the settlers to acquire wealth quickly." [3] Tobacco brought unheard-of prices in the English market. The planters took advantage of their improved bargaining position to propose to the king that he purchase 500,000 pounds annually at 3*s* 6*d* per pound. They suggested that tobacco in excess of this amount could be disposed of in Turkey, the West Indies and New England. The offer was not accepted, but it indicated the change that had taken place in Virginia. The change did not benefit the majority of the population; the profits went to a few owners of large plantations, and created social conflicts which were to come to a head in the next decade.

While the conflict between England and Spain raised the price of tobacco, it reduced the market for fish, which was largely sold at Bilboa and other Spanish ports. The depression in the fishing industry proved to be a boon to the Plymouth settlement. The reduced European demand for fish, combined with the determination of the fishing fleets to avoid any dealings with persons connected with the Council of New England, made it difficult for Abraham Jennings to make a profit from the operation of the trading post on Monhegan Island which he had obtained under a patent from the Council. In 1626, Jennings decided to sell his stock and withdraw.

The Plymouth people sent Winslow to Monhegan. David Thomson was also interested in Jenning's stock for the use of his plantation on the Piscataqua River. There were other bidders, but Winslow and Thomas agreed to buy everything and divide the goods between them. The Plymouth share came to £400. The fishermen in the neighborhood of Monhegan had salvaged some of the cargo of a French ship wrecked on the Maine coast. Winslow and Thomson agreed to purchase these goods, raising the Plymouth share to £500.

Winslow had no cash, but he was able to cover the purchase, "for ye most part, with ye beaver & commodities they had gott ye winter before." The goods received enabled the colony to increase its trade with the Indians, and secure additional furs, which were carried to Maine and sold to the fishermen for transportation to England. The Plymouth leaders had finally secured enough reserve to negotiate a settlement with the London merchants.

It was decided to send Isaac Allerton to England to make the final arrangements. However, Bradford and the small group associated with him were careful to secure the exclusive benefits of the transaction for themselves. In July, 1627, prior to Allerton's departure, the leaders of the settlement called the freemen together and insisted that they sign a document. Eight men, Bradford, Brewster, Standish, Winslow and four others, agreed to take full responsibility for the colony's debts and for the execution of any agreement that might be reached. In return, they demanded from the inhabitants an assignment of a monopoly of trade for six years. They were to be paid an annual tax of three bushels of corn or six pounds of tobacco from each freemen. The need of shoes and stockings was covered in another clause:

The said undertakers shall dureing the aforesaid terme bestow £50 per annum, in hose and shoese, to be brought over for the collonies use, to be sould unto them for corne at 6s. per busshell.

Since the majority of the colonists had no money, and since the eight leaders possessed the capital to secure an agreement in London, the freemen had no recourse but to sign the contract. It gave the little group of capitalists a monopoly of the colony's business. It also enabled them to make special arrangements with the Londoners in order to secure better terms and credits. Allerton was told "to deale with some of their speciall friends, to joyne with them in this trade upon the above recited conditions."[4]

In London, Allerton secured the cancellation of the contract. In return for £7,000 which they had sunk in the venture, the merchants agreed to accept nine annual payments of £200, reaching a total of £1,800. Allerton's ability to secure this favorable settlement was not so much due to the discouragement of the merchants, as to the special advantages which Allerton offered to the colony's "speciall friends." Four Londoners were included in the monopoly of trade which Bradford and his seven friends had secured; their influence was the chief factor in making a compromise involving a heavy loss for the less favored investors.

In the same year, Lord Baltimore manifested a renewed interest in his Newfoundland estate. England's war with France made it probable that there would be a French attack on the settlement at Avalon. But Baltimore was also having the usual difficulties with the fishermen. Although he did not endeavor to collect tribute, the competition of his fishing fleet and his control of the harbors were resented by the men from the West Country, who did everything in their power to make the colonists uncomfortable.

Baltimore left England in June, 1627, accompanied by his family and two priests. He remained only a few weeks, and went back to England. But he returned in the following spring. He wrote to his friend Wentworth: "I must either go and settle it in better order or else give it over and lose all the charges I have been at hitherto for other men to build their fortunes upon."

English and French fishermen combined to make the Avalon undertaking so unprofitable that Lord Baltimore decided early in 1629 to accept his loss and seek his fortune in another location. The French and English fishermen also proved too much for Lord Ochiltree, a

Scotch nobleman operating under a patent from Lord Alexander's company. Lord Ochiltree established a settlement at Cape Breton and levied a ten percent tax on English fishermen. Assisted by their French friends, the fishermen attacked the settlement and destroyed all the building.

Baltimore went to Jamestown in 1629. He arrived at a time when the colony was suffering from a severe depression. Overproduction had brought a sudden end to the boom; the bottom had fallen out of the tobacco market. The planters blamed the crown for their difficulties; the poorer classes, bearing as always the brunt of the depression were bitter against the English government. Feeling ran high against the Catholic royalist, with his retinue of courtiers and servants. He was in some danger of physical violence. Thomas Tindall was pilloried "for giving my Lord Baltimore the lie and threatening to knock him down." [5]

Baltimore hurried back to England, where royal favor was soon to make him the master of a province adjoining Virginia.

The troubles that Baltimore and Ochiltree encountered in the north were a blessing to the little group of capitalists who controlled the trade of Plymouth. The fishermen fighting against monopoly control were eager to establish independent economic relationships with the New England settlers. They were able to escape, at least to some extent, from English control, by carrying goods across the sea to be exchanged for furs which the Plymouth traders had obtained from the Indians.

In becoming capitalists, Bradford and his friends intensified the class differences in the colony, and prepared for the collaboration which they were soon to establish with the more prosperous leaders of Massachusetts Bay. They also found it necessary to suppress the first rebellion of indentured servants in New England.

The incidents at the settlement known as Mount Wollaston, or Merry Mount, on the south side of Boston Bay, have been described by historians as a short spate of drunken disorder, which outraged the strict Puritans. However, Merry Mount, on the site of the present town of Quincy, involved social issues which were only incidentally related to the moral code of the Puritans.

Bradford tells us that a certain Captain Wollaston founded the settlement in 1625, with "a great many servants, with provissions and other implements for to begine a plantation." After a time, finding that the plantation was not profitable, Wollaston took most of his servants to Virginia, where he was able to make money "selling their time to other men." He left the remaining servants in charge of one of his associates, intending to have them sent on to Virginia. But Thomas Morton, an adventurer who had come out with Wollaston, warned the servants that they would be "carried away and sould for slaves with the rest." Morton proposed that they throw out Wollaston's lieutenant and go into partnership with him.

The venture seems to have been reasonably successful. There may also have been a good deal of disorder and revelry at Merry Mount. Bradford writes that the inhabitants indulged in "riotous prodigality and profuse excess." [6] He says that "Morton became lord of misrule, and maintained (as it were) a schoole of Athisme." [7] However, Bradford's views were obviously affected by the fact that the people at Merry Mount were associating with the Indians and engaging in an apparently lucrative trade in furs, which interfered with the Plymouth monopoly of trade. Morton has written an interesting description of the celebration of May Day at Merry Mount.

> Upon Mayday they brought the Maypole to the place appointed, with drumes, gunnes, pistols and other fitting instruments, for that purpose; and there erected it with the help of Salvages, that came thether of purpose to see the manner of our Revels. A goodly pine tree of 80. foote longe was reared up, with a peare of bucks-hornes nayled one somewhat neare unto the top of it: where it stood, as a faire sea marke for directions how to finde out the way to mine Hoste of Ma-re Mount.

The rural springtide festival celebrated on the first day of May has had a complicated history; it would be rash to make hasty generalization concerning the social meanings which have been attached to the ceremony at various times in various places. The symbolism of the occasion has depended to a considerable extent on local conflicts and conditions. However, the culture of the common people transferred the Maypole of their English countryside to the forest clearings in the American countryside. In the New World, the sentiment and ritual of the ancient festival were to some extent forgotten, and the pole assumed a more militant significance as the Liberty Pole of the Revolution.

There can be no doubt that the tall tree standing as "a faire sea marke," (erected, it must be noted, "with the help of Salvages") was more than a center of gay revels. It was a challenge to the colonial labor system, and the methods adopted by the colonial leaders for the control of the Indians. Bradford is explicit in describing the attitude of the rulers of Plymouth: "They saw they should keep no servants, for Morton would entertaine any, how vile soever, and all the scume of the countrie, or any discontents, would flock to him from all places, if this nest was not broken." [8]

The first steps to suppress the "revels" at Merry Mount were taken by an expedition from Plymouth led by Captain Standish. The people were warned to desist from their disorders, and Morton was arrested and taken to Plymouth. However, the tall pine remained standing, the rebellious servants continued to fraternize with the Indians, and to conduct a trade in furs which Plymouth considered illegal. More drastic action was taken by John Endicott, who arrived at Salem in September, 1628, representing a group of Puritan merchants who had secured a patent to land on Cape Ann from the more or less dormant Council of New England. Endecott promptly sent men to cut down the pole. The houses, livestock and corn, were seized, and the inhabitants were told that they were henceforth under the authority of the Salem government.

The discontent of servants in Virginia, curbed by repressive legislation and the vigilance of the plantation owners, did not lead to organized protest until a later period. But there was a revolt of indentured servants in the little English colony at Nevis, in the West Indies, in 1629. The servants cooperated with a Spanish fleet in an attack which resulted in the capture of the settlement. The British landowners did not hesitate to offer their allegiance to the Spanish admiral, who guaranteed them the security of their property, and joined them in hunting down the servants who had rebelled.

In England, the uneasy peace established by the king's acceptance of the Petition of Right lasted for only a year. The old question of "tonnage and poundage," of taxation without representation, was responsible for Charles' decision to rule without parliament. On March 2, the king sent an order for the adjournment of the session. The rebels locked the door and held the speaker of the Commons in his chair, while Sir John Eliot read the three famous resolutions, stating that anyone introducing innovations in religion, or advising the imposition of illegal taxes, or voluntarily paying such levies, was to be counted an enemy of the kingdom and a betrayer of its liberties. The reading was completed as an armed force approached to break down the door. Eliot and his supporters were thrown into prison.

Yet Charles did not abandon the custom of moving in two directions at once, which had become the hallmark of Stuart policy. Two days after the violent scene in the Commons, the great seal of England was placed on the charter of the Massachusetts Bay Company. The coincidence of dates has passed unnoticed; yet it reveals the relationships of forces in England, and the unbroken power of the class that challenged the crown's power. Having suppressed the political activity of the party of the bourgeoisie, Charles and his advisers found it expedient to respect the commitment they had made to a group of prominent Puritan peers and merchants. The grant to the Massachusetts Bay Company was an admission that the Council of New England, with its dreams of feudal baronies, had faded into oblivion. The charter covered land that had already been given, under the authority of the Council, to Gorges and Mason.

Edward Sandys was sixty-eight years old. He must have smiled when he heard the news that *his* plan—the plan of his class—for transatlantic colonization, had won at last. The new corporation secured the rights and privileges for which the stockholders of the Virginia Company had fought in vain. Sandys died in October, 1629, on the eve of the great migration to New England.

Epilogue

EPILOGUE

THE STRUGGLE of the people, in opposition to the privileged class that controls the state, is the dynamic factor in our national development, the theme and meaning of our history. There have been periods when the democratic principle has found powerful affirmation in literature, art and thought; these have been periods of great popular movements, of rising tides of protest and hope among the people. But we can understand these affirmative and creative aspects of our culture, only if we recognize that they express a challenge to the class that controls the state.

A recent history of the United States, *Land of the Free,* the work of two distinguished historians, Homer C. Hockett and Arthur M. Schlesinger, asserts that, "In times so remote that their origins are obscure, certain ideas of the rights of individuals and justice in the relations of persons with one another began to take form and to govern practice among the English."

The Anglo-Saxon myth is so widely accepted today that it seems like a static generalization. But it is the product of historical change, and its development throws a good deal of light on the contemporary crisis in the nation's life and culture. A little more than a century ago, in 1847, Frederick Douglass noted the contradiction between the democratic principle and the concept of Anglo-Saxon superiority:

> The people of the United States are the boldest in their pretentions to freedom, and the loudest in their professions of their love of liberty . . . professing not merely republicanism, not merely democratical institutions, but civilization . . . claiming to be the heaven-appointed nation, in connection with the British, to civilise, christianize, and evangelize the world.

John Lothrop Motley's *Rise of the Dutch Republic,* published in 1855, is of critical importance in the American development of the Anglo-Saxon myth as a theory of history. Motley speaks of the Dutch Republic as the cradle of a movement which is "a single chapter in the great volume of human fate; for the so-called revolutions of Holland, England and America, are all links in one chain." The rise of the United Netherlands is "a portion of the records of the Anglo-Saxon race—essentially the same, whether in *Firesland,* England, or Massachusetts." The continuity is embodied in the "great science of political equilibrium," seeking a rational and "temperate human liberty," which is not "arrested in blood and tears by the madness of its worshippers." Its basic purpose is "to maintain, not to overthrow."

Motley relates Holland's imperial conquests, "girdling the world with its innumerable dependencies," to the development of England's "schemes of empire."

In the years following the Civil War, the betrayal of Reconstruction in the South prepared the way for an increasing concentration of economic power, the control of the state by giant monopolies, and the emergence of the United States as a world power competing with England and other nations for markets, sources of raw materials, territories and spheres of influences.

The change was signalized by the expanding influence of the Anglo-Saxon myth in the last two decades of the nineteenth century. As the United States moved to challenge England's imperial power, the emphasis on England's supremacy was superseded by a growing insistence on the pre-eminence of the United States. When the English historian, E. A. Freeman, lectured to American audiences in 1881-1882, he told his hearers: "When you read the history of Aryan Europe, you are reading the records of a kindred folk, in which you have the interest of kinsmen . . . As of old wherever Hellenes dwelled, there was Hellas, so we should deem that, where the English folk dwell, there is England." Freeman's influence was a principal factor in the inauguration of the "Johns Hopkins University Studies in Historical and Political Science," which began in 1882 with an introductory essay on "Mr. Freeman's Visit to Baltimore" and a monograph on American institutional history by Freeman himself. The Johns Hopkins publications inspired a generation of historians. Henry Adams wrote: "I flung myself obediently into the arms of the Anglo-Saxons in history."

The rush to "the arms of the Anglo-Saxons" was so general that a cautious scholar like Adams may have been in some danger of being trampled underfoot by his more precipitate colleagues. The advocates of the nation's "Manifest Destiny" to achieve imperial power were eager to proclaim the United States as the new center of "Anglo-Saxon civilization." In 1885, Josiah Strong wrote: "Since North America is much bigger than the little English isle, it will be the seat of Anglo-Saxondom."

The myth was closely related to the continuing oppression of the Negro in the South. The blessings and profits that accrued from the practice of Anglo-Saxon "superiority" in the South could logically be extended to all "inferior" peoples by the methods which had proved so rewarding to the rulers of England. These methods included a civilized and scholarly interest in the cultures of peoples who toiled and died to enrich the empire. For example, when England conquered Benin in West Africa in 1897, the British Museum was enriched with some of the most beautiful products of African civilization. A volume published by the Museum in 1899 entitled *Antiquities of the City of Benin* explains that the objects of art were "obtained by the recent successful expedition sent to Benin to punish the natives of that city for a treacherous massacre of a peaceful English mission."

While England pursued its civilizing tasks in Africa and Asia, the United States followed the dictates of "manifest destiny" by declaring war on Spain in 1898. The significance of this event in cultural terms is defined in Barrett Wendell's *Literary History of America,* which examines the development of "Anglo-Saxon ideals" in the United States as preparation for the period of expansion introduced by the conquest of the Philippines and American participation in the suppression of the Boxer rebellion in China.

It is customary to treat Barrett Wendell as an unimportant representative of the New England aristocracy, expressing prejudices that were amusingly old-fashioned at the time he wrote. The recently published *Literary History of the United States* observes that, "In the nineties, he was already quite reconciled to the 'provincial obscurity' into which his class and kind were vanishing." It is true that Wendell's style is stuffy, and that his literary judgments are often obtuse and naïvely expressive of the author's Tory sympathies. But there was no provincial obscurity about Wendell's belief in Anglo-Saxon supremacy. It was—and still is—the main tendency in American letters and scholarship.

Wendell's *Literary History* appeared in 1900; it is a remarkable example of the quick and powerful impact of social and political forces on the life of the mind. The book was published at a moment when there were 70,000 American soldiers in the Philippines, and 2,500 in Pekin. Wendell wrote that there had been a good deal of hostility between England and the United States during the nineteenth century. But the differences were resolved at "the moment when the guns of Admiral Dewey brought America unawares but fatally face to face with the problem of Asiatic empire." The United States "finds itself—like England, at once democratic and imperial—inevitably confronted with world conflict; either its ideals must prevail, or they must perish. After three centuries of separation, then, England and America are once more side by side. With them, in union, lies the hope of imperial democracy."

The passage has a modern ring. Few contemporary historians would use the revelatory phrase, *imperial democracy*. Yet there is no other phrase which so fully expresses the ambivalence of the dominant culture. The contradiction is given common currency in two familiar symbols—the dollar and the eagle. Both symbols came to the United States from Europe by way of Latin America.

We like to believe that the eagle of the United States is different, a distinct species found only in the New World. Scientists are inclined to doubt the uniqueness of the bird that circles over our mountains. We may assume that the eagle with great wings is stamped on our coins as a symbol of freedom, of the soaring spirit. But it is also the ancient symbol of empire.

The contradictory symbolism of the eagle is related to the dual meaning of the word, *America;* it properly designates the whole Western Hemisphere; but the people of the United States call themselves *Americans,* and describe their national character and culture as *American*. The semantic difficulty reflects social reality. To Americans of the United States, the mountain eagle may be a bird of freedom. To Americans of Mexico and Central and South America, the eagle is the imperial vulture, the bird of prey, the emissary of dollar diplomacy.

We have used the word *American* to designate the people and culture of the United States throughout this volume. Its use is unavoidable, for our language provides no other word to describe *being of the United States.*

The double-meaning of the word *American* cuts like a canyon through the greenest and most fertile areas of our national culture. The conflict enters into our life and being. Our democratic tradition is genuinely cherished; but it can have no wholeness, it can create no integral pattern of thought and feeling, for it is frustrated and mocked by the class which controls the state.

History as it is taught and written in our country is still dedicated to the concepts of property rights, state-power and the necessity of war. In accepting this prejudiced record as "the truth of history," the majority of the people lose their heritage. Yet the people are the creators of history; they have toiled through the long night of the past to create the promise that is dawning upon the earth.

In order to reveal, and possess, our hidden heritage, we must re-evaluate all the materials of history. This book will have served its purpose if it suggests the potentialities of such a re-evaluation. "All history," as Engels said, "must be studied afresh."

REFERENCES

Part I

Chapter 1: The Cathedral

1. Henry S. Churchill, *The City is the People,* New York, 1945, p. 12.
2. Plato's *Republic,* trans. by Benjamin Jowett, Modern Library edition, New York, 1941, pp. 124-125.
3. C. Osborne Ward, *The Ancient Lowly,* 2 Vols., Chicago, 1900, Vol. II, pp. 164-165.
4. *Ibid.,* Vol. I, pp. 275-332.
5. Max Beer, *Social Struggles in the Middle Ages,* New York, 1929, p. 79.
6. Cecil Headlam, *The Story of Chartres,* London, 1902, p. 120.
7. Leader Scott, *The Cathedral Builders,* New York, 1899, pp. 163-167.
8. B. D. Grecov, *The Culture of the Kiev Rus,* Moscow, 1947, p. 8.
9. Frederick Pyper, "The Christian Church and Slavery in the Middle Ages," *American Historical Review,* XXVIII, No. 1, October, 1922, p. 3.
10. Lewis Mumford, *Technics and Civilization,* New York, 1934, p. 79.
11. Karl Marx, *Capital,* revised and amplified according to the Fourth German edition, by Ernest Untermann, 3 Vols., Chicago, 1912, Vol. I, p. 643.
12. Henri Pirenne, *Medieval Cities,* translated by Frank D. Halsey, Princeton, 1925, pp. 66-67.
13. Leader Scott, *op. cit.,* pp. 3-29.
14. George Unwin, *The Gilds and Companies of London,* London, 1938, pp. 23-25.
15. Charles Gross, *The Gild Merchant,* Oxford, 1890, 2 Vols., Vol. I, pp. 107-120, 158-164.
16. Maurice Dobb, *Studies in the Development of Capitalism,* London, 1947, p. 80n.
17. Pirenne, *op. cit.,* p. 172.
18. *Ibid.,* p. 157.
19. *Cambridge Medieval History,* New York, 1924-1936, Vol. VI, p. 518.

20. Frederic Duncalf, "The Peasant Crusade," *American Historical Review,* Vol. XXVI, No. 3, April, 1921, pp. 440-453.
21. Max L. Margolis and Alexander Marx, *A History of the Jewish People,* Philadelphia, 1941, pp. 359-363; Solomon Landman and Benjamin Efron, *Story Without End,* N. Y., 1949, pp. 136-139.
22. Dobb, *op. cit.,* p. 8.
23. G. Villehandouin, *Memoirs of the Crusades,* New York, 1908, p. 65.
24. *Cambridge Medieval History,* Vol. VI, p. 502.
25. *The Education of Henry Adams,* New York, 1931, p. 388.
26. Headlam, *op. cit.,* p. 116.
27. *Ibid.,* p. 236.
28. George Unwin, *Industrial Organization in the Sixteenth and Seventeenth Centuries,* Oxford, 1904, p. 16.
29. Dobb, *op. cit.,* p. 182.
30. Miriam Beard, *A History of the Business Man,* New York, 1938, p. 76.
31. W. F. Butler, *The Lombard Communes,* New York, 1906, p. 192.

Chapter 2: HERESY

1. *Bible, Acts* 2:44-45; 4:34.
2. William Scott, *A History of the Early Christian Church,* Nashville, Tenn., 1936, p. 152.
3. Beer, *op. cit.,* pp. 149-151.
4. *Ibid.,* pp. 126-127.
5. Sreven Runciman, *The Medieval Manichee,* Cambridge, England, 1947, pp. 94, 184.
6. Beer, *op. cit.,* pp. 158-159.
7. Cited in Beer, *ibid.,* p. 132.
8. Runciman, *op. cit.,* p. 122.
9. Cited in Henry Osborn Taylor, *The Medieval Mind,* 2 Vols., London, 1911, Vol. II, pp. 298-299.
10. Cited in Taylor, *op. cit.,* Vol. I, p. 401.
11. D. C. Munro, "The Children's Crusade," *American Historical Review,* Vol. XIX, No. 3, April, 1914, pp. 519-523.
12. Beer, *op. cit.,* p. 134.
13. Beer, *op. cit.,* p. 152.
14. Paul Henry Lang, *Music in Western Civilization,* New York, 1941, pp. 112-116.
15. Margolis and Marx, *op. cit.,* pp. 392-394.
16. *Ibid.,* p. 375.
17. Charles H. Hoskins, "Science at the Court of Emperor Frederick II," *American Historical Review,* Vol. XXVII, No. 4, July, 1922, pp. 672-690.
18. Taylor, *op. cit.,* Vol. II, p. 484.
19. John Herman Randall, *The Making of the Modern Mind,* Cambridge, Mass., 1940, pp. 210-212.

Chapter 3: The People and the Multitude

1. Niccolò Machiavelli, *History of Florence,* New York, 1901, p. 123.
2. Dante, *Inferno,* Canto XXI, pp. 1-18.
3. *Ibid.,* Canto XI, p. 50.
4. Dante, *De Monarchia,* Book III, Chapter 16.
5. Miriam Beard, *op. cit.,* pp. 141-142.
6. *Loc. cit.*
7. Machiavelli, *op. cit.,* p. 99.
8. *Ibid.,* pp. 104-107.
9. *Ibid.,* pp. 114-116; Miriam Beard, *op. cit.,* pp. 143-148.
10. J. F. C. Hacker, *The Epidemics of the Middle Ages,* London, 1846, pp. 11-32.

Chapter 4: The Fishmonger's Cutlass

1. Charles A. Beard and Mary R. Beard, *The Rise of American Civilization,* 2 Vols., New York, 1939, Vol. I, p. 18.
2. Clarence Perkins, "The Wealth of the Knights Templars in England and Dispositon of it After their Dissolution," *American Historical Review,* Vol. XV, No. 2, Jan., 1910, p. 259.
3. Margolis and Marx, *op. cit.,* pp. 391-398.
4. W. Cunningham, *The Growth of English Industry and Commerce during the Early and Middle Ages,* Cambridge, England, 1910, p. 334.
5. *Loc. cit.*
6. *Social England,* edited by H. D. Traill and J. S. Mann, 6 Vols., London, 1903, Vol. II, p. 194.
7. G. G. Coulton, *Medieval Village,* Cambridge, 1925, pp. 75-142.
8. Bertha H. Putnam, "Minimum Wage Laws for Priests after the Black Death," *American Historical Review,* Vol. XXI, No. 1, October, 1915, p. 32.
9. Unwin, *The Gilds and Companies of London,* pp. 127-133.
10. *Ibid.,* p. 135.
11. Cited in A. L. Morton, *A People's History of England,* London, 1938, p. 126.
12. G. G. Coulton, *Chaucer and His England,* New York and London, 1908, pp. 47-48.
13. Geoffrey Chaucer, *Canterbury Tales,* Rendered into Modern English by J. U. Nicolson, Garden City, N. Y., 1934, p. 17.
14. William Langland, *The Vision of Piers The Plowman,* done into Modern English by Prof. W. W. Skeat, London, 1931.
15. Cited in Morton, *op. cit.,* p. 120.
16. Charles W. C. Oman, *Great Revolt of 1381,* Oxford, 1906, pp. 187-213.
17. G. M. Trevelyan, *English Social History,* London, 1944, p. 52.
18. George Sampson, *Concise Cambridge History of English Literature,* Cambridge, England, 1941, p. 61.

Chapter 5: Sacred and Profane Love

1. Frederick Engels, *Origin of the Family,* N. Y., 1942, p. 62.
2. "The Position of Women," *The Legacy of the Middle Ages,* edited by C. G. Crump and E. F. Jacobs, Oxford, 1926, p. 424.
3. Cited in Taylor, *op. cit.,* Vol. II, p. 6.
4. *Ibid.,* p. 13.
5. *Ibid.,* p. 18.
6. *Ibid.,* p. 19.
7. Chaucer, *op. cit.,* p. 15.
8. *Ibid.,* p. 316.
9. Coulton, *Medieval Village,* Appendix, *Jus Primae Noctis,* pp. 464-469.
10. Thomas Wolfe, *Look Homeward, Angel,* New York, 1929, p. 109.
11. Runciman, *op. cit.,* p. 121.
12. Jules Michelet, *Satanism and Witchcraft,* New York, 1946, pp. 34-36.
13. *Ibid.,* pp. 98-118.

Chapter 6: The Ashes of John Huss

1. Jean Froissart, *Chronicles,* New York, 1858, p. 300.
2. *Cambridge Medieval History,* Vol. VII, p. 68.
3. Machiavelli, *op. cit.,* p. 270.
4. *Cambridge Medieval History,* Vol. VII, p. 69.
5. Bernard Pares, *A History of Russia,* New York, 1944, p. 72.
6. A. V. Shestakov, *A Short History of the U. S. S. R.,* Moscow, 1938, pp. 38-39.
7. *Cambridge Medieval History,* Vol. VII, pp. 289-301.
8. Frederick A. Ogg, *A Source Book of Medieval History,* New York, 1908, pp. 476-477.
9. Lynn Montross, *War Through the Ages,* New York and London, 1944, pp. 188-189.
10. Frederick Engels, *The Peasant War in Germany,* New York, 1934, p. 186.
11. Montross, *op. cit.,* p. 189.
12. *Ibid.,* pp. 184-185.

Part II

Chapter 1: Mona Lisa

1. Cited in *Leonardo da Vinci,* edited by Ludwig Goldscheider, London, 1943, p. 26.
2. *The Notebooks of Leonardo da Vinci,* arranged and rendered into English by Edward MacCurdy, New York, 1939, pp. 1152-1153.

3. Cited in Ralph Roeder, *The Man of the Renaissance,* New York, 1933, p. 65.
4. Cited, *ibid.,* p. 63.
5. Giuseppe Portigliotti, *The Borgias,* London, 1928, pp. 115-119.
6. Karl Marx and Frederick Engels, *The Communist Manifesto,* in *Handbook of Marxism,* New York, 1935, p. 25.
7. *The Notebooks of Leonardo da Vinci,* p. 896.
8. *Leonardo da Vinci,* ed. by Goldscheider, p. 26.
9. John Addington Symonds, *Renaissance in Italy: the Age of the Despots,* London and New York, 1907, p. 155*n*.
10. Machiavelli, *The Prince and the Discourses,* New York, 1940, p. 257.
11. *Ibid.,* p. 151.
12. *Ibid.,* p. 98.
13. *The Notebooks of Leonardo da Vinci,* p. 1110.
14. *Ibid.,* p. 1113.

Chapter 2: The Union Shoe

1. Jacob Strieder, "Origins of Early European Capitalism," *Journal of Economic and Business History,* Cambridge, Mass., Vol. II, No. 1, November, 1929, p. 17.
2. Coulton, *Medieval Village,* p. 352.
3. Cited in Leopold von Ranke, *History of the Reformation in Germany,* translated by Sarah Austin, London, 1905, p. 336.
4. Mildred L. Hartsough, "Fugger Bookkeeping," *Journal of Economic and Business History,* Vol. IV, No. 3, May 1932, p. 551.
5. "Instructions of Albert of Mainz," in *Documents of the Christian Church,* selected and edited by Henry Bettenson, New York and London, 1947, pp. 260-262.
6. John T. Flynn, *Men of Wealth,* New York, 1941, pp. 40-41.
7. *Documents of the Christian Church,* p. 269.
8. Miriam Beard, *op. cit.,* p. 231.
9. *Harvard Classics,* Vol. XXXVI, New York, 1910, pp. 290-291.
10. *Ibid.,* p. 349.
11. *Ibid.,* p. 334.
12. Henry Latimer Seaver, *The Great Revolution in Castile,* Boston and New York, 1908, pp. 90-95.
13. *Ibid.,* p. 172.
14. Cited, *ibid.,* p. 185.
15. Preserved Smith, *The Age of the Reformation,* New York, 1920, p. 241.
16. *Documents of the Christian Church,* p. 285.
17. Cited in Ranke, *op. cit.,* p. 242.
18. *Ibid.,* pp. 248-263.
19. *Ibid.,* p. 309.
20. Cited, *ibid.,* p. 298.
21. *Ibid.,* p. 303.
22. *Ibid.,* p. 254.
23. Cited in Engels, *The Peasant War in Germany,* p. 69.
24. The foregoing account is based on E. Belfort Bax, *The Peasant War in Germany 1525-1526,* London, 1899, pp. 114-131.
25. *Ibid.,* pp. 133-136.

26. Cited in Engels, *The Peasant War in Germany,* p. 61.
27. *Cambridge Modern History,* Vol. II, New York, 1907, p. 194.
28. *Harvard Classics,* Vol. XXXVI, p. 332.
29. Cited in Bax, *op. cit.,* p. 141.
30. Engels, *Peasant War in Germany,* pp. 126-128.
31. *Ibid.,* pp. 138-139.
32. Bax, *op. cit.,* pp. 270-271.
33. *Ibid.,* p. 351.
34. Bax, *op. cit.,* p. 352.
35. Smith, *op. cit.,* pp. 242-243.
36. Ranke, *op. cit.,* p. 724.
37. *Ibid.,* pp. 736-738.
38. *Ibid.,* p. 751.
39. Smith, *op. cit.,* pp. 244-245.
40. Cited in Ranke, *op. cit.,* p. 754*n.*

Chapter 3: The Feast of Fools

1. E. K. Chambers, *The Medieval Stage,* 2 Vols., Oxford, 1903, Vol. I, p. 3.
2. Lang, *op. cit.,* p. 113.
3. Chambers, *op. cit.,* Vol. II, pp. 409-412, 422-425.
4. Michelet, *op. cit.,* pp. 101-103.
5. Cited in Chambers, *op. cit.,* Vol. I, pp. 320-321.
6. *Ibid,* Vol. I, p. 294.
7. Cited in Karl Mantzius, *A History of Theatrical Art,* 6 Vols., New York, 1937, Vol. II, p. 142.
8. *Ibid.,* pp. 145-147.
9. *Ibid.,* pp. 181-182.
10. Cited in Chambers, *op. cit.,* Vol. II, p. 220.
11. *Ibid.,* p. 374.

Chapter 4: The More Family

1. Randall, *op. cit.,* p. 133.
2. *Ideal Commonwealths,* New York, 1901, pp. 12-13.
3. *Ibid.,* p. 39.
4. *Ibid.,* p. 71.
5. Cunningham, *op. cit.,* Vol. I, p. 535.
6. Unwin, *Industrial Organization in the Sixteenth and Seventeenth Centuries,* p. 82.
7. A. W. Reed, *Early Tudor Drama,* London, 1926, pp. 230-232.
8. *Ibid.,* p. 171.
9. *Ibid.,* p. 210.
10. *Ibid.,* p. 87.
11. A. L. Morton, *Language of Men,* London, 1945, p. 12.

Chapter 5: Servetus at Geneva

1. Bernhard Stern, *Society and Medical Progress,* Princeton, 1941, p. 50.
2. *Ibid.,* p. 52.

Chapter 6: Shakespeare and the Famine Years

1. Morton, *A People's History of England,* p. 167.
2. E. M. Leonard, *Early History of English Poor Relief,* London, 1900, p. 71*n.*
3. *Ibid.,* p. 70.
4. Clarence Perkins, Clarence H. Matterson and Reginald I. Lovell, *The Development of European Civilization,* New York, 1940, p. 577.
5. Cited in Ima Lubmienko, "The Correspondence of Queen Elizabeth with the Russian Czars," *American Historical Review,* Vol. XIX, April, 1914, p. 531.
6. *Ibid.,* p. 530.
7. William Pierce, *An Historical Introduction to the Marprelate Tracts,* London, 1908, p. 156.
8. Cited, *ibid.,* p. 194. (The preceding material on the Marprelate tracts is derived from Pierce, pp. 144-218.)
9. Douglass Campbell, *The Puritans in Holland, England, and America,* 2 Vols., New York and London, 1892, Vol. II, pp. 187-190.
10. Louis B. Wright, *Middle Class Culture in Elizabethan England,* Chapel Hill, 1935, p. 10.
11. *Ibid.,* pp. 17-18.
12. E. K. Chambers, *The Elizabethan Stage,* 4 Vols., Oxford, 1923, Vol. I, pp. 269-294.
13. *Ibid.,* pp. 294-295.
14. E. M. W. Tillyard, *Shakespeare's Historical Plays,* New York, 1946, pp. 29-50.
15. Smith, *op. cit.,* p. 464.
16. Cited in W. Cunningham, *The Growth of English Industry and Commerce in Modern Times,* 2 Vols., Cambridge, England, 1912, Vol. I, p. 89*n.*
17. John Dover Wilson, *The Essential Shakespeare,* Cambridge, England, 1945, pp. 82-83.
18. Chambers, *The Elizabethan Stage,* Vol. I, p. 298.
19. G. B. Harrison, "The National Background," in *A Companion to Shakespeare Studies,* edited by Harley Granville Barker and G. B. Harrison, New York, 1934, p. 181.
20. Chambers, *The Elizabethan Stage,* Vol. I, p. 299.
21. *Ibid.,* p. 298.
22. *Life in Shakespeare's England,* compiled by John Dover Wilson, London, 1944, p. 18.
23. Cited in Chambers, *The Elizabethan Stage,* Vol. IV, p. 18.
24. Cited in Lytton Strachey, *Elizabeth and Essex,* New York, 1928, p. 235.
25. Cited in Chambers, *The Elizabethan Stage,* Vol. II, p. 205.
26. Cited in Strachey, *op. cit.,* p. 281.

Part III

Chapter 1: PARADISE

1. Herbert Eugene Bolton and Thomas Maitland Marshall, *The Colonization of North America, 1492-1783*, New York, 1920; *Greater America*, Essays in Honor of Herbert Eugene Bolton, Berkeley and Los Angeles, Calif., 1945.
2. Charles Edward Chapman, *Colonial Hispanic America: A History*, New York, 1938, p. 127. (Other historians give different estimates of the extent of Spanish population at the end of the sixteenth century.)
3. *Selected Letters of Christopher Columbus*, translated and edited by R. H. Major, London, 1897, p. 135.
4. *Bible, Genesis* 2:10.
5. Ralph Waldo Emerson, *English Traits*, London, 1883, p. 148.
6. Alberto Magnanghi, *Amerigo Vespucci, studio critico*, Rome, 1926; Frederick J. Pohl, *Amerigo Vespucci, Pilot Major*, New York, 1944.
7. Edward Gaylord Bourne, *Spain in America, 1450-1588*, New York and London, 1904, p. 85.
8. Stefan Zweig, *Amerigo, A Comedy of Errors*, translated by Andrews St. James, New York, 1942, p. 31.
9. Cited in Zweig. *op. cit.*, p. 98.
10. *Letters of Amerigo Vespucci*, translated with notes and introduction, by Clements R. Markham, London, 1894, pp. 8-15.
11. *Ibid.*, p. 138.
12. *Ibid.*, p. 86.
13. Thomas Hope, *Torquemada the Scourge of the Jews*, London, 1939, pp. 51-91, 123.
14. *Ibid.*, p. 192.
15. Landman and Efron, *op. cit.*, p. 147.
16. *Voyages of Christopher Columbus*, translated and edited by Cecil Jane, London, 1930, pp. 135-136.
17. Lee M. Friedman, *Jewish Pioneers and Patriots*, New York, 1943, pp. 61-72.
18. Margolis and Marx, *op. cit.*, p. 472.
19. John Collier, *The Indians of the Americas*, New York, 1947, p. 31.
20. Margolis and Marx, *op. cit.*, p. 472.
21. German Arcienegas, *Caribbean: Sea of the New World*, New York, 1946, p. 32.
22. *Narratives of the Discovery of America*, edited by A. W. Lawrence and Jean Young, New York, 1931, pp. 273-275.
23. Samuel Eliot Morison, *Admiral of the Ocean Sea*, Boston, 1942, p. 564.
24. P. M. Ashburn, *The Ranks of Death*, New York, 1947, pp. 176-190.
25. *The Northmen, Columbus and Cabot, 985-1503*, edited by Julius E. Olson and Edward Gaylord Bourne, (*Original Narratives of Early American History*), New York. 1906, p. 382.
26. Lesley Byrd Simpson, *The Encomienda in New Spain; Forced Labor in the Spanish Colonies, 1492-1550*, Berkeley, Calif., 1929, pp. 28-31.

27. *Ibid.*, p. 28.
28. *The Northmen, Columbus and Cabot, 985-1503,* p. 401.
29. Francis Augustus MacNutt, *Bartholomoew de Las Casas: His Life, His Apostolate, and His Writings,* New York and London, 1909, p. 37.

Chapter 2: The First Utopia

1. Simpson, *op. cit.,* pp. 36-37.
2. *Ibid.,* p. 41.
3. *Ibid.,* p. 47.
4. *Ibid.,* pp. 50-52.
5. MacNutt, *op. cit.,* pp. 43-52.
6. *The First Three English Books on America,* edited by Edward Arber, Westminster, 1895, p. 149.
7. *Ibid.,* p. 80.
8. Simpson, *op. cit.,* p. 48.
9. Lewis Hanke, *The First Social Experiment in America,* Cambridge, Mass., 1935, pp. 27-40.
10. Arber, *op. cit.,* p. 80.
11. *Ibid.,* p. 122.
12. Hanke, *op. cit.,* pp. 42-44.
13. Bourne, *op. cit.,* p. 272.
14. Seaver, *op. cit.,* pp. 363-364.
15. Bourne, *op. cit.,* pp. 163-169; Simpson, *op. cit.,* pp. 141-143.

Chapter 3: Anathema

1. Charles E. Nowell, "The Discovery of the Pacific, A suggested Change of Approach," *Pacific Historical Review,* Vol. XVI, No. 1, February, 1947, pp. 1-10.
2. Harold Adams Innis, *The Cod Fisheries; the history of an international economy,* New Haven and Toronto, 1940, pp. 12-15.
3. Arcienegas, *op. cit.,* p. 120.
4. Cited in Innis, *op. cit.,* p. 13.
5. *Spanish Documents Concerning English Voyages to the Caribbean, 1527-1568,* selected by I. A. Wright, London, 1929, pp. 1-57.
6. Ione Stuessy Wright, "Early Spanish Voyages from America to the Far East, 1527-1565," in *Greater America,* Berkeley and Los Angeles, 1945, pp. 59-67.
7. Pedro de Alvarado, *Conquest of Guatemala,* New York, 1924, Appendix I, p. 95.
8. *Ibid.,* pp. 62-64
9. Bourne, *op. cit.,* p. 249.
10. Chapman, *op. cit.,* pp. 73-74.
11. Cited in MacNutt, *op. cit.,* p. 429.
12. Pedro de Cieza de Leon, *The War in Quito,* translated and edited by Clements R. Markham, London, 1913, p. 85.
13. *Ibid.,* p. 159.

14. Gwendolin Ballantine Cobb, "Potosi: A Mining Frontier," in *Greater America,* p. 48.
15. Hubert Howe Bancroft, *North Mexican States and Texas,* Vol. I, 1531-1800, San Francisco, 1886, p. 97.
16. Margaret Alexander Marsh, *The Bankers in Bolivia,* New York, 1928, pp. 18-36.
17. MacNutt, *op. cit.,* p. 288.
18. *Ibid.,* pp. 316-356.
19. *Ibid.,* pp. 291-292.

Chapter 4: The Plumed Serpent

1. Salvador de Madariaga, *Spain,* New York, 1943, p. 41.
2. Chapman, *op. cit.,* p. 113.
3. Hanke, *op. cit.,* p. 5.
4. Arnold J. Toynbee, *A Study of History,* Abridgement of Vols. I-VI by D. C. Somervell, New York and London, 1947, p. 216.
5. *Ibid.,* p. 405.
6. Ortega y Gasset, *Toward a Philosophy of History,* New York, 1941, p. 59.
7. Collier, *op. cit.,* pp. 32-33.
8. J. Fred Rippy, *Historical Evolution of Hispanic America,* New York, 1945, pp. 22-31.
9. Clark Wissler, *Indians of the United States,* Garden City, New York, 1945, p. 302.
10. Collier, *op. cit.,* p. 91.
11. Paul Radin, *Story of the American Indian,* London, n.d., pp. 48-60.
12. Melville Jacobs and Bernhard Stern, *Outline of Anthropology,* New York, 1947, p. 175.
13. Radin, *op. cit.,* p. 62.
14. *Ibid.,* p. 50.
15. George F. Carter, *Plant Geography and Culture History in the American Southwest,* New York, 1945, p. 49.
16. A. L. Kroeber, *Cultural and Natural Areas of Native North America,* Berkeley, Calif., 1935, p. 219.
17. Carter, *op. cit.,* p. 12.
18. W. W. Mackie, *Origin, Dispersal and Variability of the Lima Bean,* Berkeley, Calif., 1943; Carter, *op. cit.,* pp. 77-79.
19. Cited, Radin, *op. cit.,* p. 107.
20. Collier, *op. cit.,* p. 90.
21. Sir James G. Frazer, *The Golden Bough,* New York, 1926, p. 432.
22. Collier, *op. cit.,* p. 92.
23. W. L. Prescott, *The Conquest of Mexico,* 2 Vols., London and New York, 1911 (Everyman edition), Vol. I, pp. 162-163.
24. *Ibid.,* p. 169.
25. *Ibid.,* p. 184.
26. *Ibid.,* p. 306.
27. *Ibid.,* pp. 184, 185*n.*
28. Bernal Diaz del Castillo, *A True History of the Conquest of New Spain,* edited by Alfred Percival Maudsley, 5 Vols., London, 1908-1916.
29. Collier, *op. cit.,* p. 79.

30. Woodrow Wilson Borah, "Silk Culture in Mexico," in *Greater America,* pp. 81-87.
31. Chapman, *op. cit.,* p. 116.
32. Collier, *op. cit.,* p. 151.
33. Hiram Bingham, *Lost City of the Incas: The Story of Machu Picchu and its builders,* New York, 1948.
34. Bernard Mishkin, *Rank and Warfare Among the Plains Indians,* New York, 1940, pp. 5-23.
35. Woodbury Lowery, *Spanish Settlements Within the Present Limits of the United States, 1513-1561,* New York and London, 1901, p. 133.
36. *Ibid.,* pp. 136-141.
37. *Ibid.,* p. 156.
38. Collier, *op. cit.,* pp. 190-191.
39. Lowery, *op. cit.,* pp. 165-167; Herbert Aptheker, *American Negro Slave Revolts,* New York, 1943, p. 163.
40. Morris Bishop, *Odyssey of Cabeza de Vaca,* New York and London, 1933, pp. 57-58.
41. *Journey of Alvar Nunez Cabeza de Vaca,* translated by Fanny Bandelier, New York, 1922, p. 150.
42. Bishop, *op. cit.,* p. 160.
43. Lowery, *op. cit.,* pp. 223-225.
44. "Relation of the Voyage of Cabrillo," *Spanish Exploration of the Southwest,* edited by Herbert Eugene Bolton, New York, 1916, pp. 24-35.
45. Bancroft, *History of the North Mexican States and Texas,* Vol. I, pp. 96-97.

Chapter 5: SLAVE MARKET

1. W. E. B. DuBois, *The World and Africa,* New York, 1947, pp. 120-121.
2. *Bible, Nahum* 3:9.
3. *Bible, Psalms* 68:31; *Amos* 9:7; *Isaiah* 37:9.
4. *Bible, I Kings* 10:15.
5. *Bible, Isaiah* 45:14.
6. *Bible, Ezekiel* 30:4-5.
7. DuBois, *op. cit.,* p. 173.
8. *Ibid.,* pp. 196-197.
9. Melville J. Herskovitz, *The Myth of the Negro Past,* New York and London, 1941, p. 57.
10. DuBois, *op. cit.,* p. 165.
11. Herskovitz, *loc. cit.*
12. DuBois, *op. cit.,* p. 48.
13. G. Aguierre Beltram, "Tribal Origins of Slaves in Mexico," *Journal of Negro History,* Vol. XXXI, No. 3, July, 1946, pp. 275-276.
14. Hanke, *op. cit.,* p. 23.
15. Beltram, *loc. cit.*
16. *Ibid.,* pp. 279, 346-349.
17. The most extended treatment of the problem is in Herskovitz, *op. cit.*
18. I. A. Wright, *The Early History of Cuba,* New York, 1916, p. 71.
19. Melville J. Herskovitz, *Life in a Haitian Valley,* New York, 1937, p. 59.
20. *Spanish Documents Concerning English Voyages to the Caribbean, 1527-1568,* p. 6.

21. I. A. Wright, *op. cit.*, p. 102.
22. Hanke, *op. cit.*, pp. 56-57.
23. I. A. Wright, *op. cit.*, pp. 136-137
24. Hanke, *op. cit.*, pp. 60-63.
25. I. A. Wright, *op. cit.*, pp. 201-202.
26. *Ibid.*, p. 197.
27. Herskovitz, *Life in a Haitian Valley*, pp. 59ff.
28. Cited in Herskovitz, *Myth of the Negro Past*, p. 36.
29. Wilbur Zelinsky, "The Historical Geography of the Negro Population of Latin America," *Journal of Negro History*, Vol. XXXIV, No. 2, April, 1949, p. 166.
30. Herskovitz, *Myth of the Negro Past*, p. 70.
31. MacNutt, *op. cit.*, p. 410.
32. Zelinsky, *op. cit.*, p. 163.
33. Marx, *Capital*, Vol. I, p. 823.
34. DuBois, *op. cit.*, pp. 227-228.
35. Pedro de Maghalhaes, *The Histories of Brazil*, translated by John B. Stetson, 2 Vols., New York, 1922, Vol. II, p. 41.
36. John Hiehoff, *Voyages and Travels to Brazil and the East Indies* in *A Collection of Voyages and Travels*, Vol. II, Third edition, London, 1744, pp. 8-120; Arthur Ramos, *The Negro in Brazil*, translated by Richard Pattee, Washington, D. C., 1939, pp. 42ff.
37. Girolomo Benzoni, History of the New World, London, 1857, p. 95.
38. Cited in T. L. Stoddard, *The French Revolution in San Domingo*, Boston, 1914, pp. 335-342.

Chapter 6: The Twilight of the Conquistadors

1. Francois Rabelais, *Gargantua and Pantagruel*, translated by Jacque le Clercq, New York, 1936, Book IV, pp. 62-63.
2. *Loc. cit.*
3. *Ibid.*, p. 71.
4. Jerome Vincent Jacobsen, "Educational Foundations of the Jesuits in America," in *Greater America*, pp. 106-110.
5. Arturo Torres-Rioseco, *New World Literature*, Berkeley and Los Angeles, 1949, pp. 30-31.
6. Jeanette Mirsky, *The Westward Crossings*, New York, 1946, p. 106.
7. "Potosi: A Mining Frontier," in *Greater America*, p. 54.
8. Henry Charles Lee, *The Inquisition in the Spanish Dependencies*, New York, 1908, p. 321.
9. Tom B. Jones, *An Introduction to Hispanic American History*, New York and London, 1939, pp. 143-144.
10. Chapman, *op. cit.*. p. 85.
11. Cited in William Eugene Shiels, "Gonzalo de Tapia (1561-1594), Jesuit Pioneer in New Spain," in *Greater America*, p. 127.
12. *American History Told by Contemporaries*, 5 Vols., New York, 1937, edited by Albert Bushnell Hart, Vol. I, p. 66.
13. H. C. Lea, *The Inquisition in the Spanish Dependencies*, New York, 1922, pp. 199-209.
14. *Ibid.*, pp. 216-225.

15. Chapman, *op. cit.*, p. 121.
16. Cited in Torres-Rioseco, *op. cit.*, pp. 33-34.
17. John Clyde Oswald, *Printing in the Americas,* New York, 1937, pp. 527-529.
18. Irving Albert Leonard, *Don Carlos de Siquenza Gonzora: a Mexican Savant of the Seventeenth Century,* Berkeley, Calif., 1929, pp. 182-183; Torres-Rioseco, *op. cit.*, pp. 39-67.
19. Oswald, *op. cit.*, pp. 533-561.
20. Gilberto Freyre, *The Masters and the Slaves,* translated by Samuel Putnam, New York, 1946, p. 109.
21. Oswald, *op. cit.*, p. 556.
22. Alonso de Ercilla, *Araucaniad,* translated by Charles Manvell Lancaster and Paul Thomas Manchester, Albuquerque, N. Mex., 1945.
23. Pedro de Ona, *Arauco Tamed,* translated by Charles Manvell Lancaster and Paul Thomas Manchester, Albuquerque, N. Mex., 1948.
24. Philip Ainsworth Means, *The Spanish Main, Focus of Envy,* New York, 1935, pp. 106-118.
25. Robert Southey, *Expedition of Orsua and the Crimes of Aguirre,* London, 1821.

Chapter 7: The Protestant Pirates

1. Marx, *Capital,* Vol. I, pp. 255-330.
2. E. G. Wakefield, *A View of the Art of Colonization,* London, 1849, p. 343.
3. *Spanish Documents Concerning English Voyages to the Caribbean, 1527-1568,* selected by I. A. Wright, London, 1929, pp. 64-75.
4. *Spanish Documents Concerning English Voyages to the Caribbean, 1527-1568,* pp. 92-94.
5. James A. Williamson, *Sir John Hawkins, the Times and the Man,* Oxford, 1927, pp. 122-123.
6. *Ibid.*, pp. 145-148.
7. Cited in *Spanish Documents Concerning English Voyages to the Caribbean, 1527-1568,* pp. 153-155.
8. *Ibid.*, pp. 156-157.
9. *Fugger News-Letters,* pp. 8-9.
10. *Spanish Documents Concerning English Voyages to the Spanish Main,* edited by I. A. Wright, London, 1932, pp. xix-xxix.
11. Smith, *op. cit.*, p. 157.
12. Robert F. Heizer, *Francis Drake and the California Indians, 1579,* Berkeley and Los Angeles, Calif., 1947, pp. 264-279.
13. Arcienegas, *op. cit.*, p. 148.
14. *Fugger News-Letters,* p. 42.
15. "Captain Arthur Barlowe's Account," in *American History as Told by Contemporaries,* Vol. I, p. 95.
16. Cited in David B. Quinn, "Preparations for 1585 Virginia Voyage," *William and Mary Quarterly,* Series III, Vol. I, April, 1949, pp. 212-218.
17. Means, *The Spanish Main,* pp. 90-93.
18. Quinn, *op. cit.*, p. 223.
19. Richard Hakluyt, *Principal Navigations, Voiages, Traffiques and Discoveries of the English Nation,* London, 1598-1600, Vol. II, Part I, p. 1.
20. *Ibid.*, Vol. II, Part III, p. 1.

Chapter 8: The Potato

1. Josef Marais, *Songs of the South African Veld,* Decca Album, a-471, Record 23692.
2. *Encyclopedia Britannica,* Eleventh edition, Vol. XXII, p. 201.
3. Thomas Hariott, *A briefe & true report of the new found Land of Virginia,* reprinted New York, 1871, p. 16. (The first edition was published in London, 1588; another in Frankfort, 1590. Text quoted is a modernized English version of the original.)
4. John Gerard, *Herball or generall historie of Plantes,* London, 1633, p. 927.
5. *Ibid.,* p. 926.
6. Lewis Cecil Gray, *Agriculture in the Southern United States to 1860,* 2 Vols., Washington, 1933, Vol. I, p. 4.
7. W. F. Wright, "Origin, Introduction and Primitive Culture of the Potato," *Proceedings, Third Annual Meeting of the Potato Association of America,* 1916, p. 39.
8. Shakespeare, *Merry Wives of Windsor,* Act V, Scene 5.
9. *Ibid.,* Act I, Scene 4.
10. Hakluyt, *op. cit.,* Part I, p. 13.
11. *Spenser's Prose Works,* Rudolf Gottfried, Special Editor, Baltimore, 1949.
12. *Ibid.*
13. T. A. Jackson, *Ireland Her Own,* London, 1942, p. 32.
14. William Stuart, *The Potato, Its Culture, Uses, History and Classification,* Philadelphia and London, 1928, pp. 369-371.
15. The drop in real wages is analyzed in J. E. T. Rogers, *Six Centuries of Work and Wages,* New York, 1884, pp. 392-395.
16. Stuart, *op. cit.,* p. 379.
17. Jackson, *op. cit.,* pp. 79-80.
18. Stuart, *op. cit.,* p. 381.
19. *Loc. cit.*
20. Stuart, *op. cit.,* p. 380.
21. Means, *op. cit.,* pp. 124-132.
22. Walter Raleigh, *Discoverie of the Large, rich and beautiful Empire of Guiana, with a relation of the Great and Golden Citie of Manoa,* London, 1596.
23. Marx, *Capital,* Vol. I, p. 170.
24. *Fugger News-Letter,* pp. 154-155.
25. *Ibid.,* pp. 155-156, 161.
26. *Ibid.,* pp. 168-169.
27. *Ibid.,* pp. 193-194.
28. *Ibid.,* p. 185.
29. *Ibid.,* pp. 202, 206-207, 211.
30. *Ibid.,* pp. 210-211.
31. *Ibid.,* p. 209.
32. *A History of the U. S. S. R.,* edited by A. M. Pankatrova, Part I, Moscow, 1947, p. 179.
33. Shakespeare, *Hamlet,* Act III, Scene 1.

Part IV

Chapter 1: Prologue in Venice

1. Paolo Sarpi, *The History of the Quarrels of Pope Paul V and the State of Venice,* London, 1626, First Part, pp. 3-5.
2. *Ibid.,* Second Part, p. 21.
3. Edwin Sandys, *Europae Speculum, or a View or Survey of the State of Religion in the Westerne part of the world,* London, 1638, p. A 3.
4. *Ibid.,* pp. 356-357.
5. *Ibid.,* p. 53.
6. *Ibid.,* p. 65.
7. *Ibid,* p. 234.
8. *Ibid.,* p. 94.
9. *Ibid.,* p. 32.
10. *Ibid.,* p. 205.
11. *Ibid.,* p. 199.
12. *Ibid.,* p. 188.
13. Avro Manhattan, *The Vatican and World Politics,* New York, 1949, pp. 46-47.
14. Sandys, *loc. cit.*
15. *Ibid.,* p. 226.
16. *Ibid.,* p. 139.
17. *Ibid.,* p. 138.
18. *Ibid.,* p. 169.
19. *Fugger News-Letters,* p. 199.
20. *Ibid.,* pp. 204-206.
21. *Ibid.,* pp. 218-219.
22. *Ibid.,* p. 222.
23. A. P. Morton, *A People's History of England,* New York, 1938, p. 186.
24. Alexander Robertson, *Fra Paolo Sarpi, The Greatest of the Venetians,* London, 1893, p. v; Sandys, *op. cit.,* p. 168.

Chapter 2: A Letter to the Pope

1. Helen Georgia Stafford, *James VI of Scotland and the Throne of England,* New York and London, 1940, pp. 238-239.
2. Leopold von Ranke, *A History of England, principally in the Seventeenth Century,* 6 Vols., Oxford, 1875, Vol. I, pp. 293-294.
3. *Ibid.,* pp. 408-409.
4. Arthur Percival Newton, *The Colonizing Activities of the English Puritans,* New Haven and London, 1914, p. 14.
5. *Ibid.,* p. 16.
6. Samuel R. Gardiner, *History of England from the Accession of James I to the Outbreak of the Civil War,* 10 Vols., Vol. I, London, 1905, p. 343.

7. Kenneth Bell, *Puritanism and Liberty,* London, 1912, p. 3.
8. Douglas C. Campbell, *The Puritans in Holland, England and America,* 2 Vols., New York and London, 1892, Vol. II, p. 223.
9. Gardiner, *op. cit.,* Vol. II, London, 1889, p. 254.
10. *Casebook in American Business History,* edited by N. S. B. Gras and Henrietta M. Larson, New York, 1939, p. 33.
11. Arthur Lyon Cross, *Shorter History of England and Great Britain,* New York, 1927, p. 289.
12. James Spedding, *An Account of the Life and Times of Francis Bacon,* 2 Vols., Boston, 1880, Vol. I, p. 458.
13. *Ibid.,* Vol. I, p. 461.
14. *Ibid.,* Vol. I, p. 452.
15. Innis, *op. cit.,* p. 64.
16. Cited in Dobb, *op. cit.,* p. 168.
17. Innis, *loc. cit.*
18. Cited in *A Companion to Shakespeare Studies,* edited by Harley Granville-Barker and G. B. Harrison, Cambridge, p. 184.

Chapter 3: A Shipment of Currants

1. Innis, *op. cit.,* p. 65.
2. "Proceedings of the English Colony," in *Narratives of Early Virginia,* edited by Lyon Gardiner Tyler, New York, 1907, p. 121.
3. Warner F. Gookin, "Who was Nathaniel Gosnold?" *William and Mary Quarterly,* Third Series, Vol. VI, No. 3, July, 1949, pp. 398-415.
4. *Documentary Source Book of American History, 1606-1926,* edited with notes by William Macdonald, New York, 1926, p. 3.
5. Innis, *op. cit.,* pp. 53-54.
6. *Documentary Source Book of American History, 1606-1926,* pp. 2-3.
7. Tyler, "Proceedings of the English Colony," *op. cit.,* pp. 125-126.
8. Bell, *op. cit.,* p. 8.
9. Cited in R. V. Coleman, *The First Frontier,* New York and London, 1948, p. 87.

Chapter 4: The Case of John Smith

1. Arber, *op. cit.,* Vol. II, pp. 829-880.
2. Charles M. Andrews, *The Colonial Period in American History,* 4 Vols., New Haven and London, 1934, Vol. I, p. 142*n.*
3. Cited in *Narratives of Early Virginia,* edited by Lyon Gardiner Tyler, New York, 1907, p. 5*n.*
4. Cited in Alexander Brown, *The First Republic in America,* New York and Boston, 1898, p. 55.
5. "Observations of George Percy," *Narratives of Early Virginia,* p. 18.
6. Gookin, *op. cit.,* p. 406.
7. Edward Maria Wingfield, "Discourses of Virginia," *Transactions of the American Antiquarian Society,* Vol. IV, Boston, 1860, p. 80.
8. "Observations of George Percy," *Narratives of Early Virginia,* pp. 20-21.

9. P. M. Ashburn, *The Ranks of Death,* New York, 1947, p. 120.
10. Wingfield, *op. cit.,* p. 21.
11. Herbert L. Osgood, *The American Colonies in the Seventeenth Century,* 2 Vols., New York, 1930, Vol. I, pp. 46-47.
12. Wingfield, *op. cit.,* p. 88.
13. *Ibid.,* p. 90.
14. Arber, *op. cit.,* Vol. I, p. 19.
15. *Ibid.,* p. 20.
16. Osgood, *op. cit.,* Vol. I, p. 49; *Bible, Leviticus* 14:17-21.
17. Wingfield, *op. cit.,* p. 9.
18. Arber, *op. cit.,* Vol. I, pp. 104-105.

Chapter 5: JAMESTOWN AND MOSCOW

1. Cunningham, *The Growth of English Industry and Commerce in Modern Times,* pp. 87-88.
2. Stephen H. Fritchman, *Men of Liberty,* Boston, 1945, pp. 22-39.
3. George Park Fisher, *The Reformation,* New York, 1926, p. 402.
4. Earl Morse Wilbur, *A History of Unitarianism,* Cambridge, Mass., 1945, pp. 424-426.
5. *Ibid.,* p. 424.
6. *Ibid.,* p. 427.
7. Fritchman, *op. cit.,* pp. 18-25.
8. A. M. Pankratova, *op. cit.,* Vol. I, pp. 181-185.
9. *Ibid.,* pp. 185-187.
10. Fritchman, *op. cit.,* p. 24.
11. Wilbur, *op. cit.,* p. 421.
12. *Ibid.,* pp. 437-438.
13. *World Agriculture, An International Survey* (by a study group of the Royal Institute of International Affairs), London, 1932, p. 15.
14. Fritchman, *op. cit.,* p. 24.
15. Cited in Wilbur, *op. cit.,* p. 455.

Chapter 6: MALTHUS AND THE MIDLAND RIOTS

1. *Handbook of Freedom,* edited by J. Lindsay and E. Rickword, New York, 1939, p. 98.
2. W. G. Wilkins, Jr., *History of England,* London, 1902.
3. Cunningham, *The Growth of English Industry and Commerce in Modern Times,* Vol. II, Appendix B, pp. 897-899.
4. *Essays of Michel de Montaigne,* translated by George B. Ives, 3 Vols., New York, 1946, Vol. III, pp. 922-923.
5. Robert Wallace, *A Dissertation on the Numbers of Man,* Edinburgh, 1809.
6. *Ibid.*
7. "Charles Louis de Secondat Montesquieu," *Encyclopaedia Britannica,* New York, 1947, Vol. 15, p. 759.
8. David Hume, "Of the Populousness of Ancient Nations," *Essays,* edited by T. H. Greene and T. H. Grose, London, 1875, Vol. IX, pp. 388-397.

9. Lewis J. Carey, *Franklin's Economic Views,* New York, 1928, p. 58.
10. *The Writings of Benjamin Franklin,* edited by Albert Henry Smyth, 10 Vols., New York, 1905-1907.
11. Oliver Goldsmith, *New Essays,* edited by R. S. Crane, Chicago, 1927, p. 95.
12. *The Writings of Benjamin Franklin, op. cit.*
13. Alfred Aldridge, "Franklin as Demographer," *Journal of Economic History,* Vol. IX, No. 1, May, 1949, pp. 25-44.
14. T. A. Jackson, *Trials of British Freedom,* London, 1940, pp. 45-47.
15. *Ibid.,* pp. 52-53; C. B. Roylance Kent, *The English Radicals, London,* etc., 1899, pp. 142-157.
16. Jackson, *Trials of British Freedom,* pp. 60-62.
17. Cunningham, *The Growth of English Industry and Commerce in Modern Times,* Vol. II, p. 674.
18. Marx, *Capital,* Vol. I, p. 676*n.*
19. Thomas Malthus, *Principles of Population,* London, 1817.
20. *Ibid.*
21. Vernon Stauffer, *New England and the Bavarian Illuminati,* New York, 1918, p. 233*n.*
22. Merle Curti, *The Growth of American Thought,* New York and London, 1943, p. 200.
23. Stauffer, *op. cit.,* p. 200*n,* 257.
24. Cited, *Ibid.,* pp. 248-249.
25. *Ibid.,* p. 192.
26. *The Works of Alexander Hamilton,* edited by Henry Cabot Lodge, 10 Vols., New York, 1885, Vol. X, p. 425.
27. Aldridge, *op. cit.,* p. 144.
28. William Vogt, *Road to Survival,* New York, 1948, pp. 14, 19, 78.
29. Frank W. Notestein, "Problems of Policy in Relation to Areas of Heavy Population Pressure," *Demographic Studies of Selected Areas of Population,* Milbank Fund Conference, April 12-13, 1944, New York, 1944, p. 153.
30. Kirtley F. Mather in *Science and Society,* Spring, 1949, p. 170.
31. Cunningham, *The Growth of English Industry and Commerce in Modern Times, op. cit.,* Vol I, p. 102*n.*
32. William Bradford, *History of Plimouth Plantation,* Boston, 1901, p. 13.
33. *Ibid.,* p. 14.
34. Eduard Bernstein, *Cromwell and Communism,* London, 1930, pp. 9-171.
35. Thomas J. Wertenbaker, *The Planters of Colonial Virginia,* Princeton, 1922, pp. 91-99.
36. Aptheker, *op. cit.,* pp. 164-165.
37. Irving Mark, *Agrarian Conflicts in Colonial New York, 1711-1775,* New York, 1940, p. 148.

Part V

Chapter 1: Coriolanus

1. See above pp. 128-145.
2. For example, title of Henry S. Churchill's book on architecture, *The City is the People,* New York, 1945.
3. Hardin Craig, *An Interpretation of Shakespeare,* New York, 1948, pp. 306-309.
4. Cited in Chambers, *The Elizabethan Stage,* Vol. III, p. 220.
5. Kenneth Muir, "Timon of Athens and the Cash Nexus," *Modern Quarterly Miscellany,* I, London, 1947, p. 66.
6. Craig, *op. cit.,* p. 282.
7. *Ibid.,* p. 299.
8. Gardiner, *op. cit.,* Vol. II, pp. 216-217.
9. Ranke, *op. cit.,* Vol. I, p. 477.
10. Roy Dickinson Welch, "A Discussion of the Expressed Content of Beethoven's Third Symphony," a supplementary essay in Theodore Meyer Greene, *The Arts and Art Criticism,* Princeton, 1940, p. 489.
11. Hugo Leichentritt, *Music History and Ideas,* Cambridge, Mass., 1938, pp. 181-183.
12. Lang, *op. cit.,* pp. 764-765.
13. Cited in *Encyclopaedia Britannica,* Eleventh Edition, Vol. XIX, p. 204.
14. Elie Siegmeister, *Music and Society,* New York, 1938, p. 45.
15. John Leacock, "The Fall of British Tyranny," *Representative Plays by American Dramatists, 1765-1819,* edited by Montrose J. Moses, New York, 1918, pp. 291-299.
16. Alexander Brown, *The Genesis of the United States,* 2 Vols., Boston and New York, 1890, Vol. II (Appendix).
17. Spedding, *op. cit.,* Vol. I, pp. 512-517.
18. *Ibid.,* Vol. I, p. 515.
19. *Works of Francis Bacon,* with introduction by Basil Montague, 3 Vols., Philadelphia, etc., 1841, Vol. III, p. 334.
20. Spedding, *op. cit.,* Vol. I, p. 540.

Chapter 2: The Buried Weapons

1. Lewis Henry Morgan, *Ancient Society,* Chicago, n. d., p. 6.
2. Frederick Engels, *The Family, Private Property and the State,* New York, 1942, p. 5.
3. Morgan, *op. cit.,* p. vii.
4. Wissler, *op. cit.,* pp. 55-58.
5. Cited in Francis Parkman, *Pioneers of France in the New World,* 2 Vols., Boston, 1922, Vol. II, pp. 159-161.

6. Paul Radin, *op. cit.*, p. 273.
7. Cited, *ibid.*, p. 275.
8. Wissler, *op. cit.*, pp. 110-111.
9. Paul Radin, *op. cit.*, p. 277.
10. J. N. B. Hewitt, *A Constitutional League of Peace in the Stone Age,* Washington, 1918.
11. Morgan, *op. cit.*, p. 127.
12. Collier, *op. cit.*, p. 203.
13. Cited, *ibid.*, p. 201.
14. *Travel & Works of Captain John Smith, President of Virginia & Admiral of New England, 1580-1631,* edited by Edward Arber, Edinburgh, 1910, p. 9.
15. "Observations of George Percy," *Narratives of Early Virginia,* p. 22.
16. Arber, *op. cit.*, p. 119.
17. *Ibid.*, p. 106.
18. *Ibid.*, p. 107.
19. *Ibid.*, pp. 131-135.
20. *Ibid.*, p. 146.
21. *Ibid.*
22. *Ibid.*, pp. 149-150.
23. *Ibid.*, p. 127.
24. *Ibid.*, p. 476.
25. *Ibid.*, p. 161.
26. *Ibid.*
27. *Ibid.*, pp. 163-165.
28. *Ibid.*, pp. 165-168.
29. *Ibid.*, p. 167.
30. *Ibid.*, p. 170.
31. Parkman, *op. cit.*, Vol. II, p. 178.

Chapter 3: MYTH AND MONEY

1. George Thomson, *Aeschylus and Athens,* London, 1946, p. 38. The material on Greek society in the following pages is derived from Thomson's work.
2. Gordon Childe, *What Happened in History,* New York, 1946, p. 65.
3. C. Osborne Ward, *The Ancient Lowly,* 2 Vols., Chicago, 1888, Vol. I, pp. 133-144.

Chapter 4: THE OPERA

1. W. S. Rockstro, *General History of Music,* Fourth Edition, London, n. d., p. 107.
2. Manfred F. Bukofzer, *Music in the Baroque Era,* New York, 1947, pp. 5, 26.
3. *The Art of Music,* edited by Leland Hull and Cesar Saerchinger, 14 Vols., New York, 1916, Vol. I, pp. 314-315.
4. Lang, *op. cit.*, p. 156.
5. *Ibid.*, p. 238.
6. *Ibid.*, p. 345.
7. *The Art of Music,* p. 8.

8. *Romain Rolland, Histoire de l'Opera en Europe avant Lully et Scarlatti,* Paris, 1895.
9. Bukofzer, *op. cit.,* pp. 55-56.
10. Cited, *ibid.,* p. 57.
11. Rockstro, *op. cit.,* p. 127.
12. Bukofzer, *op. cit.,* p. 358.
13. *Ibid.,* pp. 1-19. (Note the comparison of Renaissance and Baroque style, p. 17).
14. Rockstro, *op. cit.,* p. 89.
15. Thomson, *op. cit.,* p. 192.
16. *The Art of Music,* p. 45.
17. *Artists on Art,* pp. 114-116.
18. Harold D McKinney and W. R. Anderson, *Music in History,* New York, etc., 1940, p. 310.
19. *Oxford History of Music,* 7 Vols., Oxford, 1902, Vol. III, p. 97.
20. Maurer Maurer, "The Library of a Colonial Musician, 1755," *William and Mary Quarterly,* Third Series, Vol. VII, No. 1, January, 1950, pp. 39-52.
21. O. G. Sonneck, *Early Opera in America,* New York, etc., 1915, pp. 3-54.
22. Eleanor D. Berman, *Thomas Jefferson among the Arts,* New York, 1947, pp. 175-176.
23. Cited, *ibid.,* pp. 177-178.
24. Siegmeister, *op. cit.,* p. 44.
25. William Winter, *Shakespeare on the Stage,* Second Series, New York, 1915, pp. 112-122.
26. *The American Stage as Seen by its Critics,* edited by Montrose J. Moses and John Mason Brown, New York, 1934, pp. 68, 71-72.
27. Constance Rourke, *The Roots of American Culture,* New York, 1942, p. 104.
28. Leo Tolstoy, *War and Peace,* Modern Library edition, pp. 616-626.

Chapter 5: THE BEGINNINGS OF THE NOVEL

1. Ralph Fox, *The Novel and the People,* New York, 1945, p. 45.
2. James Fitzmaurice Kelley, *Miguel de Cervantes Saavedra,* Oxford, 1913, pp. 14-05.
3. *Ibid.,* pp. 56-111.
4. *Ibid.,* pp. 116-138.
5. *Ibid.,* pp. 155-156.
6. *Ibid.,* p. 179.
7. *Cambridge Modern History,* Vol. VIII, p. 547.
8. Perkins, Matterson, Lovell. *The Development of European Civilization from the Earliest time to the Present,* New York, 1940, p. 541-546.
9. Hans Rosenkranz. *El Greco and Cervantes,* translated by Marcel Arrousseau, London 1932.
10. *Artists on Art,* p. 143.
11. John Gassner, *Masters of the Drama,* New York, 1940, pp. 177-185.
12. Herbert Arthur Evans, *English Masques,* London, 1906, p. xxxvi.
13. *The Works of Francis Bacon,* with a life of the author, by Basil Montague, 3 Vols., Phila., etc., 1841, Vol. I, p. 190.

Chapter 6: The Corporation

1. Edward P. Cheyney, "Some English Conditions Surrounding the Settlement of Virginia," *American Historical Review,* Vol. XII, p. 512.
2. Cross, *op. cit.,* p. 290.
3. *Documentary Source Book of American History, 1606-1926,* pp. 9-14.
4. Osgood, *op. cit.,* p. 69.
5. Philip Alexander Bruce, *Economic History of Virginia in the Seventeenth Century,* 2 Vols., New York, 1907, Vol. II, pp. 266-267.
6. Cited in Brown, *The First Republic in America,* p. 80.
7. Unwin, *Industrial Organization in the Sixteenth and Seventeenth Centuries,* pp. 153-157.
8. William Hyde Price, *The English Patents of Monopoly,* Boston and New York, 1906, p. 83.
9. William W. Hunter, *History of British India,* 2 Vols., London and New York, 1899-1900, Vol. I, pp. 286-288.
10. Spedding, *op. cit.,* Vol. I, p. 585.
11. *Ibid.,* Vol. I, pp. 585-590.
12. Herbert Richmond, *Statesmen and Sea Power,* Oxford, 1946, p. 26.
13. *Casebook in American Business History,* p. 33.
14. Cited, Spedding, *op. cit.,* Vol. I, p. 600.
15. Cited, *ibid.,* Vol. I, p. 630.
16. Cited, Cross, *op. cit.,* p. 287.
17. Price, *op. cit.,* p. 85.
18. Spedding, *op. cit.,* Vol. I, p. 631.
19. *Ibid.,* Vol. I, p. 636.
20. Rev. James Barkley Woodburn, *The Ulster Scot; his history and religion,* London, 1914, p. 67.
21. M. A. Abrams, "The English Gold and Silver Thread Monopolies," *Journal of Economic and Business History,* February, 1930, Vol. II, No. 2, pp. 386-387.
22. Unwin, *Industrial Organization in the Sixteenth and Seventeenth Centuries,* pp. 155-163.
23. Bruce, *op. cit.,* Vol. II, p. 272.
24. Lawrence E. Nelson, *Our Roving Bible,* New York and Nashville, n. d., pp. 56-57.
25. *The Summe and Substance of the Conference. . . .* Contracted by William Barlow, London, 1638.
26. *Documentary Source Book of American History,* pp. 14-19.
27. *The Records of the Virginia Company of London,* edited by Susan Myra Kingsbury, 4 Vols., Washington, 1933, Vol. III, pp. 34-48.
28. *Narratives of Early Virginia,* pp. 76-77.
29. *Loc. cit.*
30. *Loc. cit.*
31. Price, *op. cit.,* pp. 86-89.
32. Spedding, *op. cit.,* Vol. I, p. 667.
33. *Ibid.,* Vol. I, p. 672.
34. Gardiner, *op. cit.,* Vol. II, p. 162.
35. *Ibid.,* pp. 227-228.
36. Spedding, *op. cit.,* Vol. I, pp. 678-679.

37. *The Case of Impotency, as debated in England, in that Remarkable Tryal, 1613, between Robert, Earl of Essex, and the Lady Frances Howard, etc.,* 2 Vols., London, 1719.
38. Gardiner, *op. cit.,* Vol. II, pp. 216-217.
39. *Loc. cit.*
40. Henry Foley, *Records of the English Province of the Society of Jesus,* 7 Vols. in 8 Parts, London, 1877-1883.
41. Gardiner, *op. cit.,* Vol. II, pp. 228-230.
42. Cited, *ibid.,* p. 233.
43. Cited, *ibid.,* p. 340*n.*
44. Cited in John G. Coulter, *The Story of Modern France,* Indianapolis and New York, 1939, p. 31.
45. *Ibid.,* p. 32.
46. *Oxford English Dictionary,* Oxford, 1933, Vol. II, pp. E 74-75.
47. *Works of Francis Bacon,* Vol. I, p. 175.
48. *Oxford English Dictionary,* Vol. III, p. E 75.
49. *Records of the Virginia Company,* Vol. III, p. 34.
50. Roger Williams, *Collected Works,* Narragansett Club Publications, 6 Vols., Providence, 1866-1874, Vol. III, p. 73.
51. *The Federalist,* edited by Henry Cabot Lodge, New York and London, 1888, p. 54.
52. Cited in Joseph Dorfman, *The Economic Mind in American Civilization, 1606-1865,* 2 Vols., New York, 1946, Vol. I, p. 297.
53. Frederick B. Tolles, "Unofficial Ambassador: George Logan's Mission to France, 1798," *William and Mary Quarterly,* January, 1950, Third Series, Vol. VII, No. 1, p. 7.
54. Cited in Charles Warren, *The Supreme Court in United States History,* 3 Vols., Boston, 1923, Vol. I, p. 486.
55. Cited in Lewis J. Haney, *Business Organization and Combination,* New York, 1934, p. 91.

Chapter 7: Brave New World

1. Craig, *op. cit.,* pp. 347-348.
2. Muir, *op. cit.,* p. 61.
3. *Life in Shakespeare's England,* pp. 18-21.
4. *Los Angeles Examiner,* April 30, 1949.
5. Cited in Brown, *Genesis of America,* Vol. I, p. 252.
6. *Records of the Virginia Company,* Vol. III, p. 15.
7. Osgood, *op. cit.,* Vol. I, pp. 69-71.
8. *Documentary Source Book of American History,* pp. 16-18.
9. Cited in Chambers, *The Elizabethan Stage,* Vol. II, p. 419.
10. Cited, *ibid.,* Vol. II, p. 421.
11. Osgood, *op. cit.,* Vol. I, p. 73.
12. Charles Olson, *Call Me Ishmael,* New York, 1947, pp. 39-44.
13. Herman Melville, *Moby Dick,* New York, 1930, p. 156.
14. Olson, *op. cit.,* p. 21.
15. Melville, *op. cit.*
16. *Ibid.,* p. 116.
17. *Ibid.,* p. 820.

18. *Ibid.*, p. 822.
19. *Ibid.*, p. 499.
20. The word "Negro" is not capitalized in Melville's work.
21. Herman Melville, "The Piazza Tales," in *The Works of Melville,* London, etc., 1923, Vol. X.
22. Lewis Mumford, *Herman Melville,* New York, 1929, p. 244.
23. George William Curtis, *The Duty of the American Scholar to Politics and the Times* (An oration at Wesleyan University), New York, 1856, pp. 41-42.
24. Passage previously cited, *Walt Whitman,* edited by Samuel Sillen, p. 101.

Chapter 8: LAND OF COCKAIGNE

1. Al Capp, *Life and Time of the Schmoo,* New York, 1949.
2. Gardiner, *op. cit.,* Vol. II, pp. 260-265.
3. Chambers, *The Elizabethan Stage,* Vol. II, p. 423.
4. *Ibid.,* Vol. IV, p. 372.
5. *Ibid.,* Vol. II, p. 423.
6. Gardiner, *op. cit.,* Vol. II, pp. 268-279.
7. Cited in James Ernst, *Roger Williams,* New York, 1932, p. 25.
8. Max Radin, *Handbook of Anglo-American Legal History,* St. Paul, 1936, pp. 95-97.
9. Cunningham. *Growth of English Industry and Commerce in Modern Times,* Vol. II, p. 220.
10. Price, *op. cit.,* pp. 102-106; Unwin, *Industrial Organization in the Sixteenth and Seventeenth Centuries,* pp. 181-193.
11. Cited, Price, *op. cit.,* p. 106.
12. Brown, *Genesis of the United States, op. cit.,* Vol. II, p. 772.
13. Brown, *First Republic in America,* p. 230.
14. Cited in Unwin, *Industrial Organization in the Sixteenth and Seventeenth Centuries,* p. 189
15. Price, *op. cit.,* p. 105.
16. Cited in Unwin, *Industrial Organization in the Sixteenth and Seventeenth Centuries,* pp. 191-192.
17. Chambers, *The Elizabethan Stage,* Vol. II, pp. 510-511.
18. *Political History of England,* 12 Vols.; Vol. VII, F. C. Montague, *History of England from the Accession of James I to the Restoration,* London, etc., 1907, p. 73.
19. Cited in Louis B. Wright, *Middle Class Culture in Elizabethan England,* Chapel Hill, 1935, pp. 482-487.
20. Cited, *ibid.,* pp. 488-491.
21. Cited in Unwin, *Industrial Organization in the Sixteenth and Seventeenth Centuries,* pp. 191-193.
22. *Ibid.,* p. 193.
23. Brown, *First Republic in America,* p. 247.
24. Cited in Wesley Frank Craven, *Dissolution of the Virginia Company,* New York, 1932, p. 43.
25. *Virginia Historical Register,* Vol. I, 1848, pp. 101-113.
26. *Records of the Virginia Company,* Vol. III, p. 69.
27. Osgood, *op. cit.,* Vol. I, p. 75; Bruce, *op. cit.,* Vol. I, p. 213.

28. *The Great Prisoners,* edited by Isidore Abramowitz, New York, 1946, pp. 197-198.
29. Means, *The Spanish Main,* p. 148.
30. Unwin, *Industrial Organization in the Sixteenth and Seventeenth Centuries,* p. 193.
31. Craven, *op. cit.,* p. 39.
32. Bruce, *op. cit.,* Vol. I, p. 280*n*.
33. Cited in Craven, *op. cit.,* p. 44.
34. Brown, *First Republic in America,* p. 247.

Chapter 9: THE FISHERMEN

1. Cited, Innis, *op. cit.,* p. 1.
2. William Radcliffe, *Fishing from Earliest Times,* New York, 1926, Second edition, p. 131.
3. Cunningham, *The Growth of English Commerce and Industry during the Middle Ages,* p. 396.
4. Cited, Innis, *op. cit.,* p. 11.
5. C. Pryce, *Memoirs of the Canynges Family,* London, 1883.
6. James E. Thorold Rogers, *The Economic Interpretation of History,* New York, 1889, p. 278.
7. Cited, Innis, *op. cit.,* p. 16.
8. *Ibid.,* p. 19*n*
9. Cunningham, *The Growth of English Industry and Commerce in Modern Times,* pp. 68-69.
10. Innis, *op. cit.,* p. 39.
11. Cited, *ibid.,* p. 38.
12. Cited, *ibid.,* p. 31.
13. *Ibid.,* pp. 39-51.
14. *Ibid.,* p. 52.
15. *Ibid.,* pp. 54, 60.
16. Cited, *ibid.,* p. 55.
17. *Ibid.,* p. 56.
18. Arber, *op. cit.,* p. 205.
19. Cited, Lincoln N. Kinnicutt, "The Settlement at Plymouth Contemplated before 1620," *Annual Report of the American Historical Association for the Year 1921,* Washington, 1925, p. 213.
20. *Ibid.,* p. 215.
21. Bruce, *Economic History of Virginia in the Seventeenth Century,* Vol. I, p. 230.
22. Cited in Innis, *op. cit.,* p. 57.
23. *Records of the Virginia Company,* Vol. III, pp. 242-243.
24. *Ibid.,* p. 248.
25. Innis, *op. cit.,* p. 61.
26. D. W. Prowse, *A History of Newfoundland,* London, 1896, p. 103.
27. Curtis P. Nettels, *Roots of American Civilization,* New York, 1940, p. 244.
28. *History of Wages in the United States from Colonial Times to 1928,* United States Department of Labor, Washington, 1934, p. 99
29. *The Colonial Laws of Massachusetts,* Boston, 1887, p. 53.
30. *Ibid.,* p. 266.

31. *Transcript of Appeal to United States Court of Appeals for the Ninth District,* Local 36 of the International Fishermen and Allied Workers, etc. vs. United States of America, 6 vols., Vol. I, p. 82.

Part VI

Chapter 1: The First Slave Ship

1. *Records of the Virginia Company of London,* Vol. I, p. 65.
2. Bruce, *Economic History of Virginia in the Seventeenth Century,* Vol. I, p. 280*n.*
3. *Records of the Virginia Company of London,* Vol. III, p. 105.
4. *Ibid.,* Vol. III, p. 106.
5. Craven, *op. cit.,* p. 58.
6. *Records of the Virginia Company of London,* Vol. III, p. 107.
7. *Loc. cit.*
8. Gray, *History of Agriculture in the United States to 1860,* Vol. I, p. 319.
9. "Proceedings of the Virginia Company," *Narratives of Early Virginia,* p. 266.
10. *Ibid.,* p. 273.
11. *Records of the Virginia Company of London,* Vol. III, p. 494.
12. Oliver Perry Chitwood, *A History of Colonial America,* New York and London, 1931, p. 80.
13. *Records of the Virginia Company,* Vol. III, p. 243.
14. Coleman, *op. cit.,* p. 124.
15. Craven, *op. cit.,* p. 130.
16. Cited, *ibid.,* p. 135.
17. John Hope Franklin, *From Slavery to Freedom,* New York, 1947, p. 70.
18. Gray, *op. cit.,* Vol. I, p. 317.
19. *Records of the Virginia Company,* Vol. III, p. 174.
20. Bruce, *op. cit.,* p. 593.
21. Abbott Emerson Smith, *Colonists in Bondage,* Chapel Hill, 1947, pp. 148-149.
22. Cited in Craven, *op. cit.,* pp. 193-194.
23. *Records of the Virginia Company,* Vol. III, p. 537.
24. Craven, *op. cit.,* p. 228.
25. *Ibid.*
26. *Ibid.,* p. 143.
27. *Ibid.,* p. 229.
28. Cited, *ibid.,* p. 196.
29. *Records of the Virginia Company,* Vol. III, pp. 556-557.
30. *Loc. cit.*
31. "Good Newes from Virginia," *William and Mary Quarterly,* Third Series, Vol. V, No. 3, pp. 353-354.
32. Howard Mumford Jones, "The Literature of Virginia in the Seventeenth Century," *Memoirs of the American Academy of Arts and Sciences,* Vol. XIX, Part II, 1946, p. 3*n.*
33. Richard Beale Davis, "America in George Sandys' Ovid," *William and Mary Quarterly,* Third Series, Vol. IV, No. 3, p. 299.

34. Douglas Bush, *Mythology and the Renaissance Tradition in English Poetry,* Minneapolis, 1932, p. 243.
35. *Ovids Metamorphoses,* Englished by George Sandys, London, 1656.
36. John Donne, *Works,* edited by Henry Alford, London, 1836, Vol. VI, pp. 231-232.

Chapter 2: THE ACCIDENT OF THE WIND

1. Charles Edward Banks, *The Planters of the Commonwealth, 1620-1640,* Boston, 1930, p. 32.
2. *Ibid.,* p. 30.
3. Bradford, *op. cit.,* p. 93.
4. *Ibid.,* p. 116.
5. Nathaniel Morton, *New-England's Memorial,* edited by Howard J. Hall, New York, 1937, p. 92.
6. Lincoln N. Kinnicutt, "The Settlement at Plymouth Contemplated before 1620," *Annual Report of American Historical Association for 1921,* Washington, 1925, pp. 213-215.
7. Bradford, *op. cit.,* p. 118.
8. Kinnicutt, *op. cit.,* p. 217.
9. Bradford, *op. cit.,* p. 117.
10. *Ibid.,* pp. 104-106.

Chapter 3: THOMAS WESTON'S PILGRIMAGE

1. Bradford, *op. cit.,* p. 129.
2. *Loc. cit.*
3. *Ibid.,* p. 131.
4. *Bradford's History of Plymouth Plantation, 1606-1646,* edited by Wm. T. Davis, New York, 1920, p. 122.
5. W. R. Scott, *Constitution and Finance of English, Scottish and Irish Joint-Stock Companies to 1720,* 3 Vols., Cambridge, England, 1910-1912, Vol. II, pp. 318-319.
6. Innis, *op. cit.,* p. 72.
7. Bradford, *op. cit.,* pp. 138-149.
8. *Ibid.,* p. 191.
9. *Ibid.,* pp. 143-149.
10. *American History Told by Contemporaries,* Vol. I, p. 175.
11. Bradford, *op. cit.,* pp. 152-159.
12. Coleman, *op. cit.,* p. 152.
13. Bradford, *op. cit.,* p. 159-163.
14. *American History Told by Contemporaries,* Vol. I, p. 175.
15. *Ibid.,* p. 176.
16. Bradford, *op. cit.,* p. 170.
17. Cited in Coleman, *op. cit.,* p. 150.
18. Bernard C. Steiner, "The First Lord Baltimore and His Colonial Projects," *Annual Report of American Historical Association for 1905,* 2 Vols., Washington, 1906, Vol. I, p. 117.

19. Innis, *op. cit.*, p. 64.
20. Bradford, *op. cit.*, pp. 176-243.

Chapter 4: THE MAYPOLE ON BOSTON BAY

1. Bradford, *op. cit.*, p. 246-250.
2. Lewis C. Gray, *History of Agriculture in the Southern United States to 1860*, Washington, 1933, Vol. I.
3. *Ibid.*, Vol. I, p. 260.
4. Bradford, *op. cit.*, pp. 273, 274.
5. Bernard C. Steiner, *op. cit.*, in *Annual Report, Am. Historical Association for 1905*, Vol. I, pp. 118, 120.
6. Bradford, *op. cit.*, pp. 283-286.
7. *The Roots of American Culture,* edited by Robert E. Spiller, New York, 1935, p. 62.
8. Bradford, *op. cit.*, p. 289.
9. Means, *The Spanish Main, Focus of Envy,* p. 156.

Index